Work Organisations

A Critical Introduction

Work Organisations

A Critical Introduction

Third edition

Paul Thompson
and
David McHugh

First edition 1990
Reprinted 5 times
Second edition 1995
Reprinted 7 times
Third edition 2002

Published by
PALGRAVE
Houndmills, Basingstoke, Hampshire RG21 6XS and
175 Fifth Avenue, New York, N.Y. 10010
Companies and representatives throughout the world

PALGRAVE is the new global academic imprint of
St. Martin's Press LLC Scholarly and Reference Division and
Palgrave Publishers Ltd (formerly Macmillan Press Ltd).

ISBN 0–333–94991–9 paperback
ISBN 0–333–98095–9 hardcover

This book is printed on paper suitable for recycling and made from fully managed and sustained forest souces.

A catalogue record for this book is available from the British Library.

10   9   8   7   6   5   4   3   2   1
11   10   09   08   07   06   05   04   03   02

Printed in Great Britain by
Antony Rowe Ltd
Chippenham, Wiltshire

Contents

List of Tables and Figures

Figures

Tables

Acknowledgements

It should be getting easier, but it isn't. Producing a third edition has been a lengthy and demanding process. Without the help from colleagues, friends and reviewers, it would have been a far worse one. We would like to thank Sarah Brown at Palgrave and David McDonald at Curran Publishing Services for their expertise in helping the book to see the light of day. It is less clumsy if we make our acknowledgements separately.

Paul Thompson writes:

I wrote most of the second edition during my first year of a new job at Edinburgh, and the third during an equivalent stage at Strathclyde. Rational planning is obviously not my strong point. Nevertheless colleagues at both institutions have been an invaluable source of discussion and stimulation. In this respect I cannot let the tragic death in 2000 of Harvie Ramsay go unmentioned. He was the main reason I went to Strathclyde, and I still run ideas past an imagined Harvie, for this book and anything else, to see whether they pass a credibility test.

It is a commonplace that good teaching draws on participation in research. The same can certainly be said about writing textbooks. More specifically, parts of the book have benefited considerably from my work with particular groups and individuals, and I am grateful to them for being such a stimulating source of ideas, and for allowing me to draw from materials produced in or as a background to that research. I have drawn on work on the Scottish Spirits industry by Tricia Findlay, Alan McKinlay, Abigail Marks and Jim Hine, particularly with regard to the material on teams and on innovation. Chapters discussing knowledge work and the 'New Economy' draw extensively from my collaboration with Chris Warhurst, and more recently with George Callaghan on call centres. Joint work with both Chris Smith and Stephen Ackroyd has helped shape those sections of the book that deal with theoretical resources.

Alongside and beyond matters of collaboration, I would like to thank Johanna Hofbauer, John Jackson, Inge Runar Edvardsson, Stephen Ackroyd, Alan McKinlay and Chris Warhurst (and three anonymous reviewers) for reading and commenting on all or part of the book. Producing a book is also a profoundly practical affair, and I would like to thank everyone in the HRM office at Strathclyde, particularly Linda Hill, for their support. Finally, I would like to thank Gillian Pallis for her comments and support. No doubt she will be extremely glad, as I am, to see the back of the book, at least for another few years.

Dave McHugh writes:

I would like to thank my family for their forbearance and often exclusive use of the family computer, and a special thanks to my Dad, John McHugh, for just being the best. Thanks again to all of my colleagues who have helped in the past and in particular to Hugh Willmott, David Knights, David Collinson, Martin Corbett and Gibson Burrell, whose work has so much helped to shape my perspective on organisational behaviour. This time round, distinguished mentions in dispatches are due to Linda Alker, now at the University of Derby, and to Alison Alker and Deb Groves from the University of Central Lancashire, for being brave enough to work and write with me. Alex Haslam of the Australian National University deserves thanks for allowing Paul and me an early look at his excellent text on social identity theory, of which I would have made even more use given the time.

Introduction

Our aim in writing the first edition of *Work Organisations* was to provide a critical alternative to the standard, often American, texts that still predominated in the 1980s, as well as to some of the derivative British versions. These 'standard' texts tended to combine a narrow and prescriptive orientation to issues of management, structure and organisational design, with a behavioural agenda dealing with issues such as personality and perception, where a focus on the individual appeared to have little relationship to the more 'structural' material. Since that time, more alternative texts have followed us into that gap in the market. There are now conferences on 'critical management'. All this is to be welcomed, but we still think this book has something distinctive to say, and a third edition gives us an opportunity to expand its scale and scope yet again.

There is a danger that 'critical' simply means the production of variations on an essentially managerial agenda. For us it has meant aiming to balance exposition and evaluation of mainstream writing and research with an attempt to bring together the large, but often fragmented, body of writings from organisation and management theory, labour process analysis, feminism, industrial sociology and social psychology – where they are radical and relevant to the study of work organisations. Any orientation of this sort by definition has to be interdisciplinary, pluralistic and pragmatic in the choice of sources it draws on for inspiration.

The biggest problem we encountered was the question how to link the broadly sociological and more behavioural material. We did not pretend that any form of grand integration was possible. Our aim was to ensure that the discussions in the two main parts of the book were complementary in the kind of analysis used and issues discussed. We felt strongly that organisations are places in which attempts to shape the subjectivity and identity of employees are central to the purposes of management, and that this provided an important bridge and common focus between debates in the different chapters. We have continued to look for ways of integrating material, a result of which is that this edition has two new chapters, on teamwork and on learning and innovation in organisations, which provide opportunities to bring debates and approaches together.

This new edition also gives us the opportunity further to enhance the accessibility of the book for readers. Our main innovation this time round is to break up the material into more convenient chunks. There are now 26 chapters compared with the previous 12. Within this change of format, we are still trying to balance an introduction to key debates, with sufficient depth and reflection to engage with issues and ideas in a meaningful way. We have substantially revised and extended old favourites and included whole chapters on gender and on international management issues for the first time. Current debates on surveillance, managing diversity, knowledge work, high performance work systems and learning in organisations are introduced and evaluated.

Structure of the book

It is worth reminding readers at the outset that a textbook is not like a novel. There is no narrative that requires you to start at the beginning and work through chapter by chapter until you find out 'who done it?' There are three parts to the book. The first focuses on the areas traditionally dealt with by organisation theory and more sociological and structural writings, the second on predominantly psychological material, while the third deals with more complex theoretical issues. Within these parts, most chapters have been designed to be read as stand-alone expositions and commentaries on theory and practice. We have tried hard continually to signpost links backwards and forwards from chapter to chapter.

Having said all that, it makes some sense to read Chapter 1 first, mainly because it tries to give a basic sense of the kind of approach taken in the book as a whole. It seeks to explore three main questions. Why are we interested in studying organisations? How should they be studied? And what are the general concepts and principles available to do so? These objects are achieved by contrasting the domain assumptions of mainstream and critical approaches. By this we mean some of the basic ways in which rival perspectives have looked at organisations and society. At this stage the idea is to keep it fairly simple. We do not look at theory or theories in depth, but instead at some of the underlying and underpinning assumptions. The more adventurous reader could go directly to Part III and follow this through, but it is not necessary to do this in order to follow the substantive discussions found in the intervening chapters, where we build up an understanding of theory and research in a more incremental way.

A great weakness of much organisational writing is the failure to locate analysis in its historical context. Chapter 2 seeks to show how the major characteristics of large-scale organisations in the twentieth and early twenty-first century – control, hierarchy and bureaucracy – came into being. In Chapters 3 and 4 we identify the origins and developments of the best-known 'classical' theories of organisation, notably Taylorism, Weber and the human relations movement. The focus is firmly on the attendant practices and their use by management, in the periods when the ideas emerged, the legacies left for later eras, and the continuities with management and organisation today.

Such practices, however, were never universal, at least not in the same form. A recurrent theme of the book is that different organising logics are embedded in contrasting sectoral, national and other institutional frameworks. For example, what is defined as management in Britain and North America is not necessarily the model elsewhere. This highlights the importance of the environment of work organisations. Yet such environments are often dealt with in a limited way, certainly once markets and technologies have been discussed. Chapter 5 first outlines and evaluates the mainstream literature, including contingency theory and population ecology. It then focuses on the new international environment, which gives us an opportunity to look in Chapter 6 at accounts of globalisation and its effects, and more recent institutional theories of organisation. This is part of a much wider analysis in this edition of issues of comparative organisation and international management.

The study of management rightly occupies a central place in the study of work organisations. But much of the writing has a narrow and technical conception of the nature of management and its activities. Chapters 7 and 8 contrast the extensive body of knowledge on management in mainstream literatures with radical perspectives and research focusing on analysis of management as control and as a labour process. A discussion of the extent to which management operates strategically is an essential part of this section. Traditionally, because organisations were conceived of as cohesive and unitary, the related theme of power was much neglected in mainstream writing. At best it was projected as a series of micro struggles, analogous to 'office politics'. Chapter 9 examines this literature and contrasts it with models of power drawn from radical theories. Of the latter, concepts drawn from Foucault and his emphasis on disciplinary power have become particularly influential in recent years, and such theorising is explained and critiqued. Foucauldian perspectives have made their mark in analysis of gender and sexuality, but the issues go far wider than this. Organisations are gendered in many of their everyday ways of operation. Though this is a theme that runs throughout the book, Chapter 10 enables a closer examination of the process of gendering organisational analysis, with a particular emphasis on the 'glass ceiling' debate.

In recent times many theorists have asserted that a 'paradigm break' in work systems and organisational structures has taken place under the influence of new environmental challenges. Successive models of flexible specialisation, post-bureaucracy and the knowledge economy have tried to articulate these changes. These are complex issues across a huge variety of territories. For this edition we experimented with a variety of formats to capture these debates. In the end, we found that the most straightforward was to divide the material into two chapters: the first giving an exposition of those accounts claiming the existence of a New Economy and new organisations; the second giving space to commentaries and critiques that emphasise continuity with the past as well as change. Chapters 11 and 12 therefore really do need to be read as one section.

In the 1980s, corporate culture was perhaps the main talking point in managerial literature, and was put forward as the key factor for business success. Though new themes have arisen, this 'symbolic turn' in organisational theory remains influential with theorists and practitioners alike. Chapter 13 looks critically at the merchandising of corporate cultures and examines whether it is an attempt to constitute a new form of 'organisation man'. Linking the debate to other contemporary issues such the rise of human resource management, the chapter examines the extent to which the management of cultures can be successful in generating commitment and internalising values.

In Part II we have likewise increased the number of chapters, for two main reasons. First, we have responded to readers' comments by trying to improve ease of use in making topics and issues easier to locate within a more traditional structure. Second, we have tried to consolidate what were often separate strands of argument in the second edition, for example on subjectivity, stress, motivation and groups, into single chapters. In doing this we have had to increase the number of linking references to other chapters in order to maintain our argument that all of the topics explored are accounts of interdependent processes. Similarly we continue to revisit many of the areas covered in Part I, but viewing them from an organisational behaviour (OB) perspective. Readers will note for example some repetition of assertions of the relation of psychological knowledge to managerial ideology and practice. This overlap in the issues we investigate in Parts I and II is to some extent a recognition that, since many readers will only dip into the book and not read the 'whole story' as intended, these points must perforce be made often. Thus, as with Chapter 1, we recommend that readers try to take on board the contextual discussion of what we term the 'subjective factor', which has now been gathered into Chapter 14.

We start out in this chapter by introducing the theme of Part II, which is to assess the nature and adequacy of the mainstream agenda for an understanding of our experience of organisational life, and how this shapes the construction of the identities through which we face it. We examine the deficiencies of behavioural approaches and how major theoretical areas within OB have been incorporated into agendas of regulation and control. Since we began *Work Organisations*, the content of texts in the area has moved to address many of the issues we have raised and the wider perspectives we have promoted. However the major foundations of OB are still informed primarily from the perspective of 'organisational psychology', using the subject divisions within social psychology without consistently reflecting their more humanistic origins. As such, OB is still generally subordinated to its agency in legitimating, developing and refining the social practices and techniques through which subjective identities are continuously recreated in images appropriate to the relations of social production. Thus we move on to how strategies of control are supported by what we term technologies of regulation before considering and defining the elements of the 'subjective factor' in the study of organisations. These are manifested in the experiences of organisational participants and in the identities through which they transact with others in organisational environments. Our examination of these issues as a whole is viewed through psychological approaches that tend to focus mainly on behaviour as opposed to experience. The intention here is not however to ignore the sociological and structural accounts of subjectivity available in the areas covered in Part I, but to indicate how a closer articulation of structural and behavioural explanations can benefit the understanding of subjectivity in organisations.

In Chapter 15 we introduce the topics of perception, attitudes and personality in order to uncover the reciprocal assumptions made by others and ourselves in the production of our social and personal world. Perceptual processing and categorisation underlie all of the psychological processes we discuss in Part II and lead us through theories of causal judgement in attribution theory to a consideration of attitudes in their relations to behaviour. The importance of the gaining of public commitment to attitude change provides the linkage to a scrutiny of both personality theory and its role in organisational selection, and the process of acquiring a social identity.

Chapter 16 starts by presenting an expanded examination of learning, beginning with the adequacy of learning theories in the explanation of socialisation processes and moving on to look at roles, skills and learning styles. The relation of learning to development initiatives brings us to the phenomenon of the learning organisation and how it is constructed and differentiated from the wider notion of organisational learning. The role of the learning organisation in supporting the implementation of new working practices gives us the theme underwriting a wholly new section on change. We continue to use learning and development initiatives to exemplify the treatment of change in the organisational literature, particularly in relation to the psychology of innovation and creativity. The possibilities of sustainable innovation are explored and questioned on the basis of their dependence on the subjective creativity of individuals who do not always benefit from the change processes in which organisational innovation is implicated. From here we move on to consider the interpersonal processes that to such a great extent are seen as crucial to successful change and innovation. Chapter 17 deals with communication and leadership and now includes a new section on interpersonal influence linking the ideological deployment of communications to the support which leadership supplies to the maintenance of managerial identity. Leadership in terms of personal characteristics is critiqued in favour of models that emphasise both the role-based nature of the phenomena and the reliance on networks and the psychological processes of attribution to maintain leadership and mobilise the consent of others.

Chapter 18, which brings together accounts of stress, recognises how this most contentious of psychological reactions can lead both to deleterious consequences and subjective sustenance for those who endure it. Starting with the classic notions of role stress we move quickly into a critique of modern stress management techniques, with particular attention to counselling and employee assistance. A new section on emotion management reflects developments in the study of emotional labour and links to a discussion of stress and systems of control. Chapter 19 brings together two strands of argument from the second edition. First is an exploration of the classic content and process theories of motivation, leading into an examination of the adequacy of concepts such as goals and motivation itself for understanding organisational experience. Second, we use motivation theories as a base for the investigation of the mobilisation of commitment in modern work organisations. The focus on motivation and commitment is then used to explore the internalisation of self-controls and provide linkages to the study of groups in Chapter 20.

Older material on group formation, socialisation, cohesion and resistance is brought together as an introduction to a close examination of the phenomenon of teamworking. Teams, as discussed in Chapters 11 and 12, are at the forefront of contemporary work reform, and we examine the extent to which teams can mobilise the commitment of members before moving on to a discussion of the technical, governance and normative dimensions of teamwork. We close this chapter with a critical reflection of the way in which groups and teams are often erroneously conflated in the managerial and HRM literatures.

Chapter 21 retains the basic format of its predecessor, returning to consider in more detail the nature of identity, and the contrasting approaches and resources a redefined agenda would need to focus on to better address issues of subjectivity. In particular we address social relations, such as those of domination and gender, that are central features of work organisation. A new section on impression management leads into the issue of how subjectivity is experienced, structured and transformed within organisations. This is explored through the medium of the 'identity work' performed by organisational participants as a response to pressures on the identities they secure for themselves. These are viewed firstly from the context of the individual, then through a re-examination of the manner in which managerial identity work acts to structure the experience of everyone in organisations, regardless of hierarchical position.

Part III returns to the territory of the broader theorising of organisations. The discussion draws on and links to some of the substantive issues explored in previous chapters, as well as introducing new themes such as agency and structure. Chapters 22 to 23 examine in detail the theoretical resources drawn on in mainstream and critical writing. The question of rationality is a central one in both traditions and, through an examination of new, postmodern analyses of organisations, we explore the issues at stake and conclude that rationalisation remains a fundamental principle of organisational life and that rational enquiry, in a modified form, is an indispensable part of the theorising process. Chapter 24 consolidates previous material on critical and Marxist psychologies and adds a discussion of technologies of regulation in relation to modern human resource strategies. Chapter 25 ends the book with a wider discussion on the nature and uses of organisational knowledge. How do theorists using different paradigms speak to each other? How do managers use theory in practice? How can participants at work learn from past and present to create more democratic, as well as more efficient, organisations?

Part I

1 Studying Organisations: An Introduction

Organisations and organisation society

The British government spent a huge amount of time and money on the Millennium Dome. On the night it was a disaster: tickets failed to arrive, transport routes were blocked, and over-zealous security led to long queues in the cold and rain. This led to a lead story in one newspaper headlined 'We're just lousy organisers, however much we spend' (*Guardian*, 10 January 2000). Linking problems at the Dome to a litany of other failures in schools, railways and health, Peter Preston observed that 'The alleged culprits, in short, aren't the usual suspects. They are disorganisation, profligacy, botched planning and absence of vision.'

This should be a happy, or at least pertinent, judgement for those of us who make a living from analysing organisations. Yet, as citizens of society we tend to have a love–hate relationship with large-scale organisations. We frequently berate them for being bureaucratic, wasteful and placing us under the shadow of big brother. Yet we take them for granted as providers of employment, public welfare, private services, and even charity or other voluntary activities. In the not so distant past, information, leisure, economic needs and other basic life processes were more likely to be directly and locally produced or consumed. Now, complex economic, social and political organisations provide a network of individual and social relationships through which we participate in society at local, national and global levels (Morgan, 1990).

Such organisations have therefore become a focus for academic analysis, often under the heading of 'organisation studies'. This is not a discipline with clear sources and boundaries in the manner of economics or political science. Rather it is constructed from a variety of disciplines and sub-disciplines including industrial sociology, management theory, organisational sociology and psychology, and industrial relations. This is not the place to provide detailed descriptions or historical explanations of such disciplines (see M. Rose, 1975; Hyman, 1981). What we can observe is that a common field of study around organisations has facilitated a welcome overlap in subject matter and conceptual frameworks. Though different strands will have their own more specific interests such as motivation or skill and work satisfaction, there are a growing number of common interests and frameworks. If we take management strategy, for example, it is clear that a considerable amount of research has been done from an industrial sociology perspective, within an industrial relations framework and by management studies. Similar points could be made with respect to job design, labour markets and a range of other issues. We welcome this interdisciplinary framework and its effect on organisation studies and hope that this book reflects and encourages it.

However, it would be misleading to give the impression that all is sweetness and light in this field of study. For a start, the same paradox that affects public attitudes is often reproduced intellectually. Those very 'efficiencies' that derive from the scale and structure of organisations, create conditions of domination over human liberty and democratic institutions. But even as trenchant a critic as Perrow, who notes that organisations are tools that can mobilise immense ideological and practical resources for those who control them, argues: 'If we want our material civilisation to continue as it is . . . we will have to have large-scale bureaucratic enterprises in the economic, social and governmental areas. The development of industrialisation has made this the most efficient way to get the routine work of a society done' (Perrow, 1979: 56). All commentators do not necessarily share this view today. Indeed, from popular management writers to post-modernists, organisation – at least in the sense of action to create order – has become something of a dirty word. The fashion instead is for decentralisation, disorganisation and even chaos (Peters, 1989). Big and bureaucratic is bad; but we are running ahead of the story.

The theory and practice of organisation has developed around bureaucracies, deriving partly from the work of Max Weber, who, at the turn of the last century, was most responsible for drawing our attention to the significance of large-scale organisations. As the division of labour in society and at work became more complex and difficult to manage, the responsibility and means of co-ordination of core activities became focused on specialised units. The essence of organisation is the creation of regular, standardised behaviour and orderly structure. For Weber the characteristic feature of society would be complex and highly developed administrative structures governed by rules, hierarchy and experts. Most people would work for or become clients of such bureaucracies. In current discourse, such developments are linked to the wider growth of *modernism*, in which planning, calculation and a hierarchy of authority spread to most areas of social and cultural life.

> The past fifty or a hundred years have seen a remarkable growth in the number, size, and power of organizations of many kinds, ranging through all areas of life. The extent of this change in the character and atmosphere of society can be visualized if we contrast the situation of 1952 with, say, that of 1852. In 1852 labour unions were practically nonexistent. There were practically no employers' associations or trade associations. There were practically no professional associations. There were no farm organizations of any importance. National governments absorbed – by present standards – an almost infinitesimal part of the total national product. There was no Department of Agriculture, no Department of Labour, in Washington. There were few corporations and few large businesses. Organizations outside government itself were largely confined to the churches, a few local philanthropic societies, and the political parties. There were, of course, many sporadic attempts at large-scale organizations, in almost all fields, in the first half of the nineteenth century. None of these attempts, however, resulted in the establishment of stable, continuing organizations such as we see today.
>
> (Kenneth Boulding, *The Organizational Revolution*, 1953)

As the extract above indicates, some modern writers came to believe that such an *organisation society* reached fruition in the post-1945 period (Kerr *et al.*, 1960; Bell, 1960; Prethus, 1962). The dominant themes were that private and public corporations had helped to usher in a new era where politics, ideology and conflict had been superseded by rational, scientific decision-making, guided by a new enlightened, though powerful, administrative élite. Standardised mass production and consumption went hand-in-hand with central direction of the economy and state by professional managers and politicians. A special sort of person – organisation man – was even evoked, who could be relied on to be one of the vehicles of such techniques, given that his personality and commitment was subordinated to the corporation (Whyte, 1956). As Biggart comments, Whyte was describing 'a generation of organisational workers who had been moulded by the needs of the corporation . . . conservative, impassive little grey men. Their lives in the organisation were routine and largely unemotional' (Biggart, 1989: 4). The emphasis on 'man' is not accidental. An organisation society was predicated on the assumption of male corporate warriors, sustained by women at home providing the practical and emotional support.

It was pointless to desire significantly different arrangements, as all industrial societies were destined to converge into a single, similar type. The hierarchical and bureaucratic large-scale organisation, with its particular form of technology, was placed at the centre of mature industrial society. In retrospect this kind of perspective is more of an ideology masquerading as science than an accurate description of social trends. Organisation society and 'man' are part of an imagery where:

> all the major institutional landmarks of modern industrial society – the factory, the welfare state, the business corporation, representative democracy, an independent civil service, universal education and medical care – were firmly set in place and equipped to manage any new problems which were likely to emerge in the foreseeable future. Institutional fine-tuning and technical adjustment were all that was necessary to maintain social stability and economic development. (Reed, 1986: 99–100)

At a time when there is considerable public scepticism about corporations, government and, indeed, science, this all now seems over-optimistic. It was always misguided. Grouping developments under a catch-all label of organisation society or 'complex organisations' became a means, however unintended, of stopping questions being asked about how such arrangements had come into being, how they were maintained, and whether they were necessary. In particular it obliterated real differences between organisational experiences such as being a worker and consumer of public or private services, organisations in a capitalist or non-capitalist society, and the origins and effects of different types of technology in varied cultural settings. In other words, such frameworks obscured the social contexts and social choices made about the nature of organisations – how they are structured, managed and experienced.

Defining the scope and purpose of organisations

Whether existing organisational structures and practices are necessary and efficient and regardless of which forms are dominant, it is demonstrably the case that greater power over our lives is exerted through such processes. Organisations mediate between the wider society and the individual, and joining an organisation as an employee exposes the individual to substantial direction and control. Despite the self-activity of their members, organisations as corporate bodies do have economic and political powers above and beyond those of the particular individuals that comprise them. In fact, there is every indication of a concentration of those powers in a small number of organisations, which is far from enlightened in its effects on us as workers or citizens. This was a perspective raised decades ago by C. Wright Mills (1959), who dubbed those who commanded major organisations the 'power élite'. Today, takeovers and mergers continue unabated, whether the beneficiaries are tycoons such as Rupert Murdoch or faceless financial institutions.

So, despite the limits to the idea of an organisation society, there is a case for studying organisations. But, there remain a number of unanswered questions as to *how*? The orthodox approach is to define organisations as purposeful systems characterised by co-ordinated action towards an objective. By defining organisations in this way, Donaldson (1985: 7) can link together corporations, schools, families or neighbours fixing a fence. But though work may take place within a charity or a political party, its nature and purposes are different from those that operate under market discipline. Organisation may be necessary to ensure that co-ordinated action of any kind takes place, but actions vary enormously with the type of objective. Take Buford's account of his time among extremely well-organised football hooligans:

> Extensive preparations had gone into Manchester United's last meeting with West Ham – coaches had been hired, with complex routes into the city to evade the police, the arrival times staggered so that everyone did not appear *en masse*....Problems of leadership, organisation, and 'big numbers', and a hierarchical command structure: the technocrat phrasing did not obscure that what Steve was describing was a civil disturbance involving several thousand people. (Buford, 1991: 119–20)

The problem is that only by operating at an excessive level of generality and abstraction is it possible to treat things as diverse as hooligans, scout troops and transnational companies within the same analytical framework. As Nelson and Winter note, 'There are a great many different sorts of organisations, and it is implausible that a given collection of concepts and propositions would apply uniformly, or even usefully, to all of them' (quoted in Rowlinson, 1997: 70). Salaman makes a similar point:

> a genuine sociology of organisations is not assisted by the efforts of some organisation analysts to develop hypotheses about organisations in general, lumping together such diverse examples as voluntary organisations, charities and political organisations....It also obstructs the analysis of those structural elements which are dramatically revealed in employing organisations, but not necessarily in all forms of organisation. (Salaman, 1979: 33)

We agree with Salaman here, that organisations as such are not a coherent category of objects capable of being studied in a distinctive way. This is implicitly recognised in orthodox writing, which, most of the time, is *not* about organisations *per se*. Though comprehensive formal definitions may be retained, the overwhelming amount of writing and research is about business. Why then even refer to *work* organisations? Work organisations remain a crucial meeting place of contending social forces – owners, managers, professions, and workers – which generate and reflect contradiction and change. It is also the case that it is the profit-seeking nature of business organisations that creates their distinctive forms of management, control or other social relations. Such forms of organisation remain the structural core of advanced societies, even allowing for the decline in the proportion of those engaged in manufacturing activities. It is primarily for these reasons that the bulk of this book is geared towards those events and experiences.

But in the end it is neither possible nor desirable to maintain a complete distinction between business and other forms of work organisation. Parts of the public sector have always operated in a market environment, and this tendency has rapidly increased in parts of the health service, local government and other public spheres in recent years. In addition, management methods or technologies may arise in a specific sector, but are frequently applied in modified forms in others. Finally, as Weber recognised, there are continuities of structure and practice deriving from the bureaucratic forms present within all large-scale organisations. For these reasons, while recognising the limitations, we prefer to retain work organisations as a broad framework. However, this does not mean that they are studied in isolation. Families and state structures are just two of the forces that interact with work organisations and whose links need to be examined.

Organisational analysis: problems and problematics

Even if we can settle some of the issues of the scope of organisational analysis, many unresolved problems remain which are essentially theoretical in nature. Since the 1950s, a particular approach, normally labelled organisation behaviour (OB), or sometimes organisation theory (OT), has become dominant. It is drawn mainly from management writings and organisational psychology, but enthusiastically borrows from sociology, economics, anthropology and other areas; thus laying claim to be genuinely interdisciplinary. While the borrowing of concepts may be eclectic, it is not random. Rather it is structured by specific problematics (a network of concepts oriented towards a core idea). OB focuses on social behaviour in the enterprise, directed chiefly towards problems of motivation and the performance of individuals and groups in relation to different structures and practices. OT is, according to Donaldson, primarily concerned with the trivariate relationship between structure, contingency and performance; or put another way it is 'mainly about the analysis of different designs, and their contingencies and their outcomes' (1985: 121). When both are taken into account, the result is that, 'These writers have attempted to draw together and distil theories of how organisations function and how they should be managed. Their writings have been theoretical in the sense that they have tried to discover generalisations applicable to all organisations' (Pugh, 1971: 9).

This approach is found in most American and some British textbooks and business schools. Therefore, though organisation studies has always been by its very nature interdisciplinary, this has often been on a narrow, management plus psychology basis. One of the limiting factors has been the gradual split from sociology. Organisational sociology has had a less than peaceful coexistence with orthodox approaches. In the last 25 years there has been a shift in the study of organisations from sociology departments to business and management schools (Hinings, 1988). The orientations of OB and OT have become narrower and more prescriptive. Donaldson (1985: 71–2, 119–20) defends this by reference to different levels of analysis. Issues of class and power, ideology and social stratification, and economic contradictions are the province of sociology. OT concentrates on the problems of people working inside organisations. Advocates of this approach thus seek to deflect criticism of neglect of wider concerns by moving the analytical goalposts. It is impossible satisfactorily to study something like the division of labour or hierarchy of groups in a business without an understanding of the broader social division of labour and power structure.

This is not the only or main problem with 'organisation theory' that Donaldson (1985) attributes to North American business and management schools. Despite his spirited defence, this literature continues to reproduce a largely taken-for-granted view of organisations with respect to both their structures and processes, and notions of effectiveness and rationality. The rest of this chapter seeks to open up this discussion by examining some of the basic theoretical assumptions of orthodox or mainstream approaches, before going on to outline some alternatives that inform the way we have attempted to understand work organisations in this book. So as to avoid the discussion getting too complex at this stage, we have not dealt with the theoretical resources that mainstream or critical approaches draw from. These are outlined in Part III.

Goals, diversity and interests

If organisations are consciously created instruments, then their purpose tends to be defined in terms of goal seeking. This is unexceptional and, in fact, provides a means of distinguishing organisations from social institutions (for example, families) or movements (such as feminism), which do not manifest systematic structures and processes for controlling relations between means and ends. But further definition is more controversial. Goals are seen as preferred states which organisations and their members attempt to achieve through collective and co-ordinated action: 'the planned co-ordination of the activities of a number of people for the achievement of some common, explicit purpose or goal' (Schein, quoted in Mullins, 1985: 2). In this 'goal model', action and values are seen in consensual terms. Goals are formulated, policies and objectives flow from them, inputs in the form of activities are created, which, in turn produce outputs that allow for realisation of goals and organisational success.

Though there may be vague reference to 'environmental influences', the starting point tends to be located within, rather than outside, the organisation: 'there is an assumption that the organisation has some capacity to resist environmental constraints and set its own pattern' (Benson, 1977: 5). Obstacles and variations in these processes *are* acknowledged. Members of organisations may have goals that are contradictory to senior management, creating gaps between formal and informal, official and operative, goals and actual policies (Perrow, 1961). For example, scientific and technical workers tend to be much more committed to their job than to their company, and tensions arise between employees' desire to pursue research for its intrinsic value and pressure on employers to monitor and even close down those projects (Randle and Rainnie, 1994). Furthermore, sub-units of the organisation develop a life of their own, a partial devolution of responsibility resulting in goal displacement. It is management's job to ensure the best possible fit between the goals of different 'stakeholders'. This type of thinking is reflected in standard business mission statements, such as the one in Table 1.1.

Despite some progress towards acknowledging goal diversity and uncertainty, there are huge limitations to this way of thinking about organisations and goals. Oppositional goals cannot be confined to the 'personal'. As Clegg and Dunkerley observe, 'There is no notion of rational structural sources of opposition being generated in the normal processes of organisation' (1980: 317). A sense of reification is still present, in which the organisation is treated as a thing, and the only legitimate goal-seeking collective. Problems cannot be wholly avoided by the use of the 'stakeholder' model (Donaldson, 1985: 24). While stakeholding does help us recognise a variety of interests inside organisations, in some variants it postulates a misleading pluralism in which

Extract from Pifco Holdings plc mission statement,   TABLE 1.1
August 1994

The group exists for the benefit of:

- Its shareholders – by giving them annual dividend growth and long term capital appreciation from the consistent achievement of increased profits.
- Its customers and consumers – by providing products which delight them and represent excellent value in terms of quality, design, performance, reliability and price, together with a first class service.
- Its employees – by giving them secure long term employment, a fair and equitable reward system (including performance-related bonuses, share incentives and share options for senior executives), personal career development and safe and pleasant working conditions.
- The community – by acting as a good corporate citizen by giving support to the less fortunate in society and by adopting environmentally sound policies both within the company and outside.

goals are held to be the result of a relatively equal trade-off between the preferences of competing but co-operative groups (employees, managers, owners, customers). Nor is it enough for Donaldson to assert that the higher levels of management simply 'edit and select' from competing claims. Take the Pifco mission statement set out in Table 1.1. It all sounds good: shareholders can have increased profits, consumers get first-class service, employees get secure employment, and communities get a healthy environment. Regardless of whether corporate management really means it, they may find it much harder to deliver. Value for shareholders, dictated by financial institutions, may mean 'downsizing' and job losses. Efficiency drives to increase the quantity of queries dealt with in a call centre may result in poorer-quality service for those on the other end of the phone line.

The notion that formal organisations, made up of different members, are constituted to co-ordinate wider goals as if this is a form of social contract (Albrow, 1973: 408), underestimates the extent to which dominant power groupings have set those goals and shaped the appropriate structures. In practice co-ordination or co-operation may reflect pressure, constraint or acquiescence to power as much as shared goals. Let's take an example to illustrate the problem: the Wapping dispute. In the mid-1980s, Rupert Murdoch announced plans to move production of his press titles from Fleet Street to a new site. This was planned in secret and sprung on the workforce. The subsequent strike was used as an excuse to dismiss over 5000 workers, most of whom never got their jobs back. Not much sign of a trade-off among stakeholders here. The power accruing from ownership gave Murdoch and his associates the means to enforce their objectives. Even those – notably journalists – who voted to accept the move, did so in a context of bribes (£2000 and BUPA membership) or threats (the sack). As one *Sunday Times* journalist wrote at the time, 'In a property-owning democracy, the price of the average citizen's soul is a little less than the cost of his or her mortgage'. But in one sense there is a pluralism in work organisations, albeit different from 'stakeholders'. The array of interests and interest groups that exist goes beyond a conventional management and labour dichotomy. One of the reasons that Murdoch won is that he was able to exploit divisions between journalists, mainly male printers and largely female semi-skilled workers, and white collar employees – all of whom had a history of sectional antagonism over wages, jobs and working conditions. So there is a sense in which we can refer to 'organisations' having policies or goals, but they have to be clearly recognised as frequently being the property of particular individuals or groups.

All this leads to a need to modify the orthodox definition of organisations as means of delivering collective goals. A more realistic definition would see organisations as consciously created arrangements to achieve goals by collective means. This recognises the inter-connected character of organisational practices, without any assumptions about harmonious goals and interests. A final broader point on this issue is important. As we saw earlier, to define or classify organisations in terms of goal seeking distorts the difference between them. We need to differentiate between different types of goals and the wider economic and political influences upon them; how they are constructed and in whose benefit they operate. With this in mind, it is better to think in terms of a variety of *organising logics* that arise out of those contexts and preferences. These may not all resemble the conventional bureaucratic way of doing things. For example, direct selling organisations (DSOs) such as Amway or Avon have been among the fastest-growing commercial organisations.

> Compared with traditional firms, DSOs appear loose and out of control. They repre-
> sent an apparent management nightmare that only a thick rule book and a platoon
> of managers could keep together. In fact, DSOs have almost no rules and, compared
> with most firms, few managers. Home Interiors and Gifts, for example, with 30 000
> distributors, has only 35 managers.... Direct selling has a logic too, but is radically
> different from the logic of bureaucratic organisations: a conscious alternative to
> firms as a way to organise economic activity to make a profit, as a technique for
> managing labour, and as a means of earning income. (Biggart, 1989: 5–7)

Different logic leads to the choice of particular managerial mechanisms. The scientific workers referred to earlier are subject to normative controls that attempt to mobilise commitment to the work, combined with a large degree of operational autonomy. Many other white-collar workers in conventional bureaucratic hierarchies are being managed through much more economistic methods such as performance-related pay.

Rationality, efficiency and choice

The mainstream emphasis on collective goal seeking is also sustained by a vision of organisations as *rational* instruments or tools; indeed this was a prime theme of 'classical management theory' that formed the basis of modern organisational analysis (see Chapter 8). When we talk of rationality, it normally refers to the logical nature of beliefs or actions. This is an aspect of mainstream perspectives, but the basic feature concerns the development of suitable means to reach specific ends. It therefore becomes inseparable from a notion of *efficiency*. The emphasis is on rationally designed structures and practices resting on processes of calculated planning that will maximise organisational effectiveness. Some traditional theorists have described this in terms of the 'one best way' to run organisations. A more acceptable version of the rational model recognises the contingent nature of the process: 'Organisational arrangements are viewed as the outcomes of means–end decisions to bring situational circumstances and structures into alignment in order to enhance efficiency' (Bryman, 1984: 392). Most mainstream texts continue to deny that there is one formula to fit every situation, but any serious examination of popular management writing and the associated business fads shows that the search for blueprints and formulas has not been forgotten (Pascale, 1990; Huczynski, 1993).

This can be seen by the rash of books imitating the American best-seller *In Search of Excellence* (Peters and Waterman, 1982). They all examine the activities of companies in an attempt to find the winning formula. At the level of the individual, the equivalent is the endless exhortation to become the 'successful manager', the 'one-minute manager' and so on. Interestingly Peters and Waterman attack the 'rational model' embodied in the classical theorists such as Weber and F. W. Taylor. But their objection is actually to a particular type of rational action that is based on following rules, techniques and structural devices. They approvingly quote Selznick: 'It [the organisation] refers to an expendable tool, a rational instrument engineered to do a job . . . the transformation of an engineered, technical arrangement of building blocks into a social organism' (Peters and Waterman, 1982: 98). For them, the key role is played by the distinctive values or culture of an organisation, for this has the effect of binding the various participants together. This is what has apparently made Eastman Kodak, McDonald's, Texas Instruments and other companies successful (see Chapter 13 for a full discussion). The magic formula may differ, but the framework of rational action = efficiency remains the same.

Rationality and efficiency are legitimate aspects of organisational analysis. But in mainstream theory they are presented largely in neutral terms, as if rationality was a simple determinant of organisational structures, processes and goals. Processes are reduced to a matter of technique: devising the appropriate kind of structure, or best fit with a particular environment. A cosy picture is developed of a functional relationship between rational organisations and a rational society. This perspective removes issues of politics, power and control from organisational choices, and critical questions concerning means and ends. Donaldson (1985: 101) tries to get round this by separating the latter: 'The concern with rational means rather than values is part of what makes such studies apolitical'. But there are as many contestable choices to be made about how to design jobs or authority structures as there are about the ends to which they are put.

A rational model emphasising features such as calculability is further confused with rationality or reasonableness *as such*. As Fischer and Sirriani put it:

> For the critical theorist, mainstream writers have confused the rational model of efficient administrative behaviour with organisational rationality itself...organisations must be conceptualised as tools for the pursuit of personal, group or class interests. (Fischer and Sirriani, 1984: 10–11)

Furthermore, traditional notions underestimate the role of rationality and efficiency as ideological constructs that help to legitimise the positions, rewards and activities of dominant groups (Salaman, 1979: 177–82). For example, when changes take place such as mergers or closures, they are often described in terms of *rationalisation*, as if the decision of managers or boards of directors are inevitable and the only way of doing things. It is important to acknowledge the contested nature of rationality, underpinned by the struggle for scarce organisational and social resources; and indeed, this is the direction taken by an increased range of organisational theorists (Bryman, 1984).

Hierarchy and the division of labour

Mainstream theory is strongly influenced by ideas of organisations as co-operative social systems; self-regulating bodies, tending towards a state of equilibrium and order. This, in turn, rests partly on a notion that organisations are, or should be, unitary bodies combining the activities, values and interests of all their participants. Each part of the system plays a positive, functional role in this process, for example by generating binding social values. Thus the organisation is a system of interrelated parts or sub-units – for example departments, groups and individuals – each functioning to mobilise resources towards meeting wider goals. These parts are at the same time differentiated and interdependent, aiding processes of integration and co-ordination.

The managerial requirement to integrate potentially diverse goals and activities could, of course, take place in a number of ways. But mainstream theory has tended to emphasise the advantages of a particular pattern of roles and responsibilities. Earlier we quoted Schein on the need for co-ordination to achieve goals. The extension of that sentence reads, 'through division of labour and function, and through a hierarchy of authority and responsibility' (quoted in Mullins, 1985: 2). Such an interpretation of the division of labour has always played a leading role in ideas of how to sustain the social solidarity necessary for the survival of the 'organism' of society or enterprise.

As a consequence of this line of thinking, the way that tasks, functions and jobs are divided, with the consequent specialisation and hierarchies, is all-too-often regarded as an unproblematic, technical or functional necessity. The origins and workings of the division of labour are neglected as an issue, influenced by analyses which emphasise differentiation and interdependence. As a consequence many deep-rooted features of organisational life – inequality, conflict, manipulation, domination and subordination – are written out of the script in favour of behavioural questions associated with efficiency or motivation. Some of these features may be seen as patho-logical or temporary phenomena arising from breakdowns in organisational systems, rather than a fundamental product of the structuring of the division of labour.

While conflict and struggles over scarce resources are still marginal to most writings about organisations, the situation does appear to have changed with respect to hier-archy. Current managerial rhetoric is awash with terms such as 'empowering the workforce' and 'self-managed teams', which suggest a different way of doing things. We will examine the realities of such practices in Chapters 11 and 12.

Management and managerialism

Part of management's social engineering role is to maintain the maximum degree of harmony and generate feelings of belonging in the workforce, reflecting literally the definition of organisation as 'form into an orderly whole'. Common to all versions of rational efficiency is that the logical basis of action is held to reside with the manager. In contrast, employees who restrict or oppose such action are frequently held to be acting irrationally, governed by a 'logic of sentiment' rather than one of efficiency. The more overtly managerial writers are understandably full of references to what management *should* do, and in this sense are clearly *prescriptive* in nature. For some, the role of organisational analysis is to 'help managers in organisations understand how far their behaviour can positively influence their subordinate's productivity' (W. Clay Hamner, quoted in Karmel, 1980).

Effectiveness becomes synonymous with management effectiveness, and options in debates are situated within that framework. Donaldson (1985: 86) disputes this by arguing that though both are concerned with systems effectiveness, their viewpoints are distinguishable. After all, if they were the same, there would be no point in supplying prescriptions. This is true, but the parameters are strictly circumscribed, as in the example supplied that an organisational analyst might advise greater or less socialisation into company beliefs. No question surfaces about the legitimacy of the beliefs themselves.

Not all mainstream writing is openly managerialist, but the underlying assumptions seldom stray too far. In the preface to an early version of a popular textbook (Buchanan and Huczynski, 1985), Lupton remarks that social scientists should not attach themselves to any one organisational group or its problems. But he then gives two examples of key 'puzzles'. Why and in what conditions do workgroups restrict output? What are the origins and costs of impeding technical innovation? Similarly Karmel (1980) identifies key questions. Why do people sabotage equipment? Why does the introduction of a computer make many people unhappy? Why don't subordinates obey? Alternative 'puzzles' such as why alienating technologies are designed in the first place are conspicuous by their absence. In addition, the way such problems are defined, and the recurrent use of the term *practitioners* can only refer to management practices.

Many organisational texts remain a curious and confusing mixture of analysis and prescription. Emphasis on a stream of advice and solutions to managers consistently undermines the generation of valid and realistic knowledge of organisational processes. Two qualifying points to this criticism need to be made. First, there is a need to study management as an activity. Second, an openly 'management science' servicing the needs of such groups inevitably reflects existing socio-economic relations. But such an orientation is particularly dangerous to a broader organisational analysis. As Watson (1980) pointed out, management requirements are likely to focus on short-term pragmatic relevance related to task achievement, or on the ideological expedience of unitary and consensual views of organisational life. Theorists can become in Baritz's (1960) words 'servants of power', enmeshed in restrictive client relationships within the business firm. The problem is less that of the corruption arising from lucrative contracts (though it is worrying when yesterday's advocates of participation become today's advisors on union busting) but that of knowledge and problem solving on management terms. Thus OT is helping to constitute a particular reality without critically analysing it, and runs the risk of reducing theory and practice to a technology of social control.

Not only does this limit the ability of analysis to be a resource for a wider range of participants, it has the negative consequence of ignoring lower-level employees except as objects, or in their defined 'roles' (Salaman, 1979: 47). Limitations arise from the service role itself. Reed observes, 'organisation theory has presented management with a stock of "moral fictions" (such as "managerial effectiveness") that disguise the social reality of contemporary management practice' (1986: 95). Despite or perhaps because of that role, there are frequent complaints that official theory propagated to business students and managers is out of touch with the 'real world'.

A science of organisations?

In terms of methodology, many mainstream writers take what Benson (1977) refers to as a 'simple positivist view'. That is, they tend towards the use of methods and a view of reality borrowed from the natural sciences. There are two particularly important features with regard to this. First, there is great emphasis on *measurement* of organisational phenomena, for example types of structures, technologies, leadership styles, and even the fit between them. Second, there is an attempt to discover clear cause and effect relationships. There is nothing in principle wrong with either. In fact, at a time when there has been considerable fashionable disdain for science and an intellectual retreat from a concern with evidence and careful theory building, it might be time to bend the stick back a bit. The problem with the orthodox notion of a science of organisations is that it tends to restrict the space for critical evaluation. Donaldson (1985: 84) refers to the need to 'reaffirm the commitment to valid general causal laws as the goal' and asserts the superiority of science over lay accounts. This is fair enough but is hardly the point. It is a question of the *nature* of the scientific approach, particularly the mistaken emphasis on laws. The fact that no one can actually identify any does not seem to worry Donaldson, as this is no proof that they may yet be discovered in the future!

Under this mantle of science – whether administrative, organisational or behavioural – generalisations are intended to apply to *all* organisations. On this basis, analysis and intervention can be used to predict and control events, and make prescriptive recommendations. Stress on technique rather than values matches the idea of organisations as rational instruments. The attitude towards scientific intervention into the organisation itself tends to be taken for granted, rather than treated as problematic. Organisational analysis needs to combine rigorous methods and an ability to identify trends and patterns, with an acceptance of the inherently partial and contested nature of knowledge.

A concluding comment

In conclusion to this section, we would argue that mainstream perspectives have often functioned as theories of regulation and are bound up in the purposes and practices of organisational control. This has prevented the development of 'any coherent or consensual theoretical object of the organisation' (Clegg and Dunkerley, 1980: 213). Instead organisational and societal reality has tended to be taken for granted, with emphasis on that which is prescriptive and short-term. The viewing of organisations as natural systems and as largely autonomous bodies has produced a limited capacity to explain historical changes and the political and economic contexts in which organisations operate. The overall objections of critical theory are summed up by Fischer and Sirriani:

> Common to all of the approaches is a concern over the conservative/elitist bias of organisational theory, a general absence of social class analysis, a failure to connect the organisation to the political economy of the larger social and historical context, a general neglect of political and bureaucratic power, and the ideological uses of scientific organisational analysis. (Fischer and Sirriani, 1984: 5)

An alternative and critical agenda

Having outlined some of the weaknesses, limitations and ideological functions of orthodoxy, this section focuses on the positive dimensions of the alternative to it. An outline
of a different agenda has already begun to emerge through the previous discussion, with
a concern for issues of power, control, conflict, exploitation and legitimation. Like their
mainstream counterpart, critical perspectives are based on a variety of ideas and theoretical sources, ranging from Marxian-influenced labour process theory, and radical
variants of a Weberian tradition, to postmodernism, interpretative sociology and radical
social psychology. These strands will be developed in later chapters and pulled together
in Part III. For the moment, the emphasis is on some of the basic ways of seeing and
performing organisational analysis that are shared across many critical approaches.

Reflexivity

Critical perspectives must first of all be *reflexive*. That is, they must have the capacity
to reflect upon themselves so that values, practices and knowledge are not taken for
granted. Nor can we take our own experiences for granted. A useful example is provided
in the novel *Nice Work*. Robyn Penrose, a university lecturer in English, is sent to
shadow the Managing Director of a local engineering factory. She finds the noise, dirt
and disorder of the foundry hard to comprehend:

> What *had* she expected? Nothing, certainly, so like the satanic mills of the early
> Industrial Revolution. Robyn's mental image of a modern factory had derived
> mainly from TV commercials and documentaries; deftly edited footage of brightly
> coloured machines and smoothly moving assembly lines, manned by brisk opera-
> tors in clean overalls....The situation was bizarre, so unlike her usual environment,
> that there was a kind of exhilaration to be found in it, in its very discomfort and
> danger, such as explorers must feel, she supposed, in a remote and barbarous
> country. (Lodge, 1990: 121, 130)

Despite, or perhaps because of, the lack of understanding, she blunders into actions
which spiral out of control. In fact, our inability to experience large organisations
directly in the same way as individuals or small groups, subordinates or power holders,
creates special problems for studying organisations; problems which are often resolved
through the use of unsatisfactory substitutes such as metaphors – organisations are 'like'
machines, garbage cans or prisons (Sandelands and Srivatsan, 1993).

We have referred previously to unproblematic conceptions of phenomena such as
goals and productivity. But a key example would be that of gender. Existing analyses
have largely treated gender divisions as irrelevant, or in practice invisible, despite 'the
persistent fact that women's position in any organisation differs from men in the same
organisations' (Woolf, 1977: 7). In this sense, mainstream orthodoxy has been 'malestream' (Mills and Tancred, 1992).

Instead of reflecting the concerns of established power groups, organisational theory
should critically reflect on and challenge existing attitudes and practices. It can draw on
the distinction between practical and technical rationality identified by Habermas (1971)
and subsequently espoused by many other radical writers. Technical rationality is based
on the instrumental pursuit of taken-for-granted goals such as 'efficiency'. In contrast,

practical rationality emphasises conscious and enlightened reflection that can clarify alternative goals and action based on the widest communication and political dialogue. These concepts are, in themselves, rooted in Weber's differentiation between a formal rationality concerned with calculable techniques and procedures, and substantive rationality which emphasises the values and the desired ends of action.

The embeddedness of organisations

A further guiding principle is the necessity to be *historical* and *contextual*. Organisational theory and practice can only be understood as something in process, otherwise the search for general propositions and instant prescriptions becomes disconnected from reality, as it has done in conventional ahistorical approaches (Littler, 1980: 157). It is also necessary to counter both the tendency to see organisations as free-floating and autonomous, and the concentration on the micro-level of analysis, or single enterprise. This means locating organisational processes within their structural setting, examining the interaction with economic forces, political cultures and communities. To return to the gender example, it is impossible to fully understand the emergence and development of the sexual division of labour in organisations from the inside. We have to go outside, to examine the family and patriarchal structures in society as a whole in order to shed light on internal issues.

This approach means more than diffuse references to the environment. In theoretical terms, organisational issues cannot be comprehended outside of the totality constituted by capitalist society and the mode of production in particular (Burrell, 1980). Donaldson objects to this on the grounds that locating explanations within the wider social system denies that organisational phenomena are topics of enquiry in their own right. But no convincing argument is put forward to justify the desirability or possibility of such analytical autonomy, to say nothing of seemingly denying the validity of the work of Weber, Marx and Durkheim. Donaldson raises a more pertinent point when he argues that 'the notion of totality is a reference to everything – nothing is left out' (1985: 124). It is true that that 'totality' can obliterate complexity in the search for the big picture, or reduce phenomena to a meaningless level of generality. For example, we do not always learn very much from general references to the effects of capitalism and patriarchy. There may not be a smooth fit between organisations and each part of the 'totality', but it is possible and necessary to show the concrete ways in which organisations are embedded in specific social, political and economic structures.

Multi-dimensionality

Explanations must not only be multi-layered, but multi-dimensional. Different modes of analysis are needed to deal with the complexities and levels of human behaviour in organisations. As we have seen, mainstream theories separate the behavioural dimension from employees' roles within the division of labour. Clearly people are constituted as individuals at the level of their identities and emotions, but that process is informed by the same 'structural' and collective phenomena that shape management strategies and job design, and the broader social relations of production between capital and labour, and between the sexes.

Radical writers have long been critical of the psychological component used by mainstream theory as part of the explanation of organisational behaviour. Objections

have been made to the treatment of people in organisations as 'psychologically determined entities' with abstractly and individually defined needs, for example the need to
belong or for self-actualisation. This has led some critical writers to firmly reject any
psychological orientation. Clegg and Dunkerley argue that people should be considered, 'not as subjectivities, as unique individuals or social psyches, but as the bearers of
an objective structure or relations of production and reproduction which are conditioned not by psychology but by history' (1980: 400). While sharing this critique of
psychological orthodoxy, we reject the view that people can be considered only as
bearers of objective structures. The fact that managers and workers find themselves
caught up in structural processes does not mean that they are merely passive agencies
or operate solely at a group level. Any circumstances are experienced inter-subjectively,
reconstructed and modified.

A purely structural analysis, even where it allows for human action and resistance,
fails to get sufficiently inside those routine everyday experiences in which people react,
adapt, modify, and consent to work relations. While concepts of motivation, perception
and the like inadequately address the problem, some account of subjectivity and identity
is necessary. Nor is the question of subjectivity significant solely at the level of the individual. A critical psychology should also identify the ways in which organisations act as
'people processors', through either informal cultural practices or formal managerial
strategies to mobilise consent.

That is not to say that it is easy to integrate the different dimensions. Our aim
with the book at this stage is to establish complementarity and points of connection
rather than synthesis and the solving of underlying theoretical questions. As subjectivity and psychological theories are the province of later chapters, we will say no
more at this stage.

Structure, contradiction and agency

Many critical theorists (for example Benson, 1977; Storey, 1983) utilise the notion of
dialectical perspectives as a crucial means of explaining the dynamic of organisational
change. In abstract terms, a dialectical process refers to a movement from thesis to
antithesis and synthesis, and derives from Hegel and Marx. More frequently it is used
to denote a reciprocal interaction, between structure and human agency or between
conflicting groups. It is not always usefully employed. Morgan (1986: 266) produces a
list that places 'oppositions' as varied as capital and labour, young and old, and even
sales and production on the same level. But a more focused emphasis on the interaction
and structured antagonisms between key economic actors is valuable. We refer to 'structured' because group conflicts are shaped by contradictions – forces pulling in opposite
directions – for example, between private ownership and collective social needs. These
contradictions help reproduce antagonistic relations that are built into work organisation and society, and which in turn generate conflict and change.

The most direct application to work organisations is expressed in the idea of a
reciprocal relation between managerial control and worker resistance. Management
control strategies are fundamentally a means of dealing with contradictions, uncertainties and crises in their socio-economic environment. New methods of control
inevitably provoke and shape forms of employee resistance and sometimes counter
'strategies'. Over a period of time, management responses are likely to develop into
alternative control methods, blending with and going beyond the old. For example,

piecework was introduced as means for management to set targets and control through monetary incentives. But workers on the shop floor frequently devised ways of asserting their own controls over output and earnings. In the 1970s, employers in the motor industry responded by establishing new payment systems based on 'measured day rates', but still using control techniques based on work study and measurement. Over a period of time workers developed their own methods of adaptation and resistance, so the cycle continues.

This kind of perspective puts more substance into the traditional idea of an interaction between formal and informal dimensions of organisational life. However it is formulated, we can view organisations as continually having to respond to and counter *disorganisation*: a process that is underpinned by the divergent goals and interests discussed earlier in the chapter. Those who command organisations are required to mobilise a variety of resources to counter disorganisation. While the actors themselves may not see it in these terms, we can pull together a variety of practices under the conceptual umbrellas of power, control and persuasion or consent. The factors underlying such choices regarding the different forms managerial and employee action takes, will be a key and recurrent theme of the book.

Social transformation and change

The fact that we have argued against prescription does not mean a lack of interest in the 'practical' or the applied. One of the problems of the split between organisational soci-ologists and OB/OT is that it led some of the former to believe that they were studying different objects in distinct ways. For example, Albrow argues that 'the organisation theorist is concerned to help managers and administrators. By contrast, the sociologist is "impractical". His search is for understanding untrammelled by the needs of men of affairs' (Albrow, 1973: 412). While such a view may be in part descriptively accurate, it has dangerous consequences. It tends to legitimise the separation between a narrow perspective that is only interdisciplinary to meet the needs of management problem solving, and a broader analysis that neglects the dynamics of day-to-day practices in organisations.

We have tried to approach the 'practical' in a number of ways. First, we give an account and evaluation of up-to-date empirical research into work organisations, rather than the make-believe simulations that accompany many conventional texts. This involves critically examining the interventions made by social scientists as researchers or consultants as an issue in its own right. Second, we always analyse theories and prac-tices together and as part of specific economic and political contexts. Showing how theories are used by managerial and other groups may sound unexceptional, but the dominant tradition has been to treat the major theories of organisation and management primarily as ideas systems and historically sequenced. The result is that most students do not get a realistic and informed view of the practicality of theory. In addition the impression is often given that theories developed in the past are outdated and 'wrong' compared to the latest favoured perspective. When these are inevitably replaced, cynicism about theory and organisational analysis is the likely result.

But alternative 'practicalities' have to go further than this and provide resources for social transformation. In this context, Benson adds a further dialectical perspective: that of praxis, drawing on the previously discussed notion of practical rationality. Praxis involves developing analytical resources that go beyond reflexivity and can help members of organisations, constrained by existing relations of ownership and power, to critically reflect on and reconstruct their circumstances. Though some critical theorists advocate the prioritisation of 'philosophically informed armchair theorising' (Burrell, 1980: 102), we would agree with Benson's emphasis on theory as an emancipatory guide and as a means for *empowering* a wider range of organisational participants. This needs to be distinguished from recent managerial usage. When empowerment is used to describe 'enabling' employees to chase more customers or do three more jobs, the term joins a long list whose rhetoric is not matched by reality.

A critical use of the term implies no particular form of politics or intervention, but rather empowering employees to make more choices and to act more effectively to transform workplace relations. It may be argued that this reproduces a one-sided partiality that is the reverse of the management orientation of mainstream theories. There is always that danger. But the existing realities and power relations in organisations will, for the foreseeable future, enable critical theory to maintain a certain distance and intellectual independence. Furthermore, any critical theory not testing its ideas through empirical investigation or practical intervention is ultimately arid.

Conclusion

Finally, we should make clear that our project does not involve a rejection of the idea of organisation theory, merely a particular conception of it. The view taken in this book is that there is a basis for a reformulated organisation studies which has a specific competence in the sphere of work organisations, retains the capacity to cross discipline boundaries, and which combines theoretical and practical emphases. Nor does it involve a dismissal of the whole of 'orthodoxy'. Mainstream perspectives are not homogeneous and there are tensions, as will be explained in the final chapter, between concepts derived from Weber, Durkheim and other key figures. There is also much of value in the body of ideas, in terms of both the issues raised and empirical work generated. Radical and orthodox traditions are not different on every point, and there are partly overlapping objectives for some of the strands of thought, including humanisation of work processes and non-bureaucratic forms of organisation.

It is necessary to treat mainstream theory as a series of overlapping perspectives sharing certain ideas and methods, while differing on others. Some concepts and research are useful and compatible with a critical approach; others are not. None can be considered simply as 'tools of management', or embodying the values and interests of the dominant class. Such a view wrongly assumes that there is such a clear set of interests that can be reflected at a theoretical level. The tortuous history of organisational theory and practice in fact reveals a consistent tension between different approaches to regulation, which in turn reflects the conflicting pressures to control *and* engage the workforce. All but the most unreflexive perspectives require some distancing from existing practices in order to act upon them in a way that will be a resource for management. We return to the idea of theories as a resource in Part III. Meanwhile, subsequent chapters in Part II aim to examine critically the complexities of those relations between organisational theories and practices, beginning with the historical development of large-scale organisations.

2 The Emergence of Large-Scale Organisations

he aim of this chapter is to locate and explain the formation of the large-scale industrial bureaucracies that have been the primary object of analysis for organisation studies. Our time frame focuses on the crucial period at the end of the nineteenth and start of the twentieth century, but moves backwards and forwards in order to understand the process of emergence of such organisations as the foundation of business development.

Organising the new work forms

By the start of the twentieth century, business organisations were beginning to be 'transformed from chaotic and ad-hoc factories to rationalised, well-ordered manufacturing settings' (Goldman and Van Houten, 1980: 108). This was not just a product of growth, merger and technological innovation. It was also a question of management. The New York Public Library did not have a single title on management in 1881, but by 1910 carried more than 200 (Shenhav, 1999: 17). Though the trend was in its infancy, firms were beginning to move away from particularist and uneven practices, toward the beginnings of an industrial bureaucracy. Indeed the two were intimately connected given that the increasing scale of work organisation meant that it was no longer possible to rely on personal or unspecified forms of direction. Changes involved systematising and stabilising both the practices of management and the organisation of the labour process. Job hierarchies, new patterns of work supervision, measurement and reward, as well as greater specialisation and detailed division of labour, became more characteristic of organisational life. It is important to trace the genesis and development of this industrial bureaucracy, reflecting on the theoretical issues through the work of Weber, Taylor and others. As we argued in Chapter 1, mainstream writings largely lack this kind of historical and comparative character. Moreover, they tend to treat managerial and organisational theories as ideologies with universal effects in all times and places.

Theories of management are not 'invented' and applied. Rather they form a resource through which both academics and practitioners try to understand and act. How this happens depends on different social contexts and the histories that have shaped them. Of course, we have not the space to provide a detailed business history that captures all events, variations and issues across societies. The aim is to give a broad picture that locates ideas in context and that focuses particularly on employment and labour process questions. In this and the following chapter that picture is predominantly of American and British circumstances. Nevertheless, we are aware of how specific that experience is, and compare it to the formation of management and large-scale organisation in other national contexts as part of Chapter 6.

The rise of the factory system

Work processes prior to the factory system were not characterised by an extensive division of labour, nor by directly imposed coercive authority. In handicraft and domestic production, small producers were typically involved in independent commodity production, often based on the family structure. They owned their own means of production, worked according to their own patterns, and sold the goods at markets. Some trades or crafts were organised through the guild system. This combined employer and employee, normally within the framework and traditional authority of apprentice, journeyman and master. Neither system was flexible enough to be an adequate basis for responding to the needs of an emergent market economy. Industrialisation and the new capitalist production relations developed from a variety of organisational structures, including artisan production, co-operatives, centralised manufacture and the putting-out system (Berg, 1985). We want to focus mainly on the latter.

Mainstream theory commonly asserts that the new and more complex forms of organisation, with the associated detailed division of labour and hierarchies, developed largely because they were technically required by the scale of production, technology and related factors. A number of writers, notably Marglin (1974) and Clawson (1980) have used specific historical evidence on the factory system to challenge this general explanation. Their work focuses on helping to explain why workers were deprived of control of process and product through the centralised organisation of the factory system. A common response is to argue that the impetus was the necessity to shift from hand production to power-driven machinery located in a central source. In addition, there were the benefits of division of labour, pointed to in Adam Smith's famous pin factory example.

Both Marglin and Clawson show that bringing workers together in workshops and later in the factory – for example in the weaving and spinning trades – did not necessarily involve power-driven machinery or any other technical innovation. In fact, contrary to technological determinist arguments, 'organisational change precedes, both historically and analytically, the technological revolution which is the foundation of modern industry' (Clawson, 1980: 57). The issue of the division of labour is more complicated. Marglin does not argue that it, or hierarchy, was brought into being by capitalist organisation of work. But a distinction is made between the specialisation of occupation and function that is present in any social division of labour, and the particular forms of specialisation involved in the putting-out system and then in the factory. The minute division of work was not necessarily more efficient; rather it provided a role for the capitalist to play in organising production, and enabled the capitalist to take a greater portion of the rewards: 'The social function of hierarchical work organisation is not technical efficiency, but accumulation' (Marglin, 1974: 62).

Counterpoising hierarchy and efficiency in this manner may not be very helpful and, given the time lapse, the evidence on this question is inevitably patchy. In a useful critique of Marglin from a Marxist viewpoint, Rowlinson notes that the idea that any significant movement away from hierarchy is inherently a threat to the role and power of employers is somewhat naïve, particularly when historical and contemporary evidence shows that management can live with degrees of work group autonomy (Rowlinson, 1997: 141–4). What, however, is beyond doubt is that though the new framework provided an impetus for technical innovation, efficiency and technical superiority were not the only, or even primary, reasons for the rise of factory organisation. The putting-out system allowed workers a great deal of control over their hours, rhythm, intensity and quality of work. Furthermore, there was a high level of embezzlement of raw materials, as workers sought to secure a fairer return for their labour. Historians have provided a large body of evidence showing that the workshop and the factory were utilised as a means of discipline and control in order to facilitate capital accumulation (Pollard, 1965; E. P. Thompson, 1967; Landes, 1969).

Coercive authority could also be more easily applied, including systems of fines, supervision (for instance the overlooker system in textiles), the paraphernalia of bells and clocks, and incentive payments. The employer could dictate the *general* terms of work, time and space; including the division of labour, overall organisational layout and design, and rules governing movement, shouting, singing and other forms of disobedience (G. Brown, 1977). Doray gives numerous examples of French factory regulations, including fines for faulty work, writing on walls or entering the factory through the wrong door. He does, however, point out that when applied to the labour process, regulations were not particularly detailed: 'They asserted, in repetitive fashion, the principle of the employer's authority over an unspecified range of activities' (1988: 27–8). It is not surprising that many workers bitterly resisted entry to the factory and the associated forms of discipline. In those early periods, employers were frequently forced to resort to groups such as convicts, paupers and child labour.

To break such resistance, new work habits had to be created appropriate to the discipline of labour time and cash nexus at the heart of the wage relation. Employers' concern with the moral issues of sexuality, drink, bad language and theft was directed less by fidelity to religious doctrine than to the *behavioural* characteristics – obedience, punctuality, responsibility and performance – linked to capitalist rationality and its new forms of organisational culture. As Clegg and Dunkerley observe, the triumph of the formal factory organisation was strongly determined by its 'moral machinery' (1980: 62). This term was used by the economist Andrew Ure, who was noted for his pertinent advice to employers. He and other such advisors, were clear, however, that neither the division of labour nor work values were sufficient for the purpose of achieving the goal of creating 'factory hands'. *Mechanisation* was necessary to destroy old work habits and to tie the worker to the 'unvarying regularity of the machine'.

Marx showed how workers were able to use the employer's continuing dependence on their handicraft skills and knowledge as a weapon of resistance. In turn, Ure recognised that the unity of capital and science was necessary to try to reduce skills to dexterities, create a technical framework independent of the producers, and reduce labour costs by *intensifying* work rather than the limited option of raising hours. Marglin's notion of the factory as a social control device independent of technology is therefore incomplete (Clawson, 1980: 54). Without these kinds of developments, the formal control developed in the factory could not have been adequately realised. It is always necessary to resist the temptation to describe these processes of organisational change in finished rather than relative terms. Employer control remained at a very general level and still had to be accommodated to high levels of worker skill, knowledge and self-organisation. Management as a specialist category was still underdeveloped and work was often labour intensive, with little or no bureaucratic structure. To explain the further development of large-scale organisation we need to focus more closely on the evolution of forms of control.

Modes of control in the transition to bureaucratic organisation

There were a number of obstacles to the development of a more bureaucratic work organisation during the nineteenth century. Even a more mature factory system rested on control structures that were inimical to moves in that direction. As Littler (1982: 69) argues, British industry presented a spectrum of modes of control that, despite differences, were fundamentally non-bureaucratic in nature. Using a range of evidence, three basic modes can be distinguished.

Entrepreneurial or simple control

Factories at the beginning of the nineteenth century could exercise a large degree of power and control personally. Referring to a famous foundry owner, Bendix observes, 'Boulton maintained a personal relationship with his workers, knew their names and their families, and relied upon this relationship to ensure the discipline and work performance needed in his enterprise' (1956: 57). Exercise of authority under entrepreneurial control was therefore simple and direct, and sustained frequently by legal coercion and harsh market conditions. Even at this stage, however, it was not always possible to exert control personally. Foremen could be utilised but, as Rueschemeyer points out, 'an important preliminary solution to the control dilemmas of divided authority was to rely on family ties' (1986: 57). At the required minimal level of co-ordination, the family or close friends of the entrepreneur proved sufficient. Middle managers were virtually absent; in fact, many employers were hostile and suspicious about the idea of a separate 'class' of managers.

Of course this situation could not survive a growth in the size and complexity of operations. Littler (1982) notes that the familial framework was rapidly discarded under such conditions, particularly in the US. Nevertheless, some writers argue that direct and often despotic entrepreneurial authority remained at the centre of what Edwards (1979) describes as simple control. There are important qualifications to be made to the model of entrepreneurial or simple control, particularly Edward's version. It is extremely doubtful whether it was representative of the economy until the end of the nineteenth century as he claims, rather than confined to a minority of firms (Littler, 1982: 64). In addition, though despotic authority was certainly a pervasive influence, it often had to accommodate to the power of other figures in the enterprise, such as craft workers. Hence the image of the all-seeing, all-knowing employer underestimates the struggles at the frontier of control in the workplace. There is also considerable evidence that a more significant mode of control involved contracting arrangements.

Contracting

Outsourcing functions and work to contractors is now a growth area in many companies (see Chapter 11). In the nineteenth century, one of the main reasons why management was so slow to develop was the tendency of employers to delegate responsibility for work organisation to sub-contractors, around whom the employment relationship was constructed. We are concerned here with the internal contractor rather than the independent sub-contractor who was involved, for example, in outwork trades such as clothing and boots and shoes. Evidence from historians such as Pollard (1965) on the UK, and more recently Clawson (1980) on the US, shows that internal contracting was in extensive use in a range of industries including textiles, iron and steel, mining and transport. What did the organisation of work consist of?

> The inside contractor made an agreement with the general superintendent or owners of a company to make a part of their product and receive a certain price for each completed unit....Inside contractors had complete charge of production in their area, hiring their own employees and supervising the work process...were employees of the company, and in most cases they received a day wage from the company as well. (Clawson, 1982: 71)

They accumulated considerable status and power, in both the community through patronage, and the workplace through their high income. In some cases this meant a social position and standard of living higher than company officials, and a capacity actually to pass on much of the detailed work delegated to them by the employer to assistants!

Nevertheless the intended advantages to employers were clear. Responsibility, risks and costs could be partly shifted on to contractors, thus creating greater flexibility in circumstances where managerial skills and knowledge of work operations were limited. In effect, contracting functioned as means of transition through a period of growing enterprise complexity and scale. It was certainly hierarchical, but not bureaucratic in the sense of centralised authority, rules and record keeping. Yet it proved capable of handling expanded output and technical innovation (Clawson, 1980). It did not encompass all industries or all labour within the firm. Newer industries such as service, process and railways were based on direct employment relations (Littler, 1982: 68).

Craft control

Contracting is often seen as overlapping with the 'helper system', in which skilled workers were assisted by a small number of less-skilled operatives. In some cases craft workers hired and paid them, thus reproducing contractual relations. However, the scale of operations was small, with often just one helper; the practices were exercised by craft workers normally within a trade union framework; and operated often in conjunction with foremen. In fact the helper system is the basis for a model of craft control utilised by writers such as Stone (1973) and Montgomery (1976), in which skilled workers had the power to plan and direct immediate work processes. It is important not to exaggerate this 'partnership in production', for we are talking about a system of worker-directed job controls. But though not the equivalent of employer systems, such controls had a significant capacity to resist and constrain employer authority. Craft control meant that, 'employers, in effect, gave up the right to manage' (Owen, 1994: 2). This was put succinctly by F. W. Taylor in 1911 about his experience in the steel industry:

> As was usual then, and in fact is still usual in most shops in this country, the shop was really run by the workmen, and not the bosses. The workmen together had carefully planned just how fast each job should be done, and they had set a pace for each machine throughout the shop, which was limited to about one-third of a good day's work [that is, the maximum possible]. Every new workman who came into the shop was told at once by the other men exactly how much of each kind of work he was to do, and unless he obeyed these instructions he was sure before long to be driven out of the place by the men. (Taylor, 1947: 128)

This was somewhat exaggerated in order to prove the need for Taylor's scientific management system, and particularly neglected the role and powers of the foremen. Though this varied from industry to industry, there was a far more extensive range of powers and functions than contemporaries have today. The foreman's empire included substantial influence over the manner and timing of production, the cost and quality of work, and responsibility for employees – often including hiring and firing. They operated under similar delegated authority to inside contractors, and enjoyed parallel status within and outside work. But that role must be seen within the framework of craft controls. The foreman would sometimes be a master of his trade or chief skilled worker, and would have to share or at least accommodate to the powers of craft workers and contractors.

Decay and decline of traditional controls

Despite the variety of control relationships, each in its own way functioned as a constraint to management and bureaucracy. The shift further in this direction in the last quarter of the nineteenth century must again be seen not merely in terms of gradual evolution and advance of technique. There were social contradictions as well as inefficiencies in traditional methods. Simple control is a clear case. During the period in question, the size and complexity of industrial firms increased considerably. During the last third of the century the average plant in the US more than doubled in size, and by 1900 there were 443 with more than 1000 wage earners (Nelson, 1975: 4). The impetus for change included mergers, concentration of resources, technical innovation and shifts away from local and regional markets. This leap was particularly marked in the US, given its late entry onto the industrial stage, and the relative freedom of business from social reform traditions and strong union organisation.

Such processes inevitably affected existing social relations and were characterised by an increasing separation of entrepreneurs and top managers from the daily activities of the workforce. Organisationally the crucial issue was a growing gap between the structures and expertise of management, and a more extensive division of labour, with its requirements for new forms of control and co-ordination. For capital, the solution had to go beyond the employment of more managers, towards transforming the structures of managerial activity itself.

Problems associated with internal contracts had more to do with contradictions than straightforward inefficiencies. According to Clawson, these were in two major areas. The very fact that the company had entered into sub-contract arrangements meant that it was difficult to evaluate such activities. Contractors therefore used that power to keep employers as much in the dark as possible, aided by the fact that companies seldom kept many formal records. In addition, the high income and consequent social position of contractors was also a problem in that it was difficult for employers to motivate their own officials, who often felt inferior in power, status and rewards to the larger contractors. As a result of these factors, 'many of the younger generation of employers sought to replace the contractor by a system which offered the company greater predictability and control of the workforce and the manufacturing process' (Shenhav, 1999: 22).

Craft job controls were also a serious obstacle to employers taking full advantage of mechanisation and expanded but more competitive markets. As Stone notes of the steel industry:

> At the same time that their labour costs as a percentage were rising, the labour system also prevented employers from increasing their productivity through reorganising or mechanising their operations. The workers controlled the plants and decided how the work was to be done. Employers had no way to speed up the workers, nor could they introduce new machinery that eliminated or redefined jobs. (Stone, 1973:26)

This again may be a somewhat exaggerated description, but it helps to explain why both contracting and craft arrangements came under increasing attack. Employers began to abolish internal contracting in order to shift income to the company and to create a hierarchy under their own control and acceptable to their own officials (Clawson, 1980: 119). Companies often tried to convert some of the contractors into foremen, but many preferred to quit. The power of craft workers was also increasingly challenged in the 1880s. A minority of firms tried to formulate a system of co-partnership, in the UK and France based largely on profit-sharing schemes geared explicitly to ensuring loyalty to the company (Brannen, 1983; Doray, 1988). There were other head-on clashes in the 1890s, including those between the Amalgamated Society of Engineers and their employers in the UK, and major conflicts in the US steel industry, such as the Homestead strike of 1892 (Stone, 1973).

Employers began to assert their general right to run production as they saw fit. This took a particularly virulent form in the US with its weaker unions, as manifested in the 'open shop' campaign run by some employers. The predominant measures used by capital there and elsewhere to challenge and change existing modes of control were, however, less dramatic. An important area was to modify the role of *supervisory labour*. This often involved breaking up the foremen's empire, with a shift away from traditional functions such as hiring and firing and work organisation, towards the narrower but vital sphere of task supervision and discipline. As Littler (1982) shows, this was accompanied by considerable sub-division of the foreman's role. Examples include supervisory labour carrying out quality control, rate fixers, and 'feed and speed' functions. A further interrelated change was in *payment systems*, which became more centrally determined through the office, undermining the bargaining role played by foremen and contractors. In addition, piecework and bonus arrangements spread rapidly.

Significantly, the new arrangements required some formal standards of effort and management record keeping, which were later consolidated in 'drive systems' geared towards the standardisation of labour through production controls and accounting procedures (Shenhav, 1999: 177). Payment through the office indicated a move towards a more direct employment relationship. It should, however, be noted that, at this early stage in the battle for control of output, management techniques were generally not sophisticated enough to include time study or job analysis, and were constrained by workers' initiative and knowledge. Companies frequently had to rely on the cruder measures of rate cutting and employment of 'rate busters' to prove to the workforce that quotas could be increased.

We have already noted that such changes required an increase in record keeping, given the need to specify objectives and keep track of results. The administrative aspects of a management system thus began to be set in place, including that of simple cost accounting. In some companies simple organisation manuals began to appear, complete with management principles and charts (Edwards, 1979: 30). Technological changes also accompanied administrative ones; further increases in the detailed division of labour and mechanisation were facilitated by the greater knowledge of productive processes that capital was gaining. Not only was greater output achieved, but the capacity of employers to dispense with skilled workers and exert greater controls over labour generally through standardised procedures was enhanced. As one employer remarked, 'I want machines so simple that any fool could run them' (quoted in Goldman and Van Houten, 1980: 116). Engineering principles oriented towards treating workers as simple costs of production were therefore becoming more important than personal and direct controls.

Of course these developments were part of a broader process of the creation of the modern business enterprise. Chandler (1962, 1977) stresses that viability was only achieved when the 'visible hand of management' rivalled or replaced the market as a means of co-ordinating the flow of materials through enterprise and economy. In other words, a managerial hierarchy was able to supervise a large number of operating units and to co-ordinate, monitor and plan their activities. The path to the new forms of enterprise began in the US with the railroads and the need to manage their vast regional operations, but gradually spread to other sectors, as modern big business in the decades before 1917 was able to integrate mass distribution and mass production. In this context, some firms developed from the internal growth of small single-unit firms who developed national and global networks, others from mergers. The new consolidated, multi-departmental enterprises centralised the administration of production and research facilities, and established vertical integration, attempting to control supplies and markets. Though the convergence between the growth strategies of firms and their new structures was not to reach its climax until after the First World War with the development of multidivisional, multinational enterprises, a salaried managerial class was fast rising in numbers and power (Supple, 1991: 501–2).

However, this emergent managerial revolution did not proceed in a linear fashion or purely as a result of the need to rationalise production. As Shenhav (1999) argues, management as a conscious, specialist and professional activity was given shape and force by the self-interested efforts of particular groups, notably engineers – a process we will examine in greater depth in the next chapter. They were central to enhancing the development of the new ideas through the increase of associations and journals dealing with management methods (Chandler, 1977: 464; Clawson, 1980: 167–8). Entrepreneurial ideologies were complemented or challenged by more professional concerns with the 'labour problem'; and direct recruitment from colleges grew, though specialist technical training was still relatively limited. In addition a growing army of clerical, technical and administrative employees was necessitated by new payment systems, record keeping and mechanisation, as well as the other growth functions of purchasing, sales and finance: 'at the turn of the century, the USA had the largest proportion of administrative staff to industrial workers' (Shenhav, 1999: 5). It was not just a case of management hierarchy; by the turn of the century the workforce was subject to structures of what Richard Edwards (1979) refers to as hierarchical control. As other writers put it, 'differential job statuses and wages for workers were an integral component of the hierarchical nature of the industrial pyramid' (Goldman and Van Houten, 1980: 122). Job ladders and individuated reward systems were also a means of compensating for the growing homogenisation of labour by artificially dividing the workforce (Stone, 1973).

Conclusion

It must be stressed that these measures were experimental and varied in nature (Brown, 1977: 82–3). Different countries and even sectors had their own unique characteristics and influences that added to the incoherence of transition processes (Littler, 1982), a process we will return to in the final section. Finally, though there was a great advance in managerial organisation compared to the earlier period, even in the US it was still very much in its infancy. There was still little systematic and long-term planning, and as for work organisation, management 'was unable to make the qualitative leap to a different system because it had no alternative conception of how production should be organised' (Clawson, 1980: 168). That situation was soon to change, as we shall see in the next chapter.

3 Taylor, Weber and the Bureaucratisation of the Workplace

Approaching the turn of the century, work organisations were beginning to edge towards more formal management systems and primitive forms of bureaucracy. This chapter examines how that situation was qualitatively transformed, focusing on the contributions of the two major bodies of theory and practice.

Taylorism and systematic management

The major means of change was through the work of Frederick Taylor and his 'scientific management' system. Not that Taylorism was unique or totally new; only time and motion study could genuinely be put in that category. A trend towards *systematic management* was already identifiable, as we have seen with instances of more formal management methods, cost accounting, standardisation of work, and use of less skilled workers. Nyland (1988: 56) comments that 'The "systematisers" were a diverse group of engineers, accountants and works managers who argued that US firms had grown to a size where the internal functioning of the enterprise was becoming increasingly chaotic and wasteful.'

Taylor acknowledged the influences of other innovations in management and work organisation, such as inspection systems and employment departments (Urwick and Brech, 1949: 33). However, others felt that the work of systematisers was being overshadowed, while in Britain, when Taylor proclaimed his new system as a 'science', some engineers described it as common sense masquerading under a high-sounding title (Geoff Brown, 1977: 158). Understandable though the reaction was, it missed the point. Taylor was not just in the right place at the right time; he played a crucial role in *theorising* and *popularising* the new ideas. Furthermore, his work was intimately connected to a body of practice, with Taylor 'Napoleon of the war against craft production' (Clawson, 1980: 202). Taylorism was therefore the most conscious part of the systematisation of management, and of the regulation and control of production.

Such developments met the needs of capital in that period (M. Rose, 1975: 58). This was particularly the case in the US, where larger corporations were developing higher levels of product and labour specialisation to cope with rising demand (Littler, 1982). A shift away from skilled labour towards unskilled immigrant workers was taking place, but still within the context of a relatively high-wage economy. This required new forms of co-ordination, integration and control, and methods of keeping down labour costs. The orientation of larger firms towards professional managers, engineers and consultants additionally provided a supportive framework for the rise of Taylorism. Engineers were central figures and carried out wide-ranging activities, including extensive refinements in accounting procedure (Nelson, 1975: 50). In the 1890s Taylor began to publicise his ideas about time study and piece rates, mainly through the American Society of Mechanical Engineers, and gathered round him a group of enthusiastic adherents. As Shenhav observes, engineers 'pursued an industry-wide project of standardisation and systematisation' (1999: 18). They were the key industrial group, two-thirds going on to become managers after graduating. Shenhav explains how they moved their attention from the technical to the social, quoting from a leading engineering journal, *American Machinist*: 'It is beginning to be recognised that the human as well as the non-human machine must be standardised' (quoted in Shenhav, 1999: 72).

Taylor's own work was first carried out at the Midvale Steel Works (owned by a friend of the family), in a variety of 'detective' roles ranging from unskilled labourer to machinist, clerk, gang boss, foreman, master mechanic, chief draughtsman and chief engineer. Experiments were also carried out in a small number of other firms in old and new industries. These were not confined to the US; by the First World War, 1 per cent of French firms had introduced schemes, often in new sectors such as electrical manu-facturing and automobiles (Fridenson, 1978). There were similar initiatives on a smaller scale in other European countries. In Britain, a minority of firms experienced the arrival of works engineers, rate-fixers, progress men, operations inspectors, work hustlers and other representatives of the growing army of non-producers (G. Brown, 1977: 149–52).

Principles

Many discussions of Taylorism in organisational texts discuss its defining principles around the idea of the employee as 'economic man' and are thus able to treat it as a failed theory of motivation. This is a far cry from the real basis of Taylor's ideas, which were concerned with the control of the labour process. Taylor was adamant that his system was a total package – one best way of organising work. Though affecting the activities of management and workers, the ideas were developed directly out of his obsession with combating the kind of workers' control of output – labelled 'soldiering' – observed at the steel works. He distinguished between natural and systematic soldiering: the former referring to the tendency to want to take it easy, the latter to practices deliberately geared to maximising rewards and job security. To solve the 'labour problem' a number of basic management principles were advanced:

1   Developing a science for each element of work.
2   Scientific selection and training of workers.
3   Co-operation between management and workers to ensure that the work is done according to the science.
4   Equal division of work and responsibility between management and workers, each side doing what it is best fitted for.

These sound rather bland, but their significance can only be understood when set against Taylor's description of inefficient practices. Included under this were 'rule of thumb' methods of deciding on the nature of work tasks; workers choosing their own methods of work and training; and workers' knowledge being the basis of productive technique. He was particularly critical of management by initiative and incentive, where workers were given inducements to use their skills and know-how in the most economical way, without strict managerial determination of tasks.

Scientific management started from the belief that management had to reverse existing power relations in production: 'The management assume, for instance, the burden of gathering together all of the traditional knowledge which in the past has been possessed by the workmen and then of classifying, tabulating, and reducing this knowledge to rules, laws and formulae' (Taylor, 1947: 36). The continual concern with rules and laws in Taylor's writings shows why it can be located firmly within a process of bureaucratisation of production. As Braverman (1974: 119) makes clear, it can also be seen as a control system based on the monopolisation of knowledge by management and its use to specify each step of the labour process. This 'separation of conception and execution' is clearly echoed in Taylor's comments such as: 'all possible brain work should be removed from the shop floor and centred in the planning and lay-out department' (quoted in Braverman, 1974: 113).

Other aspects of the above principles are not so prominent. Take selection: Taylor's search for workers who would follow his instructions to the letter is legendary. His tutelage of Schmidt, picked for his strength and stupidity, was repeated elsewhere, as in the selection of Pinnell – 'the hardest working man' in a railway factory – by time and motion men on behalf of British management (G. Brown, 1977: 156–7). When even his time in the lavatory was recorded, and his output only measured after breakfast when his energy was greatest, it was little wonder that Pinnell came to wish he was dead. But despite the interest of some of Taylor's followers, explicit techniques to place the right worker in the right in the right job remained an underdeveloped part of scientific management.

What about the previously-mentioned emphasis placed by OB on Taylorism as the model of 'economic man'? This is largely misleading. Like most of his contemporaries interested in management reform, Taylor *did* believe that workers were motivated by the pursuit of rational self-interest and that incentive wages – in the form of a differential piece-rate system – were the solution to most labour problems. The tendency to restrict output, however, was seen as an unnecessary product of the absence of any scientific authority for work standards. Management could ensure co-operation on the basis of a consensus established by objective work measurement. Economic incentives could be used to overcome the hostility of workers to giving up traditional job controls. This exchange proved to be a limited and fragile basis for co-operation and certainly did not ever eliminate restriction of output. But an instrumental view of human labour was a far cry from a complex theory of motivation. Taylor was far more concerned with breaking the power of the workgroup and removing the basis for collective bargaining through individualistic payment systems (Littler, 1982: 55).

Ideology and practice

The consequences of the operation of such principles were explicitly recognised by Taylor. There would be a need for: extensive work measurement to predetermine tasks; the employment of cheaper, deskilled and substitutable labour in more fragmented jobs; a large increase in the number of non-productive employees to enforce, monitor and record new work arrangements; and functional foremanship that subdivided traditional responsibilities and involved reporting to the all-powerful planning department. It would, of course, be foolish to believe that all of this smoothly came to pass. In fact there are a number of writers who believe that Taylorism was a 'practical failure' and was not widely implemented, due largely to worker resistance and employer suspicions (Palmer, 1975; Edwards, 1979; Goldman and Van Houten, 1980). This view is often complemented by arguments that its significance is as a management *ideology* which was itself later discredited (Rose, 1978; Burawoy, 1979).

What is the balance of these two processes? We should certainly not underestimate the ideological purposes. Taylor himself emphasised the pressing need for a 'complete mental revolution' in the attitudes of the two parties. Whatever success was achieved can largely be attributed to the stress on the *scientific* character of the system, which traded on the predominantly uncritical attitudes to knowledge under such a mantle. Its technical orientation was of particular appeal and use to engineers in their struggle to establish themselves as the core management group in US industry (Armstrong, 1984). But there was a potential appeal to workers and unions from the same source; 'Under scientific management arbitrary power, arbitrary dictation, ceases; and every single subject, large and small, becomes the question for scientific investigation, for reduction to law' (Taylor, 1947: 211). The theoretical separation of authority from hierarchy was an attempt to construct some level of consent in the employment relation and, with the increased productivity and wages from the system, was to be the basis for the co-operation promised in Taylor's principles.

In practice it never quite worked like this. As an ideology of science it strengthened management by providing, 'the technocratic rationale for authority in formal organisations' (Kouzmin, 1980: 68). It was also flawed and contradictory in nature. It is strange that a science of management had to be based on knowledge and skills appropriated from workers. Of course it never was a science, but rather a control system, and has tended to be seen as a set of techniques to be countered and contested by generations of shop stewards. In one of his weaker moments, Taylor even admitted the stopwatch had an element of 'guesswork'.

Most of the misunderstandings concerning the practical success of Taylorism stem from confusion of what *criteria* to employ. Many of those who see it as a failure are viewing Taylorism as a coherent and total package. This is understandable given that it coincides with Taylor's own views and his tendency to withdraw co-operation when companies refused to follow all the complexities of the schemes. But it is wrong. We need to redefine the criteria in two ways. First, as already indicated, we must consider it as part of broader movement of systematic management that was implemented in a variety of forms. Second, it was also implemented in a selective manner: 'employers looked upon scientific management exactly as Taylor insisted that they should not: as an arsenal of devices designed to simplify and improve the management of labour' (Bendix, 1956: 286). All the elements were juggled about by companies according to their needs and prejudices. A close analysis of the early literature on 'Taylor firms' by Nelson (1975: 68–78) showed that none fully represented the principles set out in *Shop Management*. References to time study can be found in every firm, and planning departments were widespread. But incentive payment schemes were patchy and employers found that functional foremanship embodied too many layers of responsibility.

It is certainly true that resistance to scientific management from key economic actors was considerable (see Shenhav, 1999: 102–31). However, even taking this and other factors into account, we can recognise a widespread, if uneven, diffusion of key aspects of Taylorist practices in industrial societies in the 1920s and 1930s (Brown, 1977; Clawson, 1980; Littler, 1982; Nyland, 1988). Taylor's death in 1915 opened the door to a variety of consultants to introduce further versions of scientific management. Some were short-cut emulators, other were Taylor's disciples such as Gantt, and the Gilbreths with their extension of Taylor's early emphasis on the study of fatigue and their advances in the use of cameras to record and time movements. This factor and changes in the external environment guaranteed that scientific management did not spread in pure form. Additionally, if Taylorism is seen as part of a wider efficiency movement, we can see that it and related principles increasingly colonised 'progressive' thinking, with even Feminists trying to develop notions of domestic engineering (Shenhav, 1999: 96).

In current managerial and sociological literature Taylorism always appears as a dynamic duo with *Fordism*. Links there certainly were. Henry Ford's innovations in technical control through the flow assembly line extended Taylorist principles such as job fragmentation and allowed for a greater level of intensity of labour through speed-up of the line and other measures (Littler, 1982: 56–7). In addition, the scale of Ford's operations and his willingness to introduce the 'five dollar day' as a means of combating labour turnover enabled another of Taylor's principles – high wages for high productivity – to be realised. Ford's plants did not use the apparatus of Taylorite time and motion study, but the management nevertheless collected a considerable amount of information on tasks, so that, for example, they had enough information to produce 7800 individual job-profile sheets (Doray, 1988: 96). This reinforces a crucial point, that we must not fetishise Taylorism at the expense of the broader trend towards 'scientific' management. The managerial regime at Ford had its own innovations in labour utilisation, stretching the semi-skilled labour by a permanent process of de-manning and flexibility: a mode of operation that challenges the stereotype of rigid machinery, products and labour under mass production (Williams *et al.*, 1992b).

Meanwhile in Europe the most extensive implementation of neo-Taylorite schemes came through the *Bedeaux system*. Charles Bedeaux was a French full-time management consultant whose schemes were based on his 'discovery' of a universal measure for all work, given the name 'B unit'. He aggressively sold them as cheap and quick methods which did not need to have major consequences for existing management structures. Like the Gilbreths, he entered the unexplored territory of fatigue through basing the measurement on the proportions of work and rest required for completing a task. Though he had considerable international success, Bedeaux had his greatest impact in Britain where employers used the circumstances of the 1930s depression to install the system and utilise it for the purposes of rate cutting and speed-up (G. Brown, 1977; Littler, 1982). This example illustrates the way in which scientific management varied in both form and timing between and within countries. Whereas Britain's late adoption differed from the US and French models, other economies such as Germany and Sweden followed distinctive paths; for example combining rationalisation measures with greater use of psychological testing (Fridenson, 1978). Contrary to some recent studies, Taylorism did influence the organisation of work in Japan, but 'was used as a vehicle for job analysis and standardised procedures rather than as a comprehensive control system' (Littler, 1982: 156–7). Aspects of the latter, notably the separation of thinking and doing, as well as individual output norms, did not fit into pre-existing patterns of fluid job boundaries, work teams and the power of foremen over production planning.

Lack of uniformity was undoubtedly influenced by the pattern of resistance from a variety of groups. There has been well-documented resistance from craft and non-craft workers, using every method from strikes to informal disruption (Nadworny, 1955; Montgomery, 1976; G. Brown, 1977). Workers were particularly opposed to effects such as deskilling and speed-up, because, as one put it, he 'never knew a rate to be raised after a time study' (quoted in Baritz, 1960: 98). But the plain fact is that resistance did not succeed in stopping the long-term diffusion of scientific management, though it certainly delayed and mediated it. This is often put down to the gradual shift in union attitudes from opposition to reluctant accommodation and occasional enthusiastic co-operation. There is a great deal of truth in this assessment, though some unions had always had a conciliatory attitude, and the behaviour of official structures should not be confused with that of rank and file members who continued resistance. Indeed, the very institutionalisation of scientific management guarantees that it is accompanied by a low-intensity war at shop floor level.

Changes of this kind were influenced by later progressive Taylorites who lacked his hostility to trade unions and were prepared to give them an institutionalised role in work study and bonus schemes. Scientific management could also be given a progressive aura by its association with planning, Nyland (1988) showing that some of its adherents advocated the extension of the system to the whole society constraining the role of markets. He also correctly points to the neglect of Taylorism's wider capacity to improve work efficiency in the spheres of scheduling, stores management and purchasing and plant lay-out. Though whether this is enough to commend Taylorism despite the control dimension is more arguable.

Supervisory and managerial resistance also continued to be a considerable constraint in both the US and Britain (Nelson, 1975: 75–6; Littler, 1982: 181–2). New schemes tended not only to change traditional roles, but to erode decision-making powers. Employers and managers often found it hard wholly to embrace Taylorism. Taylor was often bitterly critical of their competence. It challenged their traditional judgement, discretion and powers, to say nothing of Taylor's straining their patience through contract stipulations that the company must do as exactly as he told them. The high costs, disrupted routines and social antagonisms meant that failure was more often linked to managerial opposition than that of workers.

Given the evidence, the problem of Taylorism is not *whether* it was introduced, but *how*, and its *limits* as a control system. We shall return to the former later, but with respect to the latter, right from the start many employers realised that Taylor's neglect of 'the human factor' and of what Friedman (1977) calls 'the positive aspects of labour', such as know-how and goodwill, made it impossible to use on its own. We shall return to the combination with psychological methods later, but even as a means of bureaucratisation of production, Taylorism was insufficient.

Weber and administrative theories of management

For some writers, the concept of bureaucratisation of production is a problematic one. Braverman (1974: 120) objects that it endorses the mistaken view that such work arrangements are endemic to large-scale organisation rather than a product of capitalist social relations. Our argument in this book is that bureaucratisation is a universal tendency, but can only be understood through the specific forms it takes in different modes of production or specific business systems. But there is a different point at stake. Braverman's influential theory of the labour process is constructed on the implicit assumption that what we have been describing as bureaucratisation could be fully represented by Taylorism. However, what Taylorism provided was a system of detailed control over work, aided by a set of bureaucratic rules, and Clawson (1980: 248) argues that this is in contrast to Weber's stress on the remote and impersonal qualities of bureaucracy.

We will return to this question later. For now it is sufficient to observe that Taylorism had far less to say about the *employment relationship*: 'those structural conditions which surround the appointment, promotion and dismissal of individuals' (Littler, 1982: 37). Athough scientific management was meant to be able to be applied at any given level of task or technology, it 'left management in the position of having a set of principles laying down how to make its workforce more productive, whilst possessing no body of knowledge that specifically applied from supervisory levels upward in the organisational hierarchy' (Clegg and Dunkerley, 1980: 99). This was particularly important in the context of the previously observed growth of middle management; middle managers were monitoring the performance of the operating units under their command, but were not subject to systematic evaluation themselves. It is Weber and other theorists of formal management and administration who can give us a greater understanding of developments of this nature. The emphasis here is on understanding; Weber was not a theorist-practitioner like Taylor and the ideas discussed below were not immediately implemented in organisations.

In common with most other writers, we do not intend to list all the complex features of bureaucracy that Weber includes as defining characteristics, but instead to group them under two headings.

The employment relationship

The office is a vocation and a full-time undertaking. Officials are selected on a basis of technical qualification, education and expertise. There is separation of office and office holder: it is not his or her property and the employee does not possess the means of administration. Thorough and expert training is part of the conditions of employment.

A career structure is provided based on the organisational hierarchy. Tenure is for life, with fixed salary, pension rights and appropriate social status. Officials are appointed by higher authority, not externally elected, and promotions similarly regulated, for example through seniority.

Work structures and relations

There is a hierarchy of offices, with continuous and regulated activity within a fully ordered system of super and subordination. Within the chain of command is a division of labour based on defined responsibilities, rights and duties. Calculable rules and regulations, impersonal modes of conduct and a common control system govern the conduct of work. Written documentation functions as a basis of management of the office.

From these characteristics it is understandable that some may question their links to the *bureaucratisation of production*. After all, the impetus for Weber's analysis came primarily from the organisation of the state and the regulation of administrative employees. The historical context is also important for an understanding of the significance of measures such as full-time work as a vocation. In the period under consideration, it was still important to break away from patrimonial, charismatic and other relations, whereby people could be placed in position through inheritance and similar 'private' attributes. Efficiency movements among engineers and other groups in the US at the turn of the century similarly stressed the need to eliminate favouritism, nepotism and unethical practices through standardised systems (Shenhav, 1999: 92).

The emphasis on calculable rules and regulations may seem a bit abstract. But both examples highlight that the ideal type of bureaucracy is linked to Weber's wider theory of *rationalisation*. We discussed the problematic character of the idea of rationality in Chapter 1, but rationalisation is held to be the key modernising characteristic for the development of industrial societies. Authority in industrial societies was rational because it was formal and based on precise and predictable rules, calculation and accounting. For these reasons the bureaucratic organisation and administration best permitted the development of appropriate attitudes, structures and practices in public and private sectors. In this context, bureaucracies are a specific type of rational-legal authority: officials work within a framework in which command and task are based on authority derived from impersonal rules. But Weber's theories are not as separate from production as they may appear. He made it clear that they referred to bureaucratic *management* as well as administration. The Weberian 'causal chain' (R. Collins, 1986: 21–9) links the concept of rationality explicitly to the emergence of capitalist enterprise and markets. These were held to be rational because of their capacity for calculability, predictability and routinisation – through production, distribution, accounting and market pricing mechanisms. Preconditions for this 'rationalised' capitalism started from the complete private appropriation of the means of production which, Weber said, must be unhampered by 'irrational obstacles' such as workers' rights to participate in management. In addition, there was the need for common management, free labour under the compulsion of the 'whip of hunger', mass markets, minimal trade restrictions and institutional, legal support from the bureaucratic state.

Weber also argued that large capitalist enterprises were becoming 'unequalled modes of strict bureaucratic organisation' (Weber, 1984: 32). He was aware and approving of the role played by scientific management in this process. It was 'completely' the ideal vehicle for the necessary imposition of military discipline in the factory, given its capacity for dehumanisation and conditioning of work performance. Techniques such as Taylor's 'shop cards', which specified the daily routines of employees, were ideal vehicles of bureaucratisation. What is more, Taylor saw management by 'scientific' methods as a move away from traditional authority where owners and managers attempted to control by inefficient personal means. On reflection, it is therefore possible to see that Weber's schema is not only compatible with Taylorism, but also that the practices he describes can reinforce systems of work control. Formal structures of management enhance centralisation of power, and hierarchical organisation aids functional specialisation, task fragmentation and labour discipline, while emphasis on predictable performance minimises the discretion of employees.

But, as Littler (1982) argues, it is in the sphere of the employment relationship that Weber adds something new. The career structure linked to the bureaucratic hierarchy strengthened a commitment to the organisation absent from Taylorism. A specific form of bureaucratic motivation is also sustained by the identification of job security, status, rewards and performance with organisational structure. Employees may react against the bureaucratisation of control embodied in rules prescribing the way a task is performed, but welcome rules governing selection, training and promotion within the employment relationship. Nor is this necessarily confined to office administration.

Insights derived from Weberian theory have been applied in Britain and the US from the late 1940s. But companies were able to draw on parallel developments in classical management theory in the inter-war period. Other theorists of formal organisation were, like Weber, concerned to tackle the administration of the whole enterprise. By far the most significant was Fayol, a Frenchman who shared the engineering and management background of Taylor. 'Fayolism' inspired, amongst other developments, the reorganisation of railway and engineering companies, and department stores in France (Fridenson, 1978); and translation of his short text enabled him to gain wider influence. His main concern was to establish the validity of studying and training management itself, not just the management of others. Emphasis was put on formulating general features of management, first in the form of five elements – planning, organising, commanding, co-ordination and control – then through fourteen principles. The themes contained in the latter echo and extend Taylor and Weber; they include division of work, stability of tenure, authority of command and subordination of the individual interest to the general (for the full list see Pugh, 1983: 66). One principle, that of unity of command, differed sharply from Taylor's belief in functional authority.

The basis of the approach in Fayol and other similar theorists such as Gullick and Urwick was oriented to rationalising management structures, often through centralisation and specified spans of control; emphasis on the managerial role in setting and securing goals; and planning for the optimal use of resources. Modern management came to take many of these things for granted, which led some to invest Fayol's theorising with a high status and lasting effect. In fact his work was more of a practical guide with simple 'plan-ahead proverbs' (Perrow, 1979: 70) akin to today's numerous management handbooks. Later writers are more likely to prefer the judgement of Clegg and Dunkerley that 'the "principles" are neither universally empirically applicable, nor theoretically coherent' (1980: 103).

What matters more than flawed hand-me-down principles is that classical theories were engaging with real changes in economy and enterprise. When Chandler began to use the railroad as his blueprint for large-scale organisation, his emphasis was on the emergence of organisational charts, hierarchies of office and functional authority. This can be linked to a wider and related argument from Williamson (1975, 1981) that organisations emerge in the form of hierarchies when markets fail. Or to be more precise, when it is more efficient to internalise transactions – for labour, components, services and so on – within multi-divisional or vertically-integrated firms, than to have them mediated by and through the market. Because markets become increasingly complex, prices and other indicators cannot give complete information which allows individuals to cost transactions accurately. This uncertainty and complexity can often be better handled through organisations constituted as bureaucratic hierarchies, because they can monitor behaviour, establish rules and procedures and provide better information and control. Rowlinson (1997) notes that Chandler (1977) is unusual in defending bureaucracy on efficiency grounds, and is borrowing in part from Weber. The end result, however, is that managerial hierarchy necessarily supplements market power.

By 1918, the 'visible hand' that had brought the vertically integrated bureaucracies into existence was extended to defining the role and specific tasks of top management within general offices. The context was a further centralisation of administration, often within new multidivisional structures such as those at General Motors. This process included uniform accounting and statistical controls that allowed senior administrators to evaluate managerial performance and exercise long-range planning. In Chandler's later work (1990), he emphasises that investment in production and distribution that facilitated economies of scale is combined with further investment in managerial skills that lead to economies of scope and enhanced organisational capabilities. Supple comments,

> From these viewpoints, the modern industrial firm is crucially characterised by expansion overseas, by product diversification, and (most significantly) by administrative complexity – that is, by the growth in the number of its operating units, each carrying out a different economic function and all co-ordinated by a management hierarchy. (Supple, 1991: 504–5)

This focus on organisational design at the broader level is valuable, but partial. Chandler neglected the management of labour, while Williamson fails to make connections between multidivisional structures and employment relationships in his analysis of transaction costs (Rowlinson, 1999: 210).

The rise of bureaucratic control and its contradictions

Bureaucratisation also developed at the level of work and employment relationships. A number of modern radical theorists argue that in the post-war period employers increasingly turned to strategies of bureaucratic control for the shop floor. Techniques centred on stability and predictability of workforce behaviour, based in turn on enhancing rules, hierarchy and detailed division of labour are, 'recognisable to Weberian students of bureaucracy' (Goldman and Van Houten, 1977: 117). Richard Edward's research on companies such as Polaroid, IBM and General Electric points to two crucial features of the strategy: a finely-graded stratification and division of the workforce; and hierarchical structures devised to divide and conquer, which tend to 'break up the homogeneity of the firm's workforce, creating many seemingly separate strata, lines of work, and focuses for job identity' (1979: 133). In addition, impersonal rules form the basis of company policy, and detailed and specified criteria for job descriptions and performance are monitored by supervisors, rather than work tasks being directly enforced. The stress is on positive incentives in performance, not negative sanctions. When taken together with the system of job security and 'career' structure through job hierarchies, long-term identification with the company can be built.

Hence, contrary to Clawson's view, impersonality and 'remoteness' can be an effective control mechanism. It is worth remembering the point established by Edwards: that bureaucratic controls are not necessarily synonymous with close, direct or coercive authority. They rely more on *standardisation* of work processes, outputs and skills. By reducing the amount of stimuli, information and premises for decisions, behaviour can be formalised and regulated (March and Simon, 1958). The resultant indirect or unobtrusive controls are effective enough to enable the workforce to be trusted to make more decisions within established parameters, without necessarily having to change their attitudes. Popular and expert opinion points to the costs of wasteful bureaucracy. But as Richard Edwards observes: 'The core corporations survive and prosper on their ability to organise the routine, normal efforts of workers, not on their ability to elicit peak performances' (1979: 146).

We have been talking as if such bureaucratic work organisation only favours management. This is to miss part of the point. Many of its features benefit workers, or at least those who are long-term core employees. Such benefits include mobility through internal labour markets, seniority rules governing pay and lay-offs, grievance procedures, job protection and demarcation. In well-organised union workplaces, these are enforced through plant-wide collective bargaining or informal shop floor power. As part of this process there is a limited movement towards positive benefits for co-operation rather than negative sanctions: 'a system of mutually binding rules, material and symbolic incentives, and eventually the emergence of an ethos that is impersonally oriented towards performance' (Rueschemeyer, 1986: 94).

This use of Weberian categories as explanatory tools indicates their continuing relevance, but also their limitations. Clearly, bureaucratic structures have no universal rationality. Rather, they are in part consciously constructed by employers for specific purposes that cannot be reduced to 'efficiency'. A further qualification needs to be made in relation to the *legitimacy* arising from bureaucratic systems: undoubtedly they can generate loyalty and commitment, but the position of shop floor workers is not comparable to that of higher officials of a public organisation such as the civil service, which provides long-term security and stable career structures with a minimum conflict of interests. Private companies are seldom able to match those kinds of conditions, and the centrality of the effort bargain (the implicit 'contract' between employee input and reward) will always tend to introduce uncertainty and conflict into the employment relationship.

The consolidation of bureaucracy in the private and public sectors also led to a lively debate among neo-Weberian writers in the 1950s and 1960s about the variations in, and limits to, the bureaucratic ideal-type. These case study critiques have been reworked many times in texts, but it is worth highlighting some key features and issues, in part to demonstrate that many current debates on new organisations are drawing on an established track record. A central feature has been the unintended consequences of bureaucratic modes of operation, for instance in relation to *efficiency*. Writers such as Merton (1949) have pointed to the dangers of rule-following becoming an end in itself, leading to the excesses of 'red tape'. Standardisation and predictability could easily degenerate into rigidity and defensive behaviour – a kind of 'trained incapacity' resistant to innovation. This was therefore proof of the dysfunctional effects of some bureaucratic practices. *Rationality* does not escape. There is a whole sub-literature stressing the rational propensity for employees to break, bend or modify rules in order to get things done more effectively. Hence the oft-quoted adage that a 'work to rule' is an extremely damaging form of industrial action. Blau (1955) exemplifies this kind of argument through his studies of a state employment agency and a federal law enforcement agency in the US. At the law enforcement agency it was more functional to ignore rules such as those related to reporting attempted bribery, in order to be in a position of power over the perpetrators at a later date.

The case studies also indicate the existence of alternatives within bureaucratisation. The most famous derives from Gouldner's (1954) examination of gypsum mines in a closed, rural community. This showed how a form of bureaucracy based on shared knowledge and consent to rules – characterised as a 'mock bureaucracy' based on an 'indulgency pattern' reflecting the nature of the community – was challenged by a new manager acting on behalf of a cost-conscious parent company. Control was reasserted in a 'punishment-centred bureaucracy' through highly centralised authority, formalisation of rules and new technology. A theme of the above debates was the 'costs' of control, predictability and purely calculative exchange. In part this echoed themes from the then influential human relations movement (see next chapter), notably the tension between formal rules and informal practices, as well as the need for a human dimension in design.

Other well-known post-war studies have developed typologies of organisational structure, with an emphasis on different types of bureaucracy. For example, the Aston

Studies (see Chapter 5 and Pugh *et al.*, 1963, 1969) tried to identify causal relations between size, other variables and bureaucratisation, which led them to develop a structural taxonomy, focusing on three main types. *Full bureaucracies* – closest to Weber's ideal type – were based on a high level of standardisation of activities, concentration of authority and impersonal control; but were held not to exist in pure form outside central government. In contrast to this, *workflow bureaucracies* had highly structured activities such as production schedules, but more decentralised authority within the command framework. This type was found to be characteristic of large manufacturing concerns. Finally, smaller branch plants or parts of local government manifested bureaucratised employment relationships, but a low structuring of activities and control exercised in a more personal way; these were dubbed *personnel bureaucracies*.

In a later study Mintzberg (1983) identified five basic configurations:

- *Simple structure* direct supervision based on the strategic apex.
- *Machine bureaucracy* standardisation of work based on the technostructure.
- *Professional bureaucracy* standardisation of skills based on the operating core.
- *Divisional form* standardisation of outputs based on the middle line.
- *Adhocracy* rests on mutual adjustment/informal communication, with support staff playing the key role.

These configurations embody forms that pull organisations in different directions. Naturally hybrid forms can result, or different structures in different parts of the firm; but 'the organisation is often drawn toward one of the configurations in its search for harmony of structure' (Mintzberg, 1983: 288). If the five configurations are examined, we can see that all but the adhocracy are indeed variations on bureaucracy. Borrowed from Toffler's *Future Shock* (1970), the latter's design parameters are based on organic structures, low levels of standardisation and formalisation of behaviour, decentralisation and matrix-like use of specialists. This concept anticipates the arguments, examined in Chapters 11 and 12, that we are seeing a trend towards post-bureaucratic organisation.

Scientific management and bureaucratic work rules: modern legacies

The legacy of Taylorism and bureaucracy has long been sharply disputed. The former has been reviled for its apparent barbarity and economism, while the latter, as Jacques (1990) observes, has been pronounced dead and buried many times for the sins of killing initiative and crushing creativity.

There is little doubt that any burials have been premature. Scientific management was brought out of the broom cupboard by the radical theorist Braverman (1974). The argument that Taylorism constituted *the* means of managerial control in the twentieth century (see Chapter 8 for details) has been shown to be exaggerated, but there is plenty of evidence that key elements of the system have been updated and extended. Ossie Jone's (1994) entertaining account of life as a work study engineer in the 1970s and 1980s shows how the traditional techniques of method and time study were superseded by a system known as Simplified Pre-Determined Motion Time Study (SPMTS). This is merely one of a long line of innovations throughout the century. SPMTS was favoured by the engineers and would have delighted Taylor in that it promised the illusion of the removal of the 'subjective' element of rating from work measurement. Such developments may not convince all the sceptics given that they admittedly focus on a narrow, if well-known, feature of scientific management. More convincing is the rise of the influential management fix known as business re-engineering or core process redesign, whose tools – activity value analysis, time compression management and so on – and ethos are clearly rooted in Taylorism and classical theories (Thackray, 1993). With respect to the latter, as will be seen in Chapter 7, the emphasis in classical perspectives on universal principles and practices in management is also alive and well, particularly in the burgeoning genre of popular business literature.

The intimate and reciprocal interaction between the legacies of Taylor and Weber has been the subject of deservedly influential writings. In *Business Week*, Adler described the system in operation in Japanese-influenced lean production at NUMMI and other advanced manufacturing plants as a learning bureaucracy. Rules remains at the heart of the process: '[NUMMI] is obsessive about standardised work procedures. It sees what one NUMMI manager has called "the intelligent interpretation of Taylor's time and motion studies" as the principal key to success' (P. Adler 1993: 103). Even the benchmarking systems underpinning total quality management (TQM) require a concern for standardised procedures and uniform, dependable practices (Wilkinson and Willmott, 1994; Tuckman, 1994). If anything, bureaucratic rules have been spreading more rapidly in the service sector. Evidence for the *bureaucratisation of service* is most recently associated with Ritzer's (1993) 'McDonaldization of society' thesis, introduced earlier. He marshals a considerable array of evidence to argue persuasively that fast food chains are the tip of an iceberg that has extended Weber's principles of rationalisation in the form of calculable, predictable, quantified processes to an increased range of retail, leisure and media services. We should also not forget one of the central arguments of this chapter, that the distinctive contribution of Weber lay particularly in understanding the employment relationship. If current developments are examined, we can observe a number of factors that have combined to increase significantly the use of bureaucratic employment measures. These include fear of litigation in the fields of gender and race, adaptation to legislation on employment rights, and conformity to collectively bargained procedures on equitable recruitment, promotion and dismissal.

Conclusion

Whether such tendencies are dominant or 'against the grain' requires a more detailed evaluation, and we will pick up this story again in Chapters 8, 11 and 12. But we should not get contemporary developments out of proportion. One of the lessons of this chapter is that Taylorism and other management theories are not packages and, given the separable nature of their elements, any practical legacy will be diverse and uneven. Furthermore, the history of large-scale organisation shows that managers combine elements of different approaches according to perceived need and fashion. The respective traditions embody a permanent tension between different approaches to the management of work organisation. While this is frequently described in mainstream writing as technical and human organisation and the need to integrate the two, it may be more accurately thought of in terms of competing control systems. The neglect of the informal dimensions of organisational life by classical theories left gaps that had to be filled. How this was done will be considered in the next chapter.

4 Managing the Human Factor

Before 1912–13, engineering, accounting, and economics were the only bodies of knowledge relevant to systematic management. If consolidations of the 'human factor' were at all involved, they were based on philosophy, ethics and religion (Shenhav, 1999: 181).

Managers had, by the early part of the twentieth century, already drawn on the expertise of people such as Taylor and other consultants in order to develop systems of controlling the labour process. It was not enough. As Baritz observes in his brilliant account of the historical uses of social science in American industry, 'Increasingly the men who manage and direct industry, find themselves incapable of effectively controlling their organisations' (1960: 3). After the First World War, some major corporations began financing industrial psychology and endowing business schools as part of a process of research and experimentation. That interaction was eventually to result in the emergence of the *human relations* approach to management. The two approaches have traditionally been seen as opposites. Perrow's somewhat tongue-in-cheek description sums it up: 'From the beginning, the forces of light and darkness have polarised the field of organisational analysis, and the struggle has been protracted and inconclusive' (1973: 2). However the forces of darkness and light may not be as far apart as they seem. For a start, corporate co-operation with social scientists arose from the same source as links with Taylorism: the vulnerability of management to the appeal of planning and science.

This chapter explores the historical development of human relations thinking, and examines its claims to distinctiveness, and the legacies it leaves to modern management theories and practices, including human resource management (HRM).

Social science and industry: a courtship

The courtship between social science and industry began with the promise of a dowry in the form of a battery of tests and measurements offered to fit people to jobs (see Chapter 13 for further detail). While this does represent a shift from measurement of work to measurement of people, it was not wholly new. This kind of intervention represented a version of Taylor's 'scientific selection of the worker' by other means. In fact the *Bulletin of the Taylor Society* carried articles discussing issues of human personality and arguing that newly recruited workers should be tested for personality, character and temperament. In 1915, an article about one factory noted that:

> A system of cards was used, one side of each card contained information about the worker's identity, parents, ethnic origins and previous employment; the other contained a certain amount of medico-psychological information ('anaemic', 'nonchalant') and notes on the individual's degree of motivation and way of life ('father out of work', 'mother agreed to take care of child', etc.). This was followed

by his medical record (doctor, optician, dentist) and by basic health advice on the need for rest and fresh air. (Doray, 1988: 188)

This was part of a growing interest shown by engineers in the human factor and employment issues. Professional journals began to run articles such as 'Personality in the Shop Psychology of the Female Employee' (see Shenhav, 1999: 182).

This primitive psychology was openly geared towards manipulation of the 'uncertainties of human nature' (Shenhav, 1999: 174). In this sense, far from being a different academic species, it is arguable that the human relations current was partly prefigured in engineering discourses and derived from a form of Taylorist revisionism. Nor did it challenge Taylorism on its traditional territory of organisation of work. Nevertheless the battle cry of 'neglect of the human factor' did represent a partial critique that was directed against the costs of scientific management in terms of resistance and disenchantment. The simple appeal and apparent applicability of the variety of tests convinced a growing minority of employers. Problems arose when naive enthusiasm and unrealistic expectations quickly ran up against the crude nature and limited results arising from the techniques. By the mid-1920s, and in changed economic circumstances, the tests had been abandoned by most companies (Baritz, 1960: 71).

Though a similar overlap in topics with scientific management can be observed (see Table 3.1), accounts of the development of British industrial psychology (M. Rose, 1975: 65–87; G. Brown, 1977: 213–28) show it to be more sober, centralised, less consultancy-based and affecting even fewer firms. It took a particular interest – derived from experiences of the Industrial Fatigue Research Board during the war – in monotony. Fatigue was, as we have seen, an issue that also concerned the scientific management movement, linked as it was to the need for the successful measurement of work. Common interests and client relations again meant, as in the US, 'a large proportion of the their problems had to be taken over from the scientific managers' (M. Rose, 1975: 86). But despite sharing some common assumptions about efficiency,

Contents page of *Industrial Psychology*, ed. Charles Myers   *TABLE 3.1*

Source: C. Myers (1929) *Industrial Psychology,* London: Thornton Butterworth productivity and work organisation, British researchers established a distance, criticising, for instance, the anti-social and abnormal assumptions underlying notions of work rate under Taylorism (Myers, 1926: 81).

Myers perceptively noted the hostility generated among workers by scientific management through its attack on skills, and the effects of speed-up and time and motion study. He made attacks on the notion of 'one best way', rightly pointing to the greater complexity of behaviour and industrial conditions. This critique was linked to a more sympathetic consideration of the need to convince the trade unions of the validity of social science interventions, and to win more generally the consent of the workforce. The relatively progressive stance of British industrial psychologists is further illustrated by their alliance with a small group of employers centred on the Quaker families such as Rowntree, who shared their enthusiasm for 'scientific planning' and dislike for the harsher aspects of Taylorism. When those companies began to utilise psychologists, however, there was still considerable suspicion and resistance from employees, particularly when it was introduced at the same time as scientific management methods (G. Brown, 1977: 216). The Quaker tapestry firm, Lee's, divided the managerial responsibility for 'psychology' and Taylorist 'mechanics' between the owner's two sons (Johnson and Moore, 1986). Most British employers, however, still preferred to cut costs simply by squeezing wages and exploiting favourable market circumstances.

But industrial psychology was not as isolated a phenomena as it appeared. In the US particularly it was part of a wider period of experimentation involving human relations and Taylorist management, as employers chose within and between the new techniques. Richard Edwards (1979: 102) gives an interesting example of the Bancroft textile company employing a consultant to introduce welfare work in 1902, and Taylor's follower Gantt to reorganise production in 1905! *Welfarism* was a significant part of that context. A paternalistic concern for the well-being of employees in return for loyalty and hard work, had a long pedigree in some companies. Company towns were one manifestation, as employers provided houses, schools, stores, sanitation and lighting in order to attract an adequate labour force. But the rhetoric had shifted from older themes of community and improving the workingman to ones of entitlements and better working conditions (Barley and Kunda, 1992: 372).

Welfare work was also present in conventional circumstances. An increasing number of firms began to employ welfare secretaries whose role ranged from encouraging a 'proper moral atmosphere' to the provision of social and medical facilities. This interest was not philanthropic – 'Capital will not invest in sentiment', as one leading employer put it (quoted in Nelson, 1975: 104). It arose from attempts to grapple with the recruitment and motivation problems deriving from the increasing size of the labour force and a new industrial relations situation shaped by declining loyalty and rising unrest. There was a parallel development in the growth of employment or personnel departments as a means of dealing 'scientifically' with such issues – again showing an overlap with Taylorism. In the US and Britain, professional personnel bodies grew from the seeds of welfare work.

But in the latter country, welfarism was strongly connected to the study of fatigue in the laboratory of wartime factories. As in the US, British welfarism was described by one of its leading members as combining 'pity and profit' (quoted in G. Brown, 1977: 185). Lee's issued 'partnership certificates' to employees who had shown a genuine interest in the company. Many workers, particularly the women who were its prime object, saw its motivation as directed primarily towards profit, given the emphasis on improving conditions for the sole purpose of maximising output. After the war, changing economic circumstances saw the decline of welfare initiatives. But in the US, to a greater extent than Britain, there was a broader framework of 'welfare capitalism'. Companies such as General Electric, International Harvester and US Steel continued policies of off-the-job benefits in the form of insurance, healthcare, pensions, social clubs, profit-sharing schemes and other measures (R. Edwards, 1979: 91–7).

The process took many different forms. Take Ford, for example. The company had only limited social provision, but it had social control potential. The 'Sociological Department' had investigators who were empowered to visit homes to check on absentees and monitor an employee's family, values and habits. But this social control mechanism did not exist in the abstract. To act as a counterweight to the assembly line and associated problems of labour turnover and unionisation, Ford had profit-sharing schemes and the famed five dollar day. The Department could therefore ascertain the 'fitness' of workers for these generous rewards!

In a period in which space was opened up for employers by defeated industrial militancy and repression of socialist organising, welfarism in the US also had close ties to the development of company unions. This was different from the kind of enterprise unions initiated more recently by Japanese employers. The former arose primarily from wartime attempts to institute limited forms of worker representation such as works councils. After the war many large companies, often utilising their new personnel departments, were quick to consolidate this trend by initiating company unions as a focus for formal grievance procedures, thus alleviating the need for independent union representation (Edwards, 1979: 106). There was some success in delaying or undermining unionism, and employers learnt some important lessons on the importance of controlled employee involvement and formal procedures. But, as in Britain, little survived the economic changes associated with the growing depression and sharpening social polarisation. Company unionism and welfarism did not provide an adequate means of pursuing collective interests of workers, while at the same time they became a financial burden for employers without solving any of their fundamental control problems inside the factory.

Hawthorne and beyond

The Hawthorne studies occupy a pivotal place in organisational theory. Begun in the mid-1920s, the research was carried out in the large Hawthorne plant employing 29 000 workers making electrical appliances for Bell as a subsidiary of American Telegraph and Telephone (AT&T). Management regarded themselves as progressive, but this was with regard to a willingness to experiment rather than their general attitudes, for they were strongly anti-union. The significance of Hawthorne does not lie in the results of the research as such, for both its findings and methods are widely regarded as highly questionable (Carey, 1967; Silver, 1987). Rather it reflects two factors. First is the sustained nature of the intervention itself, combining psychologists, sociologists and anthropologists. In this way the courtship between social science and industry became something of a formal engagement. Second, the interpretation of the results became the core of human relations theory and subsequent managerial practices. This was partly due to the propagandising work of Elton Mayo (1946), despite the fact that he did not join the team properly until 1928 and was much more peripheral than those who actually wrote up the detailed research such as Roethlisberger and Dickson (1939, Science Editions 1964) and, to a lesser extent, Whitehead (1938).

Let us retrace these steps briefly. Early experiments centred on varying the lighting for two small test groups of women workers. The purpose was to identify conditions affecting worker performance. Unfortunately no firm conclusions could be drawn, as productivity increased under every level of illumination and even for the control group that was not being subjected to any changes at all! At the time this caused great puzzlement, but it was later theorised that the real change had been the segregation of a small group, which blossomed under special attention and treatment. Thus the 'Hawthorne effect' was born, through which it was recognised that the research intervention itself is an independent variable in its effects on human behaviour. Initially the puzzlement led to a further stage of experiments on groups of women selected for their degree of friendship with one another. Again the emphasis was on manipulation of environmental variables, this time of a greater variety: rest pauses, length of working day, group bonus schemes and so on. Observers, initially placed in a test room, were gradually encouraged to act like supervisors and become more friendly with the group. Until 1929, in almost all cases output rose, with the only consistent factor again the effects of creating a special group with its identity strengthened by the replacement of two 'uncooperative' members. However, worker interest in experiments declined and output fell with the onset of the depression. Furthermore, additional experiments with two other groups to further test the effects of incentives and rest pauses had inconclusive results, both experiments being discontinued amidst some discord.

All this confusion might appear to be grounds for giving up. But a more positive line was taken that a constant factor was the significance of employee attitudes and the influence of supervisory techniques upon them. The successful experiments were those that allowed the individuals to coalesce into a group, though it is difficult to imagine how the special conditions could be transferred.

> Right now I couldn't ask for anything better than I have. I just can't explain what it is but I sure like it in the test room. . . . I think we work for the most wonderful man in the Western Electric Company. We have no boss. Mr.___ simply waits on us. . . . We have privileges that a lot of the other girls don't have. We are allowed to go down and lie on the couch when we are tired or don't feel good, and the matron was told not to say anything to us. Of course, none of us have done that yet because we always feel pretty good and we have rest periods and can do anything we want to in those ten minutes.
>
> (Roethlisberger and Dickson, 1964: 144)

Attitudes are not simply created by interaction with management. Employee preoccupations arise from a variety of sources, so further means were found of identifying them. Even while the above experiments were going on, the company and researchers had initiated an interviewing programme to explore the relations between employee morale and supervision. 'Counsellors' were trained by researchers to play the role of the observers in the illumination phase. Over a long period of time, a variety of formal and more open-ended techniques of interviewing were utilised as a means of gaining information and of detecting, diverting and redirecting dissatisfactions. The counsellor was told by the company, 'to watch constantly for signs of unrest and to try to assuage the tension of the worker by discussion before the unrest became active' (quoted in Fischer and Sirriani, 1984: 182). Employee complaints were treated as unreliable due to their vagueness (hot, cold, damp, smoky or dusty were apparently inferior to 'the temperature in the room was 67°F'); or because they really revealed some personal, external disturbance. Even when told of grievances, management did not act on them. Aside from letting off steam, the process could also be used to adjust employees to the work situation and screen out effective counsellors as management material.

A final phase of research linked together the concern with employee attitudes and the earlier focus on the group. The famed 'bank wiring room' experiments were based on an existing workgroup carrying out wiring, soldering and inspecting tasks with a supposedly unobtrusive observer present. What was 'discovered' on the face of it was no different from Taylor's observations in the steel industry: the workgroup systematically controlled and restricted output on the basis of their own conception of a fair day's work and enforced group norms on any fellow workers who deviated by overproducing (rate-busters) or under-working (chisellers).

> One day an interviewer entered a department unobserved. There was a buzz of conversation and the men seemed to be working at great speed. Suddenly there was a sharp hissing sound. The conversation died away, and there was a noticeable slowing up in the work pace. The interviewer later discovered from an acquaintance in the department that he had been mistaken for a rate setter. One of the workmen, who acted as a lookout, had stepped on a valve releasing compressed air, a prearranged signal for slowing down.
>
> (Roethlisberger and Dickson, 1964: 386)

The interpretation and reaction were, however, sharply different. Despite the restrictions, cliques and hostilities, a more accommodating picture was endorsed of group identities. Instead of suppressing the group and attempting to individualise its members, human relations is concerned to cultivate its sentiments and switch its loyalties to management. Roethlisberger and Dickson note: 'It is as well to recognise that informal organisation is not "bad", as they are sometimes assumed to be' (1964: 559). As it is fruitless to try and destroy it, management's task is to achieve a greater harmony between the informal and formal organisation. This can be done through controlled participation, effective communication and socially skilled, humane supervision. Referring to the experience of one of the Hawthorne experimental groups, Mayo commented that, 'Before every change of program, the group is consulted. Their comments are listened to and discussed; sometimes their objections are allowed to negative a suggestion. The group undoubtedly develops a sense of participation in the critical determination and becomes something of a social unit' (quoted in Baritz, 1960: 88–9). Here we can see the seeds of every superficial consultation exercise in the managerial toolkit!

As an alternative managerial *tactic* this new way of managing the small group made a lot of sense; indeed a minority of British employers were reaching similar conclusions (G. Brown, 1977: 243). Today, as we shall see later, it is applied in new and more sophisticated ways in current teamwork practices. The problem, however, arises from how Mayo and the human relations tradition theorised their understanding of Hawthorne. They were determined to fashion a general theory of behaviour in organisations. Later management theorists have dubbed a key element of this approach 'social man' (Schein, 1965). For Mayo, this started from a critique of the so-called 'rabble hypothesis' he attributed to economists and management theorists such as Taylor, in which individuals act solely according to rational self-interest. In contrast, 'social man' proceeds from the assumption that the major human need is for social solidarity that can be satisfied through group association. Naturally, this downplays the role of economic incentives. Such associations are seen to create social routines that substitute for logical and individual self-interest. Mayo preferred the term 'non-logical' to 'irrational', but the essential message is clear: workers act according to sentiments and emotions.

Contrary to some accounts, he did not believe that management was by definition and contrast rational, for all individuals were held to be governed by the same abstract instincts and needs. Rather managers and administrators could *become* rational, precisely because they can free themselves from social routines and the accompanying emotional involvement. This is an extremely curious notion, as any analysis of management shows that it has *its own* routines and 'illogicalities'. But it indicates the uncritical attitude of human relations writers towards the economic élites. Interestingly the new theorists of corporate culture (see later and Chapter 13) manage to maintain the emphasis on emotions, symbolism and 'irrationality' without separating management and workforce in the same way.

It must also be said that the empirical basis for Mayo's assertions in the Hawthorne experience is very shaky. Group solidarity was carefully engineered through the selection and treatment of those workers involved, even to the point of replacing 'uncooperative' workers. Even this did not sustain co-operative activity. Mayo interpreted restriction of output as a combination of group sentiments and lack of trust in management. But there are alternative and simpler explanations: 'Restriction of output by voluntary norms was a rational response by primarily economically-oriented agents to the increasingly likely prospect of unemployment' (Clegg and Dunkerley, 1980: 131). Environmental influences on employee attitudes were recognised, but it was held that the consequences could be dealt with and 'adjusted' inside the enterprise.

The denial of economic factors led to some absurd psychologisms. Mayo used the curious term 'pessimistic reveries' to account for industrial unrest of any kind. Put another way, strikes and other actions that restrict output are obsessive preoccupations and signs of maladjustment, even to the point of identifying industrial unrest with mental breakdown and casting trade union leaders as psychological deviants! Not surprisingly, unions very rarely get mentioned in Mayo's writings. That did not stop later followers. The psychologist McMurry argued that not only were unions unnecessary when management acted fairly, workers joined unions not to protect their jobs and improve pay, but because of unconscious cravings to improve the emotional situation at work (Baritz, 1960: 175). Seemingly, social science had not improved much on the primitive psychology of engineering discourses, which two decades earlier had been describing striking employees as 'explosive workers' with strike-prone personalities and backgrounds of juvenile delinquency (see Shenhav, 1999: 189)!

It would, however, be misleading to view human relations through its excesses. To add to 'social man', a second highly influential level of theorisation emphasised the essentially co-operative nature of the enterprise. In fact the two were linked, as Mayo continually referred to the supposed eager desire of workers for co-operative activity. It is easy to dismiss this kind of analysis, particularly given the capacity of human relations researchers to systematically ignore or re-interpret conflictual processes. But they *had* identified significant changes in the socio-economic sphere that brought the issue of co-operation to the fore. They pointed to the disparity between the attention paid to technical efficiency and economic functions, and the absence of 'the development of skills and techniques for securing co-operation' (Roethlisberger and Dickson, 1964: 552). The need to improve the latter was especially important because, as Mayo recognised, the balance between technical and social skills had been disrupted as workers' traditional forms of craft socialisation and identity had been undermined by mechanisation and the assembly line.

Emphasis is therefore put on the role of management to use the formal organisation to intervene in the *informal*, so as to create and sustain consent. Only in this context can we understand what appear to be the superficial solutions of human relations practices, with their prescriptions of 'democratic' supervision, good communications, teamwork and socially skilled leadership. Mayo's 'lifelong obsession with social harmony' (M. Rose, 1975: 115), was not based merely on his distorted empirical observations; it was underwritten by an organic model of society in which equilibrium and stability are the natural order of things, while structural divisions and conflicts are pathological. Mayo was worried about the 'extensive maladjustment of our times' as a period of rapid change undermined values and atomised individuals. The task was to recreate a sense of community inside the workplace.

During the same period Chester Barnard, the President of New Jersey Bell Telephone Company, was developing an even heavier emphasis on the basis for human co-operation, which was to have a major impact on later mainstream theorists (Perrow, 1979). Co-operation necessary to the survival of society could be most clearly observed in organisations. Unequal power and resources were irrelevant against the 'fact' that individuals voluntarily entered and submitted themselves to a common goal unachievable without collective effort. Organisations were rational and individuals were not. But this virtual deification of the formal organisation, like Mayo, still reserved the key role for management. The rationality of the 'non-personal' organisation was in practice again located with the executive élite who, as decision-makers, had responsibility for what Peters and Waterman, in praising Barnard, describe as 'managing the values of the organisation' (1982: 26). For co-ordination was still required to make a system, particularly as a sense of common purpose was not always present amongst the 'lower participants'. Barnard therefore reinforced the emphasis, not just on co-operation, but on the balance of formal and informal. As Perrow points out, this is the most extreme identification with the formal organisation, devoid of any concern about the negative effects of power and domination, or even the stress in human relations on sympathetic supervision and controlled participation.

Consolidating human relations

Recognising the significance of co-operative activity was an advance, but it was wrong to transfer the analysis from the workgroup to the organisation as a whole. The fundamental contradiction at the heart of human relations and of Barnard is that co-operation, even of the 'spontaneous' kind, has to be created. Reed refers to an intellectual schizophrenia whereby, 'a theoretical framework is forced to reconcile the contradictions generated by a metaphysic that assumes collective moral consensus as a social given and at the same time advocates the adoption of techniques whereby this may be engineered' (1986: 6). There is a therefore a wide consensus among the critics we have discussed that the significance of the tradition is to be located in its *ideological appeal*. M. Rose (1975: 124) puts this most succinctly in his memorable comment that Mayoism was the twentieth century's most seductive managerial ideology, in which social scientists and managers fashioned each other in their own image.

There is a great deal of accuracy in the view that one of its major functions was to legitimate the power and authority of both emergent professional 'classes' of managers and industrial consultants. The problem is that such an analysis can slip into giving the impression that human relations was a gigantic, if dangerous, con-trick with no purchase on reality. In part the reverse is true, for it only makes sense as a reaction to and means of shaping new realities. The depth of economic and political crisis meant that 'by the 1930s corporate America felt under siege' (Neimark and Tinker, 1986: 25). Congress had passed corporatist legislation allowing companies greater control over markets and pricing in return for acceptance of codes governing minimum wages and maximum hours, plus guarantees of union membership and collective bargaining rights. In addition, the country was experiencing a huge strike wave of sit-down strikes and factory occupations. Large corporations bitterly resisted the 'New Deal' institutions and the union organising drive. But the more perceptive of them also realised that 'the crisis generated critical problems of social control and legitimation for management' (Boreham, 1980b: 25). A second front was opened, drawing extensively on the human relations package of better communication, democratic leadership, co-operation and social integration. This went hand-in-hand with early versions of the managerial revolution thesis, General Motors claiming that the organisation was a community of stakeholders for which management was a trustee.

The success of strikes and union organising drives only consolidated a recognition of the importance of consent and attention to employee attitudes in the more general writings of human relations theorists such as T. N. Whitehead in his *Leadership in a Free Society* (1936). Despite the weakness of the tradition in Britain, Whitehead's book was well received in progressive management circles worried about the changing position of business in a more democratic community. Human relations was able to provide greater legitimation of management authority than Taylor, because it went beyond the narrow confines of 'science' and formal organisation to address issues more in tune with the times. But it would not have made the same impact merely as a body of ideas. It had to help generate new practices.

Though it was still confined to a minority of even the largest employers throughout the 1930s, Bendix, Baritz and other researchers show that an increasing number of firms such as General Electric, General Motors and Proctor and Gamble developed programmes influenced by human relations. The Hawthorne researchers had put considerable emphasis on 'personnel work' in its broadest sense of 'adequate diagnosis and understanding of the actual human situations – both individual and group – within the factory' (Roethlisberger and Dickson, 1964: 591). With this background, greater consideration in many large companies was given to the training of managers and supervisors in the arts of intensive communication, social skills and non-authoritarian leadership that would motivate as well as command. Personnel departments grew further, alongside more use of attitude surveys. General Motors managed to neatly combine them with spying on union activists by employing Pinkerton detectives to carry out the tests! As previously, the war acted as a spur, large companies and the state finding the use of tests an invaluable means of dealing with the problems associated with the sudden employment of thousands of new workers. Despite a sustained attack by more critical academics, the diverse applications and effects of human relations theories had established a bridgehead for the social sciences in industry and, by the 1940s, the movement had gained substantial institutional support (Barley and Kunda, 1992: 374).

Legacies and continuities: from human relations to human resource management

> Many managers would agree that the effectiveness of their organisations would be at least doubled if they discover how to tap the unrealised potential present in their organisations. (Douglas McGregor, 1960: 4)

The 1950s saw the relationship between social science and industry blossom still further. This was facilitated both by the development of OB and related disciplines in business schools that specialised in the human side of the enterprise, and by the training of middle and senior executives in leadership and management development (Barley and Kunda, 1992: 375). The practices or solutions were not necessarily any less superficial than Hawthorne's. Bendix (1956: 326–7) remarks that the National Association of Manufacturer's newfound attachment to 'two-way communication' was based on the assumption that employers relayed *facts* to the workforce to promote co-operation, whereas what workers say is *information* which management can use to 'eliminate misunderstandings'.

Despite the over-emphasis on solving problems through issues of poor inter-personal relations, and the re-rise of harder managerial 'sciences' such as operations research and systems analysis with their associated quantitative and financial techniques, human relations did not disappear. The body of research and to a lesser extent practical intervention moved on to new topics. Some researchers continued to examine leadership styles or search for the qualities of good leadership (see Chapter 17). Others focused on group processes and dynamics, including the well-known socio-technical studies of the Tavistock Institute in Britain (see Chapter 5). Rhetorical claims, however, foundered on a failure to demonstrate an exact and direct relationship between theory and practice. Perrow, for example, has written sceptically of the 'thirty year history of the effort to link morale and leadership to productivity' (1979: 97). In the piece quoted at the beginning of the chapter, Perrow was dismissive of the contributions from 'the forces of light'. From the vantage point of that decade it looked as if studies of the influence of technology and organisational environments, associated with systems theory, had triumphed: 'management should be advised that the attempt to produce change in an organisation through managerial grids, sensitivity training, and even job enrichment and job enlargement is likely to be fairly ineffective for all but a few organisations' (1973: 14).

There were competitors to the new influences. The human relations school gradually became less visible, giving way, even within the territory of managing the human factor, to behavioural psychology. Mayo and others had always provided, in Bendix's words, a *vocabulary of motivation*. What developed in its wake was a fully-fledged theory of motivation, promoted by figures such as Maslow, McGregor and Herzberg, which had the additional advantage of challenging Taylorism on questions of job design (see Chapter 19). But Perrow was wrong to believe that a hard structure and systems approach had achieved a durable dominance. The earlier human relations tradition that had lain dormant and often abused for its naïveté suddenly became influential again in the 1980s. Nor was it a question of a particular soft style simply becoming fashionable again. Human relations thinking contained genuine insights within a flawed general framework. The idea that the internal dynamics of the small group could be turned around so that a degree of self-governance could favour management resurfaced in the substantial wave of interest in teamworking from the 1980s onwards (see Buchanan, 2000 and Chapters 11, 12 and 20). At broadly the same time, management theorists and practitioners were also rediscovering the benefits of creating social cohesion and value consensus through organisational 'communities'. The advocates of corporate cultures such as Peters and Waterman (1982) explicitly acknowledged the influence of earlier human relations writers (see Chapter 13).

Despite such influences, human relations theory as such is still largely regarded as a ghost from a past banquet. When people talk now of managing the human factor, HRM is what comes to mind. While there remain obvious historical, practical and conceptual continuities, we would suggest that the power of HRM lies in its capacity to escape the association of managing people purely with soft, values-driven approaches. To explain this we need to retrace a few steps. This chapter has already demonstrated that the origins of personnel work lie in the human relations tradition. As a more specific function was consolidated, the humanistic rhetoric was complemented by practices that reflected the forms of adaptation to 'local' environments. Notable in this were the dominant rule-based and hierarchical systems of bureaucratic control developed in large organisations (see Chapter 3), and the expanded legal regulation of the employment relationship established as part of the post-war settlement between capital, labour and the state. The outcome expanded the domain and expertise of the personnel function, but created practices that were largely procedural, reactive and low trust.

As part of the general shift in workplace practices and organisational restructuring in the 1980s, these orientations were put into question. The personnel function was recast as HRM, though in this incarnation it was not to be the exclusive property of a narrow functional department (Tichy et al., 1982; Beer et al., 1985). This was a matter not just of territory but of content. HRM always had a dual usage, signifying a new way of describing the field of people management, and a distinctive approach to managing the employment relationship (Mabey, Salaman and Storey, 1998: 1). Both usages are open to dispute. Some have questioned whether the approach genuinely reflects substantial shifts of policy from the old personnel, or is simply 'old wine in new bottles' (M. Armstrong, 1987). Many more have queried either the character or the delivery in practice of the management of the employment relationship (see Chapter 13).

There is some common ground, at least with respect to intent. The emphasis is on the integration of 'personnel' issues within the overall business strategy; with employees becoming a 'resource' equivalent to something like finance, with ownership of HR issues diffused down to other actors, notably line managers. 'Strategic management' is a term continually invoked to refer to the management of employees at all levels, directed towards the creating and sustaining of competitive advantage (P. M. Miller, 1989; Kamoche, 1994). Much of this espouses a 'hard' version, whereas HRM is a much more systematic, rational instrument that can support organisational change through effective mobilisation and measurement of human capabilities and performance (Devanna, Fombrun and Tichy, 1984; Huselid, 1995). There is obvious continuity here with more traditional functional practices, but it is the extent to which reward and other forms of performance management are tied in to overall strategy and bottom line outcomes that is considered to be decisive.

A softer, normative variant can be identified (Kochan, Katz and McKersie, 1986; Guest, 1987), which links HRM primarily to a transformation of employment relationships based on higher levels of employee commitment and involvement. This orientation received a considerable boost with the development of the excellence literature genre, which promoted culture change as a primary managerial resource. In many firms this enabled the HR department to take a leading role in change programmes, as the definer and measurer of value change (Marks *et al.*, 1997). The other soft pathway was through high-performance work practices. While this can be interpreted as covering all HRM territories (Huselid, 1995), it is more common for it to be associated with a workplace level and issues such as teamwork, quality and continuous improvement (Kochan and Osterman, 1994). This impacts upon the practices of employee relations. As Guest notes, the underlying goal is to get employees to go 'beyond contract' and away from old-style adversarial collectivism, 'thereby reducing the potential for the effort bargain to operate as a potential focus for conflict and grievance' (1998: 239). While the intent to restructure the employment relationship away from low-trust industrial relations systems is widely approved, the association with an attack on collectivism and trade unions is more controversial. The rise of HRM, with its unitarist philosophy, more individualistic relations between employer and employee, and direct communication between company and workforce, has undoubtedly coincided with some diminution of the significance of collective bargaining and union power (Blyton and Turnbull, 1998: 9).

Conclusion

To what extent are the levels and variants compatible? It is certainly possible to produce *models* that integrate different types of practices, of which the 'mutual gains enterprise', which combines strategic, functional and workplace dimensions, is attractive and coherent (Kochan and Osterman, 1994). However, practices on different territories and through hard and soft mechanisms are easier to reconcile rhetorically than in practice (Legge, 1995). While debates focus on conceptual tensions, they are dwarfed by the problem of holding the different facets of the HRM model together in the context of contemporary organisational restructuring. In particular, performance goals such as greater productivity and flexibility in work organisation are proving difficult to reconcile with changes in employment that undermine loyalty, career and stability. In this context, critical commentators argue that hard, cost-driven approaches are predominating over softer, commitment and trust based policies (Blyton and Turnbull, 1992; Storey, 1992, 1995). We will examine the debate on the outcomes of HRM policy and practices in Chapters 11, 12 and 13.

We began this section with a quote from McGregor, of Theory X and Theory Y fame. Despite being written at the end of the 1950s, its language is identical to that of contemporary HRM. Though he goes on to argue that the major thing holding back the efficient and scientific management of the human factor is the adolescence of the social sciences (1960: 5), we would draw a different conclusion. While the franchise for 'managing the human factor' may have changed hands, it is still proving difficult to produce a durable formula that can transform the conflicting, albeit complex, interests that lie at the heart of the labour process and employment relationship.

5 Organisations and Environments

The previous chapters provide plenty of evidence that the contexts in which organisations operate, whether they be the rise of monopoly capitalism, the ups and downs of the trade cycle, or political circumstances such as the American New Deal in the 1930s, profoundly shape their nature and development. All the great social scientists who set the agenda for organisational theory examined the workplace in a systemic context. As that theory became a specialist enterprise in its own right, such a focus was lost. Salaman argues that:

> The society in which these organisations occur, and its relation with these organ-
> isations, has been very little studied. To the extent that the outside world does
> impinge on the structure and functioning of organisations, it is conceptualised
> not in terms of interests, values, class loyalties, ideologies, market developments
> etc., but as the organisation's 'environment'. (Salaman, 1979: 32)

The idea of organisations adapting to *the* environment is not in itself problematic. It is a question of how it is conceptualised. Mullins (1985: 12) claims that organisations are viewed in their total environment. Unfortunately this does not mean that they are situated within a bigger picture, but rather that lists of multiple influences are provided. Child (1969), in examining a variety of classification schemes, notes that some utilise a narrow conception of task environment based largely on economic factors such as customers, suppliers, competitors and self-regulating groups. Child prefers a broader categorisation taking in product markets, factor markets, technical knowledge, political, and socio-cultural elements (for example, communities, social memberships and values). An even wider and more influential set of factors is employed by R. Hall (1977): technological, legal, economic, political, demographic, cultural and ecological. However, in practice, as we shall see later, most research has tended to focus on the narrower frame, particularly on markets and technology. The criticism being made by Salaman and others is that the dominant readings of 'environment' lack substance, whether broad list or immediate context, and fail to specify the local, national and systemic contexts in which organisations are located.

The chapters in this section of the book trace alternative readings of the organisational environment and discuss the issues they raise. Having given an exposition of orthodox accounts, the gaps left are filled in, notably the new transnational context and actors, as well as the changing nature of the state in capitalist societies. In particular we pose the question of how organisational theory should think comparatively in a world in which the environment is increasingly shaped by a global political economy. More recent and promising developments in organisational theory will be examined as part of this process; notably neo-institutional perspectives that see the firm as embedded in networks of institutional relationships that have different configurations across societies (Hamilton and Biggart, 1988; Whitley, 1992a).

Closed systems?

This is all a long way from early organisational theory. It is conventional wisdom to argue that classical and other perspectives took no account of the environment. Instead they were concerned with manipulating the internal variables of an organisation in the service of goal attainment. Specific emphasis tended to be put on the development of rules or principles maximising the rational and efficient application of resources embodied in work design and other aspects of formal structure. Because this treats organisations as self-sufficient entities, or systems in and of themselves, it has been retro-spectively dubbed *closed systems theory* (see Clegg and Dunkerley, 1980: 191–6). Human relations theory too has been criticised for suspending the firm in a social vacuum and ignoring the degree to which its problems were results of outside pressures (Albrow, 1973: 406). This is somewhat unfair. Researchers such as Mayo and Roeth-lisberger and Dickson did recognise the effects on employees from membership of wider collectivities, such as communities. The problem was more that they and their less discriminating followers tended to believe that the *solutions* could be found through internal adjustment.

If anything, the supposedly more sophisticated neo-human relations perspectives of Maslow, Herzberg and others were more guilty of closed system thinking. Their emphasis on a model of universal psychological needs that, once identified by the intel-ligent manager, could be harnessed through new forms of organisational design, completely isolated the individual and the firm from social structure (see Chapter 19 for further discussion). Since the 1960s, closed system approaches have largely been frowned upon. However, that does not mean that they have gone away, for two reasons. First, the focus remains overwhelmingly on the *individual* organisation and there is a tendency for theorists to highlight internal and predictable goals–means relationships that can operate as a 'buffer' to the environment (R. Hall, 1977). Second, the popular management search for the magical ingredient to organisational success which can be internally controlled also increases the likelihood of a constant reworking or accom-modation to a closed system approach.

Now this is admittedly not the whole picture. The environment *is* recognised through the notion that successful companies emerge through purposeful, though unpredictable, evolution. Though the Darwinian imagery of experiment and evolution is invoked, the message is simple. Companies survive and stay fit and well by adapting to their environment. It appears that the essence of that environment is the customer. The logic is that successful companies are those that have a large market share, long-term growth and high profits. They have adapted to the (customer) environment. Success is therefore simply read off from a diffuse concept of the environment. But we are still returned to internal organisational processes, for what made them successful in the first place, 'was usually a culture that encouraged action, experiments, repeated tries' (Peters and Waterman, 1982: 114). This is what Peters and Waterman mean by 'inten-tionally seeded evolution within companies'.

One final point needs to be made about closed systems. The use of the term 'systems' is not accidental. Mainstream writing has been dominated by varieties of *systems theory*, though greatly extending and modifying early conceptions. Organisa-tions are systems of interrelated parts or sub-units – for example departments, groups and individuals – each functioning to mobilise resources towards meeting wider goals. These parts are at the same time differentiated and interdependent, aiding processes of integration and co-ordination. Systems theory is therefore an explanation of the pattern of functioning of organisations in terms of inputs, outputs and transformations, encompassing the variety of social, psychological and technical variables.

A crucial development, however, has been the acceptance of the importance of interaction with the environment; for the survival of an organisation depends on its capacity to adapt to markets, technologies and other situations. Even the description 'closed system' is partly a label of convenience; true only to the extent that the organisation as a whole and the relation between its parts (technical and social, different departments and functions) could be seen as itself analogous to system–environment relations. True systems theory is open and adaptive in character and we need to spell this out in more detail.

Adaptation to the environment: open system approaches

There are a number of different approaches and types of research that treat organisations in terms of adaptation and as open systems, an approach pioneered by Thompson (1967) and Katz and Kahn (1970). But who is adapting and what are they adapting to? The starting point is the need for the organisation to transact with the environment, more specifically to take inputs from the environment and convert them into outputs. As Hannan and Freeman note: 'In the adaptation perspective, subunits of the organisation, usually managers or dominant coalitions, scan the relevant environment for opportunities and threats, formulate strategic responses, and adjust organisational structure appropriately' (1977: 929–30). The operation of the system in markets, and among other organisations, gives essential feedback about its performance measured by realisation of corporate goals.

Systems theory is multi-layered. At its simplest, this can be expressed as society – organisation – sub-unit (for example, department). As Elliot notes:

> This boundary can be drawn anywhere for the purpose of analysis. If the system one is studying is the whole organisation then the boundary is between the organisation and its environment; if the system being studied is the work group, then the boundary is between this group and the rest of the organisation, which in this case is its environment. (Elliot, 1980: 96)

An example of the latter is the concept of *socio-technical systems*, particularly associated with the work of Trist and the Tavistock Institute (Trist *et al.*, 1963). Primarily it is a way of identifying the key sub-systems and the relations between them in the 'conversion' process. Three sub-systems are identified: technical, formal role structure and sentient (individual feelings or sentiments). Working broadly within the human relations problematic of integrating the formal/technical and informal/social dimensions of organisation, an additional twist is given by putting greater emphasis on the technological environment. This environment of the workgroup, in the form of equipment and layout, is seen as a basic constraint on the shape of work organisation. However it does not simply reflect the technology, as the organisation has independent social and psychological properties. Management's task is to create a socio-technical system in which the two dimensions are jointly optimised and mutually supportive. There is some choice at the organisational level, but there are defined limits established by the need for 'economic validity'.

Research support has been particularly associated with Trist and Bamforth's (1951) study of the mining industry. Traditional methods of 'hand-getting' the coal had involved limited technology, short coalfaces, high workgroup autonomy over the pace and distribution of work, and an egalitarian ethos. New 'longwall' methods bore similarity to mass production, with work fragmentation and more specific job roles. Not surprisingly this led to lower work commitments, higher absenteeism and a host of other standard problems. The researchers' solution was to accept the technology and layout, but to vary the methods of work to a 'composite' approach, in which groups performed whole tasks, were paid collective bonuses and had a degree of self-regulation over job allocation. The results convinced them that management choice could be exercised in favour of methods that took greater care of socio-psychological needs, whilst accepting economic and technical constraints.

Interestingly, the mining study hardly utilised the wider environment in the analysis at all. Where the environment is mentioned, it is that of the 'seam society' immediately surrounding the workgroup. Most writers within the general approach treat the organisation itself as the system, and although the wider environment determines the general goals such as economic survival in a stimulus–response manner, the environment still tends to be defined in terms of the single unit of organisation. Attention is particularly given to achieving a proper balance of system parts. This would involve integration, co-ordination and differentiation of structures and processes, not just functions such as production or research, but activities of leadership, innovation and the like. It would be wrong to give the impression that these 'boundary exchanges' are characterised by smoothness. While the organisation generally adapts and finds equilibrium by responding to opportunities and risks in the environment, a central concept of open systems is that of uncertainty and related terms: stability, turbulence or indeterminacy. This uncertainty can arise in relations with the environment itself, through clashes with surrounding cultures, or rapidity of technological change, or internally in the organisation's members or sub-units. The interdependence of the system parts includes a measure of specialisation specifically to deal with this problem: 'we suggest that organisations cope with uncertainty by creating certain parts specifically to deal with it, specialising other parts in operating under conditions of certainty, or near certainty' (Thompson, 1967: 13).

Child (1984) identifies *variability* and *complexity* as key processes. 'Variability' refers to the difficulty of predicting changes and departures from previous conditions that will induce uncertainty. 'Complexity' is linked to the degree of diversity in organisational activities and the environments it is operating in. This may mean difficulty in gathering and monitoring information necessary for effective performance. Each organisation needs to design the structures or processes in a manner that reduces uncertainty or adapts to the degree of environmental stability.

Aside from uncertainty, the other major factor shaping boundary exchanges is held to be *dependency*. Indeed these factors may be linked, for example when dependency takes an intra-organisational form, whereby the ability of sub-units to cope with uncertainty is shaped by the degree to which a sub-unit activities are central, substitutable, or when it relies on others (Hickson *et al.*, 1973). Outside the organisation, dependency is conditioned by the fact that the environment is a source of scarce resources that have to be competed for. Dependency is the reverse of power, 'As the resources increase or expand the organisation increases in power . . . since other organisations become more dependent on the resources' (Clegg and Dunkerley, 1980: 381).

These issues have stimulated the development of the *resource dependency* model (Aldrich and Pfeffer, 1976; Pfeffer, 1987), which in turn draws on broader *exchange theory* (Blau, 1964). In this model, emphasis is on the reduction of uncertainty by managing the network of interdependencies among organisations. Organisations exchange with each other and negotiate the environment, seeking to exert power over the nature and rate of exchange. The goal of each actor in the exchange is to reduce their dependency on the other and to force the 'partner' to become more dependent on them: 'Organisations tend to comply with the demands of those interests in their environment which have relatively more power' (Pfeffer, 1997: 63).

The concept of resource dependency becomes a way of understanding power relationships more generally, which we discuss in Chapter 9. But in terms of the environment, a classic case is the 'Just-in-Time' system pioneered in Japan. This is used to control the flow of stocks and materials between large corporations and suppliers in Japan. It works on the basis that small sub-contractors are flexible on the terms of their larger 'partners'. Toyota, for example, has traditionally relied on up to 35 000 small business, most of whom exist in a totally dependent relationship. Alternatively, firms may minimise dependency by seeking alternative sources. This can be seen in the 'world car' strategy pursued by Ford and GM. By co-ordinating design, production and marketing across national boundaries, companies can ensure that components can be acquired from a considerably larger number of locations.

There is a danger of constantly talking as if organisations were 'things' adapting to the environment. However, in practice, open systems theory gives a central role to *management* to maximise a bounded rationality – in other words, to predict and design appropriate structures and responses and to manipulate resources and sub-units effectively. This highlights the connection of environmental uncertainty and dependency to issues of *decision-making*, which has long been a significant aspect of research literature (March and Simon, 1958; Cyert and March, 1963). Because of unevenness in the informational, technological and other environmental conditions, and in internal power relations between sub-units, decision-makers frequently have to cope by forming *dominant coalitions* (Thompson, 1967). As a result, 'Organisational decision-making becomes much less a matter of unquestioned command or rational appraisal and much more a process of political bargaining and negotiation in which the exercise of power plays a key role' (Reed, 1986: 41–2). The positive aspect of this type of thinking is that it begins to see the organisation in a more pluralistic light, with some, albeit limited, recognition of power, bargaining and change processes. Given that dominant coalitions have to exert choice about alternative actions, it also qualifies the emphasis in systems theory to structures as a functional imperative arising from given environmental conditions (Child, 1972).

Contingency theory

The most noted application and extension of the open systems approach is grouped under the heading of 'contingency theory'. As Reed puts it:

> Eventually the theoretical developments taking place within the systems tradition culminated in a 'contingency theory' of organisation which attempted to specify the appropriate 'functional fit' between environmental settings and the internal organisational structures which they required. (Reed, 1986: 100)

In terms of the ideas discussed so far in the chapter, this does not sound very remarkable. Its appeal, however, is in part because of a powerful *normative* dimension in which the emphasis is on practical applications (Legge, 1978). A situational approach requires a 'reading' of the firm's environment by managers and their academic helpers. Furthermore it appealed because the 'if–then' formula constituted an explicit break with the 'one best way' orientation of existing theories, while retaining powerful guidelines for what power holders should actually do to sustain effective organisation. By the mid-1970s contingency theory was the dominant approach and had been applied to specifics such as payment systems as well as to general structures (Lupton and Gowler, 1969).

Curiously, as a theory, it rested primarily on research that took place largely prior to its own development. The most noted such work was that of Burns and Stalker (1961), who studied twenty firms in Scotland and England drawn mainly from the textile, engineering and electronics industries. Management systems and structures were classified according to a range of environments differentiated by degree of predictability and stability. They found that firms operating in an environment with relatively stable and predictable markets, and to a lesser extent technologies, such as those in textiles, tended to have what they called *mechanistic* systems. This broadly resembled bureaucratic models where there is centralised knowledge, clear hierarchy, task specialisation, vertical communication, and a general emphasis on formal structures, decision-making, values and rules. By contrast, in environments where there is more rapid change, uncertain markets, and complex technologies with a requirement for constant innovation, such as in electronics, a more *organic* system predominated which was less bound by traditional structures and roles. Instead, though structures remained within a general hierarchy, they utilised dispersed information centres, lateral communication, meritocratic and expert positioning, ethos and practices, and more flexible tasks and rules.

Rather than getting embroiled in arguments for and against bureaucracy or any structural arrangements, Burns and Stalker were able to argue that both systems were suitable and rational for specific market-led situations. Successful companies were precisely ones that had adapted their strengths to environmental requirements. They did recognise that they were discussing ideal types and that relationships were not rigid. Organisations facing changes in the environment may have to move along the spectrum or mix particular characteristics. Though normally noted less, Burns and Stalker also recognised constraints to changing structures away from mechanistic models, even where it was environmentally desirable. These arose particularly from entrenched interests and routines, consolidated through the operation of internal political systems (Wood, 1979: 353).

The American writers Lawrence and Lorsch (1967) extended this type of analysis by showing that it is wrong to treat firms as homogeneous structures. Sub-units are likely to have different environments and therefore require specific structures and management in order to be successful. As a result, a crucial problem for organisation is finding a balance of differentiation and integration. Their research was based on a smaller number of firms in plastics, food and containers. So, for example, whereas the research departments of the plastics companies operated in dynamic, innovative environments that were reflected in long-term orientations and the least bureaucratic arrangements, production had a stable, technical environment and was dominated by short-term concerns and more bureaucracy. Sales departments were somewhere in between. High-performing firms were those that not only manifested a high degree of differentiation of structures and goals, but had coped by developing adequate means of integration such as specialist teams with such responsibilities. Of course, those organisations where the sub-units do not have to vary significantly can be co-ordinated through conventional command structures. As with Burns and Stalker, the emphasis is not on which theoretical model is 'out of date' but on a continuum of models suited to alternative environments.

The final piece of notable contingency research by Woodward (1958: 1965) shifts the emphasis away from market environments to technology. She started the research as a means of testing traditional propositions popular in administrative theory such as relation between formal structures or size and performance. But in studies of around 100 firms in south-east Essex in the mid-1950s, no consistent correlations were found. Instead a relationship between 'technological complexity' and organisational structure was claimed. Technologies were grouped developmentally according to supposed complexity under a variety of broad categories; eventually reduced to unit and small batch production, large batch and mass production, and process production. Woodward commented: 'While at first sight there seemed to be no link between organisation and success, and no one best way of organising a factory, it subsequently became apparent that there was a particular form of organisation most appropriate to each technical situation' (quoted in M. Rose, 1975: 203).

Among the aspects of formal organisation found to have a direct association with the technical production system were length of line of command, the extent of the span of control of Chief Executives and of supervisors, and the ratio of managers and clerical workers to production personnel. Problems of running organisations with different technologies varied. Unit and process technologies were both found to have little bureaucracy and simple organisational structures based on line specialisation of basic task functions. This is linked to the predominant problems of product development and marketing for such technologies, which put the emphasis on innovation. Woodward can be situated within a range of technological determinist writings popular in this period (Walker and Guest, 1952; Sayles, 1958; Blauner, 1964). As Michael Rose notes (1975: 202), such studies utilised fairly unsophisticated conceptions of technology as hardware and as the taken-for-granted physical aspect of production, with little or no recognition of social shaping or choice. In fact, there has been some disagreement over whether technology can be seen as part of an organisation's environment. As the dominant approaches have treated it as a factor 'out-there' determining the features of companies, it is perhaps justified to accept that it has to be discussed in that framework without accepting its theoretical rationale.

One of the attractions of the theory generally is that any contingency can be posited as the key to structural variation and business performance. Hence size is seen by some researchers such as the Aston Group (Pugh and Hickson, 1976) and Blau (1970) as the major factor. For the Aston researchers size was one of three primary contextual variables along with external dependency and technology. In turn, each predicts a series of structural variables: specialisation and standardisation, extent of concentration of authority, types of control over workflow. The Aston Group accepted the significance of technology in circumstances such as smaller companies or directly for production, but argued that increased size produced structural patterns based on impersonal control mechanisms, formal procedures, and higher numbers of administrative staff. Though there are associated problems, increased size also confers benefits through capacity to take advantage of specialisation. But the movement towards greater bureaucratisation is present in all three dimensions and it is a heavily deterministic logic where organisations 'have to adapt to adapt in particular ways to the contextual or environmental constraints which face them' (Reed, 1992b: 137).

Despite its one-time dominance, 'contingency theory has since virtually faded from the research and managerial literature scene' (Pfeffer, 1997: 158). Pfeffer attributes this to deficiencies such as its overly complex explanatory structure, which is too disconnected from decision variables available for control in organisations. In contrast, Donaldson (1995) argues that there is a bias in current American organisation theory against seeing managers as positive and controlling agents. In an earlier work he mounted a strong defence of the research programme of which he was a part, while at the same time seeking to extend it. Design strategies are focused on the familiar territory of functional, divisional, area or mixed matrix structures. Strategy might appear to imply choice, but, 'The structure which is most appropriate for an organisation depends on the situational contingencies' (1985: 172). New formulas are developed such as the adoption of functional or divisional arrangements, which depend on the extent to which product or area diversity establishes degrees of interdependency. How much this kind of thinking involves real managerial choices is open to question, as we shall see later in the chapter. What is undoubtedly the case is that organisation–environment theories have moved towards non-contingent explanations based on 'purer' economic logic. Population ecology is a case in point.

Selection theories: the population ecology approach

The population ecology approach is a mainstream theory of organisation–environment relations that shifts the emphasis from adaptation to selection (Hannan and Freeman, 1977; Aldrich, 1979). In their seminal contribution, Hannan and Freeman do not deny that adaptation takes place, but argue that it is not primary and that there is limited evidence that 'the major features of the world of organisations arise through learning or adaptation' (1977: 957). In this sense the perspective is more pessimistic about managerial capacity to respond rationally to external shifts, or exercise control over events. Change comes about largely through new organisations rather than internal transformation.

There are substantial constraints to organisations changing in order to adapt to the environment. For example, failing churches do not become retail stores and vice versa. Such constraints are based mainly on structural inertia: this includes non-transferable investments in resources and people; information blockages; the type of internal political systems identified by Burns and Stalker; conservative organisational ideologies and normative systems; plus external constraints such as legal, fiscal and political barriers. The stronger the process, the more the logic of environmental selection is likely to predominate over adaptation. A further criticism is of the emphasis on the single organisation as a focus of analysis. Instead the appropriate unit of analysis is taken to be populations of organisations; theoretical abstractions relating to classes of organisation that share some common features in terms of their relations with the environment, such as being part of a particular product market.

What is this logic of environmental selection? Over a period of time, environments are held to select some organisations or classes of organisation for survival and others for extinction. Those that have survived are proof of a successful 'fit', or at least of outperforming rivals in given environmental conditions (Pfeffer, 1997: 163–9). As can be seen, the emphasis on natural selection involves borrowing, like systems theory, extensively from biology – transferring a Darwinian survival of the fittest to organisational life, with survival paths within each sector of competing firms. There is even a species analogue for organisations; blueprints which consist of rules and procedures inferred from formal structures, patterns of activity and normative orders, for transforming inputs into outputs (Hannan and Freeman, 1977: 934–5). One 'law' is that of requisite variety; organisations need to be as complex as their environment. If they are less complex they are not likely to be adaptable enough. But over-complexity would probably mean that too much slack is being carried: 'populations of organisational forms will be selected for or against depending on the amount of excess capacity they maintain and how they allocate it' (Hannan and Freeman, 1977: 949). Furthermore the environment is an ecological system populated by sufficient organisations to allow for selection. The full process involves three stages: first are planned or unplanned *variations*, from which appropriate structures or behaviours are drawn; second, natural *selection* eliminates undesirable variations; and third is a *retention* mechanism that ensures the reproduction of those variations that have been positively selected.

The borrowings do not stop at biology, but draw from neo-classical or free-market economics. Perfect market competition tends to underlie the 'rationality' of natural selection: 'Organisational rationality and environmental rationality may coincide in the instance of firms in competitive markets. In this case, the optimal behaviour of each firm is to maximise profit, and the rule used by the environment (market in this case) is to select out profit maximisers' (Hannan and Freeman, 1977: 940). These 'natural laws' are shaped by the kind of competitive struggle over limited resources identified by the resource dependency school. Competition also produces a crucial process for population ecology theory, that of *isomorphism*. When equilibrium conditions obtain, the structural features of organisations – for example the appropriate degree of specialism or generalism – will correspond to the relevant features of the resource environment. Those organisations that fail will be selected against, though organisations can also purposefully adapt. Of course equilibrium models can be too simplistic. To help deal with this the concept of *niche* width is used. A niche consists of the combinations of resource levels at which the population of organisations can survive and reproduce themselves. It is difficult for new organisations to enter already-filled niches where they cannot compete with existing social and economic resources. In fact there is a curvilinear effect whereby competition increases as densities get higher, with mortality rates eventually rising as founding rates fall (Hannan and Carroll, 1992; Hannan *et al.*, 1995).

Despite the use of some sophisticated historical models to handle data, population ecology analysis frequently remains at a highly abstract level. Hannan and Freeman admit to a frustration with the level of empirical information (1977: 959), a problem that arises partly from the choice not to focus on particular organisations, but on populations over long periods (Clegg and Dunkerley, 1977: 376). But the problems also derive from the theory as well as the method. As Perrow (1979) argues, ecological perspectives are attractive to some theorists because behaviour and events can be interpreted as natural. Evolution through natural selection gives the impression that patterns of activity that serve society are maintained, while those that are dysfunctional fortuitously disappear. Though contingency theories generally allow more scope for individual actors to learn rationally from processes of adaptation, the remarkable thing is not the distinctiveness of population ecology but how much it has in common with adaptation approaches. Hannan and Freeman (1977: 929) admit that processes involving selection can usually be recast at a higher level of analysis as adaptation processes. We are still in the world of 'best fits', with organisations responding to environments.

Critiques and alternatives

It would be foolish not to recognise that mainstream research on organisation–environment relations has generated some useful knowledge of structural differentiation within and between organisations. The best of it, drawing on perspectives such as resource dependency, has introduced issues of bargaining and power partially on to the agenda. The appeal to 'practitioners', particularly of contingency theory, can be located in the more realistic clarification and yet expansion of managerial role and of organisational success. Indeed at one level the general argument is correct. Clearly organisations do face environmental constraints and often need to adapt to new markets or technologies to survive. For some people, the 'if–then' formula became difficult if not impossible to criticise precisely because it was based on a 'horses for courses' argument. Wood notes: 'Thus ironically an approach which began by dismissing previous work as "panaceas" became itself the new panacea, the "situational approach to management"' (1979: 336).

Contingency theory and wider adaptation and selection perspectives have, however, rightly been criticised for their *environmental determinism*. Environments are not only given determinate power, as in all systems theory, but they are literally reified through the language of environments acting on passive organisations. Somehow managerial actions to change work rules, create dual internal labour markets or hire temporary workers instead of full-timers can be elevated to a principle of natural selection which rewards flexible organisational forms (Aldrich and Stabler, 1987). Perrow notes that such reification makes it difficult to for workers to say 'I was fired by the environment', adding that:

> the new model of organisation–environment relations tends to be a mystifying one, removing much of the power, conflict, disruption, and social class variables from the analysis of social processes. It neglects the fact that our world is in large part made by particular men and women with particular interests, and instead searches for ecological laws which transcend the hubbub that sociology should attend to. (Perrow, 1979: 243)

As Pfeffer (1997: 163) observes, even organisational mortality may not reflect poor performance, but instead, a choice by successful businesses to sell while the going is good. This neglect of choice is at the heart of the general critique that can be made of the approaches discussed so far. The starting point of such critiques has often been John Child's (1972) influential concept of *strategic choice*. Strategic choice can operate with reference to the context of the enterprise, performance standards or organisational design. Most emphasis is, however, given to restoring the significance of the internal environment and particularly the degree of discretion available to power holders and decision-makers within the dominant coalitions identified earlier. Contingency and other mainstream perspectives neglect the role of policy formulation and intervention, or see it only in terms of adaptation to the environment. One of the crucial factors this ignores is the existence of multiple contingencies that affect the capacity to achieve internally consistent responses and any potential correlation between structure and performance. There is sufficient 'slack' in most organisation's position and resources to allow different strategies to be considered and pursued, without incurring performance penalties or diseconomies.

The conceptual schema used by John Child allows for important breaks with determinism compatible with a radical analysis. He explicitly distances himself (1972: 6) from technological determinism by stressing the role of decisions relating to control of work. The empirical evidence in this area has been provided in studies from a labour process perspective, including path-breaking contributions from Noble (1979) and Wilkinson (1983a). This research allows us to focus on the neglected issue of choice of technology itself, in this case the development of numerical control in engineering that allowed management to replace the direct input of craft workers by tapes and later computers that were externally programmed. Both case studies show that alternative technologies for automating machine tools existed which allowed manual data input that retained operator skills. This was passed over in part because management preferred a system that enabled them to transfer skill from shop floor to programming office and shift authority and control. A more recent example that illustrates the same point is the development of teamwork in manufacturing environments. Used primarily to facilitate labour flexibility and continuous improvement (see Chapters 12, 13 and 20), as a form of social organisation teams have often been introduced without altering the assembly or continuous process technology. In addition, the degree of self-governance given to or taken by teams means that different ways of working can coexist side by side across different lines, as research from the whisky bottling halls demonstrates (Findlay *et al.*, 2000).

At a wider level, Child's analysis moves beyond the dominance of technical criteria in organisational practices, 'recognising the operation of an essentially political process in which constraints and opportunities are functions of the power exercised by decision-makers in the light of ideological values' (1972: 22). Systems theory utilises an organicist perspective that assumes equilibrium and interdependence. For example, like their human relations predecessors, the Tavistock writers adopt a unitary and socially harmonious view of the enterprise, taking for granted that the primary task is shared by all. It is also consistent with that tradition in taking technical and formal structures for granted, the difference lying in the language of management choice rather than worker adjustment. As Rose notes, once the above constraints have been accepted, even that choice is within strictly determined managerial limits, and 'the socio-technical systems concept may be seen as a device for helping production engineers to discover better "best ways"' (M. Rose, 1975: 216). For Trist and his associates, workers' choices are seen as non-existent in the face of a determinate environment. Resistance to management plans run up against 'uncontrollable forces in the external environment' (quoted in Rose 1975: 216).

In this light, Child's early work is valuable, but how far does it take us? Certainly too far for Donaldson, who criticises his work for accommodating to the 'critical camp' by emphasising the politics of organisational action. Strategic choice theory is thus counter-productive because 'Study of effective structure requires concern for functional imperatives or systems needs' (1985: 147). Ambiguity is the enemy of design knowledge. For example, if contingencies are variables that specify appropriate structure for high performance, talk of multiple contingencies that can affect a variable makes it impossible to unambiguously specify the right structure for high performance (1985: 144).

Yet there is a good deal of ambiguity as to whether Child's work has sought to modify or supplement contingency and systems theory, or significantly depart from it. Wood notes: 'Put simply, he is arguing theoretically for the inclusion of managerial ideology as an intervening variable between the environment and organisational design' (1979: 350). At this stage, Child tended to consider strategic choice only as a variable and within management terms. Options that involve contesting existing power relations are made largely redundant. As Whittington (1988: 532–3) argues, property rights and structures of class, gender and ethnicity endow a limited circle of actors with command over resources to make strategic choices. Furthermore we need to break from the idea that environments produce situational imperatives, or from the population ecology equivalent that environments can only select out a specifically appropriate form. Child's later work (Child and Smith, 1987) from a 'firm-in-sector' perspective recognises that changes are primarily triggered by markets, but choices still remain and new strategies require an intellectual or cognitive reframing among management.

Conceptions of strategic choice have been deepened, modified and qualified within further research. Purcell (1991) has usefully distinguished between choices at different levels of decision making. First- and second-order decisions about purpose and form respectively are 'upstream', while 'downstream' decisions are third-order and refer mainly to functional activities, including employment relations. The latter are likely to be constrained by the former, as is shown in subsequent research. Kessler, Purcell and Shapiro (2000) examine the expanded discretion in the sphere of personnel practices available to public sector organisations in the UK. While some new third-order variations were found, discretion continues to be constrained by powerful external pressures from state policies and first-order, upstream decisions on mission, purpose and structure.

Research influenced by labour process theory has also extended our under-standing, primarily by situating choice within the constraints and characteristics of the capital–labour relationship. We will examine this perspective in more detail in Chapter 8 and in Part III. Early contributions on managerial control strategy (Friedman, 1977; Burawoy, 1979; R. Edwards, 1979) established an analytical framework. Child in his later work (1984: 231) refers in detail to Friedman's ideas of strategies of direct control and responsible autonomy. Direct control corresponds broadly to the scientific management tradition of close supervision, minimal responsibility and treating workers as machines. In contrast, responsible autonomy is mindful of the negative effects of worker resistance and the potentially positive gains from worker co-operation and involvement. Hence the stress on enlarged responsibilities and status, lighter controls, greater security and sometimes enriched jobs. These are not abstract choices. Responsible autonomy is more applicable to well-organised workers with controls over external or internal labour markets, who therefore need to be treated as central or core. Workers who are poorly organised, less skilled, and working for companies in highly competitive product markets are more likely to be directly controlled and treated as peripheral. This distinction, however, is too crude and does not fit all sectors.

For Child, Friedman's analysis appears to confirm the relevance of managerial choices within market environments. But this neglects the wider nature of radical expla-nations. No matter how strategies are described, and Friedman is only one variant, they are shaped not just by markets, but by the capital–labour relation itself. Management is caught in the contradiction of needing to exert control and authority over labour to secure profitability in competitive conditions, while requiring workers to be motivated and co-operative. These contradictions are also conditioned by the general dynamics of capitalist production, either in a particular sector or in the economy as a whole. The development of monopoly capitalism has enabled large firms with power over markets and access to 'scientific' planning and management to experiment without being under undue pressure for short-term profits.

Enacted environments?

Many corporate 'strategies' put adaptation to the environment in reverse. Take the example of the choices open to management over the nature and sources of labour. Labour markets are clearly part of the organisational environment and decisions about who to recruit are important ones. Employers may not always have much discretion, but the basic criteria of controlled costs, stability and minimisation of risk has been well documented (R. Jenkins, 1982). Hence employers may look for workers with characteristics such as family men with commitments, as at Ford (Beynon, 1975), or draw on informal Protestant family networks in Northern Ireland telecommunications plants (Maguire, 1986). In the former case the company hopes that mortgage and other responsibilities will mean financial dependence and unwillingness to strike, while in the latter employment of people from the same family can increase a sense of social obligation and act as a social control over behaviour such as absenteeism. But a more significant choice is over the *location* of a workplace. Radical labour market theorists (Garnsey, Rubery, Wilkinson *et al.*, 1985) rightly regard the firm as a social organisation acting collectively. In locating a plant to utilise a specific form of labour, it is segmenting the market, though such effects can also occur when employees seek to build 'shelters' round their own jobs (Freedman, 1984).

There is plenty of evidence to show that large companies have often made their location decisions with specific cheap or controllable labour sources or stable industrial relations in mind (Whitaker, 1986). When GM finally chose Spring Hill, a small town outside Nashville, Tennessee, for its Saturn plant, it was the end of a process that began with a public specification of decision criteria. The subsequent beauty contest had 38 out of 50 states offering a total of 1000 sites that would be created to the requirements (Meyer, 1986: 78). Tennessee has laws outlawing union closed shops. Locating new plants in small towns has been an increasing policy of GM, with the effect that the company *becomes* the environment.

Recruitment and location policies are examples of the power of organisations to *enact* environments. Perrow makes a related criticism of population ecology theory. He argues that to begin with the question, 'why are there so many kinds of organisation?' is to ignore reality. When we are dealing with the big corporations such as the auto giants, it is simply not the case that there is evidence of significant differences. Furthermore, the large firms very seldom die and they dominate the environment of the host of small organisations around them, as we see in the example of the Japanese 'just-in-time' system (See Chapter 11). Perrow (1979: 243) concludes, 'If there is little variation, and little negative selection, then, what is the value of the theory?'

This capacity to set limits to environments was a sub-theme of Child, who drew on Galbraith's (1967) analysis of the 'new industrial state' to argue that any significant countervailing powers to big business had broken down (1969: 54). This stands in sharp contrast to the complacency of conventional open systems theory (Thompson and McEwan, 1973: 158), which only conceives of organisations dominating their environment in extreme circumstances, which in turn will generate the countervailing powers dismissed by Galbraith.

Child also sees his own insights as indebted to the work of the business historian Chandler (1962, 1977) on strategy, previously discussed in Chapter 3. Chandler showed how a new multidivisional structure was created as a strategic response to short- and long-term market trends, and technological innovations. The refashioned structures allowed for an improved internal division of labour and resource allocation based mainly on the separation of longer-term strategic planning from operational decisions and practices. A decentralist strategy established market-type conditions within firms. There are parallels between these strategies and more contemporary attempts to extend markets within firms by creating quasi-independent profit centres which have to compete with one another and treat everyone else as customers. In addition, Williamson's related transaction-cost analysis also shows that the thrust of emergent giant corporations was to intervene in and shape economic environments in circumstances where the growth of managerial power in large corporations coincided with the declining influence of the market.

However there are limitations to how far these frameworks substantially rework conceptions of organisation–environment relations. For Chandler, though the focus is on strategy and the 'visible hand' of management, the extent to which it can incorporate real choice is open to question. The emphasis on the superiority of the multidivisional firm as a form of adaptation to new market and technological imperatives strongly resembles contingency theories. Nor does Williamson's 'transaction costs' theory allow for much diversity. The problem arises from treating the growth of firms through internalisation of the costs of transactions in an unproblematic way. As Granovetter observes, there is an implicit functionalism in the argument that 'whatever organisational form is most efficient will be the one observed' (1985: 503). It is true that firms do seek to internalise costs and for some of the reasons mentioned – environmental uncertainty and bounded rationality. But efficiency may not be the driving force or outcome. For example, if we take research on mergers and acquisitions (see Thompson, Wallace and Flecker, 1992), it would be foolish to believe that every organisation taken out of the market is less efficient or that the newly created combination is more so. Firms take over others often because their control over resources gives them the capacity to dominate their environment, including other firms. This may literally be 'the environment' in the recent case of biotechnology companies. For example, in recent years Monsanto has acquired Holden's Foundation Seeds for $1.2 billion, gaining them a 35 per cent share of the corn acreage in the US. It also holds a 40 per cent share in a second major seed company, DeKalb, and has recently acquired Asgrow, a leading soybean company, plus Agracteus and Calgene, two high-profile agricultural biotech firms (Rifkin, 1999). Such vertical integration allows a high degree of control over the production and consumption of scientific knowledge.

This inability to analyse the power resources available to the various parties in transactions is something we will return to in the next chapter. More realistic analyses do have that orientation. Teulings notes that 'large corporations do not comply with the laws of every market, but rather the other way round' (1986: 146). An organisation with a monopoly or semi-monopoly position can, for instance, create a product market through its own sales policies; or displace parts of its costs on to the environment, as with unchecked industrial pollution. The 2000 US court judgement against Microsoft confirmed exactly the former point. Equally, it would be wrong to believe that each member of a 'population' contributes equally to competition within an ecological niche (Baum, 1995). To return to the example of mergers; such processes increasingly create environments to which other organisations and sections of the community have to adapt. For example there has been a tremendous concentration of media resources through mergers and takeovers such as those initiated in many countries by Rupert Murdoch or Bill Gates. As Schiller comments with respect to the Internet, 'Smaller companies that specialised in what were initially niche markets at the frontier of the liberalisation process worked the new territory. When they succeeded, major traditional suppliers either snapped them up or rushed to develop similar applications of their own' (1999: 28). A pertinent instance is the recent merger of the world's biggest online service provider, AOL, and one of the biggest media conglomerates, Time Warner. As with other media vertical integrations, such a deal links a content provider with a new form of outlet. AOL's more than 23 million subscribers are a captive market for Time Warner's products. The outcomes not only create a new business conglomerate, but give enhanced power to shape cultural and political environments, and the ideological climate of a whole society.

A major theme to come out of this discussion is the need to take large firms seriously as economic actors in their own right (Whitley, 1987). Though there are a variety of competing options or rationalities within organisations, the subsequent actions frequently constitute market environments more than they are constituted by them. The most obvious case of the capacity to control and change environments is that of the *transnational company* (TNC). The scale of their activities usually leads to considerable impact on national economies (Dicken, 1992). The issue is less whether the TNCs are willing to adapt to the environment in the form of national conditions, than how they contribute to changes in those societal institutions.

Increasingly TNCs can call on resources and structures that are superior to many nation states. Such power is further enhanced by changing corporate forms, with a gradual shift from structures based on centre–periphery relations, to global firms which have 'foreign-based units with group-wide functions in management, manufacturing, marketing and/or research and development' (Forsgren, 1990: 9). One of the crucial powers is mobility of capital across national and international boundaries, enabling an evasion of laws on taxes and profits in a particular country. Markets can be shaped and their ebbs and flows ridden by cross-subsidisation and transfer pricing of goods, services, technology and loans between related activities in a TNC's global structure. To return to the example of the Murdoch media empire, cross-subsidisation allowed the price of *The Times* to be drastically cut to drive competitors out of the market, to the extent that News International was taking a loss of 80p on each copy sold of the Saturday paper. Domination of a product market can reduce dependence on external sources of finance. Clairmonte and Cavanagh (1981) illustrate the process with reference to textile transnationals, adding the point that those in oligopolistic positions can act as price makers, thus subordinating markets through cartels and other mechanisms. This led many countries, such as Sri Lanka and Malaysia, to create a 'friendly' environment in the form of Export Processing Zones in order to attract foreign capital. They offered virtual freedom of operations, cheap labour, bans on unions, and maximum repatriation of profits (Mitter, 1986).

Such dependency has gathered momentum in more recent times. In 1998 representatives of the world's 29 richest nations gathered in Paris to put the finishing touches to an accord devised by the OECD (Organisation for Economic Cooperation and Development) to create a level playing field for international investors.

> It amounts to a new set of investment rules that would grant corporations the right to buy, sell and move their operations wherever they wish around the world, without government regulation … it will acknowledge for the first time that corporate capital now has more authority and freedom to act than mere national and local governments. (D. Rowan, 'Meet the New World Government', *Guardian*, 13 February 1998)

Details of this Multilateral Agreement on Investment are still being debated as some governments try to hang on to their rights to regulate their own environments, but the example highlights the increasingly global context of relations between capital, labour and the state.

Conclusion

In conclusion, we have argued in this chapter for a richer, more complex and more reciprocal view of organisation–environment relations than represented in mainstream literatures. Such writings focus too much on the narrower frame of technology and product markets, at the expense both of political economy (capital markets) and cultural context. Organisations are constantly making and being made by the economic, social and political institutions around them. How many choices, at what level, and who is making them, are empirical questions influenced by factors such as different sectoral contexts and power resources. These questions can be re-addressed and further illuminated in the global arena. It is to this that we turn in the next chapter.

6 Capital, Labour and the State in a Globalising Era

Given that much popular business writing treats managers as free agents able to act in ways only constrained by their own imaginations, it is useful to be reminded of external boundaries and constraints (Morishima, 1995). However, we have argued that even when taking account of the outside world, much orthodox theory does so in an economically and technologically deterministic way. That is, it tends towards single-track notions of efficiency that can only be embodied in specific design configurations between environmental variables (product markets, technologies) and organisational structures. The environment either rules or has rules for successful adaptation and selection. Strategic choice and notions of enacted environments bend the stick back in the other direction, but we need to take the discussion further. This chapter examines theoretical frameworks that challenge narrow and limited conceptions of organisation–environment relations, in a context where capital, labour and the state are being forced to readjust their relations in an increasingly global context.

Comparative analysis: beyond the American model

It is important for organisational analysis to be comparative, to have the tools to explain patterns of difference and similarity, convergence and divergence. We have already, in previous chapters, pointed to a number of sources of variation in the way in which management theories and organisational forms developed across and within various units – sectors, countries, companies – shaped by the requirements of cultural and other forms of adaptation and pressures from key actors. However, this framework still tends to assume models that arise and are adapted to at given stages along a single line of development. Chandler's account of the rise of the 'modern' integrated business enterprise can be used to illustrate the general argument. He does give a historically-informed explanation of the emergence of the phenomenon. In general terms the US was a seedbed for managerial capitalism primarily because of the size and the nature of the domestic market (Chandler, 1977: 498–500). It was not only faster growing than other nations, but also more open and less class-divided. This encouraged the techniques and technologies of mass production and distribution.

In contrast, domestic markets in Western Europe were smaller and had slower growth. This limited the same kind of developments and kept greater reliance on middlemen to handle goods. Even where integrated enterprises did appear, they often remained small enough to be dominated by owner-managers. This kind of reasoning allows Chandler to evaluate other national experiences against this standard. British entrepreneurs are said to have failed to invest in manufacturing, marketing and management in key capital-intensive industries. As a consequence this 'personal capitalism', dependent on atomistic economic organisation such as the single-plant family firms in industries such as cotton and steel, was a pale version of its US counterpart:

'neglecting investment in administrative capabilities and research, dogged by short-termism, preoccupied with family and personal management, prejudiced against salaried managers, determined to ensure a steady income stream rather than to maximise growth and profits in the long run' (Supple, 1991: 511).

This account of stunted organisational capabilities makes an attractive link to *institutionalist* explanations for Britain's declining economic performance. Such a framework point to factors that shaped industrial development: entrenched employee job controls; the separation of the banking system from finance of industry; and educational provision that failed to provide adequately trained managerial and technical staff. As a result, managerial structures and expertise were underdeveloped and 'the British only adapted patchwork improvements to their existing organisational and productive structure' (Elbaum and Lazonick, 1986: 7). Echoes of such explanations can be found more recently in critics of short-termism and institutional failure in Britain's political economy, such as Will Hutton's (1992) influential work. But the remit is much broader than Chandler's 'internal history' of business enterprise. In emphasising the role of educational, state, legal and other institutions, such writers can demonstrate variations in industrial development.

It can also be argued that given the similarities between Britain and America's financial and industrial systems, Chandler's model of management and enterprise is even less likely to apply to other European countries. Modern American, or perhaps Anglo-Saxon, conceptions of management are built on assumptions of the superiority of a *general science* of co-ordination and control, a profession of management above particular specialisms and functions (Fores, Glover and Lawrence, 1992). In comparison, the Franco-German tradition draws on quite different sources. For example, Rueschemeyer (1986) notes the significance of public administration as a bureaucratic model for private enterprise in Germany, while the French state has developed vocationally-oriented higher education to produce generations of technocrats for the private and public sector. Germany and a number of other countries also have a tradition of engineering-based technical competence as the base for industrial progress. On the HRM terrain, there are different approaches to HRM in the US and Europe, shaped by different intellectual influences and by the fact that in the latter many aspects of the employment contract are decided outside corporate boundaries.

If the form and content of organisational structures and practices are socially constructed, Supple's comments on Chandler have more general application: 'What his assumptions make it difficult to do, however, is to generalise his results to a rounded and substantial exploration of the interrelationships and evolution of economic systems generally' (1991: 510). Our view is that socially constructed organisational diversities are the proper object of analysis for organisational theory. This is not a minor point. Measuring organisations and change against a single, linear standard rears its misleading head again later, this time with Japanese management replacing the American model. But this is leaping ahead of the story. One of the most influential challenges to the standard Anglo-Saxon textbook view of management and organisation has come from Hofstede and other cultural relativists.

The rise of cultural explanations

Contingency theory, discussed in the previous chapter, was one critical response to the idea of universal principles of management. Hofstede's promotion of the cultural relativity of organisational practices and theories has perhaps been the other most prominent. Whereas contingency research emphasised factors such as product markets and technologies, he argued that universal principles could not exist regardless of *national* environments. The accumulation of evidence about different cultures and trajectories of socio-economic development meant that by the 1970s,

> It slowly became clear that national and even regional cultures do matter for management. The national and regional differences are not disappearing. They are here to stay. In fact these differences may become one of the most crucial problems for management – in particular for the management of multicultural, multinational organisations, whether public or private. (Hofstede, 1990: 392)

Despite the reference to regional factors, in Hofstede's work culture is firmly equated with *nationality*. Nationality has central symbolic value to citizens, creating shared ideas, values and meanings transmitted through family and community. Such social conditioning becomes embedded in, 'an invisible set of mental programmes which belongs to these countries' national cultures' (Hofstede, 1990: 393). In turn, this programming predisposes individuals to act in particular ways and is reinforced by becoming crystallised in institutions such as legal systems, industrial relations and religious organisations. National character and national culture are treated as indivisible. To operationalise these assumptions, Hofstede had to identify a common conceptual currency that could map national cultures and then find a way of collecting data about them. The latter was done on the back of his work as a psychologist for IBM between 1967 and 1971. He was able to collect data through questionnaires to employees in IBM's many multinational units. The findings appeared to demonstrate 'remarkable and stable' differences between countries. There were differences in the mental programming of individuals, but an 'average' pattern of beliefs and values was identified. This and related studies have had a huge impact on scholars and practitioners (see Søndergaard, 1994).

The conceptual framework utilises a four-dimensional model for national cultures:

- *Power distance* This combines societal attitudes based on the extent to which inequalities of various kinds are tolerated, and an intra-organisational dimension related to the degrees of centralisation of authority and autocratic leadership.
- *Individualism–collectivism* Societies will vary according to how loosely or tightly social norms bind individuals into group membership. Collectivist nations are ones that require individuals to subordinate self-interest.
- *Uncertainty avoidance* There is a certain amount of ambiguity and risk in any complex society. Some societies encourage individuals to tolerate high levels of uncertainty, others create institutions to maximise security and avoid risk. Technology, laws and religion can all play a role in defining the extent and character of risk toleration.
- *Masculinity–femininity* This corresponds to the well-known distinction between tough- and tender-minded. This is said to be the outcome of the degree to which a society seeks to maximise or minimise the 'natural' division of sex roles between men and women. Masculine societies promote performance, achievement, 'big is beautiful'; feminine ones encourage quality of life, relationships and protection of the environment.

These dimensions are also held to intersect. For example, collectivist countries 'always' have large power distances. On the basis of responses to his questionnaires, Hofstede then plots where countries fall on large/strong, small/weak indexes and sometimes relates this to other factors such as gross national product. In this sense, he is doing more than description. There is an implicit normative dimension. When discussing individualism–collectivism, it is stated that wealthy countries are more individualist and poor countries collectivist. Amongst the former are the US, Britain and Sweden; the latter include Taiwan, Pakistan and Korea, with Japan, Austria and Spain in the middle. Other results show that all Latin countries are in a strong uncertainty avoidance/large power distance cluster, along with Japan and Korea. In contrast a small power distance/weak avoidance cluster includes the Netherlands, US, Britain and Sweden. Meanwhile the most masculine are Japan and the German-speaking, the most feminine the Nordic and the Netherlands.

On the basis of these results, Hofstede draws some lessons for management theory and practice. In their own terms they are fairly logical. Leadership in a collectivist society will tend towards the group rather than the individual. If there is low power distance, schemes for employee participation will flourish. Self-actualisation will be more of a motivator in highly individualistic societies such as the US than in those where keeping 'face' within group relationships is a prime social requirement. However a range of methodological problems has been identified, notably drawing strong generalisations from small samples, taken at a particular time in a specific context that may have changed. Indeed these and other criticisms focusing on the validity of the IBM sample and reliability of results taken solely from attitude surveys have been frequently aired (Kieser, 1993; Søndergaard, 1994).

While the study was undoubtedly methodologically flawed, it is unhelpful to base a critique too much on those factors. For it is perfectly possible to use a different methodology and come up with the same kind of arguments. The best-known example is the work of Hampden-Turner and Trompenaars (1993). Their best-selling management books use a more sensitive device: scenarios containing ethical and practical dilemmas that have been put to over 15 000 managers at their own multinational seminars. On this basis they identify patterns of responses that reflect different systems of values concerning wealth creation. Seven cultures of capitalism are discussed based on national cultures, including the US, Britain, Japan and Germany. As in Hofstede, there is an underlying critique of an 'American model', in this case because it is failing to respond to new forms of competition from rival cultures. Some of the value dimensions are different, such as universalism versus particularism and analysing versus integrating, while others – including individualism versus communitarianism, equality versus hierarchy – are much the same. The underlying argument also remains similar to Hofstede. Every culture is held to have a tacit dimension rooted in a subconscious set of beliefs that form the bedrock of national identity. These beliefs are the 'invisible hand that regulates economic activity' (Hampden-Turner and Trompenaars, 1993: 4).

Examples of the relationships between such beliefs and practices include the outcomes of American and British preference for universalism, analysing and individualism; in other words for generalisable rules and laws, and for breaking down phenomena into calculable parts. This is then linked to the development of scientific management and bureaucracy, the dominance of the finance function and conglomerate forms of ownership, obsession with short-term performance, high levels of bankruptcies and astronomical salaries. As for the underlying normative message, the two perspectives partly diverge. Hofstede's 'different is best' outlook is replicated by Hampden-Turner and Trompenaars' view that future economic success depends on understanding trading partners. At the same time success also involves managing these value tensions: 'economic success will accrue to the cultures which do the best job balancing the scale' (Hampden-Turner and Trompenaars, 1993: 10).

It is not difficult to see the basis of the appeal of cultural relativism. It trades on recognisable, if somewhat stereotypical, national characteristics. Normatively the approach has obvious and useful applications in terms of training to make managers more sensitive to trading partners and to local cultural conditions. Other studies have provided valuable cultural commentaries, such as Lockett (1988) on understanding the characteristics of Chinese management. Limits to theories that promote some form of universal human essence, such as Maslow's hierarchy of needs, are helpfully exposed. The progressive intent, notably to question the transferability of textbook (read US) models to circumstances, such as former Communist countries, is admirable: 'what counts is only that a country is managed according to the value systems of its people' (Hofstede and Søndergaard, 1993: 3).

Unfortunately such benefits come at a price, for there remains a massive credibility gap. By locating attitudes within a largely unvarying national character, cultural relativists tend to produce static descriptions that overestimate durability of values and practices. Many of Hofstede's pronouncements look particularly dated. Confidently asserting that the degree of individualism in a culture is statistically related to a country's wealth, the 1970 listing places Japan in the middle, and a number of the East Asian 'tiger economies' with the fastest subsequent rates of growth in GNP firmly anchored at the bottom. In a later contribution (Hofstede, 1991), he has to borrow the idea of 'Confucian dynamism' to fill the gap.

Let us also take the example of the former Communist countries. Most of them manifested high power distance, collectivism and uncertainty avoidance (Hofstede and Søndergaard, 1993). This is hardly surprising given the nature of their shared command economy and centralised party–state apparatus. In contrast, Russia is now experiencing rampant individualism and uncertainty following the collapse of the old solidaristic social norms. While the situation is not as dramatic in other ex-Eastern bloc countries, there is no evidence in either case that this reflects or is driven by changes in national mindsets.

The fact that the descriptions are often no longer accurate raises questions about the feasibility of the analysis. Such perspectives pick up on cultural differences and then believe they have explained them. For example, Hampden-Turner and Trompenaars refer to the 'psychology of short and long-term mind-sets' (1993: 139). But it is not at all clear that finance-driven short-termism derives either from mental models in general, or Anglo-Saxon ones in particular. It is equally possible to argue that the kind of 'greed is good' individualism, with associated high levels of bankruptcy and takeovers, was an outcome, not of a mental model, but specific historical and contemporary institutional arrangements in Anglo-American political economies.

Culturalist perspectives treat as universal what are the outcomes of historical struggle – such as the dominance of the finance function or conglomerate ownership. They treat as culturally specific what are universal trends, notably scientific management and bureaucracy, which were present in France and Germany in parallel with the Anglo-Saxon countries (Weber, 1968; Doray, 1988). Japan is at the top of the list for firms that take a long-term view. This is attributed to Japanese views of time, which in turn are attributed to Buddhist influences. This sounds plausible, but look at the next two countries in: Sweden and West Germany. Each no doubt could be discussed in terms of cultural history. However, what the countries have in common is also significant – institutional configurations within particular market arrangements that promote close relations between the state and major economic actors and a flow of finance between banks and business.

These debates can often get stuck in a 'chicken and egg' rut. After all, institutions can be presented as the outcome of deeply-rooted values. This ignores one very important point. As we have seen, the patterns attributed to national mindsets can and do change. Take, for example, the issue of centralisation and autocratic leadership. Hofstede says that high power distance stems from 'the psychological need for dependence of those people without power' (1990: 397). What that dubious assertion ignores is that societies or sectors within them can become more centralised and autocratic as the result of political changes, management fashions or power struggles. Not only has this got little or nothing to do with any cravings for domination, there is evidence that employees respond badly to such changes. For example a study by the Carnegie Foundation found extensive and rising dissatisfaction among academics with how autocratic their organisations had become in countries such as Britain and Australia with supposedly low power distance cultures.

Beyond a failure to explain changes in particular places, cultural relativists are unable adequately to understand more general social shifts that happen across societies, albeit unevenly. Notable in this respect has been the increase in risk highlighted by the German sociologist Ulrich Beck (1992). Contemporary political, economic and cultural processes embody greater degrees of instability and change, with consequent impacts on job and social insecurity. This would seem to imply an increase in uncertainty partly independent of any specific national mindset. Defective explanation is a poor basis for policy. Even if we knew what they were, it might not be feasible to 'manage according to the value systems of a particular people' in the contemporary political economy. One of the reasons is that other sources of cultural influence, notably of a corporate nature, may constrain or override traditional national values.

There are two ways in which corporate cultures are playing an enhanced role, with the result that multinational companies are becoming carriers of convergent practices across national boundaries. First, firms are needing to integrate an increasingly diverse number of activities and units. Many management theorists portray culture as the glue that binds those diverse units into cohesive and co-ordinated 'families' (Handy, 1984; Barham and Rassam, 1989; Rhinesmith, 1991). Second, the increasingly global nature of competition creates pressures for them to adapt to the more rapid diffusion of perceived 'best practice'. While the latter may not be primarily cultural in nature, both set limits to Hofstede's argument that 'The convergence of management will never come' (1990: 405). As Kieser (1993) notes, it is remarkable that Hofstede never considers the highly distinctive culture of IBM as a factor and how it interacts with national culture.

Modern business thus creates complex cultural environments for international managers and management. Neither the relativist 'when in Rome' view of adapting to local culture, nor the newly fashionable concept of the free-floating global manager who owes no allegiance to any country (Reich, 1991), may be adequate in this context. Knowledge and cultural competencies are forged in the interface between the corporate, functional and national, and managers face pressures to pick up the appropriate cues that signal what kind of cultural difference is operative (Jones, Thompson and Nickson, 1998: 1060; Schneider and Barsoux, 1997: 169). For example, Jones, Thompson and Nickson (1998) examined the meanings attached to terms such as the need for 'Swedish behaviour' in the constituent parts of multinationals from that country. Managers feel comfortable with talk of Swedishness, perhaps because it gives additional meaning and legitimacy. From this perspective, the prominence of Swedish managers in top positions in foreign subsidiaries is less to do with the superiority or distinctiveness of Swedishness, than the advantage such staff give in facilitating the smooth running of the 'global' management structure, with its attendant and often standardised knowledge system. For example, service transnationals need to transfer highly standardised knowledge and practice that supports a corporate brand (Child and Rodrigues, 1993: 11). However, such systems are always subject to adaptation. International firms necessarily make 'compromises' with local situations and, implicitly, with competing values and ideas of competence.

Overall the message of this discussion is that we need different, more historically sensitive and contextually bounded explanations of culture. Put simply, locating culture in ways of doing rather than thinking allows us to explain how cultures develop and change more adequately.

Institutional theories

A focus on culture is a traditional antidote to explanations that overemphasise economic and technical convergence, given that the former has more scope for grasping 'local' variation and organisational distinctiveness. However, as we have seen, culture is a slippery concept that can be applied with misleading results. Institutional theories, which have been around in organisational analysis since the 1970s (Meyer and Rowan, 1977), have been the means for correcting some of the problems associated with Hofstede and associated ideas. Organisations still adapt to the environment, but to different features of it. The emphasis is on normative adaptation and the cultural rules to which organisations conform. This arises not from the requirements for efficiency, but from the need for legitimacy and resource support that is the reward for conforming. Indeed, in some cases rules may be ceremonial and transmitted through myths rather than technical. Not only do organisations conform to the environment, but to each other. This process whereby organisations increasingly come to resemble each other is described using the strange term 'institutional isomorphism' (Di Maggio and Powell, 1983). The main factors promoting convergence across companies are key agents who adhere to universalistic standards of best practice, notably professionals such as accountants, engineers and personnel officers, as well as the state itself.

We should not be misled by the term 'culture'. This is used to mean social rules embodied in institutional processes more than mental constructs carried about in people's heads. These institutional frameworks are essentially national: as Clegg puts it, 'A stress on culture as institutionally framed and nationally diverse' (1990: 151). An important feature of this approach is to affirm the possibility of successful organisational designs to promote industrialisation in different institutional environments. The emphasis on diverse organisational rationalities is usefully strengthened through the concept of *business systems*, associated particularly with the work of Whitley (1992a, 1992b, 1999). J. Henderson (1992: 4) describes them as, 'distinctive ways of co-ordinating economic activity that give rise to particular configurations of market–firm relations'. The advantage of this concept is that it attempts to tie together in a coherent way the historical, cultural and institutional processes that shape national or regional economies. It enables a focus on the way in which state, financial, industrial relations and other systems combine together to influence organisational practices. Whitley (1992b) makes a useful distinction between background institutions (for example, family, education) that structure general social patterns and norms, and proximate institutions (for example, labour market systems) that constitute the more immediate business environment.

The role of factors such as state direction and family ownership in East Asian economies figures prominently in institutionalist accounts (Hamilton and Biggart, 1988; Whitley, 1992a; G. Henderson, 1993). Japan has received considerable academic attention for its distinctive forms of ownership and management. For example, in the influential corporate form of *keiretsu*, units are part of vertically organised enterprise groups clustered around a dominant company or companies. Interlinked shareholdings involving subcontractors and banks establish stability and mutual interest in the long-term success of the group; the joint risk-taking and access to capital avoids the short-termism associated with the Anglo-Saxon model (G. Henderson, 1993: 38–9). Crucially, this risk-taking is also shared with the state, as in the well-known example of orchestration of economic development through the Ministry of International Trade and Industry (MITI).

Japan and other Asian economies have undergone financial crises and lower growth more recently, leading some commentators to question the extent of any 'economic miracle' (Krugman, 1999). Whatever judgements may be made about current events, there is much less doubt that the particular configuration of practices discussed above was frequently a characteristic feature of late industrialisation. In Japan the commercial class was marginal to early industrialisation and the state was the primary agent in mobilising capital and mediating market forces (Littler, 1982). But the primary example of state-sponsored development is in Korea. Conglomerate enterprise groups, known as *chaebol*, are both directed and disciplined by the state through financial controls, subsidies and incentives. For example, following the bankruptcy of the leading cement producer in the 1970s, the South Korean government transferred its production facilities to another chaebol (Amsden, 1992: 15). This pattern has been repeated continually in the immensely successful restructuring process that made the country into one of the fastest growing in the world.

The state is not the only manager of the industrialisation process. As Amsden (1992: 9) shows, 'Salaried engineers are a key figure in late industrialisation because they are the gatekeepers of foreign technology transfers'. With Korean firms choosing specialised engineers over administrators, we have a further example of different forms of enterprise management within managerial capitalism. Family ownership is a key dimension of South Korea's corporate structures and familialism has been a further characteristic of some East Asian economies, particularly Taiwan and Hong Kong. Family business, particularly among overseas Chinese, operates according to particular lineage and inheritance rules, which, in turn, shape how businesses grow given that a wider sharing of trust is constrained by the familial form. More importantly for our purposes, the forms of co-ordination and direction of the enterprise are necessarily distinctive: 'there is strong patrimonial and personalistic direct control, rather than on the more impersonalised, formalised and standardised control of the rational-bureaucratic model which we are familiar with from the West' (Clegg, 1990: 164). Whatever the source of influence or configuration factors, what is being argued is that dominant social institutions generate distinctive business recipes that are relatively similar within nation states.

It is also worth remembering that there are substantial differences between those economies, as well as common contrasts to 'Western' models, further highlighting the importance of a comparative analysis of management structures and practices (Whitley, 1999). In this respect it is possible to learn from a close cousin of the above perspectives. Such *organisational* theories have a great deal in common with broader institutional perspectives in sociology, particularly the *societal effects* approach (Maurice, Sorge and Warner, 1980). Their research showed that work organisation patterns differ markedly due to nationally specific institutional logics that produce stable organisational and employment patterns. Such logics are particularly located in education, training, labour market and industrial relations structures. This helps to explain why salary structures, career patterns, management and authority relations vary among closely matched French, German and British firms. Within a similar framework Lane (1991) has looked at relations between large, medium and small firms in Germany, France and Britain. She demonstrates that the distinctiveness of 'populations' of organisations arises from their transaction with specific industrial orders. As a consequence national patterns continue to reproduce divergence rather than the homogeneity predicted by old-style convergence theory (Kerr *et al.*, 1960).

Societal effect approaches have stressed the principle of functional equivalence, thus appearing to avoid determinist or 'one best way' fallacies. However comparison is accompanied, implicitly or explicitly, by evaluation. For example, the comparisons of France, Britain and Germany in the work of Lane consistently favour the latter, particularly with reference to the organisational and technical competencies of firms and their underpinnings in educational training systems. Strong arguments promoting the positive lessons of East Asian business systems can also be seen in the work of G. Henderson (1993).

There are, however, problems within institutionalist frameworks. The earlier versions reproduce a view of 'the organisation as a passive reactor to the environment' (Bryman, 1993: 87) that is equally deterministic as population ecology or contingency, though shifting the focus to normative pressures. Even the more complex accounts run the risk of producing a mirror image of the convergence argument, focusing solely on difference. It is of course true that work organisation and other features of the industrial order will always differ from others on a local and national basis. Whether such explanations were ever wholly viable in the past, it is very doubtful that they are now. Societal institutions are increasingly subject to 'external' pressures for change. As Smith and Meiksins observe: 'Institutional analysis tended to focus on and reinforce national differences. The immediate problem with this perspective is to account for change and the dynamic nature of economies that are global, not nationally bounded systems' (1995: 3). Traditional industrial relations also tended to focus primarily on national systems or comparisons between them. This fails to engage with economic internationalisation and is inadequate in a period when those industrial relations regimes are increasingly forged at regional and supra-national levels (Howarth and Hughes, 2000).

It is inaccurate and unrealistic to go on treating organisations as 'societies in miniature' in the manner of Sorge *et al.* (1983: 54), who say that 'the differences between societies are so pervasive as to be immediately and consistently noticeable in every unit'. In reality, as we shall see later, large business organisations such as IBM are themselves carriers of distinctive financial, employment or technical practices. Sparrow and Hiltrop make a similar point with respect to the internationalisation of HRM practices: 'The "culture-bound" perspective runs the gauntlet between generalisations and stereotyping and fails to consider the equally pervasive impact of both individual differences and organisational choice over resource development' (1998: 83).

However, such perspectives are not necessarily conceptually tied to the state as an object of analysis. Neo-institutional approaches are becoming more sophisticated in their understanding of environments. As Warhurst (1997) observes, there is a growing recognition that the institutional environment does not mechanically determine organisational forms. As with conceptions of strategic choice in the previous chapter, there are still choices within constraints, and embeddedness still has to be enacted. Neo-institutionalism is also being extended to cover sectors, regions, and systems. With a small number of giant transnational firms increasingly dominating sectors and 'best practices' spreading rapidly within them, industry recipes consisting of conventions governing marketing, pricing, production methods and industrial relations can become influential (Whitley, 1987). Sectors can be conceived of as an 'organisational field' linking firms and the broader society (Di Maggio and Powell, 1983). Arias has demonstrated the value of this orientation in her analysis of the pharmaceutical industry in Ecuador. Multinationals operating in the area spread modern HRM practices from their headquarters to their subsidiaries. But local firms do not mimic the multinationals and 'seem to constitute a world of their own organised along family business lines' (1993: 24). Organisations in the two fields are responding to different normative environments and relational constraints such as rules set by government favourable to the largest players. Despite the persuasiveness of the analysis, Arias goes on to argue that the relevance of national boundaries remains paramount. But it is not enough to take the firm and the market as units of analysis, without appreciating the broader dynamics of capitalist political economy (Warhurst, 1997).

Globalisation

With many best-selling contemporary management books adding 'global' in their titles, we can be sure that a considerable amount of hype surrounds the idea. But globalisation has also become a focal point for an important debate about contemporary organisations and the economy (see for example, Smith and Elger, 1994) and for a range of serious accounts of the refashioning of key sectors such as engineering (Edquist and Jacobsson, 1988) and high technology (J. Henderson, 1989). The process can be said to consist of a number of interrelated tendencies.

The internationalisation of production and services Foreign direct investment (FDI) and industrial location have obviously been long-term developments. This is now much more prominent. FDI by companies outstripped world output by four times and trade by three from 1983–90 (Beneria, 1995). What is also newer is the organisation and co-ordination of activities by transnational companies at a global level: 'Rivals compete against each other on a truly worldwide basis, drawing on competitive advantages that grow out of their entire network of worldwide activities' (Porter, 1990: 35).

Stateless corporations Transnationals that utilise foreign direct investment to establish 'globally' integrated production or service chains are increasingly the key players. They are differentiated from multinationals that create branches in separate countries in order to penetrate domestic markets. Though genuinely 'stateless' corporations are rare, contemporary corporate structures articulate a complex network of parent–subsidiary relations, as well as direction and co-ordination of economic activities across national boundaries. Know-how which is gained centrally or in one particular subsidiary operating unit is capable of being transferred to the various sub-units of the corporation.

World markets This tendency refers not merely to the growth, but to the integration of world trade. Included within this framework are the development of relatively standardised, albeit regionally adapted, global products such as the 'world car' announced by Ford in 1994, the erosion of protected national industries (for example, European telecommunications industries or previous state firms), and the acceleration of movement out of mainly domestic markets by particular national capitals.

Increased integration into the international division of labour Within the ideal type of globalisation, 'distinct national economies are subsumed and rearticulated into the system by essentially international processes and transactions' (Hirst and Thompson, 1992: 360). This may include the development of international state apparatuses that interact with and shape the international division of labour (Pitelis, 1993). New countries (for example, China), regions or social formations, notably the new post-Communist economies of Eastern Europe, are gradually brought into the financial and corporate workings of the global economy and pressured to specialise in the provision of certain goods or services such as cheap labour.

The internationalisation of financial markets National currencies are still significant, but markets for finance have become truly global in the recent and more deregulated past, accelerated by 24-hour trading and new communication technologies (Warhurst, Nickson and Shaw, 1998: 267). There has also been closer integration with production. Transnational banks offer new services to multinationals, such as the financing of acquisitions, management of liquid assets and leasing arrangements. At the same time, increasing numbers of banks are subsidiaries of multinationals. It is therefore possible to speak of transnational finance capital in which the two actors, 'are organically linked in their internationalisation' (Andreff, 1984: 66).

Such trends are undoubtedly influential ones, with the result that the space for the national and local is squeezed as organisational forms and practices demonstrate convergent tendencies. This can be seen in Austria and Sweden, both of which are societies with traditionally distinctive national models embodied in social settlements and ways of regulating the political economy. But such arrangements are under considerable strain from the rapid internationalisation of their domestic economies. Sweden has had to cope with the dual pressures of an accelerated drift of capital abroad and competition at home from Japanese models and other variants on lean production. The closure of Volvo's Udevalla and Kalmar plants has had a particularly destructive effect on attempts to create a new 'Swedish model' based on innovative work organisation. Sandberg (1993: 8) comments that, 'The management of Volvo does not seem to be able to resist the pressure of comparisons and the possibilities of moving the production between units, that the alliance with Renault will bring'.

This convergence is aided by other processes. Supra-national state systems such as the EC, the North American Free Trade Agreement (NAFTA) and Asia Pacific Economic Co-operation (APEC) are not new, but 'What is significant today is the sheer increase in their number, the growth in their territorial scope, and their acquisition of important new functions' (Jessop, 1992: 10). The Social Chapter of the Maastricht Treaty has been just one example of the development of webs of rules involving the standardisation of qualifications, social rights, quality systems, and employment regulation (Cressey and Jones, 1991). Conservative politicians proclaimed the much-vaunted British opt-out from this dimension of the treaty. This, however, was a hollow victory. Many trans- national firms applied the provisions anyway, for example by setting up employee consultation through works councils, given that it would have been legally and ethically very difficult to exclude British employees from the new practices.

Transnational companies are significant in a variety of other ways. There is more rapid diffusion of 'best practice'. True, this is not a wholly new phenomenon. In the post-war period the giant US corporations transferred work organisation and mana- gerial techniques across capitalist countries. Firms can be effective 'social carriers of techniques', standardising the environments around them. The role of transnationals in spreading new technology and production organisation techniques across the globe is widely acknowledged, particularly with reference to Japanese firms (Edquist and Jacobsson, 1988). The more extensive integration of corporate structures noted above, allied to factors such as the internationalisation of consultancy, business schools, and the market for management literature, is enabling more rapid learning processes (Mueller, 1996). A global economic and political order 'has resulted in a transforma- tion of particular national patterns of work organisation, management and labour relations into universal standards of best practice' (Smith and Meiksins, 1995: 20). Greater convergence can result from the fact that such comparisons are coercive in a context of competitive benchmarking (Ferner and Edwards, 1995; Berggren, 1996). Finally, more advanced information technology such as computer networks for co-ordination and control are facilitating standardisation and integration of corporate activities (Marginson *et al.*, 1995).

All these trends exist and are important, but we have to add some qualifications. There is a danger of simply reverting to the earlier determinism and unproblematic notions of efficiency. This danger can be illustrated by reference to *The Machine that Changed the World* (Womack *et al.*, 1990), which has had a substantial influence on governments and companies. Drawing on the experience of Japanese production systems and extensive research into the motor industry, the authors promote the principles of 'lean production', which they claim produces efficiently with half the human effort, with considerable zeal. Such principles 'can be applied equally in every industry across the globe' (Womack *et al.*, 1990: 8), as long as auto companies adopt the necessary structures and practices to promote diffusion. An example of the latter would be 'an integrated, global personnel system that promotes personnel from any country in the company as if nationality did not exist' (Womack *et al.*, 1990: 4). We are concerned here to evaluate not the merits of lean production but its status as a universal 'best practice'. The study has been heavily criticised for getting the statistics wrong and exaggerating Japanese advantage (Williams *et al.*, 1992a). For example it does not explain how Toyota and other firms take labour out of production, ignoring the specific features of post-war Japanese labour relations, where defeated unions and malleable workforces allow high levels of work intensification. Taking a different direction, Berggren (1993) questions whether the record of Japanese manufacturers at home and in the US transplants on high work speed and employee surveillance, low health and safety standards and exclusion of union involvement in regulating production would be acceptable in the very different European context.

Though there is some evidence that aspects of production practices can be uncoupled from culture and transferred across national boundaries (Florida and Kenney, 1991), the claim of superior ways of organising *production* separates it from the supportive institutional context – the industrial relations system, the subordinate networks of suppliers, state and financial sector support. In other words we are back to the social embeddedness of economic action discussed earlier. *The Machine the Changed the World* is an extreme case of ideas of globalisation or convergence following single paths. Just like the older convergence theory, discredited for its technological and other determinisms (Kerr *et al.*, 1960), all linear models, including the popular notions of moves from Fordism to post-Fordism or mass production to flexible specialisation (Aglietta, 1979; Lipietz, 1982; Piore and Sabel, 1984) need to be treated with suspicion. This is because they work on stereotypical ideas of homogeneous, static systems and underestimate the pattern of adaptation and varied diffusion that 'best practices' go through. As we will discuss in more detail later, the patterns are still strongly shaped by the residual powers of nation states to create distinctive contexts for economic activity to which firms have positive reasons to adapt (Hirst and Thompson, 1992; Whitley, 1994). Mainstream business analysis (Kitschelt, 1992; Porter, 1990) also provides useful insights into how there are still important variations by sector in processes of industrial innovation and competitive advantage.

Understanding the comparative influences on work organisation

As with discussion of models of organisation–environment relations in the previous chapter, it has proven difficult to escape the dichotomies of determinism and choice, convergence and divergence. For transnational companies this apparent paradox is reflected through the contradictory pressures to standardise their operations, products and services so as to maximise the scale and cost benefits of global integration, while at the same time attempting to serve the needs of specific markets. It is common ground that international firms are moving beyond their traditional multi-domestic or polycentric forms in which relatively autonomous policies and practices could be geared towards differentiated local markets (Perlmutter, 1969; Porter, 1990). A favourite formula for solving this problem is the prescription for such organisations to be *glocal* (Bartlett and Ghoshal, 1990a). Bartlett and Ghoshal believe that culture plays the primary integrative role, the transnational a 'management mentality' rather than a specific organisational form.

It is certainly true that the development of complex international networks with a variety of units inside and external to firms creates considerable integration problems. A detailed examination of the co-ordination mechanisms of international firms is beyond the scope of this book (though see Thompson *et al.*, 1998), but we can make some general observations. Culture is not necessarily the glue that links the parts of a global organisation together. For example the contemporary large firm is increasingly built through acquisition, merger and collaboration; thus bringing together component parts with very different histories. While it is not impossible to extend cultural controls across the diverse units and activities, evidence shows that integration through financial controls is more likely (Thompson *et al.*, 1998). In fact there are a variety of means of integration available, as persuasively demonstrated by Duenas (1993). Drawing on case studies of a number of companies operating in global markets, he argues that only IKEA, the Swedish-based furniture dealer, operates a cohesive corporate culture that consciously transcends national and other cultural differences. Other approaches included a common framework from a technical/professional culture in a company dominated by the engineering function (Elf Aquitaine); financial planning systems used to override cultural differences (Emerson Electric); and sophisticated management information systems co-existing with local autonomy (the Dutch multinational, Buhrmann-Tetterode).

Given our emphasis on the changing relations of capital, labour and the state in the current context, to take the discussion further we need to pull together what we know of the forces that shape organisational forms and practices. A model developed by Smith and Meiksins (1995) is useful, in which they distinguish between three kinds of effects on work organisation. (See Figure 6.1.)

System effects are commonalities generated by social formations such as capitalism as a mode of production or patriarchy. All societies and the organisations within them have to operate within the parameters set by systems, for example competitive relations between enterprises, the conflicting interests of capital and labour. These processes create rules of the game that shape social relations in the workplace and constrain organisational choices.

Tsoukas (1994a) demonstrates how this operated with respect to firms in state socialist systems, utilising the previously discussed concepts of institutional theory. He argues that socio-economic systems have a macro-logic that conditions and provides continuities in the organisational characteristics of firms irrespective of particular histories and societies. In the case of state socialism, collective ownership, command planning and a heavy emphasis on ideology leave little space for autonomous economic agents. Firms therefore increase their chances of survival by displaying conformity, often of a

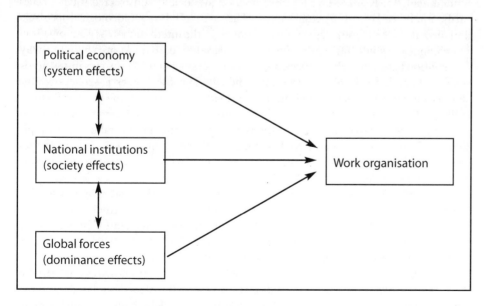

A model by Smith and Meiksins   *FIGURE 6.1*

'ceremonial' nature, to the party–state apparatus. The macro rules and institutions are isomorphically reproduced at micro level, overseen by the party structures in the workplace and a hierarchical and rule-bound style of management: 'The organisation becomes a political-cum-ideological miniature of the state' (1994a: 34). It is perfectly possible to explain the dependent relations between state and enterprise in such societies without the baggage of institutionalism and allowing for more variations (see Smith and Thompson, 1992). But the general point about system effects still stands and indicates why naïve attempts to transfer managerial techniques from West to East may fail. It is worth noting that the fact that the transition from command to market economy is still in its relatively early stages may be a more substantial barrier to such transfer than Hofstede's emphasis on national mindsets.

Under capitalism, the relations between system and organisation are more loosely coupled and there is greater diversity of institutional configurations at both levels. This is where *societal effects* are most pertinent. As we have already discussed this point extensively we need not dwell on it here, except for one observation: some nation states provide stronger and more distinctive institutional environments than others. Japan is always the example, but Sweden, Germany, or Austria would equally fit the bill. What they have in common is more densely structured institutional frameworks influenced by a strong social settlement between key actors – capital, labour, and the state – which shapes the relations between them and enhances the connections between social, economic and political institutions.

In some circumstances societies with strong social settlements can generate *dominance effects*. This is because particular societies come to represent conceptions of success and progress, with models of 'best practice' concerning labour markets, labour processes and other factors exported from one society to another. The US, Sweden, Germany and Japan have all played such a role at some time in the post-war period. You may have noticed that this term is always placed in inverted commas signalling that it is not intended to be taken literally. Best practices are socially constructed and not necessarily simply read off from actual success. They are read through ideological spectacles and mediated by a country's position and power in the international division of labour. Dominance does not indicate automatic or uncontested adaptation. There is always competition between such practices, aiding the process whereby key actors in and across societies 'search' for viable and legitimate models. This framework is useful, with one serious limitation. Work organisations are made to be the recipient of influences, embedded in contexts rather than an independent force. Given the immense power of contemporary transnational corporations this is unfortunate. To take one example, firms such as IBM, Toyota or McDonald's are also creators and purveyors of 'best practice'. The Smith and Meiksin diagram would need to be redesigned to indicate such reciprocal influences.

How the various influences of system, society, 'best practice' and organisation align themselves is not predictable or in a fixed hierarchy. This is because there are a number of complex transactions between capital, labour and the nation state within the international division of labour (Thompson and Smith, 1998: 196–8). Social scientists need to show how these transactions work and levels are linked in concrete instances.

So, when discussing how managerial and organisational knowledge is diffused, Arias (1993: 30) argues that, 'Cross national research on transfers should be done within a neo-institutional framework that allows a shifting of levels of analysis from the organisation, to the field, to the national, to the world-system level'. J. Henderson (1992) also fleshes out an institutional analysis by outlining *modes of articulation* between national and global economies. For example, most of the manufacturing economies of the EC articulate to the world economy as independent exporters, with firms distributing and marketing under their own name. In contrast some sectors of the East Asian economies and those of Central and Eastern Europe are more likely to be involved in commercial subcontracting, where production is structured in commodity chains driven by the demands of distributors and retailers rather than manufacturers.

Global capitalism remains a dynamic system in which different strategies are available to establishing competitive advantage for companies and countries. In that competitive struggle, forces of divergence and convergence are in continual tension. Different facets of societal or corporate organisation will be subject to differential pressures. For example, while there are now more discretionary powers for firms to adopt common human resource policies (Schienstock, 1991), industrial relations systems are the least likely to be internationally standardised because they are most embedded in national institutional frameworks. This may be one of the reasons why Adler and Bartholomew (1992) found that many firms did not seek to benchmark 'excellence' in global HRM practice. Production and management systems, however, are subject much more directly to dominance effects from perceived best practices and the need of transnationals to integrate their diverse activities and structures (Thompson, Flecker and Wallace, 1995). In other words, contrary to a number of writers, it is not just the existence of a 'global mind-set' that determines the likely extent of integration, but the very real pressures to standardise that impinge more on some corporate activities and in some sectors than others. Overall, the 'environment' therefore has to be conceived not as a given force within which dependent organisations adapt and transact, but as a global political economy whose levels provide a shifting dynamic within which organisations reciprocally interact.

The state still matters

Amongst all the rhetoric about borderless worlds, the state is increasingly considered to be of less and less significance. It is certainly true that the state's activities are constrained by having to operate within the existing market framework. Particularly in a world system of interlocking manufacture, trade and finance, no nation state can ignore the requirements of capital accumulation and reproduction. Capital can utilise its resource power to place unique pressure on the state's economic management processes. Within these 'new rules of the game', corporate rather than state governance has tended to become dominant. This is reflected in the drift towards 'neo-liberal', market-driven practices in which:

> Political efforts at neo-corporatist institutional design have come to a standstill almost everywhere … many governments now seem to place little hope on negotiated adjustment and no longer see it as their responsibility to protect the principle of joint regulation from the disruptive effects of a severe power imbalance. (Streek, 1987: 286–7)

However, the above discussion should not be taken to say that transnational and other large firms have total power over national and local environments. In part, this is because globalisation is far from a complete process. Rugman (2000) argues that much of the world's economic transactions are 'triadic', with trade, investment and ownership largely within regional blocs. The current situation lies between markets and states (2000: 81). It may be overdoing it to argue, as he does, that globalisation is a myth, but there are a range of qualifying factors. For example, national government policies still often support 'their' transnationals in the race of globalisation, in particular where political and military hegemony is at stake. As indicated earlier, though states can no longer act as if national economies were insulated from international competition, there are still distinctive national trajectories within globalisation (Hirst and Thompson, 1996; Boyer and Drache, 1996).

Additionally, states can still play key roles in promoting technological competence, subsidising capital accumulation or bargaining over production and investment decisions (Gordon, 1988; Jenkins, 1984; Jessop, 1992). As Whitley notes (1987: 140) the capacity of large firms to determine their own market 'niches' requires a level of analysis of the political economy of international and state agencies, yet this is seldom recognised in organisational analysis. The state also continues to act as a 'collective capitalist': attending to long-term interests even against particular business demands; providing facilities such as a national transport network or housing that single capitals cannot; and regulating and incorporating demands from subordinate classes through concessions and institutional channels which do not threaten existing class power.

As we argued earlier, these transactions are complex and may bring particular states, or supra-national formations such as the EC, into conflict with capital. The state does not function unambiguously in the interests of a single class; it is a state in capitalist society rather than *the* capitalist state, and it is an arena of struggle constituted and divided by opposing interests rather than a centralised and unified political actor (Pearson, 1986). It is possible to recognise that the state has a high level of dependency on capital accumulation for its economic resources and success, without accepting that its form or activities can be derived solely from the class relation to capital. In a more general sense, system stability, including state institutions, requires a level of loyalty, consent or even just acquiescence from subordinate classes and groups (Clegg, Boreham and Dow, 1987: 286).

Conclusion

The need to legitimise power is one reason why there will always be choices and different trajectories within and between states about how to manage the political economy. There is no evidence to show that there is any permanent or essential relation between capital, labour and the state, or between the political and economic environments business organisations operate in. Thompson and Smith (1998) recently examined the economic modernisation strategies pursued in the UK and Australia over the last two decades. Governments in both countries were trying to reposition the economy within their respective regions, with a particular emphasis on attracting Japanese FDI. Despite a common emphasis on deregulation and opening up markets, the fact that the strategies were initiated by Conservative and Labour governments respectively led to considerable differences in intent and outcome: 'State industry policies are not simply barriers or filters to the homogenising effects of corporate interests, but through their competitiveness strategies, are remaking their own "niche" in the international division of labour' (1998: 209). The state clearly still matters.

7 Management

We saw in earlier chapters that the first quarter of the twentieth century marked the emergence of professional management as social force, specialist occupational category and set of distinct work practices. This development was integral to changes in the organisation of capitalist production, with the modern bureaucratic enterprise increasingly based on the joint stock company, often in the new multidivisional form, with its separation of ownership and management. In this type of structure, middle managers headed autonomous divisions that integrated production and distribution by co-ordinating flows from suppliers to consumers in the more clearly defined markets (Chandler, 1977). Such divisions administered their functional activities through specialist departments. All this encouraged the professionalisation of management and the rapid spread of administrative techniques. However, as Tsoukas (1994b: 289) argues, despite the emergence of managerial hierarchies and increased visibility of their tasks and functions, 'it has not been easy to answer the question, what is management?'

Classical management theory

Problems of analysis have not been helped by the fact that management has often been treated as a singular, unproblematic process. Shenhav (1999: 102–5) criticises Chandler and others for treating the rise of managerial capitalism merely as a functional response to changing technologies and markets. This 'edits out' the contested rationality underlying the emergence of management systems. Particular groups, notably engineers, promoted such thinking and their own role as neutral arbiters within the systems, while some employers and many labour organisations were suspicious or hostile. Engineers worked to extend the boundaries of their profession by trading on the general rise of interest in management and planning that was characteristic of the early part of the century. However, as P. Armstrong (1984) shows, they were to find it difficult to sustain the privileged role as the focal point of management. The knowledge base of the 'profession' was to become increasingly disconnected from their productive expertise.

Management thought became intimately linked to the appearance of a distinct occupational grouping, organisational theory being used as a resource to understand the complexities of the large-scale organisation and management's role within it. A key theme underlying the contradictory and partial organisational prescriptions, strategies and tactics was the belief in principles and even 'laws' concerning the nature of managerial activities and functions. As Child observes:

> Management's claim to professionalism, for instance, was only plausible if it could be shown to possess some uniform and generalised body of knowledge upon which its practitioners could draw. The so-called 'principles of management' could

be presented as a theoretical base upon which the subject of 'management' rested. (Child, 1969: 225)

This belief in the power of professionalism has been a recurring feature of management thought, but has been sometimes difficult to sustain in the face of unethical practices and quick-fix fads. Responding sceptically to the growth of the latter, Hilmer and Donaldson (1996: 172) argue that 'good managers are more likely to emerge and gain respect if management is viewed as a profession that develops and applies an evolving body of knowledge'. Furthermore, that knowledge should be seen as 'impartial and expert'. Interestingly, one of the more perceptive pop management writers, Pascale (1990) attributes the startling explosion of fads to the idea of professional management, notably that there is a set of transferable generic management principles.

Such views have their roots in the inter-war period of 'classical management' theorists such as Fayol, Taylor and Barnard, discussed briefly in Chapter 3. As we saw, Fayol was the most concerned to elaborate common characteristics of management. These consisted of *planning* general lines of action and forecasting; organising human and material resources within appropriate structures; *commanding* the *activities* of personnel for optimum return; *co-ordination* of varied activities and *control* to ensure consistency with rules and command. These were situated within a detailed set of principles reflecting the division of labour and hierarchy of the bureaucratic enterprise, tempered by equitable treatment and personal responsibility. One of the effects of this way of thinking was to define managerial functions by a process of abstraction from specific activities into a conception of general management (P. Armstrong, 1987a). Managerial work would differ not in kind but only in the proportion that is actually 'managerial'. This would have a profound influence on management thought, spreading the idea that knowledge, skills and experience are common and transferable.

Meanwhile in Britain, Mary Parker Follet was producing prescriptions for a science of behaviour informed by the concerns of the human relations tradition. Emphasis shifted to the 'art' of getting things done through people. Management could learn this science because it was derived from situational laws governed by the needs of the system. As such, management could represent and integrate all interests through its capacity to apply optimal solutions through depersonalised authority. Classical writings have now been superseded in the post-war period by a body of more detailed studies of management. Indeed, the study of organisation has become synonymous with that of management. In the Anglo-American tradition of organisation theory, management studies has emerged as an 'intellectual field' sustained by an extensive network of educational and training institutions (Whitley, 1984). The more confident asserted the viability of a management or administrative science whose methods and knowledge could support rational activities and decision-making. A post-war generation of 'new systematisers' (Barley and Kunda, 1992: 377) ranged from those who developed techniques of operations research such as critical path method, program evaluation and review technique, to contingency theorists with their attempts to specify causal relations between environmental and structure variables, and motivational schemas based on rational calculation. Employees were either absent or objects to be acted on through the new systems. The new ground rules drew on 'hard' knowledge that could be learnt by managers in general rather than functional specialists. Such an approach competed with the influence of human relations perspectives, with their notion of training managers to learn how to exercise social and leadership skills.

This chapter aims to examine such claims through an analysis of the nature of management. It will argue that though traditional and recent research offer important insights, the perspectives are partial and flawed, presenting management as if it is neutral and de-politicised, neglecting the divisions and contradictions embedded in the managerial labour process itself. Of course, power and control are not just adjuncts to a discussion of management. The following two chapters set out the central debates about control and power in organisations in their own right.

The nature of management

The post-war literature (such as Drucker, 1955; Stewart, 1967; Mintzberg, 1973; Kotter, 1982) shared the central concern of the classical writers to identify common functions and criteria for effectiveness. There has been an even greater emphasis on the individual as a unit of analysis, a problematic of 'what do managers do?' (Hales, 1986). The answer given is a positive one. Drucker starts his well-known text by saying that, 'The manager is the dynamic, life-giving element in every business . . . the only effective advantage an enterprise has in a competitive economy' (1955: 13). Texts continually invoke as examples captains of industry such as Bill Gates of Microsoft. In this elevated role, the manager is presented almost as a free-floating centre of power. Organisations are still frequently treated as closed systems with the assumption that 'it was largely within management's own powers to fashion behaviour and relationships as might best suit their own purposes' (Child, 1969: 168). Paradoxically by focusing on the individual, management can be analysed as if it was homogeneous, leading to the conception of the 'universal manager' carrying out a generalised set of functions standing above any specific context (Mintzberg, 1973).

Theorists could agonise about whether management was science, art, magic or politics (Watson, 1986: 29), but all options rest on the analytical and practical skills of 'successful managers'. The constant struggle for competency is further linked to the assumption that management *effectiveness* is tangible and identifiable (Hales, 1986: 88). To this end anything can be quantified and learned. The focus of course changes. It may be, for instance, the fashionable qualities of managerial excellence (see Hitt *et al.*, 1986: 1011).

These various assumptions underwrite the more fundamental view of management practices as a neutral resource, the central task of which is deciding what should be done and getting other people to do it. In this view, which we describe as technicist, managers can embody and carry out the central mission of the organisation and secure its desired objectives. Such thinking, as Shenhav (1999: 1) observes, reifies management and purges its history of the conflicts that have given it distinctive shape. It also links back to the idea discussed in Chapter 1 of management as the guardians of organisations being rational tools to secure goals. By conceiving of the ends as unitary and the means as objectively rational, the socially-constructed, political character of organisational arrangements is removed (Berkeley Thomas, 1993: 37). If rationality is assumed to be unambiguously represented through formal decision-making and structures, deeper questions about ends and means in organisations are lost. So, for example, who occupies positions of authority and whose purposes managerial work serves cannot be determined by an 'impartial appeal to the requirements of an impersonal, technical logic' (Alvesson and Willmott, 1992: 6).

In mainstream writings, managers are also seen as functionally necessary in a deeper sense. The functions are 'indispensable' and are ones which 'no-one but the manager can perform' (Drucker, 1977: 39). As Willmott observes (1984: 350), this view confuses the general process of *management* of resources with the role of mana*gers* empowered to command others within specific institutional frameworks. Put another way, it wrongly assumes that 'the management function must, of necessity, reside with a particular category of agents who manage or administer other agents' (Hales, 1988: 5). In particular circumstances, work teams or worker co-operatives can equally be said to be carrying out managerial functions.

Organisational theories seldom acknowledge the wider context in which managerial work is undertaken. Whitley argues that it is better to attempt to 'specify general features of managerial tasks in terms of their functions in the organisation and change of economic enterprises as interdependent units of resource co-ordination and control, rather than identifying the characteristics of all jobs by "managers"' (1984: 343). Elsewhere, the wider theory of a 'managerial revolution' was being articulated. Part of the idea of an 'organisation society', as discussed in Chapter 1, this theory rested on a particular interpretation of changes in the nature of the large corporation. As the dominant form, joint stock companies were held to be characterised by a separation of ownership and control, share dispersal and a corresponding rise in the importance of a professional managerial élite who run the new corporations. While the growing significance of management is indisputable, many adherents of the theory (Berle and Means, 1935) took the new corporate system to be a 'purely neutral technocracy', with managers of a different background and experience exercising social responsibilities. Tougher versions (Burnham, 1945) envisaged a managerially planned and controlled society beyond the workplace, with management becoming the dominant class of all industrial societies.

The managerial revolution thesis had a wider significance for social theory, often influenced by systems thinking (Reed, 1984: 278). At its core was the view that capitalism as a system based on individual private ownership was being supplanted by a post-capitalist society in which old political disputes about ownership were irrelevant (Dahrendorf, 1959). But these theoretical developments enabled management writers such as Drucker to assert that 'we no longer talk of "capital" and "labour", we talk of "management" and "labour"' (1955: 13). Some scepticism was expressed by senior managers who referred to 'claptrap' about social responsibilities, reminding their colleagues that they remained the servants of their employers (J. Child, 1969: 152–3). Managerial capitalism had extended its tentacles. But we should keep in mind, following the discussion in Chapter 6, that such assumptions about theory and practice may be culturally-loaded. What is presented by Fayol and others as logical necessity, may be the outcome of historical development and social context (Hales, 1993: 3). Organisational life in Germany and other countries was not dominated by the search for a profession of management: 'Continentals appreciate the specialist nature of most executive jobs: they do not see why specialists should be described as "managers", nor are they notable for having occupational groups which call themselves "professionals". European business does not seem to have suffered through the lack of either idea' (Fores and Glover, 1976: 104). As Grint (1995: 5) observes, what management is 'really like' is in part a function of how we historically and cultural construct the category. *British* management and its 'rationality' is strongly linked to particular conceptions of national identity.

Researchers in this area add further objections to mainstream concepts of rationality that were raised earlier. The emphasis shifts from the political character of managerial practices to the limits of their knowledge. March and Simon (1958) introduce the concept of 'intended rationality', recognising that there are considerable constraints to the capacity to access and evaluate a full range of options. The existing structures of specialisation and hierarchy in organisations, as well as the routine practices identified in a Weberian analysis, will limit the content and flow of information and set agendas for decision-making. As a result, organisational participants are boundedly rational, having to work with simplified models of reality, and there is 'limited search' and 'satisficing' rather than optimal choices. Cyert and March (1963) point to similar processes such as 'uncertainty absorption', whereby in order to maintain stability of operations, rules and processes are geared to short-run decisions and frequent reviews. What emerges are policies and decisions by 'incremental comparison'; not a rational science, but a 'science' of muddling through (Lindblom, 1959). We discuss the question of the rationality of management at greater length in the next chapter.

Management practices: a new realism?

Demarcating the boundaries of rationality helped to extend the study of management. But discussion of the core issue of defining and classifying activities moved on to a more detailed 'realism'. Fores and Glover argue that, 'observation shows that [this] classical view is largely a convenient fiction. . . . In reality, executive work is complex, confusing to the outsider, and rarely predictable (1976: 194). What 'observations' are they talking about? By getting a large and varied group of managers to fill in diaries, Stewart (1967) drew up classifications based on how they spent their *time*. This produced emissaries, writers, discussers, troubleshooters and committee men. A later study (1976) focused on patterns of contact; this time identifying hub, peer-dependent, man-management and solo. In contrast, Mintzberg (1973) confined himself to five chief executives and classified ten roles with three headings. Under *interpersonal* come figurehead, leader and liaison; under *informational* are monitor, disseminator and spokesman; and under *decisional* come entrepreneurial, disturbance-handler, resource allocator and negotiator. Many of the categories used in these and other studies are largely interchangeable, for example leader/figurehead/spokesman (Hales, 1986). New terms such as 'network building' and 'setting agendas' correspond in substance to old favourites such as 'planning'. Hales (1993: 3) is surely right that Fayol's basic formulation endures, despite subsequent claims that it is outdated or superseded. He produces a composite list (see Table 7.1) from six of the best-known studies, which 'exhibit striking parallels with the supposedly outdated "classical principles of management"' (1986: 95). In addition, some of the variations merely reflect managerial *ideologies*, with modern writers in a more democratic era preferring to describe command as motivation (Mullins, 1985: 121).

Nevertheless, it remains the case that the new empirical studies do partly break with traditional approaches and those found in popular management books. Once the complication of producing labels and lists is set aside, more realistic insights are available. We have already referred to Cyert and March's findings on the short-term incrementalism in the sphere of decision-making. But the significant break-throughs are aided by a willingness to use a greater variety of research methods than those used in broad-brush analyses of managerial functions. Structured or unstructured

TABLE 7.1   Managerial functions

1   Acting as a figurehead and leader of an organisational unit
2   Liason: the formation and maintenance of contacts
3   Monitoring, filtering and disseminating information
4   Allocating resources
5   Handling disturbances and maintaining workflows
6   Negotiating
7   Innovating
8   Planning
9   Controlling and directing subordinates.

Source: Colin P. Hales (1986) 'What Do Managers Do? A Critical Review of the Evidence', *Journal of Management Studies*, 23. 1: 95.

observation methods, time-budget studies and self-report questionnaires can capture a greater sense of fluidity and processual factors (Horne and Lupton, 1965; Stewart, 1967, 1976; Mintzberg, 1973; Kotter, 1982; Burns, 1982).

Such studies purport to reveal that the image of the reflective strategist, thinker and planner is a myth. An alternative picture is indicated through the language of realism. Though there are variations between the studies, management practices are said to be opportunistic, habitual, tactical, reactive, frenetic, ad hoc, brief, fragmented and concerned with fixing. This arises primarily because the manager has to adapt to continued uncertainties, limited information and contradictory pressures, not least on time and energy. As a result, routines are shaped by short time spans, the domination of face-to-face interaction and lateral communication in gathering and using information. For Mintzberg, this actually corresponds to managerial preferences for use of informal structures, gossip and speculation.

Nor are such activities necessarily bad for effectiveness and efficiency. Though energy can be dissipated in conflict and power struggles between cliques, Kotter (1982) points out that patterns do emerge based on establishing and maintaining *networks* vital for co-operation and a flow of information. Finally, though the focus is on the internal world of the organisation, the new realism is not incompatible with an analysis of environmental pressures. Loveridge's (1982) study of manufacturing companies in the Midlands showed that marketing and financial pressures, plus the need to accommodate to the power of workforce job controls, led in the direction of federal structures and short-term reactive policies and a concern with implementation rather than planning.

The 'realist' challenge to the scientific and rational character of management is useful and widely accepted. It has not, however, established unchallenged intellectual domination. Not only do textbooks remain influenced by prescriptions from Fayol, preoccupations with *new* lists of functions can still be described as variations on a classical theme. Indeed the actual choice of new lists is extensive. Many pop management writers recycle a limited number of activities under new and more exotic titles, including that of jungle fighter and gamesman (Maccoby, 1977). Much more influential has been Peters and Waterman's (1982) list of eight characteristics associated with 'excellent' companies, itself influenced by the classic writings of Barnard. Lists of any kind continue to be the outward form of a belief in a universal, transferable and common *essence* of management, a disposition that has been relatively constant in the development of organisational theory (Huczynski, 1993: 98). Partly in response to the excesses of claims about new forms of organisation and management, influential voices are calling for a return to that 'essence', though it may be redefined in different ways, for example as the pursuit of rhetoric, identity and robust action (Eccles and Nohria, 1992).

Watson (1994: 37) suggests that new empirical studies have produced an over-reaction to classical perspectives. Drawing on his own research among managers he argues that there is a need to get back to basic principles, while recognising the inherent complexity of practice. Put more analytically, he is suggesting that we can distinguish between the real functions (such as planning and co-ordinating) that management has, and the activities through which effectiveness is sought. Nor is this impetus to return to some of classical themes purely theoretical. The past decade has seen the rise of a competence movement in a number of countries that aims to specify a common currency of occupational standards and develop managers with the aid of behavioural and task measurements (Burgoyne, 1993).

There are also inherent *limits* to the realist research. It is, as Hales (1988) notes, an *internal* critique, and at the heart of the problem is the fact that it is at the *empirical* level only. Realism can show us that management is not what it is made out to be. Instead it portrays the activities of managers 'as a quite arbitrary set of roles with little suggestion as to why they are as they are' (P. Armstrong, 1986: 19). The pervasive image of ad-hocery and muddling through seems to deny both purpose and coherence. Hales (1986) rightly observes that by focusing on individual jobs, rather than management as a process, behaviour is unsituated and neglects the institutional context and functions. This is worsened by the tendency of behavioural analysis to concentrate on observable activities in a non-problematical way. For all its limitations, responsibilities and functions were the focus of classical theory and many of the criticisms levelled at have been attacks on a straw man (Berkeley Thomas, 1993: 51). In this sense 'realism' marks a retreat from a broader framework of analysis.

Understanding managerial work requires questions to be asked not just about what managers do, but what they have to ensure others do: in other words, an emphasis on the *control* of particular organisational units in the labour process, albeit as one phase of the management process rather than the whole story (Hales, 1988: 5). As one manager commented to Watson in response to the question, what is the essential difference between a managerial and non-managerial job, 'Gut feel says to me: in a managerial job you have some aspect of controlling other people – directing things. I don't like the words I am using here but if I'm actually honest, it's about directing other people' (1994: 49).

Analysing management in terms of its control functions on behalf of capital is associated with labour process or neo-Marxist perspectives. These criticise the previously discussed approaches for focusing on individual activities, marginalising the neglect of the broader structural context. Or, as Tsoukas puts it, 'By reducing the study of managers to the study of individual actors on the stage, the script and the setting which enables actors to perform in the first place are neglected' (1994a: 294). However, to leap from the individual to structure runs the risk of producing over-generalised, over-deterministic accounts. Indeed, many commentators have objected precisely on these grounds, arguing that the managerial activity of making the organisation work is multifaceted, and that managers cannot be treated as 'ciphers' who simply serve other, higher interests (Alvesson and Willmott, 1992: 7). Managers may pursue their own interests and identities (Watson, 1994); act in a genuinely altruistic way on behalf of the organisation (Grint, 1995); or promote sectional interests, for example engineering, that are distinct from those of capitalists (Shenhav, 1999).

We explore some of the relations between management, strategy and control in more detail in the next chapter. However, as Grint (1995: 51) admits, labour process accounts have become subtler in their explanations of why managers do what they do. In particular, as Tsoukas (1994a: 294) notes, neo-Marxist research has tried to overcome the problem of the leap from individual to structure by introducing more complexity into the picture through a focus on management divisions of labour. The next section considers these contributions.

Bringing the threads together: management as a labour process

What is required is a structural analysis that can account for both the constraints on and complexities of managerial behaviour: a perspective that is neither deterministic nor voluntaristic. *One* way forward begins from a remark made by Braverman that 'Management has become administration, which is a labour process conducted for the purpose of control within the corporation, and conducted moreover as a labour process exactly analogous to the process of production' (1974: 267). An offshoot is that the alienating conditions attached to the purchase and sale of labour become part of the managerial apparatus itself. Though little more than an aside, it has been utilised by a number of writers, notably Teulings (1986), to produce an analysis of management's role in the administrative apparatus of industrial organisations. The very fact that management is a 'global agent' carrying out the delegated functions of capital means that it is part of a collective labour process at corporate level. As we have previously indicated, this delegation in part reflects the transfer of functions such as co-ordination from the market to management and administration.

As that role has evolved, it has also become *differentiated*. So for example, large administrative divisions are, in the case of accounting, 'producing nothing but elaborate mechanisms of control associated with the realisation of capital and its enlargement' (Johnson, 1980: 355). But it is not only a case of the emergence of specialised functions and departments.

Differentiation also takes place in terms of *levels*. Teulings puts forward a model based on the existence of four distinct management functions: ownership, administration, innovation, and production (see Table 7.2). Two major consequences of the new division of labour follow. First, though the power of the administrative machinery of which management is a part has increased, the power of *individual* managers tends to diminish due to the rationalisation and routinisation of their activities. With the development of more complex managerial structures, new techniques have been introduced to integrate, monitor and control middle and lower management (Carter, 1985: 98).

> Years ago there might be five hundred fellas but you would only have one boss. Now everyone has a chief.... You can't discuss the job with them, everything is ticked in little boxes now. The boss is scared because if they don't treat everyone

Institutionalisation of distinctive management functions   *TABLE 7.2*
at separate levels of management

Function	Levels
I the ownership function	institutional management
– accumulation of capital	– creation and preservation of legitimations
II the administrative function	strategic management
– allocation of investments	– development of objectives
III the innovation function	structuring management
– product market development	– new combinations of production factors
IV the production function	operational management
– control of the direct labour process	– direction and co-ordination of direct labour

Source: W. M. Teulings, 'Managerial Labour Processes in Organised Capitalism', in D. Knights and H. Willmott (eds) (1986) *Managing the Labour Process,* Aldershot: Gower.

in a standard way they are afraid the other bosses will report them. (Plessey engineer quoted in Thompson and Bannon, 1985: 170)

Hale's analysis of management divisions of labour qualifies Teulings by showing that some management functions – those that the latter designates as operational – have their origins in the labour process rather than the market, and that there is not an exact correspondence between functions and levels. Those divisions are vertically fractionalised so that 'there is a differentiation within the performance of management work in terms of the extent to which agents are involved in the decision-making process' (Hales, 1988: 10, and see 1993, Chapter 8). As Watson (1994) shows in his account of a major UK telecommunications firm, even senior plant level managers will frequently find themselves frustrated by centralised control in companies that takes place at cost to their strategic inputs oriented towards long-term viability. Many will be subordinated to senior management through merely providing information from which decisions are made.

The activity of managers managing other managers takes place in different forms in the modern corporation, whether it be multi-divisional structures, holding companies or conglomerates, where varying forms of decentralisation go hand-in-hand with increased accountability and monitoring. At a micro-level, techniques such as management by objectives are still important, though presented as a form of control and motivation arising from the *objective* demands of the task (Drucker, 1955), which reproduces an aspect of the relationship workers have with 'scientific management'. In other cases, managers become more literally victims of their own devices (Storey, 1983: 93), as shown in studies such as Nichols and Beynon (1977) on the chemical industry. The latter additionally note the flattening-out of career structures and exposure to redundancy, characteristic of many managers. We know from other evidence (Newell and Dopson, 1996; Scarborough and Burrell, 1996) that middle managers in particular are becoming prime victims of organisational restructuring. The corporate preference for downsizing and de-layering, though exaggerated, is seriously affecting job security, career paths and work intensity (Littler, Bramble and McDonald, 1994).

This is not wholly new. Even the detailed studies of management functions discussed earlier in the chapter had the purpose of restructuring and rationalisation. Both Mintzberg (1973) and Drucker (1979) favour using techniques to split off routine activities from senior layers, introducing separation of conception and execution within management itself. This can now be further aided by computer technology and information systems.

The second consequence of changes in the managerial labour process is the growth of structural conflicts and imbalances between the different levels and functions. Teulings argues that each level of management tends to follow a rational logic of its own, enhancing the potential for defence of specific group interests, for example between production-oriented operational management and the strata concerned with innovation in product markets. Such tendencies are worsened by the absence of, or limits to, formal mechanisms to resolve or bargain conflicts. Instead they are likely to be dealt with at the operational level, leading to a disproportionate emphasis on changing the practices of shop floor workers.

One effect not discussed by Teulings is the effect on managerial *ideologies*. The legitimatory content in management thought has traditionally been directed towards two objectives: convincing non-management groups who challenged managerial goals and activities, and sustaining common aspirations (Child, 1969: 228–9). This becomes more problematic with the development of competing claims to fashion management theories and practices. Such competition cannot be wholly understood within the kind of framework that talks of levels. It neglects the role of what Armstrong calls *inter-professional competition* (1984, 1986, 1987b). It has long been recognised that professional groups pursue market strategies based on claims to exclusivity of knowledge and monopolies over a set of practices (Johnson, 1972; H. Brown, 1980). But the examples and models have mostly come from the older and 'social' professions such as law and medicine, with professions active in business seldom figuring as prominently.

One of the reasons for the neglect is that the sociology of the professions has emphasised the traditional 'role conflict' between professional autonomy and the bureaucratic principles of work organisation (Child, 1982; Rueschemeyer, 1986). Radical writers interpret these trends in terms of the conflict between acting for capital, whilst increasingly taking on the characteristics of employees. Some refer to the growth of a new professional-managerial class (Ehrenreich and Ehrenreich, 1979), with others preferring to talk of the proletarianisation of the 'middle layers' (Braverman: 1974). While some insights can be gained from such perspectives, a primary focus on issues of class location is limited. Armstrong's model allows us to focus on the specific role of the professions in the managerial labour process.

Armstrong and inter-professional competition

Armstrong is critical of certain aspects of the idea of management as a labour process. He agrees that lower management has been subject to greater controls and its own version of the separation of conception and execution, but is concerned that attention is drawn away from that basic contradiction between labour and capital, thus legitimising the existence of any form of unproductive activity by referring to it as a labour process in its right. But as long as the connections to the dominant capital–labour contradiction are maintained, we see no reason why the concept cannot be usefully employed. Armstrong prefers to talk of struggles for control within capital, reflecting the 'tensions and contradictions within the agency relationship' (1989: 312). In other words, employers and senior managers are inescapably dependent on other agencies to secure corporate goals and policies.

So in practice, management functions for capital are mediated by competition between occupational groups. Each profession has a core of specialist knowledge and activities that can form the basis of advancement through a 'collective mobility project'. But the core can only be used effectively if it is sufficiently indeterminate to prevent parts being detached, or routinised. While the general point might apply to all professions, those active in business have to face rival claims over the carrying out of control functions. For example, drawing on the work of Layton (1969), Armstrong (1986: 26) argues that scientific management's techniques and justification for the control of labour through the 'planning department' was an expression of an ideology of engineering. Industrial engineering rests on the design of operating procedures which monitor and control labour costs (Storey, 1983: 275). But the attempt to place engineers at the apex of the firm through the diffusion of such techniques has clearly not been fully achieved, given that engineers do not predominate in the higher levels of management. At the heart of this 'failure' lies the difficulty of maintaining a monopoly over control practices that could be carried out by others.

To make matters worse, British development has taken place based on a definition of management hostile to engineering. This is because of a combination of finance and marketing as favoured specialisms, and the tendency to define management as a set of general functions and skills divorced from productive expertise (see earlier in this chapter). One commentator noted that a result has been, 'a whole generation of MBA students who will not go near a manufacturing strategy. . . . They want to be in at the gin-and-tonic end with the financial strategy' (quoted in Armstrong, 1987b: 428). Other professions have gained because of the popular belief that the education of engineers does not equip them for dealing with people and money. As a potential agency they therefore experience difficulty in establishing the vital commodity of 'trust' with those in positions of power. It is therefore not surprising that many engineers seek a route out of production into senior management through courses such as MBAs. The consequent low status of engineering identified in the Finneston Report and by Child *et al.* (1983) is, however, as we have seen, a peculiarly Anglo-American phenomenon. In contrast, German management is dominated by professional engineers, due in part to the historical relevance of engineering techniques and technical education to competition with British and other manufacturing goods, and to access to training in financial techniques.

In the case of accounting and other financial specialisms, there has been a dramatic rise from the days of poorly paid clerks and bookkeeping tasks. Some of the factors involved include the development of management accounting as cost control techniques in the industrial restructuring during and after the depression of the mid-1920s. In the United States, the control function of management accounting can be clearly identified in the following definition from the National Association of Accountants:

> the process of identification, measurement, accumulation, analysis, preparation, interpretation, and communication of financial information used by management to plan, evaluate and control within an organisation and to

ensure appropriate use and accountability for its resources. (Quoted in Wardell, 1986: 28)

Other factors include once again the need for co-ordination and control over middle managers in multi-divisional companies and the legal requirements for control through auditing. The cohesiveness of an accounting élite in business has been facilitated by the acceptance of an inevitable 'horizontal fissure' in the profession. This has allowed a range of routine tasks to be delegated to 'accounting technicians' (Johnson, 1980; Glover *et al.*, 1986), thus maintaining indeterminacy and monopoly over core practices. Accountants have also undertaken an aggressive campaign to encroach on the spheres of other professions through such measures as manpower audits and human resource accounting (Armstrong, 1986: 32). Though only a minority are closer to real power, the spread of a 'financial rationality' means that British boardrooms are increasingly dominated by those with a background in banking or accountancy, within a 'managerial culture which is often preoccupied with accounting measures and procedures' (Armstrong, 1988).

Such developments have begun to threaten the power of the *personnel* function, a segment of management that had also enjoyed a major long-term growth. From the days of its origins in company welfare workers, the Institute of Personnel Managers now has more than 20000 members. Throughout that development, personnel professionals have had a continual struggle to convince business power-holders that they could move from welfare to general management functions. They consolidated a hold over administrative functions such as interviewing and record-keeping, as well as expanding into the newer areas of staff development and determination of wage rates and incentives (Carter, 1985: 102). In a partnership of mutual convenience, the behavioural sciences have helped develop a mystique that 'the personnel manager is probably the only specialist in the organisation whose role can be distinguished by the virtually exclusive concern with the management of human assets' (Mullins, 1985: 129). But the problematic of 'dealing with people' has inherent limits in establishing a monopoly of knowledge or practice, particularly when its 'behavioural nostrums' are routinely taught to the full range of business students (Fowler, 1985). It is therefore unsurprising that surveys (Daniel and Millward, 1983) have reported a lack of qualified and trained personnel staff in many companies. Fortunately for the profession other factors have been working in their favour, notably the spate of employee legislation and codes of practice in the 1960s and 1970s, and the recommendations of the Donovan Report (1968) that firms should centralise and formalise their bargaining procedures. Both measures allowed personnel to extend and monopolise spheres of expertise, as well exercise greater authority over lower line managers (Armstrong, 1986: 37).

But deregulation of labour markets, decentralisation of bargaining and scrapping of aspects of employment law have given a further twist to the ratchet of inter-professional competition by eroding or redistributing established personnel functions. This is complicated by the rise of human resource management (HRM). On the surface it seems positive; after all personnel managers have long trumpeted the importance of treating human resources as an organisation's greatest asset rather than a cost to be minimised. HRM can then be seen as an upmarket version of personnel with a tactical name change (Torrington, 1989). This is perhaps the 'soft' version of HRM, with the harder versions stressing the integration of the management of human resources into core business strategy and practice (Guest, 1989; Storey, 1989). The significance of the latter is that it enables, perhaps obliges, other managerial groups, particularly line managers, to take HRM 'on-board'.

Whether it is *in fact* becoming more strategic or more effective is open to dispute (Guest, 1990), but the perception of greater centrality has sparked off a struggle by managers across a variety of functions to absorb the rhetoric and responsibilities of HRM (Poole and Mansfield, 1992). The efforts of traditional practitioners to defend and carve out new territories was not helped by a widely-reported study from a team at the London School of Economics that produced headlines of 'Personnel officers are a waste of time says new study' (*Independent on Sunday*, 15 May 1994). Perhaps, like other professional groups, personnel is heading for a split: 'a polarised profession consisting of a mass of "clerks of works", performing routine administrative work for a newly self-confident line management, whilst a few élite "architects" of strategic human resources policy continue to operate at the corporate headquarters level' (Armstrong, 1988: 25).

What the work of Armstrong highlights is that managerial groups have constantly to fight to establish their usefulness through the agency relationship. Given successive waves of organisational restructuring driven by the latest managerial fads or new environmental pressures, the territory for that battle is constantly shifting. Many large organisations have undergone major change programmes, often culture-led, in recent years. Companies are increasingly seeking to recruit managers who have experience of such programmes, irrespective of their function of origin. The HR function is in a difficult position, given that senior executives often aim to decentralise responsibilities to line mangers, and may be reluctant to let HR, or indeed any functional group, be seen to 'own' the change process. Research from Marks *et al.* (1997) on the spirits industry suggests that HR personnel can seek influence through their expertise as 'managers of culture'. Culture is often seen as the glue that holds change initiatives together, and culture is ultimately seen to be 'about people'. This creates opportunities for HR to influence change agendas and measure the success or otherwise of measures geared towards transforming attitudes and performance.

Change processes may set off sharp inter-professional conflicts. In a valuable study of newly privatised utilities in the UK which explicitly uses Armstrong's framework, Mulholland (1998) identifies a struggle between 'public sector survivors' and 'movers and shakers'. The former are older managers primarily from engineering and technical backgrounds within the water and electricity industries, while the latter are younger, with a graduate background, and reputations built through efficiency drives in the private sector. Mulholland demonstrates that because they are 'tainted' with public sector values, engineers have become non-preferred managers, their competencies marginalised and status diminished. In contrast the private sector experience and entrepreneurial attitudes of the newly-recruited group mean that they have become the trusted and preferred agency of senior management. As one corporate manager put it: 'Obviously the people who came into the industry aren't carrying the baggage of forty years of nationalised industry culture. . . . They are knocking aside the tribal custom for us' (Mulholland, 1998: 191).

The kind of analysis in this section usefully adds to an understanding of the complex levels and functions within the managerial labour process. As Whitley (1984) argues, there is limited standardisation across managerial tasks and this helps to explain the lack of progress in establishing management as such as a profession. The growth of MBAs and other qualifications suggests attempts to develop certification of skills and knowledges, as well as a career route. But they can best be seen as a form of individual credentialism and filter into higher paid jobs, and not necessarily a convincing one, with some employers showing considerable scepticism (Oliver, 1993). The jibe 'masters of bugger all' may be unfair, but it reflects historic tensions between generalism and specialism, as well as a feeling that the content of many courses is pitched above business requirements and the realities of middle management work.

Conclusion

A focus on competing agencies and professions also emphasises the specific historical bases and differences in the development of management theories and practices, particularly between different national traditions, though we have had little space to elaborate on them here. The discussion embodies the general purpose of the chapter: that of developing a structural analysis of management that recognises the contradictory sources of influence over activity. It should be clear that managers need not be treated as over-determined 'ciphers' in order to explain their work in a structural way. A conception of agency can be utilised that accepts considerable variation in management practices, as well as enabling us to understand the rise of new groups competing for influence. For example, business consultants, research and development engineers and IT analysts are using their knowledge to challenge the existing expert division of labour (Reed, 1992a). We have also been able to illustrate the competing rationalities of contending groups, without accepting the mainstream notion of a single, neutral rationality underpinning managerial theory and practice. Many of these issues will resurface again in different form in the following chapter.

8 Control: Concepts and Strategies

Asked what the secret of successful automotive management was, a senior General Motors executive replied, 'Control. Deal control. Product control. Labour control' (quoted in Huczynski, 1993: 185).

We can see from the discussion in the previous chapter that practically and theoretically management is intertwined with control. Yet why and how is strongly contested between mainstream and radical approaches. This chapter examines contrasting perspectives on understanding control. It is primarily about conceptualisation rather than current evidence of the outcomes of control strategies and techniques. These will be dealt with mainly in Chapters 11 and 12.

Mainstream mis/understandings

The treatment of control in mainstream writing is ambiguous at best, marginal at worst. Frameworks that assume goal consensus can often simply ignore or trivialise the issue. When it is discussed explicitly in standard textbooks, the chapters devoted to it are sometimes of a rather bizarre nature in almost omitting any reference to conflicts between groups. The talk is of technical inputs and outputs in a self-adjusting system, performance standards and feedback mechanisms. It is also seen in a unitary way: 'controlled performance' with an assumption of goal-consensus. Control is reduced to a *monitoring* device, with management's role to check progress, ensure that actions occur as planned, correct any deviation, or reassure us that what we are doing is appropriate (O'Reilly and Chatman, 1996). Some writers (Lawlor, 1976) put an emphasis on people desiring control, for example getting enjoyment from dependence on higher authority. Resistance is smuggled in occasionally when discussing the *behavioural* implications as people 'react' to control processes, requiring management to adjust strategies accordingly.

This apparent absence of control from the mainstream is, however, somewhat misleading. The issues are there but they are articulated in different language and concepts. As the influential mainstream writer Pfeffer notes, 'control is at once the essential problem of management and organisation and the implicit focus of much of organisation studies' (1997: 100). The key term here is *implicit*. When control is discussed it is often alongside co-ordination. Any complex division of labour requires mechanisms to set goals, allocate responsibilities and evaluate the effectiveness of performance. Co-ordination is a more neutral term than control and more compatible with an assumption that management is a largely neutral set of techniques and competencies.

Even when texts do have chapters with control in the title, they often pass over quickly into other issues such as job design, organisational structure or leadership. In the first instance, debate is focused on designing structures which facilitate levels of control and co-ordination appropriate to types of work that require different levels of discretion and standardisation. In the second, discussion of leadership styles such as the classic polarity of authoritarian versus democratic is a way of discussing control, but through the language of influence and motivation. So what is described in mainstream writing as technical and human organisation and the need to integrate the two could be alternatively thought of in terms of competing control systems. For example, in their historical survey of American managerial discourse, Barley and Kunda (1992) distinguish between rational (for example, scientific management, systems theories) and normative (for example, human relations, organisational culture) ideologies of control. Rather than one simply displacing another, there are successive and alternate waves paralleling broad cycles of economic expansion and contraction.

We do accept that not all control processes arise from, or are structured by, antagonistic interests. Stock inventories and financial budgeting are necessary and not always conflictual features of any system of work organisation. A written job description may under certain conditions actually allow employees to assert power or control. But most control processes remain difficult to separate from the social relations of work, even when they appear to be neutral. This was the important conclusion of Blau and Schoenherr (1971), who used the concept of *insidious* controls to highlight the way in which management can utilise impersonal and unobtrusive means. Examples include selective recruitment of staff whose sense of professionalism or expertise enables them to work without direct controls; use of resource allocation as a financial discipline; and controls embodied in technology. Thus even those staff who exercise considerable work autonomy, such as those in higher education, have a series of indirect constraints over their actions.

In practice mainstream theory is more uncomfortable with its own marginalisation of control than the above discussion might suggest. The simple indication of that can be seen in the frequency with which the death of Taylorism or bureaucracy is announced. Implicit in these pronouncements is the recognition that control does exist, but the preference that it *shouldn't*. From the human relations writers of the 1950s, with their distinctions between (bad) theory X and (good) theory Y, to the advocates of 1970s-style job enrichment, control has been presented as unnecessary and outdated. Democratic leadership styles and autonomous work groups have been seen as the basic precondition for job satisfaction and high productivity. Recent formulations have moved the debate further on. It is said that we now live in a world where change is so frequent and expertise so fundamental to the work process that 'command and control' is not merely undesirable, it is actually bad for business. Picking up on themes from the academic literature (Walton, 1985), the editor of a Scottish business journal asserts that:

> The pyramidal, hierarchical school of management is, at long last, being dragged to its knees and kicked to death. Command and control is not an option in what is rapidly becoming an economy founded on knowledge and the skills of those who have it. In such an economy it seems employees will have to be involved in strategic decision-making if organisational goals are to be achieved. (B. Millar, *Scottish Business Insider*, October 1998)

The language of contemporary management theory and practice has therefore been based around two axes: empowerment and commitment. The former suggests that organisations are delegating control to project groups and work teams, so that they become *self*-managing; the latter implies that values rather than rules have become the prime means of co-ordination. As indicated earlier, it is not our intention to examine these claims at this point. We will merely observe that they represent a continued evasion of the relevant issues. Control is either rhetorically abolished or presented in softer, more neutral terms. One of the problems with such approaches is their aspirational nature and the subsequent tendency to conflate prescription and description. Take, for example, the empowerment literature. In an incisive review, Hales (2000: 503) comments that, 'the burgeoning prescriptive or celebratory literature is replete with conceptions of empowerment which display equivocation, tautology and contradiction in equal measure'. He suggests that it is not clear whether power is to be achieved or received, what kind of powers are being enhanced (voice in decisions or choice over actions?), or the extent to which individuals or teams are expected to exercise delegated responsibilities. Such ambiguities tend to be terms – such as 'directed autonomy' – that paper over in words what is likely to be contradictory in practice (Waterman, 1988). Mainstream theory lacks conceptual frameworks that are robust enough to deal with the nature, types and levels of control. For this we have to turn elsewhere.

Radical perspectives: labour process theories of control

Pfeffer rightly observes that 'the ambivalence about the effects (if not the effectiveness) of social control is in part responsible for the development of a critical perspective on organisations and their control practices' (1997: 135). In contrast to mainstream theorists, radical writers on organisation and management frequently *begin* from an analysis of control relations. Whereas mainstream perspectives treat control and co-ordination together, radical theorists argue that management performs a *dual* function in the enterprise (Carchedi, 1977; R. Edwards, 1979). Managerial practices are a necessary means of *co-ordinating* diverse activities, but they also bear the imprint of conflicting interests in the labour process, a conflict that reflects the unique nature of labour as a commodity. This orientation was reflected in the first radical text to make a major impact as organisation theory, which began by defining the theoretical rationale of organisational analysis: 'For this volume we have proposed as such an object the concept of organisation as control of the labour process' (Clegg and Dunkerley, 1980: 1). This framework derived from Marx's analysis of the capitalist labour process, which was updated and revitalised by Braverman (1974) and a range of other 'labour process' theorists discussed below.

All societies have labour processes, but under capitalism they have specific characteristics. The most significant is what Marx referred to as the transformation of labour power into labour. In other words, when capital purchases labour it has only a potential or capacity to work. To ensure profitable production, capital must organise the conditions under which labour operates to its own advantage. But workers pursue their own interests for job security, higher rewards and satisfying work, developing their own counter-organisation through informal job controls, restriction of output and the like.

To resolve this problem, and because they are under competitive pressure from other firms to cut costs and raise productivity, employers seek to control the conditions under which work takes place. This argument is often misunderstood. Pfeffer says that Marxist analysis 'asserts that control, not efficiency, is the object of organising arrangements' (1997: 180). While radical approaches would challenge particular conceptions of efficiency, control is not an end in itself, but a means to transform the capacity to work established by the wage relation into profitable production. It is a term summarising a set of mechanisms and practices that regulates the labour process (P. K. Edwards, 1990). Richard Edwards (1979: 18) distinguishes three elements in any system of control:

1   direction and specification of work tasks
2   evaluation, monitoring and assessment of performance
3   the apparatus of discipline and reward to elicit co-operation and compliance.

Such elements may, however, be best described as *detailed* control, in that they are normally connected to immediate work processes, whereas *general* control refers to management's capacity to subordinate labour to their direction of the production process as a whole. This distinction made by P. K. Edwards (1990) and other writers is of significance in that it allows for recognition of tremendous variations in how detailed control is exercised. Such a model can even allow for employers giving workers significant discretion over tasks, as in semi-autonomous work groups, if it maintains their overall control. Control is also not absolute, but, at least at the imme-diate level, a contested relationship. Conflict is built into the wage–effort bargain, with even mainstream writers recognising that an employment contract outlining required performance runs up against employees with their own goals and wants. As each 'party' seeks to exert its influence over the formal and informal aspects of the employment relationship, the outcome is a constantly changing 'frontier of control' (Goodrich, 1975) or 'contested terrain' (R. Edwards, 1979).

What about the role of management in this process? Claims of independent actors carrying out a neutral role are disputed by evidence concerning the top strata of management (Zeitlin, 1974). By their motivation, social background and connections, rewards and share-holdings in corporations, most managers are part of the capitalist class. While a useful corrective, this 'sociological' analysis is not the crucial point. For example, a number of entrepreneurs are from a traditional working-class background. But what matter are the structural location and functions in the organisation. If anything, entrepreneurs from this background tend to identify even more closely with their new role. These roles require management to carry out functions of control and surveillance, exercising hierarchical authority over workers separated from the means of production. While it is not always clear that it is possible to distinguish between a 'neutral' co-ordination and an 'antagonistic' control, managers do act as agents carrying out the 'global functions' of capital, functions which, as we observed in Chapter 3, were delegated as part of the bureaucratisation of production. The idea of agency conjures up rather crude images of conspiracies and empty vessels: 'In the capi-talist system, the principal function of management is to exploit labour power to the maximum in order to secure profits for the owners of capital' (Berkeley Thomas, 1993: 61). But the generality 'to the maximum' is meaningless. There are only specific and diverse means through which the requirements of capital are brought about, in which management takes an active rather than predetermined role.

Radical analyses sometimes get tangled up in attempts to designate managers to precise class positions. This theme does not concern us here (though see Johnston, 1986 for a critical account). What is important is that we have available a framework for understanding management practices which provides an alternative to the dominant combination of behavioural and managerial revolution theories. The fact, for example, that executives of a large corporation have the formal status of employees is, as Braverman observes, merely the form given to the domination of capital in modern society:

> Their formal attribute of being part of the same payroll as the production workers, clerks and porters of the corporation no more robs them of the powers of decision and command over the others in the enterprise than does the fact that the general, like the private, wears the military uniform, or the pope and the cardinal pronounce the same liturgy as the parish priest. (Braverman, 1974:405)

Instead of the separation of ownership and control, radical writers distinguish between *real* or economic ownership and agents holding actual *possession* (De Vroey, 1975; Carchedi, 1977). Managerial agents are governed by the external constraints imposed by the dynamics of competition and capital accumulation, with profitability remaining the crucial criteria through which the successful management work is judged. If anything, this is enhanced by property ownership and related forms of control becoming increasingly depersonalised with the rise of finance, pension funds and other institutional shareholders. Individual enterprises become 'simply units in a structure of intercorporate relations' (J. Scott, 1985: 142), the division of ownership and possession resulting in greater vulnerability for managers who know they may be removed from office (Holland, 1975). A structural analysis does not imply that the growth of new forms of managerial labour is irrelevant. As we saw in the previous chapter, the heterogeneity of management has increased with the sheer extent and diversity of delegated functions and the competing groups, such as accountants and engineers, who lay claim to them.

Management strategies

Radical perspectives have been conditioned by Braverman's (1974) argument that the twentieth century saw the tightening of managerial control, primarily through the application of Taylorist and scientific management strategies. Detailed evidence is provided of the extension of such methods from simple to complex production and its use in the transformation of clerical labour. When allied to managerial shaping of science and technology through mechanisation and automation, work design and organisation continue to embody key Taylorist principles such as task fragmentation and the separation of conception and execution. Braverman provided an important corrective to the widespread view that Taylorism was a failed system, superseded by more sophisticated behavioural theories to be used for motivational and job design tools (see M. Rose, 1975).

But it is widely recognised that Braverman overestimated the dominance of Taylorist strategies and practices, and underestimated the varied and uneven implementation, influenced by worker hostility, management suspicion and appropriateness to given environments. In Chapter 3, we tried to reach a balanced assessment. If Taylorism is taken to be part of a broader movement towards 'scientific' management focused on fragmentation of tasks and their subjection to increasing job measurement and evaluation, as well as the structuring of work processes so that skills and planning activities are located off the factory and office floor, then particular elements remain a highly significant component of control strategies, though seldom on their own. (See Chapters 11 and 12 for a more detailed discussion of issues of modern job design.)

Precisely because Braverman confused a particular system of control with management control in general, the question of *strategy* was put firmly on the agenda because of the resulting debate on alternatives. This is not to say that issues of strategy had no place in the existing organisational literature. We have already seen in previous chapters how Chandler (1962) regarded strategy, defined as long-term planning and resource allocation to carry out goals, as the characteristic feature of the modern multidivisional firm. But control over employees was not systematically dealt with. Strategy has also been increasingly part of the agenda of the business policy and corporate management literature (Steiner and Miner, 1978). Radical perspectives differ from both in avoiding the prescriptive search for the 'best way'; remaining free to analyse what management does, rather than what it should do.

What of the alternative strategies raised in the labour process debate? Some of the best-known contributions have already been discussed in previous chapters. Richard Edward's (1979) model is based on historically successive dominant modes of control, which reflect worker resistance and changing socio-economic conditions. A nineteenth-century system of *simple* or *personal* control by employers exercising direct authority gave way to more complex *structural* forms with the transition from small business, competitive capitalism to corporate monopolies. The first of these forms was *technical* control typified by the use of the assembly line that can pace and direct the labour process. The contradiction for management is that it created a common work experience and basis for unified shop-floor opposition. In contrast, a system of *bureaucratic* control (see Chapter 3), embedded in the social and organisational structure of the firm rather than in personal authority, offers management a means of re-dividing the workforce and tying it to impersonal rules and regulations. With his co-thinkers among radical economists (R. Edwards, Reich and Gordon, 1975; Gordon, Edwards and Reich, 1982), Edwards has also argued that employers consciously create *segmented* labour markets as a response to economic crises and as a divide and rule strategy, particularly using gender and race.

In contrast, Friedman (1977) rightly eschews the notion of stages, preferring to set out ideal types or strategic poles of responsible autonomy and direct control which run parallel throughout the history of capitalism (for a description see Chapter 8). Each strategy generates its own inflexibilities in areas such as hiring and firing and task specification. The choice of strategy is governed by variations in the stability of labour and product markets, mediated by the interplay of worker resistance and managerial pressure. There is, however, an element of common ground in the belief that there has been a gradual historical tendency towards more consensual, integrative strategies; utilising internal markets, institutionalised rules and in some cases, work humanisation schemes. This is also the view of the other major control theorist, Burawoy (1979). He periodises the development of capitalist work organisation in terms of the transition from *despotic* to *hegemonic* regimes. The former involved relations of dependence and coercion that did not prove viable for capital or labour. Workers sought collective representation and social protection from the state. Capital also had an interest in state regulation of conflict and a minimal social wage that would boost purchasing power. The shift to hegemonic regimes was also based on an internal state in the workplace that provided an 'industrial citizenship', utilising grievance machinery and regulated bargaining that minimised likely resistance and class solidarity.

Subsequent events have not been kind to such models. The 1980s and 1990s have seen organisational restructuring based on downsizing and delayering, the search for flexibility in work and employment, a move away from collective and joint regulation of the workplace and a growth in job insecurity. It is always possible, of course, to adjust the model, which Burawoy does by defining the new dominant factory regime as one of *hegemonic despotism*. This is not a return to arbitrary tyranny, but the apparently 'rational' power of a capital that is mobile across the globe, over the workforce (1985: 150). But the problem is not just with specific projections, but linear thinking more generally. New conceptual categories of this nature merely illustrate the fundamental problem of the control theories we have been examining. Alternative strategies have been put on the map, but too often within what has been described as the 'panacea fallacy' (Littler and Salaman, 1982) or 'monism' (Storey, 1985). That is, the idea that capital always seeks and finds definitive and comprehensive modes of control as the solution to its problems. Admittedly, this is somewhat less true of Friedman, who in his own defence argues that responsible autonomy and direct control have in-built contradictions and are 'two directions towards which managers can move, rather than two predefined states between which managers choose' (1987: 3). But there is still a sense of a search for all-embracing categories, which have their parallels in behavioural theory, such as Etzioni's (1961) structures of compliance, or Schein's (1965) linear models of economic, social and complex man.

Nevertheless, the control debate has sparked off an extensive and useful amount of empirical work influenced by labour process theory. Early case studies tended to focus on reaffirmation of theses of deskilling and tighter controls (Zimbalist, 1979), or critiques of them highlighting mediating factors such as markets and worker resistance (Wood, 1982). Subsequent efforts were concerned to establish trends in their own right. Studies dealing with the introduction of new technology have stressed that deskilling and direct control represent only one of a range of management strategies (Wilkinson, 1986). Child's (1985) research shows even more clearly how ideas of strategy can be used, while recognising variations in goals and environments. He identified a variety of strategies including elimination of direct labour, sub-contracting, polyvalence or multi-tasking and job degradation. These were connected to an even wider set of influences, including those of national economic cycles, government policy and the culture of organisations.

Other research has applied models to specific industries, but without any claims for universality. A good example is the use by Murray and Wickham (1985) of Richard Edwards's theory of bureaucratic control. They studied two Irish electronics factories employing mainly female semi-skilled workers, showing that direction, discipline and evaluation are all carried out according to explicit rules rather than direct controls. Supervisors do not monitor production performance and enforce discipline. This is left to inspectors on the basis of statistical records that can identify the operators responsible. Supervisors, however, are central to processes of evaluating the social character of the 'good worker' in order to facilitate promotion through the internal labour market. The elaborate and artificial hierarchy created at the plants meant that one-third of workers had been promoted from the basic assembly grade, thus confirming Edward's view that employees are given positive material reasons for complying with bureaucratic rules.

A further direction was to focus on specific strategies and processes of control such as recruitment policies (Fevre, 1986; Maguire, 1986; Winstanley, 1986; Callaghan and Thompson, 2001) that were neglected in an exclusive focus on the labour process. The most extensive research has been carried out on *gender*. Socially-defined notions of femininity as a form of control have been observed in multinationals operating in the third world (Pearson, 1986). Plant management consciously exploits cultures of passivity and subordination by combining an image of the company as a patriarchal family system with the manager as father figure, Western-style beauty competitions and classes (Grossman, 1979). In the West, Grieco and Whipp's overview argues that 'managerial strategies of control make use of and enhance the sexual divisions in society' (1985: 136). Studies of office and factory workers (Glenn and Feldberg, 1979, Pollert, 1981; Westwood, 1984; Bradley, 1986) show that management use women's marginality to work, arising from the family, to frame their labour control policies.

In reflecting on the above debates, a degree of common ground emerged. Product and labour markets, worker resistance and a range of other external and internal factors are recognised as mediating control strategies and shaping power relations in the frontier of control between capital and labour. The variations in strategy that result are not random, but reflect the fundamental tension we have talked of between management's need to control and discipline, while engaging workers' commitment and co-operation. Strategies therefore contain inherent contradictions (Storey, 1985; Hyman, 1987). These are enhanced by the difficulty of harmonising the different managerial functions, sites of intervention and decision-making, which includes technology, social organisation of labour and relations with the representative bodies of employees. Hyman notes that 'there is no "one best way" of managing these contradictions, only different routes to partial failure' (1987: 30). Management of large organisations is therefore likely to try combinations of control strategies and practices, appropriate to particular environments or sections of the workforce. As one of us has remarked elsewhere:

> The most consistent weakness of existing theory has been to counterpoise one form of control to another.... No one has convincingly demonstrated that a particular form of control is necessary or inevitable for capitalism to function successfully. (Thompson, 1989: 151)

Whatever the limitations of the ideas, as Pfeffer notes, 'labour process theorists have been enormously influential in stimulating a discussion of work place control, not from the point of view of organisational efficiency or management but from the point of view of its determinants and its effects on workers' (1997: 184). The above 'consensus' fails to satisfy those within and outside the radical perspective who are critical of the explanatory power of concepts of management control strategy. For some, the problem with a Marxist-influenced agenda is that, like more orthodox accounts, it wrongly assumes high levels of rationality, this time applied to top management (Bryman, 1984: 401; Grint, 1995: 51). Others go beyond the previously noted criticism of 'panacea fallacies' to object to the treatment of management as omniscient, omnipotent and monolithic. Based on her study of chemical plants, Harris mocks the image of managers who have the attributes of deity and 'papal inerrancy' when dealing with workers, commenting that radical writers assume that senior management 'always know what is in capital's interests and unfailingly order things so that they work together for its greater good' (1987: 70). There are conflicts within management reflecting contending interest groups and the difficulty of carrying out integrative functions. Nor is it always possible to draw a neat dividing line from workers given that managers are also wage labourers subject to controls. The distortions in such analyses are held to derive from a wider determinism and functionalism in which 'managers are regarded as unproblematic agents of capital who dispatch their "global functions" in a rationalistic manner' (Storey, 1985: 195).

Capital's interests are not given and management practices cannot be 'read-off' from them. Assumptions of a 'tight-coupling' underestimate the diversity and complexity of such practices, and the significance for decision-making processes within the enterprise. It is also the case that in addition to the responsibilities that managers have to the control apparatus of the enterprise, they need to control their own personal identities and make sense of their own work in the employing organisation. Managerial work therefore has a 'double control' aspect in which there is a strategic exchange between individuals and organisations (Watson, 1994). The consequence of the above critiques is the belief that too few insights are generated into what 'flesh and blood' managers actually do.

At a general level many of these criticisms would be accepted across a wide spectrum. But some carry it much further: 'current uses of the terms "strategy" and "control" are somewhat misleading guides both to actual management conduct and to the causes of particular outcomes in work organisation and industrial relations' (Rose and Jones, 1985: 82). We can break this down into two issues: do identifiable management strategies exist and are practices centred on controlling workers?

Questioning strategy

Those who argue against the idea of coherent strategies with a fixity of purpose believe that management activities are more likely to be piecemeal, uncoordinated and fragmented, with at best a striving for logical incrementalism. Management is concerned primarily with 'keeping the show on the road' (Tomlinson, 1982: 128), corresponding with the 'realist' views discussed earlier.

Supportive research exists in areas such as work reorganisation schemes (Rose and Jones, 1985) and new technology and skills in engineering (Campbell and Currie, 1987). Any strategic capacity is held to be inevitably undermined by a plethora of sites of decision-making, varied objectives among different management specialists and interest groups, the need to smooth over diverse and contradictory practices, and the requirement of sustaining a consensual accommodation with employee organisations. The result is an unpredictable variety of managerial intentions characterised by a 'plant particularism' (Rose and Jones, 1985: 96), and control structures as merely 'temporary outcomes' (Storey, 1985). Campbell and Currie plump for the idea of 'negotiated preferences' and there is a general orientation towards explanations based on *practices* rather than strategy.

Some of these differences may reflect the sector being researched. For example, engineering is well known for its 'seat-of-the-pants' approach to management, whereas other sectors such as food or chemicals are noted for more strategic methods. Nevertheless, this kind of approach is confirmed by some writers on industrial relations (Purcell and Sissons, 1983), who note the problems created by the absence of management strategies towards their own employees, particularly ones that are integrated into overall business objectives. Instead there is a continued dominance of reactive and opportunistic practices directed towards immediate problem-solving (Thurley and Wood, 1983: 209). What *kind* of strategy is said to be absent is not always made explicit. But the basic model used is similar to that popularised by Chandler, which, like many other adaptations to the business sphere, is strongly influenced by military experience and terminology (Shaw, 1990). That is, it posits detailed and co-ordinated plans of campaign in which conscious, long-term planning based on corporate goals is supported by appropriate courses of action and allocation of resources. This can be seen in the business policy debate (Steiner and Miner, 1978; Porter, 1980) in which generations of students are warned of the negative consequences of the absence of corporate strategy, and scholars debate different models of structure, strategy and competitiveness. Similarly, standard models of strategic HRM emphasise the need for coherence and integration both within its component parts and with wider business strategy (Tichy *et al.*, 1982). Indeed, HRM is sometimes seen only to offer something new if it has strategic value (Kamoche, 1994).

The problem with mainstream notions of strategy is that it is all too easy to counter textbook ideal types of coherence and integration with the messy reality of real companies and sectors. As with the more 'realist' views of management discussed in the last chapter, the insights of social science have been applied to demonstrate how organisations muddle through rather than plan rationally. The promise of complete knowledge and controllable environments is seen as neither desirable nor feasible in fragmented, turbulent, post-modern times. As a result, in the last decade strategy has gone from buzzword to boo-word. It has been 'problematised' to the point that the concept is no longer fashionable even in strategic management circles (for a useful overview, see Whipp, 1996). Complaining that discourses of strategy are primarily about shoring up the power of senior managers and consultants, Knights and Morgan reject the concept altogether: 'Nothing new is really added by talking the discourse of strategy; on the contrary, a limit is put on our understanding of the special phenomenon because we are forcing action into a particular rationalistic and individualistic framework' (1990: 480).

But conceptions of management strategy in the above frameworks are in themselves problematic. A stereotyped polarity is set up between a conception of objective rationality that implies perfect foresight, choice and follow-through; and a bounded rationality of constrained choice in complex realities. Too often the critics collude in forcing action into a conceptual straightjacket. By adopting a straw man of 'strong' strategy, they have set criteria for strategy so stringently that it becomes impossible to meet them (Child, 1985). While it is wrong to attribute coherent, rational intent to management, it is equally mistaken to assume that strategy has to be seen as always consistent, systematic and without contradiction. Strategies may not always be effectively followed through at the implementation stage, as with the introduction of new technology. They may not constitute a coherent package for the whole operations of a company, perhaps manifesting a disjuncture between job design plans and employee relations. Coherence is an important variable, but it has to be set against the knowledge of inevitable contradictions and the likelihood of 'loose-coupling' between planning and practices. Strategies are likely to be accompanied by bargaining within management and with the workforce, so making the end result uncertain. As Friedman rightly notes, 'Irrationality, inconsistency, lack of system certainly exist and must be allowed for; however, a more useful concept to introduce is failure' (1987: 294). Even where changes are introduced without clear intent, they can establish the precondi- tions for subsequent strategy (Hyman, 1987: 47).

While managers frequently act on the world with poor information, they can and do act strategically. It is only necessary for researchers to show a degree of intent or planning, and to infer a logic over a period of time from the frequency and pattern of action, or from 'emergent outcomes' (Hales, 1988: 12). The same criteria apply to the activities of workers. Groups such as printers or doctors do not always behave in a fully conscious or coherent manner. But observation reveals a clear pattern of occu- pational and job controls, and strategies of closure aimed at excluding competitors, often women (Cockburn, 1983; Witz, 1986). The latter point reinforces research on households that shows that strategies emerge from 'bottom-up', day-to-day activities – a weaker, but still legitimate sense of strategy that relies on social scientists observing and analysing predictable patterns (Wallace, 1993).

Of course, the capacity for strategy is not random. Certain external conditions are likely to push management in that direction. Streek (1987) puts forward a persuasive case that economic crisis and rapidly changing market environments have created a 'general strategic problem' whose core element is the need for *flexibility*. However, the very nature of uncertainty and varied conditions in sectors and countries produces different strategic responses. For example, countries such as Germany and Austria with traditions of tripartite state, union and employer bargaining, have seen moves towards economic liberalisation and labour flexibility that retain a strong union role and corporatist regulation of wages, labour and product markets. The hostility of all economic actors in Germany to the prospective takeover of telecommunication's giant Mannesman by a UK competitor in 1999 is a case in point. Streek's analysis not only builds in an explanation of such variations, it provides a framework for understanding the general conditions under which strategies develop. At times of crisis and readjustment, 'the variety of strategies and structures within the collectivity of firms is bound to increase at least until a new standard of "best practice" has been estab- lished' (1987: 284). In other words, there is always ebb and flow in intensity and direction of organisational practices, but strategic patterns do emerge and can be observed, particularly in the cauldron of highly internationalised sectors where a small number of giants compete for dominance.

Questioning control over labour

The second strand of critique questions whether the centrality given to control of labour is actually reflective of managerial behaviour. It is argued that we cannot view management strategies and tactics from the vantage point of the labour process, but must consider the role of product and labour markets, and technologies. Control proceeds in a complex cycle from planning to implementation, involving groups such as accountants and industrial engineers. Analysis should focus on the 'multiple constituents' of management expertise beyond the confrontation of capital and labour in the control of the labour process (Miller and O'Leary, 1987: 10). Such a critique can be presented in a Marxist form. Accumulation and costs of production are what matter to capital and its agents, not control. If anything, managers are dominated by problems of the *outcomes* of the labour process, including sales, marketing, supply and cash flow. Kelly uses the concept of the full circuit of capital to argue that we must be concerned not only with the *extraction* of surplus value through controlling the labour process, but its *realisation* through the sale of commodities, as well as the prior *purchase* of labour. On these grounds, 'there is no sound reason for privileging any moment in the circuit' (1985: 32).

Morgan and Hooper used a similar framework in their research into the Imperial Tobacco Group in the 1970s to distinguish between three circuits of capital. *Industrial* capital refers to that used in the management and design of the production process itself; *commercial* to the sphere of buying and selling and therefore functions such as marketing and advertising; and *banking* to the process of capital used in lending and borrowing, governed by accountancy and financial controls.

These distinctions are used to argue that radical theories of the labour process have often lost sight of the role of capital and ownership because of the emphasis on management control. The case study shows a series of strategies pursued in tandem, representing the particular circuits. To break out of a static tobacco market, top management prioritised commercial and banking strategies, rather than developing existing labour processes. In particular, companies such as Imperial were drawn into investments in the share and gilts markets. These proved successful, but when the resultant money was invested in production this had disastrous results. Firms are thus conceptualised as 'sites of a complex integration of circuits of capital' (Morgan and Hooper, 1987: 623), which management must integrate and control. This takes us back to the opening quote of the chapter in which the General Motors executive was seeking control in a number of spheres.

During this period of debate, other writers questioned whether control can be regarded as the factor that distinguishes between a dominant management and a subordinate labour. Management has non-control functions and characteristics of employees, while workers exercise job controls and may be involved in the regulation of others (Melling, 1982: 249). At a more theoretical level, Cressey and MacInnes (1980) observe that workers have an interest in the viability of their own units of capital as well as resisting subordination, matching capital's dual relationship with labour as a commodity and as a source of co-operation necessary for profitable production. Some mainstream writers use their own research into the chemical industry (Harris, 1987) and those of chemicals, engineering and biscuits (Buchanan, 1986), to argue that workers basically accept managerial authority, give commitment and effort willingly, and have convergent interests with management, thus negating any preoccupation with control. This is likely to be linked to a rejection of 'zero-sum' conceptions of power in which one side necessarily gains at the expense of the other (Harris, 1987: 77). Even some radical writers believe that capital and management are not necessarily dominant, with unions having considerably more power, even in a recession, than usually acknowledged (Kelly, 1985: 49; Rose and Jones, 1985: 101).

It is certainly true that, as Hyman observes; 'If most orthodox literature on business strategy ignores or marginalises the conflict between capital and labour, most Marxist literature perceives nothing else' (1987: 34). This has a curious parallel with the virtual total emphasis in organisation behaviour on 'man-management'. So the full circuit of capital is a very useful and necessary concept for understanding the capitalist enterprise. Furthermore, change and crisis often arise from disarticulation of the moments of the circuit (Kelly, 1985), as we saw in the Imperial example. Such concepts can be combined with more orthodox accounts of the changing pattern of *corporate control* which plot how large firms seek to solve their competitive problems by reshaping structures and forms of intervention in the market (Fligstein, 1990). Such 'modes of control' have included vertical and horizontal integration, the multi-divisional form and, more recently, financial means of integrating diverse portfolios built up through acquisition.

However, these perspectives do not invalidate a specific emphasis on relations of control between capital and labour. This is not just another process equivalent to marketing or financial accounting. The management of workers and work remains at the heart of the enterprise and indeed of economic reproduction as a whole. But such an orientation need have no marginalising effect on the analysis of other social relations. As P. K. Edwards (1990) observes, the problem of 'privileging' one part of the circuit arises only if the analysis assumes that this one part determines what happens in the others.

As we made clear at the start of the chapter, we are not saying that control is normally the *goal* of management, but rather a *means* embodied in strategies and techniques. It is true that management strategies are not always developed with labour's role in mind. But it is ultimately difficult to separate a concern with 'outcomes' such as product quality of financial targets from acting on labour in some way. Strategies towards markets or technologies will often be constrained or mediated by labour policies and the practices of workers (Friedman, 1987). In addition, as Child notes, 'strategies which are unspecific towards the labour process may still have relevance for it' (1985: 110). An example is the introduction of new technology which, much research shows, is frequently used as a means of more general work reorganisation.

On the issue of the existence of co-operation and common interests, we would wholly concur. In fact we would go further. As one of us has observed: 'Workers do not always need to be overtly controlled. They may effectively "control" themselves' (Thompson, 1989: 153). Participation in routine practices to create interest or increase rewards can generate *consent* to existing structures of control and power, as Burawoy's (1979) famous studies of production 'games' indicate. What is puzzling is why some writers insist on co-operative and consensual processes being counterposed to those of control and conflict. It is increasingly recognised that all have to be theorised as different products of the contradictory relations within the enterprise. Not only do consent and control coexist; 'the mobilisation of consent' through culture strategies forms an increasingly central part of management–employee relations strategies in many sectors. This will be examined in detail in Chapter 13.

We also accept that workers exercise controls, but it would be a serious mistake to regard them as *equivalent* to those of management. This would fail to distinguish between *types* of control, particularly between the general and detailed dimensions referred to earlier in the chapter. At the general level of direction of production, managerial dominance is guaranteed by their stewardship of the crucial organisational resources. This is not 'zero-sum' because it cannot be 'added up'. Clearly, however, control of immediate work processes is largely zero-sum, in that if workers control a given item, then management cannot also do so (P. K. Edwards, 1990).

New directions? Surveillance and shifting the locus of control

Having gone through successive forms of criticism concerning ideas of control strategy, the recent period has seen the emphasis move back to new accounts of control. Some of these arise from empirical shifts in work and employment. For example, the growth of front-line service work means that the *customer* may mediate the standard management–worker dyad, providing information on employees, and directing their behaviour or values (Frenkel *et al.*, 1999; Sturdy *et al.*, 2001). The most significant challenge to established labour process frameworks, however, comes from the argument that the locus of control has shifted from external to internal. We have already identified one version of this earlier in the chapter. A move to seeking employee commitment can be seen as a form of *internalised control* that does not rely on external rewards and sanctions, or rule-following. Cultural controls rely primarily on acceptance of values and peer enforcement. In one of the earliest contributions, Ray (1986) argued that control by corporate culture was the last frontier, in that it had enabled organisations to generate sentiment and emotion, simultaneously internalising control and linking personal with corporate identity.

Issues of culture and control will be examined fully in Chapter 13. At this stage we want to concentrate on a parallel argument about a shifting locus, this time with the emphasis on surveillance replacing, or becoming the dominant mechanism of, control. On the surface this does not appear to be consistent with an internalised direction. After all, surveillance is normally associated with collecting and storing information, and using it to monitor behaviour and establish discipline (Dandeker, 1990). However, the argument is less about mechanisms than their *effects*. Case studies (Zuboff, 1988; Sewell and Wilkinson, 1992; Sewell, 1998) of high-tech manufacturing make much of the enhanced capacity of management to collect, display and attribute performance data through electronic surveillance. Because stockpiles of labour and parts are eliminated through quality (TQM) and just-in-time (JIT) systems, production arrangements are highly visible. The information is generated from and fed back through teams of employees that appear to have autonomy, but in practice internalise production norms and discipline themselves through systems such as Nissan's 'Neighbour Watch' (Garrahan and Stewart, 1992). Such information is unobtrusive and perceived to be objective, therefore accentuating its legitimacy. Teams may produce self-surveillance independently of an information-driven process. Delegated responsibilities, whether for routine production decisions or, more exceptionally, induction and evaluation of team members, mean that employees have to develop their own disciplinary 'rules', thus collaborating with management to identify and reward the 'good worker' (Barker, 1993; McKinlay and P. Taylor, 1996).

The growth of call centres has boosted new theories of control. Surveillance undoubtedly plays a pivotal role in the way that integrated telephone and computer technologies facilitate the access and retrieval of data in the service interaction between desk-bound employee and external customer. Of particular importance is a sophisticated capacity remotely to record and assess the speed and 'quality' of the work. Not only is performance data made public, a proportion of the calls will be monitored remotely and used to reward and discipline employees. As a result, the previously identified 'objectivity' of the statistics is combined with constant, but unseen surveillance. Not only do employees internalise controls, the controllers are redundant: 'In call centres the agents are constantly visible and supervisor's power has indeed been "rendered perfect" – via the computer monitoring screen – and therefore its actual use unnecessary'(Fernie and Metcalf, 1997: 29).

In the most developed theorisation of such trends, Sewell (1998) argues that the interaction of 'vertical' electronic surveillance and 'horizontal' peer group scrutiny has produced a new model of control, countering the optimistic gloss of the empowerment and team literatures, while moving beyond the limits of traditional labour process theory. The implication of Sewell's argument is that such a combination solves the direct control/responsible autonomy dilemma that has historically troubled generations of managers, to say nothing of management theorists.

Surveillance is not a new phenomenon. As we saw in Chapter 2, many writers have described the early factory in terms of the attempted subordination and surveillance of recalcitrant workers, using the work of historians to illustrate how employers used new systems of rules and control techniques to induce 'appropriate' morals and work habits. In the most detailed examination of the issues, Dandeker (1990) links surveillance primarily to processes of bureaucratic rationalisation that have developed throughout this century. By 1990, 10 million workers in the US, including many professional and managerial employees, had become subject to electronic performance monitoring (Pfeffer, 1997: 114). Given these trends and recent socio-technical systems, it is difficult to deny that *some* shift towards electronic and self-surveillance has taken place in *some* industries.

Whether this constitutes an overarching development requiring an entirely new conceptualisation is a different matter. Many practices highlighted in the manufacturing case studies were identified by earlier writers making a critique of lean production (Parker and Slaughter, 1988). Yet they were described as a form of work intensification – 'management by stress' – in other words, more a shift in the effort bargain than the frontier of control. The idea that electronic surveillance is unobtrusive is a strange one. Performance display is characterised by its visibility to management and employees. It can therefore only be unobtrusive if the information it relays is accepted as objective. Yet there is considerable evidence that employees challenge the accuracy of the data, or use it for their own purposes against management (Zuboff, 1988; Bain and P. Taylor, 2000).

Call centres *are* clearly a new development, but do we need new concepts to explain them? Callaghan and Thompson (2001) argue that Richard Edward's control framework provides better insights than recent 'electronic sweatshop' perspectives. His three dimensions of a system of control and distinction between stages of direct, technical and bureaucratic control strategies have been fully outlined earlier in the chapter. Call centres predominantly use a system of technical control. In terms of Edward's first dimension, automated call distribution systems (ACD) enable management to direct the speed, direction and character of the work tasks. Technical control in call centres goes further than assembly lines in assisting companies to operationalise the second dimension – monitoring and evaluating performance. The performance of individuals and teams can be compared within or across sites. In turn that information can be linked to the apparatus of reward and discipline through the formal assessment and review process. One of the weaknesses of Edwards' framework is its linear nature. If this is dispensed with, we can see that his 'next' system – bureaucratic control – is used in call centres to define skills and tasks, and specify behavioural and performance standards. In the Callaghan and Thompson case study, Telebank has 19 core standards of behaviour and a seven-point scale to measure the skills of operators during appraisal, which is used to generate high and low scores. This indicates that many controls in the modern workplace remain external. To take another example, normative rules in strong culture companies may be different from traditional task-based control, but they are still rules. There is still the question of whether such rules are internalised. Management's sources and use of information may have increased, but there is little evidence that they are unobtrusive or regarded by employees as objective and unconnected to visible authority relations. Far from supervisory power being 'rendered perfect', there is evidence that customer service representatives (CSR) strongly dislike the emphasis put on 'the stats' and the disciplinary uses made of them (Bain and P. Taylor, 2000; Callaghan and Thompson, 2001). Employees distinguish between the 'friendly' supervision of coaching to improve skills and the disciplinary use of performance data. As with manufacturing, CSRs challenge the objectivity of the data and turn it against them: 'I check everything, I take it away and check it, I don't just sign it. I go back into the system, you can actually remember a lot of things when you go back in and see the name. I know that people have had arguments with the research section' (CSR quoted in Callaghan and Thompson, 2001: 32).

Conclusion

One of the great advantages of LPT, as shown by Edwards, is that it has a reciprocal model of control and resistance. Given both the general nature of divergent interests between capital and labour, plus the way that any control system builds up internal contradictions, the conditions for resistance are always present and tend to develop further over time. In contrast, acceptance and acquiescence are seen as the outcomes of the interaction of external surveillance and self-surveillance. In Britain in late 1999, the first national strike of call centre workers took place on the issue of oppressive working conditions. But that is only the tip of the iceberg. Though individual, technology-paced working and remote surveillance makes resistance difficult, CSRs learn informally to manipulate the codes used to claim relief from work tasks, and become skilled in setting their own pace and variation from the company scripts when talking to customers (S. Taylor, 1998; P. Taylor and Bain, 1998; Callaghan and Thompson, 2001). The central problem in new surveillance studies is confusion of the formal capacities of technological and managerial systems with their actual usage and effectiveness. This is not a just an empirical issue. Such claims arise frequently as part of a particular theoretical perspective, derived from the work of Michel Foucault. We return to these issues within a broader theoretical discussion later in the next chapter.

9 Power, Conflict and Resistance

Power is a much used and little understood term. Take em*power*ment, which you might think is something to do with power. Apparently not: 'senior managers need to realise that empowerment is not about increasing the power of employees' (Randolph, 1995: 30). In business practice, empowerment is about increasing *responsibilities*, and employees need to be disabused of the understandable confusion that they are going to have more input into decision-making. Such confusion is unfortunate because power is becoming a 'hot' topic in current popular management literature. Successful managers are those who learn to use power, not just to get their own way, but to get things done. As Tom Peters puts it, 'Anyone who loves accomplishing things must learn to love (yes, love) politics' (*Independent on Sunday*, 15 May 1994).

> Getting things done requires power. The problem is that we would prefer to see the world as a kind of grand morality play with the good guys and the bad ones easily identified ... In corporations, public agencies, universities and government, the problem is how to move forward, how to solve the many problems facing organisations of all sizes and types. Developing and exercising power requires both will and skill. It is the will that often seems to be missing. To manage with power means recognising that in almost every organisation there are varying interests. It means figuring out what point of view those various individuals and subunits have on issues of concern to you ... and thus it is imperative to understand where power comes from and how sources of power can be developed. Finally managing with power means understanding the strategies and tactics through which power is developed and used in organisations.
>
> (Jeffrey Pfeffer, interviewed in *Business Magazine*, November 1993)

In this more favourable context there has been a rash of books seeking to legitimate power for managerial use. These include self-help manuals promising tips on how to fight the guerrilla war in the boardroom (Drummond, 1996), more substantial contributions that wisely warn practitioners that while organisational politics can be managed, it cannot be 'managed away' (Buchanan and Badham, 1999: 21). It did, however, as the next section demonstrates, take a long time to get to this point.

Power in mainstream theory

'The natural place to look for an understanding of power in organizations is that extensive body of work known as "organization theory"' (Cockburn, 1990: 76).

However, for many years Pfeffer (1981a, 1992) was something of a lone voice among organisation theorists in attempting to develop accounts of power. In contrast to control, most traditional organisational behaviour textbooks simply do not have chapters on power or, if they do, admit that it has been largely ignored or subsumed within other issues such as leadership (Luthans, 1981: 387). Cockburn's explanation is that such theory has been devised from the viewpoint of the owners and managers who control organisations. This may be less a case of reflecting the viewpoint of managers, than the conventional ways of viewing their activities that we examined in the previous chapter. Willmott (1984: 350) sums this up succinctly: 'the common sense, technical, images developed by managers to account for their activities get returned to them in the form of apolitical descriptions of the reality of their work'.

Power relations can simply be simply written out of the picture, for example by redefining 'subordinates' as 'non-managers' (Mullins, 1985: 238). They then have a shadowy existence, hidden within discussions of why management finds it 'difficult to delegate', and focusing on personal disposition rather than the structures of power that shape them. Debates on management style will contain occasional advice on when to use authoritarian methods – Hitt *et al.* writing that in today's large corporations 'fear must be used cautiously' (1986: 43). Furthermore, power is the hidden agenda when managerial prerogatives are stressed, though the ideological needs of management may blunt the directness of language. But what else is meant when the phrase 'management must manage' is used?

Some of the roots of the neglect can be traced to the historical association in organisation theory between rational, formal organisation and legitimate authority (Clegg and Dunkerley, 1980: 433–4). Rational decision-makers and efficiency maximisers should have no need for power. Reflecting a wider functionalist perspective that sees power as 'a legitimate regulation in a society based on common values' (Barker and Roberts, 1993: 195), theorists such as Parsons see authority as granting a consensual 'power to' structure the behaviour of others (Storey, 1983: 54–5). 'Zero-sum' notions of power, in which there are clear and incompatible differences of resources and interests are explicitly ruled out. Alternatively, power is linked to the breakdown of authority and the growth of informal practices. This can be seen in a standard definition of organisational power quoted in Luthans: 'the management of influence to obtain ends not sanctioned by the organisation' (1981: 389). Power therefore is seen as inhabiting the shadow side of organisations, arising when rationality fails (Egan, 1994).

In this context, it has only been possible to raise the profile of analyses of power by demonstrating its instrumental character, showing that it can act as an aid to rationality and efficiency. One of the most sophisticated accounts does exactly that. Enrolling Machiavelli as a guide, Badham and Buchanan (1999) argue that the change agent's effectiveness is considerably enhanced if she or he can indulge in some 'power-assisted steering' to complement the traditional humanistic roles of social engineer and therapist facilitator. To persuade practitioners, a contingent explanation is a useful addition to an instrumental one. In more recent writings on power, Pfeffer has filled this gap. Power as a resource is not just generally useful, it has become more necessary because informal channels of influence have been growing as hierarchy diminishes. Flatter organisation means that 'the exercise of formal, hierarchical control is less consistent with organisational values and ways or organising' (1997: 136). A disassociation of power from formal structure is both bizarre and at odds with Pfeffer's standard model of competitive struggle for resources among sub-units. The 'less hierarchy' argument is also heavily disputed, as we shall see in Chapter 12. But Pfeffer's contingent explanation is attractive to organisation theory, because it is absolutely consistent with the existing conceptualisations of power as a primarily backstage, informal phenomenon.

Mainstream models

Given the relative absence of a focus on power, organisation studies has had to rely on a small but influential number of studies. The dominant orientation is towards an analysis of the micro or internal politics of organisations, which Pfeffer defines as: 'Those activities within organisations to acquire, develop and use power and other resources to obtain ones preferred outcomes in a situation where there is dissension or uncertainty about choices' (1999: 10). To sustain this approach, organisation theory draws on a definition of power developed by Dahl (1957), which itself is based on Weber (1968). Analogous to the impact of one billiard ball upon another, power is seen as the ability of A to get B to do something they would not otherwise do, despite any resistance.

A narrow focus on power in a solely organisational setting was itself indicative of what Hinings (1988: 4) refers to as the continuing divorce of organisation theory from sociology. Within this framework one of the best-known contributions is from French and Raven (1959), who start from the concept of 'bases of power' located in organisational resources. They are available for use singly or jointly by the manager, but depend on the perceptions and responses of those 'targeted'.

> **Reward** The use of resources as rewards, where the target values the chosen method and believes it can be delivered. Can include not just money, but promotions, increased job satisfaction and social recognition.

> **Coercive** The capacity to enforce discipline. Rests ultimately on the fear of the likelihood of psychological or material punishment, whether loss of overtime bonuses or humiliation in front of the peer group for poor sales figures.

> **Referent** The personal characteristics of the manager are perceived as attractive by employees, generating feelings of identification. Similar to Weber's concept of charismatic power.

> **Legitimate** Power is made acceptable by subordinates acquiescing in the right of power holders to influence them. Linked strongly to the idea of authority.

> **Expert** The existence of power as knowledge or other forms of expertise attributed to individuals or groups, which others feel obliged to accept. It is in itself a type of legitimacy.

There is some evidence concerning the application and effectiveness of these sources of power (see Luthans, 1981: 395–401). Not surprisingly it shows that non-formal sources such as expert power impact most favourably on organisational effectiveness. But given the questionnaire methods used, this may tell us more about cultural expectations than actual work practices. This reflects genuine and broader problems in measuring power, particularly when trying to separate capacity from actual use. Researchers have had to rely on survey methods that in turn rely on respondents' assessment of factors such as the reputation of individuals or departments.

In practice, this may be measuring perceived influence, or at best the relation between influence, tactics and outcomes (Kipnis and Schmidt, 1988). That is not the only problem. The French and Raven categories are widely regarded as too individualistic, though the basic argument about individual bases of power is developed in more depth by Pfeffer (1992). Power is seen as a structural process linked to task specialisation. Given that some tasks are more central than others, the individuals involved have more chance to exert influence. However, in reality the relational structures of power are more likely to involve *networks* (Knoke, 1990) or *coalitions* (Cyert and March, 1963) which compete for resources and influence within organisations. Individuals seeking sources of power normally have to work within sectional interest groups, such as departments or specialist occupations. Pettigrew's (1973) research showed computer programmers locked into a power struggle with systems analysts. Their weapons were ideologies of expertise, exclusivity of technique by avoiding written records, and control of recruitment policies. Political *skills* are vital in these processes and, as we have seen, are increasingly viewed in a positive light in the popular managerial literature. Skills such as advocacy may be useful to the company in a competitive environment, and the management of creative contention is central to the building of alliances and informal networks that are sometimes dubbed 'dominant coalitions' (Kotter, 1982).

This political view clearly starts from the kind of 'realist' assumptions discussed in the last chapter, that 'see the manager not as a servant of the owners nor as a technocrat serving the system, but as a manipulator trying to compete and co-operate with others in order to pursue his own ends' (Lee, 1985: 206). Such a vision of sectional interests and firms as sites of struggles between different groups and coalitions is also of necessity *pluralist* in that it begins from a recognition of multiple and competing goals, as well as internal bargaining processes. Indeed, organisations can be conceptualised as politically-negotiated orders that are neither the harmonious entities beloved of managerial theory, nor the arenas for class conflict associated with radical critics (Bacarach and Lawlor, 1980). A practical spin-off can be seen in present business practice which is currently awash with references to stakeholders. Admittedly this is a 'soft' version, where companies take an inclusive approach that treats shareholders as just another group alongside employers, customers, suppliers and the wider community (RSA, 1994; Handy, 1994). Tougher varieties recognise owners as a more powerful set of players among the multiplicity of interests (Watson, 1994).

The resultant internal political systems do, however, tend to stabilise themselves through the stake in the survival of the whole system held by the competing parties, and the extra power wielded by top management. What are the dynamics of the internal power structure? A coherent explanation synthesising a range of other studies is provided through the *strategic contingencies* model of Hickson *et al.* (1973). This starts from the observation that it is necessary to treat power as being about the allocation of scarce resources and as the property of a social relationship – particularly the departmental division of labour between purchasing, marketing and so on – rather than individual action. These social relations are shaped by external and internal factors. Internally 'heavyweight' interest groups are able to influence not just matters within their own spheres, 'but beyond that in matters that would be thought to be the primary concern of other specialist units' (Hickson, 1990: 176).

At the external level, we return to the open systems model discussed in Chapter 5. Coping with uncertainty is a crucial feature in transactions between organisations and the environment. The internal institutions charged with this responsibility are the *sub-units* such as departments. Power enters the picture through the familiar frame of resource-dependency, because those sub-units that can cope with uncertainty will be able to exercise power in their competitive struggle for resources with their rivals. Hickson and McCullough (1980) use the example of purchasing agents who were trying to expand their limited power base by trying to move from merely placing orders and ensuring delivery, to the provision of information to management and planning new products. The tactics used involved building alliances with contacts in other departments and manipulation of rules. But power could only really be gained when the customer environment contained a variety of suppliers, thus increasing the dependency of other sections on purchasing.

Such examples indicate that structural contingencies constitute a number of variables that shape power. Ability to deal with uncertainty is complemented by the degree of *dependency* on other units, the extent to which activities are *substitutable*, and on the overall level of *centrality* to the organisation. Therefore power is gained through the process of exchange and control of strategic contingencies. Though the point is not often made, this kind of analysis can be extended to shop-floor employees. 'Lower participants', as Mechanic (1962) describes them, can also utilise power derived from control over uncertainty. Among his examples were hospital orderlies who exploited their skills and access to information in order to control waiting lists for operations against more senior medical staff who were not interested in administration.

A critical evaluation: three-dimensional analyses

The literature on internal politics and power is very useful, particularly when set against the traditional conceptions of rational, apolitical management. But there are costs, some of which arise from the limitations of pluralism. Talk of stakeholders and a multiplicity of interests competing for scarce resources is again an advance on images of consensus and fairness, but is too often a comfortable rhetoric that is fundamentally unrealistic about the distribution of power inside organisations. Owners hold the key stakes in corporate resources and even employees' countervailing powers have diminished sharply in recent economic, political and legal climates. There is also an illusion about management. Of course, managers represent a sectional interest, or more precisely a series of sectional interests. But they are also an agency of ownership interests, not passive prisoners, but certainly constrained actors. Even Watson's (1994) informative and determinedly pluralistic account of managers trying to assert their desires to maintain manufacturing interests at ZTC has to recognise that they are working within short-termist, cost-cutting rules set by the dominant corporate coalition.

There is also the issue of the relation between internal and external power relations. Limitations flow from the analysis being confined to a particular level of power relations. As we have acknowledged, there are problems in measuring power. Reputational methods tend to re-affirm the obvious, for example that level in the hierarchy is significantly related to a respondent's perceptions of an individual's power

(Pfeffer, 1997: 146). Alternatively, power is analysed through its symptoms, by what is observable through behavioural exchange and by identifying who the players are. As a result, any research that does exist on power concentrates on its exercise, taking, as we shall show later, the formal organisation and deeper power relations for granted. While the better frameworks allow us to observe the 'turf rules' that underlie the power game in different contexts (Buchanan and Badham, 1999), a predominantly inter-personal focus tends to trivialise power by treating it as 'office politics'. Though the 'pitch' that serves as the context for the turf game can be contextualised as comparative corporate or national contexts, it tends to be treated as particular structures and cultures within organisations (Buchanan and Badham, 1999: 32). Even when dealt with in a more substantial way, as in strategic contingency theory, the focus is primarily on *horizontal* power: 'Conventional organisation theory seldom considers the power within organisations, the power exemplified by top management, as an expression of power relations external to the organisation' (Cockburn, 1990: 77).

Vertical power hierarchies are set aside by the interpretation of the division of labour as consisting of relations between sub-units. Such neglect is reinforced by the tendency to see managerial authority and goals as always accepted by workers, or at least subject to joint regulation and negotiated outcome through the interplay of power. Substantial power differences and sources of dissension are therefore under-estimated. We need to deal with 'power over' as well as 'power to', and treat managerial authority as a form of organisational power. Though power is multi-faceted, zero-sum circumstances can and do exist, whether they are manifested in distribution of profits in dividends or wages, or the right to bargain collectively or not.

Clegg's (1977) early critique is pertinent to this debate. French and Raven and strategic contingency theory can show how managers use resources to exercise power. Neither explain the prior distribution of power – how some people come to have access to these resources while others do not. The exercise of power is premised on institutional frameworks and rules; 'the "power" of the sub-unit has to be grounded in the prior *capacity* to exercise power which managers possess' (Clegg, 1977: 27). Furthermore, managerial power has to be located within deeper structures of economic domination that underpin its use and legitimacy. A prime example is the concentration of ownership and control in the transnational company. The power to switch resources and relocate operations simply cannot be explained at the level of the single enterprise and its sub-units. Without such a structural framework, we are left with a micro-level analysis capable only of explaining the skills of 'politicking' rather than political power. We are also left with a view of managers solely as self-interested manipulators and power-seekers with little understanding of the broader dynamics and constraints which dispose management to use power in the first place.

These differences in perspective can be clarified by reference to the wider debate on power, taking the three-dimensional model of Lukes (1982) as a framework. The behavioural literature is primarily *one-dimensional* in that it focuses on the observable activities of particular 'subjects', seeking proof of power in processes such as decision-making. This formulation, which draws on Weber's definition outlined earlier, is specifically linked to *intended effects* and imposition of will: 'Power is only relevant to our understanding of behaviour and organisation, when there is conflict' (Dawson, 1986: 148). On this basis rests the behavioural assumption that power can always be observed and measured.

In the broader debate the one-dimensional view has been criticised by writers such as Bachrach and Baratz (1962), utilising the concept of 'non-decision making'. This may sound odd, but refers to the capacity of power-holders to limit those issues that are contested or even discussed. The approach usefully distinguishes between the sources and bases of power. By controlling agendas and mobilising the bias inherent in greater access to institutional resources, values and even the language of legitimacy, they can keep to safe issues and exclude others that threaten their interests. Though the research deals with political actors, there is no doubt that management actions can be seen in this light. Crucial decisions regarding investment or the introduction of new technology very seldom reach normal bargaining, except perhaps to deal with the consequences. In industrial relations terminology they are 'non-negotiable', particularly when market trends favour employers. Even with worker director schemes such as those at British Steel in the 1970s, management could manipulate the rules of the game and socialise workforce representatives to the extent that their interests were not seriously contested (Brannen, 1983).

Lukes (1974: 21) pays tribute to this 'two-dimensional' analysis, but argues that it remains too much on the terrain of observable behaviour. Élite power can prevent grievances, and therefore conflict, from ever arising by shaping the very wants and preferences of subordinate groups. This is not a question of brainwashing, but of the hidden structures of power. Market mechanisms and the distribution of wealth and property constitute power relations – such as ownership rights – which frequently come to be taken for granted. Nor should the formation of consent be conceptualised as a process distinct from the operation of power. Though there are concrete practices that arise from such relations, they are not always observable in the traditional sense. Power does not necessarily need a subject. As Clegg and Dunkerley observe, 'Much of the time the power of capital does not have to be exercised to be present . . . because this exercise is grounded in a structural "capacity" which frequently obviates the need for its exercise' (1980: 495). Put another way, power might be both the production of effects and the *capacity* to produce them. Take the previously discussed example of the diffusion of 'best practice' in large companies. What is perceived to be 'best' is largely taken for granted within existing structure of property and power. Ownership of resources thus sets the actual grounds through which agendas are set.

Though the processes cannot always be measured, the outcomes can, in terms of structural inequalities between groups. For Lukes, this indicates that a latent conflict exists, 'which consists of a contradiction between the interests of those exercising power and the *real* interests of those they exclude' (1974: 284). His three-dimensional explanation of power in general therefore coincides with radical perspectives on organisational power, which would draw on Weber and Marx's analysis of the deeper economic roots of domination. This involves a different understanding of 'dependency' in which there is a 'fundamental asymmetry of power between employers and workers' (Rueschemeyer, 1986: 76), based on workers' lack of control of the means of production. The propertyless have to 'seek access to resources owned or controlled by the few' (Fox, 1974: 284). When Nissan opened their factory in the North East of England, they had 30 000 applications for 300 jobs. Not surprisingly this enabled them to pick workers and a union wholly on their own terms. This 'structural' account of power differs sharply from the use of that term in mainstream theory, reflecting a one-dimensional focus that signifies position in the formal structure or division of labour (Pfeffer, 1997: 144).

Nevertheless Lukes' work has been subject to considerable criticism, even from other radical theorists (see Clegg, 1989). He wants to retain an emphasis on power that presupposes human agencies that make choices, but on the other hand recognises that those choices are not equally available in circumstances of differentially constraining structures. At the level of individuals it is fairly easy to attribute intentions, but much more difficult when the individual is given an 'interest' because of membership of a group, whether that be capital and labour, men and women, or professionals and skilled workers (Barker and Roberts, 1993: 210). When Lukes argues that A may shape B's preferences in a manner inimical to B, how do we know what the latter's 'real' interests are without attributing preferences to them or arguing that what they actually think or act is 'false'? How do we recognise the power to persuade without reproducing totalitarian images of agencies that control all our thoughts and desires? It may be possible, as we shall see later, to draw on a more complex notion of interests, but Lukes never adequately resolves these dilemmas about structures and agencies. The debate on dimensions of power demonstrates that there have been intractable problems in defining what power is and where it is located. A particularly intractable problem has been how to conceptualise deeper, hidden forms of power, 'Since it advantages or disadvantages individuals without being consciously mobilised' (Hardy, 1996: S8). An increasing number of radical theorists have sought refuge in the work of the French writer, Foucault, to escape those limitations.

Foucault, post-structuralism and disciplinary power

On the face of it an analysis based on surveillance techniques and forms of knowledge originating in monastic and military orders in the sixteenth and seventeenth centuries (Foucault, 1972, 1977, 1984) might seem to have limited relevance to contemporary organisation theory. But the attraction is based on the approach to power and how it can be applied to modern (or postmodern) organisations: 'deeply embedded within his detailed analyses of concrete historical situations and events there is a rich and complex model of the mechanism of power which is of direct relevance to organisational analysis' (Marsden, 1993: 108).

That appeal derives partly from restoring an idea of power as productive rather than prohibitive or solely repressive, creative and constitutive as well as limiting and constraining. This is characteristic of broader *post-structuralist* thinking. Indeed one can have post-structuralist theories of power without reliance on Foucault (see Leflaive, 1996). Such perspectives are not mere echoes of Parsons' emphasis on positive-sum rather than zero-sum relations. For power is held to be the central feature of social life from which there is no escape. Foucault uses the term 'capillary' to explain that power does not come from above, from a central source. Rather, it 'circulates through the entire social body' (Fraser, 1989: 24), into the furthest reaches and localities. Power is embodied in heterogeneous micro-practices, in everyday life rather than in a special sphere. But as particular forms become generalised in a network of relations, Foucault allows himself to use the term 'strategy' to describe the results. Resistance may break out at different points in the chain, and while that resistance recreates power, it promotes a ceaseless process of shifting alliances and tensions. Power, therefore, is discontinuous rather than stable.

Nor is power something that is possessed by an individual or group. This can be considered to commit the sin of belief in a *sovereign* power held by agents making rational decisions or attached to and formally administered by states, corporations or other groupings. From a Foucauldian perspective, power is understood without reference to agency, its mechanisms impersonal and independent of conscious subjects. In one sense this seems to extend Lukes' third, structural dimension of power in which the agency (such as capital) and its effects remain hidden. But Foucault's disciplinary power removes entirely a deliberately controlling relationship between subject and object, the imposition of A's will over B (Barker and Roberts, 1993: 216), even when conceived of as thought control and ideological hegemony (Clegg, 1989: 182). A similar argument is developed by Leflaive: if organisations or any of their members are defined as power holders, that is merely a *status* bestowed upon them; 'sovereignty, defined as the embodiment of power in the exercise of will, is not a characteristic of our contemporary environment' (1996: 43). Power lies outside its possessor, in routines and narratives that confer fluid, temporary capacities to act effectively.

This is part of a post-structuralist emphasis on de-centring the subject. Power operates not through agencies with specific interests, but through *discourses*: practices of talk, text and argument that continuously form that which they speak. Disciplinary practices produce knowledge that is inseparable from power. Language thus becomes a central feature in the discursive production of power, and power/knowledge discourses constitute norms of acceptable conduct, constructing social identities. All this sounds very abstract, but Foucault underpins his concepts by an historical account of the emergence of a distinctively *modern* power. Pre-modern sovereign power had depended on personalised bonds of obligation. In contrast, the techniques of disciplinary power were developed and refined in religious institutions, prisons, asylums, hospitals and workhouses at a local level, rather than overseen by the state. Such micro-techniques were concerned with evaluating, recording and observing individuals in an exhaustive and detailed way. During the early nineteenth century, surveillance spread from the institutions that were first faced with the mass management of large groups of people, especially to the factory:

> The dark satanic mills of Yorkshire and Lancashire simply latched on the disciplinary apparatus already let loose from the monastery into the poor house, the work house, the orphanage, the barracks and so on. (Clegg, 1989: 173)

But the prison remained the purest exemplar and microcosm of disciplinary techniques and knowledge: power is fundamentally *carceral* in character.

In the range of modern institutions, power also becomes increasingly focused on the body as an object, distinguishing Foucault's analysis from a more conventional emphasis on ideology and moulding of the mind. Developing originally in the eighteenth century, *bio-power* was aimed at the control of wider populations, their movements, gestures and routines, such as the posture of pupils and marching steps of soldiers. These processes were also facilitated by the partitioning and regulation of time and space (Dandeker, 1990: 25). Penology, medicine and psychiatry become the focal points for the development of new power–knowledge discourses that punish deviation from normative standards.

The most potent imagery of Foucauldian theory is the *panopticon* – Bentham's design principle based on a circular building with central observation tower – which, from prisons to the new model housing estates, facilitated a unidirectional disciplinary gaze. In other words the observed can be seen but cannot see, while the observers see everything but cannot be seen. So effective are such practices that individuals begin to discipline themselves to be, in Foucault's words, docile and useful bodies. The overall effect of disciplinary practices is summed up by O'Neill: 'in the bourgeois social order the prison, the factory and the school, like the army, are places where the system can project its conception of the disciplinary society in the reformed criminal, the good worker, student, loyal soldier and committed citizen' (1986: 51–2). The fact that neither Bentham's nor anyone else's panopticon was ever built has not stopped it becoming one of the most pervasive images in social science. This is, in part, because the emphasis is less on a physical manifestation, than on panoptic power expressed through electronic and self-surveillance, as discussed in the previous chapter. Surveillance constitutes organisations and their members as subjects of power (Leflaive, 1996: 25).

Applications to organisations

These perspectives have given theorists the language to interrogate past, present and future. O'Neill is one of those theorists who have used Foucault to help *reconstruct the past*. The process of the emergence of the factory and large-scale organisation is overlaid with the conceptual apparatus of the disciplinary society. Indeed much of the material discussed in Chapters 2 and 3 is represented in precisely this way. Industrial discipline was a central theme of the later rise of scientific management, which Weber praised for its military character. Equally such systems also involved an immense expansion of managerial knowledge and calculation of workers' time and motion. Theorists working in the tradition of Marx and Weber see these developments as the necessary preconditions for sustaining the appropriation of profit and the removal of the obstacle of worker control over aspects of the labour process. But for followers of Foucault, 'The causality is all wrong. New forms of disciplinary power preceded the establishment of the factory by at least two centuries' (Clegg, 1989: 188).

Foucauldian perspectives are also proving a means of *reframing the present*. The work of Townley (1990, 1993), Burchell *et al.* (1985) and Marsden (1993) focuses on identifying the social technologies of contemporary specialists in human and organisational behaviour as power/knowledge discourses. These latter day 'soft cops' in HRM, accounting and consultancy are concerned to 'observe, examine and normalise performance and behaviour' (Marsden, 1993: 118–19), carrying on a tradition established by human relations and its efforts to habituate the employee to the changing conditions of work in the large corporation. All the elaborate emphasis in organisational theory on power expressed through the politics of decision-making, inter-group conflicts over resources, regulations and rights is held to be a sideshow diverting attention from the substance of power. At the heart of that process is the monopoly of knowledge by management and its agents, a form of discursive closure that marginalises other representations and identities (Deetz, 1992).

It is in Deetz's analysis of disciplinary power in the modern corporation that we see the most complete application of Foucault. Organisational processes act to produce corporate obedience, where 'The disciplined member of the corporation wants on his or her own what the corporation wants' (Deetz, 1992: 42). Similarly for N. Rose (1990), the culture and discourses of the modern corporation have become a crucial means through which human feelings, emotions and thoughts have become increasingly managed and governed. In either case, how this is actually achieved is vague, given the need of such theory to avoid mentioning deliberate operations of directive power. But attention is drawn to an accumulation of local power/knowledge discourses that disperses into norms and standard practices of moral, medical, sexual and psychological regulation. Elsewhere in the same book of readings, reference is made to the capacity of knowledge products of personnel and organisation psychology (such as performance appraisal) to 'gaze at, scrutinize, classify and count individual characteristics and behaviours. Collected data are analysed and stored, ensuring that an individual's legacy, good and bad, is not forgotten' (Steffy and Grimes, 1992: 192). New forms of surveillance, when specified, rest largely on illustrative examples drawn from the power of information systems and the behavioural technology arising from the expansion of culture change programmes. Willmott (1994) supports Deetz's critique of the colonizing tendencies of the modern corporation, arguing that the creation of monocultures displays nascent totalitarianism. Employees are not only coercively socialised, but positively attracted to such cultures because they learn to tie their own identities to the associated norms and knowledge. Their subjectivity becomes 'self-disciplining' as individuals begin to feel secure within the corporate identities (Knights and Willmott, 1990: 550). Such analyses draw on Foucault's use of the term 'subject': meaning where an individual is made subject and makes themselves *subject* to a form of power through the association between identity and self-knowledge.

We will look in more detail at issues of corporate culture in Chapter 13. But whatever the source of new processes, Deetz argues that the effects are greater than the prison exemplar, because the modern corporation goes home with its members and colonizes competing institutions such as the media (1992: 38). Similarly, in supporting and explaining Foucault's view that all organisations resemble prisons, Burrell (1988: 232) argues that, 'Whilst we may not live in total institutions, the institutional organization of our lives is total'. Opposition is largely self-defeating since those who play the game become addicts to the rules, and the pursuit of sovereign rights through bodies such as trade unions hides the disciplinary processes that produce the struggle in the first place (Deetz, 1992: 42). In addition, resistance does not threaten power, because 'It means that discipline can grow stronger knowing where its next efforts must be directed' (Burrell, 1988: 228). Clegg is similarly pessimistic in noting the organisational outflanking of resistance, due to subordinated agencies, 'Lacking the organizational resources to outmanoeuvre existing networks and alliances' (1989: 19). As Collinson (1994) observes, this analysis draws on Foucault in arguing that knowledge and information structure access to power. Subordinates either have too little of both, or their knowledge of the likely outcome of action is so predictable that it is similarly inhibitive.

As we saw in Chapter 8, this imagery of all-powerful total institutions is reproduced in another Foucauldian-inspired literature, whose object of inquiry is new production techniques such as JIT and TQM (Sewell and Wilkinson, 1992; Delbridge, Turnbull and Wilkinson, 1992; Webster and Robins, 1993; Sewell, 1998). Marrying Foucault and Braverman, they argue that more effective surveillance techniques enhance managerial control of the labour process. Webster and Robin's alternative history of the information revolution traces a line of descent from Bentham's original conception of the panopticon, through Taylorism as a means of monopolising knowledge in management, to the contemporary flexible firm which has the capacity of IT to centralise information from an increased range of geographically dispersed units. Shop floor techniques utilise more extensive information systems that can collect data on worker performance and behaviour. This is described as an electronic panopticon that brings the disciplinary gaze to every aspect of worker activity. As we indicated in the last chapter, this orientation has been reinforced by the growth of call centres, whose sophisticated surveillance capacities have led to the label 'electronic sweatshop' (Fernie and Metcalf, 1997), which has stuck even in the popular media.

Fernie and Metcalf talk of 'perfect supervisory power' without direct supervision. Commentators on new factory regimes argue that as a consequence of such discipline and the removal of any 'slack' from the production system, 'worker counter-control (in the sense described by Roy and many others) is effectively eliminated . . . the ultimate goal of management under a JIT/TQM regime must be recognised to be Total Management Control' (Delbridge, Turnbull and Wilkinson, 1992: 105). Chapter 12 explores further current trends in the reorganisation of the labour process, but we cannot take the above description for granted, regardless of its current vogue status.

Critique

We have already critiqued conceptions of the novelty and effectiveness of surveillance. Here we want to examine in more detail some of the accompanying theorising of power. Whether Foucault's history is accurate or methodology competent is beyond our scope (but see Giddens, 1982; Walzer, 1985; Habermas, 1987), and, we suspect, not pertinent to his appeal in and out of organisational analysis. New languages to describe old realities are always attractive to academics, in this case despite, or perhaps because of, the obscure and opaque terminology. Dandeker (1990) recaps the history of the growth of the modern business enterprise, rounding up all the usual suspects – Chandler, Edwards, Clawson, Williamson, Littler – without ever demonstrating that his over-arching concept of *surveillance* depicts anything substantially new or distinctive, at least with respect to the workplace. At a more micro level, Townley (1990) repackages the personnel function as a power/knowledge discourse with the Foucauldian terminology of dividing practices (enclosure, partitioning and ranking), to similarly unconvincing effect.

Townley's work has helped stimulate some useful studies of particular HRM practices, such as appraisal (Newton and Findlay, 1996), but it also illustrates the dangers of over-privileging language and discourse. She argues that personnel can be understood as the provision of language or knowledge to reduce the space between what the formal contract of employment promises and what the employee's practice delivers. Aside from the fact that all managerial agencies operate in this gap, such conceptions distort the power resources available to and drawn on by those involved in managing the employment relationship. Language is part of that resource, but it is not, of necessity, the defining feature. Employment laws and labour markets may be more significant in empowering personnel, and may have only peripheral connection to any new power/knowledge discourse. In the context of accounting controls, Armstrong (1991) argues that Foucauldian analyses present disciplinary powers without reference to material sanctions and rewards. For example, the new accounting regime at the American company ITT was adhered to, not because those involved had internalised its disciplinary discourse, but because they were paid 25 per cent over the going rate to do so.

when confronted by resistance, the systematic surveillance and behavioural norms of disciplinary power can only work within a matrix of physical coercion, economic power, negotiated order, or some combination of these. In other words, Foucauldian representation of the manner in which accounting controls operate are incomplete because Foucault's 'microphysics' of power is itself incomplete. (Armstrong, 1991: 31)

In Chapter 1 we used the example of the Wapping dispute involving News International and print unions. A combination of bribes, threats, sackings and the use of new anti-union employment legislation was among the 'non-discursive strategies' that proved highly effective in Rupert Murdoch's victory.

When we examine capital and its managerial agencies it is clear that power is *somewhere* and its use may, in some circumstances, be rationally intended. Power is both a relationship *and* administered by individuals or collectivities. It therefore remains legitimate to refer to 'power holders', though never in an exclusive and uncontested sense. Removing 'power holders', particularly in support of the view that power is productive for all, also tends to gloss over substantive differences in sources and effectiveness of power. As we illustrated in the previous chapter, there are some circumstances in which workplace decisions may be zero sum – they cannot be 'possessed' by both management and workers. By setting aside such distinctions through arguments that power is productive for all, Foucauldian analyses run the risk of softening its substantive origins and effects. For example, Hardy seeks to move beyond negative 'power over' connotations to consider how more sophisticated multi-dimensional frameworks can help managers develop a broader array of mechanisms that facilitate successful strategic change. In particular, they can help 'those seeking to orchestrate collaborative action by preventing conflict over strategic options from emerging' (1996: S4). Negative consequences are limited to the recognition that such help may leave employees to the 'abuse' of this more sophisticated and less visible power (1996: S14).

One of the reasons why post-structuralist views are persuasive is that they trade on polarised conceptions of power. Their target is stereotypical: power as top-down, fixed and stable. Reality is considerably messier than this. Take the conflicts around the World Trade Organisation (WTO) in 1999. There is no doubt that we can identify the discursive constitution of power, through, for example, ideologies of progress and globalisation. We can also see how unstable power is, and the extent to which it can be disrupted by a variety of 'local' voices and interests. However, it remains the case that the WTO has both sovereign power holders, particularly in the agenda-setting leading nations, and the power to set rules for economic exchange that fundamentally structure social relationships across the globe.

A similar argument could be made with respect to *interests*. We have acknowledged that there are problems with this concept. If interests are attributed purely as a result of group membership, when people do not act in accordance with them, the legitimacy of those actions is unhelpfully questioned through concepts such as 'false consciousness'. Cultural affinity and identity may cut across imputed interests. It is possible to identify inequalities of power in terms of more and less successful struggles to deploy ideological and economic resources, rather than through the idea of interests (Hindess, 1982). Alternatively, interests can be regarded as structural predispositions to act collectively, which need to be discursively constituted in order to become effective. Moreover, identities *and* interests form the basis of employee resistance and misbehaviour at work, ranging from work limitation to joking rituals (Ackroyd and Thompson, 1999).

The WTO conflict is an illustration of the fact that power is not necessarily unobtrusive, invisible, 'low profile' (Fraser, 1989: 23), or used unilaterally only as a last resort (Deetz, 1992: 40). It may be said that the example is not organisational, but high-profile disputes are not the only source. As we have seen, employment relationships in this century have become progressively more bureaucratised. Yet Deetz (1992: 37) criticises Richard Edward's (1979) theory of bureaucratic control because it refers to identifiable rule and routine instead of a complex set of practices which become internalised as common sense and personal identity. This judgement is hopelessly inaccurate. Far from taking rules of payment, measurement and task allocation as given and natural, workers and their representatives have engaged in a persistent low-intensity war to use and manipulate them to their own advantage. Not only that, but there have been highly visible artefacts, such as Ford's 200-page 'Blue Book', for each side to draw on as a resource in the power struggle. Such examples confirm other evidence from shop-floor life that specific forms of knowledge are a key resource through which resistance can be mobilised (Collinson, 1994), a process illustrated with respect to call centres in Chapter 8.

A further problem is that the contested rationality between capital and labour is reduced to a local site of struggle. It is claimed that having decentred the loci of power, Foucault may be 'the last pluralist' (Clegg, 1989: 7). It is true that there is an emphasis on the dispersed and local character of power, with associated micro-technologies of discipline investigated in their own right. But the label of pluralism does not sit well with the theoretical substance of disciplinary power, which has prison and panopticon at its centre and determining force, and all organisations conceived of as total institutions, going way beyond Goffman's (1961) intentions. By treating the workplace as an extension of disciplinary practices and the factory, hospital and other organisations as paler versions of carceral institutions (Burrell, 1988), the specific character of employment relations in a capitalist society is lost. For example, control is treated merely as another version of discipline, and functionally oriented towards the creation of obedient bodies rather than sustaining exploitation (Clegg, 1989: 176). Vague and extravagant references to control over body and soul can only be justified by extreme examples such as AIDS testing in the workplace (Deetz, 1992: 140–1).

Finally, there is the problem that because power is everywhere and nowhere, the impression can be given that it is omnipresent, a force that there can never be any escape from. Resistance is part of the formal picture, but is under-theorised (Smart, 1985) and the dice loaded against it, because, 'only power is positive and productive, while resistance is simply a reaction to its production' (Dews, 1987: 99). Fragmented, insubstantial and counter-productive, resistance largely disappears from view, to be replaced by the language of docility and obedience (O'Neill, 1986: 55). In fact, the whole conceptual framework is saturated with the language of colonisation and conquest – images more appropriate to *Invasion of the Body Snatchers* than the complexities of organisational life. The problem is not so much with the Foucauldian description of new managerial techniques of power, but the assumption that they actually *work*.

A number of poststructuralist writers, noting this problem, have drawn back from some of the consequences of this 'over-disciplined' view of organisational life (Leflaive, 1996; Sewell, 1998). Unfortunately, the desire to bend the stick backs goes against the grain of their own language and concepts. There is also little sign of dissent and resistance in the case studies of writers such as Sewell (1992, 1998). A focus on talk and text away from agency tends to remove the gap between intent and outcome. What management or managerial discourse says it is doing is too often taken as synonymous with effects and effectiveness (Thompson and Ackroyd, 1995). Where studies of companies with a strong normative and surveillance agenda let us hear the voice of employees, we get a much more complex and balanced picture of power and resistance (Zuboff, 1988; Kunda, 1992; McKinlay and Taylor, 1996). This issue is returned to in Chapter 13.

Conclusion

Power gets everywhere, but it is not everything. As Fraser observes, 'Foucault calls too many different sorts of things power and simply leaves it at that' (1989: 32). It is important, for example, to demarcate a boundary with control. For radical theorists in a labour process tradition, 'Power is expressed in organisations through the control of the means and methods of production' (Clegg and Dunkerley, 1980: 476). Though power will be exercised in order to re-assert control by management, this should not mean that power is marginal or subsumed under control. The ability of employers to exert controls over labour is conditioned by a variety of different power relations. In particular companies or sectors, crucial factors will include those arising from product and labour markets, the state of employer and worker organisation, and factors identified by strategic contingency theorists such as management dependence on specific occupational and work groups. As we have seen, control structures are also shaped by broader non-industrial power relations, such as those embodied in employment laws that sustain the power of capital, or relations of social dependence in the community that are transferred into the workplace. Processes of control and power are both independent and interrelated inside and outside the workplace. More concrete discussion should reveal those complexities, not treat them as synonyms or analogues.

In the light of the evidence discussed in this chapter, power should also be accepted as inherently multi-dimensional. As with Lukes, Foucault's motives in trying to transcend the limitations of sovereign or one-dimensional power are admirable. But the result has been a conceptual and practical prison rather than a genuinely complex picture of power. Though some power decisions may be zero-sum, conceptualisations need not be. The advantage of Luke's framework is that whatever its limits, the recognition of different levels or dimensions of power remains valuable. It is perfectly possible to focus analysis primarily on one dimension, without denying the significance or influences of others. In advocating an ethnography of micropolitics in organisations, Badham notes that 'There is no presumption here that the absence of explicit or tacit attention to "deeper" structural influences on politics means that they do not exist. These factors may be manifested in or combined with an ethnography of politics focusing on political strategies and tactics' (1997: 3). Alternatively it may be possible to apply all three dimensions of Lukes' schema to explain different aspects of the same phenomenon, as Wilson and Thompson (2001) do with respect to sexual harassment. Gender and sexuality are, in fact, good illustrations of how we need to allow for the possibility that power may be a highly distinctive phenomenon inside different social relations. This will be one of the themes of the next chapter.

10 Gender, Sexuality and Organisations

No company can afford to waste valuable brainpower simply because it's wearing a skirt. (Anne Fisher, *Fortune*, 21 September 1992)

In the past decade businesses and business academics have discovered gender. Compared to other areas this has been somewhat late. There is a massive and important body of research and theory on gender, work and family (see Dex, 1985; Walby, 1986; Thompson, 1989; Bradley, 1996; Crompton, 1997; Rubery *et al.*, 1999). But that debate on the sexual division of labour focuses on occupational divisions, differential control in the labour process, female labour-force participation, segmented labour markets, or more broadly on patriarchy and capitalism. Organisations tend to be treated as passive recipients of wider social forces, with power only appearing indirectly, for example through access to employment. It is essential to 'see how organisational forms structure and are themselves structured by gender' (Witz and Savage, 1992: 8). That gap has been progressively filled with a variety of explanations and policy prescriptions.

Policy parameters and intellectual frameworks

Radical organisation theory has 'borrowed' the idea of 'gendered jobs' – ones that associate task requirements with the perceived qualities of a particular sex – and has begun to debate the extent to which organisations and their structures, bureaucracy in particular, can be considered as gendered. Empirically, the focus continues to be the 'glass ceiling' – the barriers to progress through organisational hierarchies. This narrower frame, which forms the subject matter of this chapter, has costs. Female managers are not the majority of women workers and the bigger, sociological picture can sometimes be obscured. As recent UK government figures show, the prime cause of the gender income gap is the concentration of women in lower-paid sectors of the labour market (*The Guardian*, 21 February 2000). Nevertheless, there are advantages in a narrower focus, drawing on what has been largely a 'dialogue between feminist theory and organisation theory' (Wajcman, 1996b: 262). Something new and specific has been added to an existing, powerful body of knowledge. At the same time the basic theoretical frameworks are reproduced and re-examined (see the parallels, for example, in the gender and technology debate: Grint and Gill, 1996; Webster, 1996).

That a new body of theory has had to address absences and disconnections is not surprising, as the visibility of gender in organizational analysis itself has been low. Recent surveys (Acker and Van Houten, 1992; Hearn and Parkin, 1992; Collinson and Hearn, 1994; Calás and Smircich, 1997; Alvesson and Due Billing, 1997) have trawled the major landmarks of theory and research from Taylorism to human relations and contingency theory, and have noted that though organisational processes are clearly influenced by gendered power relations, employees and managers appear to have no gender, and men and management are synonymous.

> Organisational scholarship has been, primarily, a literature written by men, for men and about men: how to gain the cooperation of men to achieve organisational ends through rationality: how to *man*/age. (Calás and Smircich, 1996: 222–3)

Weber is placed firmly in the centre of this 'malestream' organisational analysis. For him, the rise of bureaucracy brings with it an instrumental rationality in which impersonal rules, procedures and hierarchies are operated with technical efficiency. This is contrasted with traditional forms of authority reliant on individual privilege and personal allegiance. Issues of gender and sexuality are thus despatched to a private realm along with patrimonial and patriarchal relations, no longer to endanger rational–legal authority in the public sphere.

Banishing gender from the theory is far from the actual practice of organisational life, as many critics have subsequently argued (Pringle, 1989; Cockburn, 1991; F. Wilson, 1995). But by the time this conceptual invisibility was being challenged, a particular form of absence – from the management of organisations – had become the focal point of argument. The 1980s were in fact characterised by a degree of optimism that this was about to change. After all, women had been entering into the lower reaches of management and the professions, after having come to dominate the white-collar ranks in previous decades in many countries. According to 'trickle-up' assumptions, it was a question of watch and wait. To move the process along, equal opportunity initiatives were being taken by or forced upon many large companies, such as those involved in Opportunity 2000 in the UK. Progress, was, however, not wholly dependent on corporate beneficence. Optimism was fuelled by a combination of demographic, cultural and economic changes, such as the shift from manufacturing to private and public services, and from domestic to transnational companies. Taken together, they should have created a competitive imperative for companies to make room at the top (Adler and Izraeli, 1988; Adler, 1994). In other words it was not merely a matter of women getting *into* management, management were getting seriously into women.

That was the theory – the practice was different. By the mid-1990s the realisation was dawning that progress had been limited. There was movement in some specialisms (for example, human resources and marketing) and some sectors (for example, banking and finance), but by and large the glass ceiling was proving very durable. In the US a government-financed Glass Ceiling Commission estimated that women held only about 5 per cent of senior executive positions (*The Economist*, 10 August 1996). Institute of Management (1994, 1996) surveys painted a depressing picture in the UK: in 1995 the number of female managers was 10.7 per cent and that increased only fractionally during the later 1990s. Those in the senior category constituted only 5 per cent and at all levels there were differences in pay and perks, even for those similarly qualified and experienced. These trends hold true in sectoral studies, such as those in the health service (IHSM Consultants, 1994), and more detailed qualitative assessments of the position in large companies at the forefront of equal opportunity initiatives (Wajcman, 1996a, 1998). Higher up the ladder the position is worse, with less than 3 per cent of executive directors women (Caulkin, 1999). Even in Sweden

with its family-friendly social policies and high rates of female labour force participation, only 3 per cent of senior executives were female, and an earnings gap of
between 10 and 30 per cent existed (Kimmel, 1993). Australia too has a figure of 3
per cent in an economy where women make up 43 per cent of the workforce
(*Guardian*, 17 January 2000). While some, such as *The Economist* (1996), still
believed that given the different age cohorts of male and female managers it was still
a matter of time, most other commentators concluded that there was indeed something different about the 'careers' of female managers that required explanation.

Gendering organisational analysis

As Acker (1992: 248–9) observes, to document difficulties and differences is one thing,
to explain them is another. Acker herself contributed one of the most influential
concepts in this task – the gendered substructure of organisations: the frequently
implicit rules and arrangements that underlie practices taken for granted as rational.
But if the structures and practices are gendered, how are they so? The explanations
we examine in this section have contrasting answers, though they all move beyond any
account that rests on individual differences, whether these are biological (G. Wilson,
1997; Browne, 1998), psychologically based (Davidson and Cooper, 1992), or derived
from economic models such as human capital theory (Becker, 1985). Here, the cause
of unequal access to opportunity and power is located in socialisation, sexuality,
psychology or natural disposition. But gender inequality in organisations is simply
too persistent and deep-rooted to be accounted for by any variant on 'you get out
what you put in', to say nothing of the fact that women's qualifications tend to be
superior to their male counterparts.

Kanter and organisational context

The disparity between ideal type and reality was picked up earliest by one of the few
feminists working within conventional management theory. Kanter's (1993) *Men and
Women of the Corporation* was a landmark work, setting out a serious critique of the
male bias within internal power structures and an explanation for the widely-observed
'glass ceiling' restricting progress up the hierarchy (Rees, 1992; Davidson and Cooper,
1992). The emphasis on internal is important, because Kanter does not treat the
corporation simply as a reflection of the outside world: 'to a very large degree, organizations make their workers into who they are' (1993: 263). She adopts what is
described as a structural model, in the same manner discussed in the previous chapter
with respect to writers such as Pfeffer. In other words, 'structural' refers to organisational rather than societal context. Kanter identifies three central determinants of
behaviour: the structure of opportunity, the structure of power and the proportional
distribution of people or social composition of jobs. Where the distribution is strongly
skewed against women they will be marginalised, excluded and treated as 'token'.
Tokens suffer from increased visibility and their performance tends to be judged by
group rather than individual criteria.

Kanter demonstrates that no research exists that proves any sex differences in
power as manifested through leadership or management styles: 'a preference for men
is a preference for power' (Kanter, 1993: 199). In contrast, locked into the lower
reaches of the hierarchy and sex-segregated jobs, women internalise relative notions of

worth. Or, because they are playing to man-made rules, women have to resort to watchful strategies to avoid any role traps that would reinforce one of the many gender stereotypes (mother, seductress, iron maiden) that lie in wait. Cycles of power-lessness are further reproduced through the perceptions and actions of men, who use power resources to reproduce structures in their own image. This is also an informal process. Men prefer their own company and share certain language and under-standings. This 'homosociability' reproduces the existing gender order. Dominant organisational cultures and ideas of rational decision-making and effective management are overlaid with notions of masculinity, and the space for difference is closed down (Ramsay and Parker, 1992). Men are seen as making better managers because they are tough-minded, unemotional and authoritative. The 'other gender' comes to be defined as temperamentally unfit for power; Cockburn characterises this view as, 'Women are not capable of authority. And they turn into nasty people when in authority' (1991: 89).

Subsequent feminist commentators, while acknowledging its path-breaking character, have often been harsh on Kanter. Her work has been located as part of a naïve liberal feminism that was trying to demonstrate that women are people too (Calás and Smircich, 1996), and as a contingent approach that treats bureaucracy as only 'accidentally gendered' (Halford, Savage and Witz, 1997: 7). This is a little unfair. Gender is co-incidental rather than accidental – it coincides with male power in organisations. Kanter does not believe that bureaucracy is neutral, but she does think that it can be *made* rational. She works within a neo-Weberian tradition that reveals the informal and varied nature of bureaucracy. But that particular form is not fate. If women are not 'different', the acquisition of power by women could or should 'wipe out' sex, and it is organizations that have to be remade, not individuals. The boss–secretary relationship and other evidence of organizational sexuality are seen as patrimonial, pre-bureaucratic relics (Pringle, 1989). Relics can be rectified by a gender-neutral rationality.

Despite the critiques, there is contemporary evidence around that supports her core empirical arguments, rather than the broader theoretical spin given to them. In her studies of gender and culture in eight Italian firms, Poggio observes that relation-ships tend to be more egalitarian where women cease to be in the minority, 'The different sizes of the female component . . . seemingly bear out the intepretations based on the concept of "token"' (2000: 398). Simpson's (1997, 1998) studies of career barriers demonstrate that gender mix continues to be the most significant determinant of women's experience in organisations. Many women working in mixed or female-dominated environments found them supportive and enabling. 'Token' women, however continue to encounter men's networks and 'clubs' that maintain asymmetric power relations through informal mechanisms, including sexual innuendo and harassment. For example, in more evenly mixed circumstances, the demands of increased workload were often acknowledged and some balance between home and work catered for. In many organisations, however, men used their additional capacity or willingness to stay late – 'presenteeism' – as a competitive weapon, recolonising management for themselves and criticising women who left 'early'. There has also been sympathetic research on the nature and impact of male networks in organisations (see Pfeffer, 1997: 93–8).

Kanter's desire to emphasise the social construction of gender rather then the burdens of sexuality is understandable, but her analysis does lead to conceptual problems. First, that the process of social construction is conceived far too narrowly. While it is useful to locate specifically organizational dimensions, 'Curiously absent is any sense that men and women are locked, indeed formed, in an unequal gender order that spans not only work, but childhood, sexual intercourse, domesticity, street culture, and public life. There is no sense of how the organization came to take the damaging form it did' (Cockburn, 1990: 86). As a consequence neither individual nor systemic male power is adequately confronted. Kanter underestimated male resistance, in part because homosociability was treated only as a by-product of vertical occupational segregation. Second, in arguing that powerlessness, not sex, is the problem for women, Kanter fails to see the way that the two processes are interwoven, or how new forms of power and control appear around the construction of sexuality (Pringle, 1989: 88).

Part of the problem is that Kanter utilises the narrow Weberian conception of power as freedom of action and ability to get things done. As we observed earlier, though, it is 'structural' rather than individualistic and, as with French and Raven, her whole discussion covers the well-trodden territory of the first dimension of power as a relatively fixed resource, operating through the panoply of peer alliances, sponsors and the like. While insightful in its own terms, such a framework inevitably neglects the broader dimensions and relational character of corporate patriarchy (Witz and Savage, 1992: 16). Kanter's work represents the best of her tradition, but the limitations of orthodox organisation theory, particularly the tendency to separate the workplace from broader social and historical processes, are frequently reproduced. Though she opened the gate, other perspectives had to be present to establish gender as a fundamental structuring principle of power and organisations (Mills and Tancred, 1992; Witz and Savage, 1992).

Theorising difference

Most theories attempting a gendered analysis emphasise durable difference rather than potential sameness. One of the most interesting developments in this respect has been a shift in mainstream behavioural and managerial literature that has turned previously 'negative' female qualities into positive assets. In an influential *Harvard Business Review* article, Rosener claimed that a second generation of managerial women were making their way to the top, not by aping men, but by being themselves: 'They are succeeding because of, not in spite of, certain characteristics generally considered to be "feminine" and inappropriate in leaders' (1990: 120). In this, the claims of evolutionary psychology are stood on its head. Those that believe that natural selection can explain workplace behaviour argue that the 'sparse representation' of women among senior executives arises from their genetic predisposition not to be aggressive, competitive and willing to take risks (Browne, 1998). In contrast, men's testosterone predisposes them to strive for status and dominance, and only women exposed to an unusual amount of these hormones will be aggressive enough to compete in the workplace (G. Wilson, 1997).

In contrast, like Rosener, many management writers, organisations and consultants now claim to find a 'natural selection' in reverse. There is a strong similarity between how women see their leadership qualities (participative, collaborative, interactive, consensual, focused on soft skills such as teambuilding) and the new structures and styles required in the modern decentralised, post-bureaucratic organisation

(Martin, 1993; Institute of Management, 1994; Change Partnership, 1999). The editor of *Management Today* (quoted in *Guardian*, 7 March 1999) having surveyed 1000 British managers, recently pronounced that 'If men want to be successful managers, they must behave like women'. On an international stage, it is claimed that in transnationals characterised by networks of equals, women are well suited to move organisations from hierarchies to horizontal webs of relationships (Adler, 1994).

There is a surprising continuity with some of these arguments among radical feminists, though shorn of the optimism about working within the male system. Ferguson (1984) regards the structures and discourses of bureaucracy as inherently male. She locates the problem in women's exclusion from the public realm. When they do emerge, not only are their jobs marginalised, but so are the more expressive values and modes of action developed in the private sphere. Such an alternative rationality can provide a means for women and other people in subordinate positions to challenge bureaucratic, male power. Such thinking draws upon a view that has always been present within feminism, expressed by the novelist Fay Weldon, that 'women had special virtues that men had not' (*New Statesman*, 27 September 1999). Those virtues are corrupted by the system and male power and would be better directed towards building women-led or women-only structures which would be participative and non-hierarchical. There are also parallels here to eco-feminism, where science and nature are seen as in themselves masculine (Griffin, 1984). As Calás and Smircich note, 'Radical feminists have taken the traditional association of women with nature (in contrast to man with culture) and found it a source of strength and power' (1996: 226). Thus it is held that there is a different way of knowing the world that is less verbal, more emotional and spiritual.

Many other commentators, feminist and otherwise, have found the above conceptions of difference to be *essentialist*: in other words, that we can read off behaviour from some inherent essence that is, in this case, male or female. Sometimes this is biological, reducing women to their sexual and reproductive capacities, albeit as source of strength rather than weakness. Even when not *biologically* essentialist, such arguments tend to treat men and women as fixed categories, and are unable to deal with change and variation in roles and practices: 'Cross-cultural research has shown that there is no behaviour or meaning which is universally associated with masculinity or femininity: they are socially constructed and changing categories' (Grint and Gill, 1996: 5).

An emphasis on social construction of identity is typical of Foucauldian and post-structuralist perspectives. Preferring to talk of symbolic rather than material resources, such writers emphasise the existence of a bureaucratic *discourse* that relies upon a male rationality which shatters the apparent neutrality of rules and goals (Pringle, 1989). Through case studies such as the boss–secretary relationship, Pringle stresses the requirements of masculine rationality and its associated identities in the workplace to do battle with the feminine 'other'. Other contributors to the debate treat gender as a form of power/knowledge (Fineman, 1993; Putnam and Mumby 1993). It is argued that instrumental rationality within bureaucracy is defined by its opposition to emotionality. Feelings expressed by employees are either denied, suppressed or appropriated by the company for its own, instrumental ends (this overlaps into discussion of emotional labour – see Chapters 13 and 18). The potentialities of discursive construction of gender identity are highly varied. Class, age or ethnicity can cut across gender, producing different types of masculinity and femininity. Indeed, having separated sex and gender, it is then possible to argue that 'Masculinity is and can be performed by women. Women who are successful managers perform *hegemonic masculinity*' (Cheng, 1996: xii, original emphasis). It is difficult to avoid concluding from this type of argument that women cannot 'win'. If they rise to the top, they have then 'joined the other side'.

Poststructuralist writing (which we return to in the next section) is at the same time highly relativist in identifying different discourses of masculinity and femininity, but also seeks and talks of single, durable gender differences. For example, in the collection of articles by Cheng (1996), hegemonic masculinity is used as an over-arching concept to explain dominant patterns in different work contexts such as those of trial lawyers, manufacturing management teams and military colleges. An over-emphasis on gender can subsume other influences on attitudes and behaviour that may impact on men and women, notably occupational and professional identities. So, for example, nursing has traditionally promoted a preference for control over emotions in the name of professional values (Bolton, 2000). It does not take us very far to use hegemonic or any other form of masculinity to explain this. Theorising gender in organisations has to avoid over-emphasising difference, and carefully to explain the origins and impact of gender relations. As Wajcman notes, 'management incorporates a male standard that positions women as out of place. Indeed, the construction of women as different from men is one of the mechanisms whereby male power in the workplace is maintained' (1998: 2). To return to an earlier discussion, any evidence that new nurturant, soft skills are practised in organisations by women or anyone else is thin to non-existent. 'Feminine' values may be self-attributed, and tell us more about how managers like to see themselves than what they actually do. It is also notable, in Rosener's case, that her sample was drawn overwhelmingly from small and non-traditional organisations where the space to behave differently may be greater.

Of equal importance, more empirically rigorous studies show that attitudinal differences between men and women at work are exaggerated. Studies of commitment show little or no difference between the sexes (Ramsay and Scholarios, 1998: 9). Based on her research into large multinationals with ostensibly progressive HR policies, Wajcman observes that 'there is no such thing as a "female" management style and that the similarities between women and men far outweigh the differences between men and women as groups' (1996b: 333). Surveying a range of other studies, Izraeli and Adler (1994: 9) also note that 'negligible differences' were found. Both sexes are increasingly constrained by the lean and mean character of contemporary organisational life, with growing performance pressures on managers (Simpson, 1998). This is not an argument that seeks to displace gender as a key factor. Women continue to *experience* considerable constraint to career progression, while men retain greater opportunities to use formal and informal networks to advance their interests. What Wajcman and Simpson highlight is the difference between gender styles and gendered treatment. Much of the current literature is getting the significance of this the wrong way round. By over-emphasising the former, too much optimism is being generated about possibilities for women managers in a harsher, more directive corporate climate. As a senior female manager reported to Wajcman, 'The word that is being used is discipline . . . and these changes in management style favour a male style . . . management say the right things on diversity issues, but the tangible results are getting worse' (1996b: 275).

If we want to be able to understand the messy and complex picture of how men and women think and act, 'we should see gender relations within organisations as complex, dynamic and potentially at least, unpredictable' (Halford, Savage and Witz, 1997: 13). This is best explored with reference to culture and career.

Culture, careers and networks: embedding gender

The gendering of organisational analysis has brought fresh insights to existing issues, for example to conventional accounts of bureaucracies as male career structures. Public and private bureaucracies developed along gendered lines, introducing large numbers of women into routine clerical jobs. The existence of practices such as marriage bars, where a female employee would be compelled to retire on marriage, facilitated the retention and promotion of male clerks. In this sense the growth of large-scale organisations has seen the creation of mini-patriarchies where the expansion of the public sphere is shown to be 'premised on men's power and dominance in the private domains' (Hearn, 1992: 81). Even when those practices finished, evidence (Crompton and Jones, 1984) shows that internal labour markets in sectors such as banking provided alternative career routes for male clerical employees.

However, Hakim's (1995) controversial work has challenged feminist orthodoxies. Using UK data sets, she argues that women's location in lower-status, lower-paid jobs is primarily an outcome of voluntary strategy rather than involuntary imposition. Many women choose to value benefits such as flexible hours, friendly workmates and good relations with the boss rather than career advancement. While it is important to recognise differentiated motives and circumstances among women, critics have argued that Hakim pays insufficient attention to the social and historical contexts that shape preferences and may lead some women to make pragmatic adjustments and accommodations (Anker, 1997; Ramsay and Scholarios, 1998). It also remains the case that a substantial number of 'career women' face real constraints inside the organisation.

For example, our understanding of organisational culture has also benefited from a gender 'twist'. It functions as a useful gateway to gender analyses because culture focuses on the way that individuals construct the understandings and subjectivities that underpin behaviour and structure (Acker, 1992). Culturally-defined norms and values therefore crucially contribute to maintaining and reproducing the dominant patriarchal ideologies and practices (Alvesson and Billing, 1992; Green and Cassell, 1994). The argument, as we have seen, is that in bureaucracies, women are frequently strangers in a male-defined world. Culturally competent behaviour reflects largely masculine monocultures (Gerhardi, 1996; Alvesson and Billing, 1997). This goes beyond the obvious cases of resistance to women attempting to establish a presence in largely all-male preserves such as the police and fire service (Salaman, 1986; Keith and Collinson, 1994). There is evidence of women managers being perceived as threats to male self-image (Sargent, 1983; Cockburn, 1991). The latter study quotes one female senior manager: 'They certainly saw me as a huge threat when I first came. They made me feel very, very uncomfortable for six months. The woman bit. Men don't like it. They don't feel comfortable with women as superiors' (Cockburn, 1991: 141–2). Such women, as Sheppard's (1989) study found, often feel compelled to devise strategies of how to 'blend in'. The collection of essays in Colgan and Ledwith (1996) also provide numerous examples of the ways in which women in different occupational contexts devise adaptation strategies to survive and progress in male-dominated environments.

Increasingly analysis of culture has been complemented by that of networks. Access to networks has long been seen in conventional organisational theory to be a crucial factor in gaining structural advantage. Recent studies have demonstrated that women and ethnic minorities have less access to informal networks, and have different opportunities to convert their own organisational resources to network advantage (Ibarra, 1993, 1995). Whereas women feel comfortable in formal settings such as meetings, men create cultures in which in- and after-hours socialising can play a crucial role in sharing information, playing 'office politics' and securing privileges (Tierney, 1996; Simpson, 1997, 1998). Not surprisingly, women tend to use formal processes to seek promotion, while men prefer informal ones (*The Economist*, 10 August 1996). Surveys reveal that though women identify a variety of barriers to career advancement, the club or clique-like character of senior management is perceived to be crucial (Wajcman, 1996b). Interestingly a much smaller proportion of men identify informal networks as a problem, which suggests that the taken-for-granted masculinity of organisational cultures renders them invisible to the 'dominant sex'.

Cultures are, however, not homogenous. Poggio (2000) identifies a continuum of 'women-friendliness' in her culture case studies. Different types of masculinity may produce a range of managerial styles, from authoritarianism, paternalism, entrepreneurialism, careerism to informal relations where men form an in-group that simultaneously differentiates them from other groups of both sexes. The last group corresponds to the 'locker room culture' identified in a typology developed by Maddock and Parkin (1993); other gender cultures include the traditional 'gentleman's club', the 'barrack yard', and the more contemporary 'gender blind' and 'feminist pretender' arrangements, where new men affirm equal opportunities while nothing has really changed. This can be broadened further by referring to cross-cultural factors. In some national or regional cultures, such as those in East Asia where family businesses remain influential, membership of social networks outweighs credentials as a form of access. This can work for women in some circumstances, but militates against progression in the broader corporate economy (Izraeli and Adler, 1994: 8).

Halford, Savage and Witz (1997) draw useful and broader theoretical conclusions compatible with these kinds of findings. Organisations are neutral and depersonalised, but their gendered substructures are embedded within different cultural and historical contexts. Furthermore, organisations are populated by agents who reinterpret and contest existing practices and procedures. Gender, therefore, is inherently variable and continually enacted. Webster makes a similar anti-essentialist point about women's relation to technology, which she describes as 'one of exclusion through embedded historical practice, reinforced and reproduced in contemporary work settings' (1997: 25). Many of the examples and arguments drawn from such perspectives increasingly depend on analysis of sexuality instead of, or in addition to, gender. It is to this that we now turn.

Enter sexuality

Sexuality had begun to creep out of the shadows of gender in the sociology of the workplace through well-known studies of the characteristics of female (Pollert, 1981; Westwood, 1984) and male (Willis, 1977) wage labour, and the use of sexuality and gender as a method of control (see Thompson, 1989: 196–7). What such studies facilitated was a move beyond issues of sexual division of labour to those of sexuality in the division of labour. This rested largely on the fact that work behaviour was overlaid with masculine and feminine identities. In this light, homosociability is not only a rational economic action to secure collective interests, it is a way of defining and defending sexual identities. This is as true of pranks and practices of the female factory workers studied by Pollert and Westwood as of the male workers in truck plants (Collinson, 1992), or abattoirs (Ackroyd and Crowdy, 1990). While some of this might seem to be at the marginal, social end of work activity, defence of sexual identity can be intimately connected with protection of access to employment. This is most tellingly revealed in Cockburn's (1991) examination of the attitudes and practices of printworkers, who clearly felt female employment to be a threat not only to their livelihood, but to their sense of (masculine) self that had become inextricably bound to the nature of their craft.

The entry of sexuality into organisational theory, while drawing on the above studies, has also been contingent on a number of other developments. The first of these is the critique of the previously-discussed Weberian model of *de-sexualised bureaucracies*. From this absence, sexuality is suddenly to be found everywhere – in language, practices, relationships, displays, design, hierarchies and managerial strategies. In some instances it is seen primarily as a tension between a partially-submerged underlife of sexuality and the dominant calculative rationality that would seek to repress it in the name of efficiency (Burrell, 1992); in others it appears as a substantially-embedded set of practices much nearer the surface of everyday organisational life (Hearn and Parkin, 1987; Hearn *et al.*, 1989). To return to a previous example – that of Shepherd's (1989) account of 'blending in' strategies of female managers – it is clear that this frequently involved changes in appearance and body language so that female assertiveness would not threaten male sexual authority. Whether focusing on underlife or surface practice, what was being revealed was the public nature of what had been previously consigned to the private realm. In their detailed examination of sexual misbehaviour in the workplace, Ackroyd and Thompson (1999) argue that this is not merely a theoretical shift, but a practical one. The decline in gender-segregated workplaces and the increase in female employees has combined with workplace cultures that allow more elements of sociability and informality to create greater opportunities for sexual interactions. Both employers and employees have blurred the boundaries between the public and private, and between organisational and social selves.

Such trends help to explain the growing litigation and politicisation surrounding both convivial and coercive sexuality at work. In other words, companies are finding it increasingly necessary to regulate sexual interactions. While there is a growth of codes governing romantic relations, most of the emphasis has been on sexual harassment. Indeed, this has been the second route to visibility in management and organisation theory (Gutek, 1985; Stanko, 1988; Di Tomaso, 1989; Collinson and Collinson, 1989, 1994; Thomas and Kitzinger, 1997). There is no single and precise definition of harassment, in part because it is overlaid with particular legal contexts and treatments (Wilson and Thompson, 2001). Nevertheless, there are common themes focusing on the unwanted, intrusive or persistent nature of the behaviour. Such practices can 'pollute' the work environment, according to a European Commission code of practice. Again while there are contrasting explanations, there are also common themes. Whether at the office party or in promotion processes, sexual harassment can be seen as a means through which individual men exert their power over women. The varieties of forms of harassment can be seen as power plays or controlling gestures arising mainly as responses to the threat to identity and material interests when women enter male occupational territories, or from the abuse of power in supervisory and other authority relationships. Unlike Kanter's analysis of gender, sexuality cannot be confined to the organisation. Barbara Gutek's detailed and authoritative study utilises the concept of sex-role overspill to emphasise the broader social connections: 'the carryover into the workplace of gender-based roles that are usually irrelevant or inappropriate to work'. These may include conceptions of women's nurturing capacity or being a sex object, to the stereotype of men's natural leadership ability.

The third route is filtered through the discussions of sexuality and power. As Halford, Savage and Witz note, 'What has emerged from the radical feminist and radical organisation literature is a clear view that women's subordination at work is "eroticised" or "sexualised"' (1997: 21). These complex relations require a separate discussion in their own right, though themes also overlap with those already discussed in the first two routes.

Contrasting perspectives on sex, power and organisations

At one level, associations between sexuality and power in the workplace are uncontentious. Pringle's (1989) work on the boss–secretary relationship successfully established this territory, demonstrating the historical roots and contemporary features of the 'office wife' phenomenon in which women are used to enhance masculinity and authority. Analyses of service sector work have extended the argument. Adkin's case studies are used to argue that 'women employees had as a condition of their employment, the requirement to provide sexual services for male customers and employees' (1992: 214). This is not meant literally, but refers to controls over forms of dress, appearance, and engagement in being chatted-up and other verbal sexual interactions. Women's work is therefore eroticised subordination. In some ways this builds on previous discussion of emotional labour. Hochschild's (1983) study of flight attendants, as well as the later British account by Tyler and Taylor (1997), show how companies require the largely female employees to manage their own feelings to improve the 'quality' of the service encounter. Part of this process of 'acting' involves a projection of sexuality through visual and verbal display; the female flight attendant is 'part mother, part servant and part tart', as one of Tyler and Taylor's respondents put it (1997: 13). Similar patterns were identified by Filby (1992) in his account of the uses of female labour at the quality end of betting shops.

Emphasis has also been put especially on the process of *embodiment* (Acker, 1990; Halford, Witz and Savage, 1997: 25–8). Beyond the obvious examples of dress and display, consideration has been given to the routine degree of sexualised body work through interactions of doctors, nurses and other medical staff (Witz, Halford and Savage, 1994), and the associations between skill and physicality in police work (Keith and Collinson, 1994). In the latter, bodily discourses provide not only a means of keeping women officers in their proper, feminine place, but are used to make further, regional distinctions: 'In the South the people are like the landed gentry, so the police are just big girls' blouses' (female police sergeant, quoted in Keith and Collinson, 1994: 17).

While these issues pull academic and practical attention to the triangle of gender, sexuality and power, understandings of power are precisely the factors that divide many contributors to the debate. Take the question of sexual harassment. Though this is clearly *about* power, it does not necessarily involve a particular *theory* of power. Whereas Gutek does not see sexual coercion as the norm of male–female relations inside or outside work, the increasing number of radical feminists writing in this area are only too happy to do so. Admittedly much of this has nothing to do with the workplace as such. Sexuality is seen as the primary source of male power (MacKinnon, 1979), and heterosexual desire as the eroticisation of conquest and subordination (Jeffreys, 1990). Harassment is the conduit to the organisation in recent studies focusing on academia (Ramazanogolu, 1987), social work (Wise and Stanley, 1990) or professional education (Carter and Jeffs, 1992). What these and other writers have in common is the view that harassment is not aberrant, unusual or different in kind from flirtation, banter or affairs: 'it is instructive to note that "sexual harassment" and "ordinary sexual encounters" follow more or less exactly the same levels of expression' (Wise and Stanley, 1990: 20). All this is a version of MacKinnon's argument that organisations are the site of compulsory heterosexuality. As a theorisation of power, this takes us back to zero-sum notions where, in this case, men and women are erotically joined solely through mutual threat and share no common interest. Or as Carter and Jeffs (1992: 240–1) put it, 'Sexuality is always about power and is always about "us" as well as "them"'.

Others, particularly those influenced by Foucauldian perspectives, would agree that sexuality and power are intimately linked, but strongly question its characterisation. Foucault's writing sees sexuality and the body as central to power and its reproduction. Such studies 'explore how power disciplines and shapes women's bodies, movements and expressions' (Cooper, 1994: 437), though it works through internalisation and self-monitoring rather than coercion from the top or as the result of ideology. As we discussed earlier in relation to gender, seeing organisational sexuality in terms of discursive production necessarily requires an emphasis on social construction and fluidity rather than fixed and essential power relations:

> Subjectivity is constituted through the exercise of power within which conceptions of personal identity, gender and sexuality come to be generated. Thus, men and women actively exercise power in positioning themselves within, or finding their own location amongst, competing discourses, rather than merely being 'positioned by' them. (Brewis and Kerfoot, 1994: 8)

Research shows that some of these positioning processes are based on discourses of *difference*, which promote negative representations of women or men who do not play the masculinity game (Collinson and Collinson, 1989; Cockburn, 1991). But this will vary according to work situations and the available knowledge resources. Studies of local government and banking by Witz, Halford and Savage identified the deployment of discourses of gender *complementarity*. Mixed-sex work groups were endorsed by management as a means of countering the undesirable effects of all-male or all-female sociability. But employees positioned themselves too, finding fun in flirtation and romance. Contrary to the radical feminist argument, 'All the women drew an extremely clear boundary between "flirtation" and "sexual harassment"' (1994: 20).

Greater space to see the interrelationships between power and pleasure arises from Foucault's theorisation of the former as productive, relational and capillary.

Viewing events from the 'bottom-up' and through micro-practices is much less likely to result in behaviour being read-off from universal conceptions of position and behaviour. In Pringle's work, secretaries were far from passive objects of the boss's banter, deriving pleasure from imitating, exaggerating or ridiculing existing stereotypes (1989: 103). This can be supported by other studies which are not necessarily from a Foucauldian perspective. Discursive practices in which women use sexuality and 'sexy chat' as a means of acting as subjects is best exemplified in Filby's (1992) previously mentioned study of daily life in betting shops. Though management tried and partly succeeded in using women's bodies and personalities to promote the product, female employees turned the tables by developing their own aggressive 'scolding' and 'joking' routines to keep customers and managers in their place.

Evaluation: under and overpowered explanations

Foucauldian theory and research on power and sexuality has proven a useful antidote to essentialist conceptions of men as automatic power holders and women as eternal victims. It reinforces existing research that shows the workplace as a site for a variety of forms of sexual and romantic relationship (Ackroyd and Thompson, 1999). Sexuality is the most complex of social relations, and 'we need a model of power relations which can also deal with power as it is exercised in friendly or intimate encounters' (Davis, 1991: 81). Of course, all sexual relations cannot be described in this way. But even in the case of the most instrumental of sexual exchanges – prostitution – the dynamics of power and control cannot necessarily be described as men securing direct power, nor as motivated solely by the desire to affirm a masterful manhood (O'Connell Davidson, 1994a: 2).

But it is the very specificity of sexuality as a site of power that creates a problem. In different ways, both the radical feminist and Foucauldian perspectives fail to recognise this. For each theory sees sexuality as the standard template of how power works, and this has a number of negative consequences. Radical feminists cannot see sexuality without seeing power, 'both its intention and its end, its product, is power' (Wise and Stanley, 1990: 15); hence they fail to grasp its varied construction and practice. Foucauldians, at least those writing in this area, cannot see power without seeing sexuality, and therefore tend to extend the latter's reach beyond its usefulness. Much of the rhetoric about the body falls into this trap. For example, Witz, Halford and Savage comment on a woman manager who had worn a red suit in order to get noticed at a dinner:

> It really does serve to illustrate how embodied organizational participants can call up their embodiment through ways of presenting the body. The choice of a red dress is evoking a number of associations between red and the womanly body – the most obvious is the association with red and sexuality, the least obvious is that between red and bleeding. (Witz, Halford and Savage, 1994: 23–4)

Furthermore, the very fluidity and complexity recognised in post-structuralist perspectives may not be as applicable in other sites of power, particularly when we remember that the object of analysis is *organisational* sexuality. Whereas power is zero-sum in only the most coercive sexual encounters, in many workplace situations it is, as we argued earlier, often not as negotiable and is possessed and exercised by agents with a radically unequal access to power resources. Organisational sexuality is therefore influenced by the potential characteristics of both sites of power, with varied consequences for choice and constraint.

A further worry about Foucauldian theory is that it tends to overestimate the former at the expense of the latter. 'Power here is not the oppressive power implicit within liberal feminism as a zero-sum analysis where power is a possession. Rather, power for Foucault is productive, it allows us to think ourselves and our individuality as we find/fit ourselves in(to) various discourses' (Brewis and Kerfoot, 1994: 8). The problem is that organisational processes, gendered and otherwise, are not just discourses in relation to which we can position ourselves. Gender regimes are constituted through symbolic order and material practices (Wajcman, 1998: 3). The constraints to the success of equal opportunities policies, for example, are also linked to material sources of power, particularly those expressed through internal and external labour markets. Without this recognition of relatively durable structures and constraint, gender risks 'being swallowed up in the bottomless swamp of permanently shifting meanings and ambivalent discursive constructions' (Komter, 1991: 47)

In presenting bureaucracy as a discourse in general, and a discourse of male rationality in particular, current theories are in danger of throwing the practical and theoretical baby out with the bathwater. We will return to the issue of rationality and make a qualified defence of the Weberian position in the final chapter, but for the moment we want to link the theoretical discussions to more practical issues about dealing with gender inequality, not merely to add a policy dimension, but because the discussion raises key theoretical questions.

From equal opportunity to managing diversity?

Equal opportunity (EO) policies advocate formal, collective responses to gender inequalities in the workplace, marking an end to an individual differences approach that promoted the idea that women had to 'fit in' in order to succeed. In contrast, under EO the onus was on organisations to change. This ranged from targets to improve the number of women at various levels of the organisation; formalisation of procedures and specification of equitable conduct dealing with access to and treatment in jobs; family-friendly career support systems, including career breaks, job sharing and flexible hours; and additional training such as assertiveness and personal development. Overall, it can be seen as the prime policy response to the heightened visibility of gender issues outlined in this chapter, as well as a somewhat more reluctant compliance with legal regulation of sexual and other forms of discrimination.

EO was always controversial. Business critics resented 'bureaucratic' regulation of labour markets and processes. Meanwhile, radical critics (Symons, 1992; Simpson, 1997) often see it as a form of liberal feminism that encourages a superficial view that organisations could be gender neutral if appropriate procedures and policies were followed, and inequalities could be dealt with if opportunities were made available and women took them. Given the evidence examined in this chapter, it has not been difficult for critics to find problems to feed on. Even flagship progressive companies, such as those involved in Opportunity 2000 in the UK, have been shown to make limited progress (Wajcman, 1996b). An emphasis on formal procedures tends to neglect underlying structural and attitudinal factors. As a consequence, external or internal legislation may be ignored or marginalised in practice, particularly where senior managerial support is weak or operational managers are hostile (Jewson and Mason, 1986; Collinson *et al.*, 1990).

Managerial writers began to use such evidence to mount a critique of the 'ineffectiveness' of EO and US-based affirmative action policies (Blakemore and Black, 1996). An alternative was advocated under the heading of *managing diversity*. That has proven very influential in practitioner communities (see Kandola and Fullerton, 1994). The content of diversity differs, as management and policy makers struggle to come to terms with the growing heterogeneity of the labour force in terms of gender, ethnicity, age and disability (de los Reyes, 2000). In some contexts such as Sweden, as de los Reyes observes, issues of ethnicity and migrant labour predominate, though in general, 'few studies deal with the impact of ethnicity in work organisations' (2000: 260). Nevertheless, there are commonalities in the approach. As the employment policy director of Grand Metropolitan put it, 'Managing or valuing diversity differs from the conventional approach to equal opportunities in that it seeks to create a climate whereby those involved want to move beyond the achievement of mere statistical goals' (Greenslade, 1994: 28). Like many companies they prioritise the business case for any measures, notably that diversity reflects demographic change and therefore the available talent pool, enhances competitiveness by adding value to the capacity for innovation, and matches the profile of clients and customers.

The policy terrain shifts to an emphasis on personal development, support for individuals through coaching and mentoring, education to change the culture of the organisation, and broadening managerial responsibilities beyond the human resource function. This is obviously linked to and extends the scope of HRM – competitive advantage is not just through people, but their diversity (Herriot and Pemberton, 1994). Multiculturalism can be achieved without the divisiveness of EO, with its associations with conflict, exclusion and special interests (Blakemore and Black, 1996). The different perceptions, language and ways of solving problems of men and women are complementary and can both add value (Masreliez-Steen, 1989). As Kirton and Greene (2000) note, there is a shift away from norms of assimilation and towards 'positive messages' about recognising talent through and despite social differences.

Some feminists working in the management field support this. Adler argues that an equity approach assumes similarity, while MD is based on assumed difference: 'The first focuses on increasing the representation of women managers; the second, on increasing their utilisation at all levels of the organisation' (1994: 24). Such arguments clearly reflect the broader shifts in approach towards a 'soft' essentialism in feminist thought: that women can be themselves and be of value without having to assimilate. This kind of approach is superficially attractive. It draws its main explanatory power from an understanding of the significance of the kind of informal cultures and networks discussed earlier, and some of its policy mechanisms, such as mentoring, may be a useful addition.

However, MD remains limited in theoretical and practical terms. It attempts to combine what would appear to be contradictory: a focus on individuals rather than groups, yet a recognition of collective categories and change goals. The shift of emphasis towards individuals disconnects those goals from any collective force of disadvantaged groups, and regards all difference as equally salient (Kirton and Greene, 2000: 113). Measuring progress qualitatively rather than quantitatively uses the language of complementarity and depth, yet allows organisations to evade the constraints of targets and facilitate male appropriation of 'feminine styles' without substantive change in representation or progression (Wajcman, 1996a: 347). Complementarity, according to Adler, means that 'firms expect women managers, to think, dress, and act like women' (1994: 26). Aside from the fact that this is at odds with previously-discussed evidence about the much exaggerated differences between the attitudes and behaviour of male and female managers, there is 'the danger that any argument based on women's attributed differences from men will be used to reassert their essential inferiority and justifiable exclusion from certain public roles' (Webb, 1997: 163).

For all its weaknesses, EO offers a minimum defence in terms of policing procedures and behaviour. Moreover, it is consistent with the evidence we have examined that it is the formal domains of organisational life where women feel more comfortable and protected (Simpson, 1997: 126). It is true that changing informal cultures is a more difficult and long-term task, but the issue is whether it is more effective when combined with formal mechanisms. Achieving substantive equal opportunity will be a struggle, it will require more extensive legislation to encourage family-friendly policies, it will be lengthy and there will be losers. None of this fits easily into the way that many proponents of HRM view the world.

Conclusion

Despite the continued practical obstacles to career progression, some things have changed in gender relations at work. Research clearly shows shifts away from the earlier stereotypical associations of 'ideal' management with masculinity. However, while these views have virtually disappeared among women, they are still present in the perceptions of many male managers (Brenner *et al.*, 1989). Even where women are still struggling as 'tokens' in difficult environments, there is little evidence that they are falling into the role traps identified by Kanter (Simpson, 1997). In contrast, while male managers may endorse general statements about equal treatment, their views are often 'soft' and more deeply-held beliefs remain unchanged. For example, Wajcman (1996b) found that while there was no difference between the sexes when they were asked which sex made better managers, a sizeable minority of men (21 per cent) said they would prefer to work for a male manager.

Theoretically there have also been major shifts. It is unlikely that organisation theory will ever return to gender-neutral models of bureaucracy or anything else. Indeed, as we have shown in this chapter, debates on the glass ceiling and other issues have added fresh insights which complement existing knowledge of gender and work, such as on labour markets (Rubery *et al.*, 1999) and professions (Witz, 1992). The distinctiveness of that debate and its focus on organisational factors should not let us lose sight of the bigger picture. A capacity to enter the labour market and rise up the career ladder remains strongly affected by unequal domestic responsibilities, so studies of work–family boundaries need to inform organisational analysis (Crompton, 1996; Burke, 1997; Wajcman, 1998). Conflicts between job and family are particularly acute where mobility is a prerequisite for career advancement and social norms strongly reinforce the primacy of female domestic roles, as illustrated by Ng and Fosh's (2000) study of international airlines in East Asia.

In this chapter we have focused on the two key debates that have shaped that analysis, but it is worth noting that there may be tensions between the literatures on gender and sexuality. Some commentators believe that the avalanche of writing on sexuality is beginning to squeeze out attention to those many aspects of the 'gender paradigm' that are distinguishable from issues of sexuality (Witz and Savage, 1992). In relation to this, more conventional economic issues have tended to be marginalised in the emphasis on culture, discourse and identity. More controversially it can be argued that re/discovering gender has sometimes led to diminishing the importance of other interests and identities – for instance, class, occupational and professional – which may, in given circumstances, have more influence on employee behaviour. It is also worth remembering the need to differentiate within gender categories given that they will cross-cut with those other social divisions. Organisational analysis now has the conceptual resources to study the gender substructure of organisations. It remains an empirical question as to the significance and character of those structures and practices.

11 New Economy, New Organisations?

Introduction: paradigm shift or shifting paradigms?

The world of management theory and practice always appears to be changing fast, but new buzzwords and themes continue to surface with bewildering rapidity. Consistent across these twists and turns has been a widely-held belief that the days of bureaucracy are over. New 'post-bureaucratic' forms of organisation move from the 'holding' to the 'enabling' company, to collaborative joint ventures, management buy-outs, contracting out parts of the organisations, personal networking, virtual organisation facilitated by the Internet, mini-factories and industrial boutiques.

'New' organisations and economies seem to have been around for quite a long time, certainly from the beginning of the 1980s, and, arguably a lot longer in the writings of Drucker (1959, 1968), or theorists of post-industrialism (Bell, 1973). We shall return to this paradox later. For the time being we can observe that the periodisation of 'new' can be extended by identifying a systemic break. Whatever variant, the post-bureaucratic organisation in the New Economy is said to be indicative of a paradigm shift, a decisive period of transformation, and the first since Taylor, Fayol and Ford. The cause of such a shift is supposed to be our old friend, 'the environment'. New 'strategic contingencies' in a global economy marked increasingly by turbulence and volatility produce environmental shocks arising from slower economic growth, intensification of competition, and a rising rate of product innovation in new forms of knowledge and information technology. The bureaucratic structures and decision-making processes of traditionally-designed organisations cannot handle the consequent forms of uncertainty and discontinuous change adequately (Heydebrand, 1989; Pascale, 1990).

The perceived need to respond to new market conditions has not been the only 'learning experience' motivating Western business organisations and management commentators. The 'Japanese threat' changed the terms of competition in the 1980s, and in doing so has set in motion a major process of emulating or modifying the ingredients believed to be the basis of superior performance. This reading of the sources of competitive advantage has more connection to the debates on corporate culture that form the subject of Chapter 13. But if flexibility has been a central theme of the revolution against bureaucracy, then, as we shall see, the Japanese experience of intra- and inter-firm relations can be seen as an important resource for contemporary debate.

It will be tempting for some to dismiss much of the above as inflated fantasies and prescriptions from the evidence-free zones of pop-management texts. But messages about a paradigm also reflect changing theoretical paradigms amongst academics. Organisational theorists such as Clegg (1990) are also convinced that Weber's iron cage of bureaucracy – rule-driven, hierarchical and centralised organisation – is no longer a requirement for efficiency. The particular influence on such writers (see Hassard and Parker, 1993) is a theorisation of paradigm shift based on a move from modernity to post-modernity. Indeed for Clegg (1990: 2), 'organisation theory is a creation of modernity'. The latter is linked to an increasing division of labour, in which jobs, tasks and roles are highly differentiated. In contrast, 'Postmodernism points to a more organic, less differentiated enclave of organisation than those dominated by the bureaucratic designs of modernity' (1990: 181). Flexibility is once again the watchword, with organisations changing their external boundaries through chains, clusters, networks and strategic alliances, and internal arrangements such as teams and profit centres (Clegg and Hardy, 1996).

Nor must we be bound to the constraints of rationality itself, with its emphasis on calculation, direction and design. With environments ever-changing and unpredictable, organisations are more likely to succeed by being reactive. Managers will spend their time on promoting the core corporate values and symbols rather than strategic planning. This emphasis on living with chaos and managing culture echoes themes in popular management. The general account of society and organisations also resembles and overlaps with a further influential account of discontinuity, the distinction between *Fordism* and *post-Fordism*. So, for example, Mulgan (1989) refers to the replacement of 'strong power' under the Fordist corporations characterised by pyramidal structures, formal rules and close controls, by a post-Fordist order based on weak power controls and decentralised leadership, horizontal communication and self-regulating units. Though the language of environmental turbulence is replaced by more academic and radical sounding 'post' labels and phases of capitalism, the message that major changes 'out there' are producing an organisational response is common, as is an emphasis on key influences such as new forms of information technology.

While information technology, in the form of PCs, networks and email systems, can be seen as a key factor of organisational decentralisation and power-sharing, even to the point of creating 'something close to an information democracy' (Hamel and Prahalad, 1996: 238); it can also be conceptualised as the focal point of a broader socio-economic formation. Indeed the same authors refer to change from a machine age to an information age. Castells posits a new mode of development: *informationalism*. Though shaped by capitalist restructuring, it is fundamentally oriented towards the accumulation of knowledge: 'the informational indicates the attribute of a specific form of social organisation in which information generation, gathering, processing and transmission become the fundamental sources of productivity and power' (1996: 21). In current debates it is more likely that the term 'knowledge economy' will be used, but regardless of the label, we see familiar themes of networks replacing hierarchies, flatter organisations, with collaboration and collegiality displacing command and control (Despres and Hiltrop, 1995). We will return to the issue of knowledge in the economy in the next section.

Having looked at some of the overarching themes of organisational transformation and their connections to post-bureaucratic design, the chapter moves on to a more specific look at the theory and research in the main substantive areas said to be characterising and shaping change. We will give expositions of the arguments used by those advocating new models before subjecting them to evaluation and critique in the next chapter.

Firms, markets and hierarchies in the knowledge economy

Commentators on or advocates of new forms of organisation do not necessarily locate them in a coherent 'big picture'. But when Heydebrand refers to an 'intrinsic elective affinity' between post-industrialism and post-bureaucratic forms' (1989: 349), he raises the issue of the drivers of change. One of the most sophisticated accounts has been provided by theorists of flexible specialisation (Piore and Sabel, 1984). This is the term given to efforts, 'to convert the traditional highly integrated, corporate structure into a more supple organisational form capable of responding quickly to shifting market conditions and product demand' (Piore, 1986: 146). In its earlier form, Sabel's (1982) analysis preferred to speak of corporate attempts to maintain continuity with mass production, deskilling and labour controls, while moving away from standardisation. This *neo-Fordism* was seen as coexisting alongside a new high-tech cottage industry that combines craft forms of production with computerised technology (Smith, 1987: 1).

Later work declared a general crisis of industrial systems or 'second industrial divide'. In this formulation, the Fordist system of mass production is held to be incapable of permanent innovation. Flexible specialisation works on a kind of *design chain* that works downwards from changes in markets and technologies, through firm structures, to work organisation and employment relations (see Figure 11.1). Though rival purveyors of the big picture may contest the detail, we discuss it in some detail because it is characteristic of much contemporary theorising.

It starts with increasingly specialised demand for customised quality goods, which renders the old economies of scale redundant. The shift to new market conditions is facilitated by production and information technology such as flexible manufacturing systems (FMS) and manufacturing automation protocol (MAP) which are general purpose and programmable, allowing switches within and between families of products on more of a small-batch basis (Williams *et al.*, 1987: 409). Once such choices are made, manufacturing economies are seen as being locked into a technological trajectory. Large corporations cannot adequately handle the flexible markets and technologies, therefore networks of small firms grow in significance. As Harrison observes,

> a multitude of writers continue to preach the virtues of small firms as engines of contemporary economic growth. We are told that ... consumers increasingly seek more customised fashion-oriented goods and services. Mass markets become saturated, the demand for such commodities as clothing and furniture becomes increasingly fragmented. ... These developments are said to conjoin to favour technically adroit, well-informed small enterprises. (Harrison, 1994: 6–7)

Further down the chain, fragmented and repetitive work organisation characteristic of Taylorism is no longer appropriate. Collaboration between designers, producers and managers is both feasible and necessary, while craft skills and 'the production worker's intellectual participation is enhanced' (Piore and Sabel, 1984: 278). In turn, that creates the need for high-trust work relations in which there is an exchange between participation and greater job security.

This kind of analysis of the logical fit between flexible forms of technology and flexibility in skills and work structures is paralleled in Kern and Schumman's *The End of the Division of Labour* (1984). This talks of the reprofessionalisation of production work and new production concepts; and also finds support from some other writers on advanced technology. (Gill, 1985; Francis, 1986). There are also parallels with accounts of post-Fordism and related concepts such as disorganised capitalism (Lash and Urry, 1987); but advocates of flexible specialisation see differences and problems (Hirst and Zeitlin, 1991).

THE FIRST INDUSTRIAL DIVIDE
Mass production era

THE SECOND INDUSTRIAL DIVIDE
Flexible specialisation

FIGURE 11.1 The flexible specialisation hypothesis

Source: Thomas Bramble (1988) 'Industrial Relations and New Management Production Practices', *Labour and Society*, vol. 112, June.

Flexible specialisation is said to allow transnationals in some instances to begin to reverse the international division of labour, in which assembly processes are located in low-wage areas of the Third World, while maintaining research and design at home. Technical innovation, capital-intensive manufacturing and far higher levels of productivity from smaller workforces enable redomestication of activities; though the developing countries are likely to still utilise the low-skill, mass production methods. In the advanced economies, decentralised production will be the order of the day, as smaller plants can operate efficiently within the same range of products and be close to the customer to save transport and other costs.

Piore and Sabel admitted that working economic models of flexible specialisation based on networks of small firms are limited to regions such as Veneto and Emilia Romanga in Italy. But it is certainly possible to identify firms or sectors that appear to qualify. General Motor's Saturn Plant utilises flexible equipment to produce specifically tailored products, without retooling and with a high level of worker participation (P. B. Meyer, 1986: 74). Technology such as computer-aided design systems have enabled clothing firms to both create and then speedily respond to customer demands for a greater range of design and colour. Standardisation and long runs are said to become uneconomical. Computerisation also helps large firms such as Benetton to centralise marketing and skilled processes such as design and dyeing among its small core workforce of less than 2000 people, while decentralising its other production work to small subcontractors, and franchising its sales outlets (Fergus Murray, 1983; Mitter, 1986). Small IT firms have been found to be geographically and structurally mobile, utilising their lack of hierarchy and pervious boundaries to adapt successfully to new competitive challenges (Ackroyd, 1995).

Though each of these claims remains prominent in the business and social science literatures, flexible specialisation as a package does not. The 'big picture' franchise has passed to theories of the knowledge economy (Nonaka and Takeuchi, 1995). Similarly, some of the leading lights of post-Fordist theories such as Leadbetter (1999) are now prominent advocates of the new model. Picking up on themes associated with post-industrialism (Bell, 1973), exponents promote the trend as a virtuous circle in which empowered, creative employees work for collaborative, innovative firms, meeting the needs of intelligent consumers in a dynamic, socially inclusive society. Knowledge has been used in two ways as an explanatory device. On the one hand, it is seen as a *reflection* of societal change. In particular, its association with professional and technical work means that an increase in such categories in the occupational structure is held to signal the growth of creative, intellectual labour (see Barley, 1996). On the other, the distinctive characteristics of knowledge, now the prime factor of production rather than land, labour or capital, are seen as *triggering* economic transformation. This side of the equation is expressed somewhat apocalyptically by Despres and Hiltrop:

> Many analysts surmise that the nature of life and work will thus be fundamentally changed for this and all future generations. Since the late 1980s, then, various authors have advanced the idea that the knowledge age is breeding knowledge workers who are employed in knowledge-intensive organisations. (Despres and Hiltrop, 1995: 9)

It is the 'weightlessness' of knowledge that is held to be decisive or, as Leadbetter put it, 'Most of us make our livings from thin air: we produce nothing that can be weighed, touched or easily measured' (1999: vii). In the knowledge economy service, judgement, information and analysis, from call centres to the science lab, is what employees provide. The core workers are what Reich (1993) labels symbolic analysts, people such as designers, marketers and engineers. The association of knowledge with services is believed to make a crucial difference. The intangible nature of services means the transformation into a product of cognitive manipulation in which rules, routines and machinery are secondary.

As Blackler (1995) observes in a useful overview, the dominant view is that while there are a variety of forms of knowledge, the key growth areas are conceptual (embrained) and encultured, rather than residing in lower-level knowledge that is explicit or embedded in systematic routines. Knowledge, then, is seen as having caring and sharing qualities. It cannot be developed or managed within relations of command and control. Its ephemeral quality is held to facilitate all the distinctive and benign features of the 'New Economy' – for example the move towards networks and creativity and the break from control and hierarchy. Given that knowledge work is too complex to be vertically controlled, management has to throw out the rule book and develop horizontal co-ordination, with collegial, collaborative methods (Hamel and Prahalad, 1996; Barley, 1996). Knowledge work generalises across increasing territories the kind of employment relationships and task structures that allow for creative application and development of that knowledge. It provides the main engine of growth in the modern economy, spreading high-skill, high-expertise employment outside the traditional professional high-tech heartlands. In particular, the search for more creativity and participation from routine employees through devices such as teamworking compels employers to devolve responsibilities and increase trust (Frenkel et al., 1995). We will return to these issues in the later section on high performance work systems. Meanwhile, the flexibility theme moves downwards towards the firm and its boundaries.

Post-bureaucratic organisation: restructuring the corporation

For mainstream organisation theory, challenging bureaucratic designs ultimately rests on change in the sphere of *structure*. In earlier times, organic structures or ad-hoceries were one way of adapting to the environment. Now it is frequently presented as the norm, a permanent condition of organisational life.

To explain these arguments, it is useful to return to the (four) Ds with which we began this section of the chapter. Big is no longer merely not beautiful, it is seen as positively dangerous and anachronistic. As part of a process of *decentralisation*, companies are said to be breaking up their bureaucracies and setting up smaller or independent units, or developing new corporate structures where divisions operate as autonomous profit centres with delegated decision-making powers. Heydebrand (1989: 330–1) argues that profit centres overcome the market–hierarchy dichotomy and reduce the need for CEO control, while encouraging direct negotiation among sub-units. Integration will be provided by overall strategy, information technology and corporate cultures. After this organisational revolution, the more autonomous units will be 'guided by a coherent vision rather than by memorandum and managers-as-cops' (Peters, 1989: 31). Units will therefore be more loosely coupled and decision-making more dispersed, as in matrix systems with multiple accountabilities. 'External' surveillance and control will be increasingly replaced by new forms of market

Old	New
stability	disorganisation/chaos
rationality	charisma, values
planning	spontaneity
control	empowerment
command	participation
centralisation	decentralisation/disaggregation
hierarchy	network
formal	informal/flexible
large	downsized/delayered

A post-bureaucratic organisation?   *FIGURE 11.2*

disciplines between the autonomous units, or even work teams, who are each other's customers (Clegg, 1990: 180).

The break-up is linked to *disaggregation* or *de-integration*, which goes beyond the internal redistribution of power by reducing the corporation to a relatively small core as central functions are dispersed to small firms, are outsourced to specialist units and franchises, sub-contracted to telecommuters in electronic cottages or other forms of virtual organisation (Jackson, 1999). Handy (1989) refers to such trends as a move towards federalism, or beyond to the 'donut' organisation that has nothing in the middle. The centre has only to keep a broad watching brief on finance and longer-term policy. This deconcentration of capital (Perrow, 1992) puts into reverse the historic trend towards vertical integration: 'If the old model of organisation was the large hierarchical firm, the model of organisation that is considered characteristic of the New Competition is a network, of lateral and horizontal interlinkages within and among firms' (Nohria, 1992: 2). Such a characterisation of current trends connects to the vision promoted by flexible specialistion theorists, of industrial districts populated by small entrepreneurial firms coexisting happily in a new division of labour with their scaled-down, larger sisters. The growth in franchising is also sometimes linked to such development trends (Labour Research Department, 1986b; O'Connell Davidson, 1994b), though the motive is primarily to transfer risk in uncertain markets while retaining control of supplies, prices and business style.

The combined effects of these two trends are that 'new organisations are small or small sub-units in larger organisation' (Heydebrand, 1989: 337). Peters (1992) makes the most sustained assault on previous orthodoxies about organisation scale. Technology and brainware are taking the scale out of everything, while networks can create the efficiencies that vertical integration once did. As proof, he cites data showing that the average size of firms is getting smaller. Even when they stay large, big firms are trying to act small, because the latter are winning the innovation game.

Networks appear in another form, an alternative to internal hierarchy, as organisations go through a *delayering* process. 'Downsizing' may sound like another term for the same process, but its normal meaning is slightly different. While downsizing is often a cynical euphemism for sacking people, claims are made for a trend towards flatter, less hierarchical forms where whole layers of middle management have been removed on the back of new, horizontal communication channels and devolution of responsibility to self-managing and project teams, a trend enhanced by single status deals that remove barriers between categories of employees. Quinn Mills (1993: 8) even invents a new label: the post-hierarchical firm.

He is also typical of many recent managerial writers in attributing to new forms of information technology a determinant role in facilitating many of the above changes. As the New Economy has a 'techno-logic' transforming it (W. Taylor, 1994: 66), the design chain has a different driver, though with broadly the same outcomes. 'It's a voyage that begins with technology and leads inexorably to trust' (Webber, 1993: 24). As we saw earlier, anything from fax machines to new computer link-ups is a key and benign driving force of new ways of working: 'Today, technology is following its own dynamic direction toward distributed computing of greater and greater power and diffused, not centralised information' (Quinn Mills, 1993: 15).

Finally we have *disorganisation*. Peters, for example, has travelled from 'thriving on chaos' to 'necessary disorganisation' in the ephemeral world of the 1990s. Bureaucratic structures and rationality are based on planning. In contemporary unpredictable environments, attempting to plan, predict or control the future is pointless when there is no way of knowing what it will be. As a result, 'The era of strategic planning (control) may be over; we are entering an era of tactical planning (response)' (Moss Kanter, 1993, 2nd edn). It is not just scientific management, but science *in* management that is held to be out-of-date and 'positively counterproductive' in a 'world of perpetual novelty and change' (D. Freedman, 1992: 26, 37). As we saw in Chapter 7, even in more mainstream academic spheres doubts are being cast about the utility of concepts of business planning and strategy.

Indeed, this is only one way in which popular management writing is reinforced by postmodern perspectives that emphasise the reactive nature of organisational behaviour in circumstances where there is inherent uncertainty and disorder in a multiplicity of local situations (Cooper and Burrell, 1988); and also lay stress on new chaos theories of science in which nature appears as random as a throw of the dice (D. Freedman, 1992). Organisations are 'out of control' (Kelly, 1994) but that's fine because that is part of the continual cycle of creation and destruction undertaken by 'mobius strip' organisations that have no identifiable top or bottom, beginning or end (Sabel, 1991).

Flexibility, work and employment

As we have seen, flexibility has been the dominant language of organisational and economic change. Work and employment relations have been no exception. During periods of significant change in work organisation, attention is often directed towards a particular phenomenon that is seen as an obstacle to efficiency. In the past it has been 'overmanning' or unofficial strikes. Since the 1980s, within the general reference to the defects of Taylorism and Fordism, it has been *work and employment* rules: regulatory mechanisms established by workers and managers to govern the workplace. At the start of that decade, *Business Week* (1983) celebrated a revolution against rules that place constraints on management's right to allocate and organise labour. As we have seen in previous chapters, under systems of bureaucratic organisation and control, employers had gained from rules by being able closely to specify job assignments and operate internal labour markets. Unions could restrict arbitrary power and enforce adherence to rules that benefited workers. In addition to such areas as task demarcation, seniority rules governing job protection, lay-offs and promotions were established. Because work rules were embodied in contractual relations, rights and grievance procedures, they gave unions bargaining power. Employment protection in law also enhanced status rights that limited what employers could gain from contractual exchange (Streek, 1987: 241–2). The flexibility offensive was directed not just against the 'rigidities' of work rules; but their high, often fixed, costs in terms of compensation and movement (Mangum and Mangum, 1986). Flexibility therefore requires the firm's internal and external boundaries to be redrawn, bringing into question employment contracts and the location of work, as well as the previously mentioned work rules (Guest, 1987).

The rest of this section discusses the flexibility issues through two prominent sources of influence: Japanese production regimes and the flexible firm model.

Japanese production regimes

Flexibility within markets and between organisations in networks is facilitated by new forms of supplier relationships. This has been particularly associated with the Japanese-derived just-in-time (JIT) system. This depends on a set of relations between large corporations and suppliers, normally characterised by tightly-controlled multiple sourcing through layers of subcontractors. In this system it is primarily the suppliers who have to be flexible, the large firm having passed on the risk in order to gain from the efficiencies of low stocks that can be used only when needed.

However, the influence of Japan as a design model is more associated in the public mind with the *demonstration effect* of 'best practice' in work and employment (Turnbull, 1987: 2). For the UK, this was first illustrated through the Nissan example (Garrahan and Stewart, 1992). A Nissan plant was set up in May 1986 in Washington, Tyne and Wear. The then UK Employment Minister, Norman Tebbit, stated that 'We want them to demonstrate to our auto makers . . . these aspects of Japanese industrial management' (quoted in CAITS, 1986: 20). The Nissan effect can also be identified in the desire of British and other companies to *emulate* Japanese practices. An early 'After Japan' initiative at Rank Xerox based on quality circles, an 'employee involvement' programme and a new management culture and structure foundered on workforce opposition (Giles and Starkey, 1987). The second attempt to achieve a 'Japanese' restructuring of jobs and shop floor practices culminated in the 1988 dispute at Ford. Explicit reference was made to Ford's plethora of grades compared to Nissan's two: manufacturer and technician. But Ford is by no means the sole example. In a similar period, Jaguar and Lucas introduced extensive experiments featuring JIT and employee involvement (Turnbull, 1986); while among the joint ventures, the Rover–Honda link-up was notable for its use of 'zone circles' and 'zone briefing groups' (Smith, 1987).

A further 'Nissan effect' derived from the single-union, 'no-strike' deal. In fact it is not a no-strike deal because the Amalgamated Engineering Union is not a negotiating partner! A company council deals with all matters of wages, conditions and company business at plant level, with direct worker representation conditioned by company veto. However an initial deal was struck specifying complete flexibility and managerial prerogative. Teamworking, temporary workers and an intense work pace were also prominent features – the latter causing low morale and drop-outs (*Daily Telegraph*, 6 May 1987). We return to issues of lean production later in this chapter and, more critically, in the next.

The flexible firm model

The most widely used analytical framework for understanding the moves by employers to vary their workers and work was provided by the *flexible firm* model developed by Atkinson (1984) and the Institute for Manpower Studies (IMS). It is based on a break with existing unitary and hierarchical labour markets, relying on organisation of internal means of allocating labour, in order to create a core workforce and a cluster of peripheral employment relations. Though not in itself a macro, big picture model, it has been associated with post-Fordist perspectives. And, while derived from British experience, it has had a much wider influence, in part because the growth of flexible and non-standard labour has been global, though of course varied in character (see Felstead and Jewson, 1999). Three types of flexibility are identified: functional, temporal and financial, and numerical. We shall look at each in turn.

Functional Core workers gain greater job security in return for managers' right to redeploy them between activities and tasks as products and production requires.

   Functional flexibility is often assumed to lead to higher levels of skilled labour (Ackroyd and Proctor, 1998: 179), though the most used terms tend to be multiskilling or polyvalence. Clearly any increased focus on a core workforce is likely to enhance the need for training and retraining, though this will be in-house and often limited to

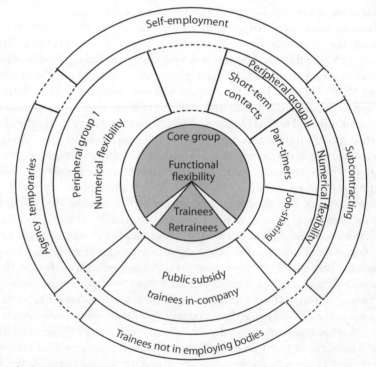

FIGURE 11.3 Model of the flexible firm

Source: C. G. Magnum (1986) 'Temporary Work: The Flipside of Job Security', *International Journal of Manpower*, 17. 1: 14.

firm-specific skills. Surveys reveal that senior managers believe that there has been a significant increase in these kinds of functional flexibility (Burchell *et al.*, 1999: 13–14). It has never been difficult to find high-profile examples of workplace agreements concerning functional flexibility. The most extreme, such as those at Nissan and at Sony, specify complete flexibility, even to the point of managers and clerical staff working on the production line if necessary (*IPM Digest*, 1986). Beyond general statements of manpower utilisation, agreements are mostly directed towards removing 'barriers' between grades and categories. This may be achieved by merging production grades or ensuring job rotation. But a crucial goal of 'multiskilling' has been the erosion of distinctions between production and other categories such as indirect, maintenance and even craft work. For example, production workers at Cadbury and Findus have to carry out maintenance work, while skilled engineering construction workers on oil and gas platforms must undertake semi or unskilled work if there is no craft work for them to do.

Emphasis has also been put on creating flexible craftsmen or 'crafticians' by focusing on the interfaces between crafts and non-crafts, craft assistants, supervisors, and other trades (Cross, 1985). Even clerical groups have not been exempt. Lucas Electrical amalgamated many clerical with manual tasks under a new grade of materials controller. The growth of teamworking has facilitated functional flexibility, as job rotation and additional training has enabled many companies to move towards complete interchangeability of labour (see Proctor and Mueller, 2000: 11–13). We shall return to such practices later.

The most touted carrot, however, is job security, which is linked to 'the difficulty of implementing productivity programmes without the full co-operation of the employees' (Clutterbuck, 1985: 2). Prominent examples are drawn from the US, notably the 'job banks' at Ford and GM in which an equivalent number of jobs are created if production is outsourced. If workers are laid-off, they are promised retraining, relocation and income support (Mangum and Mangum, 1986: 12). However, there have also been British examples of rolling job security deals such as UDV (Marks *et al.*, 1997).

Temporal and financial flexibility This has been associated with changes to functions. Reductions in grading have allowed the simplification of pay structures and bargaining. Companies such as Shell have linked rewards and career progression more closely to individual appraisal and performance-related pay, thus undermining the traditional notion of a specific 'rate for the job'. Not surprisingly this often has the intention or effect of undermining trade union organisation, which has to adapt to a weaker, enterprise-based orientation based on single or reduced representation, local bargaining, and a shift from an industrial relations to a 'human resource management' framework (Streek, 1987: 299). There are also alterations in the use of time, as employers seek to vary attendance in order to meet fluctuations in workload and gain general control over time scheduling. Some high-profile cases of zero hours contracts, such as those in the Burton Group and Burger King, have received considerable publicity. But instances where employees are required to be available for work solely at their employer's discretion are the exception (Cave, 1997). More frequent practices have included buying-out overtime and breaks or ending them as rights, and introducing round-the-clock, round-the-shift systems, with the use of part-time and temporary labour to cover peak demand (Yates, 1986; CAITS, 1986; Wainwright, 1987).

Numerical This is the capacity to vary the headcount according to changes in the level of demand so that there is an exact match between the numbers needed and employment; or as one senior manager bluntly put it, 'A workforce that can be picked up and put down whenever I need them' (quoted in Burchell *et al.*, 1999: 8).

Early UK surveys for the IMS showed that most larger firms claimed to have increased numerical flexibility, though sectoral variations indicated a predominance in service work (Atkinson and Gregory, 1986). Substantial, if uneven, growth was confirmed by the Confederation of British Industry (Yates, 1986), ACAS (1988), Hakim (1990), Casey (1991), Marginson (1991); and more broadly by the International Labour Organisation (Standing, 1987).

The growth of non-standard forms of employment has been linked with the post-bureaucratic agenda of eroding formal and rule-bound modes of recruiting, mobilising and regulating labour (Felstead and Jewson, 1999: 9). While such forms are seen as growing throughout Europe, they are 'most established in the UK, where, of all EU member countries, employment is least regulated' (K. Purcell *et al.*, 1999: 1). However, it is also widely recognised that accurate comparative mapping of changes is difficult, given different methods of data collection, varying legal and academic definitions and overlapping of categories.

Even within national contexts, it is important to disaggregate the categories and look at long-term trends. For the UK, Robinson (1999) has produced some important correctives to over-generalised images of numerical flexibility. Using Labour Force Survey data from 1979–97, he shows that full-time permanent employment has indeed declined from around 75 per cent to 62 per cent. The share of part-time employment rose correspondingly by 8 per cent, self-employment by 5 per cent and temporary work by 2 per cent. However, the small print indicates that the decline of full-time work occurred most sharply during the 1980s recession and has now slowed considerably, while the non-standard categories all show different patterns. Part-time employment has not only been growing throughout the period, it has been doing so steadily from 1945. Self-employment grew rapidly in the 1980s, but has now come to a halt, while the growth of temporary employment is largely a 1990s phenomenon.

So what has happened? With respect to part-time employment, the proportion of women has remained largely stable, but it has doubled among men. However, much of this can be accounted for by the emergence of students onto the labour market as higher education has expanded in the 1990s. The rise in self-employment to 13 per cent of the UK labour force affected most sectors, rather than those that have traditionally used such arrangements, suggesting that contracting out functions and services was a general, though limited, trend (Clutterbuck, 1985). There has been a big growth of temporary help service agencies in a number of countries, notably the US. While some firms, such as Control Data, have used 'supplementals' on short-term contracts with poor conditions to act as buffer to their permanent staff (CAITS, 1986: 32), the growth of temporary contracts is no longer confined to marginal or manual workers in manufacturing, or to seasonal work. The sharpest increases are in among professionals in financial services and the public sector, such as lecturers on renewable or rolling contracts.

Robinson's interpretation of the data, like other recent work, challenges a number of the received wisdoms in the flexibility debate. First, 'the more dramatic assertions about the arrival of a "core–periphery" model in employment relationships find relatively little backing in the data' (1999: 90). Second, non-standard does not necessarily mean casual or low-skill. Rosenberg and Lapidus (1999) demonstrate that for the US, while contingent workers often lose out comparatively in terms of pay and benefits, there is huge diversity, including independent contractors who have relatively beneficial work and employment conditions. This is linked to a third point, that while part of the strategic rationale for numerical flexibility was to externalise some of the uncertainty, costs and risks to a variety of holders of labour service, we should not assume that potential employees do not see benefit in some of these arrangements. For example, UK Labour Force data shows that only 12 per cent of part-timers would prefer full-time work. In contrast, 39 per cent of those in temporary employment were 'involuntary'. Both had risen by small amounts from the 1980s. This appears to support the argument of Hakim (1990, 1996) that many women choose employment that social scientists have often labelled as peripheral or belonging to secondary labour markets (though see critique in Chapter 10). Fourth, there is no consistent relationship between the degree of regulation of labour markets and the extent of non-standard employment. Regulated markets such as those in Southern Europe and Scandinavia have higher rates in many categories of flexible employment than the more deregulated UK and US. This is not as surprising as it appears. The huge variations in patterns of standard and non-standard employment derive from complex 'incentives' given to employers and potential employees alike to engage in different types of labour market action. Tight regulation of standard employment may benefit those in work, but therefore encourage firms to take people on a temporary or other flexible basis (Cousins, 1999).

Home and teleworking

Images of this kind of work have ranged from manufacturing homeworkers, for example women domestic outworkers in sectors such as textiles, electrical components and toys (Mitter, 1986; Allen and Workowtiz, 1987), to glamorous networkers from Rank Xerox, F International and ICL linked by computer in 'electronic cottages' (Control Data Corporation, 1985). While the former pattern has involved up to one in twenty firms (ACAS, 1988), it has been easy to dismiss the latter as exotic exceptions. However, advances in communication technology and the Internet have put virtual working more firmly on the agenda, with commentators highlighting the benefits for the co-ordination of teleworkers (Mirchandani, 1999) and professionals in 'virtual', cross-functional teams in and across work units (Nandhakumar, 1999). This move of the debate from margin to mainstream is a reflection of its strong link to the wider theme of knowledge work and employment, discussed below.

Knowledge work and portfolio people

As Felstead and Jewson note of the above trends, 'A common feature of all these types of employment is that they diverge from the pattern which became regarded in mid-twentieth century advanced capitalist economies as the "norm"' (1999: 1). 'Standard' employment tended to be full-time, reasonably secure, and formally regulated through contracts and legislation. Flexibility models, though they differ in their degree of endorsement of the product, have presented the outcomes primarily as employer-initiated attempts to deregulate labour, moving more employees into various forms of 'peripheral' and 'precarious' employment.

If we return to the logic of the earlier claim about knowledge work, that it belongs to and moves with the employee rather than the organisation, this kind of interpretation can be contested on grounds of extent and character. Rather than seeing numerical flexibility as a management strategy, contracting out and homeworking can be viewed as a choice of individual employees, cashing in on their knowledge, and the dependency of organisations upon it. Hamel and Prahalad (1996: 238) refer to 'a world of independent labour contractors'. While this may be something of an exaggeration, plenty of other commentators would regard it as a trend. Handy (1995) and Leadbetter (1999) link the emergence of a knowledge economy to the growth of portfolio workers, who will work either simultaneously or sequentially for a number of employers. In this context, short-term contracts no longer have a negative connotation, as they reflect the rapidly-changing business environment, with its emphasis on projects and teams.

Handy (1995: 6–7) does accept that there will be casualties in this restructuring of the boundaries between work and home, short- and long-term employment. In addition, there is wide recognition that employee adjustment to new realities is likely to be slow and painful. This is not just a question of changing employment status, but a transformation of the employment relationship itself. A quote from one of Heckscher's interviewees sums it up with considerable clarity:

> My basic mindset was, there's an implicit contract, I expect that the company will provide me a career, development opportunities, and reasonable pay and benefits: and they, in turn, should expect from me that I'm willing to work very hard for them. When either one of us is unhappy with that situation, the contract is broken. And up until the past few years, as a corporation I had faith that that would occur. (Heckscher, 1997: 18)

In other words, the social, or what some commentators call the 'psychological', contract is no longer based on large, hierarchical companies providing stable employment, internal labour markets and long career ladders. Knowledge workers will increasingly be empowered to manage work and career themselves (Birchall and Lyons, 1995). While these discussions are pitched in the language of universality, such trends are predominantly about professional and managerial employers. After all, not that many routine manual and clerical workers had such conditions to be changed in the first place. On the surface this new social contract and the end of loyalty as a bond between organisation 'man' and the corporation seems somewhat lop-sided. However, there is a mutual gain as long as notions of opportunity and advancement are re-imagined. For Heckscher (1995) the new arrangements will have the benefits of being based on open negotiation and the promise of equality between organisation and individual, rather than paternalism and effort–security bargain. The individual will not have to subsume his or her personality in the organisation, and the breakdown of paternalism will allow more women and minorities to enter the ranks of management. Finally, there are new obligations: rather than provide employment, firms provide opportunities and transferable skills to help people become more employable, thus furthering a career across organisations and within occupational communities rather than up a single corporate ladder (Barley, 1996). We will return to some of these issues in Chapter 13 on corporate cultures.

If these, then, are regarded as trends in the labour market, what about work itself?

High performance and work systems: restructuring the division of labour

The labour process is a vital arena if the promises of the anti-bureaucratic revolution are to be fulfilled. Employees' attitudes have to be transformed from grudging compliance to high commitment, while practices change from narrow, demarcated tasks to fully flexible, interchangeable labour. In the original 'design chain' of flexible specialisation, the last steps in the sequence were a high-trust strategy based on skill upgrading and worker autonomy. Similar themes reappeared in talk of the primacy of horizontal co-ordination in knowledge work, as well as the growth of functional flexibility. In more recent times they have been packaged in a broader guise of 'high road' strategies for workplace transformation and competition based more on quality than cost, with the 'highs' being commitment, involvement, skill, and performance, in addition to trust (Applebaum and Batt, 1994). We will return to claims of a high performance work *system* (HPWS) later, but before that we need to look at how such ideas and practices have travelled along this 'road'.

Description or advocacy of participation, autonomy and collaboration is hardly new. In particular, on the surface the language and practices are continuations of the 1970s quality of working life (QWL) or work humanisation initiatives. QWL had long been a generic or umbrella term subsuming anything from job enrichment to participation schemes. Yet we know that despite the extensive publicity for high-profile cases such as Volvo Kalmar and some reports of gains in productivity and quality (Daniel and McIntosh, 1972), by the end of that decade most of the work reform initiatives had diminished or disappeared (Ramsay, 1991). It is therefore tempting to dismiss the new language and practices as a rebranding exercise. Yet the supporters of such approaches would argue that the speedy reappearance of new forms of employee involvement through quality circles, team briefings and other initiatives in the early 1980s, showed the persistence of attempts by employers to create new work paradigms that could move beyond the limits of Taylorism and Fordism.

This was not a direction chosen on the basis of values, but conditioned by a combination of opportunity and threat. New forms of involvement derived in part from technology such as flexible manufacturing systems and production processes, notably JIT (Sayer, 1986; Tailby and Turnbull, 1987). While it would be over-deterministic to ascribe 'needs', there is little doubt that both operate more effectively with higher levels of co-operation, knowledge and flexibility than previous configurations of technology and work organisation. Under JIT workers are expected to do on-the-spot problem solving. Indeed they have little choice given that reduced buffer stocks mean that subsequent activities would break down without such action. In turn this requires *multiskilling* and the incorporation of inspection, maintenance and support activities into production operatives' tasks, or vice versa. These processes also require increased *knowledge*, both of details of the work process such as quality control, and a wider range of jobs.

That such systems are largely Japanese in origin indicates where the threat was coming from. The spread of quality circles and mid-1980s initiatives such as GM's QWL and Ford's Employee Involvement programmes in the US indicates the extent to which emulation of a perceived Japanese model was high on the agenda of Western manufacturers, though some, such as Rover in the UK, tried to avoid a 'Japanese' tag by relabelling initiatives as zone briefings and circles (D. Smith, 1987: 23). The comparatively short-lived nature of many such initiatives by no means ended the influence. Since that period the spread of Japanese transplants into the US and Europe has been extensive, and their apparent success has lead to further pressures that combine demonstration effect and emulation. The transferable ingredients of Japanese productive expertise have been repackaged as the system of *lean production* pioneered by Toyota, particularly in *The Machine That Changed the World* by Womack, Roos and Jones (1990). We discussed the issue of transferability in Chapter 6, but as a design template, lean production conforms to the anti-bureaucracy menu by stressing that in this brave new world, firms will employ teams of multiskilled workers whose jobs will be more challenging and productive, and carry more responsibilities.

The range of new involvement and communication practices had limited impact and sustainability, not simply because they were often imitative, but because 'these schemes tended to be "bolted-on" rather than integral to the work process' (Marchington and Wilkinson, 1998: 16). For example, many companies used quality circles as a catalyst for a period of organisational restructuring and dispensed with them once the goals had been achieved (Dunford and McGraw, 1987). This absence of a systemic character is addressed in some of the next phase of 'new management practices'.

TQM programmes promised a broader, more holistic approach than localised quality circle techniques (Hill, 1991). In the pursuit of the goal of continuous improvement in the production of goods and services, TQM differs by starting from the top and cascading through the organisation. Flatter structures and reduced hierarchy develop as workers take increased responsibility. Hierarchy is also reduced by a network of interdependencies arising from the necessity for employees to treat each other as internal 'customers'. Changes to job design are not the add-ons of old, but a genuine re-integration of conception and execution that is integral to the work process. Though TQM began by focusing on the 'hard' elements of capturing information about processes, it gradually shifted towards a 'softer' orientation to employee commitment and appropriate cultures (Wilkinson, 1992).

The consultant-driven (Hammer and Champy, 1993) emergence of business process reengineering (BPR) continued a holistic approach, promising that a focus on processes rather than functions would flatten hierarchies and produce complex jobs for smart people. Though BPR spoke the standard language of HRM and post-bureaucracy, its route to competitive advantage lay in an integration of work and technical system redesign (Greenbaum, 1998: 136). Given the history of organisational change, it is hardly surprising that BPR initiatives squeezed out 'slack' with little consideration of the human dimension or consequences. Subsequent criticism and retreat meant that the management fad had reached burn-out in about five years (Buchanan, 2000: 26). Buchanan notes that, in contrast, though teamwork has been continually 'rediscovered' over three decades, the current wave is proving more durable.

It is not that teamwork is short on superficial prescription. The managerial literature is full of inflated empowerment rhetoric and exhortations to create self-managing teams so that 'no boss is required' (Dumaine, 1990: 40). There is, in fact, a wide consensus that current teamworking is distinguished from its 1970s predecessor by its much more instrumental, pragmatic orientation, with little concern for job enrichment and industrial democracy (Jenkins, 1994; Applebaum *et al.*, 2000; Proctor and Mueller, 2000). At the same time it is seen as the core of work reform, and the 'heart of the lean factory' (Womack, Roos and Jones, 1990: 99). Mathews argues that such elements of new production systems are not passing fads and differ sharply from QWL, which only grappled with the symptoms of workplace problems. Contemporary initiatives fundamentally reorganise the process of work: 'In place of command and control structures designed to enforce rigidity and compliance, the new production systems call for management that offers facilitation, guidance and co-ordination between self-managing groups of employees who are capable of looking after the details of production themselves' (1993: 7).

There is certainly considerable evidence for the spread of initiatives, as 'teams have progressively replaced the individual as the unit of work organisation' (Adler, 1997: 62). Adler notes that the proportion of leading US firms claiming to utilise self-managed work teams has risen from 6 per cent in 1979 to 28 per cent in 1987 and 68 per cent in 1995. In Britain, the WERS survey reported 65 per cent of all workplaces with over 25 people had teams (Cully et al., 1998). Interestingly there is also some agreement across managerial and radical commentators that management in an increasing number of companies is having success in devolving responsibilities to the group, getting employees to think and act like managers, and thus generating a genuine sense of shared values (Wickens, 1992; Barker, 1993; Sewell, 1998). In this way the workgroup can be used to redirect collective goals towards the company in a way that fulfils the old human relations dream; though for the critics, as we saw in Chapter 8, this is more like a prison of peer pressure and self-surveillance.

The evidence on value internalisation is critically evaluated in the following two chapters, but it is the case that both teamworking and TQM require attention to what Wood (1986: 432) calls 'attitudinal restructuring'. In other words, it requires a much more explicit focus on shaping employee attitudes in spheres such as co-operativeness and self-discipline. As Sayer notes with reference to JIT, 'profitability can depend quite heavily on the performance of workers who are technically unskilled or semi-skilled but behaviourally highly skilled' (1986: 67). This helps explain the paradox that many companies are engaging in detailed and intensive selection and screening processes for relatively routine jobs, often recruiting young 'green' labour. When the NUMMI plant was established, all candidates for employment undertook three days of interviews, job simulations and discussion on the firm's philosophy and objectives (Wood, 1986: 434).

Conclusion

For all the spread and significance of teamwork, not everyone would consider it the bedrock of organisational redesign. The idea of HPWS, developed primarily in the US (Osterman, 1994; Applebaum and Batt, 1994; Lawler et al., 1995), is based on the *interlocking* character of the management of work, organisation and employment. Work organisation, as already outlined, depends upon 'the decentralisation of the gathering and processing of information to non-managerial employees' (Appelbaum and Berg, 1999: 1), with participation and problem-solving enabling front-line workers to contribute to operational decisions and performance. Work-based teams are supplemented by off-line problem and project groups are needed. Such practices are reinforced by skill formation strategies based on enhanced training in social and technical skills, plus more rigorous and selective recruitment, and incentives that make rewards contingent upon team or company performance, whether that be merit pay, profit sharing or group incentives.

Finally, trust is enhanced by employees being encouraged to become stakeholders in the firm, primarily by the development of a mutual gains approach that, among other things, seeks to replace adversarial industrial relations by partnership and participation (Bluestone and Bluestone, 1992; Kochan and Osterman, 1994).

There are other versions of systemic interlocking, such as Huselid's (1995) emphasis on the combination of employee skills, organisational structures and motivation, but the continuities are strong, and all versions claim that effectiveness resides in the 'bundling' of different practices that can lead to high commitment and positive employee behaviours (MacDuffie, 1995). Not only have such bundles or clusters been identified, a number of the studies have found a positive association with company performance (Huselid, 1995; Ichinowski *et al.*, 1996; Applebaum *et al.*, 2000). British research on similar lines has been more circumspect. Wood and de Menzes (1998) found a widespread adoption of high commitment practices, though of a diverse rather than 'packaged' nature; and also did not identify significant performance differences. However, the WIRS survey (Millward *et al.*, 2000), and other evidence on European trends (Sisson, 1997), does confirm that there has been a spread and some clustering of a number of direct participation practices.

We have now worked our way right down the 'design chain' of organisational change, outlining claims and evidence about the specific dimensions, as well as the interrelations between them. Do these add up to a paradigm break: new organisations in a new economy? This is the theme of the next chapter.

12 Continuity and Change at Work

We have seen in the previous chapter that there are a number of overlapping organisational themes from the 'models' established through flexibility and other restructuring discourses. This chapter returns to each set of issues and uses contemporary research to subject the associated theory and evidence to a critical evaluation. In one sense this is not difficult. The quality of evidence in new economy, new organisation (NEO for short) arguments is often poor and frequently relies on relies on stereotypical polarities between old and new. Academics, consultants and a growing band of policy entrepreneurs have a vested interest in proclaiming and promoting the 'new', largely as a way of differentiating their own intellectual products. In fact a strong case can be made that leading purveyors of NEO, such as Drucker, have been making essentially the same argument about a rapidly changing economic environment compelling organisations to break up their bureaucracies since the 1950s (see Eccles and Nohria, 1992; Thompson and O'Connell Davidson, 1994). Similarly, knowledge economy perspectives sound remarkably similar to those put forward by writers such as Daniel Bell (1973) over a quarter of a century ago (see Smart, 1992). Yet each is predicated upon a supposed link between new market or technological conditions and new structures. Despite these weaknesses, it would be a mistake simply to deny the 'new' as frothy rhetoric. The really difficult task for organisational analysis is to grasp the patterns, dynamics and characteristics of continuity *and* change. This is our aim in this chapter.

Hierarchies, networks and knowledge revisited

There is no polarity that has been used more extensively than mass production and a variety of 'flexible' or knowledge-based successors. We focus on two of those successors – flexible specialisation and the knowledge economy – in this section, which deals primarily with macro market processes rather than organisational issues.

Though flexible specialisation is less fashionable these days, its account of changes in firms and markets remains typical of NEO arguments. The theory rapidly became a new work organisation paradigm and therefore a target for extensive critique (Smith, 1987). A number of studies, notably Williams *et al.* (1987), convincingly argued that the conceptual polarity between mass production and flexible specialisation is misleading. Traditional mass production is still widespread, particularly where semi-skilled women workers doing labour-intensive assembly and packing jobs remain a cheaper or more reliable option (Pollert, 1988a). In addition mass production does not always use dedicated equipment to make standardised products, but can handle diversification within flow lines. Wood (1989b) has shown that the world car – the archetypal example of mass production within the international division of labour – remains prominent, albeit in modified form. Economies of scale have fallen, but the break-even point is still high. Japanese and other companies have established variety within mass production with the use of JIT and not always with advanced technology (A. Sayer, 1986). Even the identification of flexibility with manufacturing itself neglects the service sector as the major growth area of such practices (Hyman, 1988). The flexible specialisation thesis and post-Fordists also made exaggerated claims for the use of programmable technology (Jones, 1997). Advanced technology such as FMS (flexible manufacturing systems) is very expensive, particularly for the small firms that should be in the forefront of customised production. Furthermore, not all new technology is either inherently flexible, or being used in a flexible way. The emphasis is more likely to be on control and co-ordination of the labour process, quality and routing rather than product flexibility (Wood, 1989b: 9).

Nor are mass markets necessarily saturated. There are a huge range of industries still based on mass and large batch production, and the pattern with goods such as colour TVs and video recorders is for production to be based on families of inter-related models. Fragmentation of demand, or what companies call 'positioning strategies', is more often an attempt to create a market rather than reflect new consumer tastes. Big firms can produce for mass and niche markets, as the ugly phrase 'mass customisation' indicates. Notwithstanding this hybrid capability, key industries, such as food, are actually destroying regional, craft production in the march towards global standardised products and marketing (Levitt, 1991; C. Smith, 1991). Indeed, it is ironic that the most explosive global growth is in fast food, which is 'dominated by homogeneous products. The Big Mac, the Egg McMuffin, and Chicken McNuggets are identical from one time and place to another' (Ritzer, 1993: 155). Ritzer may sometimes overdo the extent to which production and service has been McDonaldised, but the uniformity of high streets and shopping malls is testimony to the continued dominance of standardised commodities, mass markets and large firms. This is particularly the case in Britain, where large manufacturing firms have tended to 'eschew the production of complex products' in search of diversified production activities and standard products for mature markets (Ackroyd and Proctor, 1998: 166, 170).

The obsession with the Fordist stereotype also ignores inconvenient facts about the past. On the one hand the operations of Ford's key plants, such as those as Highland Park, never corresponded to the description of inflexible Fordism (Williams et al., 1992b). On the other, the spread of Fordism has been exaggerated. Most plants in modern economies have never contained assembly lines, and Fordism never travelled far outside mass manufacturing (Williams et al., 1987; B. Jones, 1997). As Bryn Jones has noted, there is a persistent tension in production paradigms between Taylorist bureaucracy and Fordist integration, and pressures for product versatility (1998: 11). This tension has been reproduced in different ways within and across national economies. Japanese flexible manufacturing systems tackle capital and skill utilisation in ways distinct from European and American practices. But none resemble anything that resembles a flexible specialisation or post-Fordist model: 'on the key measures of product-range, system-versatility and worker polyvalence, most FMSs operate within Fordist and Taylorist pre-conceptions' (1998: 21).

This same observation, Jones notes, also applies to Italy, where flexible specialisation theory draws much of its inspiration. Even on their 'home-ground' in Emilia-Romagna, the majority of production is still Fordist in nature, while quality craft work is the preserve of the majority of middle-aged men: 'Semi-skilled assembly work, plastic-moulding, and wiring work is carried out by women, while heavy foundry and forging work is done by Southern Italian and North African workers' (F. Murray, 1987: 88). Overall, as the work of the William's team demonstrates, the statistical and case study evidence used by Sabel and Piore was frequently poor or non-existent.

There is a wider message about small firms here. As we noted in Chapter 11, there are sectors where innovative networks of such firms are playing a significant role in economic development. As usual, however, discontinuity perspectives have oversold the message. Across the globe, manufacturing and services remain dominated by large, indeed increasingly larger, firms. Counting the numbers of firms is misleading. It is true, for example, that in the US, 85 per cent of all individual enterprises in the computer industry employ less than 100 people. But the 5 per cent that employ 500 or more accounted for 91 per cent of employment and sales (Harrison, 1994: 5). Such trends are repeated sector by sector. In the UK, more than half of all employees work for organisations with more than 500 employees (Teasdale, 2000: 7). Even a persuasive advocate such as Perrow has to admit that the output of small firm networks on a global scale is 'probably trivial' (1992: 445). Moreover, small firms have been less technologically innovative than large ones, and their profitability often rests primarily on long hours and low wages (Amin, 1991; Harrison, 1994).

Knowledge in the economy

The basic pattern identified above, of stereotypical polarisation, limited evidence and neglect of diversity, tends to be reproduced in each new generation of macro arguments, and is certainly observable in relation to knowledge economy theories. As we saw in the previous chapter, the 'weightless' character of knowledge is said to make the economy fundamentally different from the old, hierarchical predecessor. Despres and Hiltrop argue that the crucial ingredient – knowledge – lies in the heads of producers: 'it remains with the employee and in no real sense is it ever of the firm . . . it is impossible to separate knowledge from the knower' (1995: 11). Relations inside and between firms therefore have to be of a horizontal, network kind.

However, this formulation is factually inaccurate and conceptually confused. What gives weight to an object or idea in a market economy is its status as a commodity. Its physicality or otherwise is wholly irrelevant. Knowledge can be calculated, rationalised and ultimately commodified (see Yakhlef and Salzer-Morling, 2000). A simple example is the emergent intellectual property regime in biotechnology. Global corporate players have been rushing to establish patents on genetic material, so that they can 'own traditional knowledge and take advantage of the privatisation of life forms' (J. Vidal, *Guardian*, 13 April 2000). Value can and is being assigned to these so-called intangible assets. Furthermore, though companies are dependent on scientific, knowledge workers to 'mine' this gene pool, the transformation into saleable commodities relies precisely on separating that knowledge from the knower. That, after all, is what 'knowledge management' systems are about. The language of knowledge economy theorists such as Nonaka and Takeuchi (1995) speaks of 'capturing' or converting knowledge as if that process is neutral and benign. As with our previous macroeconomic discussion, this is partly a temporal confusion. Autonomy and creativity are maximised during periods of pursuing knowledge and creating systems. Yet the commercialisation of the products of knowledge takes the form of standardised, highly-structured systems in areas such as software design or surveying. There are few detailed empirical accounts of how new knowledge management systems work. McKinlay (2000) shows the tension between creativity and control in his case study of Worldrug, a large pharmaceutical company. Mechanisms for the former, such as electronic cafes and intranets, sit alongside much more bureaucratic measures, such as data warehouses and other IT-led support tools with little dialogic character, to store and codify tacit knowledge. Knowledge management systems may also be geared towards standardisation to meet customer requirements:

> For example, a lot of the engineer's knowledge can be captured using knowl-edge-based (or expert) IT systems to map out design and installation processes, by following a conventional rule-based approach. The outcome is that customers get consistent specifications, price quotations and quality from any company in the group. (David Bell, Chief Knowledge Officer at Clyde Bowers, quoted in *Scottish Business Insider*, October 1999)

The impact of the valorisation of knowledge is not merely on employees. Corporate power places constraints on the process of independent, collegial knowledge production, as universities become ever more dependent on private sources to finance scientific research. For example, 37 per cent of biotechnology scientists who are members of the American National Academy of Sciences have industry affiliations (Rifkin, 1999). Nor in market terms do the fast growing knowledge intensive industries behave any differently from more traditional sectors. Rifkin details how, contrary to the network myth, the concentration of capital (and vertical integration) is unabated. Global pharmaceutical companies have recently spent $3.5 billion buying up biotech firms. When they are not buying them up they are tying them to licensing agreements (at the cost of $1.6 billion expenditure).

We can see similar trends with respect to the Internet. It is true that many new e-commerce companies have come into being, backed by venture capitalists and making a lot of money for their founders. However, the trends in what Schiller calls 'digital capitalism' are also towards concentrated ownership and vertical integration.

> Smaller companies that specialised in what were initially niche markets at the frontier of the liberalisation process worked the new territory. When they succeeded, major traditional suppliers either snapped them up or rushed to develop similar applications of their own. (Schiller, 1999: 28)

Huge mergers such as that between Time-Warner and AOL merely confirm the direction of change. With this in mind, the association of knowledge production and acquisition with new forms of ownership is a mixture of wishful thinking and confusing the early stages of market formation in an emergent sector with its mature, normally oligopolistic characteristics. As their predecessors before them, knowledge economy theorists are unwilling or unable to explain such trends. In *The Last Days of the Giants*, Baldock (1999) asserts that the current merger wave is the 'last throw' of the big corporations as they try to fight off the threat from e-commerce. A decade earlier, Tom Peters (1992) had described mergers as 'madness'. The fact remains that the global boom in mergers and acquisitions continues unabated. Despite relatively poor returns for shareholders, United Nations figures show that cross-border mergers and acquisitions drove foreign investment volumes to a new record of $856 billion in 1999 (Mark Atkinson, *Guardian*, 10 October 2000). With market expectations of double-digit growth per year, such activity is the quickest way into mature industries. In addition, economies of scale and scope are more important than ever, particularly for knowledge intensive firms with huge research and development costs. Responses vary from strategic alliances to link-ups such as the £110 billion merger of Glaxo Wellcome and Smith Kline, but the message remains the same – big is still beautiful.

Finally, what about claims that knowledge work is the engine of growth in the new economy? As Warhurst and Thompson (1998) demonstrate, at the heart of NEO arguments are a host of conceptual and empirical confusions. Proponents exaggerate the scope of knowledge work. Occupations requiring 'thinking' skills will expand, but that expansion will be limited in scope and potential for employment growth. While there are certainly high tech clusters (Finegold, 1999), only 7 per cent of the fastest growing occupations in the US – the imputed model of economic transformation – could be classified as knowledge workers who manipulate symbols and ideas (Harwood, 1996). It is easy to conflate the production of high-tech goods with the need for a workforce of highly skilled workers (Keep and Mayhew, 1999). Even knowledge-intensive firms 'actually require quite small numbers of highly skilled employees once the major information transfer technologies have been put in place. A very small élite of system designers and strategic managers is required, whilst the globally dispersed plants and offices can be serviced by workers with very much less training and knowledge' (Ackroyd and Lawrenson, 1996: 157).

Further down the occupational hierarchy there is a further and consistent conflation of knowledge and information. Lists of 'knowledge workers' (for example, Handy, 1995: 4) consist of heterogeneous occupations who have little in common other than handling information. Financial services, for example, frequently require little more of workers than information transfer – the inputting of customer details onto pre-programmed screens and software. As even an exponent of the knowledge economy, Robert Reich, observes, 'The foot soldiers of the information economy are the hordes of data processors stationed in back offices with computer terminals linked to worldwide information banks' (1993: 23). Many of these foot soldiers no longer belong to Western armies. Locations in the Caribbean or the Philippines are promoted as 'digiports' with high tech infrastructures, and 'skilled' but low-paid staff.

Most employment growth, actual and projected, is in service work, and within that predominantly at the low end in serving, guarding, cleaning, waiting and helping in the private health and care services, as well as retail and hospitality industries – both in the US and the UK (Crouch, 1999). Much of this constitutes a growth in 'no knowledge' work, at least as measured in conventional terms. Recent skill surveys reveal that 41 per cent of personal services, 62 per cent of sales and 80 per cent of 'other occupations' require no qualifications for entry (Brown and Keep, 1999). When managers were asked what proportion of their workforce could be described as skilled (such as professional, associate professional, technical or craft), there were some startling results. For example, 40 per cent of managers in wholesaling/retailing and 57 per cent of managers in financial services said that they had no skilled non-managerial employees (Cully *et al.*, 1998, and see Keep, 2000). There is an increasing emphasis from many employers on employee attitudes and even their 'aesthetic' qualities rather than formal knowledge and skills (Nickson *et al.*, 2001). Such facts are almost completely unacknowledged by NEO theorists, who fail to recognise the diversity of employment and skill trends. We will return to the issue of the growth of knowledge-ability in work in the final section of the chapter.

Corporate structures: organised capitalism

The rhetoric of replacing centralised bureaucracy by decentralised, 'disorganised' networks does not rely solely on the balance of large and small firms, but on the nature of modern corporate structure. Hierarchical structures are more durable than the business literature would have us believe. In fact a consistent theme of previous studies has been the gap between the potential for decentralisation and skill enhancement, and the reality of subordination to traditional functional structures, narrowly defined cost efficiency and conservative cultures (Cummings and Blumberg, 1987; Child, 1987; Williams, 1988).

However, there is little doubt that there have been considerable changes in organisational structure. Traditional bureaucracies are, in one sense, being broken up with the creation of a myriad of smaller units such as profit centres and internal markets within large firms. Business periodically adjusts the balance and mechanisms of central control as it seeks to adapt to new economic and political conditions, though these vary considerably by sector and country. In the UK, current changes are part of a longer-term shift away from 'Americanised' strategies and structures which were relatively unresponsive to market flexibility and product and process innovation (McKinlay, 1999). However, both the intent and the outcome of such changes have been misunderstood and misrepresented. We have to distinguish between the delegation of operational autonomy, and strengthened financial and other controls by the central structures.

Just as studies of the labour process such as Shaiken et al. (1986) show that the primary managerial concern remains that of centralising control and reducing unpredictability, so analysis of new corporate structures demonstrates that decentralisation of the form is accompanied by centralisation of the substance of power. At companies such as GEC and British Telecom, the system of profit centres relies on accounting structures, marketing forecasts and limits on the discretion of plant managers to control and monitor costs (Hallet, 1988; McKinlay, 1999). As Hallet observes, 'District managers, supposedly freer than ever in the age of devolution, complain of now being more tightly restricted by budgets imposed from above over which they have less influence' (1988: 35). Research into newly privatised utilities in the UK report a large gap between the rhetoric of autonomous units transacting with each other and the reality that profit centres are mostly monopoly suppliers to each other. In addition they are closely controlled through corporate business plans, capital expenditure, employment and revenue allocations and targets (O'Connell Davidson, 1993). 'Empowered' managers are often equally as sceptical as their shop floor equivalents:

> I'm going to be constrained by my management. My management is going to be constrained by their management. And so on up the ladder. The chairman of the board is going to be constrained by the board and the financial market. (Product manager quoted in Potterfield, 1999: 84).

The sheer spatial and functional diversity of units at national and international level, particularly following complex patterns of merger and acquisition, has led to a considerable strengthening of financial control systems that give corporate headquarters much more sophisticated means of monitoring and regulating the management of subsidiaries (Thompson, Wallace and Flecker 1992; Ackroyd and Proctor, 1998). A survey of the largest companies operating in the UK revealed that in a substantial majority, 'headquarters exerts tight controls over business unit operations and profitability targets are not devolved' (Armstrong *et al.*, 1994: 13). This may vary by function, with more autonomy devolved in areas such as human resource policy, though constrained by strict budget allocations (Sisson and Marginson, 1995; McKinlay, 1999). In such areas the route to centralisation is likely to be indirect. As we saw in Chapter 6, the capacity of transnational companies to establish standardised management systems and production organisation is facilitated by their ability to transfer know-how and 'best practice' within the organisation. The real networks are increasingly globally integrated production or service chains, with standardisation rather than local autonomy the main feature (Thompson *et al.*, 1998).

Disaggregation or de-concentration of functions and operations is another real trend, though, as we have seen, the evidence for some of its supposed forms such as flexible specialisation and industrial districts is vastly exaggerated (Amin, 1989). A much more characteristic and bureaucratic mechanism of disaggregation has been franchising. Case studies (Felstead, 1994) demonstrate that business formats imposed by the central company dictate precise procedures and criteria governing operations, finance, and transfer of 'know-how'. In the case of the shift from direct employment to franchised operations in milk delivery, managers contradicted the new philosophy of partnership between company and franchisee. They admitted that the system of supervising roundsmen was exactly the same as before, and that their work was closely prescribed by the franchise contract, with the added 'bonus' that the franchisees had lost all previous employment rights and benefits. Like the self-employed workers studied by Rainbird (1991), any autonomy was largely lost in longer days, intensified labour and other signs of self-exploitation. Even where groups such as freelance media workers have a reasonable degree of telework autonomy, research shows that almost half are dependent on a single client for business, often their former employer (Baines, 1999). UK Labour Force Survey data reveals that 12 per cent of the self-employed had only one customer and that 7 per cent were previously an employee of their main customer (Teasdale, 2000: 9).

The reality of dependency has also been established in Rainnie's (1988) authoritative study of small–large firm relationships. In industries such as clothing, the large firm is able to dictate methods and profit margins, transfer costs and uncertainties to the smaller unit. This is similar to supplier networks in JIT systems. Nissan established the first British and possibly European example of a spatially concentrated production process (Crowther and Garrahan: 1987). A large site enabled the company to maximise influence over the industrial environment and the supply of components. Car manufacturers have been able to put a similar squeeze on component suppliers. The Fiat Melfi plant in Southern Italy includes 22 component makers who simply run their products onto the production line.

Benetton has been held up as the archetypal post-bureaucratic firm. In fact, such companies indicate the existence of a new type of *extended hierarchy* that takes in decentralised and desegregated units, but still has the powerful large firm at the centre. As Wood (1989a: 24) observes, 'the Benetton case does not match up to the image of a nexus of firms all flexibly specialised and employing highly committed, skilled workforces. It appears if anything more like a network dominated by the large firm along the lines of Atkinson's flexible firm'. Harrison (1994: 25), too, refers to Benetton's complicated layering of high-end design in the core, sub-contractors and homeworkers as a hierarchical production system. For him, this is just one example of 'concentration without centralisation'. Instead of dwindling, concentrated economic power is changing shape through downsizing and disaggregation, networks and alliances. But at the centre remain big players: 'production may be decentralised, while power finance, distribution, and control remain concentrated among the big firms' (1994: 20).

What about the other sense of hierarchy – removing the middle layers? Again, this is undoubtedly a significant trend. But delayering is not synonymous with the destruction of hierarchy, at least not if it means any diminution of centralised power. Paradoxically, the thinning-out of middle levels of command can actually lead to the power of strategic decision-makers increasing. In an organisational world constituted through line management, direct reporting and accountability, the removal of intermediate levels, with their attendant committees and other structures, also removes the potential for removing obstacles to central control and coalitions of countervailing power. For example, in some firms, 'radical delegation of decision-making also had the explicit objective of reducing the power of divisional "barons" and sharpening executive responsibilities' (McKinlay, 1999: 155).

McKinlay also details the growth of qualitative measures, such as rates of new product and process innovation and customer satisfaction that complement budgetary controls. This is particularly the case in the public sector, where forms of control and co-ordination based on professional autonomy and self-regulation have been under attack from expanded corporate and state influence. In higher education, universities have had to respond to research and course evaluation exercises through external funding agencies by greatly increasing the monitoring and control of performance at departmental and individual level: 'increased bureaucracy becomes necessary to cope with the proliferation of control, audit, monitoring, reporting and accounting functions that carry out the tasks previously undertaken by academics themselves' (Parker and Jary, 1994: 7). In schools, a recent survey showed 91 per cent of teachers and 95 per cent of lecturers identified a growth of bureaucracy as being one of the main factors shaping their recent experience of work (*Guardian*, 7 and 14 March 2000).

IT has a powerful role in all these processes, for example when automated purchasing cuts out the need for specialised functions. But the idea that technology automatically redistributes power and democratises information flows is both naïve and deterministic. Though IT is flexible enough to allow for varied uses, the vast increase in information available on work activities can in itself reproduce managerial power to monitor, control and predict performance. Giordano accurately observes that this means 'the development of an industrial organisation whose planning and financial decisions are centralised and whose operations are frequently decentralised and highly interdependent' (1985: 11). The chairman of the international conglomerate ABB, whose global information system helps control the 400 companies and 240 000 employees gives an example of this:

> We also have the glue of transparent, centralised reporting through a management information system called Abacus. Every month Abacus collects

performance data on our 4500 profit centres and compares performance with budgets and forecasts. You can aggregate and disaggregate results by business segments, countries and companies within countries. (Taylor, 1991: 100)

The practices described in this section are incompatible with images of disorganisation and firms being 'out of control'. In contrast to the rhetoric of 'disorganisation', capitalism remains 'organised', whether at the macro or micro level; though structures of control and co-ordination change. While greater complexity is undoubtedly being introduced into those processes, there can be little doubt that whether it is TQM, financial monitoring or integrated computer-based models to predict yield and return, standardised central *planning systems* remain an essential feature of business practice.

A new flexible firm?

The less theoretical cousin of NEO perspectives has been the flexible firm model (Atkinson, 1984) that laid out a core–periphery explanation based on maximising the possibilities for functional and numerical flexibility. Though less sweeping in its range, the model made claims of sufficient strength and visibility to attract a degree of criticism similar to that of flexible specialisation/post-Fordism. Pollert (1988a, 1988b) argued that both share vital commonalties, including a celebration of the market and consumer sovereignty, legitimation of the view that the solution to organisational and economic problems lies in altering the behaviour of labour, the resurrection of a dual labour market analysis, and a futurological discourse underwritten by a post-industrial analysis in which flexibility marks the vital break from the past. In a memorable phrase, Pollert observes that both flexibility arguments fuse 'description, prediction and prescription' (1988a: 43).

These points are widely accepted, and a considerable scepticism is now attached to the claims of strategic intent and novelty surrounding flexibility. Legge (1995) notes that there have been three types of problem raised by critics: empirical support, conceptual clarity and ideological agenda. With respect to the latter, though the IMS did function indirectly as intermediary between employers and government policy in the labour market, description was always more important than any prescriptive message. How accurate, then was the description? We tried to summarise the evidence on extent of change in the previous chapter. Teasdale's analysis of UK Labour Force Survey data sums the picture up succinctly: 'there is little sign of irrevocable long term trends or of recent dramatic shifts . . . [People] will continue to spend most of their working lives in "conventional" jobs as full time permanent employees. Indeed with women spending more of their life in the labour market, the conventional job will be the experience of a greater proportion of the population' (2000: 26). But what of issues of conceptual accuracy in flexibility models?

The idea of a new *core* workforce has attracted a significant body of critical comment. A central point has been that the multiskilling at the heart of functional flexibility represents a modest enlargement of the range of tasks required rather than any more fundamental change in the direction of skill enhancement (Elger, 1991), and that the pace of change has been slowed by worker resistance (Turnbull, 1986; Storey, 1992). Geary (1995) argues that employers have been seeking to change the work–effort bargain through removing demarcation boundaries rather than instituting a new model of skill. The novelty of flexibility agreements can be challenged by making comparison to the productivity deals and general manning agreements of the 1960s that also reduced demarcation and restrictive practices in exchange for greater rewards (Towers, 1987; MacInnes, 1987). Others have pointed to the somewhat underwhelming evidence collected by the IMS itself, for example in the NEDO study (1986). This found that though changes were widespread, they were uneven by sector, there was little evidence for any extensive flexibility, and that the changes themselves were mostly the result of short-term cost-saving and threats of job loss, without sinking deeper roots or employment cultures at the 'core'.

Such observations coincided with scepticism in other commentaries (Elger, 1987; Hakim, 1990; Hunter and MacInnes, 1992) which raises the possibility that talk of flexibility may often be a post-hoc managerial rationalisation, rather than a product of the valued goal of strategic planning. Research on FMS confirms that in most cases new arrangements were piecemeal, improvised and contained a variety of forms of skill utilisation (Jones, 1998). The degree of strategic intent may, however, vary across countries, demonstrating the 'societal effects' we discussed in Chapter 6. O'Reilly's (1992) research on banking contrasts functional flexibility accompanied by training and upgrading in France, compared to its ad-hoc manner and orientation to work intensification in the UK.

A highly critical examination of the evidence in relation to the peripheral category was made by Pollert (1988a, 1988b). She pointed out that evidence has tended to conflate long-term changes and standard practices to vary production with genuinely new employment patterns, an argument supported by Marginson's (1991) distinction between high level of use and change in use of non-standard employment. Pollert went on to use a variety of sources to show that most of the figures for temporary, part-time, homeworking, self-employment and subcontracted work were greatly exaggerated. Again, where there has been an increase it is often on the basis of already-established practices, and on the basis of state sponsorship in the public sector rather than management strategy in the private. Finally, the use of 'peripheral' itself does not really do justice to the centrality of such forms of work, particularly that done by women, to a modern capitalist economy.

Most of the worst aspects are at the 'periphery'. Trends towards decentralisation in industries such as clothing are resulting in a modern 'burgeoning sweatshop economy' based on women and ethnic minority workers (Mitter, 1986). In an inter-related way the purpose of some policies is not flexibility per se, but the avoidance of remaining legislation that protects employee rights. For example Italian laws giving job security can be avoided in firms with less than 15 on the payroll. The reality of homeworking is more likely to be superexploitation and casualisation rather than the happy, autonomous employee in the electronic cottage (Allen and Wolkowtiz, 1987; Phizacklea, 1987). In fact flexibility analyses largely set aside the issues of gender and ethnicity by recasting dual labour markets as benign, progressive or inevitable (Pollert, 1988a).

A precise differentiation between sectors is not always possible. Fast food chains are one of the fastest growing parts of the economy. But this 'core' sector, employing mainly the young, black people and women on part-time and unsocial hours, has workers with decidedly peripheral employment conditions (Transnationals Information Centre, 1987). Alternatively, one can have regular, continuous employment such as that experienced by contract cleaners, but still be insecure due to the particularistic choices available to clients and incoming management (Allen and Henry, 1994: 9); or be performing core functions such as research and development, but gradually be losing privileged status due to competitive, external contracting (Whittington, 1991a). Taken together with the problem of whether the model is a strategy to aspire to or a description of existing practices (Legge, 1995), this illustrates the conceptual ambiguities involved in identifying and operationalising the central categories.

These critiques have provided an important corrective to exaggerated flexibility claims and to weaknesses in the flexible firm model. However, for all the unevenness of theory and practice, looking back on the last two decades it is uncontestable that functional and numerical flexibility are significant global trends. While full flexibility was always likely to remain a 'holy grail' that is desired but never quite attained (*IPM Digest*, 1986:.11), employment dualism is a reflection of increasing reorganisation of person–power resources and control over the headcount. Proctor *et al.* (1994) rightly point out that it is too easy to adopt stringent criteria for strategic intent by employers that prevent a recognition of emergent strategy demonstrated through consistent patterns and decisions. This judgement reflects the broader argument about strategy and control made in Chapter 8.

Furthermore, commonalties between flexible firm and flexible specialisation can be overstated. Precisely because one is a management policy model and the other a grand theory, the flexible firm can be utilised in some instances as an explanatory tool, without the burden of any wider conceptual and historical baggage. This argument has been forcefully extended by Proctor *et al.* (1994), who note that almost all contributors to the flexibility debate carefully distinguish between their descriptions and critiques of flexible specialisation (or post-Fordism) and the flexible firm. It is perfectly possible to accept that employers may find the labour control potential of the latter more attractive and more feasible than ushering in the return of the craft worker.

Once universalistic empirical claims are scaled down, it is possible to identify more 'local' flexibility strategies. While, as we saw in Chapter 12, there is no automatic link between labour market deregulation at national level and the incidence of non-standard labour, it is perfectly possible to recognise state or employer action aimed at shifting the balance of power through flexibility in labour markets. The embrace of labour market deregulation and legal weakening of employee protection has been particularly prevalent in countries such as New Zealand and Australia where the state has traditionally played a significant role. Under right-wing governments in both countries, there has been a reciprocal growth of employment insecurity and some forms of non-standard work, notably of a casual and part-time nature (Ryan, 1992; Burgess and Strachan, 1999)

We have already indicated the limited progress towards any form of job security in large firms. In some sectors it has been the reverse. For example, the British and American steel industries have both re-hired redundant workers under subcontractors with significant loss of pay, benefits and health and safety protection (Fevre, 1986; Mather, 1987). The most dramatic example is provided by the Burton Group in the UK who announced in 1993 that they were turning most of their retail employees into part-timers who had to wait each day for a phone call to indicate whether they would be needed! Such concern for the casualties of flexibility echoes experience from Japan, where the commonly referred-to six 'pillars' of company practice are lifetime employment, company welfare, quality consciousness, enterprise unions, consensus management and seniority-based reward systems. Even taking this sympathetically as an ideal type, evidence suggests that it applies at best to the 20 per cent of core employees in large private and public corporations (Briggs, 1987; Dickens and Savage, 1987). The 80 per cent working in smaller firms and for subcontractors are largely excluded from fringe benefits, company welfare and job security, as (obviously) are the large number of those on temporary contracts, and casual and part-time workers within both sectors. Such secondary labour market characteristics are indeed found within the big companies themselves, as Kamata's (1982) graphic account of life as a temporary worker at Toyota illustrates. Contemporary accounts indicate that the deliberate measures to erode employment security and increase the number of workers on non-standard contracts are characteristic of a growing number of large Japanese corporations (Kyotani, 1999).

While many researchers would probably be happy to accept a scaled down, less prescriptive version of the flexible firm, there have been attempts to recast the model. Using evidence from a database of large British manufacturing firms, Ackroyd and Proctor (1998) argue that a distinctive pattern of production at plant level can be identified and described as 'the new flexible firm'. They agree with the 'old' model, that labour is a central source of flexibility, but can see no evidence that it is associated with highly skilled polyvalence. Influenced by their diversified activities and finance-based forms of control, such firms have substituted flexible labour and organisation for capital investment. Managers work within a framework of reorganisation and re-regulation of existing resources, focusing on elimination of unproductive activities, broadening roles and responsibilities and adjusting external relations, rather than constituting qualitatively new practices.

While this contribution is valuable, it is a description of a particular 'local' strategic approach that may not be as accurate for the manufacturing regimes of other countries, or indeed in the service sector. We also have to be able to identify the varied and sometimes new ways in which flexibility, work and employment are constructed.

Changing employment relations and the new insecurity

NEO arguments recognise that employment relations may be less secure than in the past and that increased flexibility for firms has disrupted the old 'psychological' contract-based job tenure and long career ladders. It is widely accepted that downsizing and delayering have had an impact on middle managers. However in NEO writings, the consequences are seen in predominantly benign terms, the new scenarios creating opportunities for a bargain to be struck between organisations wanting expertise and commitment, and highly mobile professionals who can use their knowledge to increase employability and build portfolio careers within occupational communities (Heckscher, 1997). There are certainly some glowing reports of the work conditions and employment packages of highly mobile net workers in the US, of whom 15 per cent are apparently offered free massages and 31 per cent free dry cleaning (*Guardian*, 21 September 2000). But how typical are they?

Given the somewhat diffuse nature of the 'portfolio' category we do not really have any reliable indication of the numbers involved. Census data in the UK suggests an upper limit of about 2.5 per cent of the total workforce involved in teleworking (see Baines, 1999: 20, for more detail). But there are problems with how to calculate numbers from the diverse composition of people who work in some way from the home. Taking a narrower definition of those whose main work is in the home, Teasdale argues that 'homeworking proper' constitutes just 600 000 people. Noting that these numbers have not changed, he notes that, 'It would appear that teleworking has changed how homeworkers do their job rather than making more homeworking possible and moving jobs from larger workplaces' (2000: 24).

On another front, while temporary help agencies are growing, particularly in the US, the figures do not tell us whether those involved are reluctant conscripts or enthusiastic adherents. What we can say is that there is a huge difference in significance between the casualties or survivors of corporate restructuring, and the smaller number of people with scarce skills who can set themselves up as independent contractors. The little evidence available suggests that the growth in contingent work is primarily driven by changing *employer* preferences (Goldin and Applebaum, 1992; Burchell *et al.*, 1999).

The problem with the benign view is that the new social or psychological contract is a somewhat one-sided 'bargain'. Employees are being asked unconditionally to invest more of themselves and work collaboratively in the job, while any employer promises are purely conditional; the result is a 'collectivisation of effort and decollectivisation of risk' (Burchell *et al.*, 1999: 60). This is recognised by some NEO theorists: 'In all the talk about the new responsibilities of employees, there is little talk about the new responsibilities of managers . . . the fact is that most employees feel that they are the company's most expendable resource' (Hamel and Prahalad, 1996: 239). Furthermore, there is little indication that employers are living up to expectations of return investment. Not only are employees being asked to take over responsibility for career development, studies show that employers are making less investment in training and skill development, in part because of fear that such investment will be lost through redundancy or exit from their firm (see Cappelli, 1995: 576–7). Contrary to the portfolio worker argument, management frequently tries to convert contractors with the most knowledge into permanent workers, precisely because of this (Ó Riain, 1998: 294, 298).

The impact on employees goes far wider than the '"casualties" expelled from core to periphery because they cannot add value' (Handy, 1995: 6–7). As Cappelli (1995: 589) notes, decreasing job security, job switching and flatter hierarchies, contrary to the flexible firm model, are not a core–periphery issue. Downsizing and delayering have become central to successive waves of corporate restructuring, as firms seek ways of cutting costs to improve financial performance and meet competitive pressures. There is a threefold impact on employees, especially in middle management: the removal or diminution of career ladders, greater insecurity, and intensification of work for the survivors of restructuring. This holds good across a number of countries, including the US (Cappelli, 1995); Australia (Bramble, Parry and O'Brien, 1996); New Zealand (Inkson, 1993), Britain (Institute of Management, 1995, 1996) and Japan (*Japan Labour Bulletin*, 1 May 1994), though there are variations, such as slightly increasing job tenure among women and the retention of internal labour markets and career structures in the public sector.

While a number of studies of job tenure have shown greater than expected stability (Burgess and Rees, 1996), and an increase in tenure for women (Teasdale, 2000: 17), it is important to distinguish between job stability and insecurity. As Burchell *et al.* (1999: 21) observe, their survey and others demonstrate that professional workers have gone from the most secure to the most insecure group between 1986 and 1997. Yet greater uncertainty in the external labour market influences employees to stick with their downsized organisations. As these are general trends, it is not possible for employees to 'act out their frustration with the break in the psychological contract' (Cappelli, 1995: 588). Given that overt resistance is small and corporate performance on balance improving, it would seem that organisations have not incurred any significant 'costs' from this broken bargain. This interpretation, however, would be mistaken. Both case studies (for example, Newell and Dopson, 1996) and surveys (see Cappelli, 1995: 586) show sharp declines in employee commitment and morale, particularly in downsized companies. Moreover, demotivation and lack of identification with company goals are directly related to feelings of job insecurity (Burchell et al., 1999: 53–7).

Among the consequences of such changes are increased defensive behaviours and attitudes, with emphasis put on securing the positional advantage of individuals and functional groups, and exacerbation of competitive struggles to 'impress' the corporate hierarchy between generational, gender and professional groups among managers (Collinson and Collinson, 1997; Hallier and James, 1997; Mulholland, 1998). In one sense, employees have got the message: individual ambition, not organisational loyalty, is what matters. As Sennett (1998) eloquently argues, whether this is a solid basis for the kind of trust relations that can sustain creativity and commitment in organisations is another matter.

Participation, control and commitment in the labour process

The labour process is at the heart of any transformative ambition of NEO perspectives given the emphasis on the move from command and control, low-trust relations and fragmented tasks, towards creative, high-commitment, participative work. Empowerment has been the dominant rhetoric for change at this level. Yet, analysis of survey data (Harley, 1998) and case studies (Potterfield, 1999; Hales, 2000) shows that little connection exists between managerial mechanisms of empowerment and employee autonomy. Neither employee 'voice' in decisions nor 'choice' in work arrangements show any sign of substantive improvement, nor organisational hierarchy any sign of diminution. What empowerment does mean in practice we shall explore at various points in the rest of the chapter.

However, we have seen the argument shift from particularistic claims, such as those about enhanced involvement, to ones based on a general, strategic combination of high performance work practices (for example, Osterman, 1994). At times it can sound as if management has reached the pot of gold at the end of the rainbow, with better soft (for example, trust) and hard (performance) outcomes. For example Huselid (1995: 635) argues that the combination of high-performance practices can improve knowledge, skills and motivation, and enhance retention of good employees, while reducing shirking and 'encouraging' non-performers to leave! However, in their favour, HPWS theorists, unlike pop management writers, are relatively hard-headed about what 'high road' practices consist of and have empirical tests for their presence. There is recognition that new work systems are not about general empowerment, but much more localised involvement, and are contingent in their positive and negative effects on workers (Applebaum and Berg, 2000). We saw in Chapter 11 that there is evidence for the existence of clusters of innovative practices in American and UK surveys.

Claims concerning HPWS should, therefore, be taken seriously, but they do remain open to question. Scepticism focuses on two main areas. First, there is alternative evidence for the persistence of traditional 'low-road' managerial practices. Evaluating a range of British evidence, Marchington and Wilkinson (1998) observe that a range of direct participation measures have been implemented in a half-hearted, limited and ad hoc manner rather than in a holistic and integrated way. This is confirmed in a number of surveys (Millward, 1994; Wood and Albanese, 1995; Edwards *et al.*, 1996). Many British firms continue to rely on labour flexibility and reorganisation of existing resources (Ackroyd and Proctor, 1998). Milkman (1998) reaches similar sceptical conclusions that most firms remain wedded to a low-trust, low-skill road from her own and other research on US workplaces. There is, of course, a variety of forms of research being considered here, which sometimes makes it difficult to make comparisons. Quantitative research that examines HPWS in its own terms is therefore of particular importance. Using large data sets from the British WERS and Australian AWIRS surveys, Harley, Scholarios and Ramsay (2000) examine the relationships between various high-commitment variables and employee outcomes such as job discretion and management relations, and the impact of such relationships on commitment, satisfaction and stress. Their findings give little comfort to HPWS theorists, as such management practices are only weakly related to outcomes such as greater discretion, and have limited links to any positive attitudinal data.

The second area of scepticism concerns the methodologies of many HPWS studies. While recognising that useful general pictures can be created on the spread of practices, it remains the case that the information gathered might also be superficial and therefore potentially misleading. The main drawback is the reliance on mail questionnaires or telephone surveys to managerial informants for data on practices and their impact. Such informants are being asked to report practices in which they have a role or status, and may slip into a normative or intentional mode (Guest, 1999a). Reliability is also problematic because in many case studies, 'high-road' companies are being identified as 'transformed' if a certain number of practices are present, telling little about the substance of any of the changes, or the extent to which they have really challenged traditional structures or correspond to employee experience (Biewener, 1997). Finally, in assessing performance outcomes, it is hard to disentangle the effects of direct participation from that of other variables and to determine the direction of causality (Marchington and Wilkinson, 1998). None of these factors are reasons for not doing survey work, and there have been attempts to overcome some of these limitations (for example, Guest, 1999b; Applebaum *et al.*, 2000). They do, however, point to the need for extreme caution about interpreting the results. It is helpful for such approaches to be complemented by qualitative, case study methods, and to disaggregate the component features of high commitment or performance. With this in mind, the rest of the section focuses on three areas: autonomy, control and surveillance; skills, tasks and rules; and the effort bargain and work intensification.

Autonomy, control and surveillance

Scepticism concerning specific claims in the area of enhanced autonomy is informed by negative experience of previous waves of reform. Evidence from varied contexts, including Australia and the UK (D. Smith, 1987; Dunford and McGraw, 1987), showed that quality circles, briefing groups and other two-way communication devices were wound down after they had achieved their initial aim as change catalysts, leaving behind a workforce cynical and hostile to any similar initiative in future. Such initiatives at Rover, Ford, Lucas, Reckitt and Colman and other plants engendered little enthusiasm from supervisors or workers, given the limited content and lack of genuine two-way communication. Programme failures partly reflect the difficulty of grafting high-trust practices onto low-trust cultures and environments.

In a broader sense, what happened with Japanisation and flexible working arguably had more to do with a reappropriation of the *language* of participation, job redesign and even humanisation. Wood rightly notes that though QWL practices signalled a move away from low-trust, low-knowledge systems, they do not signal a transition to any form of industrial democracy. This would be to demean the concept and to detach it from any conception of power relations. Whatever participation was created tended to exist within a management decision-making process concerning issues of cost, efficiency and product quality (Giordano, 1985: 31). Though Meyer refers to real powers invested in work groups at Saturn, this is qualified by the comment that these 'represent actions which have already been routinised to the point at which machines could execute the functions' (1986: 84).

With respect to TQM, recent evidence shows that while workers do respond positively to attempts to draw on their expertise and reductions in close supervision, existing hierarchies still constrain attempts to delegate power and expand involvement for employees (Dawson and Webb, 1989; McArdle *et al.*, 1994; Kerfoot and Knights, 1994; Wilkinson, Godfrey and Marchington, 1997) and even managers (Munro, 1994). Both TQM and BPR involve substantial continuity with Taylorist and bureaucratic traditions through the use of technology as an instrument of change and the separation of system design from execution (Grey and Mitev, 1995; Blair *et al.*, 1998; Knights and Willmott, 2000), and the accompanying techniques of work process measurement and codification tend to counter any emphasis on enhancing employee discretion (Adler and Borys, 1996: 61).

Patterns do not necessarily repeat, and it has been argued that current forms of teamworking represent a more fundamental change. For example, using her own case study, Batt (1999) argues that TQM had no discernible effects on performance, whereas self-managed teams significantly increased impact. There are a number of 'textbook' cases of self-managing teams, such as the two US sites investigated by Cutcher-Gershenfeld *et al.* (1994). They are not, however, representative. Critics have from the inception outlined a familiar range of criticisms that stress the relatively limited nature of delegation of authority (Wood, 1989; Boreham, 1992). Other case studies and small-scale surveys of the amount of autonomy across key decision rights in teams shows that the empowerment rhetoric is often empty and managerial prerogative largely intact, with, for example, only a small minority of teams electing their team leader (Fucini and Fucini, 1990; Turner and Auer, 1994; Murakami, 1997; Danford, 1997). Significantly, this judgement is supported by larger studies. A survey of over 5 000 European workplaces revealed that only 4 per cent corresponded to standard definitions of strong, high autonomy teams (Benders and Huigen, 1999). These limits on team autonomy have been confirmed in other studies. The latest WIRS survey showed that only 5 per cent of the 65 per cent of workplaces that had teams were self-managing based on appointment of team leader, task responsibility and co-decision over how work was done, (Cully *et al.*, 1998); while a cross-national survey in the autocomponents industry demonstrated that the role of operators in many decisions was minimal, whether in lean or traditional work environments (Delbridge, Lowe and Oliver, 2000).

It is important, however, that such evidence is about *limits* to, not absence of, change. One of the major sources of dissension between supporters and critics of a lean production model is the extent to which modern work systems can be efficient with extensive team autonomy, as well as more holistic jobs and long task cycles (see Sandberg, 1995). The critics prefer a more European socio-technical systems model, such as that practised at Volvo. For the supporters, the closure of the flagship Kalmar and Udevalla plants is proof that such arrangements are inimical to efficiency. Adler admits that at lean production plants such as NUMMI in the US, 'the emphasis on standardised methods meant that workers had no autonomy whatsoever in how they performed their tasks' (1995: 213–14). Lean production teams, inside and outside Japan, are about participation and continuous improvement, not autonomy. Beyond national differences, even within industries such as motors, there are significant differences between companies. Mueller's (1994b) comparison of Ford and GM showed that teamworking had been superimposed on Ford's tradition of controls over the shop floor, which meant that they had developed more hierarchical arrangements which allowed for little autonomy, while GM had moved more genuinely away from traditional supervisory structures. In addition, much of the research, even that of the harshest critics (for example, Robertson *et al.*, 1992; Danford, 1997), demonstrates that employees prefer working in teams and welcome the chance to exercise greater discretion, and are disappointed when promises of increased participation and responsibility prove empty (Milkman, 1997; Wilkinson, Godfrey and Marchington, 1997).

Other critics of teamwork tend to be those influenced by Foucauldian frameworks, who see the new arrangements as opportunities for management to extend control through electronic surveillance and peer pressure (Sewell and Wilkinson, 1992; Barker, 1993, 1999; Sewell, 1998). The argument rests on the assumption of extensive self-governance, which, in turn becomes self-policing. We have already critically evaluated such views in Chapter 8, but it is appropriate to add three further points here. First, if we take the overwhelming weight of evidence considered above about constraints on autonomy, it is difficult to see how such claims can be sustained, or at least generalised very far. Second, peer pressure in teams is not necessarily linked to self-governance. Small workplace groups in Japan have long had a strong element of compulsion, yet we know that teams have little or no autonomy. Itoh's (1984) account of Matsushita brings out a common theme that 'voluntary' activity in quality circles is founded on being forced to give suggestions: in this case, three a month ranked on a scale of one to nine. Loyalty is also cemented not only through peer group pressures, but also through cheap loans to buy houses and other financial inducements related to the process of creating company man (Briggs, 1987). Third, surveillance is not necessarily linked to teamwork, self-governing or otherwise. Ironically, the workplace sites where surveillance does appear to be most strongly entrenched are call centres, yet teams are largely formalistic in character given the individualistic nature of the tasks.

The discussion so far has been about various types of routine work. Surely the argument, promoted particularly by knowledge work theorists, that professional and technical labour is governed increasingly by collegial and horizontal forms of co-ordination, is nearer the mark? In some senses, the answer is yes. It is true that knowledge-intensive organisations, among others, require much higher levels of autonomy and trust from particular groups of employees. Whether this is new, increasing, or consistent is another matter. A tension between creativity and control has always been at the heart of expert labour, a fact often forgotten in recasting discussion through the language of 'knowledge flows' and 'stocks of knowledge (Hull, 2000). Current market and organisational conditions are, if anything, exacerbating those tensions. We have already noted earlier in the chapter the negative effects of increased bureaucratic and managerial control in the work of public-sector professionals.

Where quasi-markets are impacting on groups such as teachers, direct market pressures are increasingly constraining the time for creative experimentation among technical workers in the pharmaceutical industry (Randle, 1995). McKinlay's (2000) case study of knowledge management at Worldrug shows that the major corporate goal in the industry is to reduce the life cycle of molecule-to-market projects from 14 to eight years. This requires an attempt to facilitate the creative process as a learning resource *and* exerting greater control in development and documentation. Time is, in fact, at the heart of the management of knowledge work. As recent studies of software developers (Greenbaum, 1979; Beirne *et al.*, 1998; Ó Riain, 1998; Sharpe, 1998; Kraft, 1999) demonstrate, project teams, experimentation, trust and creativity are essential preconditions of the creative phase. But as projects move beyond the development phase, managerial control is reasserted through targets and deadlines. In addition, control is exercised through performance metrics, project monitoring procedures, packaged software products and automation. If all else fails, software production can be 'exported' to another part of the global production chain. The software technology parks of India not only provide cheaper expert labour, but a standardised software production pattern (Sharpe, 1998: 370). Taking these elements together, Ó Riain (1998: 289) refers to 'a system of time–space intensification' in the global workplace.

Skills, tasks and rules

Earlier we argued that, while there is an increasing proportion of knowledge-intensive work, most employment growth is in low-skill, service work. However, many of the most interesting developments are taking place in between these two ends of the spectrum, and if some of the more inflated claims are set aside, a reasonable degree of consensus can be established about trends in manufacturing and white collar work. While there is considerable continuity with past patterns, there are new elements, notably in utilising increased employee knowledgeability.

While skill variety or functional flexibility is necessary to exploit arrangements such as JIT and modular production, variations or new responsibilities such as self-maintenance may be small and it is more accurate to speak of an enlarged number of interchangeable tasks carried out by substitutable labour (Elger, 1990; Pollert, 1991; Delbridge, Turnbull and Wilkinson, 1992; Geary, 1995). This emphasis on continuity with the past is given partial endorsement by more realistic management writers, such as Peter Wickens, formerly of Nissan. He admits that 'lean production retains many Taylorist elements' (1992: 84), and notes that the work of line operators is still 95 per cent prescription and 5 per cent discretion. While multiskilling and multiactivity jobs are a significant change, it is much harder to argue that they constitute the end of Taylorism. Putting these together, adding on further deskilled tasks (NEDO, 1986), or extra ancillary duties such as inspection, does not normally make a substantial difference to their content. As a worker at Lucas Electrical commented: 'The jobs are just the same, you just do more of 'em' (quoted in Turnbull, 1987: 17). Studies by Shaiken *et al.* (1986) and Jones (1998) refute the flexible specialisation thesis by showing that, in a small minority of cases of firms using FMS and numerical control machinery, management did grant workers a central role in innovation and debugging. Within teamwork, the capacity to rotate workers across tasks is predicated on their prior fragmentation, rather than combining them into something more holistic (Findlay *et al.*, 2000).

Obviously, manufacturing environments vary considerably in their patterns of skill utilisation and not all practices are based on 'taking complexity out of jobs' (Biewener, 1997: 13). Among higher-level technical employees a detailed division of labour can be an obstacle to creativity and flexible response, and managerial strategies, for example in the computer industry, have ebbed and flowed between various ways of dividing and combing labour, supporting both deskilled and upskilled jobs (Greenbaum, 1998; Beirne *et al.*, 1998). An alternative way of addressing the problem is to fragment the work into new hierarchies of labour, as is shown by studies of computer programmers (Kraft and Dubnoff, 1986) and software developers (Sharpe, 1998).

There has been confusion about the discussion that increased flexibility means fewer rules. In fact it means the reduction of one type of rule, demarcation between tasks. Rules still govern organisational life. American surveys show that 'the vast majority of employees work in establishments with extensive formal procedures' (Adler and Borys, 1996: 61). Tasks themselves, at least in routine jobs, are still subject to high degrees of standardisation. What is more, the techniques for ensuring this – worksheets, performance codes and job evaluation – are classically Taylorist (Williams *et al.*, 1992a; Thompson *et al.*, 1995). Slaughter (1987) shows that teamworking at NUMMI involved specifying, measuring and timing every move in greater detail. Interviewed by the *Wall Street Journal* (18 May 1999), a plant manager admitted that standardisation poses problems for workers who thrive on developing their own personal style: 'To be true to these ideas, you're really supposed to dictate everything', from which knee to kneel on, to how far an arm should be moved to carry out a task. Nor is this confined to factories. Warehousing increasingly uses computer-based systems to produce 'engineered work standards' that can specify tasks and maintain 'real-time' control over workers (Wright and Lund, 1998). As we have noted earlier, the benchmarking systems underpinning TQM and BPR require a concern for standardised procedures and uniform, dependable practices (Wilkinson and Willmott, 1994; Tuckman, 1994).

Such instances would not surprise some supporters of lean production. In an influential *Harvard Business Review* article defending Taylorist time-and-motion discipline and bureaucratic structures as essential for efficiency and quality, Adler notes that '[NUMMI] is obsessive about standardised work procedures. It sees what one NUMMI manager has called "the intelligent interpretation of Taylor's time and motion studies" as the principal key to success' (1993: 103). Would it be justified, then, to describe lean production, teamwork and TQM as a form of 'superTaylorism'? (Slaughter, 1987). We do not think so. Whether Taylorism and bureaucracy are 'necessary' or not, Adler's description of the arrangements at NUMMI and other advanced manufacturing plants as *learning bureaucracies* is useful. Though standardisation and rules are central and workers' knowledge continues to be appropriated by management, the move away from narrow specialisation toward devolved responsibilities, problem solving and continuous improvement, however limited, marks a significant break from those parts of Taylorism based on a clear separation of conception and execution. More generally, the conception of skill needs rethinking in circumstances where the relation between a person and a machine is being replaced by the relation between a team and an integrated production system.

Research into changes in the commercial vehicle industry illustrates the point (Thompson *et al.*, 1995). Many of the *individual* tasks continue to be further deskilled under the impact of standardised procedures and uses of new technology. This is allowing management in the UK to dispense with expensive and 'inflexible' craft workers. But the *collective* labour of the group involves expanded cognitive abilities and extra-functional skills, for example in the form of greater need for problem-solving and decision-making powers, or qualities such as communication and co-operation. However, the situation with respect to 'new production concepts' is never static. Even in Germany, where 'participative rationalisation' was based on some degree of consensus between capital and labour and progressive forms of autonomy and job enlargement, commentators are noting a re-emergence of more traditional forms of Taylorism. Planning and optimisation are once gain the property of rationalisation experts inside and outside the plant, with 'forced standardisation' and short job cycle times (Springer, 1999; Schumann, 2000).

Manufacturing is not the only terrain on which change in the form and content of bureaucracy has been taking place. Despite the dubious association in NEO perspectives between the spread of the service sector and the rise of the knowledge economy, it is widely recognised that task rules have been spreading into the service sector. Evidence for the *bureaucratisation of service* is associated primarily with Ritzer's (1993) 'McDonaldisation of society' thesis. He marshals a considerable array of evidence to argue persuasively that fast food chains are the tip of an iceberg that has extended Weber's principles of rationalisation in the form of calculable, predictable, quantified processes to an increased range of retail, leisure and media services. This echoes earlier research such as Gabriel's (1988) study of a variety of catering jobs. He demonstrates that the industry has shifted from reliance on the social and technical skills of the workforce to an industrial model that rests on standardised organisation of tasks and a technologically determined work pace. While not all jobs in the sector are as routine as fast food, the standardisation of the service encounter is widespread, including in upmarket hotel chains (Jones, Nickson and Taylor, 1997). A prime reason for this is that many retail and service outlets believe that to maintain a competitive edge, a friendly, high-quality service encounter must be produced over and over again. Consistency of product is ensured by training, monitoring through report cards, and surveys on employee attitudes and behaviour through real and company-employed 'shoppers'. Service can also be bureaucratised by increased monitoring of employees, either through information technology such as the EPOS system in supermarkets or through 'control by customers' (Fuller and Smith, 1991).

The tendency identified by Fuller and Smith approximates to a further and more radical development in the bureaucratisation of service – *feeling rules*. This term draws on the work of Hochschild on flight attendants and other employees involved in emotional labour, briefly discussed in Chapter 10. From fast food and insurance work

Henry's table order of service   *TABLE 12.1*

1   Customer greeted at reception.
2   Customer accompanied to table and given menu and special cards.
3   Waitress asks for drinks/wine order.
    Glasses for wine put on to table.
4   Drinks/wine dispensed.
5   Waitress takes food order (and wine) acknowledging specials.
6   Waitress offers:
    – choice of jacket potatoes or chips
    – degree of cooking for steaks.
7   Waitress reads order back to customer.
8   Waitress takes order for pitta bread.
9   Glasses for wine and wine to table.
10 Starter cutlery to table.
11 Starters taken.
12 Appropriate starter accompaniments.
13 All starters cleared.
14 Main course served.
15 Appropriate main course accompaniments.
16 During main course:
    – 'Is everything alright?'
    – 'Would you like more wine/drinks?'
17 Main course cleared.
18 Customer invited to go to sweet display or given details.
19 Sweet and coffee orders taken.
20 Liqueurs offered with coffee.
21 Bill to customer – invite to pay at reception.
22 Customer pays.
23 'Goodnight' – acknowledge.

(Leidner, 1993), to supermarkets (Ogbonna and Wilkinson, 1988) and call centres (S. Taylor, 1998), service increasingly requires scripted interactions and standardised displays of feelings through smiles, forced niceness and other forms of verbal interplay and body posture. Putnam and Mumby note, 'When emotions are incorporated into organisations, they are treated as commodities' (1993: 43).

Though this tendency is not as pronounced in manufacturing, new normative controls have been introduced whereby management ask for and reward conformity to behavioural rules, particularly governing attitudes and action inside the team. An increased emphasis on selecting and training 'the appropriate worker' shows that a traditionally neglected part of Taylor's agenda is being renewed (Wood, 1989b: 11). To return to the service sector, it is also worth noting that there is a parallel to the attempt to tap into employees' tacit knowledge to improve competitiveness. However, interactive service work, such as call centres, 'draws on capacities and attributes located (often unconsciously) within each worker. These workers draw on limited technical knowledge during their work, but they do have to develop a consciousness of their social skills and awareness of when and how to deploy these' (Thompson, Warhurst, and Callaghan, 2000: 128).

The effort bargain and work intensification

NEO perspectives, and the lean production variant in particular, have promoted the idea of 'working smarter not harder', and this has received some support from extensive plant studies such as those carried out by Applebaum *et al.* (2000). However, this has to be set against a substantial body of research that identifies a rising tide of labour intensification associated with new forms of work organisation and management. This is certainly the message from a variety of critics of lean production, some associated with trade unions (Turnbull, 1988; Parker and Slaughter, 1988; Elger, 1991; Garrahan and Stewart, 1993; Fucini and Fucini, 1990). Intensification has been associated particularly with advanced work arrangements such as JIT, which rely on continual and controlled pressure (Turnbull, 1987: 13), internalising disciplinary pressure within the group (Sayer, 1986: 66), and conforming to new behavioural rules. In one of the most influential contributions, Slaughter gives a vivid account of 'management by stress' at NUMMI, where the goal is to stretch the system like a rubber band. Breakdowns and stoppages of the line are encouraged as this can indicate where weak points are and how they can be corrected, fine-tuned and further stressed. Workers who fall behind may have video cameras trained on them to 'help' in this process. TQM is also partly geared towards eliminating slack and waste in the system, and workers have reported that 'empowerment' involved considerably harder work (McArdle *et al.*, 1994). Flexibility itself has always involved employees bearing extra burdens. When *Business Week* (1983) discussed job flexibility, most of the examples were simply of enlarging jobs by adding extra duties, cutting the size of work teams, or eliminating breaks. Many employees feel that management 'abuse' the extra flexibility and efficiency gained through teamwork by cutting the size of teams or by applying extraordinary performance pressures (Springer, 1999; Findlay *et al.*, 2000).

Task restructuring is, however, not the only source of work intensification, nor are manufacturing workers the only recipient of its effects. Customer service representatives suffer intense stress and emotional exhaustion as they try to balance the twin pressures of demands for quality and quantity in high surveillance environments (P. Taylor and Bain, 1998; Batt, 1999; Deery *et al.*, 2000). Rising stress levels and work intensification as a result of re-engineered jobs, staff cuts, internal markets, and greater external assessment have also been reported by public sector professionals (Willmott, 1993b; Dent, 1993; Leverment *et al.*, 1998). Institute of Management (1995) surveys and qualitative case studies in the UK (Collinson and Collinson, 1997) provide confirmation of increased time pressures and workloads. Intense work demands may also arise from trying to take advantage of co-ordination of projects across time zones in increasingly globalised industries such as software production (Ó Riain, 1998). This is one example of the way in which at particular times in the production cycle, highly autonomous teams in more 'virtual' conditions can find themselves under external and self-imposed pressures to meet deadlines. It is also an indication of the way in which, contrary to futuristic visions of automation and leisure, the amount of time that employees of all kinds spend at work has been rising steadily; 'overwork' appears to be a basic condition of modern economic life (Schor, 1993).

As a leading British survey has noted, taken overall, the combined effects of work reorganisation and downsizing have led to 'an extraordinary intensification of work pressures' that, in turn, 'are strongly associated with tension in the home' (Burchell *et al.*, 1999: 60, 51). This should come as no surprise given that UK statistics show that 'people at both ends of the employment hierarchy work excessively long hours' (Perrons, 2000: 284). Contrary to the flexible firm model, a key part of burden of securing extra performance has fallen on the core workforce. This is confirmed in some US studies: 'By downsizing, the company is not just trimming the so-called "fat" from the organisation, it is making deep cuts in its regular workforce, and then bringing people back into the organisation under new employment arrangements' (Biewener, 1997: 18). Those that are left bear the burden of such changes in extra workload, often under the heading of 'empowerment'. This is damaging the basic effort bargain – employees' perception of a fair day's work for a fair day's pay – as well as the broader psychological contract (Burchell *et al.*, 1999: 31).

Conclusion

The message of this chapter has been that there remains a massive gap between the rhetorical claims for the end of bureaucracy and the realities of organisational life. Bureaucratic forms are certainly not confined to a few residual institutional niches such as the public sector (Heydebrand, 1989: 324), and where change has taken place it is often in the direction of *more* rules, hierarchy and centralisation. Yet we are under no illusions that the hype of the anti-bureaucratic revolution is going to go away. Bureaucracy has few friends, and some of its enemies have a vested interest in proclaiming the virtues of the new and the necessities of permanent revolution. We are referring here particularly to popular management discourse which, in order to sell the latest formula for firms, has continually proclaimed new forms of organisation in new turbulent environments, back at least to the 1950s (see Eccles and Nohria, 1992; Thompson and O'Connell Davidson, 1994).

Though it is sometimes difficult to distinguish pop management and academic writings on management and organisation (see Clarke and Clegg, 1998), it would be unfair to tar some of the academic critics with the same brush. Debates about flexibility and new production concepts are more serious and substantial. Nevertheless the evidence concerning contemporary developments in organisational design does not justify a new paradigm or general theory of work organisation. Nor does change at firm level warrant the term 'post-bureaucratic'. Even among serious scholars there is a blurring of the boundaries of description, prescription and prediction, sometimes for ostensibly good reasons. For example progressive management writers and social scientists, particularly in the US, want to promote positive messages about change and the benefits of 'high-road' strategies; and flexible specialisation theorists often advised left-of-centre administrations. Nevertheless, too much has been invested in flagship or exceptional cases and paradigm breaks, with the result that the examples and concepts cannot bear the conceptual and empirical weight placed upon them. Continuity in organisational structure, work and employment might not be as exciting a message, but it is often a more accurate one.

This is not to deny that very important changes, for example in the areas of decentralisation and disaggregation, are taking place, but their character is either misinterpreted or the significance exaggerated. With respect to the first tendency, horizontal, network-type relations can coexist with vertical hierarchies. Indeed, as Warhurst and Thompson argue, we are increasingly seeing the emergence of a 'dual structure which combines the search for innovation with enhanced financial and operational accountability' (1998: 17). While the subsequent tensions can be creative, as we have seen they can also involve substantial conflicts of interest between senior management and various groups of professional, clerical and routine employees.

With respect to the second, too many contributors to the debate have taken bureaucracy to be a static ideal type, instead of a living, changing and diverse set of practices. This is often as true of defenders of the abstract and unchanging benefits of hierarchy such as Elliot Jacques (1990) as of the paradigm breakers. We need to restore some of the features of past debates, discussed in Chapter 3, where researchers identified some of the variations in bureaucratic form and content, as organisations engaged with new environments and influences. A good modern example of this is Considine's (1996) account of how a new organisational form, market bureaucracy, has developed in the public sector to deal with changing conditions of risk and taste. Yet it still coexists and competes with other administrative regimes such as procedural, corporate and network bureaucracies.

Whatever the constraints to change, while new organisational arrangements may not live up to the rhetoric of management and management theorists, they have no essence; the form and content remain open to influence by the major organisational actors. Such factors are one of the driving forces behind the continued organisational diversity, allied to traditional factors such as product and labour markets, and institutional context. This brings us back to our main theme of the balance of continuity and change.

Debates about the shifting conceptions of competitive advantage and corporate restructuring have become polarised: Fordism or flexibility, mass production or flexible specialisation. There is little sense of the contrasting experiences of sectors or firms, of the importance of administrative heritages in shaping contemporary strategic choices and structural options (McKinlay, 1999: 149).

We will return in the final part of the book to issues of the theoretical understanding of bureaucracy and rationality.

13 Corporations and Culture: Reinventing Organisation Man?

Culture, as we have seen throughout the book, is a high-profile issue in managerial thought and practice. Nor is this confined to the workplace. Commentators (Sayer and Ray, 1999) refer to a more general 'cultural turn' away from a concern with the economy and structure. It was not always like this. In 1956, William H. Whyte wrote the influential *The Organisation Man*, a vituperative attack on the 'social ethic' shaping the values of those in the middle ranks of private and public corporations. This oddly-named ethic was a collectivist nightmare that morally legitimated the powers of society against the individual. Among those blamed were Mayo and his obsessive concern for belongingness and group adjustment. Whyte's solution was for the individual to fight a rearguard battle against the organisation, with the aid of some useful advice such as 'how to cheat at personality tests'. As Peters and Waterman note (1982: 105), the association with grey conformity made corporate culture a taboo topic. Culture was only acceptable as an issue when it was associated with the necessity for managers to be sensitive towards national diversities in the 'collective programming of the mind' (Hofstede, 1980).

But by the end of the 1980s, organisation man was back in fashion. Though some continue to doubt the idea of people 'belonging' to the company (Lessem, 1985), IBM's 'corporate fascists' with their historic emphasis on conformity and commitment could get their overdue kudos as well as smile politely on the way to the bank (Pascale and Athos, 1982: 186). Despite all the hymns of praise to corporations, the credit for reviving the issue largely goes to American academics and management consultants, notably the two mentioned above, plus Ouchi (1981) and Deal and Kennedy (1988) – all except Ouchi connected to the McKinsey consultancy company. However, it was filtered, as we began to discuss in Chapter 11, through a reading of the Japanese experience that located their success in the existence of strong cultures and 'turned-on workforces'. In other words, cross-national competitive advantage was seen to be linked to cultural factors (Dahler-Larsen, 1994).

Corporate culture was put on the agenda. This can be defined as the way in which management mobilise combinations of values, language, rituals and myths, and is seen as the key factor in unlocking the commitment and enthusiasm of employees. To the extent that it can make people feel that they are working for something worthwhile, it is projected as part of the solution to the historic search for meaning or the holy grail of commitment in the study of organisations. For work humanisation theorists such as Herzberg and Maslow, that search was connected to the provision of intrinsically satisfying tasks through job redesign. The ground shifted to the psychosocial benefits from identification with the company and its superordinate goals. There may be characteristics that make companies successful, as in the famous lists of Peters and Waterman or Goldsmith and Clutterbuck – autonomy, zero-basing, productivity through people – but corporate culture is the core and the glue that binds the increasingly diverse activities together. When the project is defined as developing a non-deified, non-religious 'spiritualism', it is to be expected that advocacy often takes on a distinctly evangelical tone, with managers and workers exhorted to love the company. Such acts of will can break the 'attitudinal barriers' that hold firms back (Goldsmith and Clutterbuck, 1985: 5).

More conventionally, there is an emphasis on culture strategies, with senior management taking the process of value-shaping seriously. But perhaps strategy is the wrong word. For as we discussed in Chapter 11, corporate culture is part of a proclaimed shift from the hard S's of strategy, systems and their quantifiable objectives, to the soft S's of style and shared values. So, has this been another fad of pop-management or a doomed attempt to transplant culture-specific Japanese systems? Certainly, corporate culture is less prominent now as other panaceas such as business process re-engineering have taken centre stage. But it has by no means been entirely displaced. The management of culture is recognised as one of the central features of HRM, given that employment relationships are seen as moving away from bureaucratic hierarchy and low-trust industrial relations towards securing real *commitment* (Guest, 1987; Legge, 1989, 1995). Culture has become the main ingredient of broader change programmes, as well as providing normative and behavioural scripts for more specific initiatives in areas such as customer care and TQM (du Gay, 1996; Reed, 1996; Thompson and Findlay, 1999). Similarly, the battle to introduce private sector styles and methods into public services and the widespread adoption of mission statements indicate that the identification and transmission of values remains on the organisational agenda. Finally, as we saw in Chapter 6, corporate culture is also advocated as the solution to the problem of integrating global companies that are too diverse and complex to be run by rules from the centre.

Nor should we underestimate the shift in management theory, and to a lesser extent practices, that has been going on. Changing people's emotions or what they think has mostly been off-limits to the dominant strands in OB. It is summed up in Herzberg's answer to a question about the problems of employees at a seminar: 'Don't worry about their attitudes or personality, you can't change them' (Carr Mill Consultants, 1973: 7). Similarly, when commenting on March and Simon's views, Perrow argued that, 'to change individual behaviour, you do not have to change individuals' (1973: 147). Under systems of bureaucratic or unobtrusive control, what had to be changed was the structure of communication, rules or selection, along with provision of the appropriate rewards and sanctions. As Perrow said, somewhat tongue in cheek, 'after manipulating these [structural] variables, sit back and wait for two or three months for them to take hold' (1973: 27).

Managerial and professional employees were subject to moulding and socialisation processes, though how seriously or effectively is open to question. But for all the unitarist rhetoric about goals, routine manual and clerical workers were not really expected to identify with the company. It was more a case of 'if you've got them by the balls, their hearts and minds will follow'. *Normative regulation* changes this: 'It is only with the advent of the "excellence" literature that management is urged to become directly involved in determining what employees should think, believe or value' (Willmott, 1992: 72). How this is supposed to work can be seen in the statement from a manager at a famous high-tech US company: 'Power plays don't work. You can't make 'em do anything. They have to want to. So you have to work through the culture. The idea is to educate people without knowing it. Have the religion and not know how they got it' (quoted in Kunda, 1992: 5).

Product and perspective: the corporate culture merchants

'In culture there is strength' is the ominous-sounding new law of business life proclaimed by Deal and Kennedy (1988: 19). What such writers are actually talking about is a specific product: 'a culture devised by management and transmitted, marketed, sold or imposed on the rest of the organisation' (Linstead and Grafton Small, 1992: 332). But what is it that gives such strength? One of the most recurrent themes is *attention to employees*: ownership in a shared vision rather than changes in work or working conditions. The notion of 'pillars' occurs again, this time in creating a committed workforce. The British personnel writers Martin and Nichols (1987) name three: a sense of belonging to the organisation, a sense of excitement in the job, and confidence in management. In general terms 'the notion of employee commitment is built on the internalisation of the norms and values of the organisation' (Kelly and Brannick, 1987: 19).

Interestingly there is explicit recognition of the benefits of *emotional* engagement: affectiveness more than effectiveness. As 'man is quite strikingly irrational' (Peters and Waterman, 1982: 86), employees can be appealed to through symbolism and the ceremonies and awards of 'hoopla'. In the new corporations it is the role of those at the top to act as symbolic rather than rational managers; scriptwriters and directors of the daily drama of company life (Deal and Kennedy, 1988: 142). By symbolising the organisation internally and externally, heroes become a crucial component of the leadership process. For Deal and Kennedy, John Wayne in pinstripes is an appropriate role model. Leadership is invested with a large burden in cultural management, reflecting in part research that has identified the *founder's* influence in shaping values (Schein, 1985). Indeed, for Schein, culture and leadership are simply two sides of the same coin: cultures are created by leaders, and a key function of leadership is the creation and occasionally destruction of cultures. A notable example is Anita Roddick's pivotal role in the Body Shop organisation. The underlying message of the publicity is 'Work for the Body Shop and you're on a permanent high', and that high is sustained by training schools, roadshows and videos with the founder to the forefront. According to one trainer, 'Staff get desperate for the fix of Anita' (*The Times*, 28 September 1991).

In addition, the focus of such organisations is on disseminating values through stories, myths and legends about the company, its products and heroes, backed up by rites and rituals which reinforce cultural identification. The latter also helpfully facilitates the goal of a large dose of Skinnerian positive reinforcement, where *everyone* is made to feel a winner. Management in general is expected to use non-authoritarian styles to create a climate of trust. Some writers make a nod in the direction of feminism by referring to nurturing qualities and androgynous managers (Naisbitt and Aburdene, 1985: 207). Others are content to report the aim of shifting from an aggressive, confrontational and macho style at companies such as Ford and Rank Xerox (Giles and Starkey, 1987).

Though the package of corporate culture is new, some of the ideas are not. Pop management writers seldom discuss theoretical sources, but Peters and Waterman acknowledge that 'The stream that today's researchers are tapping is an old one started in the late 1930s by Elton Mayo and Chester Barnard' (1982: 5). Human relations influences can most clearly be seen in the focus on managing the informal organisation, workers as irrational creatures of sentiment, and social needs to belong, whereas the shadow of Barnard looms over conceptions of the organisation as a co-operative social system and on the role of the executive in articulating and disseminating values and superordinate goals. This is, however, given a harder edge. The predisposition to consensus and identity sharing gives way to a more conscious harnessing of needs and promotion of cultural mechanisms to secure common values.

But there may also be deeper, less direct roots: 'it is in the various writings of Durkheim that a conceptual framework for discussions of corporate culture may be found' (Ray, 1986: 290). Ouchi is one of the few corporate culture writers to accept the need for a macro-sociological analysis that breaks from the interpersonal level so favoured by many organisational writers. His article with Johnson (1978) draws directly on a Durkheimean framework which sees a modern division of labour involving a loss of moral community and mutual obligation, with a decline in the role of the family, Church and other institutions. Durkheim believed that the necessary function of social control and cohesion could be played by professions and occupational groups, a theme echoed later by Mayo. Ouchi and Johnson argue that Japanese work organisations have provided the necessary primary relations. Ray (1986) extends the analysis by pointing out that the corporation is expected to take on the functions embodied in Durkheim's realm of the sacred. Hence the emphasis both on faith in the firm and binding rites and rituals. Most corporate culture books draw on such assumptions. Deal and Kennedy do so explicitly: 'corporations may be the last institutions in America that can effectively take on the role of shaping values' (1988: 16). In this sense it is not entirely true that for the first wave of managerial writers, it was as if the idea of organisational culture had 'sprung from nowhere' (Martin Parker, 1999). But Parker is right in his broader point that writings on *corporate* culture had conveniently 'forgotten' the rich history of work on the informal side of organisations in Weber and Taylor, let alone human relations; as well as other contributions such as industrial psychologists on 'organisational climate'.

Such complexities got in the way of the dumbed-down version of culture presented in that first wave. The *evidence* for the dual claim that strong cultures exist, and that they constitute the primary reason for better or even excellent performance, is also somewhat dubious. Though more companies sought to join the 'culture club' (Thompson and Findlay, 1999: 163), many of the same names tended to appear across the range of US books: IBM, Proctor and Gamble, Hewlett Packard, McDonald's, Delta Airlines. So do some of the 'baddies', notably Harold Geneen and ITT who seemed to get it in the neck consistently. In the UK the roll call has included Marks and Spencer, Plessey, Sainsbury, Burton and Schweppes. As for the information about the companies, the opening sentence of Deal and Kennedy begins, 'S. C. Allyn, a retired chairman of the board, likes to tell a story' (1988: 3). With the partial exception of Ouchi, stories, vignettes and anecdotes about the dedication and commitment of corporate heroes and managers, or the devotion of ordinary employees, constitute a large proportion of the evidence presented.

Of course they are not the only sources. Across the books, it is possible to find interviews with top management; testing the culture by conversing with the receptionist; profiles based on company documents; use of formal statements of objectives and philosophy and of biographies and speeches; and questionnaires filled in by chairmen asked to rank their firm according to 'excellence' criteria. Occasionally, as in Goldsmith and Clutterbuck (1985), there is reference to interviewing people on the shop floor, but there is no sign of the results.

There is considerable positive reference to slogans such as Delta airline's 'the Delta family feeling', IBM's 'IBM means service' and 'respect for the individual', or GE's 'Progress is our most important product'. Apparently *everyone* knows and believes in Tandem Computer's slogans such as 'It's so nice, it's so nice, we do it twice' (Deal and Kennedy, 1988: 9). McDonald's has an extraordinary quality assurance and level of care for its people (Peters and Waterman, 1982, xix–xx). The slogans of privatised utilities in the UK, such as BT's 'We answer to you', and the numerous statements of supermarkets and other companies about customer care could be put in a similar category (Legge, 1995). These kinds of statement about 'qualitative beliefs' are then linked to a second set of quantitative information detailing the superior financial and economic performance of the given companies over 10 or 20 years. Strong cultures are the assumed link, but there is no direct evidence, or real discussion of other market or environmental variables. A rare statement of this kind comes from Deal and Kennedy: 'we estimate that a company can gain as much as one or two hours of productive work per employee per day' (1988: 15). No criterion or proof is ever given.

Mini 'cases' are also developed in the popular literature, for example of Hewlett Packard's 'HP Way'. Open-plan offices, open managerial styles, extensive formal and informal communication, and team and workforce meetings are just some of the mechanisms to generate the high commitment that is the key to quality and innovation. Something like the 'HP Way' is a classic rhetorical device: a communicative symbol whose goal is primarily to mobilise organisational commitment and project community of interest. Stories about the heroic exploits of founders Bill and Dave reinforce a collective identity and organisational goals. Peters and Waterman found it impossible not to become fans. A more serious academic account of a similar organisation is given in Kunda's (1992) *Engineering Culture*. The mostly male engineers at 'Tech' operate in what appears to be an informal, egalitarian, work and play hard environment, sustained by a commitment to job security and technical innovation. Slogans and metaphors permeate working life – 'do what's right', 'he who proposes does', 'having fun', 'tech is a bottom-up company', 'we are like a football team' – and there is a mini-industry of meetings, rituals and workshops that reproduce company culture. Unlike managerialist accounts, Kunda actually demonstrates how culture permeates the everyday language and perceptions of employees, though, as we shall see later, the range and impact is uneven.

Much of the debate about corporate culture, particularly with reference to companies such as HP and 'Tech', is notable for the fact that the descriptions and debate frequently overlap with HRM. What is the link?

HRM and the management of culture

In Chapter 4 we discussed the move from personnel to human resource management (HRM) practices. There are two key connections to culture. If the managerial role is seen as shifting towards the symbolic sphere, HR managers are the central resource and functional gatekeeper of these processes. As Michael Peretz of Apple Computers in Europe put it:

> The role of the Human Resource Manager, the 'priest' in whose hands the company's 'Ten Commandments' lie, is to ensure the survival of its soul. Far from merely providing a functional service determining salary rises and fringe benefits, the human resource management function forms the very heart of a company, and its manager exists to confirm the company's particular values and try and apply them in practice. (Schneider and Barsoux, 1997: 128)

Second, if employees are the key strategic resource, then commitment is the key to unlocking the untapped human capital. In turn, that requires conscious development of the value base of companies, such as mission statements, and new and expanded means of communicating them; as well as the battery of participative measures such as team working and team briefing to generate a high trust culture associated with 'soft' versions of HRM (Storey, 1989; Guest, 1989). The imputed strategic character of HRM thus facilitates the development of strong cultures by integrating policies of recruitment, reward and retention. Across how much territory this integration can take place is debatable. For example, those advocating culturalist perspectives influenced by the work of Hofstede and others (see Chapter 6) argue that HRM must be made meaningful across cultures. Multinational companies 'must discover and pick their way through these national differences' in norms associated with recruitment, training, performance and so on (Schneider and Barsoux, 1997: 135).

Notwithstanding this qualification, in many national contexts, culture has become a shorthand for a new ideology and rules of the game accompanying a shift from collectivism to individualism in the management of the employment relationship (Sisson, 1990). Collective bargaining and unions are bad words in the new world of *unmediated* relations between the organisation and the individual. An example of such practices is that of direct communication with the workforce. Winning companies have a culture that enables 'a passion for disclosure of information' (Goldsmith and Clutterbuck, 1985: 73). Hence the rash of briefings, videos, house magazines, open days and consultative forums. Trade unions are not given much of a part in strong-culture companies. At best they are considered a recalcitrant junior member, and at worst an unnecessary obstacle. The HRM advocates Kelly and Brannick deliver a blunt warning: 'The ability to organise will be curtailed, if not openly challenged by management, and the role of the trade union as an element of the communication network will lose its significance' (1987: 20). In fact such employment practices already constitute a significant part of strategies by a growing number of companies to make themselves union-free by removing or substituting for any employee desire for collective representation (Basset, 1989). Any independent, 'sub-cultural' source of alternative values, trade unions, profession or occupational groups is therefore an obstacle to the development of a unitary, cohesive culture.

Certainly there are prominent companies that fit this picture, notably the major US computer firms such as IBM (Dickson *et al.*, 1988) and Hewlett Packard. They carefully construct their employment practices to individualise employees' relations with the company. Prominent features of this approach are personal wage 'negotiation' and performance evaluation, immediate grievance accessibility to management, and an internal labour market that provides for mobility and job security. But the typicality of such practices in foreign transplants or greenfield sites is in doubt. We know from case studies (for example, Martinez Lucio and Weston, 1992; Marks *et al.*, 1997) and wider survey evidence such as the Workplace Employment Relations Survey (Millward *et al.*,

1992, 2000) that HRM practices, in the UK at least, exist extensively in unionised workplaces. Raising such questions about the character and extent of HRM and strong cultures is part of a much wider critical evaluation, to which we now turn.

Critics and questions

Questioning the novelty

The extent of strong-culture companies is exaggerated. These are trends within some, but not all organisations. Many companies, small and large, will carry on with 'weak cultures' and would not recognise a culture strategy if it landed on the MD's desk. However, it does happen, though how new or novel current initiatives are is open to question. As Jacques (1996) has demonstrated, corporate capital has always been concerned to 'manufacture the employee', for example in the 1920s through welfare programmes, company unions and workplace social communities (see also R. Edwards, 1979). Companies such as Cadbury and Marks and Spencer in the UK do have corporate cultures of a highly distinctive nature, but there have always been strong-culture companies. Such organisations have often used management styles based on 'sophisticated paternalism' which combine high levels of employment security and social benefits with careful screening of recruits, direct communication and in-house training, wrapped up in a 'philosophy' of respect for the individual (Miller, 1989). And all this before any thought of corporate cultures and HRM!

Accounts by historians and sociologists show that we can trace paternalism back to older patterns. Joyce (1980) shows that from the mid-nineteenth century many Victorian firms, particularly those influenced by religious non-conformism, developed a social paternalism embedded in the interwoven fabric of work and community life. Though often associated with small firms, paternalism survived and changed form as size and scale increased, though family ownership still played a key role. At Lee's Tapestry Works on Merseyside between the wars, considerable efforts were made to develop 'a sense of belonging and a feeling of loyalty to the firm' (Johnson and Moore, 1986). There was an 'exceptional' family atmosphere, company saving schemes, a holiday camp and partnership certificates issued to employees or 'members' as they were called from 1931. Glucksman's study of factories in the inter-war period gives an account of the Peak Frean biscuit factory in South London. Though Peak Frean was not characteristic of the majority of firms, it prided itself on its welfare provision, had 'a large sports ground and games room, dances and social events were organised, and the house journal, The Biscuit Box, was distributed to all workers' (1990: 96). Both the companies were non-union. But this is not an inherent characteristic of such firms. Ackers and Black's (1991) overview and case studies in the development of paternalist capitalism demonstrate that major players – Pilkington, Rowntree, Cadbury – came to accept a form of unionism and collective bargaining in their own paternalistic image.

Even after the war many large workplaces generated employee identification based partly on stable employment, as well as being a focal point in and for local communities. A typical example is English Electric in Liverpool (Thompson, 1994). Worker identification with the firm was enhanced by almost all promotions coming from the shop floor, thus creating a strong internal labour market, though top management tended to be imported. The company owned houses and had its own hospital and dentist on site. There was an extensive company social life, including an annual sports day which catered for 10–12 000 children and a flower show, a variety of clubs, dances and shows. These were all organised on a voluntary basis by a combination of management, staff and workers. The firm, though paternalistic, was not anti-union and officially recognised a number of appropriate trade unions. Though managers did not always like it, they worked within an industrial settlement in which a system of bureaucratic controls over work and employment relationships empowered shop-floor union organisation.

In the late 1960s, the company was taken over by GEC, their main competitor. They began to run down production and transfer products out of the place almost immediately. A new layer of senior management was brought in with very different attitudes. Within a short time the whole social side of the factory apparatus was wound down. What happened at English Electric was indicative of the breakdown of the old culture paradigm under the impact of the first major wave of post-war restructuring of capital in the mid to late 1960s. Under the impact of this concentration of capital, firm mobility, mergers and acquisitions and the decline of company towns and occupational communities, old forms of identification tended to break down. British management responded in a variety of ways. There were many measures designed to tighten controls on the wage–effort bargain, for example the replacement of piecework by measured day work. Others changed the pattern of accommodation and attempted to further institutionalise the factory-level union organisation. A smaller minority tried progressive work redesign schemes such as work humanisation, but 'Anyone who talked about employee "loyalty" and "all pulling together for the good of the firm" was regarded as a nostalgic crank who did not understand modern industry' (Ackers and Black, 1991: 30).

Paternalistic cultures became a minority phenomenon, though they continued to exist in different forms, often in smaller firms. One such traditional paternalist company of 300 workers is described in a case study by Wray (1994). 'Ourfirm' built on local traditions of company welfare provision and a dependent, quiescent labour supply. Its management articulated a paternalist philosophy, high pay and profit sharing, and links with the local community. Even here, steady growth led to difficulties in maintaining 'the personal touch' that underpinned paternalist relations. Middle management and demands for a union on the shop floor have grown in tandem. Despite the breakdown of old patterns, both case studies project continuities between paternalism and the rise of a new unitarism in the form of corporate culture and HRM, so that 'the future may look more like the past than the present' (Ackers and Black, 1991: 55). But how reliable are the contemporary claims in the wider literature?

Questioning the evidence

Given the reliance of the product on stories, myths and other forms of 'organisation talk', what executives and managers say in words or on paper tends to be taken as proof for the existence of string and distinctive cultures. There is little critical reflection on this. Martin and Nichols are at least honest in admitting that:

> we cannot be sure of the extent to which the companies we studied were *actually* successful in creating that commitment or whether that commitment

contributed to their success. All we can say is that the managers in question *reported* that their efforts to create commitment met with a positive response and produced a significant improvement. (Martin and Nichols, 1987: ix, our emphasis)

In addition, they present some useful, if brief and largely propagandising, cases. As for most of the literature, much of the time even corporate slogans are taken as virtually incontrovertible evidence of culture and effects, because they are taken to be synonymous with superordinate goals.

With this kind of evidence, so much of it resting on bland management statements, unattributed quotes and plain assertion, it is tempting to dismiss the whole enterprise as a fairy tale. Drucker, the best-known management writer, pulled no punches in describing *In Search of Excellence* as 'a book for juveniles' and a fad that would not last a year (quoted in Silver, 1987: 106). The lack of rigour in research methodology has been a persistent theme of critics (Hammond and Barham, 1987: 8–14; Guest, 1992). Samples of companies, for example those used by Peters and Waterman, were selected and treated in a cavalier and uncontrolled manner, dropping some from the original list and using evidence from others not in the sample at all (Silver, 1987: 113). The tenuous link between cultures, excellence and performance turned out to be highly fragile. Companies were included whose performance was far from excellent, and a significant number subsequently ran into difficulties as *Business Week* (1983) reported under a headline of 'oops!' An important book on IBM (Delamarter, 1988) – by a senior economist who had worked in the US Justice Department on the anti-trust case against IBM – pointed out that the company built up its dominance by undercutting its competitors in vulnerable market sectors and paying for it through excess profits from customers who had little choice. Commenting on *In Search of Excellence*, the author argues that:

> According to the authors, IBM has benefited from a strong central philosophy that was originally laid down by its charismatic leaders, the Watsons. They present a simple, appealing model for IBM's success – excellence in management. But this view is dead wrong. IBM's success comes from the power of monopoly. (Delamarter, 1988: xvii)

Follow-ups such as Peters and Austin's *A Passion for Excellence* (1985) have failed to quell the doubts, particularly as the same author has apparently decided (Peters, 1987) that there are now no excellent companies in the US. The treatment of theory and evidence is similarly suspect, with eclectic and uncritical use of parts that suit particular arguments, even if they are not compatible with the general perspective. The use of Skinner in *In Search of Excellence* is a case in point. A further remarkable aspect is the failure to learn from their main inspiration, the human relations tradition. There is no sign of recognition of the central flaw that arose from the Hawthorne Studies, that intervention based on 'attention to employees' produces independent effects on performance. At least some of the hoopla and contrived events could produce a stream of Hawthorne effects of a short-lived and superficial nature.

Of course expectations of high-quality evidence from popular management texts would be somewhat naive. What is more disappointing is that a number of academic theorists appear to making similar mistakes in confusing what managers and companies say they are doing with the more complex and messy reality on the ground. This is largely a by-product of the influence of post-structuralism in organisation theory (see Part III). While accounts of corporate discourses are often fascinating for what they reveal about managerial values and intentions, a theoretical approach that makes no distinction between these 'representations' and reality runs the risk of exaggerating their coherence and influence. In reviewing these accounts (for example, Rose, 1990), Thompson and Findlay (1999: 172–4) found that there was a large gap between strong claims and weak evidence. The stated goals of senior management and other power holders, whether in documents or through interviews, is frequently the only evidence. Evidence of how discourses are operationalised outside the text, or how intent is turned into concrete influence over behaviour and attitudes, is hard to find, particularly as detailed primary data on employees is largely absent.

Finally, is there anything more conclusive from the more varied studies of culture change programmes, particularly those associated with HRM? Legge (1995) attempts to evaluate that research and finds it inconclusive, owing to a range of methodological and conceptual problems. There has been little research on the explicit links between culture and commitment, particularly of an in-depth and longitudinal kind. Even more importantly, both culture and HRM tend to have been treated as generic headings for a variety of interrelated changes, from which it is impossible to disentangle the key variables. While it is not surprising that managers may have absorbed the message, given their centrality as focal points for the articulation and dissemination of values, there is less evidence that this has worked its way fully through to the shop and office floor. Or, if it has, the effects are on manifested behaviour rather than internalised values. This is a crucial distinction to which we will be returning later.

Questioning the concepts

The previous discussion illustrates the need for a complex understanding of culture. Too often the corporate culture debate has working with impoverished conceptions of culture which mistake style for substance. A complex and realistic analysis would avoid treating culture as a catch-all for the soft aspects of management (Hammond and Barham, 1987: 10), or as a reified and monolithic phenomena. There is some recognition of *sub-cultures* on functional or gender lines, but not enough, and anyway these can be *managed* to produce a healthy tension within the corporate framework (Deal and Kennedy, 1988: 152–3). Martin (1992) identifies this perspective as an *integrationist* one, viewing organisations as mono-cultural and bound by homogeneity of purpose. In contrast, a proper recognition of sub-cultural cleavages and conflicts of interests would reflect a *differentiation* perspective.

It is precisely the assumption that culture can be managed that is called into question by a range of critics that Willmott dubs 'culture purists'. Such critics take their cue from the influential paper by Smircich (1983), which argued that it is better to regard culture as something an organisation is, rather than something an organisation *has*. It is a process not a checklist, and something continually being creatively remade by all participants, rather than fixed (Wright, 1994). As a result, in the context of a variety of often contradictory influences, cultural development is just not as amenable to direction or use as an integrative device as believed (Martin and Siehl, 1983: 53). Nor can it be simply fitted into overall strategic goals. As Ackroyd and Crowdy (1990) illustrate in their study of the highly-distinctive informal interactions of slaughtermen, many of the meanings attached to work behaviour are embedded in particular class or regional culture. Their very externality adds to the lack of feasibility of managerial influence. Such instances emphasise the variety of identities that employees bring to or affirm in the workplace. Martin (1992) dubs this a *fragmentation* perspective, drawing on post-modern ideas of shifting contexts and meanings.

Whether it can be managed or not, it remains the case that the complexity of organisational cultures has been neglected and employees treated as an 'empty space' within which values can be inserted. There is, 'a tendency in the organisational culture literature to treat workplace culture as independent of the labour process' (Alvesson, 1988: 3). Without a recognition that the labour process is fractured by a variety of social cleavages, organisational analysis will continue to neglect the dimensions of conflict, power and even consent. For example in Chapter 10 we looked at the way that workplace cultures were gendered and acted as barriers to the success of equal opportunity policies (Cockburn, 1991). Using such a framework, we can avoid nonsensical ideas that strong cultures produce conflict-free organisations (Kelly and Brannick, 1987: 1). After all, despite IBM's worldwide strategy for a union-free environment and sophisticated industrial relations system, it still has to contend with an international organisation of IBM workers opposed to its policies (Howard: 1985). Even where IBM has been successful in securing employee identification with its individualistic culture, as in the West of Scotland, those same workers had collectivist attitudes towards general social issues and supported trade unionism, even if they felt a union was unnecessary in their particular circumstances (Dickson *et al.*, 1988). This illustrates a further important point, that any analysis should show what is unique about organisational as opposed to national, regional, family or other cultures; something that is largely absent from the management literature (Hofstede, 1986). On that basis it would be possible to examine how the societal and organisational cultures interact.

Given the numerous flaws it is tempting to dismiss most writing on corporate cultures as simply the emperor's new clothes. In *Management Today*, Thackray (1986) argues that the American manager needs a language that goes beyond particular functions. Buzzwords therefore come and go and culture has entered on the scene as Western pride has been shaken by Japan and old certainties have been eroded by economic and occupational shifts. New ideas are required to motivate the troops and a 'gaggle of culture consultants', as well as human resource and personnel teams and others whose empires expand with the literature, are feeding at the honey pot. It appeals to managers because it proclaims that their activity and skills can produce the results, as Mayo once did in relation to early human relations. Silver (1987: 123) also argues that corporate culture is the latest attempt by management consultants to 'wrap each new technique in packaging slightly different from that of its predecessors'. If it is a fad and one that vastly overestimates its capacity as a change mechanism, then the whole trend is destined to go the same way as others: 'Culture appears to have been reduced to the status of yet another concept, which, like many before it, has reached the decline stage of its "life cycle"' (Ogbonna, 1992a: 6).

But all this is bending the stick back too far. Willmott (1993a) criticises the 'purist' position for moving from a judgement that the corporate culture literature is so deficient that it is unworthy of serious attention. Meek is an example, when she argues that if culture is embedded in social interaction, 'it can *only* be described and interpreted' (1988: 293, our emphasis). This may be underselling its potential as a control mechanism. There may not be a definitive authentic culture in organisations, but there clearly are 'official' ones which power holders can at least attempt to impose on others. Having questioned the largely managerial evidence about companies and culture, the rest of the chapter looks at alternative and more critical explanations of what is happening inside organisations.

Culture: commitment or control?

Corporate culture writers like to present their prescriptions as an *alternative* to control (Naisbitt and Aburdene, 1985: 53; Kelly and Brannick, 1987: 8). But the perspective is riddled with glaring contradictions. We are told that 'in institutions in which culture is so dominant, the highest levels of autonomy occur' (Peters and Waterman, 1982: 105); while Deal and Kennedy assure us that companies with strong cultures can tolerate differences (1982: 153) and that outlaws and heretics are encouraged in companies such as IBM (1982: 50–1). At the same time the latter authors tell us that managers do not tolerate deviance from company values and standards (1982: 14), and that middle managers as well as blue-collar workers should be told exactly what to do (1982: 78). The books are so anxious to convince us that these are anti-authoritarian, 'no-boss' set-ups, that we are expected to accept that calling workers cast members (Disney) or crew members (McDonald's) in itself banishes hierarchy and class divisions. In Silver's (1987) brilliant demolition of the excellence genre, he reminds us of the reality of McDonald's 'people-orientation': 'Behind the hoopla and razzle-dazzle of competitive games and prizes lies the dull monotony of speed-up, deskilled Taylorised work – at McFactory. And McFactory's fuel is cheap labour – part-time, teenage, minimum wage, non-union workers' (1987: 110).

Reconceptualising the process in terms of new forms of management control is not entirely foreign to the more academic of the culture literature, which openly describes the process as a form of organisational control (Ouchi and Johnson, 1978; Martin and Siehl, 1983). Nor is it inconsistent with many of the statements from the more popular works, such as, 'Strong culture companies go into the trouble of spelling out, often in copious detail, the routine behavioural rituals they expect from their employees' (Deal and Kennedy, 1988: 15). Cultural or *normative* control is essentially concerned with the development of an appropriate social order that provides the basis for desired behaviour (Kelly and Brannick, 1987: 8). Indeed, in order to let people loose to be 'autonomous' they have to be programmed centrally first, with a central role played by more intensive selection and training (Weick, 1987). Tandem Corporation's exhaustive selection process is likened to an 'inquisition' by Deal and Kennedy (1988: 12). One of the offshoots is that those who are chosen are likely to have a much more positive image of themselves and the company. It is not surprising, given such developments, that some management writers have begun to worry that corporate culture produces conformist thinking inimical to creative organisational development (Weick, 1987; Coopey and Hartley, 1991).

Cultural controls also operate through expanding the sphere of social activities in the organisation. Communicating company goals can take place outside the workplace. Part of GM's Hydra-matic Division's QWL program includes week-long 'Family Awareness Training' sessions at education centres (Mike Parker, 1985: 17–19). This does not refer to the employee's nearest and dearest, but to the notion of company as family. Once outside the normal environment and in circumstances where everyone is individualised, psychological exercises and techniques are used to break down old identities. GM questionnaires rate those with limited scores on loyalty to the company as having a low quality of work life. Breaking down the boundaries between economic and social activities is something that is often characteristic of Japanese corporations' methods of using the peer group as a means of integrating both shop floor and managerial employees. Broad (1987: 11) notes that 'Social gatherings organised by team leaders and foremen are regularly held amongst all male employees'. The link to Japan is also made in Goldsmith and Clutterbuck's jolly account of management japes at Asda's social events: 'The schoolboy activities in these companies [are] strongly reminiscent of Japanese companies, whose evening carousals have traditionally been part of the cementing of the managerial team' (1985: 82). Many of the other books are similarly full of accounts of cultural extravaganzas that function to develop a sense of community through a form of *compulsory sociability*.

How should we understand the significance of this trend? Some radical theorists go further than simply analysing culture in terms of control by arguing that corporate culture represents an alternative and dominant mode. The key theoretical influence is the work of Ray (1986), who utilises a Durkheimean framework discussed earlier. She points out that bureaucratic control, though an attempt to integrate employees positively through internal labour markets and the reward system, is still control by incentive. This may generate contradictions around the struggles of the workforce to establish work rules and job guarantees. In addition, 'while bureaucratic control may prompt individuals to act as if the company is a source of meaning and commitment, that is an entirely different matter from seriously believing it. In other words control remains externalised rather than internalised' (1986: 292–3). Even humanistic controls deriving from the various branches of the human relations tradition do not possess the real tools to generate sentiment or emotion. The difference is that *normative* control works less through formal structures and mechanisms than through informal processes, value systems and management of the emotions.

Ray's analysis is complemented by like-minded empirical studies such as Alvesson's (1988, 1991) account of a medium-sized computer consultancy firm in Sweden. The founders established an open and charismatic managerial style capable of generating strong emotional ties among the consultants employed. A particular problem for the management was that the work was by its very nature variable and flexible, and therefore could not be controlled by conventional means. It was also largely carried out at the client's workplace, potentially undermining the consultant's sense of identity with his or her own firm. This is compensated for by a large number of social and leisure-time activities with the emphasis on fun, body contact, informality and personnel support; which in turn build social and emotional ties and a sense of company as community. Some of these are consciously linked to presentations of corporate performance to enhance favourable perceptions.

Further support comes from research on the retailing sector. Employees have to be subjected to engineering the soul so that they can automatically deliver the quality service required by the new, more enterprising customer (du Gay, 1991a). Ogbonna and Wilkinson (1988) and Ogbonna (1992b) detail that engineering in a supermarket where management have initiated a substantially expanded staff training and development programme that ranges from the recruitment of 'like-minded' people to a 'smile campaign'. Supervisors claim that 'We are able to detect when a check-out operator is not smiling or even when she is putting on a false smile . . . we call her into a room and have a chat with her' (Ogbonna, 1992b: 85).

Not only does this perspective counterpoise control through conventional rules and regulations to changing the way that employees think and feel, the latter is seen as 'considerably extending' the scope and penetration of managerial domination (Willmott, 1993a: 522). Willmott makes a forceful case that in combining normative rules with the erosion of alternative sources of identity:

> Corporate culturism extends the terrain of instrumentally rational action by developing monocultures in which conditions for the development of value-rational action, where individuals struggle to assess the meaning and worth of a range of competing value-standpoints, are systematically eroded. (Willmott, 1993: 3)

Monocultures are designed to avoid contamination by rival ends or values and, to the extent that they succeed, become the vehicle of nascent totalitarianism, accompanied by classic 1984-style doublethink of 'respect for the individual' in organisations where employees are seduced into giving up any autonomy. This analysis is wrapped up in the kind of Foucauldian terminology discussed in Chapter 9, where corporate culture programmes exert self-disciplining powers that trap people within the promise of secure identities and personal development. Similar Foucauldian themes of cultural 'seduction' and discursive colonisation of self are pursued in Casey's US case study of the Hephaestus corporation. Put more simply, through team practices and family rhetoric, the company produces 'designer employees', who buy into the secure identity offered by the simulated community.

The limits to cultural influence

In criticising culture purists, Willmott persuasively argued that we should take corporate culture seriously. But perhaps he has taken its significance and effectiveness *too* seriously. In arguing that the 'governance of the employee's soul' (1993a: 517) is a key ideological element of a new global regime of flexible accumulation, he is in danger of over-extending the concept and maintaining a separation from traditional forms of control associated with Fordism, Taylorism and bureaucracy. Corporate culture should not be isolated as *the* defining feature of contemporary forms of control. While Willmott rightly says that management is trying to extend the sphere of instrumental action to rules governing emotions and the affective sphere, traditional controls, as we have seen in recent chapters, remain important in a number of ways.

Even within those organisations that do implement cultural controls, they are intended to complement not eliminate the need for bureaucratic, technical or other systems. In the supermarkets described earlier, employees are subject to the surveillance of TV cameras in the manager's office looking for deviations from the desired behaviour, as well as controls through new technology that can record productivity such as the EPOS (electronic point of sale) system. In Kunda's excellent ethnography of 'Tech' we are given examples of both normative and technical controls. With reference to the former, managers evaluate subordinates on personality criteria: 'Jim has a people problem. He is gruff and angry with people and says exactly what is on his mind. . . . I want him to control himself. Next year he is going to be evaluated on that.

I'm watching him. He knows it' (manager quoted in Kunda, 1992: 187). But employees are also aware that managers check up commitment by looking at who is logged onto the computer after hours. Though he sees a shift in focus from bureaucratic to normative controls at Tech, Kunda rightly acknowledges that systems of cultural control, 'build on, rather than replace one another' (1992: 220).

This continuity can be ignored or misunderstood by making culture into an overarching concept. For example, Wright talks of the 'culture' of Fordism, which 'is converted from a mission statement into detailed practices, dividing each task into tiny details and specifying how each should be done' (1994: 2). In contrast, the culture of flexible organisations relies on empowered, self-disciplined workers. Culture in this sense, however, should not be seen as *everything*, but rather as managerial attempts to mobilise values and emotions to support corporate goals. An expanded array of often-traditional rules and sanctions is then used to enforce the new moral order and extend levels of identification between employee and organisation. Academic confusion about how far to extend the use of culture reflects similar trends among managers. In their studies of the Scottish spirits industry, Marks *et al.* (1997) noted the deployment of two rhetorics: the first signified culture as a vision or set of shared values intended to guide the change process; the latter as a much more diffuse way of describing 'the way that we do things round here'. The problem with the latter usage is that almost any change in practices can then be subsumed under the 'culture' label. The other thing worth noting is that the practice-led usage can exist independently of any explicit attempt to change values.

Additionally, we only have to return to previous examples of IBM and Hewlett Packard to see that their respective 'Ways' are sustained by careful structuring of the employment relationship around individualistic means and ends. Like the studies referred to earlier, Harrison and Marchington (1992) also examine the growth of customer care programmes in retailing, but argue that 'The preoccupation with culture may blind us to the enduring importance of promotion structures, remuneration incentives, and working hours in shaping employees' acceptance of managerial initiatives' (1992: 18).

What about the second element, the effectiveness of corporate culture as social engineering? We should keep in mind that Ray (1986), the inspiration for many extravagant claims about culture as the ultimate control, distinguished between intent and outcome, and was very circumspect about the extent to which it would work outside the US and independently of other managerial techniques. Beyond the ranks of post-structuralism, there is a large degree of scepticism in case studies and surveys on the limits to culture, or at least to the extent to which commitment has been internalised (Guest, 1992; Ogbonna, 1992b; Scott, 1994; O'Donnell, 1996; McKinlay and Taylor, 1996; Wilkinson, Godfrey and Marchington, 1997; B. Jones, 1997). Take the British Airway's manager quoted in Höpfl (1992: 10): 'We know it's hype – they know its hype. It's okay. It's reassuring. It makes you feel good. But do I believe in it – well that's a totally different question.' Employees may be conceptualised as empty vessels in which to locate corporate values, but that is not how it works in practice.

Employees may comply with demands for adherence to the language of mission statements, appearance and demeanour in the sales process, or participation in quality circles *without* internalising the values and therefore generating the 'real' commitment. Though studies record a diversity and unevenness of responses, the prominent themes are distancing behaviour, cynicism, deep acting, and resigned behavioural compliance rather than value internalisation. Employees may go through the motions of cultural conformity while remaining sceptical that, for example, supposedly distinctive 'Ways' are any different from the methods used by rival international hotel chains (Thompson *et al.*, 1993). The dramaturgical theme is continued through employees developing a variety of means of disengagement or distancing from corporate values through cynicism, parody and irony. Advocates such as trainers for Body Shop may claim that cynicism cannot survive the participative culture, but that is belied by interviews with staff: 'They want you to feel part of a team, but you're not. They want you to feel important when you're just a shop assistant. If you want to stay there, you do better as a Roddick clone' (quoted in *The Times*, 28 September 1991). Considerable evidence of cynicism and distancing was also observed by Kunda. Many employees used an alternative language to describe the culture – 'the song and dance', 'pissing contests', 'Tech strokes', 'burnout', 'doing rah-rah-stuff' – or rival slogans – 'I'd rather be dead than excellent', 'There is unlimited opportunity at Tech, for inflicting and receiving pain'.

All this is not to imply that attempts at culture change have no effect or are viewed in an unambiguously hostile manner. As Rosenthal *et al.*'s (1997) supermarket case study shows, systematic exposure to change discourses may impact on attitudes, particularly when employees identify with some of the aims of quality, or customer care programmes. However, the authors make clear that this is a long way from total acceptance or control. What comes over in this and many other studies is that, far from seduction, employees are highly aware of the complex aims and outcomes of managerial action. They may be aware that they are acting as a form of coping strategy (Ogbonna and Wilkinson, 1988; S. Taylor, 1998), or staff may use the rhetoric to try and bring management into line with what they have been told about the way that customers and employees should be treated (Rosenthal *et al.*, 1997; Callaghan and Thompson, 2002 forthcoming). These examples take us back to the idea that culture cannot be treated as the property of management. If it is embedded in social interaction, employees produce as well as absorb meanings, transforming culture in the process (Meek, 1988).

As these studies and earlier ones such as Kunda (1992) illustrate, much of this ambivalence is directed towards maintaining a private self, or showing that they understood the real politics and status processes underneath the official surface; a process that Collinson (1994) refers to as 'resistance through distance'. Employee awareness of the nature of the dominant culture will vary, for example, by position in the organisational hierarchy. As our discussions of gender demonstrated in Chapter 10, women managers could 'see' the informal masculinity of values and practices, whereas men largely took them for granted.

Even more controversially, we can ask whether the predominance of behavioural compliance without commitment actually matters. Supporters may point to a time lag whereby behavioural precedes attitudinal change (Schein, 1985). But in the light of serious research, this seems optimistic. Are we back full circle to Perrow's view that to change individual behaviour, you do not have to change individuals? Some critics would appear to agree. Drawing on their research customer care programmes, Harrison and Marchington argue that, 'management does not actually have to achieve value change among the workforce to successfully implement customer care' (1992: 18). The conventional armoury of management control and remuneration measures, or indeed the coercive effects of fear of job loss, may be sufficient. While there is evidence that initiatives focusing on changing behaviour have been far more successful than those on transforming values (Hope and Hendry, 1995; Marks *et al.*, 1997), there is no need to question the distinctiveness of 'hearts and minds' programmes. Our disagreement with theorists such as Willmott is not about whether some firms try to develop monocultures, but with the extent to which they can ever be successful. Willmott (1993a: 538–40) argues that the very process of role-playing and cynical disengagement entraps employees in the insidious controls of the culture and confirms the appearance of tolerance and openness.

Such interpretations risk underestimating both the fragility of corporate culture and the creative appropriation, modification and resistance to such programmes. Corporate culture cannot eliminate the powerful informal group norms that are the bedrock of organisational life. Work groups are just one of a number of sources of competing claims on commitment and loyalty. Attempts to prioritise an aggressive corporate identity may disrupt the delicate balance between these specific and super-ordinate allegiances. This is particularly the case in the public sector where traditions of professional autonomy and an ethic of service are increasingly at odds with a new managerialism bent on central direction and enforcement of the bottom line (Anthony, 1990; Harrison and Marchington, 1992). Increasingly bitter conflict between general managers and staff in the NHS, universities and the BBC is indicative of the tensions arising from attempts by senior managers to impose a 'strong culture' and a web of rules to enforce it. In any organisational context, but particularly where competing professional, commercial and personal goals are present, employees will face difficult value conflicts and behavioural choices.

Resistance may also be generated by the selective or partial nature of participation in the culture and its attendant reward systems. Such programmes are aimed often only at the 'core' workforce, as Kunda's case study demonstrates. Class 2 workers, mainly clerical and temporary, received inferior benefits and were treated as non-persons, 'just not techies' as one manager put it (1992: 209). Unsurprisingly they only gave a minimal self back. This example reinforces the point that culture is sustained by material, institutional supports. Senior management may be taking greater risks with such initiatives because employees are being asked to invest more of their public and private selves, thereby raising the possibility of enhanced resentment when the promises of large-scale culture change programmes prove difficult to deliver, as at British Airways (Höpfl, Smith and Spencer, 1992). This is but one of the trends in corporate development which are working against the stability of cultures of company loyalty and commitment. Contradictions are raised by the clash between concerns for individual development in organisations and the continuous pressure for rationalisation of resources and for more effort. In addition, what the management pundits are calling 'downsizing' – the cutting out of middle layers of the company discussed in Chapters 11 and 12 – is hurting most the 'organisation men, conditioned to look to large corporations as the fountainhead of security' (Thackray, 1988: 80). Hope and Hendry (1995) argue that in this context research into imposed culture-change programmes does not demonstrate they have been effective as change mechanisms or control devices.

Loyalty, obedience and goal identification are not easy to sustain when companies are scrutinising their policy manuals to remove implied promises of job security or even termination benefits:

> How the hell can you preach this flexibility, this personal and business develop-
> ment at the same time as you are getting rid? As someone said to me yesterday,

an operator, 'Why am I in here now doing the best I can getting this product out when tomorrow morning you are going to give me a brown envelope?' I had no answer. (Manager quoted in Watson, 1994: 209)

In essence this is no different to the tensions identified between 'hard' and 'soft' versions of HRM, where workers are expected to be both dependable and disposable (Legge, 1989). Ackers and Black raise the question of whether it is possible that new forms of corporate paternalism can ever reproduce the depth of social relationships fostered by firms embedded in local communities and stable markets: 'The impersonal, footloose multinational, with its mobile, diffuse, high-turnover workforce, and even more transient management team, appears ill-equipped to fashion an emotional nexus with its workforce' (1991: 56). This may be exaggerating the difficulty, but current trends at the very least expose the highly contingent nature of any culture–commitment link.

Conclusion

In this chapter we have tried to set out both the significance and the limits to attempts to reinvent 'organisation man'. Given the theoretical faults and practical constraints, it is sometimes difficult to see why the product has been so influential. Undoubtedly, it fitted the mood of a certain period. Silver (1987) adds a wider ideological and political dimension to the explanation. He describes the excellence genre as 'Reaganism writ small', a glorification of entrepreneuralism and the capacity of America to stand tall again. It is certainly true that a clear subtext of Peters and Waterman and Deal and Kennedy is that the discovery of excellent companies in the West means that all good things do not come from Japan. It is also the case that the ideological content of most of the books often shows a sharp break with the old 'liberal' consensus. Deal and Kennedy say that the society suffers from too much uncertainty about values and that managers should have the conviction to set standards and not undermine them by being humane (1988: 22, 56, 76). In Britain, similar links existed between the rise of corporate culture and a broader ideology celebrating the market and the spirit of enterprise (du Gay, 1991b).

But it is not simply a sign of a particular time. Cultural differences between organisations do matter, and culture strategies have become deeply embedded in the corporate consciousness. The contemporary management of meaning has become inextricably linked with culture as the language of change, though, perversely, survival is likely to be aided by the previously-discussed confusion of culture as changing values and practices (Thompson and Findlay, 1999: 183). Within this complexity, managers will be able to find benchmarks for progress or a rationale for 'another go' at changing employee attitudes. Indeed, there is evidence that managers are the group who invest most in change programmes and have most to lose if they go wrong (Watson, 1994; Hope and Hendry, 1995; Webb, 1996; Mulholland, 1998).

Moreover, for all the absurdities of content and presentation, the corporate-culture literature has touched on genuine issues that, as we argued at the start of this chapter, were partly neglected in the past. These need looking at in a context free from the merchandising process. The tragedy is that we have a lot to learn from studying organisational cultures (Frost *et al.*, 1985; Pheysey, 1993), particularly as culture mediates all change processes. Creating a culture resonant with overall goals is relevant to *any* organisation, whether it be a trade union, voluntary group or producer co-operative. Indeed it is more important in such consensual groupings. Co-operatives, for example, can degenerate organisationally because they fail to develop adequate mechanisms for transmitting the original ideals from founders to new members and sustaining them through shared experiences.

Examples of this kind indicate that there may be more promising settings for the development of strong cultures. This may even be the case in a business context. As Biggart (1989) demonstrates, direct selling organisations (DSO) such as Amway and Tupperware are unique in their combination of commercial imperative and non-bureaucratic mode of operation, though the kind of corporate culture involved has recently been described as a mirror of the Communist conformism officially feared in the US (Horwell, 1999). As we saw in Chapter 1, DSOs work through informal social networks, affective bonds between members and a degree of operational autonomy: 'Even the most upbeat corporate culture of traditional American business, however, pales beside the daily round of direct sales distributors. Relations in most DSOs are not just friendly, but highly personal. Distributors become involved in each other's private lives and often describe themselves as "family"' (Biggart, 1989: 4).

Such an emphasis by no means rules out studying specifically corporate cultures as management strategies. But this has to be within the plurality of cultures and interest groups in the workplace. Luckily, as well as the case studies referred to in this chapter such as Kunda, there have always been rich sources to draw on such as Salaman's (1986) study of the occupational culture of the London Fire Brigade; accounts of making-out on the shop floor (Nichols and Beynon: 1977; Burawoy: 1979; Delbridge, Lowe and Oliver, 2000); and gender at work (Willis: 1977; Pollert: 1981; Westwood, 1984; Kondo, 1990). Organisation 'man' may be back on the agenda, but the cultural agenda cannot only be set in the boardroom.

Part II

Part II

14 Understanding Organisational Behaviour: Issues and Agendas

The purpose of this chapter is to explore how psychology approaches issues of organisational behaviour: what is the mainstream agenda, what are its limitations and what alternative approaches might be useful? We will not survey industrial/organisational psychology as a whole (for a good account see Hollway, 1991); rather we will use historical and contemporary examples to explore what kind of knowledge organisational psychology produces. Our argument is that while there is much of value, mainstream approaches tend to offer a fragmented, partial account of the human condition, and moreover, one that is frequently distorted by a managerial agenda.

In a review of the 'discipline' of organisational psychology as a professional practice, Blackler describes it as follows:

> The subject 'organisational psychology' can legitimately be understood to include all aspects of behaviour in organisations that may be studied from a psychological point of view. By common usage, however, the term is normally used to refer to applied social psychological studies of organisation. Important areas of practical and theoretical concern have included motivation, attitudes and job satisfaction, job and organisation design, interpersonal and group behaviour, leadership studies, approaches to participation and industrial democracy, conflict, decision-making, and the planning of change. (Blackler, 1982:203)

This is by no means exhaustive of the work undertaken by organisational psychologists. Topics could be added from those more usually associated with occupational psychology such as selection, placement and counselling. If we ask the question, 'what is the study of OB about?', then as a subject it initially establishes a territory via which we can generate a list of topics as above. But such a list is not very helpful in understanding the distinctive character of the discipline. To do this, it is useful to begin from where it actually comes from.

Technologies of regulation?

Historically the subject has manifested a problem-centred approach dealing with the major perceived difficulties of organisational society at the time:

> Industrial Psychology thus covers a wide field. It deals with the human, as contrasted with the mechanical and economic aspects of labour. Its chief aim is to reduce needless effort and irritation and to increase interest and attention throughout the workers in industry. (C. S. Myers, 1926:11)

In a similar vein, Hollway (1991: 4–5) cites Alec Roger in the 1950s as giving a neat definition of the paradigm for occupational/industrial psychology as 'Fitting the man to the job and the job to the man', (FMJ/FJM). The issue here is one of the quality and integrity of the psychological practice and knowledge applied in the area, and the FMJ/FJM paradigm gives us a client-centred definition which from the start has given a technical orientation to work in the area. Such a definition relies heavily on the notion of a value-neutral, objective science that is independent of the power relations in the organisations and societies within which it is practised. The reality is, of course, that both power and knowledge are not singular, unitary or completely objective. Even a person believing he or she is a value-free carrier of fully objective scientific knowledge has to utilise and exercise that knowledge in the real world, and the one thing we do know is that power relations in organisations are seldom, if ever, completely equitable.

Without such awareness, new practical and theoretical knowledges from the repertoire of organisational behaviour can function as *technologies of regulation*, used to control and discipline employees. Such practices were inherent in the origins and early development of the sub-discipline of *industrial psychology*. In the first two decades of this century, employers drew on the variety of psychological theories on offer (Bendix, 1956: 200–1). For example, *behaviourism*'s orientation towards 'human engineering' was a particularly useful source of advice for managers seeking to manipulate environmental stimuli in the form of penalties and incentives, in order to produce appropriate worker responses. At the same time, rival schools such as *instinct psychology* could suggest means of employers meeting 'innate' needs such as self-expression, which were being distorted by evil Bolsheviks and union organisers. Perhaps most practically, *vocational psychology* could provide a battery of tests and measurements for applications to selection and placement. It was in this latter sphere that industrial psychology really took off in the US, boosted by the extensive use of tests for intelligence and other factors during the war.

Psychology in industry had in fact begun in the area of advertising, but it soon shifted from manipulation of consumers to workers. Most concepts and techniques were extremely primitive, but psychologists such as Munsterberg promoted the idea that they could be applied to the 'labour problem'. The accumulation of knowledge about individual differences provided the basis for a varied apparatus of testing and measurement techniques geared to vocational counselling, placement testing and job analysis, with suggested correlations between factors such as intelligence, personality and potential work performance. Munsterberg summed up the general aim as finding 'those personalities which by their mental qualities are especially fit for a particular kind of economic work' (quoted in Baritz, 1960: 3). There was a widespread tendency to claim bogus relationships between national or racial characteristics and suitability for jobs (Kamin: 1979). In Britain, organisational psychology was relatively isolated from its American cousin. The National Institute of Industrial Psychology, founded under the leadership of Charles Myers in 1921, took a painstaking and broader interest in the related issues of training, rest, monotony and fatigue at work (see quote above and Hollway, 1991, for an analytic account of this venture). But even here consultancy pressures dictated programmes of vocational guidance, selection and testing.

It was these kinds of development that led Baritz (1960) to develop his famous analysis of psychologists and other industrial social scientists as *servants of power*. The science of behaviour was seen as giving management 'a slick new approach to its problems of control' (1960: 209). Included in the 'bag of schemes' were attitude surveys, selection devices, motivation studies, counselling and role-playing. Events in the 1930s Hawthorne studies, discussed in Chapter 4, were a particularly powerful confirmation of the social engineering role that could be played by social scientists, in this case under the framework of human relations theory. Those kinds of superficial and manipulatory practice are still being recycled today. For example, the reaction to objective problems that employees face in their work, recognised in the modern stress research literature, has led to the astonishingly innovative introduction of employee counselling programmes! Baritz's great insight was to recognise that the service provided by social scientists to industry meant that 'control need no longer be imposed. It can be encouraged to come from within.' Workers could be manipulated to internalise the very ideologies and practices that ensured their domination.

A perfect modern example of this is the role played by industrial psychologists in some of the new human resource management techniques. The American writer Grenier (1988) worked as part of a team hired by Johnson and Johnson, the medical products company, to create the required conditions for the setting up of a new plant on a greenfield site in New Mexico. This involved many of the elements discussed in Chapters 11 and 12: quality circles and semi-autonomous work teams, status and symbolic harmonisation of conditions, extensive socialisation into a corporate culture facilitated by psychological testing at the selection and hiring stage. None of this of course is necessarily negative or manipulative, even the secret tape recordings of work team meetings to help identify success in fostering group identity and dynamics. But the hidden agenda of the whole project was a 'union avoidance' campaign, and this came to light when some of the workforce began an organising drive. The social psychologists became active and central participants in the struggle inside the heads of employees. All the supposedly innocent information collected became a means of screening workers and their attitudes. Team meetings in particular played an important role in identifying pro-union workers, and Grenier was asked to develop an index through which to rank workers in their degree of support. Grenier later publicly revealed this process and himself became subject to surveillance and intimidation.

Not all social scientists of course have been concerned with such manipulatory practices, and there has been a considerable amount of useful work done on employee satisfaction. The modern equivalents of Baritz's servants of power are not necessarily 'on the payroll', but still have a tendency to accept managerial norms as the parameters of their activities. In the same way as the newspaper owner does not have to threaten journalists to toe the editorial line, mainstream behavioural scientists generally internalise controls, and largely unacknowledged self-censorship becomes the order of the day. In other words, the institutional relationship between the disciplines and their client groups remains a crucial problem.

Later, in developing out of industrial and human relations psychology in the 1950s and 1960s, organisational psychology brought to the study of work organisations an emphasis on descriptive and experimental research incorporated from social psychology. This was allied to the concern with applied psychology that had given impetus to industrial psychology in the early part of the century, and the human relations tradition discussed in earlier chapters. Later inputs to organisational psychology from areas such as socio-technical systems theory and operations research have further cemented the relationship of the subject with the interests of power groups in organisations.

FIGURE 14.1 'Psychological warfare'

Source: CAITS (1986) *Flexibility, Who Needs It?*, London, p. 34.

That the practitioners of organisational psychology and organisation theory are mainly located in such institutions as business schools, rather than in industry or psychology departments, also reinforces the conception of the subject as a discipline in its own right, with its own client groups and professional concerns. At the same time this distances them enough from their clients and subject matter to enable them to concentrate more on the theoretical understanding of organisations than was the case with the more strictly application-led industrial psychology. In turn, this enabled retention of much of the humanistic theoretical orientation derived from social psychology. Theoretical ideals of this nature do not, however, often survive exposure to the needs of the main client group. As with industrial psychology before it, this results in the subject becoming chiefly directed towards the practical needs of management. A humanistic perspective fully cognisant of the effects of organisational work on the interests and identities of employees is unlikely to promote harmonious relations with clients whose major tasks include the deployment and control of an organisation's 'human resources'. Nor would an organisational psychology that grounded its theory and practice in an understanding of the politics of production be likely to be in a position to fully give itself over to the demands of these clients. The upshot of all this is that the explanations, instruments and techniques developed from mainstream theories often function to sustain and implement a culture of domination in the workplace. Organisational psychology, though paradoxically informed by humanistic concerns, has both a role as an agent and a vested interest in mobilising the consent of organisational members.

Topics and texts: subjects and subjectivities

Given the above discussion, it is not surprising that the areas from social psychology that have been enlisted into organisational psychology's project of understanding human behaviour are often limited to those having functional utility. As we indicated above, texts tend to be presented under chapters or headings focusing on topics such as learning, perception and motivation, reflecting psychological explanations of individual personality; and topics such as leadership and group processes, which incorporate social-psychological explanations of interpersonal dynamics. However, topics in the sphere of aggression, affiliation and prejudice, which within social psychology are assumed to deal with influential determinants of human behaviour, have not been assimilated routinely into organisational psychology.

This is an odd separation, given that such factors may be expected to have at least some bearing on practices within organisations. The difference is largely that the latter set reflects areas of subjective experience which, although of importance to individuals and groups in organisations, are not of direct relevance to the production process, except insofar as they might interfere with it. Rather, the factors are treated as external to what is considered necessary and appropriate behaviour at work. Similarly, issues of discrimination, though a structural feature of organisational life, have long been marginalised and not constituted as significant objects of study. Aggression has been addressed obliquely in OB through the issue of organisational conflict, but the perspective used examined conflict, for example, as a problem to be resolved or avoided rather than to be understood as a possible consequence of inequalities of power and resources.

Since the first edition of this text, researchers have begun to look at issues of anti-social and aggressive behaviour in organisations in more detail (see Giacolone and Greenberg, 1997). They are producing evidence to show that factors such as downsizing, role diversity and increased reliance on part-timers are increasing the levels of emotional disturbance and aggression in the workplace (though the aggression is often indirect, passive and verbal, with the glaring exception of 'going postal'). Likewise there have been moves of late to address issues such as discrimination in general OB texts, but this has generally been under headings such as *managing diversity* (see Chapter 10 and Weightman, 1999: 225–6). This, along with the issues of workplace bullying and 'dealing with problem people', is probably being addressed in the context of managing organisational liability to litigation on the basis of equal opportunities and employment legislation.

The competing mainstream explanations of psychological and social processes are treated in OB texts almost as if they were discrete accounts of human development and activity. Take an area such as learning (see Chapter 16) which must be integral to any account of psychological development; the mechanisms and processes of apparently mutually exclusive perspectives such as the cognitive and behaviourist models are categorised through the assumptions about human nature that underlie them. Thus we get the 'models of man' approach to OB, where theories are assessed through the assumptions they make and the implications of those assumptions for social behaviour. There is nothing intrinsically wrong with this as a method of analysis, but it does tend to reinforce the exclusivity of differing approaches, which are in fact no more than varying conceptions of the basic processes by which we all develop and negotiate our changing identities.

We will return to the general limitations of the mainstream agenda in Part III. In its content, that agenda can be thought of as a journey through the processes by which individuals become social participants who perceive, learn and are motivated beings with individual personalities. Our intention here is to treat the mechanisms and processes identified by competing approaches as inputs to, rather than exclusive accounts of, this developmental process. This is because the fragmented treatment of subjectivity in OB means that the implied journey through an individual's development into a social being never explicitly takes place.

Defining the 'subjective factor'

While there is undoubted value in a topic-based approach, it tends, as we have noted, to miss out many issues and experiences, notably those of subjectivity and identity. The importance of the way that people feel about their selves and their organisational roles are demonstrated in the following:

> I have a reputation for getting people's backs up who work for me. I will help them if I consider they need it, but sometimes I give them the impression that I can't be bothered. I prefer them to learn by looking for themselves. So I'm fairly abrupt and indifferent. I'm not worried if they like me but I do want their respect. …I don't like them to take advantage …they often say, 'Oh we can't understand you, Allan, we try to be nice to you but you're not nice back.' I think there's only one I've not made cry.…I don't think I have to do the job. My job is to keep them as busy as possible. I'd rather me be bored than them, otherwise if you do bring work for them again, it just leads to moaning and groaning. You can't keep all six happy at the same time. With some you can tell their monthly changes, even the other girls say so. Sometimes when they're having a good chunner about the inspectors I have to impress on them that if it was not for the men, there'd be no jobs for them, if the blokes don't go out and sell insurance. (Knights and Collinson, 1987: 158)

Socially produced identities are a central factor delineating people's experience of work. As the authors of the Insco case study argue, Allan views his hierarchical position as a reflection of his own personal status and dignity. In his dealings with his female 'subordinates' he utilises a mixture of patronising humour, sarcasm and indifference in order to maintain a symbolic distance of authority and 'motivate' them to work independently. His proud boasts also indicate the significance of gender to his work identity.

The case itself addresses the gendered aspects of job segregation and the social construction of skill in the insurance industry where 'Conventionally, the task is described in terms of an heroic drama in which intrepid and autonomous males stride out into the financial world and against the odds return with new business'. These 'almost mystical perceptions' of male skills are contrasted to the 'internal staff of women clerks whose work is assumed to be dependent, supportive and secondary' (1987: 148). Far from the aggressive instincts of the hunter, success in selling is seen to be dependent on the *gendered interpersonal skills* that are employed to maintain 'exclusively male relationships' with insurance agents. At the same time the devalued work of the female clerks is essential in the maintenance of long-term client support

and after-sales service. Thus the success of the 'heroic' male is paradoxically dependant on the 'stock of working knowledge' possessed by the women, which allows
them to maintain their own personalised telephone relations with clients. The unacknowledged and differentially rewarded 'tacit skills' employed in the administrative
support role are 'further emphasised when women also act as caring ego-masseurs or
office wives for sales inspectors who sometimes return to the office dejected after
unsuccessful appointments' (1987: 150).

> The continuation of such gendered job segregation is seen as being dependent
> on the continued acquiescence of the clerical staff to their subordination, even
> in conditions where Allan's highly coercive approach generates a level of anxiety
> or frustrated resentment which is expressed in internal conflict, poor standards
> of work, indifference, disenchantment or even resignation. (Knights and
> Collinson, 1987: 168–9)

These reactions from the women underwrite the prejudicial attitudes used by the male
managers to exclude the women from promotion to the sales force on the basis that
they are 'naturally' unfit to handle such macho work. But such 'reactions' are not
in fact problems in themselves; they are in effect the range of coping responses open
to the women in that they themselves have internalised the view that they are unfit to
be sales 'reps'. By accepting the gendered definition of themselves they are limited
to striving for personal material gain or 'symbolic security expressed either in resignation, indifference or the search for future promotion within the clerical ranks'
(1987: 169). Such necessarily individualistic strategies are said merely to reproduce
the contradictions of job segregation, and effectively to block any moves towards
collective action that would challenge their institutionalised subordination.

Issues of identity raised in the Insco case are therefore central, but cannot be dealt
with without concepts deriving from the study of structural processes such as organisational design, control strategies or the impact of wider social formations. But they
in turn will be incomplete without reference to the factors surrounding the *construction* of the subjectivity and experience of those involved. Organisational psychology
should allow us to enter these areas necessary for a fuller account of 'organisational
behaviour'. But as the discussions in Chapter 13 have begun to argue, the relation
between organisational psychology and the subjective factor in the study of work
organisations is by no means clear. Though organisational psychology and its practitioners might be expected to have a natural concern with the identities and subjective
experience of participants, the range of issues and topics traditionally presented in the
area do not consistently address these concepts. Explaining Allan's relations to 'his
staff' would thus be difficult using the theoretical models and concepts currently
employed in introductory OB texts.

A further complicating factor here is the treatment of psychological knowledge in
the literature. Hosking and Morley (1991) for example, give three types of dominant
theoretical orientation. They cite Gordon Allport (1963) on the first two, which he
terms the *individualistic* and *culturalistic* fallacies. The individualistic fallacy focuses
on personal characteristics at the expense of cultural and contextual factors. The
culturalistic fallacy turns this on its head to focus on social and situational forces at the
expense of the person. The third approach they identify is the 'more complicated
without becoming more sophisticated' (1991: 4) *contingency* approach, which is said

to give weight to people and context but is merely a 'statistical interaction' between 'inputs' from person and context. This argument allows that an attempt has been made to take account of variables affecting individual and group psychology and action in organisations, but that it does not have an adequate account of the social interactions through which people produce their contexts and are shaped by them. Hosking and Morley (1991: 40–2) take this further in a critique of the top-down, *entitative* approaches (based on Meyer, 1985) that have dominated OB and HRM literatures. These are essentially reified perspectives relying on assumptions of the independence of person and organisation rather on their interdependence. Entitative approaches to persons focus on characteristics, traits and behaviours of individuals, while they treat organisations as entities in their own right with their own values and goals.

In an interesting commentary on such issues, Nord and Fox (1996) reviewed the linkages between organisation studies and psychological factors and processes. They found that the focus on the individual in organisational psychology has gradually moved away from the *essentialist* view of the individual found in approaches emphasising personality, motivation attitudes and so on. The shift has been towards 'sociology, literature, communications and other disciplines consistent with a more macro conceptual orientation' (1996: 170). This is somewhat at odds with the previous arguments of Henriques *et al.* (1984), whose view was that mainstream writings persist in an *individual/society dualism*. Even in attempts to provide accounts of how individualistic and culturalistic factors (cf. Allport and Hosking and Morley above) interact in shaping behaviour, there is still a tendency to come down on the side of explanations which emphasise biology and/or individual rationality as causative agents. Social and structural factors are tacitly acknowledged as having some effects, but these are seldom treated in an explicit fashion. They are generally reduced to the status of intervening variables that complicate the action of the individually based mechanisms and determinants of behaviour.

It may be that this dualism means that shifts from *micro* to *macro* OB, as Nord and Fox identify, can never produce a satisfactorily integrated *meso* level of analysis. This does not prevent us however from attempting to increase the level of articulation between contextualising and essentialist factors. Our approach to the 'subjective factor' in organisations tries to do this by focusing on the experience of people in work organisations through the common themes of subjectivity and identity. Both concepts present problems of interpretation, and there is considerable overlap in their usage. Our use of 'subjectivity' follows Henriques *et al.*'s (1984: 2–3) twofold definition (though see Pritchard, 1998 for a critique of our usage of this). First is the '*condition of being subject*': the ways in which the individual is acted upon, and made subject to the structural and interpersonal processes at work in organisational life. Second, the '*condition of being a subject*', possessing individuality and self-awareness. Thus the term encompasses the fundamentally contradictory experience of work and the subjective development and regulation of people's 'emotions, desires, fantasies, a sense of self' (Banton *et al.*, 1985: 44).

The concept of identity commonly involves the notion that there is an irreducible core of social and individual being that uniquely identifies each of us. Psychologically, identity variously incorporates concepts of self and self-esteem, structures of values, attitudes and beliefs, personality and associated traits. Sociologically, it includes concepts of self and of roles and reference groups. Lasch (1985: 31–2) notes a shift of meaning that does not admit a fixed or continuous identity, but a '*minimal self*' which, because of our need for an 'emotional equilibrium', retreats to a 'defensive core, armed against adversity' (1985: 16).

Our usage then, incorporates the notion of *self-aware* and *participative* subjects, who maintain a valued part of their identity against the unpredictability of the external world, while being acted on and constrained by organisational ideologies and practices. These themes of subjectivity and identity are examined in the context of interrelated arguments, together providing a framework capable of addressing issues of structure, agency, individual action and experience. We are concerned to maintain a perspective rooted in a materialist conception of social production and existence. Capital, and management on its behalf, manipulate, direct and shape the identities of employees. This reflects the need to mobilise the consent and co-operation of workers in order that effective control may be maintained over the work process. We also maintain a focus on the development of identity in individuals and the *reproduction* and *transformation* of those identities in the context of work organisations. Individuals are not the passive recipients or objects of structural processes but are constructively engaged in the securing of identities (Knights and Willmott: 1985), and the development of capacities (Leonard, 1984). These, although influenced and shaped by organisational contexts and practices, are at the same time the unique products of each person's history.

Conclusion

In any account of individual history and experience we need an appropriate starting point. Our problem in emphasising the thoroughgoing interdependence of concepts and issues in understanding behaviour in organisations, is that they should be treated in an integrated way. However, that is not the reality of standard discussion of behavioural issues. We have therefore maintained many of the traditional topic and conceptual divisions in order to engage with the existing forms of explanation. The final chapter on identity work acts to re-integrate our main themes and bring the conceptual threads together.

It is appropriate to begin with perception and its relations to attitudes and personality. In this way we can both make topics easier to identify and follow for the reader, at the same time as recognising that all of the psychological and relational processes we will discuss are dependent on the development of the perceptual processes which shape our view of the world.

15 Masks for Tasks: Perception, Attitudes and Personality

In this chapter we give an account of the processes through which we comprehend the world and the other people with whom we interact, and those processes by which others make judgements about us. In our exploration of perception, attitudes and personality we find that the reciprocal assumptions made by others and ourselves produce a social world where we actively transform ourselves according to our context.

Perception: learning what to see

Perception can be defined in terms of 'the dynamic psychological process responsible for attending to, organizing and interpreting sensory data' (Buchanan and Huczynski, 2000: 212). This is usually explained within a perspective that emphasises information processing and seeks to explain how our perceptions of ourselves, others and our environment shape our attitudes and behaviour. The utility of understanding perceptual processes lies in the fact that people's perceptions of themselves and others can be manipulated to change attitudes and behaviour in the situations and contexts within which work takes place. The practices which were associated with the 'Japanisation' of British industry in the 1980s, such as single-status canteens and clothing, provide an example of this, in that they are intended to alter perceptions of the divisions between management and labour, in order to create attitudes (see below) more compatible with organisational goals.

Perception, then, is the umbrella heading for the processes through which we organise and interpret the range of visual, aural, tactile and chemical stimuli that impinge on us. As these processes enable us to comprehend and order the world around us, they must also underlie the manner in which we go about constructing identities.

Perceptual processing

The organisation, processing and interpretation of incoming stimuli are the basic subject matter of *cognitive* (knowing through sensation or perception) psychology. Much material in this area deals with the neurophysiology of perceptual systems. But as our focus is on organisational psychology we do not intend to deal with the detailed cognitive processing of information, as the ordering and organisation of these systems are not wholly determined by their structure. In social, interpersonal and self-perception, the determinants we are concerned with are the past and present influences and constraints on us, and our actively directed interests. Perception, then, is not just the process of seeing, but involves our other senses and is intimately connected with the notion of intention. In other words, what we see and hear is transformed according to how our system of values, attitudes and beliefs informs our actions. The formative content of identity could, in this light be viewed as produced by the filters through which our perceptions pass in order to select out what is of value to us.

Basically, to perceive something we have to be attending to it. This does not mean that we only take in those stimuli that we notice. Rather, we take in everything our particular range of senses allows us to. What it does mean is that we only actively process and act upon those parts of the incoming data that concern us. This concept of *perceptual selectivity* or *selective attention* can be illustrated by a crowded and noisy office, where we cut out much of the background noise in order to concentrate on the people we are listening to. Yet we can still pick out and shift our attention to references to ourselves, or to other things that interest us coming from other parts of the room, temporarily or permanently cutting out the immediate conversation we had been intent on a moment before. Hence we appear to have some mechanism that can shift our attention and select the stimuli to which we attend, according to which appear of the greatest current relevance. Thus having to concentrate for long periods on a single type of stimulus, for example components being inspected on a production line, requires effort in face of the distractions coming from other stimuli in our environment.

Perceptions are often classified as primary or secondary on the basis of whether they come from actual or vicarious experience, though it may be more proper to view these classifications as related to forms of attention. Keltner (1973) claims that we attend primarily to strong or unique stimuli and secondarily to learned selection patterns, but we may also depend upon 'derived primary attention' where secondary perceptions become habitual and unconscious. Hence the notion of perceptual selectivity underlines the *intentionality* of attention. We may not be consciously aware of directing our attention, because we are predisposed to notice some things rather than others. Our perceptual systems are structured to pay attention to things that change and things that stand out from their surroundings, and we might also perceive information as being more valid when it comes from what we consider to be an 'authoritative' source. Thus criticism of our work from a respected peer or a superior responsible for evaluating it will be taken more seriously than that from sources less close to our own interests. These filtering processes are summarised in Figure 15.1.

Environmental stimuli ⟶ **Sensations** ⟶ **Attention** ⟶ **Perception**

Sources	*Sensory filters*	*Attention filters*	*Perceptual organisation*
Light	Range of sensitivity	Stimulus	Categorisation
Air pressure	and threshold	characteristics (e.g.	Figure-ground
Heat	values of senses	size, intensity,	Proximity
Chemicals	(e.g. not being	frequency, contrast,	Similarity
Gravity	able to see UV	motion, rate of	Closure
	or IR light)	change, novelty)	(see later)

The perceptual process   *FIGURE 15.1*

Source: based on D. J. Cherrington (1989) *Organizational Behaviour: The Management of Individual and Organizational Performance*, Boston: Allyn and Bacon, pp. 82–6.

The outcomes of these processes are seen in the notion of the *perceptual set*, which refers to our individual and unique readiness to perceive what we expect to perceive. Our perceptual set reflects our perceptions of ourselves and our social position and is, in effect, the outcome of our socialisation processes (see the next section). For instance, we often appear to be set to perceive people of lower status to ourselves as less competent, inferior and more generally inadequate. This type of set extends to social groups and to wider social divisions – men for example generally perceive women as less competent than themselves, reflecting the social value placed on gender rather than any reliable sex differences. Likewise men tend to attribute competence shown by women to luck rather than skill (Deaux and Emswiller, 1974), showing that their subjective adaptation of their perceptions will tend to reinforce the security of their male identity.

The consequence is that we put actual effort into interpreting the world around us, rather than simply taking it all in as a camera might. But a haphazard interpretation of the myriad stimuli coming to us would be worse than none at all. We need a system of interpretation; our perceptions need to be organised. Wertheimer and the 'Gestalt' School identified the classic principles of perceptual organisation up to the 1920s (see McKenna, 1994 or Mullins, 1999 for applications and examples). These principles show that we tend to place organisation on stimuli, by focusing on significant or moving rather than background factors, by associating stimuli that are close together, similar, moving in the same direction or that appear to be a continuation of other stimuli. According to the principle of *closure* we fill in gaps in perceptual input to give meaning to apparently disorganised information. This underlines the notion that we actively *transform* our perceptions in order to make sense of our environment.

The importance of the gestalt principles for providing insights into how we go about constructing our personal and social world is not generally given great emphasis in the organisational psychology literature: apart, that is, from the extent to which they can be utilised in the construction of the kind of test instruments used in recruitment and selection procedures. That our perceptions are ordered to extract and construct meaning out of our environment both helps to engender our individuality and makes us vulnerable to those who seek to limit or channel the kind of information we receive. By placing perceptual stimuli, people and events, into categories, we effectively take shortcuts in our comprehension of the world. We enable ourselves to deal with the numerous stimuli that impinge on our senses by reducing the necessity to analyse each new stimulus as a unique object. This does however mean that we treat the things and people with which we interact through their relation to the subjectively determined, but apparently objective, categories into which we place them. Thus, to some extent, we *reify* everything and everyone we come across. We produce them as mental representations of our own creation, yet we treat them as if these images were in fact real. The images and slogans associated with corporate cultures and missions are precise examples of attempts to channel our perceptual organisation into acceptance of a dominant reality through supplying a ready-made basis on which to apply closure to contexts and concepts on which we might not have accurate information.

Perceptual categorisation

It is through this process of *categorisation* (see Augoustinos and Walker, 1995: 106–9) that the major perceptual processes dealt with in organisational behaviour texts can be understood. Categorisation involves an *accentuation effect* (1995: 106), which acts to increase both perceived similarities within categories and differences between categories. Categorising people on the basis of limited cues, such as gender, skin colour, bodily characteristics, social, regional and national identity, and then treating an individual as having the generalised traits associated with that category, is the pervasive phenomenon known as the *stereotype*, identified by Lippman (1922). This enables us to make quick assessments of others and of situations. You can, for example, have a stereotype of what a particular kind of person or meeting will be like and react accordingly, or you may need quickly to assess the intent of someone who enters your office or wants to come into your house. Although it has psychological uses to the individual, stereotyping can also have negative social consequences: for example, men in secretarial work might be seen as only seeking temporary employment, unambitious or gay (Callan Hunt, 1992). Stereotyping, then, is one of the mechanisms through which racism and sexism are socially enacted and given ideological justification. Thus a branch manager in a case study of the insurance industry comments on his perceptions of why women are unsuitable for sales work at 'Insco': 'Yes, it can be a soul destroying job, and women are either not hard bitten enough to ride off insults or those that can are pretty unpleasant people' (Knights and Collinson, 1987: 155). It would appear that in the face of an established stereotype, you just can't win!

Another process given force by our categorisation of stimuli is the so-called '*halo effect*' identified by Solomon Asch in 1938, which is essentially another process of producing a stereotype. When we come across new persons or situations we can only assess them in terms relevant to our own experience and the limited cues we have about them. This initial assessment, whether positive or negative, tends to be carried over into the attitudes we build up to that person or thing because of the powerful categorisation effects of *first impressions*. Thus if we rate a new workmate in a positive fashion on the basis of our first impression, we would tend to continue to rate them positively in the future. Of course, the fact that we rate them positively will probably in itself improve our relations with them. This may produce a *self-fulfilling prophecy* (Merton, 1949) from our first impression and probably improve our opinion of our ability to judge others. The halo effect can work against stereotyping, in that meeting a member of a group about whom we hold stereotyped views, who makes a good first impression on us, may weaken a negative stereotype. On the other hand, we may simply view the person as an exception, and perceptual selectivity may bring us to focus on the aspects of their appearance or behaviour that fulfil the prophecies of our stereotypes. These processes might, for example, have powerful effects on new recruits in organisations, since stereotypical attitudes can be socially communicated. This is backed by evidence such as that of Salancik and Pfeffer (1978), whose *social information processing model* of job design implies that our reactions to our work are significantly influenced by cues picked up from our co-workers. In an organisation where the prevailing experience of power relations is unitarist and hierarchical, we might expect new managers or workers to hold stereotypes about each other that will heavily reflect categorising processes, in that their experiences will tend to be interpreted through the dominant attitudes of their peers.

We also have a tendency to categorise others in the same light in which we categorise ourselves. Suspicious or aggressive persons, according to this principle of *projection* – or more properly, *assumed similarity* – will view others as being more suspicious or aggressive in nature than will people who tend to be more trusting or placid. We can apply this notion to the kinds of attitudes and values in the 'new realism' identified in industrial relations since the 1980s. To someone who sees themselves as 'looking after number one', those who stand for the values of class solidarity and union loyalty might be seen as stupid, unrealistic or hiding a lust for personal power behind a facade of caring for others. Identity in this sense becomes the standard of social comparison by which we judge the world and those in it.

To project categorisations onto others, we must be categorising ourselves. We can produce stereotypes about ourselves, perhaps regarding our probable or favoured responses to certain people or things. We can also apply the halo effect to ourselves. If we perform well at a particular activity the first time we try it, we will tend to rate ourselves better in the future, and vice versa. The major source of the categorisations we use are the various groups to which we belong, as the membership of these groups provides us with the basis of the identities which we take up in various situations. Thus the norms and standards of conduct of a group to which we belong will inform both the kinds of stereotypes we use and the identity which recognises our right to make such judgements. If a group can be said to have an identity, then that identity is communicated to its members in their self-perceptions and becomes part of, possibly a major part of, their own identities. Given that the major groups that many of us belong to are related to work and work organisations, our identities will be constructed in terms of our perceptions of ourselves within work organisations. Even the identities of the unemployed might be defined to a great extent by their lack of attachment to work groups.

The major theoretical position on identity from social psychology itself, Tajfel and Turner's social identity theory (see Tajfel, 1982; Fiske and Taylor, 1991; Haslam, 2000), is essentially a theory of intergroup behaviour as it relates to personal and social identity. (See Chapters 17 and 20 on leadership and groups.) We should be careful not to place too much emphasis on group influences, however, as social identity theory in particular has been criticised for not accounting for the individual adequately. This has led to the development by Turner and also Oakes *et al.* (in Augoustinos and Walker, 1995: 127, 213) of self-categorisation theory which accounts for the levels of necessarily stereotypical abstract categorisation we apply to ourselves within particular contexts as follows:

- superordinate – for example, self as part of humanity
- intermediate – for example, self as part of a group
- subordinate – for example, self in personal terms.
  (see Augoustinos and Walker, 1995; Hogg and Abrams, 1990)

Attribution theory

Organisation and categorisation of our perceptions enable us to comprehend and interpret our world in a contextual fashion, and on this basis we are able to make judgements dependent on how we interpret the intentions of others. This is a crucial task for any individual, as it is linked to the fashion in which we identify the links between cause and effect in events. *Attribution theory*, initiated by Heider (1958) and developed by Kelley (1971), shows how we tend to be biased in our judgements of others' intentions. It is founded on the notion that we calculate whether the reasons for actions are due to internal (or dispositional) factors or to external (or environmental) factors, based on our assessment of the *distinctiveness, consistency* and amount of *consensus* of any particular action. It appears that we have an inclination, termed the *fundamental attribution error*, to judge people's intentions in terms of dispositional factors (see Arnold *et al.*, 1991: 288). We tend to attribute the causes of their actions to their personality or nature. In the Insco case, women office workers are seen to require high levels of supervision and control. This is not attributed to their 'experience of subordination and blocked mobility but to their gender'. The 'discontented and moody' behaviour they are seen to exhibit is thus attributed to their gender-based disposition, and is further used to disqualify them from jobs in sales (Knights and Collinson, 1987: 151).

Another form of perceptual error identified by attribution theory is that of *self-serving bias*, which is the propensity to attribute our successes to internal factors and our failures to external ones (vice versa for those we disapprove of). Heider also identified the *discounting principle* which indicates that in social perception we may pay more attention to strong situational cues and ignore a person's disposition: for example we may distrust the overtures of an insurance seller who asks about our heath, regardless of what we think of him or her as a person.

According to Martinko (1995: 11) in a survey of OB texts, attribution theory is generally only considered in detail in chapters on perception, and attributional studies are sometimes cited in chapters on leadership and selection. In UK texts, where attribution is covered, the apparent emphasis is on achievement and performance appraisal, though there is also a tendency to relate it to a person's locus of control (for example see Johnson and Gill, 1993: 72–3). Martinko is keen to emphasise the role attribution theories have played in the development of work on areas such as learned helplessness, achievement and expectancies in the study of intrapersonal motivation. At the same time Martinko emphasises the problems involved in the study of attribution in organisations, particularly regarding its measurement and application. (See Martinko, 1995, for extended discussions of these issues.)

Attribution theory does imply, however, that the more information we have about other people, the greater our capability of making accurate environmental attributions about their actions. We are better able to see things as not necessarily intentional or inherent in their nature but due to their social and personal circumstances. The choice to initiate a strike may be attributed by employers or managers whose knowledge of their employees consists mainly of stereotypes, to bloody-mindedness or their militant nature. In Lane and Robert's (1971) account of the long strike at Pilkingtons in St Helens, the tradition of paternalism meant that management could only interpret the action in terms of intruders such as scousers, revolutionaries or both. One would hope that attribution theory implies that managers who know something of life at the lower end of an organisational hierarchy might be more likely to attribute workers' decisions to factors relating to the workplace or its environment, making a more realistic assessment of the situation in the process. Of course attribution processes are just as prevalent in managerial activities themselves, as noted by Leavitt and Bahrami (1988: 65): 'managers are both blessed and cursed by that tendency to ascribe causality, because the causality – either way – is often ascribed to them rather than to other aspects of the situation'.

As an example, judgements on the performance, ability and effort of others, that is, of their behaviour and characteristics, are nowadays routinely subsumed into judgements of a person's commitment. Thus the concern is not just with what we do or who we are, but whether we 'mean' what we are doing and what we present ourselves as. In traditional OB terms, this would be reduced to judgements of whether individual satisfaction, motivation and so on tend to be derived mainly from intrinsic, social or extrinsic sources. It is possible, however, that the outcomes from judgmental processes are both more dependent on, and more faithfully reflective of, attributional process than they are of any activity or characteristic of the person under judgement. For example Dejoy (1994: 3) in a study of safety work, notes that 'actions to manage safety derive more from attributions than from actual causes'. Likewise Gronhaug and Falkenberg note that:

> Attribution and attributional research serves as a point of departure to capture how managers and organizations make sense of their internal and external environments, enabling them to act purposefully. (Gronhaug and Falkenberg, 1994: 22)

To some extent we are, in making attributions, making assessments of the personality or identity of others. But our ability to make consistently valid attributions is questionable. We constantly have to make judgements on the basis of too little or inaccurate information. On this basis we are assumed to carry around our own implicit personality theories (Asch, 1938) about how people look and behave. These act as barriers to the kind of new information we will take in about them. Also, according to Langer (1981), we often behave in a less rational manner than assumed by attribution theory, using habituated scripts which we act out in appropriate situations (see Chapter 19). In sociological terms this notion of scripting is linked to the 'habitus-project' distinction made by Bordieu in his 'theory of action' (1977, 1994). *Habitus* equates to our dispositions, our 'embodied history' which we bring with us from our past personae and which act as a set of cognitive and motivating structures, without however impinging on consciousness or will. This 'internalised second nature, forgotten as history' distinguishes the notion from purely behavioural mechanisms and from the value free judgements of more rational-cognitive explanations.

These factors, coupled with our tendency to make dispositional attributions, make both our perceptions of others and ourselves highly subjective and prone to fallibility. We can add one last layer to the barriers to accurate perception, one that is receiving increased attention in these days of global markets and information exchange, namely ethnocentrism. This is the tendency to view the world through the values norms and roles of our own culture or even subculture, and to devalue or show hostility to those of other cultures (see Jackson, 1994). Because our perceptual worldview is learned, we can come to an understanding of other cultures by exposure and, in the case of modern export management and 'international management', by specific training. Our sensitivity to those in other cultures depends on monitoring our reactions to information filtered through our own ethnocentrism. Thus, in our construction of identities out of our perceptual world we need to make constant reference to sources of knowledge and comparison that we have built up over time. In social terms, among the major sources of such knowledge are the attitudes which we and others espouse and through which we make the categorisations on which we depend for comparisons.

The attitude problem

All that we see, learn, are and do is not just part of ourselves, but part of the social world around us. Others can judge us on what we do, what we appear to be, and can attribute the reasons for our actions; but to predict how we are likely to react to situations, there are a limited number of possible avenues to be explored. In social and interpersonal terms, we depend a great deal on the verbal statements of others to estimate their likely responses to situations and events. Likewise we communicate our own position in regard to issues, objects, events and our social transactions and negotiations. Such statements of belief, evaluation and feeling are of necessity a major component of socio-psychological study, and this study of attitudes has correspondingly been one of the main sources of data and practice in the development of OB.

When we consider the structured environment of the workplace, performance can be measured, though an employee could be a hard worker and a 'troublemaker'; personality can be assessed, though this may often produce counter-intuitive results not trusted by the client (see next section); and behaviour itself can be regulated in attempts to ensure future compliance. However, such information as can be generated through such techniques does not necessarily provide the requisite depth of information for the planning and systematic control desired by modern organisations. Rothwell and Kazanas (1986: 15) argue that even 'sophisticated quantitative techniques' are 'generally not superior to the kind of structured expert opinion that can be gleaned from survey results'. They see attitude surveys as fundamental to the process of human resource strategic planning in procuring 'a means of tapping employee creativity and knowledge about the organisation and of building genuine commitment to future success'.

Defining attitudes

In the 1870s Charles Darwin referred to attitude as the facial expression of emotion (Petty and Cacioppo, 1981: 20), though these days attitudes are most commonly regarded as consisting of three main components: the conative (behaviourally-oriented), cognitive (belief-oriented) and the affective (emotion-oriented). This is based on Rosenberg and Hovland's (see Ajzen, 1988) model, which more correctly identifies these 'components' as abstractions, based on verbal and non-verbal responses, from which the construct of attitude is inferred. The implication here is that the evaluations implicit in the components can differ while at the same time leading to a unified expression of 'attitude'. For example, an employee may dislike the kind of work undertaken in a new department he or she is being asked to move into (negative affect), but believe that the workers in that department are a cohesive and effective team to work with (positive cognition), and thus agree to make the move (positive conation) (based on Ajzen, 1988: 20). It is important to note that in the example given, the enquirer could infer a wholly 'positive' attitude from the conative component alone, unless the negative affect was actively expressed by the employee. More commonly it is the cognitive component which is subjected to measure; for example Taber (1991: 598) claims that in one major area of attitudinal measurement, 'current job satisfaction assessments may be assessing what workers think about their job satisfaction, rather than how they feel about their jobs'.

Though discriminations between such components have been made in depth in the socio-psychological literature (see Ajzen, 1988: 21–3) these distinctions are rarely carried through into the design or analysis of studies in the wider literature making use of attitudinal measures. In essence, attitudes are often taken as indicative of an undifferentiated consistency of response, which is in turn predictive of behaviour or intention. An implicit assumption of much research involving attitudes is that they are informed by and reflect value systems. The distinction between attitudes and values is generally that attitudes are directed toward specific objects and that values are evaluative standards. In effect this makes them an output of the filtering and ordering processes by which we perceive and learn. As such, attitudes have been considered as embodying psychological functions for individuals:

- **Adjustment:** utility of object in need satisfaction; maximising external rewards and minimising punishment.
- **Ego defence:** protecting against internal conflicts and external dangers.
- **Value expression:** maintaining self identity; enhancing favourable self-image; self-expression and self determination.
- **Knowledge:** need for understanding, for meaningful cognitive organisation, for consistency and clarity.

(from Katz, 1960, in Kahle, 1984: 18)

There is not a great deal of confirmatory evidence for this model and this may in some part be due to its being merely descriptive rather than prescriptive or diagnostic. It says little about the measurement of attitudes, or the relation of attitudes to behaviour that has generated much of the research in the area. According to Eiser (1986: 13), 'an attitude is a subjective experience involving an evaluation of something or somebody'. This active experience of perceiving, interpreting and evaluating experiences with a public reference to others should be contrasted with the more general usage of attitude as an object to be measured, correlated and tabulated. As subjective experiences, attitudes must have some consistent linkage to social behaviour or, as Eiser notes, 'it would be difficult to know what such verbal expression *meant*' (1986: 13). The problem really arises when it is assumed that attitudes can predictably cause behaviour.

Attitudes and behaviour

The failure of socio-psychological research to find strong correlative links between attitudes and behaviour led to a decline in attitude-based studies in the 1970s. However, work on the specificity of behaviour as related to attitude, notably by Ajzen and Fishbein, brought the subject back into focus. Ajzen and Fishbein argued (1980) that attitudinal measures have to correspond with the particular components of a behaviour in order for prediction to be possible. These component elements of behaviour are the specific *action* itself, the *target* of the action, the *context* in which the action is performed, and the *time* the action is (to be) performed. The assumption is that the more of these components that can be measured accurately, the more likely that the attitudes will predict behaviour. The problem once more is that many attitude surveys only measure the cognitive target component, that is, the attitude to the thing itself – rather than the attitude to the use or doing of the thing or to the when, where and how in which the behaviour would be expected to take place. In other words, they ask, 'what do you think of this?', without asking 'what about doing it under these specific conditions?'

Ajzen and Fishbein in their 'theory of reasoned action' link the prediction of behaviour to what we know of the person's *intention*, which is a function both of the attitude toward the behaviour and of their *subjective norm* regarding the behaviour. Thus we have to take into account not only their positive and negative feelings, but also the social pressures surrounding the particular behaviour. Attitude here has two subcomponents: beliefs about the consequences of the behaviour, and affective evaluations of (in other words, feelings about) the consequences (Perloff, 1993: 95). Likewise, subjective norms have two subcomponents: normative beliefs about whether significant groups or individuals approve or disapprove of the behaviour, and the person's motivation to comply with such normative beliefs (1993: 97). In addition to such qualifications it should be noted that the Ajzen and Fishbein model has been criticised for being too rational/cognitive in nature and that the effect of more 'mindless' behavioural associations, such as the accessibility of an attitude and the effects of past behaviour, selective perception/direct experience and habit (Triandis, 1980; Bentler and Speckart, 1981; Fazio, 1985) are also important determinations of the attitude–behaviour correlation.

Attitude change

Because of the presumed effects of attitudes on behaviour, there is a concomitant concern with the possibility of changing attitudes (and hence behaviour). The possibilities of changing attitudes are often linked to the persuasive characteristics of persons as *sources* (attractiveness, trustworthiness and expertise); as *targets* (high or low self-esteem); and of *messages* themselves (levels of threat). The routes to attitude change are generally explained in terms of Kelman's (1961) three sources of attitude change, *compliance, identification* and *internalisation* (discussed further in Chapter 19), and through the reduction of psychological tensions as conceived in balance theory (Heider, 1946) and cognitive dissonance theory (Festinger, 1957). (See McKenna 2000, chapter 8 for an extended discussion.) Perhaps the most important aspect of attitude change in organisations is the gaining of public commitment (Deutsch and Gerard, 1955; Tedeschi, Schlenker and Bonoma, 1971), where 'whenever one takes a stand that is visible to others, there arises a drive to maintain that stand in order to look like a consistent person' (Cialdini, 2001: 72 – perhaps the most readable source on influence processes).

Public commitments are seen to produce more enduring effects in changing attitudes and behaviour than private commitments (see Eiser, 1986). Corbett (1994: 56) gives an example of this need for consistency in what he terms 'Internal Marketing': in competitions where tie-break questions are used to give a reason or slogan for buying a product, 'tens of thousands of people testify in writing to the product's appeal and they experience a powerful psychological pull to believe what they have written'. The discussions below on attitude surveys and personality tests, and those in Chapter 19 on goal-setting and development profiling, all concern attempts by organisations to gain public commitment to corporate objectives. The overall effect of such systems is to reinforce individual responsibility for fitting in to organisational objectives. This can be linked to the currently popular practice of 'project-based working', where individuals are steered towards or allowed to follow their own initiatives in developing and implementing solutions to organisational goal barriers, with appraisal being based on the success with which they carry their projects through.

The paradoxical possibility that if attitudes are consistent and predictive because they reflect predispositions, then it will be very hard to change them, is seldom exercised to any great degree in the management literature which makes so much of attitudinal research. The likelihood is, however, that attitudes are much more variable than is often assumed, and that even if changing core values is difficult, the changing of more operational attitudes and more particularly the generation of new attitudes can be controlled by the use of agenda-setting devices, including attitude, morale and opinion surveys.

Hollway (1991: 90–1 and 146–50) cites various examples which indicate that the interpretation and use of surveys has, since their inception in the 1930s, often been more of a public relations than a human relations exercise, and that they 'could be used to produce a self-fulfilling prophecy effect' (1991: 91). Rather than surveying and analysing individual and cultural diversity, they are largely tools of cultural conformity. Referring back to the earlier notion that norms and habits affect the translation of attitudes into behaviour, we might suppose that the best strategy for changing attitudes is to embed them in self-enacting scripts which people are forced to internalise as a necessary part of their social and organisational functioning.

The usage of attitudinal measures in the workplace can be more readily understood with reference to the focus that Zimbardo *et al.* note in looking at attitude change from the perspective of populations rather than individuals:

> Even though we cannot predict the behaviour of single individuals, we should be able to predict that people (in general) will *change* their behaviour if we can *change* their attitudes of greatest relevance to the behaviour in question. We cannot predict which people will change or how much they will change, but a change in the attitudes of the population should be accompanied by a change in the behaviour of the population. (Zimbardo *et al.*, 1977: 52)

In this light, the utility of assessing attitudes as a cultural technology of regulation can be demonstrated by Boddy and Buchanan's advice on managing 'change projects':

> Assess attitudes. What evidence was there about the enthusiasm and commitment of those working on the project? Were there signs or hints of resistance, which might suggest a change of approach? Were staff becoming frustrated by delays, difficulties or changes to plan, which the manager needed to do something about? Or were they enthusiastic and positive about the activity, and going out of their way to make it work? (Boddy and Buchanan, 1992: 150)

This is presented as an element of 'managing the control agenda', a major facet of the 'continuous monitoring process to keep variances acceptably small' (1992: 149). The important notion here is the status of attitudes as evidence: even if not the 'enduring entities' they are so often assumed to be, they reflect the psychic status of persons within evaluative hierarchies and the choices of individuals to show whether they intend to collaborate or not with managerial practices.

The values we internalise, the attitudes we exhibit, will all reflect the choices, however limited, we have made and the learned constraints within which we act. Our unique history of learning and socialisation (see next chapter) enables us to produce a subjective identity which is malleable in both our own terms and those of the others and the organisations we encounter. We produce something which others see as our 'personality' but which in effect is simply an actively managed and continually rehearsed manipulation of our identity, fitted to what we have to do and what we want to do.

Personality: masks for tasks

Personality is defined in terms of 'the physical, mental, moral and social qualities of the individual' (McKenna, 1987: 11), or as whatever makes you different from other people. It is understood as a complex of characteristic features or traits that describe the particular types and/or dimensions through which personalities are categorised. This may be the ultimate contradiction in organisational psychology, in that the study of 'unique' personalities is placed almost wholly in the service of the production of standardised measures aimed at the categorisation and selection of individuals so that they can be fitted into their appropriate niches in organisational cultures.

The psychological understanding of how an individual develops a distinctive personality depends, like that of perception, on the notion of categorisation. Because personality is generally understood within a series of categorisations, its relationship to the construction of identity cannot be separated from the activities of those who produce the categories. Hence the explanation of personality in an organisational setting is more directly connected to the use of personality theory by managers than is the case with perception.

Describing personality as that which makes an individual different from others essentially defines it as that which sets the boundaries of what you are and what you are not. However, the way the notion of personality is used in OB highlights this type of definition as an idealised, liberal conception that is in direct contradiction to operational concerns with the controlled performance of work. The study of personality from this angle centres around the identification and prediction of *consistent* and/or *distinctive modes of response* in individuals. Some of the more recent approaches, which attempt to account for the interaction of personality with situational factors, would term these modes of response as dispositions, which include emotions, cognitions, attitudes, expectancies and fantasies (Clark and Hoyle, 1988). Distinctive behaviours in this sense are not the same as uniquely individual behaviours. They would be typical ways of reacting to people or situations which would distinguish an individual as belonging to a category of persons. Thus people who are seen to react in a consistently uncooperative fashion may be placed into a stereotypical category whereby their future behaviour will be assumed to be typical of that sort of person who is 'difficult' or a 'problem person'.

Behaviour, then, is assumed to be inherent in the individual's personality, biologically or genetically fixed. Being fixed, it is possible to predict, and being possible to predict it becomes a useful tool in controlling behaviour. Personality theory becomes an exercise in discovering how these various modes of response vary over time and between situations, in order to refine the levels of categorisation and prediction possible. For example, what kind of observed behaviour in a person is sufficient to label him or her as a troublemaker? Or what type of situation will influence a person to reveal different aspects of or levels of his or her 'undesirable' behaviour? Approaches such as that of Clark and Hoyle (1988) and that of Aronoff and Wilson (1985; see Hosking and Morley, 1991: 9–13), which attempt to contextualise personalityin the social process, do acknowledge that dispositions can be modified by situations and experience, but still focus on how these variables can be combined to predict behaviour.

Types, traits and tests

For OB as a 'science', this process frequently results more in a battery of methodologies and techniques for selecting the 'right person for the job' than in an account of personality. These are used to select prospective employees or candidates for promotion into categories which show how well they fit into organisational culture, thus making it easier to take decisions about them. Personality tests and inventories effectively perform the same function for an organisation as stereotypes do for an individual or group. They help to sort out the bewildering variety of information available about organisational members into categories which can be easily comprehended and dealt with. The last thing with which a science of personality of this sort is concerned is that which makes us subjectively unique individuals. There may be interest in what makes a particular individual different to others, but only to the extent that it might be a pointer to a characteristic useful or damaging to the organisation.

In delineating categories of personality characteristics, psychologists tend to fall back on two main sets of concept. The first of these, personality *types*, are predetermined categories into which we 'fit', and which represent broad generalisations of character such as 'moody' or 'lively'. The second, personality *traits*, are habitual behaviours or tendencies to behave in particular ways: for example tendencies to react in an anxious, reserved or outgoing fashion. Types or personality factors are generally used to refer to patterns or clusters of traits or personality variables, which can be used to map the profiles of individuals using factor analysis of responses to self-report questionnaires. The Eysenck Personality Inventory (EPI: Eysenck and Wilson, 1975) groups clusters of variables – such as reserved, unsociable, quiet, passive, careful – into factors, in this case introversion. The factors used by Eysenck, introversion–extraversion and stability–neuroticism, are based on Jungian psychodynamic theory, as are those utilised by the Myers-Briggs Type Indicator and Cattell's 16PF (Personality Factors). These days types are generally reduced to the 'Big Five' personality dimensions characterised by tendencies to extraversion, emotional stability, agreeableness, will to achieve and openness to experience.

Personality inventories are still used by organisations on tens of millions of people every year in selection and to determine who will make good managers or will be eligible for promotion. Cattell's 16PF scale, which is based on the same basic types as the EPI, is widely criticised on both its content and generalisability, and yet still is used because it appears to select people who will make good managers. Hollway (1984) notes that it does not really matter whether the 16PF tells us anything realistic about personality, as it actually works by fulfilling the expectations of existing managers about what makes a good manager. That is, it identifies people like themselves, who are in the main 'male, middle-class and middle-aged' and, in the West, most often white. Since it is possible to work out which are the appropriate types of answer to the questions, it does not really matter if the respondent does not actually belong to the same social groupings as the dominant organisational culture he or she is trying to enter. It will help if he or she does, as it makes 'correct' responses easier to identify, but the ability to lie correctly is just as good a sign that the candidate is capable of becoming, and willing to become, the kind of person who will fit. Candidates who are unwilling to frame the right kind of responses, or are incapable of doing so, automatically select themselves out, regardless of their actual managerial potential. For example, graduates going through the 'milk-round' career selection may sit similar tests up to five times in the course of their applications. The conclusion that such tests are used for 'people processing' rather than individual treatment of personal characteristics and differences is hard to escape, and produces the conclusion that they are more effectively 'gate-keeping' rather than selection methods. Indeed, such tests were originally used in the UK in the First World War to screen out 'neurotic' soldiers: that is, those who did not want to fight! Current doubts on the use of tests have led to recommendations on using techniques such as structured interviews and role-playing in *assessment centres*, though the expense and effort involved makes it unlikely that these would be used extensively in smaller organisations.

Charles Johnson and Steve Blinkhorn (a designer of tests himself) claimed in *Nature* that tests lack validity and are difficult to replicate, and that there is not much evidence that tests predict job success except at the extremes of the range tested. In any case, the scores obtained are often not influential or even used in actual selection decisions, and of course, job seekers being questioned are unlikely to respond dispassionately. Their conclusions were that many different types could actually be successful in any particular job, and that much of personality testing is in fact no more than 'pseudoscience'.

Personality testing is however currently undergoing something of a revival, as a new generation of computerised personality profiling systems are coming onto the market. Their ease and speed of use, combined with neat computer printouts detailing managerial potential, reinforce an air of spurious objectivity in their validity as managerial tools. Most of them are still of course based on systems such as the EPI, but do not impose the same levels of cost in terms of licensing and training for their administration and interpretation as the older paper-based systems. In the US, the polygraph was for a long time a staple in the testing of employees due to its claim to be able to detect lying, based on changes in the electrical conductivity of the skin. However the reliability and ethical implications of its use has led to restrictions since 1988. *Voice Stress Analysis* (VSA) has been touted as a method which can replace the polygraph, though with a fine irony the American Association of Police Polygraphers cite a 1996 Department of Defense study to the effect that there is 'no credible evidence to validate voice analysis as an effective instrument for determining deception'. Employers have returned to the use of personality style tests claimed to measure an employee's *honesty* or *integrity*. If these in turn are banned, employers may turn to techniques like graphology (popular in Europe) and astrology (popular in the Far East) for selection and gatekeeping purposes.

Personality and selection

In utilising tests, employers are essentially clutching at straws, and on this basis will probably use anything that will help them make some kind of systematic decision.

Other forms of selection/screening that may be influential in the future include *genetic screening*, used to detect tendencies to congenital disease (and possibly stress through tendencies to heart disease), and *lifestyle screening*, used for detecting hazardous elements of personal lifestyles, for example dangerous hobbies, addictions and so on. These are driven mainly by the possible reduction of insurance costs that could be achieved through their use (as is also the case for the smoke-free workplace), and by the costs of retraining replacements. Overall the value of all of these developments is in their capacity to reduce complex factors to simple stereotypical categorisations. Thus, they make the decision-making process for personnel departments simpler, more cost-effective and less dependent on skilled staff – a veritable Taylorism of recruitment.

The underlying assumption behind techniques such as the 16PF, that managerial ability is somehow related to personality factors, would almost certainly ignore the kind of managerial ability it takes to, say, hold down a job, run a household and bring up children. But of course the dominant cultures in most organisations and institutions are not composed of the working women who have to display such abilities. The assumption is not about personality as such, but about having, or aspiring to, the right kind of personality. In contrast to managerial assessment, the assessment of shopfloor workers has traditionally focused on *psychometric* tests of *capacities* and *aptitudes* rather than personality. Psychometric tests examine factors such as verbal, logical and mathematical reasoning, and are said to have high test–retest validity, in that they yield similar results over time for the same subjects, which is not necessarily the case with personality inventories. Both are tests of the ability to do the job, the difference being that it is assumed that only in the higher levels of organisational hierarchies does personality become a relevant factor. The utility of psychometric tests is in essence their cost-saving ability to predict who is capable or willing to be trained. Hollway (1984: 50) also notes that where psychometric tests are used in assessment centres, the more objective information they yield is still contaminated by the subjective preferences of decision-makers, possibly on the basis of photographs and biographical details attached to assessment forms. It is again the pragmatic psychology of Taylorism that is at work here: as long as the person can do the job, who they are and what they are is of little importance. The personality of a manager is not important, as long as he or she has a 'managerial' personality.

Other personality factors and characteristics employed in assessment include *locus of control*, *self-monitoring*, *self-efficacy* and *positive/negative affect*. Locus of control (Rotter, 1972) refers to whether we believe that we control events (internal) or events control us (external); likewise self-monitoring (Snyder and Gangestad, 1986) refers to how attentive we are to internal states (low) or to appropriate situational and inter-personal cues (high) in determining our behaviour. High self-efficacy (Bandura, 1977) is the extent to which we believe we can overcome obstacles and get things done, whereas positive and negative affect represent the extent to which we accentuate the positive and negative in ourselves. In managerial selection, assessment and development, the preference is for the person who demonstrates an internal locus of control, low self-monitoring, high self-efficacy and positive affect. Thus supplicants for managerial status are measured against what is effectively a stereotype of an 'ideal' manager, mainly attentive to the demands of managerial identity and practice. In personality and attitude assessment, as in stereotyping, projection and attribution, the assignment of categories on the basis of limited information can lead to damaging consequences.

For example, the assigning to personality of a biologically-fixed nature that can be assessed through the identification of types and traits can reinforce the notion that problems within an organisation are rooted within the pathological personality characteristics and behaviours of individuals. Thus the interpersonal, social and organisational problems that arise can be blamed on bad attitudes and in turn on bad personalities. The end result is blaming bad personalities on genetic inheritance, and then we are one step from the attitude that says that to resolve the problems you need to remove the people who cause them. (See Chorover 1979 and Henriques, 1984 for extended discussions of biological and cognitive determinism in social theory and practice.) At a less extreme level, the branch manager at Insco commenting on the traits appropriate to sales work in insurance delineates them in a sex-typed fashion which acts to render problematic the employment of women in this area:

> I'm looking for whether they've got drive, initiative and are basically a self-starter. So he must want to get on, and get on by his own efforts. (Knights and Collinson, 1987: 156)

The focus on traits and types in OB is a function of their utility in making personality amenable to classification and manipulation. Yet personality to a great extent is simply the observable manifestation of identity. It is essentially similar to the notion of social identity, which a person develops and constructs through negotiation and interaction with others. In this sense, personality cannot simply be a cluster of traits; it is a process. It is not something that can be measured in terms of the ways in which people tend to react. Personality is a proactive process in which people present to others the image that will most benefit them in the situation in which they are. This is reflected in the use of development profiling systems that ask you to outline your strengths, weaknesses and career-related goals, as well as how, and by when, you intend to achieve them. They use techniques such as 'domain mapping' and self-report questionnaires similar in style to the Occupational Personality Questionnaire from the Saville and Holdsworth consultancy firm. The OPQ is claimed to be a way for people to indicate their own perceptions of self, and such self-descriptions are validated on the basis that they relate well to expert descriptions of respondents. Such systems have the added utility of producing a public commitment from the respondent, as well as reinforcing individual responsibility in the same fashion as 'project-based working', as noted in the section on attitudes.

The focus on 'self-report' and its links to disciplined and goal-oriented behaviour gives us insights into what testing and the panoply of related measures, for example, assessment centres, are really about. The whole point is to sell yourself to a prospective or present employer on the basis of how well your personal agenda and goals line up with objectives at organisational, departmental and group/personal levels. This means that selection, gatekeeping and appraisal are more to do with the management of impressions than with the FMJ/FJM paradigm (see Chapter 14) assumed in HRM practice. The process of acquiring a personality, a social identity, is itself influenced by filling out personality inventories or going through an assessment centre. It necessitates putting over an impression of your personality that is appropriate rather than accurate. The personality exhibited in this situation would be a mask appropriate to the task at hand and is achieved through *impression management*, which we will examine in more detail in Chapter 21.

Conclusion

Though the mask we present might be appropriate to our own reading of how to cope with a situation, it might not fit others' expectations of how we should react. Argyris (1967) examined the extent to which the demands of managerial and organisational practices were inconsistent with the drive towards greater independence, self-control and complexity in the maturing personality. For employees, especially at the lower levels of organisational hierarchies, the imperatives of managerial control and decision-making may lead to frustration of their desire to actively pursue meaningful goals and to the employment of defence mechanisms to protect their personal identity. These include regression to less mature behaviour, daydreaming, apathy and aggression, and may

FIGURE 15.2 The 3Cs model of context–content–conduct and individual differences

Source: T. Jackson (1994) *Organisational Behaviour in Management*, Oxford: Butterworth-Heinemann, p. 42.

be interpreted as personality characteristics by others. This might lead to the kind of 'assumption trap' attributed to Theory X attitudes (see Chapter 19), prompting managers to be even more directive and coercive. Likewise our assessment of the personality we need to exhibit might be inappropriate to guide our conduct in face of unfamiliar cultural contexts. Jackson (1994) proposes a '3Cs' (context–content–conduct) model of the factors which need to accounted for in linking our individual differences to our behaviour in social processes (see Figure 15.2). This model indicates that personality, like perception, is interdependent with our socialisation and intention. It is constructed in relation to what one is trying to achieve, to developing strategies to survive the circumstances one has to endure. It is a tool that allows individuals to manipulate their own environment, even at the same time that it allows others to manipulate them in organisations. The personality component of our identity indicates the types of influence to which we are open, but whether such influences actually have an effect on us is determined by whether we learn from them, and the extent to which that learning changes us. We need to learn in order to check on the validity of the identity we have secured for ourselves, and its appropriateness in our current context.

16 Learning, Change and Innovation

> Given further acceleration, we can conclude that knowledge will grow increasingly perishable. Today's 'fact' becomes tomorrow's 'misinformation'. This is no argument against learning facts or data – far from it. But a society in which the individual constantly changes his job, his place of residence, his social ties and so forth, places an enormous premium on learning efficiency.   (Toffler, 1970: 374)

Whether modern occupational patterns have changed to the extent that Toffler predicted 30 years ago is debatable, but the focus on *learning* he forecast has most certainly come to pass. Toffler was perhaps most prophetic in asserting that we will have to 'learn how to learn' (1970: 374), a phrase that is by now familiar to many in educational and business organisations. Learning is commonly defined in relation to the individual in such terms as 'a relatively persistent change in an individual's possible behaviour due to experience' (Fontana, 1985: 64). The use of learning theory in organisational behaviour (OB), on the other hand, is tied to refining the processes by which individuals are socialised into the behaviour patterns required by organisations. Such socialisation is accomplished through prescriptions aimed at increasing the effectiveness of training programmes (see Arnold, Cooper and Robertson, 1998: chapter 15, for a good account), and in team and cultural initiatives aimed at achieving organisational change.

In this chapter we will first look at how learning and associated socialisation processes have come to have such importance in the mainstream OB agenda. We then examine current managerial practices in systems of staff and managerial development profiling, and move on through these to critiques of so-called organisational learning. Using as an exemplar the phenomenon of the *learning organisation*, in which learning how to learn is supposedly a way of life, we argue that learning organisation initiatives are essentially technologies of regulation aimed at facilitating change processes. Lastly, we move from considering the rather eclectic change literature to the more substantial literatures on innovation and creativity, bringing in the issue of sustainability to link the themes and topics we explore to the previous discussion of learning.

Learning and socialisation: seeing what to do

Our perceptual organisation enables us to comprehend our experience, but if we do not learn from it then our experience is of little use. The concepts and mechanisms of individual learning are of fundamental importance to understanding how we build up both unique identities and common behavioural patterns out of perceptual experience. Accounts of learning might then be expected to focus on how and where we acquire the behaviours appropriate and necessary to our social functioning and survival. In the psychological literature, this is usually presented in terms of models based variously on *behaviourist*, *cognitive* and *social learning theory*.

The behaviourist model focuses on *associative* and *instrumental* learning. In the former process, proposed by Pavlov and refined by Watson (1930), we learn to behave in a certain fashion because we identify and associate that behaviour with a particular stimulus. For example, a bell or buzzer signalling the end of a tea-break can cause us to stop what we are doing and go back to work even if there is no supervisor present to tell us to do so. We do this because we have identified the stimulus as signalling the danger of punishment for non-compliance and associate it with the behaviour of returning to work. We are thus *conditioned* to obey the buzzer. The process of instrumental learning or *operant* conditioning takes this a stage further, and provides more explanation of why we learn, in that it focuses not on the stimulus, but on the consequences that follow the behaviour. This process, pioneered by Thorndike and refined by Skinner (1971), focuses on the way in which the rewards and punishments which are the outcomes of a behaviour become associated with that behaviour. If we do not go back to work when the buzzer sounds and get away with it, then we are rewarded by extending our rest period and by avoiding the associated punishment. Thus the likelihood of our doing the same thing in a similar situation is *reinforced* by the positive consequences of the behaviour.

These two mechanisms have been used at one time or another to explain the learning of just about every type of behaviour by the process of *shaping*, being repeatedly conditioned to close approximations of the desired behaviour. They do not however tell us very much about the mental processes which allow us to associate stimuli and behaviour or to expect and assess consequences, given that behaviourism does not regard mental processes as open to examination. The positive (reward) and negative (punishment) aspects of reinforcement schedules do however, neatly fit into what we term the *technologies of regulation* which back up the processes of control in organisations. The incentives to work harder and the disincentives to social and collective interaction with other workers which a piecework system encourages present a good example of these strategies of control. McKenna (2000: 193–7) notes that the techniques of organisational behaviour modification which use conditioning and reinforcement principles to attempt to 'shape' the behaviour of workers (for example in areas such as safety practices and absenteeism) are mainly confined to 'highly controllable situations', the basic flaw in such techniques being that they ignore the 'interaction between situational and personal factors' which is 'encapsulated in social learning theory' (2000: 198).

The theoretical base of behaviourism does not really explain how we acquire new behaviours. It does not explain how someone would ignore the warning buzzer the first time, beyond doing it accidentally. Theorists such as Chomsky have constructed damning critiques of behaviourism in terms of the inability of conditioning, reinforcement and shaping to explain phenomena such as the acquisition and use of language. Social learning theory, on the other hand, explains novel behaviour on the basis of observing and imitating the behaviour of others. Thus we could become socialised into ignoring the buzzer and pushing the limits of how long we can take for a tea-break as part of a social process whereby we both reinforce our own actions and are reinforced by the successful actions of others in our workgroup.

To explain this we need some recourse to cognitive theory, which emphasises the role of insight and the building up of *schema*, mental maps which allow us to act on the basis of imperfect knowledge and expectation, rather than the trial and error approach of the behaviourists. For instance, we could learn to ignore the buzzer in the right circumstances on the basis of what are known as 'TOTE' units. These *Test–Operate–Test–Exit* units (Miller *et al.*, 1960) represent the stages in which we learn a behaviour or a skill and process the information relating to it. The process involved is a simple feedback mechanism whereby we continuously monitor (test) the results of our actions (operations) until we successfully complete them (exit). TOTE units build up behaviours as part of subplans which feed into wider plans. Thus we might continually test out the limits of how far we can extend our tea-break as part of trying to increase our time away from work we dislike, or as part of attempts to annoy a hated supervisor, or even as a formally constituted plan to resist management controls. The importance of Miller's work is in establishing the importance of feedback in the dynamics of the learning process, although as those of us who endure annual appraisal know, feedback of poor quality can turn learning into a chore rather than a dynamic opportunity.

The behaviours we learn can be built up into scripts, so that we use learned knowledge through applying categories of particular activities. This is the process involved in the notion of *action regulation* (Hacker and Volpert, cited in Resch *et al.*, 1984), whereby all action is hierarchically organised into units representing sub-goals of the planned action. 'Actions are continually adjusted to changes in the environment' (Frese, 1982: 213), and are initially performed and learned at an *intellectual* level under conscious control. After time and practice they become more 'automatised' and are controlled at the level of *flexible action patterns*, which are the intermediary level of control and represent standardised scripts that can be somewhat modified in the face of situational change. At the final or *sensorimotor* level, actions become stereotyped, automatic responses. Thus when learning to drive we start out having to perform all actions consciously and often err in them. With practice we rehearse patterns of behaviour for changing gear, approaching junctions and so on, to a standard sufficient to pass our driving test, though novel or unexpected situations can throw us back to the intellectual level. Eventually we get to the point where we can drive to work at speed, unconsciously negotiating all manner of obstacles, while at the same time rehearsing our arguments for an important meeting with our boss. Thus when actions are learned to the sensorimotor level, the higher levels are made available for pursuing other goals and tasks. Of course in highly routinised work, although actions may be made at the sensorimotor level there is no concomitant 'freedom' to pursue personal goals. At the intellectual level such work only frees us to be frustrated or at best to daydream.

We can explain how we go about learning from the above perspectives, but it is more difficult to explain how we know what we need to learn, and what the appropriate behaviours are in any given situation. If we are to link learning to the construction of identity in organisational settings, we need to know how the demands of that setting are communicated to us and why we internalise them. When we join an organisation, there are demands on us to learn certain things (how to do our work, 'correct' attitudes and behaviour) and we need to learn how to survive in a new and possibly unfamiliar environment. This process can occur in a formal fashion, as in induction programmes where we learn about the work itself and the rules and procedures that surround it. But more importantly it can proceed in an informal fashion, stemming not from training but from our interaction with those we work with. Most people learn about work through observation and questioning of their workmates. One of the major industrial training methods has for a long time been the 'sitting with

Nellie' approach where the recruit works with a trained operative to learn the skills necessary to the task. An unlooked-for consequence in this may also be 'learning the ropes', how to cope with work, utilise short-cuts, or learning to 'make-out' by manipulating bonus systems. A modern analogue of this approach is the practice of *mentoring* where 'entrants' or candidates for promotion are guided and counselled through their career development. Kram (1983) identifies stages of *initiation, cultivation, separation* and *redefinition* in this type of relationship, mentors effectively leading their chargse to a stage where they can define their own relationship to the demands of their 'career cycle'.

Hosking and Morley (1991: 100–4) comment on how 'evaluative beliefs' contribute to mentor/sponsor relationships, in that as projects/organisations become larger, more reliance has to be placed on ideological belief structures, with both positive and negative results. They widen this discussion to the relations between scripted behaviour, cognitive dissonance, self-justification and rationalisation in network building, which is essentially a process of what we might term self-socialisation in support of career and personal goals.

Socialisation

The models and mechanisms of learning relevant in the above contexts are those that offer some account of the process of *socialisation*. Socialisation as a process reflects our general theme on the construction of subjective identity, in the sense of an individual both becoming a subjective entity and becoming subject to external influence. These two aspects of the socialisation process are not separate, although they are conceptualised differently in organisational literature and are generally explained through psychosocial mechanisms rather than subjective experience. On the one hand there are the aspects of socialisation that deal directly with the psychological process of learning, notably the 'social learning' models characterised by Eysenck (1947) which focuses on inherited differences in a person's ability to build up conditioned responses, and by Bandura and Walters' (1963) model which focuses on how conditioned responses to external stimuli are mediated by internal psychological processes. On the other hand, there are those aspects of learning dealing with the ways in which a person is tied to the demands of the groups to which they belong through social identity theory, which is discussed further in Chapters 20 and 21.

Social learning theories combine elements of cognitive and behaviourist theory to produce a model of learning which focuses on interaction. From this the basic process of learning is the observation of the behaviour of others: the *selection, organisation* and *transformation* of the stimuli provided through observation, and the subsequent identification with, and imitation of, selected parts of the observed behaviour. This process, known as *modelling*, goes further than mechanisms such as associative or instrumental learning, as it involves people generating their own rewards and reinforcements, and selecting behaviours in line with their own expectations and desired consequences. We do not slavishly imitate the behaviour of those about us, or even those appearing to act in the most appropriate fashions. We select those aspects of the activity we observe which we can usefully incorporate into our own repertoire of appropriately scripted behaviours. By modelling our behaviour in this fashion we avoid indulging in wasteful and possibly embarrassing attempts to fit ourselves to our surroundings by trial and error, while managing to exert some control and influence over our own activity.

Roles

The modelling process guides us to the appropriate behaviours demanded of us in our organisational 'role'. The concept of 'role' has had too much interpretation for us give a full account (see Biddle, 1979 or Mullins, 1999: 470–6). But for our present purposes, roles can be seen as sets of self-categorised, stereotyped and scripted behaviours enabling us to act in a contextually consistent manner. The effect of the *role expectations*, both formal and informal, placed on us by our work and peers are seen as so important to effective management that diagnostic instruments such as the Belbin Team Role Self Perception Inventory (1981) have been developed to aid people in effectively scripting their own differentiated roles in groups and teams (see Chapter 20). Through modelling, our behaviour can be influenced by that of those we select as *role models*, those whom we perceive to be acting in a 'correct' or desirable fashion. By building our own behavioural repertoire out of selected actions of role models we can fit our actions to those required by the organisational culture. Thus close associations with role models can effectively form an informal mentoring relationship. We also utilise negative role models to define for us the types of behaviour we do not wish to imitate, generally based on those we perceive as acting in inappropriate or socially disapproved fashions. In other words, what individuals gain from the social learning process are guidelines and frameworks for action and self-evaluation in the production of an identity which can cope with and blend into its surroundings. Examples might be found in the way that newcomers are socialised into sexually-stereotyped occupations. In the Insco case, for example, the branch manager explains that 'we try to keep people coming in at the bottom so that we can train them to our ways, get them used to the company' (Knights and Collinson, 1987: 161). The models who newcomers are most likely to emulate and compare themselves to are those who appear situationally competent, who fit the appropriate stereotypes and who hold the right attitudes, thus reproducing, for instance, the 'macho' image of the construction worker.

Socialisation through social learning does not, however, simply transform an individual into an image of what an organisation requires, notwithstanding Handy's definition of socialisation in OB terms as 'the process by which an organisation seeks to make the individual more amenable to the prevalent mode of influence' (1976: 134). We certainly do learn to produce in ourselves normative characteristics and produce identities with consistent social meaning, but at the same time we acquire and produce distinctive characteristics, those which define our identities. Even though social learning enables us to take on a normative role, our observations can just as easily lead us to enhance those things about ourselves reinforcing our personal rather than social meaning.

The role models we use are not only those people with whom we are in immediate contact. In producing an identity we also use individuals and *reference groups* with whom we may have little or no interaction. We may base the image we present not only on those behaviours and models appropriate to our present context, but on those pertaining to roles and perceived identities to which we aspire. We may act in a way consistent with other shop floor workers, but at the same time adopt some behaviours which link us with superiors if we desire promotion, or perhaps the representatives of a professional or trade union organisation if we perceive enhanced meaning and identity as lying in that direction.

Skills and styles

As intimated earlier, much of the work on learning theory has been linked to increasing the effectiveness of formal training programmes, the key concepts here being the *transfer of learning*, the *acquisition of skills* and adapting training programmes to the *'learning curve'* of the trainee. (See McKenna, 2000: 571–2 for a useful discussion.) Learning transfer relates to the conditions under and extent to which stimuli can be generalised to new situations. Skill acquisition is generally approached through prescriptions about the nature of feedback to be given (developed for example from Miller's TOTE model), and how learning tasks should be broken down into assimilable chunks prior to practising the integration of the whole task. 'Learning curves' indicate that the rate of assimilation of learning tends to reach a plateau after a while, and that careful setting of objectives is needed to get the trainee to the next stage of his or her learning. This latter notion can be related to our earlier comments on action regulation, in that as action patterns are learned we need to go back to the intellectual level of learning before we can script new action patterns and get to the next stage of integrating the total activity into sensorimotor action. Where we have to learn consciously again, clear objectives become critical variables in our motivation to learn. (See the section on *goal-setting* in Chapter 19.)

Pressures continually to update employees' skills are becoming greater in this era of 'continuous professional development' (CPD) and quality standardisation in initiatives such as ISO9000 and Investors in People (IiP). This has consolidated the interest in management development circles on the notion of *'experiential learning'*, derived from Kolb's (1976) work on the *'learning cycle'*. This suggests that learning takes place in four stages, all of which are necessary to effective learning:

1   Seeking concrete experiences related to goals.
2   Reflective observation and interpretation of experience.
3   Forming abstract concepts and generalisations related to goals.
4   Active experimentation on concepts, leading back to 1.

Kolb's evidence on management learning claims that personal preferences and learning goals will lead individuals to focus on particular stages of the cycle in learning styles which can be identified through use of the 'Learning Styles Inventory' (LSI). On this basis, Starkey (1996: 262) notes that 'In general managers tend to emphasise active experimentation over reflective observation. . . . Theorists of management tend to stress reflective observation and abstract conceptualization.' This is indicative of the fact that Kolb's learning styles actually relate to combinations of preferences for particular stages as follows: convergent (3 and 4), divergent (1 and 2), assimilation (2 and 3) and accommodation (1 and 4).

Kolb (in Starkey, 1996: 279) then links these styles to a model of the problem-solving process so that the full process requires all four styles to be enacted. Style preferences are not simply related to personality characteristics, but to the context of, and the skills or strengths needed in, the learning situation. Thus managers would tend to an accommodation style which Kolb links to executing solutions and choosing models or goals. Management theorists on the other hand would tend to an assimilation style which Kolb links to problem selection and considering alternative solutions.

It is still the case that in much of the mainstream OB literature, learning styles are linked directly to personality traits in stages 1 to 4 above, rather than to Kolb's style typology. This can be seen in an often-cited application produced by Honey and Mumford (1982) who classify the stages themselves as styles:

- activist (1)
- reflector (2)
- theorist (3)
- pragmatist (4).

Honey and Mumford's styles are used more as predictive personality traits than as analytic or diagnostic categories, and are claimed to explain why 'given the same experience . . . some people learn while others do not' (promotional brochure for Honey and Mumford's 'Learning Styles Questionnaire'). The probability is, of course, that given the same experience, what some people learn is that they do not want to assimilate the material their trainers are giving them. When CPD becomes '*compulsory* professional development', learning itself becomes a chore which will promote either resistance or resigned acceptance to learning initiatives.

Learning and development

The predecessor of systems of continuous improvement or professional development was *staff development*, the theoretical base of which Miller and Verduin (1979) place in perceptual psychology, assuming attitudinal and behavioural changes to be dependant on changing perceptions, as argued in Chapter 15. The element of *goal-setting* involved (see Chapter 19) made staff development the natural heir to Drucker's earlier *management by objectives* (MBO), but took the notion one stage further. Instead of setting goals monitored by senior managers to ensure compatibility with organisational objectives, individuals were required to set goals compatible with their own aspirations and 'needs'. By emphasising the intra-organisational construction of individual goals, staff development provides an effective gloss over managerial strategies for transforming learning, motivation and identity into influence and productivity.

Personal development forms and similar tools for profiling our work relationships are an integral part of organisational learning and development practices. They act as self-administered, continuously assessed personality, attitude and aptitude inventories, providing feedback to both management and staff. They facilitate the moulding of operational identities through the integration of functional activities into social comparison processes and hierarchical relationships. Profiling can be further reinforced by courses, trips and exchanges which act as rewards for correct behaviour, and the internalisation of group and organisational norms. Employers such as Ford Motors have offered exchanges to production workers: they visit and work in plants employing new production processes and those which are said to have good productivity and industrial relations records. Return visits presumably imbue others with the values that have made particular plants successful and of course highlight workers' perceptions of their dispensability within the international division of labour. Exchanges can produce facilitation effects similar to those of team-building exercises where members of the same group or organisation are required to dress similarly and/or indulge in activities designed to increase group identification (see Chapter 20).

What systems such as staff development and CPD are predicated on is the belief that individual change within processes of organisational change is facilitated by behavioural technologies such as the LSI, profiling systems and so on. In the same fashion, organisational change is facilitated by strategic approaches to learning which emphasise generating the 'right' *learning climate* in organisations. There are many forms of organisational learning initiative, but we wish to focus on phenomena of the learning organisation as it is founded on the links we wish to go on to make between learning and change.

Learning organisations

The literature on what has come to be known as the 'learning organisation' is characterised by themes of strategic and self-managed change as a way of dealing with environmental uncertainty. The notion, which can be traced back to the work of Argyris and Schön (1978) on *theories of action* in *organisational learning* and to the work of Lewis (1984) and others on *open learning* and computer-based training, is based on the recognition:

> that members of organisations must be equipped to create and sustain values, knowledge bases, processes, skills and systems which promote effective responses to change. This dictates the need for higher trust cultures, for responsive systems and knowledge workers who are capable of participating in making decisions and solving problems at point of discovery and without reliance on complex command and control systems. (West, 1994: 15)

Numerous writers including Senge, Lessem, Honey and Burgoyne have been involved in promoting the idea of a learning organisation, a phenomenon that John van Maanen of MIT has described as 'what management in the twenty-first century will be about' (MCB University Press circular advertising *Learning Organisation* journal).

Research on learning in social psychology was in the main individually-based, and the assimilation of such knowledge into a more collective notion such as the LO was difficult and only achieved at some cost. Analogies to individual learning used by leading organisational psychologists such as Argyris (1967) tended to rest on a physical/mental progression from infant passivity, dependency and submission to control, through to the maturity of reflection, foresight and responsibility for others. However as Mathews notes (1994: 288), the concept of the learning organisation is distinct from the learning processes of individual employees. Thus people embody learning in their own minds, but organisations have no 'mind' except in a metaphorical sense. Organisations need to develop institutional structures embodied in organisational routines through which experience can be gathered and accumulated. Such organisational memory can be manifested informally through culture or formally through official records, minutes of meetings and so on.

Organisational learning versus learning organisations

The critique of the learning organisation literature presented above is not, however, the whole story. Much of the discussion of learning in organisations nowadays comes under the heading of *organisational learning*, which like the learning organisation sounds on the surface like simple reification; organisations are not entities –

therefore they cannot learn. However, as complex interactions of individuals and groups, and as flows of information and resources, organisations can be considered as 'communities of practice' (Brown and Duguid, 1991). As such they are arenas where both formal and informal learning takes place, where relevant knowledge is constructed, stored and transferred. How and whether organisational learning and learning organisations differ in relation to such a concept of organisation is seldom explored in mainstream texts.

Where differences are noted, they seem to centre on the formal/informal distinction as exemplified in the work of Jones and Hendry (1994). They associate organisational learning with traditional training regimes and HRM initiatives, and learning organisations with Pettigrew and Whipp's (1991) notion of *organisational capability*, which is more in line with informal socialisation and experiential learning as discussed earlier. The important point here is to what extent both are instances of managed versus self-managed learning. We know that significant numbers of people in modern organisations learn to appropriate information technologies to their own use, learning much more than is required of them in their work. Thus the development of capabilities by organisational members will proceed in a tacit manner even where no formal training is given.

In the light of such self-directed empowerment, McHugh, Groves and Alker (1998) note that in operational terms there appears to be little in learning organisation initiatives that provides any real commitment to HRM strategies of mobilising consent:

> The linkage to strategy demands support for flexibility of organisation and open-ended intrinsic commitment, but for the learner the 'locus of control' is still exogenous in that learning must be shown to achieve objectives related to their task and role. (McHugh, Groves and Alker, 1998: 218)

Thus, although characterised by factors such as emphases on self-management, matrix type structures, dedicated training support and flexibility in working practices (Sims, Fineman and Gabriel, 1993: 198), there is little practical difference between learning organisation initiatives and the content of traditional organisational learning. As such, the use of practices under these banners can also be viewed as yet another vehicle for achieving organisational change, or more accurately as Swieringa and Wierdsma (1992: 1) put it, for 'the changing of behaviour'.

This can be exemplified by reference to earlier notions of open learning via computer-assisted learning (CAL). Fuller and Saunders (1990: 32–3) note three basic rationales to open access learning: the *instrumental*, based on simple access to training opportunities; the *prescriptive*, based on empowerment of individuals and groups; and the *functional*, based on cost-effectiveness. They argue that the prescriptive approach (that closest to the ideal of the learning organisation) is 'likely to be inconsistent with company objectives' and 'inevitably constrained by commercial and organisational factors': in other words, it will be *managed learning*. The implication here is that learning organisation initiatives will be dependant on *ad hoc* instrumental opportunities and functional imperatives. Thus even a sincere attempt to promote a learning organisation will face a tendency to slide back into Jones and Hendry's organisational learning approach, all that is left of the learning organisation being the legitimating rhetoric of employee empowerment.

The idea of a learning organisation now becomes similar to the 'morally sustaining ideas' and 'socially integrating myths' through which Selznick characterises leadership (see Chapter 17). This is to be expected in that implementation of organisational learning can be firmly linked to that of 'new-wave' manufacturing techniques. Winfield and Kerrin (1994), in a survey of 60 Midlands manufacturers and a case study of Toyota in Derbyshire, note that the 'continuous improvement programmes' associated with organisational learning are deployed directly alongside TQM and JIT programmes. The introduction of such programmes is criticised for a lack of attention to 'human resource issues' (1994: 8), and learning systems and techniques complete the 'whole package' necessary for the effective utilisation of 'new' production practices. In a similar vein, Seely-Brown and Duguid (in Tsoukas, 1994c: 165–87) make important distinctions between 'espoused' and 'actual practice' in working and learning, Shrivastava (1983: 25) earlier noting a link between organisational learning and the development and introduction of new management information and control systems. The failed implementation of such systems was identified with a lack of concern by designers for existing socio-cultural norms and learning practices.

In its ties to the introduction of new working practices and disregard for subjective learning, the learning organisation would appear to devolve 'into a simple goal-setting exercise underwritten by an appeal to the superordinate goal of organisational survival' (McHugh, Groves and Alker, 1998: 218). As such it has little respect for the learning theory from which it claims descent, and is more properly seen as a tool of change and development practices, attempts to change behaviour and working practices through cultural initiatives, and more straightforward attitude change techniques. This is a reciprocal relationship in that the tools employed, for example Lewin's unfreezing–refreezing model, are essentially developments of learning theory, in this case the notion of the learning curve. The identification of the individual's 'training needs', in systems such as development profiling, provide the mechanisms through which public commitment to change is acquired. That such technologies of regulation are seldom related to any real concern for individual development is evidenced by the argument that learning initiatives can be short-circuited by what Easterby-Smith characterises as an 'obsession with activity' (1992: 28), and Senge (1992: 38) as a concern with *performing rather than learning*. This bias towards productivity and 'bottom-line' definitions of growth once again confirms the paucity of claims to increase the motivational content of work and refocuses commitment as simple compliance (see Chapter 19).

The difficulties and self-defeating nature of linking strategic organisational demands to learning and motivational factors must in the end lead us to question the extent to which systematic control of such factors is ever possible. However, such systematic control is exactly what is sought in the study of how we learn to collaborate with organisational transformation through the planning and implementation of *change*.

Changing the people?

Change, in both individual and organisational terms, provides the linkage between learning and attempts to harness the *innovation* processes regarded as critical to organisational success these days to the 'bottom line'. Just as the exploration of learning in organisations requires consideration of socialisation processes, our accounts of innovation and change require us to consider issues of *creativity* and *sustainability* as in Figure 16.1.

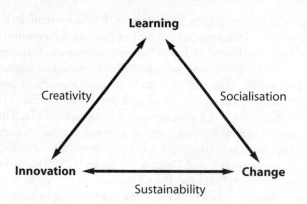

FIGURE 16.1 Learning, change and innovation

Models and processes

Most models of change are developments in one way or another of Lewin's and/or Leavitt's early models. Lewin's (1951) force-field analysis of driving and restraining forces has found widespread practical application in its unfreeze–move–refreeze model, which itself is also applicable to learning and attitude change. Newer models seldom do more than add new variables to the list of factors assumed to influence responses to change (see Martin, 1998: 589–91). Rather like the content theories of motivation we will discuss in Chapter 19, they tell us about the *what* of change but little about the *how*. When the how of change processes is discussed, it is generally in prescriptive terms and concerned with managerial responses or styles. While employee resistance is continually invoked as a barrier to change (see Martin, 1998: 583–6), the issue of managerial resistance is rarely mentioned.

Other models such as that of French *et al.* (1985) specifically develop Lewin as a mechanism for planning and evaluating change processes. Unfreezing here involves *preparing for change* by gaining trust and developing team awareness. The movement phase *evaluates* the current position, developing aims, objectives and action plans. *Implementation* can overlap the unfreezing phrase, where for French *et al.* the important courses of action consist of stabilisation and review of the situation.

Leavitt's (1965) people–task–technology–structure model is widely used to illustrate the interdependence of organisational variables in the process of managing change. Like the Lewin model, new variables such as strategy, environment or culture are routinely added to reflect current concerns (see Martin, 1998: 587, or Rollinson *et al.*, 1998: 612–3). Strangely, one of the few developments of Leavitt's model to highlight explicitly the role of the individual is the McKinsey 7-S framework of organisational analysis. Despite its genesis in the work of Peters and Waterman (1982, see Chapter 13) this model does highlight skills, staff and style as being of greater importance to change processes than strategy, systems and structure (shared values being the linking factor).

Collins (1998, Chapter 4), in his review of sociological perspectives on change, produces a cogent critique of what he terms the *n-step* models of change abounding in the literature. N-step models act as programmatic, recipe-style guides to the change process much as the French model cited above, Collins giving a typical simplified example as follows (1998: 83):

1   Develop strategy.
2   Confirm top-level support.
3   Use project management approach.
4   Communicate results.

These models are described as *undersocialised*, 'in that they fail to acknowledge change as a social activity, involving people from diverse social groups, who will tend to interpret issues in different, and often quite divergent ways' (1998: 82). Their rational, sequential and prescriptive nature (1998: 84) focuses mainly on the co-operative elements of organisation (1998: 87), where the 'futile resistance' of workers is centred around 'poor communications or deficiencies in worker psychology' (1998: 91). Opposition to 'new business realities' is ideologically recast as resistance by workers who are 'lacking the psychological make-up to deal with change' (1998: 92). Thus, according to Collins, real people are absent from n-step models (1998: 96) or appear to be 'docile, malleable and altruistic . . . while managers appear to be strong, creative and decisive' (1998: 97).

What is apparent here is that, as with the study of personality (see Chapter 15), the concern is not for the uniqueness of the individual experience of the change process but for consistent modes of response that can lead to predictive and/or prescriptive categories. Such categories are judged against outcomes and these in turn are judged against increasingly standardised sets of criteria, for example, 'benchmarking' (see Rollinson *et al.*, 1998: 614–15). Where models (such as Lewis, 1991) do attempt to account for subjective factors of individual feelings, skills and knowledge, they still tend to set subjective and personal factors against objective and task-related aspects of the change process. Thus they are still intended as tools to aid managers to 'imbue the person with the courage to confront his or her feelings about the change' (Rollinson *et al.*, 1998: 614–15).

Such examples illustrate why reading the change literature is such a frustrating experience. There are many models, innumerable prescriptions and case studies, but little that is truly informative. It also embodies a recurring tension between self-directed and imposed change. As Hollway notes in her commentary on Argyris's work on interpersonal skills training:

> How do you ensure change without imposing it? You convince the individual who is the object of the change that they are choosing it. This is what I mean by subjectification. Argyris calls it growth. (Hollway, 1991: 95)

An organisational capacity for change is often reduced to an individual's willingness to 'be motivated' or to 'accept ownership'. Such thinking neglects the complex mixture of identities and interests at work.

Staff and managers within public organisations are often trying to deal with change on many levels at once, trying to balance conflicting demands, trying to sustain a sense of personal worth and purpose within large and confusing organisations, to construct an identity out of the elements of professional, manager, citizen or activist that make sense of trying to feel good about what they do. They are working within the constraints of

> organisations that don't work well with creaking systems and not enough money. For many staff and managers, old realities exist. They do not experience change as transforming the everyday job, simply making it more difficult.
>
> (Goss, 2001: 154)

As the extract above indicates, employees may reject or resent the 'subjectification' process. That is not to say that change does not or should not take place, merely that we need a deeper, more balanced understanding of it.

Change and stability

What is often lacking in both theoretical models and real-world change processes is an awareness of the importance of continuity to individuals and groups involved in change. Alvin Toffler (1970: 342–3) argued that to cope successfully with change we need *zones of stability*. Toffler, who was one of the first advocates of managing rather than suppressing or adapting to change, identified factors such as close family ties and habits as 'patterns of relative constancy' (1970: 435) which provide us with what we would term a redoubt against the relentless pressure to change. However in organisational terms, such zones of stability might represent the very factors managers and change models identify as sources of resistance to change. Thus we have a catch-22 in the fact that the implementation of change demonstrably lacks concern for the very factors that might make individuals tolerate it. It is often held that people prefer technological to cultural change, and in zones of stability we can see why.

The management of change rather than the experience of change is the focus we find in mainstream OB. Hosking and Anderson (1992) cast doubts over this perspective, arguing that it produces an 'illusion of manageability'. They cite Ernecq on interventions often being 'usurped by outcomes which were neither expected nor intended', and Crouch *et al.* on their study on the 'myths of managing change' to the effect that:

> a common response to environmental change was for managers to initiate endogenous changes in their own organisations, which often result in pleasant feelings of coping with anxiety-provoking events. (Hosking and Anderson, 1992: 7)

Change as conceptualised by OB appears to be a process of attitudinal adjustment, behavioural change and outcome evaluation. Change processes are presented as value neutral in much the same way as decision-making processes. Such political neutrality has an ideologically normative value for management (see Hosking and Anderson, 1992: 8–9). This reinforces the value to be had from cost and efficiency benefits, but ignores the problems raised by the tensions between stability/pressure to change, strategy/execution and autonomy/interdependence noted above. According to King and Anderson (1995: 86), what managers will increasingly demand in the future is 'evidence of rigorous evaluation of different intervention strategies'. From our point of view, this should bring us full circle to the concerns of those such as Rowntree and Myers noted above. Constant change programmes, coupled with the constant experiential change to which individuals and groups are exposed, should put change fatigue to the fore as the focus of the study of change. However King and Anderson argue that managerial demands will lead instead to more research on factors such as team building for innovation and creativity training

Innovation: necessity or luxury?

Defining innovation

The typical response to 'hitting the wall', as one senior manager in a case study company put it, is to reinvent the programme: a perspective driven by a problematic of 'change' rather than innovation. Yet innovation is regarded as increasingly important, primarily because it is taken to be a key indicator of how successful organisations are in adapting to more rapidly changing and complex environments. The innovation literature is overwhelmingly focused on the problems of initial design and development, and then of implementation and diffusion (Slappendel, 1996). In part, this is because of the continuing bias towards products and technologies. But even in the organisational sphere, the distinguishing feature of innovation is conventionally seen as newness or novelty, partially as a means to make distinctions from conventional change. As Anderson and King observe, 'By far the largest proportion of research into the organization as innovator is concerned with identifying factors which help or hinder the introduction of innovations' (1993: 7). In practice, this results in problems of poor implementation. As a leading consultant with Arthur Anderson said of UK managers, 'They're good at leaping into new ideas, not so good at finishing them off' (quoted in *Financial Times*, 'Innovation Does the Rounds', 18 September 1995).

This theoretical orientation is at odds with the practical experience of organisations. The main priority for management strategy is to create the conditions – institutional and cultural – for sustainable innovation through self-generating processes and learning mechanisms in the workplace. Yet organisations often do not get through to this stage of development. Instead they get delayed and diverted by problems of diffusing innovation through organisational layers, functions and units. Typical definitions reflect the concern for newness and novelty:

*   'the commercial application of knowledge or techniques in new ways or for new ends' (UK House of Lords Select Committee on Science and Technology).
*   'innovation at the organisational level is defined as the adoption of an idea, or behaviour new to the adopting organisation' (F. Damanpour, 1996).
*   'the intentional introduction and application within a role, group or organisation of ideas, processes, products or procedures, new to the relevant unit of adoption, designed to significantly benefit the individual, group, organisation or wider society' (West and Farr, 1990: 9).

We can also distinguish between potential and actual innovation: 'Potential innovation occurs when an agent or system alters its dominant schema. . . . Actual innovation occurs if this alteration is beneficial to the agent or system'(Stacey, 1996: 288). 'Beneficial' in these terms is regarded as the delivery of what is considered the 'price for further interaction'. Additionally, while it is useful to distinguish between phases of innovation, we should also recognise that there are key organisational domains with distinctive tensions and choices: most notably the labour process, employment relationship and governance. In other words, innovation does not take place abstractedly in *the* organisation, but on particular territories that do not necessarily operate with the same dynamics and agents. Moreover, as we outlined in Chapters 11 and 12, private-sector research has shown that it is in the 'interaction effects' between these spheres that innovative work organisation is most effective.

Diffusing innovation: change agents and agencies

As Anderson and King observe: 'By far the largest proportion of research into the organization as innovator is concerned with identifying factors which help or hinder the introduction of innovations' (1993: 7). This emphasis on the nature of the diffusion process has traditionally been researched in terms of inhibitors and facilitators.

There is considerable emphasis on the characteristics of innovators themselves, who are frequently seen as self-directed agents guided by a clear vision, or champions of products and processes. Often this involves trying to identify personal qualities: 'this "trait approach" assumes that certain individuals have personal qualities which predispose them to innovative behaviour' (Slappendel, 1996: 110). Again this indicates a bias towards science and technology; innovators are akin to the 'heroic inventor' of the past. More broadly, as Mathews notes, 'in the business and management literature, organisational innovation is still conceived generally in terms of the characters, personalities and qualities of the people involved . . . this is equivalent to the "great man" perspective of scientific and technological progress' (1994: 299). There are clear parallels also with the change literature. As Buchanan and Badham 1999: 23) note, 'change champions' are often presented as heroic figures at the expense of the wider cast of characters.

While key individuals are important, this way of looking at things separates individuals from their context and neglects other participants. The latter are only brought into the picture as potential 'resistors to change' with a predisposition to be hostile to novelty. Whether we are identifying the positive (for example, teams) or the negative (professional or functional groupings) it might be more accurate to talk in terms of agencies, as well as agents. Successful diffusion tends to require that action moves from specific projects and 'change champions' to durable networks and alliances between organisational functions and interests (Marks *et al.*, 1998).

Climate and culture

As Anderson and King note (1993: 14): 'The lessening of interest amongst innovation researchers in leader characteristics and structural variables has been matched in the last decade by a growing emphasis on the role of organisational climate and culture in facilitating or inhibiting innovation'. A focus on the wider climate and culture for innovation is a way of emphasising the collective and contextual nature of action. The conventional wisdom of research is not surprising: climates should provide support for new ideas, willingness to tolerate failure and challenge convention, freedom to act, constructive controversy and risk-taking.

It may also be useful to examine the way in which successful change projects are based on the formation and diffusion of cultural capital. Adapting the concept of Bourdieu (who uses it to explain comparative educational advantage), the spirits industry research referred to previously (Marks *et al.*, 1997) found that United Distillers recruited managers who had experience of leading change programmes, rather than for their technical or sectoral experience. This infusion of managers constituted a key cultural resource. The change programme, Towards World Class (TWC), was conceived by the senior operational executive team and defined through 18 months in often gruelling meetings, facilitated by consultants. This constituted both a crucial learning period for senior operational managers and an intensive socialisation into the new expectations of United managers. Six cross-functional project teams – Assets, Competencies, Standards, Service, Suppliers and Culture – acted as the foci of an integrated change effort, tied into matrix reporting. TWC became a vehicle that compelled managers at all levels to become embedded into networks whose triple purpose was improved performance, learning and innovation. The cultural capital accumulated by key agents at the beginning was diversified across plants and functions, TWC compelling managers to 'reinvent' themselves, delegating to wider layers and promoting changes in values.

Sustaining innovation

Diffusion, successful or otherwise, is not the end of the story. Where does innovation go from here? There have been various attempts to conceptualise the stages or evolutionary sequence of innovation. For example, Anderson and King (1993) note problem recognition, idea identification, initiation, adoption, implementation and routinisation; West and Farr (1990) similarly cite recognition, initiation, implementation and stabilisation. There seems to be a problem here about the 'final stage' of innovation. Even when a model moves away from a simply linear sequence, it is essentially cyclical. In other words we are back to the problem of what to do when you 'hit the wall'. This implies that organisations are condemned to replay and reinvent change programmes. Even organisations with some success in diffusing innovation will be faced with a distinct set of problems in sustaining it. The only literature routinely addressing these issues is that on the learning organisation. Whatever its weaknesses, as outlined above, it picks up where the innovation debate tails off by focusing on the need for an internal dynamic of continual transformation. However, in the next section we suggest that the literature on creativity might be a useful source of 'added value' to the innovation debate.

Creativity

Forester notes that innovation 'has been used interchangeably with the term "creativity"' (1995: 3), though fundamental differences exist, for example, over the question of novelty. The role of newness or novelty is seen by Bouwen *et al.* (in Hosking and Anderson, 1992) as part of the 'dialectic process between old and new' (1992: 124) and as one of the three tasks of innovation management. These tasks exemplify the tensions between dominant logics, characterised by continuity – and inclusive of culture, structure and task strategies (1992: 127) – and new logics, characterised by novelty. These are resolved in the innovation process through the third task, transition, characterised by emergent, shared meanings and organisational learning. Novelty is likewise a key definitional component of creativity, although it is qualified by situational appropriateness and the degree of uniqueness as judged variously by the creator or by relevant social groups (King and Anderson, 1995: 12–13).

The critical point here is that creativity/innovation is endemic in both formal and informal work organisation. We have to be creative both to 'make out' and to perform labour, and much of our creativity is deviant in the view of organisational hierarchies, coming under the heading of what Ackroyd and Thompson call *organisational misbehaviour* (1999: 4, 29, see Chapter 21). At the other end of the scale, the everyday fate of creative outcomes is to be appropriated routinely by colleagues and management with no guarantee of mutual gain for the creator. In this sense, any strategy for the promotion of innovation/creativity is another form of intervention aimed at what we refer to as 'engaging the intellect' in Chapter 20.

This notion of creativity as a product of tension is reiterated by Stacey (1996: 256) who talks of the 'space for creativity' as a 'state of tension between an organisation's dominant schema, which is embodied in its legitimate system, and its recessive schema, which is embodied in its shadow system'. Stacey conceives this shadow system as interactions outside the legitimate systems of organisations, in which members 'pursue their own gain, but also the arena in which they play, create and compare innovations' (1996: 290). The utility of this view from the perspective of organisations as complex, adaptive systems is that it separates creativity and the innovation process from the purely institutional. This is similar to the way in which Ackroyd and Thompson (1999: 29) posit the 'dialectic of innovation' as existing between directive and self-organising systems in the production of misbehaviour at work. What Stacey adds (1996: 178–83), is identification of the control parameters mediating the tension between dominant and shadow systems as comprising:

- rate of information flow
- degree of diversity
- richness of connectivity
- level of contained anxiety
- degree of power differentials.

What this gives us, however, is a feel for the role of creativity in the process of innovation in organisational but not subjective terms. Ford (in West, 1997: 2) asserts that creativity is subjective, context-specific and judged on outcomes. The creative outcomes of both individuals and groups are necessary to the innovation process, but organisational innovation does not require involvement of all participants. For many, organisational innovation is at best adaptive learning as opposed to the generative learning supposedly found in learning organisations (see McGill *et al.*, 1992 or McHugh, Groves and Alker, 1998) and at worst non-participative change. Experiencing innovation without creative involvement is likely to be simply the 'exchange of one obligation for another' – the meaning of innovation in Scottish law. Whether innovation is an inclusive experience will be dependent on factors such as the role of intrinsic motivation (Amabile, 1996) and discretion (King and Anderson, 1995: 61–4). These factors will in turn be contingent on perceived levels of ownership of the process as a whole, and on mutual outcomes – in terms of both interaction as noted by Stacey and mutual gains. This again follows Ford (West, 1997: 3) in that innovation is intentional and dependent on expected benefits, which may possibly substitute for the lack of creative involvement for many involved in change initiatives.

Social and organisational creativity

The most cited works on creativity are those focusing on techniques used to 'increase' creativity in decision-making, for example, variations on group-based techniques such as brainstorming and Synectics (see Hicks, 1991). Associated with this type of work is that of Adams (1979) on conceptual blocks to creative thinking, which he divides into:

- *perceptual* – for example, stereotyping, tunnel vision, problem isolation
- *emotional* – for example, preference for judgement, lack of motivation, fear of mistakes
- *cultural* – for example, logic versus intuition, taboos, management style
- *environmental* – for example, distractions, monotony, lack of communication
- *intellectual and expressive* – for example, inadequate language, skills and strategies.

(See Hicks, 1991: 41–50)

These same factors are also directly identified as blocks to change (see Rollinson *et al.*, 1998: 617). In the same vein of socio-psychological research are the conceptual tools called KEYS developed by Amabile (1996), which are 'designed to produce an inventory by assessing stimulants and obstacles to creativity in the organisational workplace' (Roffe, 1999: 10). Once again we see the legacy of the Lewin Force Field model in organisational psychology, with the driving and restraining forces here being reified into conceptual categories of environmental factors. Perhaps more important in Amabile's work is her focus on the role of intrinsic and extrinsic motivation, which with relevant skills are the foundation of creative performance.

Her experimental work shows that creativity is fostered in environments where intrinsic motivation is high (1988) and where people are free from concern about social approval and evaluation (1987). A focus on extrinsic motivation or instrumentality is seen to hamper creativity, as can the presence of explicit contracts for rewards (1986). In terms of innovation, the main contribution organisational strategy and policy can make to enhance creativity would, according to Amabile, be in giving people time, freedom, support and interesting work. As Goss (2001: 169–70) notes of innovation and learning in the public sector, 'Managers and staff need time to think, and spaces within which to try out new ideas, to experiment and test themselves'. The other major requirements are those of participative decision-making and flexible structure. Here, though, we must query at what participation and flexibility are directed; if they are directed simply at the strategic and operational ends of the organisation, then there is no guarantee that levels of intrinsic motivation will be high enough to encourage creativity. The real lesson from this strand of creativity research may be that flexibility has to exist for the employee, and not just for the employer.

The emotional climate in organisations is also cited in relation to the promotion of creativity. Tran (1998: 99) sees emotionality affecting 'organisational dynamics such as idea generation, creativity, adaptability to change, and facilitation of or inhibition of learning processes'. Lofy (1998: 5) 'stresses the importance of attention to the affective dimension of employees' lives as a factor in empowerment and creativity'. Rationality, and in particular critical thinking, also has a role here; Nickerson (1999: 397) notes that creativity and critical thinking are often thought of as opposites, but are best conceived of as independent dimensions. In other words, we need both at once for creativity to flourish. This concern has penetrated institutional thinking in the US to the extent that 'many prestigious bodies, including the American Assembly of Collegiate Schools of Business and the Accounting Change Commission, have asked accounting educators to improve their critical thinking skills' (Reinstein and Bayou, 1997: 336), which gives a whole new spin to the notion of 'creative accountancy'.

Conclusion: creativity, learning and sustaining innovation

The ability to sustain innovation and reproduce the conditions for creativity is inherently complex and fragile. Innovation in each of the domains thus develops its own dynamic, reflecting genuine differences in management requirements, workforce expertise and interests. Changes and uncertainty in the external environment, for example, takeovers and rationalisation programmes, may undermine both zones of stability and mutual gains. Yet there is a paradox here, in that we also have to recognise that an exclusive focus on sustainability may be deleterious to the creative aspects of innovation. The reasons for this can be discovered through research on identifying conditions under which creativity is seen to flourish. Pillinger and West (1995) identify low market share and teamworking, with classic organisational innovation supplying ways of dealing with such factors. The more prosaic factors of job cycle time, variety and responsibility for quality problems cited by West (1997: 87–8) usually produce responses of individual or group creativity, as in the kind of covert job design described by Runcie (1988, see Corbett, 1994: 33–4). Thus success in dealing with external threats or internal job design might remove the very spark needed for creative endeavour to contribute to sustainable innovation on anything other than a formal basis.

Further to this, Ward, Smith and Finke (1999) raise the role of imagery in creative cognition, citing evidence from Finke (1990: 204–6) that creativity is higher when faced with unexpected rather than predetermined categories through which to interpret data. This leaves us with the possibility that uncertainty may be as important to innovation as sustainability, and that systematised innovation processes may again hamper creativity. The difficulty here is in planning for long-term competitive advantage while providing the time, autonomy and support necessary to creativity. The upshot of this is that it may be possible for innovation to be best viewed as a necessity when situations are unfavourable, and a luxury in more favourable times.

Change, then, whether dependent on mechanisms of learning or innovation, seems to require the routine unfreezing or creative destruction of current attitudes and practices surrounding work. At the same time, there is no guarantee that this will not unfreeze the very values that led to identification with the organisation in the first place, even in the case of managers. Indeed many of the *systems of action* (Limerick *et al.*, 1994) which operate to recognise environmental discontinuities and overcome what Argyris (1976) termed *defensive routines*, are aimed at managers:

> Such routines 'enable managers and others to stay within the relative comfort zone of the current deep structure' (Argyris, 1976: 34) and it is the skills and feedback from the learning community which are proposed as the transformational trigger which can bring down such barriers to change. (McHugh, Groves and Alker, 1998: 210)

If 'deep structure' and defensive routines equate to Toffler's stability zones, then change through learning and innovation must be backed up by participation and support to succeed. The further tensions we have identified, between autonomy/direction, strategy/implementation and stability/contention, may make change a speculative enterprise at best, unless creative and innovative learning opportunities are provided for all involved. Unfortunately the factors most often employed in such endeavours represent the exercise of power through attempts to change perceptions rather than any mutual process. They are themselves phenomena which are regularly diagnosed as the source and solution of many organisational problems: *communication* and *leadership*.

17 Open to Persuasion: Communication and Leadership

> An implicit assumption underlying these (sensitivity training) groups is that very little can be gained if someone tells us how we are supposed to behave, how we are supposed to feel, or what we are supposed to do with our lives. (E. Aronson, *The Social Animal*, 1972: 240)

Aronson's comments on the role of leader communication in awareness training accurately reflect the disjunctures between what we know about openness of communication and leader–follower relations, and the way these topics are often presented in mainstream organisational behaviour (OB). The role of the 'leader' in change and innovation processes is often in communicating precisely what Aronson indicates we should not: in other words, the vision of how things should be for the 'good' of the organisation. This chapter explores communication and leadership, with an emphasis on how fundamental psychological processes are turned to the task of moulding our understanding and behaviour within organisational contexts.

The power to communicate

In Chapter 15 we noted that perception and attribution processes can systematically determine or alter people's interpretation of events, others and the attitudes they develop. Our understanding of this in the social world and the workplace is based mainly on the concomitant effects on the *communication process*: effectively, the way we send and receive messages. Such messages can be exchanged between individuals or groups, and can convey information, ideas or feelings. The problems that occur and the means of developing more effective communications have been a major component of the techniques through which the knowledge base of OB is applied in pursuit of organisational effectiveness. At its most basic, this relationship can be seen in the effects on the amounts and complexity of information being transmitted, or *communication load* (Gibson and Hodgetts, 1986). Both individuals and groups can be seen to undergo conditions of *underload*, *overload* or *appropriate communication loading*. These conditions are moderated by personal variables such as the ability and desire to communicate, and organisational variables such as levels of co-ordination, physical proximity, routineness of tasks, time constraints and the number and quality of decisions to be made. Appropriate loading is seen to enhance motivation and productivity, underload to lead to alienation, apathy and demotivation, and overload to cause increased stress, uncertainty and the tendency to make mistakes.

The study of communication in organisations traditionally examines the processes and flow of communications through channels and networks, and the content, sources and nature of messages sent, these last being particularly relevant to the study of persuasive communications. The variables involved in the basic interpersonal communication process are given in Figure 17.1. The level of variability possible at each stage makes it surprising that any successful communication happens at all. The characteristics of senders and receivers, coding, transmission and decoding systems are further complicated by the directions of flow and the levels of formality of the communications, as well as the various kinds of 'noise' that can interfere with communications at any time.

Such a model of communication has its drawbacks, in that it tends to view communication as a step-by-step rather than a simultaneous process, and consequently ignores the interpersonal dynamics of communication. This type of model needs to be augmented by sensitivity to the perceptions of the sender and recipient, as well as the overall social and organisational contexts that give rise to the shared meanings which allow communication to take place. The perceived status, competence and intentions of the sender and, for the receiver, the various factors that we earlier identified as possibly distorting perceptions (for example, halo effects and projection) need to be accounted for. Notions of shared meaning relate precisely to Schein's (1985) model of organisational culture in that shared assumptions, beliefs and rituals constrain the communication patterns of organisational members, especially where cultural beliefs are embedded in notions of openness or those of formality. Conditions of openness and informality may reinforce open debate, rapid and effective communication and loyalty, but at the same time may increase interpersonal conflict and reduce the ability to set and maintain goals and schedules. Conditions of formality and closed, hierarchical

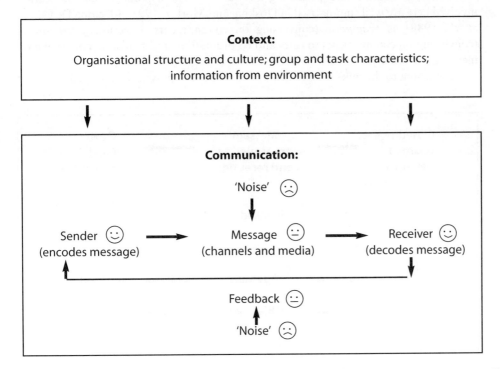

Context and the communication process   *FIGURE 17.1*

Source: based on D. Fisher, *Communication in Organizations*, 2nd end, St Paul, Minn.: West Publishing, pp. 6–21.

communication may lessen debate and conflict along with the ability to express new ideas, while communications will be more precise and deliberate and policies and standards easier to formulate and monitor.

The assumptions and inferences made by senders and receivers in conditions of open versus closed communication have been analysed by Sussman (1991) in terms of the variables given in Figure 17.2.

As the extremes of the closed condition are approached, the level of *meta-communication* is said to increase so that all messages are scrutinised for the hidden agendas and meanings they might convey. At such a level the interpersonal politics of linguistic gameplaying might become of greater importance than the overt content of communications themselves. This in turn links the study of communication directly into debates on the dimensions of power in organisations, which can be seen in Kirkbride's (in Hartley and Stephenson, 1992: 77) discussion of power in the employment relationship. Kirkbride cites various sources to illustrate the point that the use of rhetoric and argument are part of the 'tactical dimension' of power by which meaning is manipulated, both in the pursuit of legitimising control mechanisms and in underwriting political resistance. In particular he cites Czarniawska-Joerges and Joerges who examine 'organisational talk' as a form of 'unobtrusive control' in which linguistic devices in the form of labels, metaphors and platitudes can 'enable [management] to manage meaning by explaining, colouring and familiarising, as opposed to the traditional methods of commanding, fighting and punishing' (1992: 77). The aspects of communication involved here are well summarised in Hosking and Morley (1991: 30, citing De Cindio *et al.*, 1988) as *pragmatic* (conversing on commitments to actions), *structuring* (conversing on commitments to roles and co-ordination) and *semantic* (conversing on meanings of words).

Returning to the links between communication and power, the oft-cited notion of

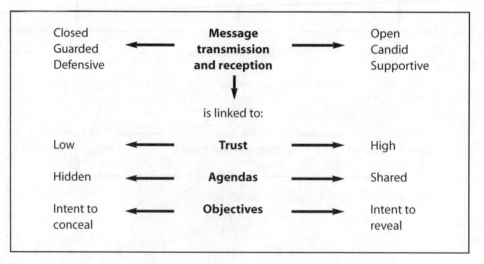

FIGURE 17.2 Communication openness

Source: P. Hellriegel, J. W. Solcum Jr and R. Woodman (1992) *Organizational Behaviour*, 6th edn, St Paul, Minn.: West Publishing, p. 400.

communication as the 'energy' of an organisational system has led to much research directed towards understanding organisational rather than interpersonal communication, particularly in relation to management information systems (MIS). Saunders (1981) has proposed a theoretical linkage between the use of MIS, communication and the relative power of organisational departments or groupings. The use of MIS in critical tasks is said to increase power by their ability to decrease *uncertainty* stemming from lack of information, to increase *nonsubstitutability* (the extent to which activities cannot be carried out by some other group), and to increase the ability to cope with higher levels of *pervasiveness* (the number of communication links with other departments). Though largely untested, this model does point to the importance of communications in maintaining power and role relationships in increasingly complex organisational structures.

The relation of managerial roles to communication has been seen as intimately associated with systems of shared and – more often than not – informal meanings. In her powerful study of computerisation in the workplace Zuboff (1988) traces this relation back to Chester Barnard in the 1930s (1988: 101–2), who characterised organised communication in terms of the *means* (that is, the people involved) and the *system* (the positions they hold). From this, Zuboff argues that managerial executives are responsible for communicating their 'action context' from their own particular facet of the organisation to other executives and 'so contributing to a shared sense of the whole' (1988: 102). Such 'sharing' demands a high degree of informal and face-to-face contact. For Barnard this requirement underwrote the notion that, regardless of formal competencies, the selection and promotion of executives was driven by the interpersonal politics of whether a candidate would 'fit' into the community they must perforce interact with (as we argued in Chapter 15). Zuboff's analysis of the computerisation of managerial information/control systems indicates that managers, in becoming dependent on these systems, may become insulated from 'organisational realities' outside their own networks and community of interest. Through this they might become less adept at the reciprocal communicative relationships they need to maintain up and down the organisation for effective control. She argues that not only do workers face new demands from new technologies, but that:

> Managers also are likely to face new communicative demands – for sharing interpretations, problem-solving, and making sense of complex and interdependent forms of data about people and events. (Zuboff, 1988: 361)

Perhaps the most enduring view on research into communication comes once again from Whyte in *The Organisation Man*. Whyte was so unconvinced by the state of knowledge on communication at the time that he argued that 'it has no business whatsoever as a basic undergraduate discipline'. Notwithstanding the many advances in the area, his remarks on the 'technicians' who 'mentor' this process still ring true today:

> Many of these people don't even *like* the language. They torture it with charts, they twist it with equations and they have so little respect for the devices they recommend as the avenue to the masses that they never demean themselves with their use. Rarely has brevity been advocated so interminably. (Whyte, 1957: 94)

What we need here is an approach that can get beyond the problems Whyte raises and begin to place communication in the context of the relations of subjectivity we highlight. Though there is no fully formed perspective that can do this, insights from social identity and self-categorisation theory (see Chapter 16) at least give us a start in this area. Haslam (2000: 144) argues that from these perspectives communication is a 'complex intersubjective achievement' and that:

> Only when individuals define themselves in terms of a common sense of 'we-ness' will their motivation and attempts to communicate ultimately ensure a full transfer of meaning. In this way *communication produces and is produced by* a shared cognitive network that has the capacity to transform potentially idiosyncratic inputs into co-ordinated action. (Haslam, 2000: 145)

Haslam, in a detailed exposition of the social identity approach to communication, asks, 'Why do people in organizations communicate?' (2000: 125) and concludes that it is 'necessarily oriented towards and structured by our social self-definition in any given context' (2000: 130). The key function of communication in self-definition is seen in exerting influence over others, along with reducing uncertainty, gaining feedback, co-ordinating group performance and serving affiliative needs. Organisational communication, on the other hand, is often these days a tool of ideological influence, and relies heavily on the ability of individuals to underpin their actions within systems of belief. Ideological systems are important to groups as well as individuals (see Chapter 21), but for the moment we turn to the ways in which the capacities, techniques and skills of interpersonal influence are employed to provide self-definition through the effort of surviving and pursuing our personal agendas in organisations.

Interpersonal influence

Influence can be pursued through coercion, the exercise of various forms of power and so on, but the success of such endeavours is in turn reliant on the interpersonal skills of the participants. Arnold, Robertson and Cooper (1998: 45) identify leadership, assertiveness, negotiation, group working and relationship-building as key interpersonal skills, though the implication here is that influence is essentially a set of characteristics which people either have or can acquire. Likewise, persuasion is most often viewed through its effects on the communication process and on attitude change (see Chapter 15). The other main area in which interpersonal influence is considered in OB is that of leadership (for example, in terms of leadership style or the management of meaning for subordinates, see Chell, 1993: 143, 157). Our interest here is more in the techniques, tactics and strategies used to influence others. These can vary from the deployment of argument, rhetoric and metaphor, to the less obvious but equally important skills of impression management, through which we negotiate a consistent image to the world (see Chapter 21).

The basic tactics of influence have been summarised by Forsyth (in Martin, 1998: 521) as:

- promising
- bullying
- discussion
- negotiation

- manipulation
- demand
- claiming expertise
- ingratiation
- evasion.

More complex models of influence in terms of 'political behaviour' have been proposed (for example, see Rollinson *et al.*, 1998: 399) and cross-cultural comparisons have also been put forward (for example, see Fisher, 1993: 416). The former still tend to be lists of tactics, and the latter to be little more than stereotypical continua of characteristics. All the same, managers, organisational consultants and theorists have become more aware of the tactical importance of influence strategies at the same time as individuals and groups have become more adept at using them to pursue their own goals (for example, in interviewing and testing, and communication and presentation skills). Books on how to influence others through self presentation and psychological technique are becoming ever more common, the best being Cialdini (2001), who examines the social psychology of influence and compliance, taking experimental and participant observation research and using examples from a wide range of 'influence practitioners' from the police to consumer and marketing agencies. He takes a wide-ranging view of the practical strategies of influence and the theories underpinning them:

- fixed-action patterns; scripts; compliance
- reciprocation; obligation; repayment (even if uninvited); rejection–retreat; unequal exchange
- consistency; initial commitment, 'foot-in-door'; rationalisation; low-ball
- social proof (consensus, modelling); uncertainty; ambiguity; similarity
- liking; physical attractiveness; similarity; praise; familiarity; association
- conformity pressure; socialisation; adaptivity; symbols
- scarcity, limited edition, deadlines; reactance and loss of freedom (teenagers!); access; newness, competition.

Cialdini notes that most strategies rely on the simple observation that people can usually be pushed into making decisions based on very limited information, and by gaining small commitments it becomes possible to manipulate a person's self-image (2001: 74). Others link influence to meticulous preparation for interpersonal encounters and more recently to nonverbal behaviour. An example of both of these is McCann's (1988) notion of influence through *psychoverbal communication*, which is in turn largely based on the therapeutic techniques of *neuro-linguistic programming* (NLP), which is itself becoming popular in the area of management development (from Bandler and Grinder, 1976, or see Knight, 1999 for a good introduction). McCann links the NLP techniques of strategic and operational pacing to a traditional model of personality (1988: 8–9) based on the Margerison and McCann *Team Management Wheel* (1986) to produce prescriptions on how to achieve influence in different situations. Strategic pacing involves the planning of conversations based on knowledge of your subject, and operational pacing involves techniques originally taken from hypnosis and relying on establishing a feedback rapport with the subject which then allows you to take a leading role in the interaction. NLP has moved on from the therapeutic arena and continued to grow in popularity. What is seldom emphasised in the management and training literatures, however, is the amount of training needed to utilise pacing techniques successfully, and that they work best in highly controlled situations. There are also a plethora of 'airport' style books on offer which indicate that when uncertainty and contingency make it difficult to predict what will work best in any given situation, the only recourse is to the interpersonal skills and techniques which underwrite social and organisational politics.

As noted above, those most dependent on the power of communication and the application of influence are perhaps those who need to convince us that their construction of reality is somehow more powerful than our own. All managers need to do this to some extent, and the most successful are those who appear to be able to achieve this through the exercise of the mysterious power known as leadership.

Leadership, might or myth?

Leadership is defined by Buchanan and Huczynsci (1985: 389) as 'a social process in which one individual influences the behaviour of others without the use or threat of violence'. Explanation in this area has focused on personality traits, styles of leadership and more recently on situation-contingent styles and relations between leaders and group members. It is assumed that the threat of violence is not commonly relied upon nowadays to maintain positions of leadership, though the continuing use of threats to, and sanctions on, financial and job security in organisations means that the 'social process' of leadership must be understood in its intimate relationship with the exercise of power (and possibly in the continued existence of bullying, sweatshops and slave labour). According to Fiedler (1967: 108), 'the acid test of leadership theory must be in its ability to improve organisational performance'. The study of leadership is then directly related to the improvement of management control strategies and to the refinement of the tactical options open to managers in the day-to-day practice of regulating workplace behaviour. This can be seen in the notion that managers, in dealing with problems and subordinates in differing situations, can adopt various 'leadership styles'. In addition, leadership also serves as an almost perfect exemplar of how behavioural theory is incorporated into managerial discourse only up to the point where it becomes too complex for easy assimilation into ideology and practice, with the consequence that the managerial literature then tends to fall back on prescriptive generalities based on theory and research that has been long discredited or overtaken.

Katz and Kahn (1978) refer to leadership in terms of three sets of meanings that are often used simultaneously: first, there are the attributes of the *occupancy of a position* in a social structure; second, the *qualities or characteristics* of a particular person; and last, the *categories of behaviour* associated with a particular person. Occupancy of position essentially refers to the *position power* (see section on '*Contingent leadership*' below) of a person in an organisational hierarchy: for example, regardless of their characteristics, soldiers are to obey officers, no matter who and what they are like. Characteristics and behaviours associate particular qualities with individuals in terms of their recognition as a leader by a particular group. Thus an officer may have the power to lead but may not be recognised as a leader.

The historical study of leadership tended to focus on the habits, sayings and characteristics of those recognised as great leaders, hence the *Great Man* notion of leadership theory that is also referred to as the *Zeitgeist* (literally: 'Spirit of the Age') theory. According to this notion, leaders were born to lead and would rise to power and influence like the cream on the milk, or the scum on the pond, depending on whether you were a follower or a victim of their cause. People could 'rise from the ranks' if they had the necessary qualities, but of course this view did tend to favour those already in positions of social dominance in that they would be better fed, housed, educated and have access to resources and social networks unavailable to others. However the search for what leaders had in common only managed to establish the range of variation possible in leaders, from the short, balding French Emperor to the handsome, gay Macedonian one.

Traits and characteristics

The failure of the search for common physical characteristics led to an effort to find common psychological factors in the *trait approach*. The ideas that particular traits can predict leadership ability and that leaders can be selected still hold fast in conventional wisdom, though in effect all this approach did was to further establish the wide range of possible characteristics that leaders can have. Stodgill's (1974) review of research on traits did not bring up any reliable correlations between leadership ability and particular traits, and found that traits in general were ambiguous and ill-defined. A good contemporary example of this is the so-called 'helicopter ability' (Handy, 1980: 109), which is taken as the ability to 'rise above the situation and see the big picture'. Where we still see lists of leadership traits in the managerial literature, their most abiding feature is that they are generally more representative of those traits thought to be stereotypically male, such as dominance, aggressiveness and rationality, rather than traits stereotypically associated with women such as passivity, nurturance and emotionality. This emphasises the point that leadership qualities can function as legitimising ideological support for the notion that it is the duty and obligation of the manager/leader to direct those not blessed by access to their particular sources of power. When viewed through the kind of assumptions made by managers in McGregor's 'Theory X' (see Chapter 19) and the managerial control imperative of scientific management, the continuing popularity of this largely discredited approach is completely understandable. Indeed Selznick (1957) identified leadership as partly founded on 'morally sustaining ideas' and 'socially integrating myths'. The former mobilise support for the notions of compromise and restraint underpinning management's search for meaning and security. The latter are the *superordinate goals* which leaders appeal to in order to unite organisational members behind managerial strategies.

The fashionable 'Japanese' management styles of the 1980s (discussed in Chapters 11 and 12) worked to lock both managers and workers into appearing to make the organisation successful for the good of all. This was manifested in the single-status canteens and dress, and the workgroup-based discussion circles that channelled perceptions of the organisation towards superordinate goals. Possibly the most interesting pieces of evidence from the trait line of research were the somewhat disconfirmative findings on the acceptability of leaders to group members, which appear to show that groups prefer high-status members as leaders and that the characteristics of followers determine the acceptability of leadership characteristics (Stodgill, 1974: 208–14). The most predictive factors in the characteristics of any given leader would then be their apparent status and the values, interests and personalities of their followers. What is indicated here is that leadership is a relationship with a group of followers or subordinates, a *role* and not a set of characteristics.

Styles and roles

The work of Likert at Michigan, and more significantly Stodgill's work at Ohio State, meant that that rather than being limited to selecting people with leadership traits, leaders could be trained in the form and style of their behaviours and relationships with their followers or subordinates. The Michigan work followed on from the work of Lewin, Lippitt and White (1939) which related three styles of leadership to the emotional climate and hence the assumed effectiveness of work groups. This followed in the trait tradition in that the styles are assumed to be universal or at least enduring attributes. The first of these styles, *autocratic* leadership, continues the tradition of strong personal control and rule-bound relationships, while *democratic* leadership is less regulatory and emphasises collaboration and responsive relationships. This latter style can be firmly linked to the human relations tradition in OB and shifts the view of leadership away from duty and direction towards responsibility and co-ordination. The managerial assumptions here are perhaps best exemplified in McGregor's 'Theory Y' and human relations in general, though interestingly Stodgill (1974: 365) relates 'Theory Y' more closely to the third style, *laissez-faire* leadership. This third style did not provoke as much research effort as the first two, which is easily understood in that it is described as a style in which the leader 'fails' to accept the responsibilities of the position.

The Ohio work stepped away from the trait approach in describing leader behaviour which was open to modification and not an attribute of a person. Two specific forms of behaviour were identified: *initiating structure*, aimed at defining roles, patterns of communication, organisation and action; and *consideration*, aimed at developing working relationships, trust and respect. The only essential difference between these and the autocratic and democratic styles was that any given leader could rate high or low on either or both forms of behaviour. Overall, these bodies of work led to research and training programmes aimed at changing the leadership climates of organisations and the behaviour of leaders – climate being found to have more enduring effects on behaviour than training. This led to assumptions about managerial behaviour shifting for a time towards the notion that it was the duty of managers to co-ordinate rather than direct effort.

Other work, such as that of Vroom and Mann (1960) found that style preferences depended more on the situation, autocratic styles being preferred where objectives centre on task accomplishment. Further developments in this direction appeared to show that autocratic styles were more acceptable in stressful or crisis situations, where the speed of decision-making may be more important than the quality of the decision. Stodgill's impressive review and summary of these approaches (1974: 403–7) concluded that 'In view of the complexity of leader behaviour and the variety of situations in which it functions, a conditional and multivariate hypothesis seems more reasonable than a simplistic, bipolar view of the leader–follower relationship' (1974: 407). In general, then, no one form of leadership could be guaranteed to produce increases in group productivity.

The notion that leadership is a role performed in a group context can be related to work such as that of Benne and Sheats (1948) on group roles, Tuckman (1965) on group formation, Bavelas (1950) and Leavitt (1951) on communication networks and Bales (1950) on the interaction analysis of group performance. Though these bodies of work tend to suffer criticisms stemming from the artificiality of their methods, a synthesis of their general principles rather than their detailed prescriptions can provide useful insights into the processes by which leaders may emerge from newly formed groups.

This is especially the case when related to the often-disregarded notion of leadership 'acts', where leadership is seen as a series of acts or behaviours that can be performed by any member of a group regardless of status and power. Acts tend to fall into two major categories, as in Bales' group functions or Benne and Sheats' group roles, which are *task maintenance* and *group maintenance*. The first of these relates to preventing irrelevant behaviour, overcoming goal barriers and rewarding performance. The second emphasises defusing tensions, offering support and encouraging and rewarding participation. The consistent and competent performance of acts in these categories increases the likelihood of particular individuals emerging as either task or group-oriented leaders as they internalise the success of their actions.

The performance of leadership acts within the arena of group formation could be seen as an input to Tuckman's process of role differentiation in the group (see Chapter 20), and similarly as a mechanism by which members come to have differential access to and control of communication networks. In this sense an emerging leader would be the group member who most consistently performs leadership acts in the *forming* stage and influences the setting of interaction patterns in the group in the *norming* stage. From the development of Bales' work we also get the notion that a group may effectively have two leaders. Since both task and group maintenance roles are necessary to group functioning, even where a formal leader is appointed to a group, an informal and subsidiary leadership role or 'second-in-command' may emerge. This would be occupied by the member most consistently performing leadership acts of the opposite type to the formal leader (in this case most probably the group maintenance or *socio-emotional* role).

Another strand of often-ignored work adding to this synthesis is Hollander's (1964, also see Katz, 1982) notion of *idiosyncrasy credit*. Here the consistent compliance of a leader with the norms and expectations of a group (and consistent performance of leadership acts?) gains 'credit' from the group which subsequently permits them to deviate from group norms. This is a simple concept with great explanatory power, again viewing leadership as a specifically group-oriented role, but a role that allows the leader to act outside the normal social and task maintenance processes of the group in order to serve its interests. A leader may have to represent the group outside its own context, or bring demands to the group that do not fit its norms or expectations. As such, the ability to act idiosyncratically and innovatively may be of benefit to the group as a whole. This concept could be extended to include the acceptability of leadership behaviours such as the selective reward and punishment of group members. As long as they have credit with their group, leaders can act in a manner that might not be acceptable from other members. When a leader is seen to act incompetently or deviates too far from group norms, 'credit' may pass to the member performing the subsidiary leadership role and shift the power relations in the group.

Contingent leadership

Many other elements could be added to a synthesis of the kind introduced above, which though grossly overgeneralised does highlight the notion that leadership is a *process* in which power, influence and role definitions are conferred on or competed for by group members in the mundane performance of tasks and getting on with others. A major fault of such a synthesis is that it cannot easily account for situational and contextual variables, and in considering these factors alongside leader behaviour, leadership theory moved towards *contingency models*, best exemplified in Fiedler's (1967) theory of leadership effectiveness. This was based on his use of his *least-preferred co-worker scale* (LPC), with research based on real-world groups of many kinds from bomber crews to basketball teams. Leaders were asked to rate their most and least preferred co-workers (MPC and LPC). Those rating them similarly were designated 'high LPC' and found to be less controlling and more group-oriented, those rating LPCs more negatively were designated 'low LPC' and tended to be more autocratic and task-centred. (For a discussion of this see McKenna, 2000, or Smith, 1991.)

Leadership effectiveness was seen as dependent on *situational favourableness*, which was in turn contingent on levels of *task structure* (the more structured, defined and routine the more favourable), *leader–member relations* (the more trust and liking for the leader the more favourable), and the leader's *position power* (the more power to coerce, reward and punish the more favourable). Of these factors, leader–member relations were assumed to be the most significant and in situations of mixed favourableness the high LPC, employee-centred leader was found to be most effective. In very favourable or very unfavourable situations the low LPC, task-centred leader was more effective. Additionally, Fiedler also noted that groups might tend to have more than one leader, and in stable or mature group structures the best combination might be for a low LPC leader, with a high LPC second-in-command.

Though many studies have cast Fiedler's conclusions into doubt, the model does sit well with the notions that democratic leaders are preferred in most situations and that autocratic leaders will be more acceptable in crisis situations. What is less understandable in Fiedler's model is why the autocratic leader should be more effective in highly favourable situations. However, the notion that a leader's behaviour could be adjusted to fit the situation or that conditions could be adjusted to fit the leader remains a powerful influence in the field of study, offering as it does the idea that leadership is a variable that can be manipulated to achieve organisational objectives. Other models which extend the themes of situational and behavioural contingency are those of House and Mitchell (1974) and Vroom and Yetton (1973), which both bring in factors relating to the acceptability of leaders by subordinates. House's path–goal model is termed a *transactional* theory as it considers the balance of exchange between leaders and followers, accounting for follower attitudes and expectations. It gives four dimensions of leadership behaviour, subdividing the traditional autocratic–democratic split into *directive*, *achievement-oriented*, *supportive* and *participative*.

Vroom and Yetton's model extends the notion of leader–member relations to consider the quality of leader decisions and the information and skill requirements of subordinates. They give four styles similar to those of House and Mitchell: *autocratic*, *delegative*, *group dominated* and *consultative*. The achievement-oriented and delegative styles offer a partial explanation of Fiedler's finding that autocratic leaders could be more effective in highly favourable situations in that a mature, effective and cohesive group might prefer a leader who simply sets goals or delegates tasks and leaves them to get on with it. This form of leadership might represent the return of the laissez-faire leader to the extent that it is exemplified in the 'hands-off' approach often used with high skill or status groups such as research and design teams.

The style elements of leadership will also be significantly influenced by the ideological elements of organisational climate or culture. Purcell (1987) has summarised such effects on employee relations in a model of management style in which dimensions of individualism versus collectivism give rise to a range of behavioural and strategic options for managers. (See Rollinson, 1998: 693 for a discussion of this.) (See Figure 17.3.)

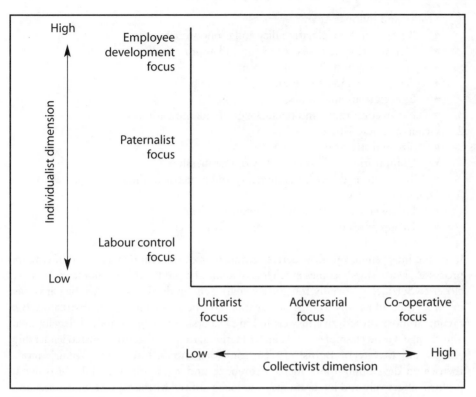

Purcell's scheme for mapping management styles   *FIGURE 17.3*

Source: reproduced from D. Rollinson, A. Broadfield and D. J. Edwards (1998) *Organisational Behaviour and Analysis: An Integrated Approach,* Harlow, Essex: Addison-Wesley. After J. Purcell (1987) 'Mapping Management Styles in Industrial Relations', *Journal of Management Studies,* 24. 5: 535–48. © Blackwell Publishers Ltd.

The Purcell model serves to remind us that the contingent nature of managerial behaviour is itself routinely exploited in the regulation of employees and that managerial labour itself has to be transformed in the face of situational contingencies.

Transforming leadership

The Vroom and Yetton model is known as a 'normative' or 'prescriptive' model in that it specifies leader behaviours further than the four basic styles and links these to decision-making approaches to be used in relation to a range of individual or group problems and situations. The decision-tree methodology used to decide which approach is the most appropriate is still in use as a heuristic to explain how decisions might be reached, but has less practical applicability in that it is complex to use because the variables are difficult to map onto real situations and produce few non-obvious results. The increasing complexity of leadership theory and research was recognised in Stodgill's conclusions to his review (1974: 411–29), where he noted that directions for future research would best be pursued under a conditional or contingency model, but warned that studies would have to account for interactions between more than 30 variables summarised below:

1 Leader and follower characteristics:
- Background (race, nationality and economic condition).
- Identification (age, sex, physique and appearance).
- Status, responsibility, authority and power.
- Personality and behaviour.
- Expectations and values.
- Norm conformity and reference group identification.
2 Group characteristics:
- Size and structure.
- Composition and homogeneity of membership.
- Task nature, difficulty, complexity and time constraints.
3 Outcome criteria:
- Follower satisfaction and acceptance of leader.
- Group productivity, motivation and cohesiveness.

If we add intervening variables derived from context, structural factors and interaction processes, leadership becomes much less of a unitary, predictable phenomena. It moves closer to Selznick's 'socially integrating myth', the multiplicity of variables involved meaning that numerous strands of research have been sidelined in mainstream OB in favour of more prescriptive models linking leadership to organisational development and change. Good examples are Adair's functional model of 'action-centred leadership' (1979) and McGregor Burns' (1978) 'transformational leadership'. Adair's model focuses on developing the leader's awareness, understanding and skills in order to perform effectively and integrate the functions required by the task, team maintenance and individual needs of the group. Leadership here resides in the function and not in the person, and so is close to the notions of role-based leadership discussed earlier.

However, group processes are conceived non-developmentally and the model mainly deals with how formally-appointed managers can be trained to be reflexive about the way that their behaviour affects group commitment and goals. Adair's model embodies some elements of transactional leadership and in its emphasis on achieving change can be linked to Burns' model, which highlights the leaders' need to transform their followers through a focus on their intrinsic or higher-order needs rather than on a particular style. This is essentially a form of motivational 'consciousness raising' which attempts to highlight for individuals how they can satisfy their needs and desires through commitment to group (and of course managerial) goals. Though presented as where 'leaders and followers raise each other to higher levels of morality and motivation' (1978: 20), it is effectively a group-based behavioural technology for turning self-gratification into a superordinate goal. It is unsurprising that this technique enjoyed great popularity in the 1980s, and indeed both this and Adair's model have served as the basis for numerous leadership initiatives in the area of organisational and managerial development.

Charisma?

The development of Burns' transformational model by people such as Bass (1985) and Tichy and Devanna (1986) has brought back into the managerial literature on leadership the concept of *charismatic leadership*. This was brought forward by Weber in the 1920s and had fallen so far out of favour by the 1970s that it rated only six lines and no index entry in Stodgill's opus:

> The *charismatic leader* operates with a staff of disciples, enthusiasts and possibly bodyguards. He tends to sponsor causes and revolutions and is supported by charismatic authority, resting on devotion to the sanctity, heroism or inspirational character of the leader and on the normative patterns revealed or ordained by him. (Stodgill, 1974: 26)

Stodgill does note that Weber's ideas on legitimate authority and leadership were becoming more influential in the US at the time, but this most probably referred to interest in the transition from patrimonial to bureaucratic forms of leadership and authority. The portrayal of the charismatic leader and its discourse of sanctity and disciples is a classic 'morally sustaining idea' that underwrote many of the sermons on visionary leadership from the corporate culture merchants of the 1980s. Causes and cultural change, heroic identification and the idea that everyone can turn themselves into a winner if they will only believe, were the stock-in-trade of Tom Peters and his numerous imitators; only the bodyguards were missing! Hollway's discussion of this phenomenon (1991: 140–4) notes that it attempted to reverse the trend of subsuming leadership into a management function or skill and reintroduced 'soft' human relations ideas into the harder world of professional management training, using the claim that such an approach was capable of capturing for management the 'intractable and intuitive side of the organisation' (1991: 143). Hollway further suggests that in the end rationalistic management practice would find it 'hard to embrace' this cultist version of people management principles. All the same, the 'socially integrating myth' aspect was useful to many organisations to the extent that rationalisation could easily be disguised as revolution. In terms of changing attitudes through culture, whipping up some enthusiasm, even if it is mainly engendered by fear of being on the downside of downsizing, can beget the minimum public commitment necessary to get people on your side for long enough to achieve your desired changes.

Under the models discussed above, from House to Burns and beyond, the duties and obligations of management have shifted considerably. From directive and co-ordinating leadership we have moved to a model that is underwritten not so much by duties or obligations but rather by a desperate casting about for methods of controlling the motivation and commitment of workers. This is achieved mainly through strategies emphasising the manipulation of situations and the management of meaning. Leadership has come down to the management of employee self-control, a problem which Hollway claims has never been solved to the satisfaction of senior management (1991: 143). Johnson and Gill (1993) cite the work of Mantz and Sims (1989) as a major contribution to leadership strategies aimed at producing self-regulation in pursuit of the 'self-controlling organisation'. They suggest that *extrinsic control mechanisms* (that is, traditional controls, external to the individual) should be judged effective to the extent that they 'influence self-control mechanisms based on the internalisation of norms within individual organisational members' (1993: 121).

The focus of leadership behaviour here is to encourage 'self-reinforcement, self-observation, evaluation and control; self-expectation and goal-setting and rehearsal and self-criticism' (1993: 131). This is not of course the 'abdication of responsibility' of the *laissez-faire* leader of old, but is more a recognition of the type of power that needs to be exercised to ensure the mobilisation of commitment necessary to labour processes embodying work intensification and reduced supervision. However, just as Hollway was dubious about the acceptability of such an approach to management, Johnson and Gill are also pessimistic about the advent of the self-controlling organisation, depending as it does on the 'democratisation of society in general and its institutions'. Of course it is always possible that in an attempt to maintain their cultural acceptability workers could present themselves as intrinsically motivated and committed to self-control when the real source of their commitment is greed, guilt or fear – followers just cannot be trusted!

Networking

We now return full circle to the notion that leadership is about legitimating the exercise of power at both the strategic and interpersonal levels. It is not simply the wielding of power, but an inherent component of the armoury of tacit and open skills employed in the negotiation and brokerage of individual and group hegemony. This is exemplified in the approach taken by Hosking and Morley (1991, chapter 9) who see leadership as 'a more or less skilful process of organising, achieved through negotiation, to achieve acceptable influence over the description and handling of issues within and between groups' (1991: 240).

Their critique of leadership in HRM and OB centres around the entitative approach (based on Meyer *et al.*, 1985, see chapter 14) they see as endemic in these literatures. These are exemplified by the treatment of person and organisation as separate entities, persons being theorised independently of their contexts with the result that 'the concept of organisation is implicit and underdeveloped in the treatment of individuals and groups' (1991: 40). Because of this, leadership processes are under-emphasised in favour of a focus on leaders and their manipulations of others in pursuit of 'organisational goals' (1991: 241). Rather than talking about leaders and followers they speak of *participants* in relationships who perceive 'each other as achieving influence in different ways', with varying degrees of acceptability in particular contexts and in line with our earlier comments on leadership acts, that all participants may 'come to be expected to make contributions' (1991: 240). Hosking and Morley highlight the social construction of relational exchanges in terms of *social*, *cognitive* and *political* processes. They argue that cognitive processes need to be understood as 'sense making' rather than as instruments for diagnosing and selecting appropriate behaviours (1991: 247). The political processes and power should be viewed as mainly resident not in structural factors and interpersonal influence but in the 'quality of relationships' and 'the context of interdependence' (1991: 249). Finally they examine the cognitive and political aspects of the organising process of skilful leadership through the 'vehicles' of *networking*, negotiation and enabling.

The political quality of *networks* lies in their influence on commitments to shared understandings, lines of action and the projection of shared valuations. 'Networking' is the process of relationship-building by which persons build up 'organisational intelligence'. Leaders would be those who build enabling relations through negotiation with other participants (with networks of their own?) who can act as their 'eyes and ears' and on whom they can depend for specialised skills. Leaders' networks would probably be small and cohesive, as more diffuse networks might jeopardise the quality of relationships (1991: 252).

We should note that for all that Hosking and Morley's work is detailed, dense with examples and carefully constructed to avoid the failings of mainstream OB, what they conclude is most akin to a more rational and contextually-grounded version of transformational leadership. Networking needs to take place in conditions of 'open-minded thinking' and participation, negotiation through 'acceptable influence' and enabling in respect of the valuations and projects of all participants and not just leader-derived goals (1991: 258). They speak of a 'culture of productivity' where 'all participants take responsibility for the relational processes through which they may help and be helped', a laudable aspiration which is ignorant of the constraints of ideological structures and defensive identities. After all, in the end leadership is no more than what you do with it!

Attributing leadership

A good example of the legitimacy and power attributed to managers as individuals is the way in which attributional bias (see Chapter 15) affects us all. As is the case for any organisational member, managers work within a series of role and informational networks and under both myriad situational influences and, as noted by Lord and Maher (cited in Brotherton (1999: 66), the cognitive context of perceptions of past behaviours and performances.

So personal meaning and influence for managers derive in large part from consistent performances of group roles, but it is also the case that anyone can perform group and task maintenance acts and that these vary between cultures. The expectations placed on managers with formal leadership roles might aid managerial labour by working to mask the visibility of such acts by others. In this sense power and legitimacy are dependent on the shaping of cultural meanings within groups in the direction of dispositional rather than situational attributions. These would enable perceptions of competence to be ascribed to specific individuals rather than to the group as a whole.

Returning to Hosking and Morley's view that leadership is contingent on the networks that can be activated and maintained by managers, we have also to note that networks can be seen as an example of what Feldman and Klich (1991: 76–7) identify as inauthentic social relations. Thus the managerial influence and perceived competence that underwrite leadership may depend, both in their production and maintenance, on creating perceptions of co-operative behaviour, while the reality of the relationship is essentially self-serving. According to Bolman and Deal:

> Leadership, therefore, is less a matter of action than appearance. And when leaders do make a difference in a more proactive sense, it is usually by enriching and updating the script for the organisational drama – by constructing new myths that alter beliefs and generate faith among members of their audience. (Bolman and Deal, 1994: 105)

Creating such perceptions will depend on the maintenance of an illusion of the non-interdependence of intra-group relationships. Such an illusion could be essentially derived from follower 'tact' (Goffman, 1971, see Chapter 21) in that continued group membership would necessitate the collaboration of group members in allowing others to produce consistent performances. Tact may break down in circumstances where there is a loss of perceived legitimacy and/or competence, activating self-serving bias so that group attributions would tend to shift towards situational factors placing the competence of the group over that of the manager/leader role. Shifts of this kind are seen to occur in performance appraisal processes (Tennen and Affleck, 1990) whereas breakdowns in situational tact might again best be observed in organisational change interventions, where managers may have to place task maintenance over group maintenance factors. In a similar vein, variations have also been noted in the task/group orientation of both leaders and subordinates in terms of cross-cultural comparisons, for example, those of Hofstede (1980) and Misumi *et al.* (1989), although once again we need to beware of the stereotypical characterisations embodied in such comparisons.

Finally, the implications of attributional theories of leadership also show that those in leadership roles carry significant advantages in the social perception of their actions by others. For example if we believe that it is possible to affect events, then a 'leader' taking action will be more likely to be perceived as causing the event (Calder, 1977). Meindl *et al.* (1985, 1987) also note that when causes are not clear we are more likely to attribute leadership as the cause (though this might not be unilaterally favourable to leaders) and that organisational success was rated more favourably when attributed to leadership than when attributed to the situation (both cited in Jewell and Seigel, 1990: 432).

Conclusion

Of all the problem areas addressed by psychology in organisations, it is possibly the question of what constitutes leadership that has most influenced the construction of managerial identity. Groups are a tool (see Chapter 20), and communication is a vital skill, but it is the status of the manager as leader which most acts to mobilise the commitment of managers to endure the role conflicts which are the inheritance of their hierarchical position. The commitment of managers, who of necessity must buy into ideologies of control, is more or less taken for granted. It is primarily the ability of managers to infuse motivation and commitment in others that is the common external measure of their fitness for leadership. Internal recognition of such fitness among managers themselves will nevertheless be mainly reflected in factors serving to buttress managerial identity against the contradictory role expectations placed on them by their status as managers and leaders. A crucial factor here is the extent to which managers can withstand and capitalise on these very pressures, and such resistance needs to be understood in terms of the topic we turn to next. This is a phenomenon which we all increasingly recognise in our lives and which is often borne as a badge of honour by managers, *stress*.

18 Putting the Pressure On: Stress, Work and Emotion

The recently-renewed popularity of *evolutionary psychology* has seen any problems we have with work, stress and emotion (and most other organisational behaviour (OB) issues) attributed to mismatches between our 'ancestral psychology and our contemporary environments' (Nicholson, 1997: 1056). This is because 'having left behind our ancestral social systems, we have spent our history experimenting with new social structures which achieve imperfect compromises between our unchanging human nature and our changing environmental conditions' (1997: 1056). Particular evidence on stress and ill health, for example, is related to the physiological effects of occupying subordinate positions in status hierarchies (1997: 1071). However such claims are based in the main on evidence from animal studies, and the fact that human cognition relies heavily on past experience, expectation and imagination means that our experience of stress and emotional upset is very different to that of animals. Arguments such as Nicholson's can in fact be interpreted as using organisation theory to legitimate evolutionary psychology rather than to provide useful insights into the former. What we could get from the evolutionary psychology viewpoint, however, are ways of examining to what extent the scripting of our behaviour is linked to 'hardwired' responses which are difficult to ameliorate or change through experience and learning. The 'fight or flight response' for example (see below) is still with us in the everyday stress reactions we experience, and there may be other automatic responses that we have to deal with in our interactions with others. What we examine in this chapter are the various conscious and unconscious reactions we produce to the pressures put on in the work environment.

Stress: the force to adapt

> There's a lot of tension now, and that makes people mean. We had more control before and less confusion. You could get things done. Every once in a while my head starts to throb. I can't take it. (Stock and bond transfer assistant cited in Zuboff, 1988: 143)

Managerial work was one of the first areas to be associated with the negative effects of stress, especially through personality traits linked with supposedly high rates of coronary heart disease (Rosenman *et al.*, 1964). These are associated with high levels of personal investment in work, as is expected to be the case with those in managerial grades. Although it has since been established that stress-related illness is more likely to vary inversely than positively with organisational status, position and job-related skill (Cooper, 1985), there is still a great concern with managerial stress and its possible effects on organisational effectiveness.

Stress is an all-pervasive phenomenon the effects of which are detectable from the

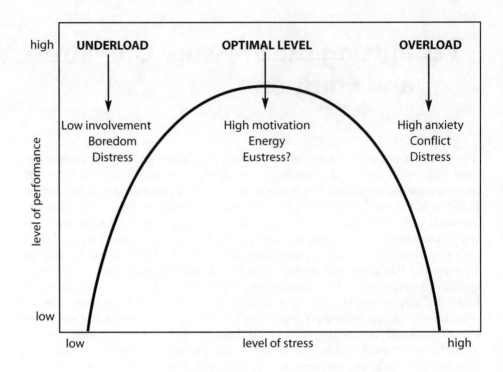

FIGURE 18.1 Stress and performance

biological level, through the psychological and the interpersonal levels, right up to sociocultural systems of values, knowledge and technology, as recognised by C. D. Jenkins (1979). Jenkins' illustrative model identifies the capacities that can help us resist stress, the stimuli or stressors that can lead to a stress reaction, the type and form of those reactions and the possible consequences of the stress continuing. It focuses, however, as does most stress research, on the negative connotations of stress such as heart disease and other illnesses. This is so despite the fact that Selye, a pioneer of stress research, as early as the 1930s identified two main forms of stress, *distress* (often termed strain),which is the negative form found in conventional wisdom, and *eustress*, which is the 'healthy, normal stress' that leads to positive feelings and possibly to what have been termed 'peak experiences'. These forms of stress are possibly better thought of as positive and negative consequences of what is termed *arousal*, or the level of drive or motivation we put into a task. This notion arose from the work of Yerkes and Dodson (1908, see Fisher, 1986: 94–6) on the relation between drive level and learning ability, the idealised results of which are summarised in Figure 18.1.

These results were mainly generated from exposing animals to deprivation or painful stimuli and went on to distinguish two functions of arousal, the *cue* function, which serves to guide behaviour and the *vigilance* function concerned with the amount of energy expended. The continuation of this line of research into the effects of various stimuli on performance has received both confirmation and qualification in work on humans, using incentives as well as negative stimuli. In general, three dimensions of arousal can be distinguished (Schonpflug 1983, cited in Fisher, 1986: 109):

- *Arousal* – facilitating performance.
- *Interference* – trying to ignore the stimulus.
- *Compensatory effort* – putting in extra effort to the task.

Thus, from the start, research into what we now term 'stress' has focused on the facilitation and inhibition of performance. Further, the definition of stress has been problematic both in terms of whether stress causes illness directly (*aetiological*) or indirectly (*non-aetiological*) and because of the range of stimuli and other factors often cited under the catch-all definition of stress, for example, anxiety, fear and frustration.

In 1936 Cannon was the first to make the important link between behavioural changes in individuals and physiological responses to stimuli that upset the organism's homeostatic balance of energy provision. In order to avoid or defend against threats, the organism's circulatory, muscular and digestive systems react similarly to what is commonly termed a 'fight or flight response'. Heart and respiration rates increase, blood supplies to the skin and intestines are reduced while that to the muscles is increased, hormones such as adrenaline are released which both heighten arousal and promote the increased uptake of blood sugars to meet energy demands. However, it was Selye in 1956 who really promoted what we now know as *stress-related illness* in his identification of stress as 'the body's non-specific response to any demand that is placed on it, whether that demand is pleasant or not' (from an interview with Selye: Cherry, 1978: 60).

Selye had been working since the 1930s on physiological stress in terms of his '*general adaptation syndrome*', which identified three phases in the body's response to stressors. The first phase, the *alarm response*, is where a stressor is perceived and the physiological responses given above take place. The *resistance phase* is where the organism adapts to the particular stressor though at the same time becoming less resistant to other stressors. The final phase, *exhaustion*, is where the symptoms of stress-related illness develop (or the 'pathological end-state' according to Jenkins, 1979), where prolonged exposure or overload means that adaptation or resistance could not be maintained (Selye, in Clarke *et al.*, 1994: 398). The problem for the organism here is that the stress response is both cumulative and additive: small stresses or prolonged low-level stress adding up to a larger effect, and different stressors adding to the overall level of stress. The classic relation of stress to heart disease can now be understood in relation to long-term increases in heart rate and blood pressure, and likewise the proneness when under stress to other illnesses such as bacteriological and viral infections through the long-term depression of the body's immune responses. Indeed this model can be used to explain a multitude of phenomena from 'cold spots' in haunted houses (reduced bloodflow to the skin when something scares us) to 'butterflies in the stomach' when apprehensive or in love (reduced bloodflow to, and contraction of, the intestines).

Selye was attempting to distinguish the aetiological, causative factors in the stress reaction from our generalised responses, though Beech *et al.* (1982: 10) note that this has not been followed up by most researchers who refer to both causes and responses as stress, further adding to the confusion as to what stress actually is. Likewise the distinction between eustress and distress is not followed up greatly in the modern stress literature, even though it provides the basis for the most important element of most contemporary models of stress and techniques for stress 'management'. This is that the outcome of the stress response in positive or negative terms is linked to the cognitive perception, interpretation and attribution of the stressors concerned. What one person perceives as stressful may be pleasurable to another. We may change our interpretation of a stressor from something that causes us distress to something we might perhaps look upon as a challenge, or we might react differently to a stressor depending on our locus of control and on whether we attribute its cause internally or environmentally.

Role stress

The cognitive aspect of stress is most commonly identified with the 'cognitive appraisal' approach of Lazarus (1966), who emphasised cognition over the previous medical and physiological approach. However Lazarus, like Cannon, acknowledged that stress was a result of person–environment interactions and it was this factor which led to possibly the most popular modern approach to stress, promoted by the social psychologists Katz and Kahn (1966), which examines stress as a question of '*person–environment fit*'. For Lazarus, individual differences in cognitive appraisal of what is stressful are accompanied by differing psychological strategies or approaches to how we cope with stress: *problem-focused coping* concerns trying to alleviate or manage the stressor itself, whereas *emotion-focused coping* (or *affective regulation*) tries to manage our internal responses to the stressor. These two categories of response describe almost the full range of modern approaches to managing stress, the question for most organisations being the cost-effectiveness of the approach. The latter category seems to be preferred (see 'Counselling' below), even though affective regulation tends to be a short-term strategy on the basis that subjective, emotional coping has diminishing returns in the face of objective problems.

For Katz and Kahn, psychological stress in social situations was linked to how well a person's skills and abilities matched the expectations of their social roles. In the OB literature, expectations are routinely dealt with through the notion of role: the roles we wish to play ourselves, the roles others wish or expect us to play, and the roles set or demanded of us from our relations within work organisations. The total number of *role expectations* that impinge on any individual is referred to as a *role-set*, and can comprise contradictory demands from workmates, supervisors, management, customers or clients, and from what is nowadays referred to as the *home/work interface*. Where the demands of a role or roles are unclear and norms and standards of social comparison are lacking, people may experience *role ambiguity*. The negative consequences of such ambiguity are evident in the importance given to clarity of roles and objectives in management development and employee learning initiatives. Where competing role expectations (for example, those that play a part in determining an individual's intra- and extra-organisational roles) cannot be fulfilled, we come into *role conflict* and such pressures may also originate in *role overload* or *underload*, where the demands of a role are greater or lesser than expected. Role conflicts existing between expectations from the differing parts of a person's role-set are inevitable with the level of pressure that most of us are exposed to in or out of work these days, as people cannot always fulfil all the demands of their role-set. In addition, we may experience role conflicts between external role demands and personal values and beliefs, or between a person's gender, ethnic or skill identity and their treatment by other workers or management.

The cognitive appraisal approach provides crucial links between stressors, attribution and loci of control. This can be illustrated by reference to the work of Winefield *et al.* (in Blau *et al.*, 1993: 147) on unemployment in young adults. When compared with employed adolescents they had lower self-esteem, more likelihood of being depressed or having negative moods, and were more likely to have a high external locus of control. The attribution of the cause of their unemployment had a mediating effect, however: those who attributed it to environmental factors such as bad luck had higher self-esteem and less feelings of helplessness than those who gave internal attributions such as lack of ability (see Blau *et al.*, 1993: 147). It would appear that where stressors are perceived as having internal causes this could bring about a form of self-fulfilling prophecy that in itself adds to the level of stress we feel. This is simply the other side of the coin to the situation where success in overcoming stressful situations can lead us to believe that we can achieve anything at all.

Stress management

Contemporary accounts of the stress 'process' in the work place often follow this notion of stress as 'resulting from a misfit between an individual and their particular environment' (Arnold, Cooper and Robertson, 1998: 422), where internal or external factors push individuals' adaptive capacities beyond their limit. This view has been widely popularised by Cooper and his many co-workers, who have found confirmation for their general model in studies covering a wide range of occupations and organisations. The model proposed by Cummings and Cooper (1979), a 'Cybernetic Framework for the Study of Occupational Stress', reprises many elements of the homeostatic medical model proposed by Cannon, as can be seen from the summary below:

- People attempt to keep their thoughts, emotions and relationships in a homeostatic balance or 'steady state'.
- For any individual the various elements of their physical and emotional makeup will have a balance he or she is comfortable with, or a 'range of stability'.
- Stressors are forces which push physical or psychological factors beyond their range of stability, producing strain and provoking behaviour which attempts to restore the balance or feeling of comfort.
- The various behaviours individuals use to maintain their state of balance constitute their 'coping strategies' or 'adjustment process'.
- Knowing that a stress might occur constitutes a threat to the individual and threat can itself produce strain.

(See Arnold, Robertson and Cooper, 1998, chapter 17)

Derivations of this model, typologies of sources of stressors and the forms of pathological end-state to be encountered, as seen in the Jenkins model above, account for much of the modern stress literature. This tends to emphasise the amount of productivity lost due to stress, its inevitability and the benefits for the enterprise of managing stress. Costs are examined socially in terms of rates of heart disease, mental disorder and social dysfunction, and in the workplace through effects on job satisfaction, performance and absenteeism rates, and more recently in the costs of compensation claims and health insurance (see Arnold, Robertson and Cooper, 1998). Estimates have varied on the cost of stress-related illness to industry, and figures have varied in terms of how they are measured, from in excess of 40 million lost working days in 1986 (Lucas, 1986) to £12 billion in costs to industry in 1996 (Earnshaw and Cooper). These have led to an increasing concern with organisational programmes to help individuals to cope with work-related stress and conflicts over the home/work interface.

Examples of these 'wellness' programmes include Pepsico's multi-million dollar 'fitness' centre, and the stress management programmes developed by the Trustee Savings Bank and Digital Equipment in the UK (Cooper, 1984). The 'Staywell' programme and Employee Advisory Resource of the Control Data Corporation in the US offered 24-hour advice on assessing health risks, medical screening and health education to help people to change life and work styles in healthy directions (Lucas, 1986; McKenna, 2000). 'Companies have a major stake in promoting a healthier life style for employees, because of the potential benefits in reduced insurance costs, decreased absenteeism, improved productivity and better morale' (McKenna, 1987: 403). McKenna (2000: 626–9) refers to a number of UK and US-based health promotion programmes, but also cites Ivancevich and Matteson to the extent that 'quite a large percentage of employees who took part in wellness programmes stopped doing the exercises and showed an inclination to return to their old lifestyles' (2000: 629).

In contrast to the wellness view, the Labour Research Department (LRD) concluded that 'only a minority of organisations are tackling the problem directly' and that the main effort is towards management rather than prevention:

> Where they exist management 'stress control' programmes peddle individual victim-blaming approaches to stress problems that in reality can only be solved by changing workplace organisation and relations. (LRD, 1988: 2)

This individualisation of organisational problems as personal pathological reactions is effectively demonstrated by the use of stress inventories in the diagnosis and 'treatment' of stress. Such inventories commonly rely on identifying the extent to which the individual fits the 'Type A' behavioural pattern which Rosenman *et al.* (1964) labelled *coronary-prone behaviour* owing to the correlation with increased rates of coronary heart disease. The traits associated with Type A behaviour include achievement orientation, status insecurity, time urgency, competitiveness and aggression, traits often erroneously associated with managerial or leadership ability. The inventories themselves are problematic, as indicated by Selye who claimed that 'all stress inventories in common use are somewhat flawed because they fail to give enough weight to individual differences' (Selye, in Cherry, 1978: 63). It is likely, however, that the mere use of a stress inventory does serve to educate and inform respondents as to the nature of their problems. In the main, attempts to modify Type A behaviour tend to concentrate not on relieving the source of the strain but on modifying behaviour through goal-setting and time-management techniques, so that the stress is in effect being actively managed though personal self-control. The result of this is a reduction of the strain felt by the individual into a managerial control variable determining fitness to the required organisational role.

This is further demonstrated by the differential focus on coping in mainstream accounts. Again the emphasis is not on dealing directly with the problem but with emotion-focused coping and what is termed *cross-resistance*. This latter is the notion that increasing adaptive capacities in one area, for example health and fitness, will increase resistance to other stressors, and is the foundation of the corporate wellness programmes discussed earlier. Emotion-focused coping is seen mainly in the popularity of relaxation training, and indirectly in what is possibly the most common corporate response to stress, counselling. Relaxation training and its derivatives including meditation and biofeedback are individual-centred techniques using exercises to reduce muscle tension and reduce stress through improved relaxation and identification of stress symptoms. Murphy and Sorenson (1988), in a quasi-experimental study of highway maintenance workers who were given either relaxation or biofeedback training, found that although the workers felt better both physiologically and mentally, the expected improvements in absenteeism and productivity were not manifested. What they did conclude however was that:

> Stress management may be most useful as an adjunct to organisational change interventions e.g. increased participation in decision-making, improved worker autonomy, task identity and feedback and implementation of flexible work schedules. (Murphy and Sorenson, 1988: 181)

Stress counselling

Counselling is an even less direct approach to stress, and at its best is effected by '*cognitive redefinition*' of the 'problem' in much in the same way that psychoanalysis requires patients to redefine their identity and world-view within a framework that makes their difficulties understandable. However, this kind of technique, like the 'talking cure' of psychoanalysis, would be expected to work best with long-term chronic problems and would not be cost-effective on a large scale due to the intense one-to-one relationship required. At its worst, employee counselling often consists of a short interview with a hired-in consultant in response to episodic or acute problems which cannot be solved in this fashion. What is taking place is, in effect, the location of the problem in the context of 'organisational reality', as in, 'you need to pull your socks up or you'll be in trouble'. There is nothing new here, of course. Baritz's interpretation of the Hawthorne study points out that the outcomes of the research on employee counselling led some to the conclusion that 'workers did not have compelling objective problems' (1960: 201). The rationale for this, according to a counsellor cited by Baritz, was that their grievances could be dealt with by allowing them to 'talk them out':

> It may not be even necessary to take any action on them. All that they require is a patient and courteous hearing, supplemented when necessary, by an explanation of why nothing can be done.... It is not always necessary to yield to the worker's requests in order to satisfy them. (Baritz, 1960: 201)

It is the ability of this form of counselling to address, albeit on a superficial level, individual differences and subjectivity that makes it highly cost-effective in the stress management stakes, with the added benefit that it again persuades the individual that it is *his or her* problem. However it is unlikely to actually remove the source of the experienced strain and does not necessarily increase adaptive capacities. The role of the organisation in producing unhealthy systems and conditions of work is in danger of being ignored. In its place we get systems reinforcing the self-attribution of stress and anxiety as personal problems to be coped with in the fulfilment of our various roles rather than structural issues to be contested.

Employee assistance programmes

Such systems are in direct contrast to the early welfarist tradition (cf. Hollway) of industrial psychology, which focused on fatigue and working conditions and on organisational and job design as solutions. The modern focus is less likely to lead to environmental attributions of the causes of stress, and thus defuses possible sources of hostility and resistance to the organisation. Work in this area concentrates on the operation of *employee assistance programmes,* or EAPs, which manage the care of employees. Over 2 million employees are covered by EAPs in the UK according to the Employee Assistance Programmes Association (IPD, 1997). They state that 'the rapid increase reflects the growing appreciation amongst employers that, as stress levels increase, an EAP is an attractive staff benefit which also has advantages for the employer'. EAPs are provided either in-house or by external contractors, the reasons given for their introduction being given in surveys by Cooper (cited in Magnus, 1995) and Berridge *et al.* (1997: 188–92) as primarily humanistic, helping employees deal with change and stress and giving the image of a 'caring organisation'. Alker and McHugh (2000) argue that EAPs are primarily introduced for instrumental reasons, dealing with the consequences of change and the introduction of new working practices, and that:

> there may at least be a 'residual role' for welfare and/or counselling in modern HRM practice as evinced by reported difficulties in handling counselling and similar problems and even in the enthusiasm for the EAP itself. In this sense managers and their organisations could be seen to be turning to EAPs in much the same way that they turn to personality tests in the selection and recruitment process – not because they work but because they provide an objectivised frame-work for the activity and a reduction in uncertainty for the sponsors of the activity.
> (Alker and McHugh, 2000: 316)

Wider critiques of EAPs reviewed by Carroll (1996: 19–21) are summarised in Table 18.1. These criticisms, coupled with increasing concerns about the cost of EAPs, have led to a focus on external, agency-led 'managed care', often run from remote call centres according to Bacharach *et al.* (1996). These systems 'have become institution-alised in the American workplace as a mechanism for managing employees' personal problems' (1996: 262), with EAP professionals becoming 'essentially management personnel' (1996: 264). The response to this according to Bacharach *et al.* has been the rise of peer-based *member assistance programmes,* or MAPs, sponsored and run by labour unions and having greater levels of commitment to collective identity, peer support and issues of confidentiality. Although there is limited evidence of MAP-style programmes in the UK there is also evidence that systems of managed care are becoming more cost-attractive to UK institutions. At a meeting of the Scottish branch of the UK Employee Assistance Professionals Association (1998), a senior HRM director of a major Scottish bank and a director of a US/UK counselling provider responded to questions on managed care by saying that in future his organisation wished to focus its efforts on the 'twenty most problematic areas' identified by its coun-selling services. Apart from horrifying the counsellors present on the basis of the ethical issues of confidentiality raised, this response highlighted the fact that EAPs are about managing costs and not employee stress.

To deal directly with stress requires problem-focused coping, where individuals or groups might actively design their own working environments and methods, negotiate their own roles or acquire new capacities. Such an approach, though highly effective in managing stress, would necessitate the vertical integration of control over work design

Criticisms of counselling and employee assistance programmes

TABLE 18.1

Involves:	Leading to:	Seen as:
Individualising problems	Politics and faction fights	Tool of management
Decontextualising problems	Shelving responsibility to employees	Weakness
Making problems apolitical		Deflecting justified emotions
Emotion management and social control	Absolution from compassion	Not integrated into organisation
Ignoring environment/causes	Not facing implications of action/policy	Anti-collective

Source: L. Alker and D. McHugh (2000) 'Human Resource Maintenance? Organisational Rationales for the Introduction of Employee Assistance Programmes', *Journal of Managerial Psychology*, 15. 4: 303–23, based on M. Carroll (1996) *Workplace Counselling*, London: Sage.

and costs, and is consequently not highly popular. External experts could be brought in to design similar programmes that might have more wide-ranging effects than approaches based on emotion-focused coping, but costs would still be high, as with job redesign. Furthermore, the likelihood of being able to deal adequately with individual differences, as with home/work conflicts, would be low. They would also work less well with situational stress factors such as role conflicts, as these are in general less directly identifiable as consequences of the organisation of work than are environmental stress factors (noise, chemicals or working with VDUs). This is precisely because they are attributed to an individual's incapacity to cope with the demands of work. The work of nurses and social workers provides a good example of organisations exploiting a person's ability to cope with untenable situations to the limit, and only becoming concerned when the rate of turnover or lack of efficiency of skilled staff becomes difficult to manage.

Contesting stress

In contrast to the stress management techniques outlined above, the Labour Research Department offers guidelines for dealing with stress on a collective basis, urging union members to research stress-related workplace issues which could be negotiated with management, and to communicate results to all members and appropriate officers and institutions. The negotiation strategy itself gives the following advice:

- Concentrate on one, preferably winnable, stress issue to gain confidence.
- Do not be afraid to consider a long-term strategy.
- Don't think of stress in isolation from other workplace hazards and issues.

(LRD, 1988: 22)

Such collective attempts to alter conditions for the individual and the organisation are in direct contrast to the individual-centred methods that invoke the 'psychological fallacy' that 'since the organisation is made of individuals, we can change the organisation by changing its members' (Katz and Kahn, 1978: 391). The LRD approach again high-lights stress as an issue of workplace control, not only of job performance, but also of personal lifestyle in support of this. Commentators such as Steele and also Handy support this view in relation to worker assistance and health programmes, while Orlans notes that counselling often only deals with problems at the individual level (see Wheeler and Lyon, 1992: 48–9). For models of stress which go beyond individual level approaches and account for perceived levels of control, we need to go to work such as that of Karasek and Theorell (1990) or Fisher (1986). Karasek and Theorell link job strain to dimensions of *demand* from the situation, and the level of control, autonomy or *jurisdiction discretion* available to the individual in the workplace.

High job demands and loads can be perceived positively in situations of high control, but where control is low high demand is associated with strain. The outcome of this is that in hierarchical, authoritarian conditions, the best available coping response may be the reduction of effort (see Fisher, 1986: 157, 238), which raises the possibility of Taylor's 'systematic soldiering' as a coping mechanism. Karasek and Theorell (1990) also give evidence that low levels of social support may exacerbate the relation between high demands and low control. Wheeler and Lyon (1992: 47) note that Karasek's approach, 'effectively recognises the relationship between the subjective experience of stress and the social conditions which may give rise to it'. Fisher takes this a step further in examining coping responses to stressful conditions as strategic responses, the range of which are constrained by life experiences and personal style. The implication of this trend in research is that not only are work and organisational designs significant sources of strain, but they may also limit our adaptive capacities to cope with it.

In studying stress at work we must not, however, forget the person who feels the emotions and strain created. Fineman claims that though organisations can be seen as 'emotional arenas', the persons within them are presented as 'emotionally anorexic', their emotions reduced to managerial control variables, 'the feelings of *being* organised, *doing* work and organising are hard to detect' (1993: 9). At the same time he asserts that stress has 'come out' as an issue, in that counselling is at least provided by some and also that there is a tacit acknowledgement that 'being sick or off work for reasons of stress is acceptable – up to a point' (1993: 219).

Emotional labour

The psychological pressures on individuals have been well documented, not only in terms of pressures to mould behaviour and identity, but in terms of the intrapsychic conflicts they can produce. Interpersonal conflicts and conflicts between role expecta-tions are seen as causative factors in producing anxiety and stress. An example of the conflicts which fulfilling a role may induce is seen in Hochschild's (1983) notion of *emotional labour*. Hochschild characterises emotional labour as 'a covert resource, like money or knowledge, or physical labour, which companies need to make the job done' (1993: xii). This was originally identified in occupations where individuals have to manage their emotions in order to serve the commercial purposes of the enterprise. Other writers on emotional labour (see Fineman, 1993) have extended such notions to the full range of behaviour in work organisations and most recently to resistance (see Sturdy and Fineman, 2001 for a comprehensive discussion). It should be noted that emotional labour is about the valorisation of human capital; it is not a 'catch-all' phrase for anything to do with emotions and work (Fineman, 1993). Furthermore, Hochschild does make some differentiation between 'deep' and 'surface' labour, a construct that could link emotional labour directly to the questions of identity and impression management discussed in Chapter 21.

Using flight attendants and bill collectors, Hochschild (1983) showed how people are constrained to maintain emotions in their work – friendliness for the stewardess; suspension of trust and sympathy for the debt-collector – which relate only to the requirements of the job. This requirement extends beyond individuals and includes collective emotional labour:

> It is not simply individuals who manage their feelings in order to do a job; whole organisations have entered the game. The emotion management that keeps the smile on Delta Airlines competes with the emotion management that keeps the same smile on United and TWA. (Hochschild, 1983: 185–6)

In such situations, where management attempts to mould the social identities of individuals and groups into images consonant with commercial demands, people often become estranged from their own feelings. As an interdependent process, emotional labour requires both the collaboration of the client and the adjustment of personal feelings to accommodate the client's demands. For the emotional labourer, identification with the job itself can lead to difficulties in making constant adjustments to situations, and considerable socio-emotional costs may be incurred. Work in the 'caring' professions, for example, requires that people identify closely with their work or clients, and also that they exercise self- and emotional control over their role-based work. This may bring them into conflict with the levels of commitment required in their work, in that they have to constrain emotional responses to an extent that has serious consequences for their mental health and social relationships.

In order to respond to conflicts between commitment and capacity to act, people may *burn out*. Storlie (1979) argues that this occurs where the individuals confront an intractable reality that cannot be changed, so that the only effective response is to change themselves. The end result is that they continue to 'go through the motions', but remove any emotional or identity investment they had in their work. This acts as a defence mechanism against the stresses that may result from the conflicts between their own tendencies and their role demands. Emotional labour can thus lead the individual into a removal of emotion, labour being reduced to mere activity. This may have some benefits to the employer, but for the employee such numbing of emotional response leads to a loss of a central source of meaning for them. (See Kunda, 1992: 198–204, for an extended discussion.)

Emotion management

The control of labour in emotional terms has been explored in a number of case studies in the service sector, including a study of call centre work at Telebank by Callaghan and Thompson (2002). They use a distinction from Bolton (2000) which differentiates between *pecuniary* (according to reward) emotional labour, and *philanthropic* (according to endowment) emotional labour, which they illustrate in Telebank workers as follows: 'At the weekend, on a Saturday, you get old women or men phoning and they just want to talk. It's great, I love getting these calls.'

That such chats require emotional labour is evident, but these emotions are not directly part of the remunerated emotional labour enacted in normal dealings with clients, as in Hochschild's original conception. Rather, they are given as what Bolton terms a gift, which could also be given to others as an 'extra', even in formal organisational interactions. However, at the same time as such giving such emotional gifts, Telebank workers have to be aware of the other forms of labour they perform:

> I'm quite happy to chat to them, but it's always in the back of your mind, got to watch my average handling time. I think you set a better example for the bank. (Callaghan and Thompson, 2002)

This example serves to illustrate the other two categories of emotional labour which Bolton distinguishes: these are *prescriptive* (according to organisational or professional rules of conduct) and *presentational* (according to general social rules) emotion management, reflecting the demands of the work itself (handling times) and those of the culture that surrounds it (identification with the image of the bank). Bolton observes that 'Hochschild's concept recognises that employees' private emotional systems have been appropriated by management as a renewable resource' (2000: 163), but makes her categorisations on the basis that Hochschild does not recognise emotional labour in the 'unmanaged spaces' in organisations. It is not the nature of emotional labour which changes in Bolton's formulation, but its range and scope in terms of what people have do to their emotions in order to survive and cope with their work. Philanthropic emotional labour is especially important here, as it illustrates how part of emotion management actually contributes to employees being able to make space for the expression of their own identities, or possibly to just get a breather in the relentlessly computer-paced modern workplace.

A more utilitarian typology of emotional labour is given by Mann (1999) in her discussion of what she terms the 'have a nice day' (HAND) culture endemic in the service sector. The HAND culture is of one what Mann claims are a number of scripted cultures which companies are 'frantically foisting' on their staff and customers (1999: 38). These scripted cultures and their associated display rules are discussed further in Chapter 21. The typology of emotional labour Mann puts forward is based on the work of Briner (1995) and reflects the fact that emotional display in work does not always match our own feelings, nor is it always in line with social and organisational expectations. On this basis emotional labour can be categorised as:

- *Emotional harmony*, where 'displayed emotion is the same as expected emotion and felt emotion'.
- *Emotional dissonance*, where 'displayed emotion is the same as expected emotion but different from felt emotion'.
- *Emotional deviance*, where 'displayed emotion is the same as felt emotion but different from expected emotion'.

(Mann, 1999: 68–9)

Of these, *emotional dissonance* is the only area where true emotional labour is involved. In comparison with Bolton, all three of Mann's categories could be classed as pecuniary, whereas only emotional harmony could be philanthropic in organisational terms. Both harmony and dissonance would be both prescriptive and presentational, while emotional deviance would be neither, and might better be classed as a coping mechanism or low-level burn out. Mann has extended her work on emotional labour through the Mann Emotional Requirements Inventory (MERI),which claims to 'work out how much emotional labour you perform, on average, in your day-to-day working life' (Mann and Ward Dutton, 1999: 115).

With the kind of typologies put forward by Bolton and Mann, we may be seeing the first step in the process of emotional labour being seen as a necessary skill in employees. As such, it might be operationalised into a technology of regulation to be accredited and appraised alongside all of the other explicit and tacit work skills appropriated as competencies by management and OB practitioners. The Mann inventory is at present a self-report technique, and we do not yet have to fill in 'emotional development forms' in our appraisals, but Callaghan and Thompson (2002) do give the example of the 'rapport training' given at Telebank which attempts to 'recognise and extract worker emotions'. Such regulation is itself problematic, however:

> The system of work makes building effective rapport difficult, workers are asked to produce both quantity and quality, to combine strength and stamina with emotional labour to deliver 180 second units of 'bubbly personality' one hundred and twenty times a day. (Callaghan and Thompson, forthcoming)

Even with rapport training, such pressure means that absenteeism is rife and that two years' work out of an employee is seen as a 'reasonable return on investment' for some call centre operators. Emotional labour of whatever form appears to have the same problem of diminishing returns as emotional regulation does, as a mechanism for coping with stress (see section on 'Role stress' above). Under the conditions of work intensification inherent in much modern job design, emotional labour has its own catch-22 in that the more it is required, the more it can become a prelude to burn-out.

It is clear that emotional labour needs to be distinguished better from and contextualised within the other forms of labour we perform on ourselves and others in pursuit of organisational demands. McHugh (1997) identifies these other forms of managerial work as follows:

- *operational labour* – regulation of behaviour and discipline
- *emotional labour* – regulation of affective responses
- *intellectual labour* – regulation and construction of meanings and symbols
- *dramaturgical labour* – regulation of impressions and advocacy
- *attributional labour* – regulation and ascription of intent and commitment.

These categories need refinement and consideration of whether they apply to self-management in terms of non-managerial work, but they do serve to illustrate that it is not just our emotions that we control in our working lives. The latter two categories in particular are discussed further in Chapter 21, but for now we simply need to note that each of these forms of labour carries its concomitant stressors and contributes to the role conflicts we suffer.

Stress and control

The psychological and physiological pressures which impinge on us are generally seen these days as being manifested as stress, though in other times and using other terms they have been linked more to notions such as fatigue, anxiety, alienation and even to neurotic and psychotic disorders. In fact, some commentators claim that stress is an artefact (see Briner and Reynolds, 1993 for an introduction to this debate), much in the same way that Seivers (see Chapter 19) claims motivation to be a product of the relations between psychologists and managers. Regardless of its status as a phenomenon, stress-related pressures and the individualisation of attributions of stress mean that we all face normative pressures, not the least of which centre around fitness to work. Such normative expectations form one basis of what is termed the *psychological contract* (Argyris, 1960, or see Schein, 1980: 22), and act as a form of control over the identities we are capable of constructing for ourselves in the workplace.

According to Kunda (1992: 11), 'under normative control, membership is founded not only on the behavioural or economic transaction . . . but, more crucially, on an experiential transaction'. Although the expectations that arise originate within the interactions, goals, strategies or policies of the various individuals and groups in an organisation, in subjective terms they can also appear to originate in the organisation itself. Thus role expectations (see 'Role stress' above) are not separate and neutral consequences of status, position or skill. Rather, they are specific and interdependent products of a social organisation of work which itself depends for effective production on the internalisation of role demands. The divisions of labour resulting in fragmented work are likewise dependent on role specialisation being perceived as a natural social order.

Role socialisation and control

Salaman (1979: 133–6) raises the possibility that variations in role discretion and role expectations may be linked to strategic decisions on the forms of control exercised over different categories of workers. Professional employees face contradictory expectations arising from their peers, their external professional associations, and from the organisation itself. These have to be handled by the individual and managed by the organisation. Direct control by managers over professionals, involving rule-bound job definitions and tightly regulated behaviour, may conflict with the latter's values and socialisation. A more effective form of control can be achieved through a focus on their roles as professionals, performing their organisational duties to the satisfaction and benefit of their masters or clients.

In contrast to the forms of control appropriate to professionals, 'Role type control is less commonly employed with workers because senior members of organisations (and, possibly, the workers themselves) see the workers as being in conflict with the goals and reward system of the enterprise' (Salaman, 1979: 136). The moulding of workers' attitudes and behaviour can be identified with 'adjusting one's perspectives on what one will be able to achieve' (Frese, 1982: 210). Since such 'adjustments' necessitate at least some internalisation and legitimation of structures of regulation, it may be expected that role-type control would be possible at most levels of organisations. But of course, not everyone in an organisation 'knows their place' or is resigned to powerlessness and helplessness. The informal socialisation of workers, or 'learning the ropes', will consist largely of learning the shortcuts around, and resistance to, organisational controls. Such knowledge and its associated activities confer at least some small sense of personal autonomy, meaning and hence identity to workers. Consequently, direct controls combined with elements of technical and bureaucratic control where possible or appropriate, are more often employed by management at lower levels of organisations.

Socialisation within work is not necessarily directed at the technical aspects for other grades. When examining the socialisation of skilled manual workers into their workplace identities, Penn argues that such socialisation is more directed at 'instruction into the appropriate actions of the trade' (1986: 4). Such instruction and the identities it produces are aimed at generating scripts for interaction in the workplace. They deal with 'Norms and procedures held to be appropriate for dealing with three groupings found in the workplace: fellow workers, other workers and management' (1986: 4).

This process builds on anticipatory socialisation into work in the home and at school, in that apprentices require a commitment to deferred gratification and continued learning after the end of formal schooling. Hence there is a form of preselection for skilled manual work in that those who have previously internalised appropriate forms of meaning are preferred: 'A certain degree of seriousness and moral uprightness is required by a sponsor who already works in a firm' (1986: 4). In contrast, 'tearaways' who define their identities as inimical to authority and those who seek immediate extrinsic gratification in work are not wanted (Willis, 1977). Organisations, then, try to get the right kind of material to mould into the images they require.

The types of assessment techniques used in recruitment and selection procedures also reflect differential concerns, this time with the personality dimension of identity. The study by Hollway (1984) cited in the section on personality in Chapter 15 shows that the assessment of managers, and hence the forms of control used over them, is related to the 'fit' of their personalities into dominant organisational cultures. When reviewing organisational recruitment procedures in the British Army and Ford UK, Salaman (1979) also notes that this 'fit' is shown by the candidates' willingness to demonstrate an 'appropriate' range of attitudes. Today, the need to fit has become so transparent in the recruitment process that the tactics used in attempts to control the impressions others gain of us in such a process are both an object of study (see Feldman and Klich, 1991) and a topic for training. This is explored further in the section on 'Impression management' in Chapter 21, but for the moment serves to illustrate the extent to which we are involved in the construction of our organisational roles.

In the above sense, roles are scripts which are themselves as essential to the labour process as the working practices, labour and machinery through which they are played out. Attempts to increase worker 'participation' can thus be seen not only as efforts to place individual goals more in line with organisational goals, but as attempts to produce role-based control of workers. The aim is to produce workers who will themselves initiate the enactment of the correct scripts, rather than having to be directed to do so. This produces savings for the organisation in terms of the amount of direct supervision necessary, and of course in terms of the number of supervisors needed. There is currently a parallel emphasis on the operational skills 'content' seen as necessary to make management education more responsive to the 'needs' of business. The management trainee is assumed to have the necessary role commitment and motivation to consent to organisational control structures. Thus 'education' becomes a process of exposing trainees to the 'skills', techniques and attitudes that will be required of them, and then teaching them how to recognise the appropriate contingencies in which particular scripts should be enacted. If we learn such scripts to the sensorimotor level (see Chapter 16) they may even become so automatic that they may be experienced as 'natural' or emotional responses to pressure, and such emotional responses have become a major object of study in recent years.

Stress in the labour process

The problem with role-based stress as an explanatory concept is that it has the effect of portraying the process as natural and individually based, instead of a product of the historically produced conditions of work. In his study of responses to the pressure of work in 'Powerco', Sturdy (1987) notes that management was aware of the negative effects that such pressures had on employee morale. At the same time managers would not want completely to remove backlogs of work as that would portray their sections as overstaffed, and on occasion leave people with little or nothing to do. The anxieties and pressures of work at Powerco led to the practice of 'shifting' in the employees, where people, even in conditions where motivation and commitment might not be expected, indulged in 'unceasing effort beyond what would be expected from even the most committed worker' (1987: 35). Their compulsion to keep ahead of the work and not let backlogs build up, to relieve pressure by getting work 'shifted', extended to refusing breaks and feeling frustrated rather than relieved when interruptions such as computer breakdowns stopped the work. Though partially based in the desire to increase security in work, shifting, according to Sturdy, acts for individuals not only as a relief for the helplessness they feel, but also as a mechanism which obscures the experience of subordination itself. By using shifting to cope with the pressure of work, the individual co-operates with the structures of workplace control to produce a sense of identity that offers some level of autonomy and responsibility. At the same time, shifting paradoxically increases the pressures employees feel, as both management and themselves come to depend on the gains stemming from their increased productivity. Identities can, then, be reactively moulded as a response to situational stress factors, and in directions that reproduce the experience of subordination and domination in work.

In order for any stress 'management' programme to succeed, it has to change both attitudes and cultural factors in the workplace and become part of managerial strategies for moulding the identities of workers. The Control Data Corporation (see earlier) placed great emphasis on group sessions where 'eventually group members learn to help one another to sustain the changes in their behaviour, and they practise various techniques and strategies to avoid failure' (McKenna, 2000: 628). The feeling that a person can cope with adverse situations can be a source of both meaning and danger to them in, for example, working in difficult and dangerous occupations such as construction or agricultural work. The result would be the divorcing of a person's view of their working conditions from their desire for personal safety, to the extent that they take unnecessary risks or adhere to dangerous practises.

As noted in the previous chapter, the ability to deal with or actually relish a high-pressure working environment is seen as a valued characteristic in managers. The person who is able to cope with the conflicting demands of a managerial position is encouraged to view this capacity as a personality trait that indicates his or her suitability as a leader (see Chapter 17). Through such a process, it is no surprise that organisational élites come to view themselves as those most fit to lead and survive in the given environment. Such legitimations, though active in the securing of managerial identities, are not necessarily part of any conscious conspiracy of control or domination. They may simply be the habitual response managers have learned, to cope with the stress they feel or threats they face to their individual or collective identity. Domination and control would thus be manifestations of the scripts managers enact in their daily activities.

It does appear that material on the moulding of identities in organisations tends to focus on professional, skilled and managerial workers. However, such concepts as emotional labour and the utility of 'wellness programmes' would indicate that organisations may routinely attempt to mould the identities of all levels of employees. Aichholzer and Schienstock (1985) examine opportunities for maintaining identities in the face of the intensification of control surrounding the introduction of new technologies. Such intensification is seen in 'tighter binding of human actions with machine processes, an increasing transparency of the labour process as a whole, a rising vertical integration and extension of technological control to white collar work' (1985: 20). They also note a number of apparent 'counter-tendencies' to increased control. These include the reintegration of fragmented work roles, the revaluing of 'marginal' human functions in work, and an emphasis on problem-solving activities. Aichholzer and Schienstock argue that these counter-tendencies in effect pressurise workers to internalise controls in order to soften the problems of control raised by new forms of technology and work organisation, and that this questions the 'maintenance of individual and collective identities in the modern labour process' (1985: 81). At the same the kind of approaches coming from the Labour Research Department and the advent of MAPs do offer some hope that stress can be managed for the individual as well as the organisation.

Conclusion

If the negative consequences of stress are our bodies' way of telling us to slow down, then stress management is the organisation's way of telling us to keep up. Just as health and safety legislation recognises the concept of 'contributory negligence' in attributing the blame for accidents, stress management communicates the nature of power relations in the workplace by bringing home to us our negligence in not being 'fit for work'. This phenomenon now seems to extend to how well we fit our emotions to our occupational roles and identities, and we may be left with the view that work is just plain unhealthy in physiological and emotional terms. As such, we are probably as guilty as the mainstream literature in ignoring the eustress aspect of the stress paradigm in our lack of emphasis on positive arousal and feelings.

It is true that work can be a joy, but that is usually when our intellect and emotions are fully engaged in 'learning the ropes' of work that is rewarding in personal or material terms. Once anything becomes a chore, in that it is both unpleasant and compulsory, then the only 'eustressors' available to us may be based more in misbehaviour and bloody-minded resistance to control than in the work we once loved. In the next chapter we will approach the notion of positive arousal from another direction, which we will use as an extended exemplar of both managerial and self-control much as we utilised stress in this chapter. The project remains the same, but we move on to assess the extent to which psychological knowledge can deliver changes in employee behaviour in the direction of greater commitment to corporate objectives through the magic of *motivation*.

19 Motivation: The Drive for Satisfaction

In this chapter we explore the journey from the notions of instinctual drives governing our behaviour, through the content and processes of our motivations, to a final consideration of issues of identity and commitment in modern organisations. We begin by introducing the motif we employ throughout the chapter: the question of whether the abstract conceptions of motivation theory as found in mainstream organisational behaviour (OB) literature can be distinguished from the more pragmatic processes of influence and coercion.

Motivation or motivating?

William F. Whyte, writing in 1956 on economic incentives and human relations, spoke of the 'Five M's of factory life: men, money, machines, morale and motivation' (1956: 1). The last of these, coupled with the aspects of satisfaction contained in the notion of morale, has driven the primary interests of organisational management in psychological knowledge. Motivation, according to Dawson (1986: 7), 'refers to the mainspring of behaviour; it explains why individuals choose to expend a degree of effort towards achieving particular goals'. It is explained in terms of biologically-based *needs* and *drives* and the selection of *goals* (content theories) and cognitively-oriented notions of *information processing* on the rewards, costs and preferences for particular outcomes of action (process theories). Knowledge of human motivation is linked to the service of organisational 'needs', in that motivation is understood in terms of the process of *social influence*. Even though Herzberg (1968) pointed out that in attempting to influence someone to work harder it is the manager who is motivated and not the worker, it is still the case that one of the principal concerns of organisational behaviour is to increase 'motivation' in the search for greater productivity.

Motivations are viewed as perceived predispositions to particular behaviours and outcomes, reflecting the things we want and the strategies we choose to achieve or obtain them. Originally they were explained in two ways. The first was in terms of instinctual drives which we are motivated to reduce: for example when are thirsty we are driven to seek drink. Second, they were described in the mechanistic terminology of *stimulus–response*, when we seek out those things which satisfy or reward us and avoid those which punish or cost us. However, since motivation also concerns choice and hence intention, it is necessary to explain how such choices are made. This is explained within cognitively oriented models that examine either the *content* of motivations, or the *process* through which they are expressed. The former examine what motivates people through concepts such as goals, needs and 'motivators', and is exemplified by the work of Maslow, Alderfer, McClelland and Herzberg. The latter examine how behaviours are selected, directed, initiated and maintained, as in the work of Porter and Lawler, Adams and also Vroom (see below).

Both types of theory are concerned with the notion that humans direct their behaviour towards goals. In the case of content theories the concern is with the source of the goals, while process theories focus on the decision-making process by which goals are selected and pursued. We must also consider motivation in terms of the process of social influence by which external agencies try to direct the selection and pursuit of desired goals by individuals. This aspect of motivation theory, into which both content and process theories are incorporated, is the practical focus of organisational behaviour as a whole, practitioners being concerned to understand the strengths and directions of human motivations in order to increase control over the performance of work-related behaviours.

An example of this is found in McGregor's (1960) conception of 'Theory X' and 'Theory Y', often presented as a need or content theory of motivation. Students, and some texts, often represent theories X and Y as showing that there are two types of people, those who dislike work and responsibility, focus on economic security and need to be coerced into effort (Theory X), and those who like work, will accept responsibility for their own effort and are capable of innovation (Theory Y). However these theories are more properly understood as a continuum of managerial attitudes to workers, whereby Theory X views held by managers will produce an 'assumption trap' which leads to coercive behaviour on their part and thus a vicious circle leading to Theory X behaviour by employees. Likewise Theory Y assumptions should lead to Theory Y behaviour, though of course there would probably be no 'virtuous circle' here as it would eventually lead to the complete abdication of managerial control. The practical parallel here is in the fate of scientific management and the human relations movement. Both were assumed to increase motivation and performance, and both could be said to fail on the basis of ignoring the effects of the assumption traps they produced: scientific management via assumptions of coercion through economic rationality and the managerial appropriation of control and expertise, and human relations through the assumption that managers would give anything but lip-service to employee participation in decision-making.

Enriching the content

The goals to which we direct our behaviour constitute a formative influence in the identities we construct for ourselves. But this aspect of goal-related behaviour is not examined within organisational behaviour as a discipline, except to the extent that individual goals can be moulded or 'set' to fulfil organisational ends. The branch manager in the Insco case provides relevant commentary:

> I'm looking for someone who will work with me. So I look for some one who I think I can mould to my own ways, but they must already have the necessary spark and drive. (Knights and Collinson, 1987: 154)

Identity and related goals are thus treated as external to the position of workers in the productive process, in that goals are usually related not to intentions but to biologically-derived drives, or more often, needs such as those identified by Maslow (1954). Maslow's typology of human needs has been discredited to the extent that the 'prepotency' of 'lower order' physiological needs (in other words, these needs must be fulfilled before 'higher order' social and psychological needs) is not supported, yet

'Maslow's hierarchy' is still given prominence in most OB and management development texts. The probable reason for this is that theories which actually tell us
something about motivation are too complex and too dependent on contingent factors
to have any simple predictive application in management practice. These 'needs' for
food, shelter, affection, self-respect and individual growth are more accurately seen
these days as operating on the basis of either *intrinsic*, *social* or *extrinsic* stimuli or
rewards. Intrinsically motivated persons are assumed to be influenced through their
attachment to their work itself, through the enhancement of skill, responsibility, status
or authority; socially motivated persons through their social relations in the workplace
to peers, colleagues and group membership. It is assumed that extrinsically motivated
persons will only be influenced by aspects of their work that facilitate their 'outside'
interests such as pay levels, perks and increased leisure time. Though particular motivations may be more forceful for an individual at any one time, positive feedback from
all three types of factor will have some bearing on how they direct their goal-related
behaviour.

Content theories

As noted above, organisational behaviour texts almost always refer to Maslow and
his 'hierarchy of needs' but very seldom consider the satisfaction of needs within the
organisational environment beyond the extent to which they can be manipulated to
increase productivity. They are once again seen as external to the place of the worker
in the productive process. Those in positions of control in work organisations do not
see themselves as being in the business of comprehensively supplying the needs that
Maslow hypothesises. They exchange financial and sometimes material benefits for
the labour of employees, but beyond a minimal concern that workers should be sufficiently satisfied with the conditions and rewards of work to improve performance, or
at least to not disrupt production, little else is provided. Indeed McClelland's (1961)
typology of needs as *affiliation*, *power* and *achievement* does not take the lower order
needs into account at all.

The hypothesised need for 'self-actualisation' (based on the work of the therapist
Carl Rogers) and individual growth has repeatedly been incorporated into prescriptive packages such as Herzberg's (1968) notion of 'job enrichment', which seek to
improve the content of work to the point where workers will be self-motivated to
improve their performance. However such initiatives tend to fail on the basis that no
real improvement is made in factors relating to the conditions of work and the job
context or environment. For example, in Nichols and Beynon's (1977) study of job
enrichment at Chemco, managers were motivated to pursue the 'New Working Agreement' on the basis that they were convinced that they would get at what makes
workers 'tick' and thus be able to coax more work from them. For most of the workers
involved, all that came out of this was an inadequate system of job rotation which was
worse than the system they had evolved for themselves. Hence managers in this study
were easier to 'motivate' because the context of their work was adequate.

Herzberg himself recognised this in saying that job rotation constituted 'job
enlargement' rather than enrichment, and this could result in no more than short-term
improvements in productivity as it represented 'adding nothing to nothing' (1968:
263–4). Such prescriptions are still offered by organisational consultants and still
bought by organisational management, however, possibly because even short-term

improvements in productivity offer some kind of competitive edge in the market. Motivation, in the above example, is reduced to the status of things or techniques that will motivate, a manipulative rather than an explanatory concept. The outgrowth of Herzberg's notions in Hackman and Oldham's (1980) *Job Characteristics Model* links job redesign and enrichment to a diagnostic scheme which analyses work in terms of four variables *(skill variety, task identity, task significance* and *feedback)* indicative of the extent to which a job could or should be redesigned. Although this scheme is widely cited in the literature, Hollway (1991: 107) reports that it was not popular with managers in that its focus on the job rather than the individual did not fit the managerial ideology of the day.

The drive for satisfaction

The key concerns in these theories and related applications are to a great extent those that relate task performance to the concept of *job satisfaction*, which is difficult to define or measure in the first place. Thus the application of techniques based on the assumed relation between satisfaction and performance tends to ignore the operation of social, cultural, organisational and environmental factors which will all intervene to make a simple 'more satisfaction, more performance' relationship less likely. Argyle (1974) examined the relations between satisfaction and productivity, absenteeism and turnover, concluding that while absenteeism and turnover did have a direct relationship to levels of satisfaction, productivity only did so for highly skilled or intrinsically motivated workers and that even in these cases, individual differences were highly significant. (See Figure 19.1.)

It appeared that while, on average, people did work harder when satisfied, some people worked harder when less satisfied and some less hard when more satisfied.

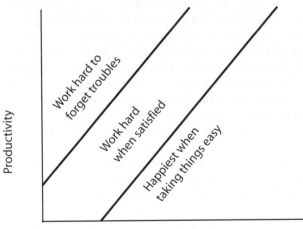

The relation between productivity and performance   *FIGURE 19.1*

Source: M. Argyle (1974) *The Social Psychology of Work*, Harmondsworth: Penguin, p. 239.

Working hard to make the time go faster in an unsatisfying job or just to forget about one's troubles is a familiar experience to many of us, and 'skiving' or systematic soldiering is a classic response to fragmented or meaningless work. The only aspirational rewards available in such situations are those we can gain from controlling our own time and playing our own games (see discussion of Roy's work, page 302).

Beyond these considerations, any meaningful view of the relation between job satisfaction and performance would have to recognise that alienated responses are rooted in the estrangement of workers from their creative capacities in the act of production, from ownership and control of the workplace, and from fellow workers. As the condition and responses derive, at least in part, from the basic structures of the capitalist labour process, changing them would require more than tinkering with peripheral aspects of work design. This does not mean that individuals will not report some sort of increased positive satisfactions. For example Frese (1982) states that:

> much of the work on job satisfaction has tapped an attitude which could be labelled resigned job satisfaction. Because of the unavailability of other jobs and ways to change the job situation, a worker has reduced his aspiration level over time and has become resigned to his job. (Frese, 1982: 212)

Such feelings are directly related to powerlessness and lack of control over the job situation. Reduction of aspiration levels does not necessarily imply a lack of aspiration, however; it could simply mean resignation to progression as defined by the rules and procedures of the organisation, an acceptance of bureaucratic methods of control and the ideologies which underlie them. In Knights and Collinson's Insco case, for example, one of the female clerks who was continually discouraged from applying for a position as a sales inspector decided not to risk her position as senior clerk, and redefined her aspirations in terms of 'a woman's idea of going higher up within the company on the inside' (1987: 166). By considering the idea of progression into office management rather than sales, she has started the process of redefining her goals in line with the gendered job segregation fostered by the company.

People experiencing passive satisfaction with their lot rather than active satisfaction with their work may still be open to the types of influence exemplified by attempts at job enrichment or similar schemes. Herzberg's (1968) two-factor theory of motivation suggests that the 'motivator' factors associated with job *content* and satisfaction are separate from the 'hygiene' factors associated with job *context* and dissatisfaction. The content factors, such as *growth*, *responsibility*, *recognition*, *achievement* and *variety*, are similar to those assumed to motivate people who value intrinsic rewards and the status and esteem components of social rewards. The context factors, such as *salary*, *conditions*, *security*, *relationships* and possibly *policy* and *status*, are similar in effect to extrinsic and social rewards in that they make work either easier or more rewarding as they improve. Techniques such as job enrichment assume that if content and context factors are adequately met for individuals in organisations, then the motivation to work will be maintained. More importantly, they rely on the notion that people are passive recipients of organisational influences. If people do construct for themselves a passively resigned workplace identity, then the chances will increase that they will accept the redesign of their jobs on the basis that it will eventually improve their lot. The developments in flexible working practices and unitarist industrial relations in the 1980s may indicate that what was identified as a 'new realism' was nothing more than the kind of coping engendered by having to adopt a passive workplace identity in response to environmental constraints such as high unemployment.

Job context and content factors are seldom, if ever, met adequately for everyone within the work environment, so attempts to influence individual motivation levels will always run foul of factors they do not take account of. Thus in addition to active attempts to 'motivate' individuals, organisations take advantage of the socialising pressures of work to create a climate where people are open to these kinds of influence. However, attempts to motivate or socialise individuals into accepting the managerial direction tend to ignore the decision-making aspect of the process of becoming motivated. If motivation is indeed the 'mainspring of behaviour', then it refers not only to the selection of goals but to the selection and development of the coping strategies and skills that individuals use to achieve those goals. Lee and Lawrence (1985) identify four factors that underpin all 'political' models of motivation that focus on decision-making:

- *Goals*: relating to values, interests and perceptions of individual opportunities and possibilities.
- *Strategies*: formulated to achieve goals or to react to threats to capacities to achieve them.
- *Coalitions*: exchanging commitment to group interests for support for goal strategies which cannot be achieved on an individual basis.
- *Power*: assessing success of goal strategies and membership of coalitions, arriving at estimates of personal power to affect events and revising goals in line with this.

The first three factors are dependent on the fourth, in that 'An individual's perception of his power will affect the goals he sets, the strategies he chooses and the nature of the coalitions he joins' (1985: 78). Likewise in the construction of identities, perceptions of a person's *situational power* (see Chapter 21) will determine the sources of meaning that are appropriate to the maintenance of a secure identity.

Motivation may be influenced by either interfering with, or facilitating, the individual's capacity to perceive, formulate or implement one or more of these factors. Organisational strategies that simply restrict the employees' capacity to act in these areas will, however, probably lead to individual and group attempts to circumvent them. Techniques aimed at the 'motivation' of groups and individuals may not in this sense achieve their aims. They may exacerbate the situations they were designed to ameliorate by reproducing or reinforcing existing areas of conflict, by reopening old issues or by introducing new topics of dispute.

Aimed at increasing production quality, overall productivity, workforce flexibility and job satisfaction, strategies aimed at enhancing group motivation depend on the production of workgroup identities consonant with the collective goals of management. These in the end can only be sustained to the extent that the organisation enables group members to maintain comparative material benefits and secure identities. This however, has long-term implications for job security which are in direct contradiction to the aim of producing a flexible workforce responsive to the short-term demands for changes in product lines, working practices and manning levels. The threat of a reserve pool of unemployed labour is not sufficient to maintain the levels of commitment required by these programmes. Commitment based on the fear of losing one's job is only equivalent to the type of motivation achieved by holding a gun to someone's head. As soon as the threat is removed, so is the motivation. All that is achieved is an increase in the likelihood of retaliatory action.

In essence, then, the study of motivation in OB is the study of the processes of organisational influence and a study in the exercise of power and domination. No matter what the intent of consultants and practitioners in the area in terms of increasing job satisfaction and the elusive 'quality of working life', to management these techniques are effectively 'technologies of regulation' aimed at increasing control over behaviour and performance. Unfortunately, from a managerial point of view at least, in the long run such programmes cannot survive exposure to the contradictions inherent in trying to control subordinates who are actively attempting to control their own environment. Before moving on to consider process theories, we wish to reflect in more detail on the role of organisational behaviour and organisational psychology in motivational technologies of regulation. To do this we will consider Herzberg's (1968) pragmatic critique of motivational practices, which is still germane in modern OB.

The 'kick in the ass' life cycle

> The problem arises when managements come to believe so firmly in their so-called motivation techniques and theories that they incorrectly attribute the behaviour they see with the attitude ('highly motivated') they impute with the source behind that behaviour. The very term 'motivation' in its shopfloor context, implies that workers are not intrinsically inclined to behave in the way their managers would want. (R. Hershey, 'A Practitioner's View of 'Motivation', 1993: 10)

Herzberg in 'One More Time: How Do You Motivate Employees?' (1968) addresses the strategies available to the manager who answers the question, 'How do I get an employee to do what I want him to?' with the age-old response of 'Kick him!' (1986: 256). Herzberg used his analysis to examine his notion that most attempts to 'motivate' workers produce nothing more than short-term movement towards a reward or away from a punishment, and through this to argue that to produce self-motivating workers, jobs must be enriched. More interesting for our present purposes, though, is his analysis of the development of the techniques available to achieve these objectives, the so-called *KITAs*. Herzberg argued that the basic technique of the kick, or *negative physical* KITA, failed due to the problems of image and retaliation associated with a regime of punishment. Psychologists naturally came to the rescue by uncovering 'infinite sources of psychological vulnerabilities and the appropriate methods to play tunes on them', that is, *negative psychological* KITA (1986: 257). Herzberg moved on, then, from this form of KITA (coercion, and not motivation), to consider positive KITA.

Management found that, due to the failure of the traditional range of rewards they had employed in that they were subject to diminishing returns, they once more had to listen to the 'behavioural scientists who, more out of a humanist tradition than scientific study, criticised management for not knowing how to deal with people' (1986: 258). The self-replicating string of KITAs resulting from this collaboration gave us, according to Herzberg, *human relations*, *sensitivity training*, *communications* and *two-way communication*, *job participation* and *employee counselling*. If we extend the role call of positive KITAs we can include everything from Herzberg's own critical output in job enrichment to autonomous working, sociotechnical systems, management by objectives and all the rest of the 'bag of schemes' routinely employed to increase motivation. That these offer no more than temporary influences towards greater commitment and goal consensus, rather than avenues towards self-generated motivation to work, is not important to management, as long as they give rise to short-term productivity gains. This reinforces the status of the products of OB as an integral part of the labour process itself. It is almost as if the techniques and approaches coming out of behavioural science have their own version of the marketing concept of the 'product life-cycle'. As soon as one KITA is reaching its diminishing level of marginal utility, the research and development process of critique and hypothesis testing gives rise to a new one. That all that is new about them is often only the name is unimportant, as long as the 'improved product' is sufficiently distinctive enough to carry out its function as an ideological cover story for yet another technology of regulation.

The attractions of KITAs to managers parallel their attitudes to new technologies. They have an intrinsic marketing advantage over their target audience in that if the competition has them, then they feel that they have to have them too. The similarity goes further, in that like new technologies, KITAs are often brought in by management who do not fully understand them or their possibly deleterious effects on cultures based on established procedures and working practices. Worse still, they only ever work effectively so long as management remain committed to resourcing them properly and do not use them as levers for unilaterally increasing levels of control and productivity.

Process theories

The content theories of motivation only ever really sought to explain motivation in terms of its directions, and lacked the sophistication to explain the strength of motivations. To be really useful in terms of selection or developmental training it is the relative force of motivation that needs to be measured; this being seen in 'process theories' such as *exchange theory* (Homans, 1961), *equity theory* (Adams, 1965) and *expectancy theory* (Vroom 1964). Equity theory is based on notions of cognitive social comparison and exchange, expectancy theory on comparison of outcomes and preferences. These are reinforced by techniques that actively intervene in the selection and pursuit of goals and personal agendas such as goal-setting (see below), which is based on comparison and reinforcement of behavioural standards. All extend the basic notion of cognitive comparison to attempt greater levels of accuracy in prediction and control. Though in general empirical support for these theories is positive, expectancy theory in particular has been singled out for some criticism (see Arnold *et al.*, 1998: 252–4).

This effort to integrate 'human resources' more fully into the production process, typical of content theories, is similarly present in the usage of process theories of motivation. The difficulties in using motivation theories as a basis for 'people processing', can be seen in the application of the expectancy theory of Vroom (1964). This seeks to quantify and predict the strength of an individual's tendency to behave in a particular way as an assigned probability which is given by the *simplified expectancy equation* (see Thompson and McHugh, 1995: 301–4 or Huczynsci and Buchanan, 2001:

248–52). On the surface, this appears to be a simple and powerful tool for predicting behaviour, but the assumptions made in such a measurement present a number of problems. The first is that expectancy theory provides a *rational–cognitive* explanation of individual behaviour. Can we assume that individuals make rational calculations based on their cognitive input in deciding whether to act in a particular way? Even assuming that this is the case, do these form the major determinant factor in their subsequent actions? These questions are sometimes posed in organisational behaviour texts, but no adequate account is generally given of whether such assumptions are warranted. The question is simply stated prior to a discussion of what can be done with expectancy theory in terms of understanding motivational goals, in order to influence and alter people's behaviour.

An objection arises from those, including Langer (1981), who suggest that many of our behaviours, rather than being acted out in analytic, rational fashion, are carried out in what they term a 'mindless' manner. We follow unconscious 'scripts' analogous to sensorimotor learning (see Chapter 17) in much the same way as we do not consciously think of the complex series of actions we go through in making a cup of tea. Although we may consider the options open to us and the best way of going about a task, the underlying motivation may simply be that we are following the script which we have come to learn as appropriate to that situation. The work of Roy (1973) provides examples of how both labour and social interaction in the workplace can take on the attributes of ritual. Roy's monotonous and fatiguing work of 'mincing plastic sheets into small ovals, fingers and trapezoids' (1973: 208) was made 'relatively satisfying' in Baldamus' (1961) terms, by turning the production process into a series of 'games' which varied the colour, shape and ordering of the components turned out. The self-induced scripting of the work itself was accompanied by the breaking-up of the working day into 'times', such as 'peach', 'banana' and 'pickup time'. 'Times' were constructed around the ritualised social interactions and verbal interplay in the brief interruptions to production, which were repeated on a daily basis. Thus the behavioural scripts built up around eating, drinking and visits from outsiders reintroduced some level of meaning and interest for the machine operators into a deskilled labour process. Interest was further enhanced by the continuous repetition during work of 'serious' and 'kidding' verbal 'themes', centred around the characteristics and problems of the operators involved. In this sense, then, scripted behaviours become an effective, though not necessarily actively planned, mechanism for coping with the mundanity of working life.

A related problem for models of motivation is the narrow and over-deterministic series of accounts of experience that rational–cognitive theories of human behaviour produce. These accounts place the responsibility for action on individuals, rather than on the contexts in which they find themselves. This tends to reinforce the view that the pathology of organisations is based on the irrational actions of individuals. In this view, the problems and uncertainties faced by organisations are caused by the self-serving behaviour of those who do not appreciate the 'big picture' of organisational life.

Even if the behaviour of individuals in organisations is largely carried out in the context of scripts which their socialisation into organisational life has taught them, they still bring to their working life an actively constructed identity which has been transformed within the organisation into an appropriate image. These behaviours and scripts do not exist in isolation. Even considering the possible outcomes of working harder on one particular task, as is done in expectancy calculations, this would involve an almost endless series of ramifications and secondary consequences. Thus to obtain a realistic prediction about how motivated a single individual would be to behave in a particular way, we would have to provide a basis of comparison. This would involve taking into account not only most of the behaviours applicable to a person's work and home life, but also those of similar individuals inside and outside the organisation. The project of fully understanding how people are motivated would from this perspective necessitate identifying and explaining all of the subjective and structural influences on their lives and those of the others surrounding them.

The relative lack of success of process theories in managerial terms is due to the very complexity that makes them more powerful in explanatory terms than content theories. Most management development texts still present content theories in the main because they are simple, easier to demonstrate, and they sound powerful, whereas cognitive/process theories suffer from the very fact that they are multifactorial and multivariate, with the implications that:

- there are too many factors which can affect the relations between effort, performance and outcomes
- too many value associations have to be made in assessing outcomes
- it is too difficult to place accurate values on variables
- models require assumptions of complex mental calculations which are hard to reproduce and demonstrate.

We will return to this theme below in considering new developments in motivation such as control and self-concept theories. At present, however, we wish to summarise and reflect on some the problem aspects of the account we have given of motivation so far. In doing this we especially wish to query the uncritical use in mainstream OB (and by ourselves!) of the ubiquitous concept of *goals*.

The goals of motivation

Motivation as presented above lies at the heart of the explanatory project of organisational psychology, and as such can be used to reflect on the limits and contradictions of mainstream theories and practices. At one level, motivation is a classic case of Adorno's concept of '*identity thinking*' (Rose, 1978), where a concept is used as if it denoted instances of something, when it does not. For example, individuals are not 'motivated' to perform well at a particular task or 'satisfied' with their job when the underlying goal of their performance is to maintain a reasonable level of subsistence and not to lose their job. In this sense, OB and organisational psychology assume an identity between being motivated to do something and being constrained to do it by physical and social necessity. In Adorno's terms one can only make proper use of a theoretical concept or construct in the context of the 'theory of society' through which it is itself constructed.

In taking the situational contexts in which behaviour in organisations takes place largely as given, concepts such as goals in mainstream analyses are often reified, involving 'the conversion of concrete social relations of production into abstracted, quantitative measures' (Wexler, 1983: 66). Reification in this sense can be viewed as a dual process, and is productive of entitative relationships as identified by Hosking and Morley (1991, see Chapter 14 and below). First, the products of human thought and activity are treated as things in themselves; and second, socially produced concepts are treated as being intrinsic to individuals and organisations. In relation to the first part of this process, organisations are often treated as actual entities or organisms with their own needs, drives, goals and characteristics analogous to those of people, rather than as the continuously recreated products of human labour and organisational ingenuity. The second element of the reification process is illustrated by the content theories discussed above in their use of highly generalised typologies of needs such as that of Maslow (1954). These are developed into measurement packages that seek to typify the range of needs applying to individuals in order to establish the minimum conditions for their compliance to the goals of the organisation.

Thus the concept of motivation is applied to organisations themselves in that they are seen as having their own internally derived goals that can change to accommodate the environmental contingencies which the organisation is faced with. At the same time, individual goals are conceptualised as a subset of those organisational goals. For instance, the currently fashionable 'continuous development' programmes designed ostensibly to meet the 'training needs' of organisations, serve mainly to locate organisational problems at the individual rather than the structural level (see Chapters 15 and 18). Such systems could be seen simply as extensions of social facilitation though the medium of the technique of *goal-setting*.

Goal-setting

Goal-setting as a technique is said not only to be effective with scientists, managers, and blue-collar workers, and thus assumed to extend earlier techniques such as management by objectives in that it is claimed to work beyond supervisory and managerial grades; it is claimed by Locke and Latham to be a core motivational technique (1984: 121) that can underpin job enrichment, behaviour modification or other processes. It operates through attention to levels of:

- commitment to goals
- acceptability of goals
- difficulty of goals
- specificity of goals
- participation in setting goals.

It is seen to affect the choice of goals, the effort put into them and the strategies selected in pursuing them. The outcomes are assumed to be thoroughly positive in managerial terms: human resources are fully utilised by directing attention and action; energy and effort are mobilised; persistence is increased and the development of appropriate task strategies are encouraged. It works by breaking down goal-related behaviour into simpler sub-routines in the way that scientific management does with physical operations, thereby reducing the stress of dealing with complex goals. Locke and Latham portray it as a tool which 'gets results', but when used improperly can result in 'conflict, feelings of failure, increased stress, dishonesty' (1984: 171).

Arnold *et al.* (1998: 259–620) give a useful account of the limits of goal-setting, noting that it 'could be criticised in its early days for being a technique rather than a theory' (1998: 261). Regardless of subsequent developments, goal-setting is still an example of the extension of technologies of regulation that replaces 'impractical models and theories' with 'a technological approach to using human resources effectively for the creation of industrial wealth' (Wellin, 1984: 4). These are essentially contingent strategies for increasing effectiveness, or 'a practical bag of tools for solving human problems in organisations' (1984: 183). However, it is probable that such strategies will probably never work as intended. Even if individual subjectivity can act, as Knights and Willmott (1985) argue, to separate people and blind them to their collective interests, it will still operate to motivate and enable them to circumvent technologies of regulation for their own purposes. You can in no way guarantee that staff will develop the goals set for them, only that they will develop goals, just as you cannot guarantee what staff will learn, only that they will.

Goals versus identity projects

Goals themselves have been queried as a useful concept, especially in Hosking and Morley's (1991, chapter 2) comments on top-down, *entitative* approaches to persons (that is, the characteristics, traits and behaviours of individuals) and groups in organisations, through topics such as motivation, attitudes, job design, leadership and group dynamics. These are essentially reified approaches that depend on assumptions of the independence of person and organisation. Hosking and Morley identify (1991: 72) the focus on goals in such approaches as a major sticking-point that pervades the organisational literature, and argue for an emphasis on projects rather than goals to explain the interlocking nature of personal and social processes. They illustrate this with the following example:

> Consider the projects of three academics. One has reached a certain point in his career and now actively is seeking promotion; another wishes to build a network of persons whose research interests are the same as hers; another wishes to get more favourable publicity for her subject. They join forces in organizing a conference; not one of them has resources sufficient for organizing the conference on their own; and each has different reasons (grounded in their different projects) for coordinating their actions in this way. (Hosking and Morley, 1991: 74, based on Weick, 1979)

The important point here is that we need others to pursue our projects or *personal agendas* regardless of their congruence or divergence. This frees us somewhat from abstract concepts of goals and complex motivations, and may also help to explain why changing circumstances affect individual motivation differentially. Hosking and Morley (1991: 29–32) refer to personal projects as a series of *conversations*, which have aspects that are variously, but not exclusively, *pragmatic*, *structuring* and *semantic*. These are said to define culture for groups, and are the arena in which individual and group subjectivity are constructed and transformed in organisations.

Though Hosking and Morley produce a powerful critique of goals as a motivational concept, there is a sense in which it comes too late, since goals are thoroughly pervasive in the literature and more importantly are embedded in common usage. Even if the goals of individuals are divergent and/or incongruent with organisation 'goals', they are still assumed to be necessary for organisations to exist at all. In other words, we utilise at least some implicit sense of shared goals or values and some notion of how goals are developed in motivational terms in much the same way as we utilise implicit personality theories (see Chapter 15). Goals are perhaps best viewed in the end as a variable in the process of setting our personal agendas and pursuing our personal projects (see 'Control theories' and 'Self-concepts' below).

Motivation as an artefact

It appears, then, that the functional utility of motivation models is in establishing the minimum conditions under which workers can be *mobilised* to consent to the nature of work that is demanded of them. This is achieved through a narrow conceptualisation of motivation which is useful in engaging consent for working practices by actively manipulating perceptions of expectations, preferences, social and material rewards, and threats. What is effectively happening here is that extrinsic factors largely outside the control of the individual, such as pay and conditions, are being translated into intrinsic factors. These include those processes assumed to be under individual control, for instance satisfaction and motivation, thus making employees personally responsible for their own objective situation, much as we have argued is the case in the attribution of stress. Seivers (1986) goes further by arguing that motivation is not an intrinsic factor of individual personality, but an artefact produced by the science of organisational behaviour; which acts as a surrogate for the meaning that people have lost from fragmented and dehumanised work:

> Motivation only became an issue – for management and organisation theories as well as for the organisation of work itself – when meaning was either lost or disappeared from work....In consequence, motivation theories have become surrogates for the search for meaning. (Seivers, 1986: 338–9)

That management has become such a great consumer of theories and techniques of motivation is in itself an indication that there is little in much work which can in itself act as a source of meaning and the basis for a secure identity. Attempts to introduce greater levels of participation, to 'humanise' work, to 'enrich' jobs, are in part a recognition that at least some level of commitment from workers is necessary to valorise capital efficiently. Attempts to 'motivate' are founded on the assumption that workers need to be led, as in Theory X, but their theoretical bases do not examine the corollary that they need to be influenced to co-operate because of their essential alienation from the productive process. However, the use of motivation as a manipulative concept implies not a lesser but a greater unitarism of outlook from management. The integration of individual and organisational 'goals' not only binds people ever closer to the productive process, but creates the climate where programmes such as TQM make them responsible for monitoring their own performance. The 'motivations' served are the managerial aims of greater unit productivity; the drive for more work and less waste, operating under the cover story of a consensus-based participation provided by motivational techniques which have not moved on much since the days of Herzberg and McGregor.

Control theories

Whether motivation theory can move on to a more considered view of the social relations of production will depend to a great extent on whether theories can begin to incorporate both the objective and subjective dimensions of work. One attempt to do this is in what is probably the most powerful development in motivation theory to appear in the last 15 years: Klein's *Integrated Control Theory of Work Motivation* (1989). What this theory manages to do is to integrate cognitive motivation theories, theories of scripted response, theories of causal perception and attribution and cybernetic theories. These latter, combining information processing and the control of action, are based on Wiener's (1948) cybernetic hypothesis and the notion of feedback, and are similar to Miller's notion of TOTE units given in Chapter 16. The main elements of behavioural control theories are given below:

- cognitive   internal goals
               information on current state
               comparison of goals and state
- affective   perceived discrepancies
               behavioural resolutions.

Klein's model (Figure 19.2) is essentially a metatheory aimed at accounting for the hypotheses generated by the various approaches it incorporates, and according to Klein (1989) it is consistent with the propositions of social learning, equity, expectancy and satisfaction theories. However, it also claims to focus more on individuals' self-regulation in response to external influences than on the effects of those influences, such as providing goals and incentives, as is the case with most motivation theories.

If we imagine that many of these processes, for example the continuation of previous behaviour (1989: 7), might themselves be organised into hierarchical systems of goal-directed action, the theory's potential explanatory power becomes enormous. (See Arnold *et al.*, 1998: 263–4, and McKenna, 1994: 93–6, for more detailed expositions.) Since the model does acknowledge the influence of individual and situational factors such as ability, past experience, social comparison processes, situational constraints and reward structures, this theory offers some hope of reconciling cognitive/rational theories with approaches emphasising subjectivity and its construction. However, the propositions that Klein derives from control theory are still to be tested in any detail. Even so, as Klein demonstrates with his extended example of a salesperson trying to meet a quota, it does offer considerable insight into the dynamic processes of self-regulation in individual action and of how 'automatic and conscious processes operate simultaneously to initiate and direct behaviour' (1989: 168).

On the basis that Klein's model represents an even more sophisticated and multivariate theory than previous accounts of motivation, any predictions would have to view practical applications as still a long way off. A similar view on control and integration to Klein's is advocated by Brotherton (1999: 38–43). This is Ford's *motivational systems theory* (1992), which seeks to integrate factors such as goals, emotions, personal agency and behavioural schemata in a fashion which, according to Brotherton, conceptualises motivation in a fashion which emphasises that 'facilitation, not control, should be the guiding idea' (1999: 40). In support of Ford, Brotherton notes that 'Psychology makes a fundamental error if it adopts the

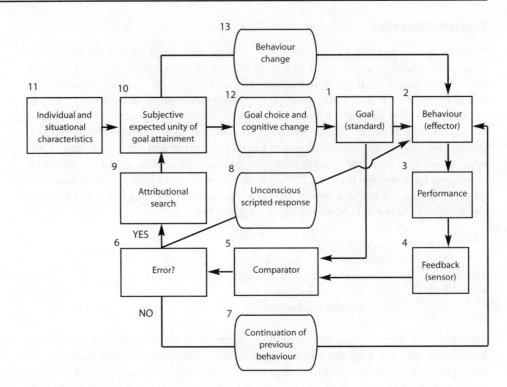

An integrated control theory model of work motivation   FIGURE 19.2

Source: H. J. Klein (1989) 'An Integrated Control Theory of Work Motivation', *Academy of Management Journal*, 14. 2: 1451.

proposition that managers need oversimple models of what are actually complex processes', but at the same time, 'there is too much pressure on managers already to have them accept the quick fix' (1999: 42–3). As such, it appears that managers are caught in a cleft stick, needing simple techniques to attempt continually to gain a competitive edge in motivational terms, but suffering the consequences of employing inadequate conceptualistions of workplace motivation. Brotherton argues that future shifts in values and training are key factors in being able to utilise more complex approaches. In the meantime, it is probable that the blunt instruments of Herzberg's KITAs will remain the dominant techniques to be employed and redeployed in the process of mobilising commitment.

Self-concept theory

Though models such as Klein's make a comprehensive attempt to integrate content and process theories, they are still open to the kind of critique put forward by those such as Shamir, who claims that,

> current motivational theories are restricted in certain respects due to their over-reliance on individual–hedonistic assumptions and their over-emphasis on cognitive–calculative processes. (Shamir, 1991: 405)

According to Shamir, the kind of influence strategies employed by 'transformational leaders' (see Chapter 17), who try to 'persuade their followers to transcend their own interests for the sake of the team' (1991: 407), cannot be explained from the point of view of theories which highlight individual satisfaction. It is possible that the concept of *subjective expected utility*, as found in expectancy theory and incorporated by Klein, could account for such phenomena through the delayed gratification rewards attached to superordinate goals. This could not, however, counter the second strand of Shamir's critique, in that process theories may have their greatest explanatory power in what Mischel (1973) characterised as strong situations where there are clear goals and expectancies tied to performance incentives. The inability to explain weak situations where there may be large variations in individual behaviour is tied to what Shamir argues is a tendency of content theories to 'emphasise easily and measurable and observable and relatively discrete behaviours' (1991: 408).

Shamir further asserts that motivation theories tend to embody limited concepts of intrinsic motivation and to exclude values and moral obligations. Such conceptions are said to ignore the fact that a task may have no intrinsically satisfying properties and yet might still be 'motivating due to its meaning for the individual, for instance in terms of the affirmation of his or her identity and collective affiliations' (1991: 409). Even where motivation theories do make strong distinctions between intrinsic and extrinsic motivation, Shamir notes that the task-oriented focus tends to 'neglect the symbolic and expressive aspects of human beings' (1991: 409). This is especially true of the notion of *denotic motivation*, which examines the possibility of a drive towards discharging one's moral obligations (from Schwartz, 1983, and Etzioni, 1988).

Shamir's *self-concept* theory of motivation attempts to produce both a theory of general work motivation (investing effort in the work role) and general job motivation (investing effort in your current job). It does not attempt to explain the motivation to perform specific tasks but, like Klein, Shamir integrates material from a number of sources, notably Bandura's (1986) social cognitive theory, 'structural symbolic interactionism' from Stryker (1980), and Gecas' (1986) self-concept theory. The assumptions driving the theory are given below:

1   'Humans are not only goal oriented but also self expressive.' They 'choose to spend time in situations that allow them to express their dispositions, attitudes and self-conceptions'.
2   'People are motivated to maintain and enhance their self esteem and self-worth.' This is reflected in that 'both competence standards and cultural values are internalised into the self concept in the form of evaluative standards'.
3   'People are also motivated to retain and increase their sense of self-consistency. . . . In a sense, the self-concept is an ideology that people attempt to express and validate in their behaviour.'
4   Self-concepts are composed, in part, of identities. . . . People derive meaning from being linked to social collectives through their identities', and may operate on an 'authenticity motive' (Gecas) to reflect their 'true identity' in their actions.
5   'Self-concept related behaviour is not always related to clear expectations or immediate and specific goals.' They may be motivated by faith and 'the imagined possibilities of the self'.

(Shamir, 1991: 411–15)

Overall, general job motivation is seen as determined by the extent to which the person's self-concept is congruent with their current job and its situational context. Job-related identities are seen as central to the self-concept, though other identities (for example, national, ethnic and family) must be acknowledged (1991: 417). The theory is said to be most powerful in 'weak' situations (see above) where goals and the means for achieving them are unclear and there is no explicit linkage between performance and external rewards (1991: 416). However, Shamir does claim that the theory may be useful for explaining some 'strong' situations, for example, 'deviant, non-conforming behaviour such as whistle-blowing' (1991: 416), presumably on the basis that these activities have strong identity salience.

Control, self-concepts and identity

The need for such a synthesis of control and self-concept theories can be demonstrated through Jackson's (1994: 83) summary of the influence of cultural factors on motivation. Jackson argues that in international comparisons, process theories are more portable due to their focus on 'universals' of motivation and since 'static-content theories do not travel very well between cultures' (1994: 83). Self-concept theory might thus provide useful insights into how general work motivation is subject to cultural variation, while control theory can provide explanation of the 'universal' processes by which persons choose specific courses of action.

If, as in self-concept theory, we can link both the content and processes of motivation to identity, we can focus on these as inputs to situationally determined strategies that people adopt to enhance the identities they have constructed. People would not be 'intrinsically' or 'extrinsically' motivated. Rather, they would take meaning from whatever sources are available and use it to enhance both the image they have of themselves and the images that others hold of them. In a work environment where possibilities for securing meaning were scarce, people might still be capable of taking meaning from the situation to the extent that they can gain some personal or collective control over their work. Strongly cohesive workgroup cultures might in this sense actually identify with working practices to the extent of feeling that they, and not management, 'own' them. Attempting to redefine working practices in such situations might only detract from the sources of meaning available in the workplace, and in essence, attack whatever portion of identity resides there. If this is the case, then compensations, even assuming they are designed to satisfy both intrinsically and extrinsically derived motivations, would probably not overcome hostility to changes and would make them difficult to implement. Whatever the case, it appears debatable that motivational interventions actually manage to mobilise any real *commitment* to organisations, a contention we wish to explore in our final section.

Mobilising commitment

As far as the practical use of motivation theory at present is concerned, identity is essentially an *intervening variable* acting to complicate applications that attempt to mobilise worker commitment. Taking account of individual identities introduces subjective factors that make motivations difficult to assess with standardised test inventories such as interest questionnaires. But it is already the case that social identity measures are being used almost as predictive personality traits. For example James *et al.* (1994) use measures such as self- and collective esteem, value differences, expressiveness and perceived prejudice in assessing the health of minority workers. The relative degrees of prediction and attempted control available to managers are illustrated by the model proposed by Myers and Myers (1982, in Jackson, 1993: 73) in Figure 19.3.

It is evident that the processes described in control and self-concept theory operate mainly at the 'psycho-social' level, where the possible degree of managerial control is said to be only moderate to low. As with Herzberg's commentary on motivational techniques and the statement from Hershey above, the problem is an imperfect control of intrinsic motivational impulses which can only partially be corrected by the deployment of extrinsic rewards. To achieve systematic control over commitment, were this even possible, would require that psycho-social factors be regulated through social and organisational processes. However these must be considered in relation to effects of environmental variables (politico-legal, socio-cultural, market-economic and so on), which even in relation to Leavitt's (1978) basic model of the interaction between people, task, technology and structure could

Factors	Examples	Degree of management control
Organisational	Nature of jobs Physical/technical environment Reward system Supervision Available information Organisational goals Organisational structure	High
Social	Reference groups Peer groups Work groups Role-set	Moderate
Psycho-social	Needs Perceived abilities Aspirations Personal objectives Perceptual set	Moderate to low
Psycho-biological	Genetics Nurture	Nil

Management control of motivating influences   *FIGURE 19.3*

Source: M.T. Myers and G. E. Myers (1982) *Managing by Communication: An Organisational Approach*, New York: McGraw Hill, reproduced in T. Jackson (1993) *Organisational Behaviour in International Management*, Oxford: Butterworth-Heinemann, p. 73.

be seen to produce a welter of mediating variables. Thus, the main burden of such change in the end falls on people, as they are the factor over which management has the least reliable control.

Such structural and cultural pressures, ideologically legitimated by the 'need' to change tasks and technologies, coupled with the long-term failure to control intrinsic motivation, have produced the whole panoply of modern-day KITAs. Ranging from desperate attempts to reassert control over rewards in performance-related pay and share schemes, through group-based initiatives, to the bludgeon-like tools of restructuring and corporate culture, what success these initiatives have is not in producing general job and work motivation. It is merely the production of short-term movement towards increased effort on specific tasks. The only routes that appear to be left for increasing general motivation are in the control of meaning and of group-based socialisation into work roles (see Chapter 20) as the main psycho-social factors subject to external manipulation.

Internalisation of commitment

To achieve this form of change requires that practices that have evolved into scripted behaviours be 'unfrozen' in Lewin's (1947) terms, so that re-socialisation can take place. As scripts are based on the kinds of flexible action patterns and sensorimotor learning discussed in Chapter 17, what would be sought here is the constant re-engagement of the intellectual level of learning. Behaviour would not be directed by learned patterns of experience, desire or collective obligation, but by adaptive behaviour in response to constant uncertainty. This situation is reflected in Hopwood's (1974, cited in Johnson and Gill, 1993: 34–5) model linking social and administrative controls. Social controls, such as group norms, aimed at regulating output, and administrative controls, such as reward systems, aimed at increasing productivity, require enactment through their internalisation as self-controls. Johnson and Gill (1993: 34–6) extend this by reference to Kelman's (1961) work on conformity and Kanter's (1968) comments on organisational identity. In Kelman's eyes, internalisation is one form of conformity whereby the individual adopts the norms and value structures of 'significant others' in the development of their 'internal moral imperatives'.

Compliance is conformity based on the motivation to gain rewards and avoid costs, which may be linked in organisational terms to Hopwood's administrative controls. Identification also involves 'significant others', but is conformity to the social influence they exert on the basis of our becoming emotionally attached to them, wishing to be like them or perhaps to be identified as one of the group or cultural community to which they belong. The role of compliance and identification is finally linked to the idea of internalised self-controls through Kanter's concepts of 'mortification' and 'surrender': the former involving the 'exchanging of a private identity for one provided by the organisation', and the latter the 'attachment of one's decision-making prerogative to a greater power' (Kanter, 1968, cited in Johnson and Gill, 1993: 35–6). The importance of this for Johnson and Gill is that:

> it draws our attention to the processes that can disengage the individual from prior social and ideological attachments by redirecting his or her beliefs and norms towards those that predominate in any organisational context – whatever those might be. (Johnson and Gill, 1993: 36)

This is linked to the development of organisational commitment through reference to Brown (1965) on the nature of conformity and moral development. Individuals are seen to initially obey external demands and sanctions and then to develop emotional attachments in 'everyday social interactions' that produce identification and eventual internalisation (1965: 36).

The dilemma here is that the context within which internalisation takes place is as important to the outcomes as the process itself. As Hosking and Morley (1991: 5) note, 'people are both products of their contexts and participants in the creation of those contexts'. The relation between person and context is one of 'assimilation' by changing the context and 'accommodation' by changing oneself. Relationships of this kind would make attempts to promote the internalisation of controls appear to be a one-sided process. Accommodation and compliance would be the normative valuation for those instituting control systems, whereas assimilation and identification would be the desired outcomes for those subject to control. Since the opportunities for assimilation of context are limited for most employees, it is likely that any accommodation that takes place is rather a case of resigned acceptance more analogous to mortification than 'empowerment'.

Institutional commitment?

> Why is it that when a company wants people to direct their purchasing behaviour in a particular direction, they turn to advertising agencies for their expertise in *persuasion*, but when they want to direct their own employees' behaviour in a particular direction they call it *motivation*? (Hershey, 1993: 10)

Hershey's concern essentially devolves to an appeal for line managers and HRM practitioners to employ the techniques of persuasive communication used by advertisers to compensate for the lack of success of motivation theory, reflecting the focus within the Myers model above on the extent of managerial influence at the psycho-social level being limited to training and communication. Commitment, on the other hand, implies both a condition of personal commitment to courses of action or belief as aspired to in the mainstream literature, and one of 'being committed'. This latter, in the sense of being locked into a system which is somehow beyond our control, is more representative of the critical literature on management. It presents organisations as institutions to which we are committed against our will and where persuasive *therapeutic* techniques are used on us in order to produce a good 'organisation person'.

This view harks back to Goffman's notion of a total institution in his 1961 book *Asylums*. Such institutions – exemplified by prisons, mental hospitals and so on – were seen to have extensive if not complete control over their inmates lives, backed by systems enforcing their formal rules. This does not imply that inmates are passive recipients of control; both Goffman and later Becker (1963) noted that these institutions also embody informal rule systems enacted by both inmates and staff, which can work against the formal rules but which are necessary to the continued performance of their respective roles. The picture here is of total compliance to control, but of resistance to, and lack of internalisation of, control systems – almost the opposite of Kanter's notions of mortification and surrender as outlined above.

Kunda (1992) addresses the extent to which modern work organisations can be likened to total institutions in his case study of control and commitment in 'Tech', a hi-tech US engineering company. On the surface, the resemblance to a total institution is slight, employment at Tech being economically rewarding and desirable and members being continually involved in 'reflective discourses' that openly embody irony, cynicism and humour. But at the same time there is a pull towards an escalation of commitment to the corporation, towards corporate definitions of reality, and continual pressure on the boundaries of personal privacy. The outcome, according to Kunda, is that 'people over time are submerged in a community of meaning that is to some extent monopolised by management: a total institution of sorts' (1992: 224). The self is not surrendered or captured in Kanter's terms, but the foundations on which the self is built are continually undermined as the authenticity of experience is continually appropriated by corporate ideology.

The effect of such an appropriation of meaning overlays rules of belief onto the systems of rules regulating behaviour, imperfect articulation between the two giving rise to manufactured uncertainty and insecurity. This insecurity is a classic precondition for the exercise of power through self-discipline as exemplified in Grey's (1994) study of professional accountants. The uncertainty produced by exhortations on the superiority of accountants, coupled with a secretive employment and promotion policy, led to constant self-surveillance. This was characterised by a search for 'signs of grace' signalled by formal indications such as salary, job ratings and allocations and informal signs such as working and social relationships with superiors. Where 'grace' is found this reinforces the self-confidence of the individual and hopefully engenders a self-fulfilling prophecy of success. Thus to gain, in Whyte's (1957: 404) terms, 'the peace of mind offered by the organisation' and to reduce levels of manufactured uncertainty does not require abject surrender to the formal restrictions or beliefs of the total institution. At the same time, though, it will require the same types of tacit collaboration and 'tactful' behaviour that Goffman saw as necessary to the continuation of organisational 'performances' and which we explore further in chapter 21.

Conclusion

Motivation is a chimera, a hybrid concept that owes more to science and organisational necessity than to nature, human or otherwise. It is often linked to that other organisational chimera, the so-called 'psychological contract' (see Guest's 1998 review and critique), which some now associate with similarly suspect notions of 'organisational citizenship' (see Brotherton, 1999: 44). Like the psychological contract, motivation seems to be noted more in the breach than its observance, and managers often appear to be better at demotivating workers than at enthusing them with the spirit of the enterprise. From short-term productivity initiatives based mainly on social facilitation, influence or coercion, we now have a huge ramshackle edifice which constantly reshapes and renames itself to accommodate the changing contexts of work.

In consultancy and management development work we often hear managers complain that 'my workers are not motivated' and the stock response has become: 'No, only dead people aren't motivated, they're just not motivated to do what you want them to'. To a great extent, in this era of short-term contracts and demands for continuous development, we are now expected to be responsible for our own motivation to work. Now that we cannot have a comfortable progression up a job ladder to mobilise our commitment, and the diminishing returns of reward and autonomy are recognised everywhere except in the case of CEOs, organisations are turning elsewhere for inspiration. The area of psychological knowledge that is being mined most extensively for the raw materials of motivation is nowadays that which supplies most of our social facilitation in the first place: the group. In the next chapter we explore the regulation of organisational behaviour through the nature and dynamics of groups or, to be more in line with modern usage, through teamwork.

20 From Groups to Teams

As we saw in Chapters 11 and 12, teams are at the forefront of contemporary work reform. Some of the management writers and organisational psychologists who once wrote about groups have now dusted down their material and applied it to teams. This chapter seeks to outline and evaluate that journey, considering the traditional behavioural literature on groups, before looking at the extent to which the equivalent writings on teamwork adds to, distracts from or distorts it.

The authority of the group

Groups are defined in terms that vary according to the aspects of the topic that are being studied. However, a composite definition could describe a group as 'a collection or coalition of people who interact meaningfully in the pursuit of common goals or objectives and who have at least a tacit sense of agreed standards, values and common identity' (based on Schein, 1965, and Drake and Smith, 1973). Groups are often referred to as the 'building blocks' of organisations and are studied in terms of the roles and associated norms generated within them, their role and communication structures, their interpersonal dynamics and their relations to other organisational coalitions and interest groups. Whether formally or informally constituted, cohesive or loosely associated, groups could be viewed in many situations as responses to pressures. We live out much of our existence in the contexts of varying coalitions to which we are attached for a purpose, whether this is by individual design, accident or external determination. Groups in this sense are social and interpersonal tools, or even possibly technologies of action through which we achieve ends that are beyond our perceptions of personal power. At the same time, our activities are circumscribed by, and directed towards, whatever goals or ends the group exists to serve.

In organisations, groups tend to be formed around the divisions and stratifications inherent in structural and or social processes. Thus they can arise around and within sectional, divisional and hierarchical boundaries, and also out of the interactions of groups of peers, workmates or social interests. Any individual is likely to have allegiance to any number of such groups at the same time, even though they might not actually consider themselves to be a member of any particular group. In the same way our allegiances may change and shift without this registering in a conscious fashion. Numerous typologies of groups are in use, which classify them, for example, as *membership*, *affiliation* or *interest*, *formal* or *informal*. More useful classifications for the study of groups in the workplace examine them on the basis of levels of *skill* and *interaction*, closeness/type of *relationships*, and the levels of *control* the group has over factors such as *methods and pace of work*, *membership* and *adherence to norms*. The various typologies of groups are often used very loosely in the organisational literature and even more so in the HRM literature, which often assumes global effects of group membership that are not always true of all types of group. For example, typologies which give groups as *task* (sometimes *project*), *team and command* (sometimes *technological*) can be interpreted as classifying groups according to the levels of control that the group itself has over the factors given above. Task groups would have high levels of control and latitude for decision-making, command groups little or none.

Though the distinction between formal and informal groups is well-rehearsed in the literature, it is false in the sense that even the most rigidly constituted formal groups still have informal processes surrounding the interactions of members both within and without the group. By the same token, even loose informal coalitions have their behaviour formally constrained to some extent by evaluative standards such as norms. In reality this distinction should be restricted to whether the group has been formally or informally constituted and to levels of control as above. Hollway (1991: 70–1), for example, notes that the focus on the informal group in Mayo's Hawthorne studies did not lead to practices based on the informal interactions of friendship or social affiliation, but rather to the genesis of the training group, 'temporarily constituted of strangers in isolation and permanently under the control of the trainer' (1991: 71). Likewise, distinctions based on the closeness and type of relationships in the group, normally given as *primary* or *secondary* groups, are again misleading. The closer, mainly face-to-face interaction of primary groups such as families, teams or groups of colleagues working on a task is not of necessity any more influential than the more distant and impersonal secondary group such as a company, union, professional association or a public institution. There are certainly more opportunities for influence to be effective in the primary group, but secondary groups very often act as *reference groups* (see McKenna 1994: 314–16 for a discussion). These we use as a source of personal or group standards or as a basis for comparison; they can be significant in determining the social and organisational roles that we aspire to or are constrained by. As such, they may have greater effects on our individual norms or values than the groups to which we presently belong, and even be a source of conflict between our values and such groups.

Of particular importance within organisations are what Alderfer and Smith (1982) refer to as *identity groups*. These are a special case of interest groups that can cut across sectional and hierarchical divisions and generally originate outside of organisational boundaries. In fact they can often be organisations themselves, professional associations, pressure groups and most notably unions. When they form a significant source of norms and values they can exert considerable influence on workplace attitudes and behaviour, often in a fashion counter to organisational objectives. As such, it is possible to see much of the culture/HRM movements of recent years as an attempt to undermine the influence of external identity groups and to shift the focus of reference back towards the employing organisation.

Group formation and composition

In terms of the definition given above, a given collection of people is not immediately a group, and the process of group formation and maturation is seen as important in determining the eventual role relationships and the performance effectiveness of the group. The most often-cited model of group formation is Tuckman's (1965), in which four stages of *forming*, *storming*, *norming* and *performing* lead to effective teamwork; a fifth stage, *adjourning*, was added to cover temporary groups and committees (1977).

This model has been adapted by Wanous *et al.* (see Cherrington, 1989: 390–2) to relate it to Feldman's notions on organisational socialisation as shown in Figure 20.1.

What this work establishes is that group roles are a function of group processes and are not necessarily dependent on the personalities of specific group members. Many groups, of course, never actually reach the stage of the mature, collaborative group, and many groups fall apart in the earlier stages. For example, if group cohesion (see 'Group cohesiveness and polarisation' below) does not develop, then the attractiveness of other social attachments might undermine the commitment of members to the purpose or task of the group. The command group described above has obvious barriers to ever being able to develop into the final stages owing to its formalised communication hierarchy. The way in which new members of organisations (for example, first-year students) form many group attachments before finally settling into a particular friendship group illustrates how competition for particular group roles may lead prospective members to abandon the group rather than take up a role they are not prepared to play.

The reasons for individuals maintaining group membership are given by Schein (1985: 150–2) as rooted in their socio-psychological 'functions'. Thus they act to provide a sense of belonging and identity, affiliation with others, guidelines for behaviour, and as a means for altering the formal structures of an organisation to suit group members better. An example of this is seen in Nichol and Beynon's (1977) 'Chemco' study (see Chapter 19) where a formal job rotation system was introduced under a job enrichment programme which only allowed workers to move from one routine job to another. Yet the workgroups had already organised informal job rotation which allowed members to rest whilst others covered for them.

The fact that the internal dynamics of groups impact on their effectiveness has led to group *composition* receiving a great deal of attention in management development circles, especially in relation to the skills necessary to produce a *balanced* team. This has produced some of the most overtly manipulative technologies of regulation in the organisational behaviour (OB) bag of tricks. Best known are the Belbin *Self-Perception Inventory* (1981) and its typology of personality-based team roles, and the Margerison and McCann *Team Management Wheel* (1986), which links team roles to job functions. (See Furnham, 1997: 456–61, or McKenna, 2000: 341–7, for

	New group	$\longrightarrow$	Mature group	
Developmental stage	Forming $\longrightarrow$	Storming $\longrightarrow$	Norming $\longrightarrow$	Performing
Group/role process	Orientation	Confrontation	Differentiation	Collaboration
Characteristics	Uncertainty Developing relationships	Conflict over power and influence	Shared expectations	Cohesiveness Commitment

FIGURE 20.1 Group development process

Source: based on D. J. Cherrington (1989) *Organizational Behaviour: The Management of Individual and Organizational Performance*, Boston: Allyn and Bacon, pp. 390–2.

extended discussions.) Both of these have limited reliability and validity as tests, and the Belbin inventory in particular has attracted extensive criticism, not least because it is based 'on data obtained from training courses run for senior management' (Hosking and Morley, 1991: 197). According to Hosking and Morley (1991: 199) and Furnham (1997: 458), Belbin's work does however establish the importance of the leadership role, creativity, support for group members and open communication in effective teams. Hosking and Morley further note that 'Belbin's theory is most useful when firms lack systematic working procedures and rely too heavily on informal methods of communication' (1991: 199). At the same time, the contradictory nature of using inductively derived personality constructs to develop processes dependent on group interaction rather than individual characteristics (as noted above) is not acknowledged by users of the Belbin typology. This, along with difficulties in matching individuals to required roles (see McKenna, 2000: 345) is why this 'would-be' technology of regulation is difficult to use outside training sessions and is mainly useful as a heuristic device for scripting managerial behaviour (see section on 'Roles' in Chapter 17).

Group socialisation

Groups can also be highly effective mechanisms for making out, and directly instrumental for their member's capacity to control the wage–effort bargain, as research such as Burawoy's (1979) shows. On the other hand, however, groups also have formal, instrumental functions for organisations as a whole, and by implication for the dominant power groupings within them. In this sense they are the basis for the distribution of work, the units of monitoring, control and data collection and an integral part of many organisational decision-making processes (Schein, 1985: 149–50). Groups and looser coalitions are also the arenas within which individuals secure identities, and of management attempts to regulate them. As identity groups, such as trade unions, professional or employers' associations, they set the contexts within which individuals and smaller groups compete for power over the structures and processes of organisations and for access to the material and psychic rewards they can supply.

In terms of making out, groups can also be viewed as sites of socialisation and as a major venue of attitudinal change, as indicated by Lewin's (1956) experimental research showing the greater impetus to attitude change in group versus individual techniques. The identity constructs that are of great importance to individual meaning and social definition based on class, race, gender, or religion are communicated to us through the behaviours and beliefs we internalise (see Chapter 19) by participating in groups. The processes of socialisation through which the appropriate behaviours an organisation demands are developed are dependent on the operation of intra-group processes for their effectiveness. Thus individuals entering an organisation become attached, or are assigned, to particular groups, wherein they 'learn the ropes' of how to survive and what is expected of them. As direct influence and hierarchical control is a possible source of threat to identity, it is possible that such moulding into appropriate images could better be pursued through the influence of peers. This can be seen clearly from the examples of use of peer-group pressures as a form of social control in Japanese management techniques. Similarly, when using the 'sitting with Nellie' approach to job training, companies would be foolish not to ensure that 'Nellie' is someone whose own workplace identity is at least roughly compatible with managerial objectives.

Group cohesiveness and polarisation

The extent to which we are influenced or affected by the particular groups to which we belong is generally seen to be associated with the relative *cohesiveness* of different groups. Cohesiveness is both a function and consequence of the individual's attraction to a group. The motivation to remain a member stems from the individual's subjective expectations concerning the personal, social or material rewards to be gained. It is not necessary, however, that we rationally calculate differential attractiveness and available rewards. We might become members of various groups simply as a result of following appropriate scripts for making out in various social situations. Calculations of advantage and disadvantage may only actually apply when we become self-reflexive about our membership of a particular group. Most of the time we will probably construct our own identity in line with the identity of the group, on the basis that it is appropriate to the behaviours the group carries out. When a group becomes something to cope with, rather than something that helps us to cope, we may reflect on the possibilities we have of rejecting one group membership for another. Alternatively we may try to redefine our own position in the group and thus our own identity within it, or even attempt to redirect the group itself and thus reconstruct group identity in line with our own interests.

Hosking and Morley (1991: 106–7) cite Janis (1972) on *interpersonal* versus *task-based* cohesiveness, which can respectively produce an 'illusion of unanimity' among group members and feelings of commitment to task-based norms. High interpersonal cohesiveness may lead to people suppressing personal doubts and bowing to group consensus through self-censorship, high task-based cohesiveness to selective perception, and convergent thinking, especially in conditions where openness of expression is not encouraged. These are the kind of conditions under which Janis' (1972) notion of *Groupthink* occurs, where moral judgement and 'reality testing' are suspended, particularly in the face of high-risk decisions in high-status groups. A good example of this was the decision of the Thatcher government to prosecute in the 'Spycatcher' affair, where concerns for secrecy and solidarity outweighed the opinion of the rest of the world that it could not win the case. Groupthink is said to be a special case of Moscovici and Zavalloni's (1969) notion of *group polarisation*, where social comparison processes and persuasive arguments can lead to groups shifting towards higher risk or more caution in decision-making discussions. Haslam (2000: 149–55) provides an excellent overview of research in this area which queries the extent to which polarisation effects are universal and rooted in individuals rather than being the social products of particular groups. Further, an analysis from the social identity approach leads Haslam to agree with Fuller and Aldag (1998) that 'groupthink' as a concept has led to serious limitations in research on group-decision making. Coined by Janis to utilise the Orwellian metaphor of 'doublethink', groupthink applies a negative spin to psychological processes within groups, which can, according to Haslam (2000: 177):

- be psychologically efficient and creative
- be grounded in group members' social reality
- have the potential to be socially enriching.

Hosking and Morley (1991: 100–12) provide further insights into the relation between individual and group coping and group context, learning and cohesion. In a discussion of Janis and Mann's (1977) conflict, commitment and choice model in decision-making processes, they too conclude that psychological processes are not necessarily negative in their effects:

> Fortunately the process is not inevitable. . . . If a cohesive group has norms and working procedures which require a 'primary commitment to open-minded scrutiny of new evidence and a willingness to admit errors' the tendency to cling to unsuccessful policies may be replaced by 'a careful reappraisal of the wisdom of past judgements'. (Hosking and Morley, 1991: 111, citing Janis and Mann, 1977: 18)

Much as stereotypes have a negative image but a vital psychological function, polarisation effects may have a vital part to play in all group-decision processes and may not be universally negative for group members or the wider organisation. Regardless of this, the perceived dangers posed by such effects to the efficacy of group decision-making have prompted a great deal of research on methods to avoid them and to make decision processes more effective. The techniques evolved include classics such as brainstorming, the 'Delphi' technique, the use of 'devil's advocates' and even 'dialectical inquiry' (Sweiger *et al.*, 1986). Whether such techniques produce more creative or effective decisions is a moot point; their effect however is less ambiguous. What they are aimed at, along with the teamworking initiatives discussed below, is the translation of interpersonal into task-based cohesiveness, much as motivational techniques attempt to translate extrinsic into intrinsic factors (as discussed in Chapter 19). It would appear that from the point of view of organisational effectiveness, the interpersonal and political processes taking place in groups can become too powerful. The decision-making capacities they are often employed for must be restrained lest they lose sight of the 'common good' of the enterprise.

It seems possible, then, that it is the efforts we make to adapt to the groups to which we belong that, in the end, make organisation and organisations possible. Further, the strength of group effects themselves has a role in the construction of the organisational 'need' for regulation and discipline.

Group responses to pressures on identity

The consequences for the individual of not adapting to the authority of the group can lie in physical or social sanctions from the group itself and/or in increased feelings of stress and anxiety. At the same time, just as group polarisation might produce positive effects, individuals can use groups actively to transform their personal and social identities. For example the reflexiveness involved in raising consciousness of disadvantage in social groups can be the spur for responses to pressures that direct the use of groups as technologies of action. Thus interest groups can actively promote not only the material interests of members, but also their development of positive identities as mechanisms for making out. The patriarchal nature of power relations in organisations were contested throughout industry, commerce and the professions in the 1980s by women's groups that relied on their own systems of *networking* to counter the male cliques who controlled their destinies.

Such networks provide fora both for ideas and information and to heighten awareness of the position of women in organisations. Their capacity for social transformation is dependent not only on the extent and nature of the contacts they build up, but also on the extent to which they empower women to develop strong individual and group identities. On this basis, such groups are often more than promotional or defensive interest groups, in that they act to foster the recognition and self-development of the capacities of all women. 'Our purpose is to help women to develop their potential – not to foster elitism' (North-West Women into Management, 1987).

The recognition of group identity by members and those outside group boundaries will be a major determinant of the kinds of responses groups will make to threats to their identity. In addition, the social components of our identities are highly dependent on the meanings we ascribe to objects, persons and events, and which we assimilate through our interaction with and accommodation to 'reference persons and groups' whose behaviour and attitudes have particular 'salience' for us. The importance of groups, according to Hosking and Morley, lies in the fact that 'social actions are inherently ambiguous' (1991: 98), and what we get from such persons and groups are systems of evaluative belief including attitudes and ideologies which:

> focus our attention on the need to justify our actions, so that they appear reasonable to members of our reference groups. This would generate modes of behaviour that are more consistent, more selective, and more characteristic of the person considered as a member of that group. (Hosking and Morley, 1991: 98)

The better-defined the identity of a group, the greater the value of the group to its members as a source of social support, comparison and evaluation. The more effective these processes are, the greater the range of external pressures which can be perceived as affecting the group, and thus the more likely that some kind of collective response will be demanded. Haslam (2000: 305) notes that 'identification with a group increases an individual's sensitivity to injustices against it'. Likewise, the stronger the identity of a particular group, the more the likelihood of other competing groups perceiving its members and their actions as sources of threat, and thus the more likely that competitors will take action which once more demands some form of response.

An important factor is the extent to which group identity is constructed around a coherent set of values: common instrumental strategies for maximising extrinsic rewards or the needs and desires of group members for affiliation and interaction. This is most visible in the contestation over control of the labour process between management and workers, but that conflict is also manifested within intergroup relations. Thompson and Bannon (1985) show that the instrumental and anti-authoritarian attitudes of the better paid 'high-flying' groups in their case study of telecommunications workers caused friction not only with management, but with lowly-rewarded and traditional craft workgroups. Each group identity was strengthened by the conflict, and the prime target of resentment was more often other workgroups, rather than management. Individual identities can of course suffer in intergroup struggles, but this is a measure of the extent to which group membership provides powerful means of resisting pressures from outside. The pressure to conform can outweigh the pressure to secure oneself against uncertainty and damage. Brown confirms the above example, arguing that intergroup conflicts act to strengthen group and intra-group identities, and when groups do resist management, 'the psychological satisfactions an individual may gain from his group membership may be more potent than the rewards (or threats) the management can hold out' (1980: 167). For management, the problem of how to disrupt, short-circuit or redirect group identities is central for securing organisation goals, mobilising consent, exerting influence and promoting 'motivation' and organisationally-directed goals.

Group resistance and conflict

Group resistance needs to be considered in relation to groups as sites of socialisation and as technologies of action. Group reactions are often along the same lines as those available to individuals, but with the added facility of being able to join in cohesive coalitions where group identity can be secured or enhanced. Of course at the same time as such responses can enable us, they can also be utilised as the basis for managerial strategies for controlling workplace behaviour. Even when there is only a tacit, unacknowledged sense of group identity, the stereotyped judgements of power-holders about particular groups may lead them to form sub-cultural units. They are likely to be based around resistance to managerial activities rather than in a coherent ideology of their own. Individual cohesion within such a group may be low, and resistance may not be co-ordinated in any sense. It may not even be visible as such, but manifested in jokes at the expense of superiors, general stubbornness and lack of co-operation (Nichols and Beynon, 1977). At this level, pressure on individual identity may be no more than disapproval at not joining in or, at worst, definition as being somehow different. Over time, the benefits of belonging to such a group in terms of access to sources of meaning may cause it to coalesce into a true subculture with the ability to protect members against threats to identity.

Haslam (2000, chapter 7) explores a similar theme on social identity in intergroup negotiation and conflict management. He introduces a wide range of evidence to show that identification with sub-groups, for example same sex groups, can be beneficial in negotiation and conflict situations. By bringing conflict out into the open, sub-groups have the potential to:

- explore issues fully (clear the air rather than paper over the cracks)
- identify parties' real concerns
- consider more options
- avoid false optimism
- enhance feelings of empowerment and justice.

(Haslam, 2000: 205)

Such effects are dependent on the development of a superordinate social identity which 'frames subgroup differences' and provides social motivation to participants (Haslam, 2000: 205). This focus on superordinate identity reinforces the arguments in the section on cohesiveness and polarisation above, in that group processes are not necessarily of negative import. However, in the absence of a superordinate identity, conflict might escalate, and this where the skills of negotiators themselves come into play if the process is not to run out of control. Hosking and Morley discuss these skills at length (1991: 161–9), especially noting the importance of cognitive and political processes in avoiding unnecessary or unrealistic conflict. Cognitive processes 'help negotiators to match their intellectual capacities to the demands of the task', and reduce unnecessary obstacles to agreement. Political processes 'help negotiators to organize disagreement so that it is seen as a natural part of a business relationship', rather than requiring a 'defensive response' (1991: 167). Once again, we have a process whereby potential contestation of issues is appropriated in such a manner as to place the responsibility on individuals and groups, rather than the organisation. Here informal processes are being transformed into formal relationships in negotiation.

Many informal organisational processes, including subcultural groupings, are generated within the free areas that groups and their members carve out for themselves within the division of labour. Whether formally or informally constituted, such groups have to in some fashion reduce the possible internal tensions that might develop out of any contradictory goals and identity concerns of their members. The internal dynamics of groups have been seen to consist largely of role-based mechanisms and processes directed at the maintenance of the group, and according to Breakwell, 'group dynamics are the most frequent sources of threats to identity. These threats need not be personalised: they are directed at the individual as a group member, a cipher in a social category, not as a personality' (1986: 128). The detailed operation of such processes will be group-specific. But like the actions of individuals, it will be oriented towards identity-securing strategies. Just as the construction of individual identities depends in part on competition with others for sources of meaning, the production of group identities depends on gaining access to symbols and resources or behaviour patterns which serve to distinguish the group from others. We will return to the issue of what distinguishes groups in behavioural terms after first exploring the area in which this issue is of most contemporary concern, *teamworking*.

Teamworking

As we saw in Chapter 13, there is little doubt that, in manufacturing at least, teams are replacing individuals as the basic unit of work organisation, and project teams are increasingly used as a means of co-ordinating managers and professionals. What is it that managers and management writers see as particularly advantageous in teamwork? Much of the enthusiasm for teams and teamwork can be traced back to the fashion for reorganising production processes into semi-autonomous work groups in the 1970s and 1980s. Such work groups, based on notions of job enrichment and redesign (see Chapter 19), gave employees some latitude of decision-making over operational matters, and integrated different levels of production-related skills into more flexible working on more 'natural' units of work. This effectively turned production-line assembly into a semblance of unit or small-batch production. Wall *et al.* (1986), in a long-term study of autonomous work groups, identified the justifications underlying their implementation as being in their assumed effects in increasing intrinsic motivation to work. These included enhancing employee satisfaction, improving group performance and reducing labour turnover, as well as suggested increases in organisational commitment and improvements in mental health.

The results of this study indicated that 'employees clearly appreciated the autonomous work system. On balance managers did too, though clearly there were costs in terms of personal stress arising from the difficulties involved in managing and maintaining the system' (1986: 298). Of the assumed effects, only intrinsic job satisfaction and productivity were significantly increased, along with reported perceptions of increased autonomy. Labour turnover actually increased, through increased dismissals of those who could not or would not fit in to the new systems. The enhanced productivity was not due to employees working any harder. If anything, their individual productivity was lower in comparison with those working on more traditional lines. Improvements largely flowed from reduced indirect labour costs, due to decreases in the need for direct supervision of the work groups. This organisational benefit can be seen as a gain at the expense of increased managerial effort, with greater responsibilities being generated in monitoring and managing the new system.

In part, then, companies have been persuaded of the 'bottom-line' advantages of teamwork: less a case of enhancing the quality of working life and more that of enabling greater flexibility, problem-solving and continuous improvement. Yet behind these technical rationales lay further assumptions that teams can reproduce much of the dynamics of groups, while turning the goals and outcomes in a managerial direction. In other words, team members can be persuaded to think like managers by delegating responsibilities that were once the preserve of management. Supporters of teams, largely from an OB tradition, see this positively in terms of group cohesion facilitating co-operative and productive units (Eby and Dobbins, 1997); critics present this more negatively as peer pressure, and self-surveillance as socialisation into corporate identities (Casey, 1996; Sewell, 1998). Both, however, seem to accept that teams are effective sites for socialisation and vehicles for normative integration (Findlay *et al.*, 2000). Restated in the language of group theory, teams can be *sentient* as well as *task* groups. This is a distinction drawn by Miller and Rice (1967), with task groups being based on the human resources necessary for work activity, while sentient groups are those to which individuals are prepared to commit themselves and on which they depend for emotional support (see 'Groups versus teams' below).

Re-engaging the worker

Most of the interventions to which members of organisations are periodically subject are based around either simple social facilitation or attempts to re-engage the intellectual level of learning (see Chapter 16). In current terms, teamworking interventions are among the most common attempts to *re-engage* the worker. They are often necessary due to the legacy of downsizing and flattening of hierarchies, with their concomitant increases in spans of control. This means that managerial skills (and what might be termed the *organisational locus of control*) need to be driven downwards in the hierarchy in order that control can be maintained.

A particularly influential article that appears to provide support for the above arguments, albeit from a critical perspective, comes from Barker (1993). We have already made reference to Barker's work in Chapters 8, 11 and 12, but will recap and comment further here. Barker offers evidence that the values of control systems appear to be internalised by some groups of workers in specific circumstances. This is exemplified in the concept of concertive control taken from Tompkins and Cheney (1985). This fourth form of control:

> represents a key shift in the locus of control from management to the workers themselves, who collaborate to develop the means of their own control. Workers achieve concertive control by a negotiated consensus on how to shape their

behaviour according to a set of core values, such as those of a corporate vision statement. (Barker, 1993: 411)

Here, though, it is both the organisation and its members that are seen to adopt a 'new substantive rationality' and a 'new set of consensual values'. It would appear that this represents the translation of Hopwood's (see Chapter 19) administrative controls into social controls, and thus the achievement of accommodation, assimilation, identification and finally internalisation. Barker's case study was of ISE Communications, a small US manufacturing company which adopted a structure based on self-managed teams in the late 1980s. The structural changes in the company are detailed in Table 20.1.

The process by which concertive control came into being was first through the development of a value consensus based on the company 'vision statement', then the emergence of normative rules driven by the addition of new teams:

> Members of the old teams responded to these changing conditions by discursively turning their value consensus into normative rules that the new workers could readily understand and to which they could subject themselves. (Barker, 1993: 424)

The final stage was the formalisation of these rules into a system that resembled in

TABLE 20.1 Structure of ISE before and after the change of teams

Before the change	After the change
1 Three levels of managerial herarchy between the vice president and the manufacturing workers.	1 Managerial hierarchy extends directly from the manufacturing teams to the vice president.
2 Manufacturing assembly line organises the plant. Workers manufacture boards according to their individual place on the line.	2 Team work areas organise the plant. Teams are responsible for complete fabrication, testing and packaging of their assigned circuit boards.
3 Line and shift supervisors form the first managerial link.	3 Teams manage their own affairs, elect one person to co-ordinate information to them.
4 Workers have little input into work-related decisions. Managers make all decisions and give all directions.	4 Team members make their own decisions within guidelines set by management and the company vision statement. Teams have shared responsibility for their own production.
5 Management disciplines workers.	5 Team members discipline themselves.
6 Management interviews and hires all new workers.	6 Team members interview, hire and fire their own members.

Source: J. R. Barker (1993) 'Tightening the Iron Cage: Concertive Control in Self-Managing Teams', *Administrative Science Quarterly*, 38: p. 417.

some ways the old bureaucratic structure. The formalisation of abstract values into specific behavioural guidelines was seen to provide a sense of stability, and was not interpreted as the creation of a bureaucracy, in that though they represented a rational, rule-based system, the rules were formulated and enacted by the teams themselves. The teams were thus said to be 'their own masters and their own slaves' (1993: 433) and even though managing the concertive system produced a great deal of strain in team members, they were reluctant to give up their control of their working practices, uncommitted workers not lasting very long. Barker's conclusion is that in the end even a self-managed rational apparatus only serves to bind employees further to Weber's 'Iron Cage', resistance being at the cost of risking their human dignity by 'being made to feel unworthy as a "team-mate"' (1993: 436).

The self-managed responsibilities produced by the concertive system themselves begin to enact the construction of a rational apparatus, in that the formalisation of consensual values into rules could be seen as an adaptive mechanism to relieve the levels of stress induced by autonomous decision-making. Thus team members become, in Willmott's (1994) terms, 'responsible individuals' who seek the stability of a rational apparatus in that they 'are spared the anguish of choice because feelings of anxiety and guilt associated with this responsibility are contained within organisationally defined boundaries' (1994: 26). However, here it is the uncertainty produced by the move to self-management which unfreezes team members to the point where corporate ideals can be identified with, rather than the generalised uncertainty Willmott associates with the 'indeterminacy and finitude of human existence' (1994: 26).

The Barker study demonstrates that re-engagement of the intellectual level of learning (see Chapter 16) can be achieved through collective obligations that guide adaptive behaviour in response to manufactured uncertainty. But once again the identification here is not directly to administrative controls and managerial values. Identification with the corporate mission is dependent on the continued abdication and transfer by management of responsibility and control to social consensus. Management has changed the context of control by changing the structures through which it is enacted, but the extent to which this represents any real measure of internalisation, rather than simple compliance to a new locus of control, must be questioned. What this form of self-management achieves are constant self-monitoring and environmental scanning by the team, and learned changes in behaviour that are not necessarily accompanied by increases in either general or specific job motivation. As indicated in Chapter 19, what appears to be important here is not genuine motivation, but the mobilisation of commitment. Even this is not commitment to intrinsic values, but to the expenditure of effort in required directions. The mechanisms for accomplishing this may rest on appeals to values and the construction of meaning, but their aim is the attainment of strategically-directed change.

Team dimensions

There are, however, grounds for scepticism about how far teams are sentient and characterised by high levels of normative cohesion. Part of the problem is that both advocates and critics of teams tend to present them as a 'package' in which task functions, value-orientations and capacity for self-governance are all mutually reinforcing. Along with other recent commentators on teamwork (see Proctor and Mueller, 2000), we prefer the view that teams can take many different forms dependent on context, in part because teamwork has different components. A widely-used example of such an approach is the *team dimensions model* (Thompson and Wallace, 1996; Findlay *et al.*, 2000). This uses a threefold distinction between the technical, governance and normative dimensions of teamwork. (See Figure 20.2.)

The technical dimension is at the heart of the current wave of managerial interest in teams, and is concerned with issues directly related to the actual tasks undertaken by team members (for example, problem-solving and flexibility). Teamwork must, however, also rest on changes in the normative (for example, socialisation of team members and changes in attitudes and behaviours), and governance dimensions (management of teams including increased responsibilities and decision-making). In turn, the dimensions are influenced by wider support systems such as reward and industrial relations arrangements.

A multi-dimensional approach enables the variety of managerial objectives and configurations of actual practices to be identified and more adequately understood. Two such trends have been identified in earlier discussions of teamworking (see Chapters 11 and 12). First, the overwhelming rationale for the introduction of teams is instrumental and pragmatic, focusing on benefits in the technical sphere such as functional flexibility. Second, only a small number of teams have a high degree of autonomy. Companies tend to initiate only that degree of involvement in decision-making

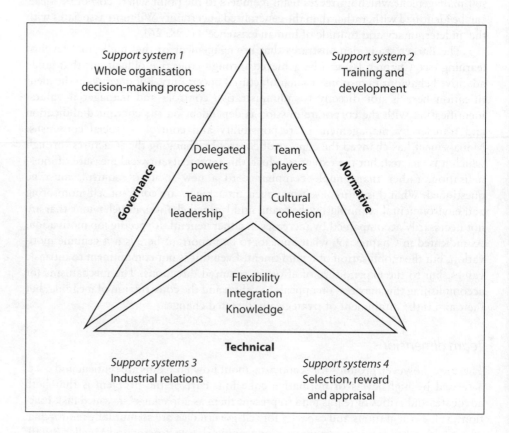

FIGURE 20.2 The team dimensions model

necessary for more effective use of workers' tacit knowledge and skills to improve efficiency. It follows that the precondition of an association between self-governance and positive normative behaviours, identified in parts of the OB and critical literatures, is not present or is underdeveloped in many contexts. There is no identifiable trend for teams acting like groups as effective sites for socialisation and normative integration, though this will vary considerably across and within particular companies and countries.

This is not to say that the normative dimension is absent or irrelevant. Even those organisations with limited, largely pragmatic objectives require that employees change some of their behaviours and attitudes in order to become better 'team players'. Emphasis may be put on co-operativeness, willingness to listen and learn, or acceptance of collective responsibility and avoidance of a 'blame culture'. Some companies therefore invest in soft skills training to back up these objectives, using teams as additional vehicles to spread awareness of business goals and conditions of competitiveness. In case studies in the Scottish spirits industry, Findlay et al. (2000a, 2000b) found that the two companies had some success in developing positive attitudes and normative competencies in areas such as communication. Team members were also more aware of business issues. However, they were far from simply internalising company values through teams. If anything their experience militated against it. Awareness of business made many them more critical of the gap between corporate rhetoric and shop-floor reality. Many team members felt disillusioned with teamwork, complaining of abuse of flexibility and intensification of work pressures. Most importantly, they were very aware of and sceptical towards any perceived attempt by the company to indulge in extensive socialisation through soft skills training or other means, labelling it 'brainwashing'. Interestingly, similar reactions have been picked up in other case studies (Pollert, 1996; McCabe, 2000). More generally, many studies have found that team sub-cultures continue to provide sources of dissatisfaction, resistance and distancing from managerial objectives (Robertson et al., 1992; Stephenson, 1994; Sharpe, 1996).

What the above discussion reveals is that the different dimensions of teamwork may not only vary, but also pull against each other. If, however, the purpose of a multi-dimensional model is to identify different configurations of practices, we have to allow for the possibility that there are indeed a small number of companies that have much more ambitious normative agendas. They may even be more successful in the resultant social engineering. Even if Barker has identified the conditions for concertive control in his case study, he gives little consideration to the extent to which it is typical or generalisable from what may be a highly specific context. Even companies with similar ambitious agendas of socialisation and self-surveillance have found that they may unravel under employee suspicion and resistance (McKinlay and P. Taylor, 1996). We will briefly return to Barker in the next section, which examines our understanding of the compatibility of group and team dynamics.

Groups versus teams

This section attempts to reflect on and tie together some of the issues raised by our respective discussion of groups and teams. If groups are the building blocks of organisations and the ability of groups to modify individual behaviour is what in the end makes hierarchical organisation possible, then what of teams? Can we assume they have the same characteristics and psychological effects as groups, or are they a special case that is dependent on context for their specific functioning? Relating to the assumed effects of group membership, Brown (1992: 73) notes that the studies of the textile industry and coal mining associated with the Tavistock Institute in the 1950s recognised the difficulties of generalising conclusions on the benefits of reorganising groups on sociotechnical principles. These difficulties are what led to the Miller and Rice (1967) distinction between task and sentient groups discussed above.

The task/sentient distinction parallels the classic formal/informal group differentiation with the added dimension of identifying the sentient/informal group more strongly with the classic psychological group. The problem is that the boundaries of task and sentient groups often do not coincide in temporal, spatial or organisational terms, and it may prove impossible to bring them into alignment. There is no necessity for task groups to exhibit the attributes of emotional closeness accruing to the sentient group, and even if they do, this may result in resistance to change through attachment to existing structures and practices. Attitudes to participation, for example, are seen as determined by group membership rather than occupational category (Brown, 1992: 51). In addition to this, Haslam notes that:

> in most of the situations where researchers have drawn inferences about the behaviour of individuals in groups, their research has failed to study groups that are psychologically real and engaging for those individuals. (Haslam, 2000: 271)

The major focus of concern with groups in labour process analysis has tended to be on their role in the restriction of output and in the production of group solidarity. Beyond the recognition that there are internal dynamics that alter behaviour, the tendency has been to treat groups as simple aggregates rather than as negotiated collectives with their own logics of conflict, control and resistance. Overall, consent, commitment and compliance are conceptualised as individual relationships, mitigating against accurate interpretation of how related practices are reproduced as a social phenomenon and how the rules of consent are communicated.

The acknowledgement of groups as sites of resistance and concomitantly as bearers of sectional and cultural interests has over time tended to reinforce the conception of groups as conveyors and communicators of oppositional values. Studies such as Thompson and Bannon (1985) and Egri (1994) typify the parameters of this treatment. Thompson and Bannon exemplify the task group as the site of sectional contentions within a factory culture, while Egri examines organic versus traditional farming, treating groups as social movements contesting the cultural transformation of work organisation both within a particular industry and in society at large. Because of links between sectional interests and wider identity groups, such distinctions can only be made in the account of particular cases, but they are repeated constantly within the labour process and wider sociological literatures.

The labour process collections on skill and consent (Sturdy, Knights and Willmott, 1992) and on resistance and power (Jermier, Knights and Nord, 1994) provide many good examples, notably in the studies by Yarrow, Sturdy and Collinson. Yarrow's (1992) study of Appalachian coal-mining communities in particular highlights how concerns with 'group unity' and elementary notions of group socialisation are often incorporated into issues that mainly focus on gender competition and degradation of relative status (1992: 35–7). The hostility of male miners and managers to women coming into the mines during the 1970s is understood here in terms of male sociali-sation into the values of solidarity, competition, physical strength and courage. These produce psychological resistance to the degradation of status posed by women being able to do the work. But at the same time Yarrow reports that 'miners have typically made accommodations to maintain the unity of the crew' (1992: 36).

The most difficult thing to explain in this study is that there was any acceptance of women at all within groups where gender and class consciousness were so deeply embedded. But from the perspective of the working group, especially in a case such as this where Yarrow acknowledges that safety considerations acted to heighten the import of interpersonal dependence, it is understandable that women could quite quickly come to share in group unity. In such highly cohesive groups where effective collaboration and communication is paramount, the group exercises a power of its own. This harks back to Minard's classic 1950s socio-psychological study where black and white mine workers lived segregated lives on the surface while co-operating and exhibiting group solidarity downshaft. The ability to demonstrate that members can effectively fulfil their role demands appears to outweigh other considerations during the performance of the task. In this sense the lack of preoccupation with group process leads to an undertheorising of why we might not exhibit resistance in the conditions of a particular labour process, which is surely as important to a holistic account as why we do!

If we consider now the converse of resistance as exemplified by worker commit-ment, Marchington's (1992) analysis of consent and co-operation in labour relations highlights how the lack of a group perspective might make labour process analysis itself dependent on rational-cognitive explanation. Marchington notes (1992: 158–9) how a conception of individual relationships in terms of hierarchical position fails to account for personal motivations and objectives such as the more basic prospect of 'doing a good job'. This is said to be central to much of our socialisation into work, and in support of this Marchington cites work as diverse as that of Peters (1986), Nichols and Beynon (1977) and Knights and Collinson (1985), who raise the notion that workers often voice critical appraisals of managers based on their mistakes, lack of understanding, commitment, and failures to communicate.

The theme of groups as regulating mechanisms is more familiar in labour process analysis than is the theme of the group as a medium of individual and collective expression. The debate around the latter conception was raised by Whyte (1957) in his analysis of the relations between individuals and groups. Whyte recognised that the concept of 'groupness' was often incidental in many situations (1957: 50) but that even where people might not think of themselves as a group, for example in a committee, the aggregate could still function as a 'disciplining vehicle' in the produc-tion of acquiescence. Whyte was sceptical of the role of the group as a creative vehicle, however, and referred to the false collectivisation characterised by managerial attempts to treat formally constituted groups as if they embodied the attributes of what have been later termed as mature collaborative groups. The often unwarranted managerial assumptions made about the effects of cohesiveness on group behaviour and group effects on performance levels almost appear as a form of 'wishful group-think' in the desire to reproduce the illusion of unanimity in task groups.

This is typical of the uncritical approach to groups and the 'common interests' of organisational members taken in the HRM and quality literatures, in other words, the instrumental and socio-psychological functions of groups are taken as unilateral phenomena, applicable to all group members regardless of personal agendas and identity projects. This is evidenced in the claims of Armstrong in 'HRM: Strategy and Action' (1992), where the eliciting of commitment in HRM practices is dependent on promotion of 'mutuality' of goals, influence, rewards and responsibility, which are said to produce benefits in terms of productivity and individual development.

The fallacy involved in such assumptions of mutuality and homogeneous commitment is essentially that teams and task groups might naturally develop the same levels of role differentiation and collaboration as a settled and cohesive psychological group might be expected to exhibit. The problem is that while psychological or sentient groups presuppose at least some level of interpersonally negotiated role differentiation, teams only presuppose a limited level of negotiated task differentiation, and task or command groups nothing more than prescribed task specialisation (see the section on 'Team dimensions' above). Unless teams or task groups are allowed the time and space for action, confrontation and autonomy that allow them to develop into sentient groups, the probable outcome will be no more than a heightened sense of domination within processes of control. The greater likelihood is, however, that teams will be broken up long before they can develop such dangerously high levels of confidence and awareness of their own capabilities and situational power. Managerial teams may of course be subjected to 'development' in the form of the Belbin inventory, or related techniques, to remind members of their scripted roles in task performance.

Conclusion

As with our discussion of motivation in the previous chapter, we might also posit the assumed similarities of groups and teams as another instance of Adorno's *identity thinking*. What we need are analytic tools that will allow us to gauge the extent to which teams and task groups do exhibit the psycho-social effects of groups. One such is found in Haslam's (2000) summary of his chapter on group productivity and effectiveness, where he concludes that a social identity approach has the following implications:

- Individuals in groups will tend to underperform when a relevant social identity is not salient or a group goal is prescribed by an outgroup.
- Labour will be divided more effectively if group members share a relevant social identity.
- Productivity on a group task will increase to the extent that group goals are congruent with a salient social identity.

These might be seen as the minimum conditions under which teams or task groups might be expected to exhibit any of the characteristics of sentient groups and any of the benefits which group working is assumed to have. The problem here is that much of what we have described as teamwork in this chapter precludes the congruence of social identity and group goals in anything but a prescribed fashion. Coupling Haslam's work with the team dimensions model might at least allow us to gauge the extent to which there is room for identity salience or superordinate identity in a teamworking system, and thus what chances there are of teams being able to perform like sentient groups. What we have to beware of is the tendency to emphasise the technical over the normative and governance dimensions of teams, as this constrains the extent to which identity salience can be generated within a team. Without cognisance of such constraints, teamworking becomes little more than another form of domination and control, and will suffer from the attempts of groups and their members to establish and secure identities that are psychologically real for them.

The dialectic between the shaping of identities and the forms of resistance and coping arising out of initiatives aimed at domination and control is, for many of us, the experience of being organised. In the next chapter we move on to examine how the construction and maintenance of identities is implicated in the production of control and self-control in employees and managers alike, and the contrivances through which such *identity work* is achieved.

21 Identity Work

Social organization is both means and bar to control. The concrete physical and biological settings in which actions occur are crucial. It is thus the outcomes and contentions among identities which is what cumulates into social organisation. (Harrison, 1992: 16)

Explanations of identity

As argued in Chapter 14, the mainstream agenda in organisational behaviour (OB) can be shown to refer to common and basic processes through which individuals develop identities. Through these processes, notably learning, perception and socialisation, the individual is seen to develop a distinctive personality and patterns of motivation. There has been much that is useful to learn from examining that journey, but as an account of the development of subjectivity and identity within an organisational context, it has distinct limitations. It fails adequately to understand individual identity as a social reality through which we transact with our environment. At another level, the sociological stream of organisation theory is much more comfortable with notions of groups acting according to economically determined interests. That is indeed part of the picture. But objective reality is filtered through *subjective constructions* which interpret and shape our whole world in terms of what we value about ourselves. Our focus on subjective identity lies in this process, because as individuals we guide our actions according to what will in our view best defend, enhance or substantiate our identities. As Knights and Willmott (1985) argued, we are all effectively engaged in securing for ourselves identities which provide both personal stability and a basis for directing our activity. Identity is thus a tool that we use to present ourselves as, and possibly transform ourselves into, images appropriate to our social, cultural and work context.

Unless personality and identity are exclusively genetically-determined phenomena, there can be little doubt that social contexts and pressures shape an individual's identity. In researching differential socio-emotional development in male and female children, Lewis (1975) found that parallel to the earliest distinguishable biological influences, there are differences in the treatment of the two sexes by adults and other children. Thus, though biological influences undoubtedly have some effects on personality in the same way that they have an influence on hair colour and general bodily characteristics, these effects are cannot easily be differentiated from social or environmental influences.

According to Weigert *et al.* (1986: 31), 'identity is a definition that transforms a mere biological individual into a human person. It is a definition that emerges from and is sustained by the cultural meanings of social relationships activated in interaction'. To extend the above example, if someone dyes or changes their hairstyle, they have taken steps to place a self-directed social construction on the body they were born with. They are taking for themselves an identity produced out of what they select as attractive or appropriate out of the social values, expectations and fashions of their time. The tradition of sociological social psychology represented by Weigert and others tries to avoid the contradictions between notions of personal and social identity. They take the view that identity is a *social product* both bestowed on the individual by others and appropriated by individuals for themselves. It takes the form of a *typified self*, any of a number of self-produced categorisations of what is available to the individual within the various situations in which they participate.

Shifting the focus from personal to social identity, we can see that we constantly represent our subjective selves to others in our social environment. In the way we dress, speak and behave we present a changing image of who we are. Identity is in this sense a negotiated construction. Depending on who we are dealing with, we present images intended to appear appropriate to both the situation and the expectations of others. Using a symbolic interactionist framework, Erving Goffman (1971) explored this conception of self within a dramaturgical metaphor, representing social identity as a performance analogous to that of an actor. The image presented is not necessarily the 'real' self of the person but a situationally appropriate image sustained by the 'actors' and those observing and/or interacting with them. The 'audience' collaborate with the actors to enable them to present a consistent performance, and hence a social identity consistent within the situation. The students in a lecture theatre collaborate with the lecturer to maintain an image of authority for the latter and of subordination for themselves, even though they may not consider themselves socially or intellectually inferior to the lecturer. They simply exercise '*tact*' in order to continue participating in the production of a performance that fits the perceived rules of the situation.

The interface between social and personal identity lies in this act of interpersonal negotiation. A social identity does not simply spring fully formed from the demands of the situation, but requires effort and practice from the individual and appropriate feedback from others. Thus the contexts from which we are able to construct unique subjective identities for ourselves consist mainly of 'rationalised' performances where we construct personal identity out of the strategies and responses we devise to deal with contingencies. The idea that we each possess a core identity relating to what we value about ourselves is examined in the *social learning* conception of identity (Miller, 1963). As a source of meaning, identity links us to others in the social structure through perceived similarities and processes of identification. As a definition or typification, identity sets us apart from others; it is the basis of social comparison, showing us the things and people which our particular personal meanings debar us from identifying with. Personal, subjective identity consists of the meanings and images we have found to represent us accurately in the past. Social identity, where it is different to the former, consists of the negotiated position between our personal identity and the meanings and images demanded of us in our current social context.

This leads us to a final aspect of identity as a linking concept between differing levels of explanation. We gain identities through interaction and association with the social and cultural groupings to which we belong. These groups provide us with points of reference and comparison out of which we can define ourselves, and through this route are in turn directly shaped by social structure. For this reason Miller (1963) saw identity as the foundation of the links between social structure and personality, and fundamental as such to the explanation of socialisation, motivation and psychological conflict. Likewise, the *social identity theory* of Tajfel and Turner (1979, 1986) links intergroup relations to social conflict and through *self-categorisation theory* (Turner, 1985) to the interpersonal dynamics of groups. Our personal transactions with social structures are conducted in the great part through the organisations we belong to, work for, and with which we have to deal. Organisations attempt to socialise people into their particular workplace cultures. Management attempts to influence individual motivation to its advantage. The amelioration of the psychological, interpersonal and group conflicts engendered by these activities is a major rationale for the involvement of social and behavioural scientists in organisations.

Redefining the agenda

To understand more adequately the individual's development towards an organisational participant who is active, yet acted upon, we need to further redefine some of the issues and agenda. For example, because so much of OB takes the structures, workings and goals of organisational life for granted, it underestimates the degree to which the environment restricts sources of meaning for secure identities and imposes costs on individuals. The resources that individuals can bring to an identity project will depend on their *situational power* in the organisation (see Chapter 19). Situational power does not depend simply on a person's place in an organisational hierarchy: a shop floor worker can construct an identity just as, or even more, secure than that of someone with more position power. An individual's perception of his or her own situational power, whether at an interpersonal, group or organisational level, conditions how secure he or she feels, mediated by factors such as *self-monitoring*, *locus of control* and *self-efficacy* (see Chapter 17). These identities are not necessarily situation-specific, providing meaning and support outside of the context they were constructed within, though there are of course limits. The 'organisation man', secure in his identification with organisational goals and objectives, may generalise associated attitudes and behaviours to situations where such an identity may be inappropriate.

The treatment of identity in mainstream psychology also neglects contextual issues in treating identity in an everyday fashion as being inherent in the person. Breakwell (1987: 95) argues that psychologists 'tend to treat identity as the origin of action'; they use it as a 'motivational variable'. In contrast, we see identity as the outcome of interaction within particular material contexts which act as constraints on available sources of meaning and on the process of identity construction. The central limiting factor on available sources of meaning is the context of *fragmented* and *commodified* work. Labour is reduced to abstract capacities which serve the ends of production rather than those of the person, as in the appropriation by work organisations of the *use-time* available to individuals for developing and pursuing their own capacities, abilities and interests (Seve, 1978). Subjectively this reduction of the relations between people and things to their value in a system of exchange increases powerlessness and decreases personal responsibility. In an externally controlled environment, the most individuals can often hope for is to maintain or increase their situational power and material resources. Our relationships with, and our attribution of motives to, others are reduced to their instrumental function in the process of 'accumulation without regard to need' (Wexler, 1983: 122). Socio-psychological models of motivation continually reflect this, as in the rational calculations of personal advantage we are assumed to make in process models of motivation (see Chapter 19).

Gender and ethnic identities

The instrumentality of relationships also extends into the definition of gender identities in the workplace. As we saw in Chapter 10, writers such as Hearn and Parkin (1987) identify the *desexualised* nature of work organisations as reinforcing patriarchy and sexism. Instrumentality in the continuing forms of fragmented, Taylorised work relations defines masculinity and reproduces organisational work as a male concern:

> The workman is, potentially at least, nothing more than the doer of the task, without feelings and emotions. The ideal workman would appear to almost lose physical presence, or be a mere disembodied bearer of role, in effect part of a machine system. (Hearn and Parkin, 1987: 19)

Women workers have been excluded from the predominantly male culture of organisations, and feminine gender identity suppressed or marginalised. Women managers especially are often required to adapt to masculine models of management, or risk being viewed as exceptions to women in general. Likewise domestic labour is not viewed as 'real' work in the fashion that paid work is; the identity construct of 'worker' is reserved for those carrying out the latter. Women's labour in organisations has often been an extension of domestic labour, as in the example of secretaries who act as 'office wives, protecting their charges from unnecessary interference and strain, making tea, buying presents, even cleaning their bosses' false teeth' (1987: 92).

Sexual, and racial, discrimination in labour markets is reinforced by stereotypical categorisations of women and black workers that portrays them as 'naturally' inferior in various abilities or only suited to certain types of work. Notions such as women being better suited than men to boring, repetitive tasks serve to legitimise restricted access to labour markets. Black workers in particular have been discriminated against in recruitment and selection processes on the basis of a stereotyped lack of acceptability in white workplace cultures. Jenkins (1986) notes that the causes of racism are often attributed to those who are discriminated against: 'managers do, in the main, see black workers as posing problems for their organisations. These problems were typically seen to be created by black workers, not by white racism' (1986: 114).

Predominantly white, male managers, with workplace identities closely aligned with organisational goals, would not be expected to attribute problems to either their own or 'institutional' racism. Rather the problems would be seen to reside in those who demonstrably deviate from 'natural' cultural standards. White workers are viewed as individuals, whereas black workers are perceived as groups characterised by often contradictory stereotypes: 'if you've got a problem with one of them, you've got a problem with all of them, whereas with the whites, you're just dealing with an individual' (1986: 99). Of course, that people tend to fall back on the resources of group identity in the face of discrimination and situational powerlessness is wholly understandable, but it often unfortunately acts to reinforce stereotypes. Falling back on group identity is also a perceived problem with white workers, especially when that identity is crystallised in trade union activity. But this type of resistance is at least seen as acceptable in the sense that its source is a competing power structure, based on the same socio-cultural framework. Thus their actions are legitimised, though disapproved of.

Domination and security

It is important to recognise that organisational domination does not rely only on overt coercion such as threats to job security. Consent has to be mobilised, because domination by coercion is often 'inefficient', requiring constant reinforcement of coercive pressures and extensive monitoring of reactions to them. Domination of the individual through self-limitation and constraint is far more effective. This is engendered through individual assimilation of, and accommodation to, dominant workplace cultures and ideologies. At its most visible level, this process can be seen in the internalisation of norms and accepted standards of behaviour that occurs in organisational and group socialisation (see Chapters 16 and 19). If consent is not present, pressures to shape ourselves in appropriate images may not be perceived as legitimate, and could promote active resistance. In Westwood's (1984) 'Stitchco', women participated in a patriarchal labour process which management viewed as 'harmonious' in its appeals to common, progressive goals and paternalistic values. The women, however, had a 'clear understanding that there were sides in industry and that these sides maintained an uneasy truce which was easily broken' (1984: 25). Westwood argues that the 'deprivation, pain and waste that black and white working class women live with on a daily basis' can be 'a spur to action rather than defeat'. Domination can thus become the source of identity projects empowering creativity and resourcefulness, sisterhood being the focus of resistance that does more than enable survival in a hostile environment.

In attempting to construct identities offering us protection from uncertainty (Knights and Willmott, 1985) we often find ourselves in competition with others for sources of meaning and the 'possession' of the material resources and symbols on which we place value. To maintain identities we attempt to control our environment and those in it, and to resist those pressures that act to define our identities for us. Identity gives us a basis to resist external manipulation, but can place us in competition with those who could aid us in our resistance. Thus we could both resist attempts to shape our identities within groups, and yet use our positional or situational power in those groups to enhance our identities at the expense of others. This separation may act to blind us to organisations as structures of *interdependence*, and thus reinforce systems of control dependent on our compliance with managerial demands. By neglecting the context in which we compete for sources of meaning we can become estranged from one of the major sources available to us: the collective identity and power of those with similar interests.

Of course the contextual issues raised above are not necessarily simply sources of constraint. They may for some be the very factors which allow them to secure identity. Workers with worries over job security may find meaning in defining themselves through nationalist or traditionalist sentiments, giving expression to their fears through hostility to 'immigrant' workers or women who should remain at home. Likewise, hostility and resistance to organisational goals and practices may arise out of the conditions of exploitation, domination and alienation which render others submissive. It would appear that identities are constructed out of whatever meanings are readily available, and are constrained by the individual's ability to sustain them. Thus the construction of identity is a continuous process that has to be understood in the context of the workplace, where it is maintained and reproduced on a daily basis.

Organisations and identities

If society is characterised by the involvement of individuals in organisational structures, then organisations are characterised by their attempts to *control the performance and behaviour* of the individuals of which they consist. It is this rule-bound control of individual behaviour that distinguishes organisational behaviour from other forms of social organisation. Home and family life, for example, are undoubtedly organised, and controls and sanctions are placed on the behaviour of family members. But this control is in no sense as systematic as that existing in even a small commercial organisation. On this basis, for work organisations of any type to maintain their present forms of authority, hierarchy and control, it becomes necessary to produce some kind of change in the types of regulation to which employees will consent (see Chapter 19).

However, organisations do not simply transform individual identities at work by some form of brainwashing. Neither do they simply depend on individuals' recognition of economic necessity to ensure their consent to the control of their performance in their work. The concept of 'economic man' is not adequate to explain workers' consent to change. Rules and procedures constraining work-related behaviour may conflict with attempts to secure stable and favourable identities. Alternatively, workers could construct viable identities out of the very rules which restrict them, becoming 'organisation men', or setting themselves up in opposition to their employers – or perhaps distancing themselves from the whole affair and concentrating on external interests. Whatever the survival and coping tactics employed by individuals, they may in time transform themselves into an image that functions in a way that is useful to the organisation they work for. Even the 'deviant' or militant worker may provide images of what the 'good' employee *should not be* (see Ackroyd and Thompson, 1999: 21–8, for a discussion), as well as providing a focus for the attribution of blame (see Chapter 15).

Identity is the basis of individual involvement in organisations, and the basis for manipulation achieved through negotiated transactions between organisational strategies of control and individual strategies for securing identity. The consequences of this are not always positive for the organisation, and we all have to cope in a creative fashion with the constraints of work or unemployment. Strategies used for survival can become powerful tools for extending our own abilities and capacities. Those who try manipulating our behaviour must face the fact that they are interfering with the self-perceptions and judgements that make us what we are. If manipulation goes too far, it may do no more than to encourage employee identities more resistant to organisational control.

Identity work and situational power

Subjective experience in organisations consists of *lived relationships* bounded by social, organisational and workgroup cultures in the context of structural and ideological constraints. These form the three basic contexts within which individual identity is continually reproduced. Lived relationships are the subjective arena of identity construction. Even though our subjective 'now' is informed by our past experience and moulded by the pressures brought to bear on us, we still act as if we are independent and self-directed entities. Thus our everyday existence can continue as if it largely bypasses the influence of cultural and structural constraints on our behaviour. Thus *situational power* is central to explanation of organisational behaviour. This is recognised in what Azjen and Madden (1986) term 'perceived behavioural control', which, according to Augoustinos and Walker (1995: 25), links behavioural attitudes and norms in the 'actor's perception of the ease or difficulty of performing the behaviours'. The extent to which we can control our behaviour and estimate our ability to act will determine the kind of strategies available for achieving our personal agendas or identity projects.

Social, organisational and workgroup cultures are, then, the arenas in which 'fitting behaviour' is moulded and regulated and in which we perform *identity work* (Goffman, 1971; Cohen and Taylor, 1978). Just as our perceptions of the world are simplified by the use of stereotypical categories, the activities we carry out in the workplace are simplified by the use of stereotyped categories of behaviour. These various cultural contexts also represent the medium of communication and translation of structural contexts to everyday existence. These are the limiting factors on identity construction in work and social life. They act to define possible sources of meaning and activity in hierarchical organisations and also provide the contextual limitations on what is acceptable practice for those who study, design and intervene in organisations.

Individual and group concerns with job security, status, promotion, conflict and satisfaction, can be characterised under a number of related categories:

- the prediction and control of reality
- coping with uncertainty
- retaining autonomy and discretion
- maintaining or enhancing situational power.

These represent the tensions created by trying to maintain and monitor the *strategies* through which we enact behaviours. An identity secure in the ability to control these tensions both forms a bulwark against threats and provides personal standards for social comparison and action. The strategies utilised by individuals and groups to secure or appropriate identity will thus seek to control sources of power and meaning. As a consequence, identity construction may threaten the organisation of work (Knights and Willmott, 1985; Weigert, 1986; Breakwell, 1987).

Organisations, in trying to reduce uncertainty, are willing to allow room for the maintenance of worker identities insofar as they make the control of behaviour and production processes more effective. In implementing the introduction of CNC machine tools, firms such as Westland Helicopters allowed an element of manual input from operators on the basis that human intervention is necessary in automated processes because they are not absolutely error-free (Corbett, 1985a). Such decisions allow operators to exert some levels of skill and discretion within labour processes with increasing tendencies towards deskilling. Thus alongside gains in the reduction of uncertainty in the production process, there may also be benefits to the organisation in reducing the level of threat to skilled identities implied by automation.

The greater the effort put into attempts to define employees' work lives, the greater the use of undefined areas by workers to develop 'informal work group cultures'. Cultures of this type can provide workers with a degree of autonomy and a basis for active resistance (see Chapter 19). By the same token, membership of sub-cultural groups in organisations may provide the same benefits to threatened identities as they do for subcultures in wider society: 'the threatened can regain self-esteem, generate positive distinctiveness and promote continuity' (Breakwell, 1986: 141). Although Breakwell argues that societal subcultures have virtually no impact on power structures, they are, she maintains, the focus of possible social concerns and the associated 'moral panics' (Cohen, 1973) that identify them as being 'scheduled for control'.

This is not to say that managers never recognise this tendency and take steps to short-circuit the development of informal groups that may become hostile to organisational goals. Drago and McDonough (1984: 67) quote from a management planning document that was part of a 'controlled participation experiment' at the General Food's Topeka plant: 'No power groups will exist within the organisation that create an anti-management posture.' In trying to predict and control reality, it is our subjective concepts and values that are most amenable to change, as we cannot on our own hope to change the structural framework of the organisations within which we work. Even for those with the power to effect change, there is still no absolute security of position or certainty that their actions will produce results fully in line with their projects. Thus, in coping with the uncertainties of organisational life most individuals are forced either into a strategy of accommodation which necessitates a gradual redefinition of self and subjective reality, or a strategy of assimilation which requires these to be subjected to the superordinate identity of the group.

Responses to pressures on identity

The production of ideologically justified and scripted behaviours enables the individual or collective enactment of situational power and resistance. This does not however explain *why* individuals and groups try to resist organisational controls. Resistance is in itself both a source of meaning and a pressure on identity. This is founded on the perception by individuals of contradictions between the goals, ideologies, approved identities and required behaviours manifested in organisational settings. Leonard (1984: 116–18) identifies four sources of pressures leading to resistance, avoidance and dissent:

- *Contradictory consciousness* This arises from competing ideologies based on the material interests of groups and classes. Because dominant ideologies partly clash with people's actual experiences of everyday life, they can never have more than an imperfect influence on identities. Leonard cites class, gender and ethnic struggles as examples of the conflicts that produce psychological disturbances in individuals and can produce acts of deviance, while at the same time still resulting in a general submission to the demands of the dominant order. These acts of deviance may be directed towards material gains, individual protest, or to fulfil particular values not acceptable to the social order. There may be important consequences for organisations in the form of theft, industrial sabotage or other 'destructive' actions.
- *Unconscious resistance* Leonard represents this partly in Freudian terms as the

struggle of id against ego and superego. The individual attempts not to repress or bury those impulses which 'are unacceptable or inconvenient to dominant social forces' (1984: 117). However, impulses to act against the social order may be renounced and buried in the unconscious, because the obstacles to action are too great or perceived situational power is too little. Anxiety and frustration are the likely results of everyday unconscious resistance. At their extremes, internal conflicts could result in forms of mental disorder; Leonard identified tendencies to neurotic and psychotic illness with social-class position. In organisational terms, neurotic reactions could be characterised as consistent with the frustrations caused by conflicts around the role-based control and supervisory responsibilities of professional and managerial classes; Kets De Vries and Miller (1984) noted neurotic syndromes in managers of failing firms. Psychotic reactions, characterised as escapes into alternative realities, are associated with the working classes. In a parallel concept, the Hungarian psychologist, Laszlo Garai (see Eros, 1974), refers to individuals having recourse to 'fictive satisfactions', when the specifically human 'need' for self-realisation and non-alienated activity is blocked. These can take the form of destructive impulses, cynicism or the ritual affirmation of helplessness, all of which are likely to be perceived as unmotivated or individually deviant.

- *The development of individual capacities* This arises from the attempt to avoid the dehumanising effects of alienated labour. It may lead to the development of personal activities either within work or outside of it, which are directed at benefits for the individual rather than the organisation. Outside of work, individuals may develop artistic, literary, craft or sporting skills (these also being fictive satisfactions) that 're-humanise' their lives, making active and identity-enhancing use of their time, rather than merely recuperating from work. Within the workplace, people can develop capacities from the exploration and development of their skills that extend beyond what is demanded by wage labour. Wilkinson (1983b) provides an example of CNC machine tool operators, some of whom effectively redefined the technology that had deskilled them and brought some interest back into their work by teaching themselves to programme the computers.

  However, just as the world of fashion or popular music, where people's creative and autonomous control over their own image and expression are eventually incorporated into commercial products, the smart company will incorporate the efforts of individuals to indulge in non-alienated activity into the organisation of the labour process. In the world of the work organisation, the 'revolt into style' may be transformed into the instrumental rewards of the suggestion box.

- *Participation in collective action* This 'contains contradictions between hope and despair, optimism and depression, depending on the balance of political forces at any given time' (Leonard, 1984: 118). Capacities are further developed through joining informal coalitions to pursue some more or less specified goal, or becoming formally involved in unions or professional and other associations. The immediate benefit is in an enhancement of situational power through collective strength. Leonard sees benefits in collective resistance in that it counters individualistic impulses and moves towards altruistic activity which attempts to transform social relations into forms beneficial to the individual and group. It also raises consciousness about forms of change that are available, associated with a redefinition of self that can counter subordination.

These forms are neither exhaustive, nor mutually exclusive. Nor do they mean that resistance is inevitable, even though it may be structured into the forms and processes of organisations. Where there are no overt conflicts, it is possibly easier for individuals to accept managerial definitions of reality; to become 'organisation people' and to gain meaning from their appointed roles. It must be remembered, however, that these responses are interdependent processes, which can be conceptually separated, but which are all part of the cycle of organisational control and resistance. In securing and maintaining a stable and meaningful identity, individuals are faced with the difficulty of presenting consistent images to the other people with whom they must deal. When threats arise, they are left with the choice to submit or resist. Both involve possibly substantial redefinitions of the identities they have secured.

Impression management and scripting

The management of identities has been explored in work such as that of Goffman (1959) on *impression management* (IM). The individual, like an actor on stage, attempts to maintain a consistent and believable performance for the audience: those who have a significant influence over the role they play. When used in this sense, identity is malleable and instrumentally defined. However active and manipulative such identities are, they are still dependant on the collaboration of others not to interfere with the performance. We know that the performance of an actor is not real. But according to Goffman we exercise 'tact' to allow the performance to proceed, as in the case of a management 'pep-talk'.

Goffman's *dramaturgical* model (1959, especially chapters 3 and 7) established the basics of informal rules for interaction and the relations between personal and social identity. It makes the distinction between *frontstage* (the arena where the performance is carried out and interaction is primarily with the 'audience' or 'client') and b*ackstage* where the interaction is primarily with other 'actors' and the 'resources' for performance are created. Goffman essentially sees IM as a form of self-presentation and ongoing self-definition of what he called the *personal front*. A similar notion used by Harré is that of *persona*, though this implies more of a conscious choice in selecting appropriate persona than Goffman would admit to. IM was further popularised by Schlenker (1980), when he defined it as 'the conscious or unconscious attempt to control images that are presented in real or imagined social interactions' (cited in Russ, 1991: 220). One caveat we should note here is that although we all use IM, we do not necessarily do it as well as others or rely on it to the same extent; this appears to be based on the extent to which we are skilled at self-monitoring.

Giacalone and Rosenfeld's excellent set of readings on *Applied Impression Management* (1991) discusses the widespread and significant implications of IM in areas such as organisational development, careers, appraisal, negotiation and conflict, gender and culture. They also provide useful summaries of the major models of IM. Leary and Kowalski (1991: 87–8) focus on the concepts of *impression motivation*, 'the desire of individuals to generate specific impressions in others' minds in order to maximise social and material outcomes, self-esteem, and/or cultivate a particular public identity', and of *impression construction*, 'the process of choosing the kind of impression to create and deciding exactly what behaviours would be effective in transmitting such an image'.

Tedeschi and Norman (1991: 105) conceptualise the IM process as a reward exchange where, 'each party is providing reinforcements to the other for his or her ultimate gain'. Baumeister (1991: 197) similarly views the goals of impression management as audience pleasing and constructing the ideal self, particular practices being mediated by normative and cultural pressures. Martinko (1995: 259–77) provides a detailed applied model that, while recognising 'many IM behaviours may be unconscious and unintentional', views IM 'as a systematic and purposive process of behaviour self-management that is both conscious and intentional'. The specific issues Martinko sees as being of future interest to IM are the extent to which IM behaviour is *plastic* or malleable or is conversely located in traits, and thus to what extent we can be trained in IM. Martinko also raises questions of ethics and credibility, individual, group and cultural differences and, perhaps most important of all, the relation of IM to self-monitoring as conceptualised by Snyder and Copeland (1985). The Martinko model is essentially prescriptive, but like many such models it acts better as a description of the processes involved than as practical guidance because of the multitude of variables involved.

The extent to which IM works in a practical sense is documented by Baron and Byrne (1997: 67–9), citing experimental studies which stress the importance of other-enhancement (for example, ingratiation, see below) as a key factor in gaining higher performance ratings at work. They also cite evidence (1997: 503–6) pertaining to IM in job interviews, especially with reference to effects of appearance, gender and the role of expectations in interviewer style and behaviour. Arnold *et al.* note the importance of IM as a set of skills in their commentary on Goffman's work (1998: 243–4). Examples of the type of skills and associated contexts involved are in interviewing, testing, communication and presentation. Such techniques are discussed in more detail by Feldman and Klich (1991: 69) who summarise them as:

- Ingratiation: flattery, agreement, doing favours
- Intimidation: veiled threats, appearing dangerous
- Self-promotion: embellishing accomplishments, overstating capabilities
- Exemplification: appearance of dedication or self-sacrifice
- Accounting: denying responsibility, assuaging problems
- Supplication: promoting sympathy, nurturance or allegiance from superiors.

Such *protective* impression management including excuses, apologies and damage control is seen as important by Rosenfeld, Giacolone and Riordan (1995), who cover its measurement and relations to HRM in some detail.

The management of impressions is thus one example of the processes of identity work referred to earlier. Kunda's study of 'Tech' (1992, chapter 5) provides numerous and excellent examples of related forms of identity work. (Also see Van Maanen, 1992 on the linkage of identity work to discourses of masculinity.) These include routine *identity displays* of behaviours which either embrace or distance the worker from organisational roles, and *artifactual displays*, for example, of signs and posters, in personal workspaces which supply the image of 'a strong individual surviving in a hard, competitive, often irrational world' (1992: 196). Artifactual displays are a particular form of *non-verbal communication,* which itself is a specific aspect of IM and includes Goffman's notion of *signing* in relation to the tactics and techniques we use to register impressions on others. Both types of display are seen as dramatic performances which balance the display of the successful organisational self with an image of ability to meet organisational concerns, giving oneself some space for manoeuvre.

Such performance may break down in the context of threats and constraints in the work environment, and we may be forced to respond with impressions and performances which are 'out of character' for the expected role. Kunda characterises these as *enlargement dramas*, where in formal or informal circumstances the routine order of role playing is allowed temporarily to break down, and individuals are allowed to enlarge upon the selves they generally present, exhibiting attitudes or capabilities beyond their required roles. Such dramas are often associated with temporary or marginal members of organisations. Similarly, individuals may experience difficulty in coping with situations where their projected images are not adequate to achieving some measure of control or meaning. For example Hochschild, in examining the supervision of emotional labour, cites the reaction of a flight attendant whose pay cheque had been mishandled: 'I can't take this all day and then come back here and take it from you! You know I get paid to take it from the passengers, but I don't get paid to take it from you' (1983: 18).

The IM element of Kunda's identity displays is analogous to the *display rules* noted by Mann (1999) (and see the section on 'Emotional control' in Chapter 18). These rules are generally organisation-specific, but they can be related to the scripted cultures such as the 'have a nice day' (HAND) culture which, she argues, are spreading out from the service sector. The HAND culture is characterised by the *fast-food server* script which is used by waitresses, shop assistants, receptionists and flight attendants to guide IM and emotional labour to encourage customers to come back. The rules are not however homogenous across cultures, the rule about smiling for example being contrary to expectations in Japan and some Muslim cultures. They are even stronger than in the US/UK in some Mediterranean cultures such as Greece (1999: 24–6). The 'have a rotten day' culture, on the other hand, though again familiar from Hochschild's conception of emotional labour, is characterised by the *debt collector* script, where people such as bouncers, security staff and police use displays of anger, irritation or disapproval 'to discourage re-use of the service' (1999: 45). The final script Mann notes is the *lawyer* script characteristic of the 'have a cool day' culture used in many professional and social settings to mask emotions. Doctors, managers and politicians might use this script, which emphasises lack of warmth and emotion, in order to maintain an image of 'detached concern' (1999: 43). The importance of these scripted cultures is both in their integration of IM and emotional labour, and in the extent to which learning them is crucial to the development of careers and the professional identities associated with them.

Careers have traditionally been a central source of identity formation, and indeed career development seems to be undergoing something of a renaissance as an OB topic. However, this is a little odd, since for many people what was considered to be the main avenue of career development, the internal job ladder, has all but disappeared in many organisations. Perhaps because careers are seen to be less linked to bureaucratic controls (for example, see Herriot, 1995; Adamson *et al.*, 1998), then in some ways the management of careers becomes more problematic, from the point of view of both the organisation and the individual. Without the framework of a job ladder or a clear career structure in a profession, it is possible that staff could become demotivated or demoralised about their expectations, or become highly instrumental and competitive about pursuing personal agendas. The latter orientation is exemplified by the notion of a 'careerist orientation to work' as proposed by Feldman and Klich (1991) and in the increasing concern with impression management through presentation skills and techniques. Of course, we must not overestimate the extent to which trends towards flexibility and 'new working practices' have actually been adopted by organisations (see Chapter 13). All the same, the job for life is not now seen to be the rule, and we are led to believe that flexible careers and multiple job-holding are apparently the wave of the future; for example see the account in Arnold *et al.* (1998, chapter 16).

Career development is in effect a misnomer for many in modern occupations. In the Telebank case (Callaghan and Thompson, 2002) call-centre work was characterised as a routine job with modest pay and a flat promotion structure. Here there was no development as such, merely training in conformity to scripts and techniques of conversation control. Scripted impression management effectively is the job, the employees carrying out *dramaturgical labour* (McHugh, 1997), involving both regulation of their impressions and advocacy for the organisation. Within such strictures, identity work for those at Telebank must be carried out in whatever spaces a scripted culture leaves to them.

Identity work and 'making out'

The identity work we perform seems to depend a great deal on our ability to utilise and manage the scripts available to us. Conversely we need to break free of the habituated scripts we use to 'make out' when the conditions under which we employ them become untenable. Opportunities to secure new or enhanced meanings, symbols, capacities and goods are as much pressures on our identities as are threats to them. Breaking free from established patterns of identity work can therefore be difficult, as Sloan's (1987) study of sales work illustrates. The salesmen had invested a great deal in a conception of professional identity that could legitimate the arduous work and their manipulative relations with customers. Professionals did not need unions. There was also a gendered dimension whereby masculinity was central to the identity: 'A little alcohol and a lot of imagination reproduced a culture in which reps were not only professional salesmen, but were also professional lovers' (1987: 31); the 'heroic' males of Insco are apparently not alone!

Such responses to the identity concerns of individuals are difficult to locate in frameworks solely based on different categories of resistance or dissent. The relatively unconscious coping strategies identified by Roy (see Chapter 19) can be seen as responses to identity concerns, but are essentially strategies of accommodation rather than resistance. Typical forms of individual response to pressure contain a combination of coping strategies, instrumentally derived tactics and accommodation to the dominant culture, as well as different types of resistance. As far as individuals are concerned, they are making out in the best fashion possible in the given circumstances, the form of response being determined in subjective terms by available scripts and what appears to work.

Strategies or responses of this kind could in one sense be said never to fail entirely. With the capacity to redefine meanings and manage impressions, human beings are capable of creating their own self-fulfilling prophecies and self-attributed judgements, shifting the ground on which they stand to justify both success and failure. In counterpoint to strategies which lead to negative consequences for the individual, there are forms of making out which can lead more unambiguously to social recognition, approval and self-justified identities. For example, pressure to define identity in line with assumed leadership qualities can lead to subjectively supportive behaviours and self-perceptions. The failure of others to recognise an individual as a leader, or attempts to undermine their leadership, might lead to perceived contradictions with the leader's self-justified role. These could be handled by more autocratic attempts at control, justified by attributions of deviant characteristics to those causing the disturbance. Conversely, if strategies to cope with the situation fail and put the identity of the ostensible leader at risk, he or she could distance him or herself from the role on the basis that dealing with such people was impossible or not worth the effort.

Identity working: strategies for organisational survival

The strategies suggested in the example above are by no means restricted to leadership roles. Nor are they simply abstract categories of identity work, but basic strategies of *domination* and *distancing* which Knights and Willmott (1985) identify us all as performing in order to reduce anxiety, secure identities and survive our working existence. Strategies of domination can involve anyone with power over the distribution and possession of scarce resources using those resources to give him or herself the partial illusion of independence and security. Such reliance acts to obscure the interdependence of social relations. Managers or others can then ignore the fact that their power is dependent on the compliance of their colleagues or subordinates. Compliance in this sense is related to Rotter's (1972) notion of internal and external *loci of control*. People who feel that they are externally controlled may also put themselves into a state of *learned helplessness*, where the tendency to comply becomes part of the way individuals define themselves (Seligman, 1975). To subordinates, however, compliance may simply be their way of making out and avoiding 'identity damaging disciplinary controls' (Knights and Willmott, 1985: 25).

According to Knights and Willmott, strategies that employ the 'cynical distancing of self from the activities and social relations within which individuals are immediately involved' (1985: 27) act to reinforce individualism and subordination. At the same time, distancing is also one of the main patterns of identity work identified by Cohen and Taylor (1978), whose focus is not on power and interdependence, but rather on 'escape attempts'. Escape from, or resistance to, the mundanity and unpleasantness of everyday life is in this sense crucial to our subjectively 'making out'. However, the strategies they see as employed in identity work can still have relevance to the understanding of how making out is incorporated into the social relations of production. Cohen and Taylor start out at the level of the 'regularities which we happily accept as part of life' (1978: 26). These regularities are not necessarily tedious behavioural repetition, but are scripts to which we *unreflexively accommodate* as a method of managing the 'paramount reality' of our objective world. Scripts in this sense are more than the 'mindless' behaviour posited by Langer or the 'sensorimotor' activity posited by Hacker and Volpert (see Chapter 16).

The habitual dependence on scripts referred to by Cohen and Taylor can be a defence against uncertainty, as well as providing meaning through their very regularity.

However, our capacity for self-reflection allows us to create a *zone for self* or *identity domain* (1978: 32), which enables us to distance ourselves from those who appear to be committed to the scripts by which they live. The capacity to be self-reflexive can effectively remove the need actually to do anything about the conditions of our existence, because we critically separate ourselves from them in our thoughts. At the same time we often deprecate those we see as not having our own level of critical self-awareness, defining them as something less than ourselves. The paradox here is our fellow workers are likely to have the same thoughts about ourselves, since they do not see our thoughts, only our regulated actions and routine behavioural displays.

A concomitant capacity with which self-reflexiveness endows us is the release of the *escape into fantasy* where we can alter the conditions of our life to our own satisfaction. This form of escape is akin to the strategy of unconscious resistance identified by Leonard. Leonard's identification of these escapes with position in the organisational hierarchy can now be understood, in that fantasy is free. Cohen and Taylor also note socially institutionalised routes of escape which are seen as legitimate self-expression, where 'assertions of meaninglessness of the activity are virtually taboo' (1978: 95). These *activity enclaves* give us free areas in our lives, where, in the terminology of Seve and Leonard, we can develop 'personal concrete capacities'. Such socially approved escapes from work or the lack of it include hobbies, games, sports, holidays and the attractions of mass culture.

On the other hand, there are less socially approved activity enclaves which more resemble Garai's fictive satisfactions in that they are often socially viewed as self-obsessive or destructive. 'Preoccupations' with sex, gambling, drugs and even dependence on therapy are examples of this form of escape. They are, however, only different to other forms in terms of the social, legal and historical contexts in which they are carried out. Again self-reflexiveness carries its own internal contradictions. Distancing ourselves from the roles we play is, in the end, another limited and passive strategy which tends to confirm existing organisational structures, separating the individual from the possibilities inherent in social relations.

Finally, to escape from this vicious spiral of making out through reconstruction of identity concerns, Cohen and Taylor identify the strategy of *self-conscious reinvestment*. Individuals become recommitted to aspects of the very regularities – language, rituals, clothing – from which they are escaping. Within work organisations this represents the return to the fold, making something of one's life, or the rescue of career. All of these means of psychic escape can be utilised to further managerial control, either by employees' dependence on the financial and social supports necessary to pursue them or, in the case of reinvestment, the cleaving-back to the very structures of control themselves. For those who run organisations, the problem is to monitor and control the identity work of employees to ensure that they do not overstep the bounds of the acceptable. For the employee, the problem is to discover the appropriate mode of escape, enjoyment and making out for the subjective and objective conditions pertaining at the time.

Identity, ideology and technologies of regulation

The strategies and identity work of groups are likewise incorporated into organisational processes. This is achieved through ideological legitimations supplying positive self-attributions. Organisational ideologies thus play a crucial role in underpinning identities, particularly those of management. Salaman (1979: 199–212) locates five:

- *Structuralism*: political neutrality, achievement based on merit, focus on internal hierarchies and markets.
- *Psychologism*: individual responsibility for performance, people as resources, moulding identities, objective assessment procedures.
- *Consensualism*: specialised division of labour, differentiated rewards, consensus, individual pathologies of conflict.
- *Welfarism*: integrating commitment, concern for well-being, emphasis on personal relations and relaxed supervisory methods.
- *Legalism*: the 'right to manage', binding contractual agreements, negotiation, appeals to obligations, rights and duties.

Whether or not such ideologies act in practice as coherent guiding principles of organisations, they do present some common themes, notably the neutrality of managerial practices, the rational and consensus-based form of organisations and the emphasis on individual responsibility for exhibiting appropriate behaviours and identities. We cannot, however, simply equate ideology with domination. As Billig puts it, we cannot see people as 'passive and gullible pawns, duped by an array of ideological managers and institutions which serve the interest of dominant classes' (in Augoustinos and Walker, 1995: 296).

If internalised by employees, ideologies have the effect of reducing uncertainty for dominant groupings and thus increasing their situational power in securing strategic identities. They risk failure in the light of the contradictory consciousness raised by perceived conflicts between espoused values and actual practice. Knights and Collinson give the example of a US-owned firm in Britain which directed its communicative efforts through a house magazine that:

> simply exacerbated the 'them and us' attitudes since the harmonious and effi-
> cient image of Slavs depicted by it conflicted dramatically with the experience
> of shop floor workers. The shop floor was insulted by what it saw as the decep-
> tive 'propaganda' in the magazine. (Knights and Collinson, 1987: 9)

Ideologies of this sort survive in part because dominant groupings have the power to shape cultural meanings on the workplace. They can, in turn, call on the expertise of their peers and outside professionals to justify them or supply the technologies of regulation to make them applicable to changing circumstances. The technologies of regulation employed include the development initiatives, team reviews, performance counselling and redesign of jobs discussed in earlier chapters. These largely depend on social facilitation effects, pressures brought to bear on individuals through the effects of social comparison processes, group norms, and the perceptions of expected rewards. An important aim is the achievement of a 'best fit' between the policy goals of the organisation and the workplace identities of both employees and those who manage them. The latter is important in that successful interventions have to convince managerial clients that they have bought the right strategy (Evden, 1986). Any doubts, or sophisticated ideas such as failure being a valuable learning experience, undermine the positive identities such interventions can reinforce.

All interventions to some extent work by encouraging self-attributions reinforcing organisational objectives, and by focusing social comparison on functional activities. They break down managerial, professional and supervisory work into operational units just as scientific management does with production work. Instead of appeals to ideologies of rationality, neutrality, objectivity and efficiency as noted above, they appeal to the subjective ideologies supporting individual identities. The success of technologies of regulation are thus dependent on the expectation effects that can be induced in participants; consultants, for example, need to become 'evangelists' who can sell vision rather than working techniques (Evden, 1986).

Managerial education outside organisations is likewise based on reinforcing the ideological identity work required of managers. The content of managerial education is effectively directed at making concrete the notion that systematic control over complex and variable processes is possible, making management essentially a reified construct. The reduction of uncertainty provided by the ideas themselves, backed up by the demonstration of techniques which purport to provide reliable diagnostic and control procedures, acts as a powerful enabling factor in the maintenance of ideological structures. The expected rewards in financial and career mobility terms are bought through a process of personal identity work. This increases self-perceived competence at handling the contingent uncertainties of organisational life, with the concomitant organisational gains of increased effort and commitment in overcoming goal barriers.

Managerial labour and identity work

The form and content of control processes are influenced by the responses of managerial groups to pressures on the identities produced in their role as agents of capital. Mobilising their consent to expose themselves to the threats and pressures of management roles has its own particular place in the labour process. It also underpins the mobilisation of consent of production workers to comply with that supervision. Resistance and contestation by other individuals and groups are threats to managerial identity, which are only somewhat ameliorated by the situational power managers wield:

> Managers, though suffering from frustration and a perceived lack of strategic control, provide operational and systemic flexibility in organisations through their labour...it is the buffering provided by managerial labour between strategic policies and productive labour itself that is necessary to provide the continuance of structured forms of organising work. (McHugh, 1997:2)

McHugh draws on Teulings' (1986) argument that the reactive nature and routinisation of managerial activities have diminished the power of individual managers. Teulings divides managerial function into *institutional*, *strategic*, *structuring* and *operational*, and on this basis we might expect to find differing forms of managerial labour dominating the activity of managers at different levels (see Chapter 7). This will depend, of course, on the position and situational power of the managers involved; but it does point to the fact that managerial work has its own levels of alienation and fragmentation. If this is so, then dominant organisational groups will also expend effort and devise strategies to secure and defend their identities.

Hochschild (1993: xi), for example, notes that managers are involved in emotional labour in regulating both their own feelings and those of others. This dual responsibility can have mixed effects.

In delineating forms of managerial work, McHugh (1997) (see Chapter 19) argues that managers, as well as being involved in operational, emotional, intellectual and dramaturgical practices, perform attributional labour in regulating and ascribing intent and commitment to themselves and their subordinates. Causal judgement in attributional terms (see Chapter 15) is thus claimed to be a significant factor in managerial impression management and identity work, especially in processes such as performance appraisal and locating the pathology of organisational problems. The implication here is that managerial activity may be derived more from attributions about causes of events than from simple responses to circumstances. As such, there may be a managerial bias to dispositional attributions in defining performance objectives for employees, and an environmental bias in defining such objectives for themselves. At the same time McHugh (1997: 8) cites Leavitt and Bahrami (1988: 65) to the extent that 'managers are both blessed and cursed by that tendency to ascribe causality, because the causality – either way – is often ascribed to them rather than to other aspects of the situation'.

Effective managerial identity work can thus utilise worker resistance and associated damage to productivity and profitability as an ideological justification for managers' own strategies to enhance identity. The discussion of autonomous work groups and teamworking in Chapter 20 provided examples of the way in which interventions by management act to both secure managerial identities and short-circuit potential worker resistance. Although suffering increased stress, the fact that managers thought the effort of introducing teams worthwhile indicates that associated productivity benefits provide enough possibilities for enhanced situational meaning to offset personal costs.

However, in one of the most widely-studied implementations of autonomous working, conflicts with ideological conceptions of managerial control were seen to interfere with the factors that made such systems of work more effective. In a case study based on this material, the experimental assembly of trucks within an autonomous work group system in the Volvo company conducted between 1974 and 1976, Blackler and Shimmin (1984: 117–19) note that workers finishing their daily quota of work were allowed some relaxation around their work station. Senior managers however saw this relaxation as 'slack' which could be taken up and controlled by decreasing job timings, producing demoralisation in the workforce. Allowing slack time is contrary to the managerial conception of how productivity is to be maximised, even though it may be one of the major factors that produce the sense of autonomy for workers that allows the system to succeed. An enhanced source of workplace meaning for one group appears in this case to be an unacceptable threat to the processes of control that supply meaning to another group.

At the same time, managerial responsibility for shaping the identities and emotions of employees can threaten managers' own identities and emotions. As we discussed in Chapter 13, managers make considerable emotional investments in the design and outcomes of culture change programmes. Yet those programmes tend to be predicated on unrealistic expectations that employees will 'buy into' or 'take ownership' of the objectives and practices. When that does not happen, it is managers who have to carry the 'culture burden' (Thompson and Findlay, 1999). They are caught in the middle between selling the message to the troops and explaining why it is not working to the board. Their identity as effective change agents can only be secured by taking responsibility for redoubling efforts to 'communicate effectively', or alternatively becoming cynical about and partially disengaging from the change process itself.

Managerial misbehaviour

Strategic choices about organisational design are often reinforced by indoctrination into dominant organisational goals. This is a primary level of response to the attempts of members to secure a measure of autonomy and discretion within their work, and to create free areas where they can develop their own identities and capacities. Lynn (1966) argues that managerial prescriptions to maintain warm and friendly relations with subordinates go hand-in-hand with maintaining a social distance between managers themselves and the group.

> We see here the dual role of the brainwasher: the aloofness corresponds to the threatener role, the friendliness to the protector role. The authoritarian leader is only playing the threatener role and misses out on the friendliness. Vice versa with the laissez-faire leader. It is the brainwashing, democratic leader who plays both roles who is the most effective. (Lynn, 1966: 270)

Such inauthentic relations are present within both formal and informal socialisation, functioning to reinforce self-control rather than self-management. Neither is indoctrination necessarily consonant with the stated aims of the organisation. The study of bakery salesmen by Ditton (1974) showed how the salesmen were trained to cheat their customers in order not to lose out when they ended up short in their takings. Supervisors both tacitly and overtly encouraged this activity as it short-circuited possible conflicts caused by the firm trying to recoup losses from the drivers' pay. The socialisation process also worked to weed out salesmen who would not or could not collaborate in theft and legitimise it to others as a means for making out in the job. Hence there was no objection to them making a little for themselves on top of balancing their books. Comments from a sales manager such as 'They're not real salesmen if they can't make a bob or two on the side, are they?' (1974: 36) indicate that the ability to steal was linked to job competence, the same manager being noted for encouraging valued salesmen to 'use fiddled cash personally'.

This socialisation into theft was, of course, only sanctioned by management to the extent that salesmen did not begin to steal from their employers as well as their customers. Mars (1983) has claimed that fiddling can increase job and group satisfaction, and raise work rates and productivity by making the process of work more interesting. Management can use it as a reward, as in Ditton's example, as long as they 'turn a blind eye', or it can still be used as a method of 'cracking the whip'.

> The final irony for management is that they lose control of the fiddle that they themselves have started. The workforce then seize it, and use its unofficial and unsanctioned ability to increase their wages (especially in times of national restraint) as a basic condition of employment. (Ditton, 1974: 36)

Managers, then, can misbehave in ways that serve their interests at the expense of the organisation. Ackroyd and Thompson (1999) present an analysis of how misbehaviour as a category produces managerial practice. They argue that social science has generally concentrated on aspects of *organised non-compliance* in industrial relations, class struggle, resistance to control and deviancy. They propose an integrated 'map' of 'misbehaviour' from which to begin an analysis. (See Figure 21.1.)

It is argued that OMB is not to be understood simply as the result of control (1999: 29) but as a reciprocal relationship that analyses directive and responsive behaviour by both management and workers. This is directly reflective of the way in which we have considered the various forms of identity work to operate and offers a neat way of conceptualising the identity projects carried out by all members of organisations.

Ackroyd and Thompson consider topics such as resistance, self-organisation, subcultures and sexual misconduct in detail, though here we only follow up on the relations of management to misbehaviour. They look at the factors influencing managerial decisions about and responses to misbehaviour (1999: 81) and the kinds of managerial strategy these are typically related to (1999: 88). Especially important here is the concept of 'controlled autonomy', which is what HRM policies pursue but seldom achieve because of the barriers placed on change, not least by managerial identity. Ackroyd and Thompson offer a useful account of how the dynamics of control act to produce and amplify misbehaviour, adding detail to classic concepts such as the 'vicious spirals' associated with McGregor's Theory X and Y (see

	3 Appropriation of time	1 Appropriation of work	2 Appropriation of product	4 Appropriation of identity
Commitment Engagement	Time perks		Perks	Goal identification
Co-operation	Time wasting	Work activity		Joining rituals
		Effort bargaining	Pilferage	
Compliance	Absence	Soldiering	Fiddling	Subcultures Sex games
Withdrawal Denial Hostility	Turnover	Destructiveness and sabotage	Theft	Class or group solidarity

Dimensions of misbehaviour   FIGURE 21.1

Source: reproduced with permission from S. Ackroyd and P. Thompson (1999) *Organizational Misbehaviour*, London: Sage.

Chapter 19). Though this is schematic and stylised, it does offer insights into the process of control, rather than using control as an abstract determinant concept like authority or power. It also raises the notion of two effects that intensify the 'impulse to control' (1999: 95–6). The first, the *measurement effect*, is the area in which classic organisational psychology serves managerial strategy in producing technologies of regulation, and is resonant of our arguments on personality testing in Chapter 15. The second, the *innovation effect*, where 'increased managerial attention will cause behavioural innovation' (1999: 95), can be related to the idea of 'engaging the intellect' we raised in Chapter 20. Thus processes of surveillance, environmental scanning and self-monitoring produce new behaviours and practices to identify, subvert and constrain them. Ackroyd and Thompson thus provide linkages from managerial labour and identity work to specific psychological processes such as learning, group dynamics and attribution.

Conclusion

Identity work is conscious and unconscious, individual and collective, competitive and collaborative. It is the vehicle of self-expression and enactment, and at the same time binds us to systems of ideological self-legitimation through which we accede to systems of control, both internal and external. The networks we access and the roles we are expected to take on in the workplace provide the scripts, our interactions and negotiations with others the arena in which we act them out. It appears that what we strive towards in producing consistent role performances and in maintaining a secure identity is a situation where we do not have to negotiate who and what we are with others, where our concerns, actions and status are automatically legitimate. In this sense, identity work is the medium through which we express power over ourselves, others and situations.

We buy into systems of control in order to increase our situational power, and at the same time we resist pressures to make us completely controlled by our role and the demands of others. In many ways identity work is the primary work of organising, if not of organisations themselves. As such, it must also be the primary work of those who structure the processes of organising towards corporate ends. One appeal of management, beyond the extrinsic rewards, is that just being a manager automatically affirms and protects identity, at the expense of diminishing the manager's capacity to resist the role demands the position confers. The manager as a communicator of role demands has in effect committed him or herself to controlling the identity work of others, which in turn commits him or her to one or another form of response to such pressures.

It is through identity work that the conditions of being a subject and of being subject gain substance for managers and workers alike. The negotiation and pursuit of identity concerns and projects make up the drama of everyday organisational experience. As we have seen, the psychological processes underwriting that drama cannot give an adequate account of it in purely mechanistic terms. Neither, though, can interpretative or structural accounts afford to ignore the influence those processes have on us in our journey to becoming fully-fledged participants in the modern work organisation.

Part III
Theorising
Organisations

Introduction: the story so far

In Chapter 1 we set out some broad principles or ways of seeing organisations and society that inform a critical approach, and that have guided our efforts in this book. These include the need to be reflexive in not taking organisational processes for granted, to locate theory and practice in their historical and comparative contexts, and for explanations to be multi-dimensional. We have tried to utilise an approach that can explain the embeddedness of organisational action. Throughout the book we have been highly resistant to any variety of deterministic, 'one best way', or single, over-arching explanations for complex processes. Yet clearly action is not random. The reciprocal interaction of different structures and agencies still produces specific patterns and these need to be theorised.

In earlier chapters we have, of course, discussed theory, whether that is Weber's account of bureaucracy, a labour process analysis of control, or population ecology explanations of organisation–environment relations. So what is different here? Many of the theories we have looked at are specific to particular issues, such as the resource dependency theory of power. Others, such as institutional theories of convergence and diversity, have broader application but are still specific to the organisational sphere. The purpose here is to dig a little deeper and look at the resources provided by more general social science theories.

So what is the state of play? When concluding his entertaining 'short and glorious history of organisation theory', Perrow (1973) hit an optimistic note. The forces of light (human relations) and darkness (scientific management and other mechanistic perspectives) had fought each other to a standstill. Out of the debris, all schools of thought agreed that organisations should be understood as complex, open systems in which environmental variables, including technology, explained most of the variation within and between industries. Solutions based on better interpersonal relations, good leadership and job redesign had no scientific basis. Changing the structure of rewards or authority remained the most effective route to success: 'after manipulating these variables, sit back and wait for two or three months for them to take

hold. This is complicated and hardly as dramatic as many of the solutions being ped-
dled, but I think the weight of organisational theory is in its favour' (1973: 27).

Viewed from the beginning of the new millennium, this optimism looks decidedly
odd. As Reed had earlier commented, 'contemporary students of organisation find
themselves at a historical juncture and in a social context where all the old ideological "certainties" and technical "fixes" that once underpinned their "discipline" are
under attack and seemingly on the retreat' (1997: 32). Nor is this new. The field had
begun to fragment and become more contested within a decade of Perrow's original
musings, and such trends accelerated thereafter. We hope in previous chapters to have
captured some of the ebb and flow of such debate. But as an introductory text, we
could not let the shadow of grand theory fall too heavily across the pages. Part 3 pulls
in the other direction, though nothing too ambitious is attempted. Instead, the emphasis is put on examining more of the theoretical resources that underpin organisational
research and analysis, reflecting back on some of the substantive issues we have dealt
with elsewhere.

Later in Part III we turn our attention to examining the relations between theories, and between theory and practice. In doing so, we evaluate the usefulness of treating general theories as competing paradigms, an approach pioneered by Burrell and
Morgan (1979). A paradigm is a conceptual map that draws on basic differences in
the philosophy of science and social theory to enable us to see the world (and the place
of organisations within it) in a distinctive way. Particular groups of theorists develop
common conceptual languages that are different from and hostile to other paradigms.
Parker and G. McHugh comment that:

> For Burrell and Morgan, paradigms are incommensurable belief systems that con-
> tain the core assumptions to which a research community adheres. Along with
> Kuhn (1962), they argue that these are not merely 'opinions' on a particular matter
> but the ontological and epistemological grounds on which theorists build their
> particular conceptions of a discipline. (Parker and G. McHugh, 1991: 451)

Leaving aside the controversial 'incommensurability' question for the time being,
ontology refers to the assumptions we make about what we know and the nature of
reality, while epistemology concerns assumptions about how we know things, the
grounds of knowledge that influence that often underpin the methodological choices
researchers make.

22 Resources for Orthodoxy

If one were to examine the contents of some of the leading organisation theory journals, particularly in Europe, a quite different picture of orthodoxy would emerge from that described in this chapter. Such journals abound with postmodern and other critical perspectives. What, then, is the justification for regarding systems theory and its related ways of thinking as orthodoxy? It is in part historical: this was constructed as the mainstream. It is also geographic: North America remains dominated by what one of its leading defenders describes as a 'functionalist-positivist' approach (Donaldson, 1996). Most of all, it is about the unique relationships that organisational analysis has with a practitioner community. Mainstream approaches continue to provide theoretical resources that range from standard academic research to simple 'how to do it' manuals. If we were to take a narrower version of management theory, it would be accurate to say that practice has drawn unevenly on two basic traditions: a rational, mechanistic one that came to the fore with Taylor and scientific management, and a stream of more normative, organic thinking that is particularly associated with human relations (Barley and Kunda, 1992). But management thinking, on the surface at least, draws lightly on theory. What are the deeper roots and means of explanation?

Weber, bureaucracy and rationality

We outlined Weber's views in some detail in Chapter 3, and his writings on bureaucracy reappear in a variety of contexts. Yet his intellectual legacy is, as we shall see, not straightforward, for it is claimed by both mainstream and critical traditions. The basis of the former claim is not difficult to identify. Donaldson affirms that 'much of Organisation Theory derives from Weber's (1968) work on authority and bureaucracy' (1985: 6). If, as one of its advocates asserts, mainstream theory 'has as its central problematic the design of efficient organisations' (Hinings, 1988: 2), Weber's model of bureaucracy remains the template. Donaldson goes on to argue that 'Organisation Theory seems to be distinguishable as a body of thought by a concern for internal characteristics such as differentiation, standardisation, specialisation, integration, coordination and the like' (1985: 118). Weber's characterisations of functional specialisation, hierarchy, depersonalisation, formal rules and the like tend to be projected as general laws, though open systems ideas of transacting with the environment have added in arguments concerning the key contemporary and determinant variable: size, technology or any other factor.

Weber also provides orthodoxy with the theoretical sinew of rationality. Rationalisation was a theory of the transition from traditional to modern societies. For Weber, social stability was established through acceptance of authority as a form of control which people regarded as legitimate. Previous societies had been dominated by limited forms of authority based on charisma (personal qualities of leaders), or tradition (established rights and customs of dominant groups). Weber's theory went beyond economic life. Rationalisation was held to encompass processes as diverse as law, politics, religion and scientific method itself. All were becoming governed by impersonal objectives, procedures and knowledge, embodied in structures and processes which confront 'individuals as something external to them' (Brubaker, 1984: 9). The modern world is thus characterised above all by the spread of this *formal* rationality. Its elements provide a framework for coping with uncertainty, In this sense, mainstream theory draws on the idea that rational calculation makes the world more purposeful and manageable (Clegg, 1990: 32–3).

More specifically we saw in Chapter 3 that Weber believed that the rational organisation of labour required its disciplined subordination to management and organisational goals. In this Taylor was a resource. Weber saw in his schemas for the potentially 'scientific' character of management, echoes of the themes of rationality and formal control. Paralleling Weber's work, Taylor saw management by 'scientific' methods as a move away from traditional authority, where owners and managers attempted to control by inefficient, personal means. Orthodoxy also sustains its conservatism through Weber's emphasis on the market embodying rationality because it was the classic example of a disenchanted, impersonal realm dominated by the calculation of advantage, without intrusion of moral considerations (Holton and Turner, 1989: 179). Alternatives were dismissed: 'More and more the material fate of the masses depends upon the steady and correct functioning of the increasingly bureaucratic organisations of private capitalism. The idea of eliminating these organisations becomes more and more utopian' (Weber, 1984: 36).

However, Donaldson and other mainstream writers fail adequately to acknowledge that for Weber rationalisation was a morally and politically problematic development. Weber makes important distinctions between types of rationality, notably *formal* and *substantive*. The former refers only to the constraining features of structure and the calculability of techniques and procedures: 'What makes modern capitalism rational is not its ends but the unprecedented extent to which actions of its economic agents are calculated' (Sayer, 1991: 96). In contrast, substantive rationality emphasises the dominance of norms and values in the choice of means to ends (Ritzer, 1996: 576). The key point is that while formal techniques are of a specific type, such values and ends inevitably differ. Thus space is opened up for recognition of contested rationalities between groups and individuals. Indeed Weber acknowledged that the formal and substantive were always potentially in conflict, frequently making pessimistic comments about human needs being subordinated to the former. The formally rational, such as the pursuit of profit by merging and 'asset stripping' companies, may be substantively irrational in terms of its social consequences. For example, downsized companies may improve short-run profitability but find that they have lost the tacit and organisational knowledge necessary for long-term efficiency and innovation. In this sense Weber does make some separation of rationality and efficiency, not only for the above reason, but because there could in principle be different views of what constitutes either category. For example, workers' co-operatives and private ownership could both be regarded as efficient on the basis of different value criteria.

These kind of points form part of the basis of a defence of Weber by some writers (such as Albrow, 1992) against the normal way his ideas are used in mainstream theory. But though this has some validity, it is not clear how significant it is. Aside from the fact that Weber is not always clear about the separation and its consequences (see Storey, 1983: 26–34), from the viewpoint of evaluating mainstream perspectives as a whole, most theorists influenced by Weber have acted as if rationality and efficiency are the same thing. As a result they have tended to be rather uncritical of existing organisations. Reed notes:

> The causal link which he is thought to have identified between rational bureaucracy and technical efficiency provided a substantive focus and theoretical bone of contention from which a general theory of organisations, based on a systems frame of reference, could be constructed in the course of the 1950s. (Reed, 1985: 17).

Weber's model of bureaucracy has of course been endlessly refined and renewed. As we saw in Chapter 12, some neo-Weberians have sought to offset its simplicities by developing alternative designs within bureaucracy, such as those influenced by contingency models (Fischer and Sirriani, 1984: 9). Others, such as Blau and Gouldner, have built from the distinction between formal and substantive rationality in order to uncover the neglected aspects of the functioning of bureaucratic organisations, their empirical research revealing two key processes. First are the inefficiencies arising from the following of impersonal rules, such as the displacement of the original goals by obsession with narrow interest and ritual by the office holder. Second is the dependence of bureaucratic organisations on informal, innovative behaviour and consensual human relations. These writers have greater affinities with social action theory, which we will examine later. We will also return to examine the alternative, radical structuralist reading of Weber in the next chapter.

Durkheim, human relations and social needs

The other 'founding father' of sociology to have a significant impact on organisational analysis has been Durkheim, though there is a marked contrast to Weber. Durkheim's contribution to understanding the transition to modernity centres on the significance of the *division of labour* in sustaining the social solidarity necessary for the survival of the 'organism' of society or enterprise. Writing in the late nineteenth century, he observed that the more complex division of labour in industrial, urban society was undermining traditional values and social order of a 'mechanical' kind held together by faith in a common morality. But at the same time it was laying the basis for a more effective integration of individuals in society, which was labelled 'organic solidarity'. This advanced industrial, technological division of labour was inevitably based on specialisation, hierarchy and functional interdependence between tasks and occupations. Durkheim recognised that the new arrangements and formal structures contained sources of social disorganisation, conflict and harmful individualism; summed up in the term *anomie*. Any effective division of labour could therefore only take root and bind people together when it was sustained by new social values, by moral communities such as professional or occupational groups, and when workers had an understanding of their place within the overall scheme of production.

This kind of formulation was later interpreted through mainstream theory in terms of the permanent tension between the technical and formal needs of the organisation and the social needs of those who worked in it. It was therefore management's role not just to organise the former, but to carry out running repairs on the latter. This necessitated paying specific attention to the *informal* side of the organisation, particularly to the primary groups to which people belonged, such as workgroups. In the 1920s and

1930s this theme was taken up and popularised by Elton Mayo, who had identified problems arising from the breakdown of traditional skills and values associated with the rise of mass production. Researchers could help management to reintegrate the worker by identifying social needs and relating them to common values that led to identification with the company. Human relations analysis also drew from a Durkheimean framework, when it 'defined the anomic consequences of capitalism as abnormal, as a deviation from the ideal circumstances of organic solidarity' (Hamilton, 1980: 70).

Barnard (1938) extended the original analysis with emphasis on how large-scale organisations could become 'co-operative social systems', based on specialised competencies and common goals. He more clearly defined the role of the executive and the specialised managerial function in terms of defining and communicating goals, and securing workforce effort. A key feature of the human relations approach is the social engineering role given to management through maintaining equilibrium and integrating the parts of the organisation. The vehicle is not formal structures of co-ordination and command, but values, informal practices and the 'logic of sentiment'. Though a subordinate aspect of organisational analysis for considerable periods, as we saw in Chapter 15, it has recently reappeared within a new socio-economic context and new management writings on corporate culture such as Peters and Waterman's *In Search of Excellence* (1982). Attention is being focused once again on employees' social needs, the human side of the enterprise, and on creating and sustaining unity through common cultures.

Interestingly, the emphasis on corporate culture clashes with some central features of Durkheim's perspective that depended on the existence of professions and other intermediary groups to generate moral communities. For Durkheim, the modern individual must be equipped to question moral systems, not just to need to identify with the collective or its symbols (Dahler-Larsen, 1994: 10). In addition, Durkheim provided a critique of market rationality, which tends to foster excessive egoism and acquisitive individualism. This is just one example of a growing trend in social theory to see a different, more critical legacy from Durkheim's work (Pearce, 1989; Starkey, 1992). But, even more so than Weber, it remains the case that this is not how Durkheim has been used as a resource for orthodoxy.

Systems theory

The roots of systems thinking go back a very long way. As we saw in Chapter 2, engineering 'systematisers' were a driving force in the construction of early management theory and practice. Human and non-human entities were seen as interchangeable and manipulable (Shenhav, 1999: 19). While such thinking was limited as theory, its focus on organisations as purposeful, interdependent systems resembles the basic organic analogy used by Durkheim and others, in which all social systems have to adapt to the environment to survive. In such biological analogies, system parts (or sub-systems) are interconnected, and each is functional to the viability of the organisation, for example by generating binding social values. This became a theme of *functionalist* social theory (Parsons, 1951) which regards social systems as self-regulating bodies, tending towards a state of equilibrium and order. This has long had an influence in organisational theory. In their description and theorisation of the Hawthorne experiments, Roethlisberger and Dickson (1964) talked of industrial organisation in terms of functioning social systems striving for equilibrium under the influence of environmental factors (Reed, 1998: 37). Donaldson (1985: 29) argues that there *is* movement within equilibrium, but it is a process of internal adjustment between the sub-systems and to the environment over time, normally triggered by external change such as those in technologies or markets. Nevertheless any breakdown of order tends to be treated as pathological, and the non-rational elements confined to the informal organisation.

The classical theories, including scientific management and human relations, can be conceived as *closed system* perspectives, previously discussed in Chapter 3. By treating the organisation as a structure of manipulable parts that could be regulated internally, it appeared as if a rational means–ends relationship could be optimised. It was a question of re-balancing the human and technical, or formal and informal components, when one changed more rapidly than the other (Brown, 1992: 45). This can again be related to functionalist analysis, whose primary assumption is that the components of the structure must be integrated to ensure system survival. Change is likely to occur when 'the functional contributions of a given structural arrangement are exceeded by dysfunctions associated with the arrangement' (Tolbert and Zucker, 1996: 176).

The focus of manipulating the parts, as we know, shifted to an *open systems* approach – organisations coping with uncertainty through exchange and transaction – with *contingency theory*, with its emphasis on 'designing organisations rationally so that their internal coherence and external match to their environments are both maximised' (Tsoukas, 1994c: 4), the most popular variant. As Donaldson (1996: 63) notes, 'Fit is the underlying key'. While, as we saw in Chapter 5, contingency theorists identify a range of factors that might couple structure and environment, the common theory is structural adaptation to regain fit. In other words, there is a positive performance outcome of a fit between each contingency and one or more aspect of organisational structure. If an organisation moves into misfit, a new phase of structural adaptation begins to regain the desired relationship. Despite such transactions, mainstream organisational analysis has increasingly presented itself as divorced from broader theory. One of Donaldson's (1985) central arguments is that organisations can be studied as an independent realm. If the outside world comes into it, it is as the 'environment', a backcloth against which it is possible to specify relationships between contingencies, structure and performance. As Willmott observes, the various factors in this environment 'must be registered and controlled if strategic adjustments are to be successfully achieved. There is minimal consideration of the relevance of social theory . . . for the study of organisations' (1990: 45).

Woodward, one of the most noted contingency theorists, sums up the intellectual confidence felt by those pursuing this approach from the 1950s onwards:

> Even more important from the point of view of ultimate theory building is the fact that various schools of thought are beginning to see themselves as concerned with the study of systems...the starting point is the identification of a system and the subsequent questions asked are very much the same: what are the objectives and strategic parts of the system under review and how are these parts inter-related and interdependent? One result is that those concerned with the study of organisation are beginning to develop a common language, on whatever discipline their work is based. (Quoted in Eldridge and Crombie, 1974: 93)

Donaldson (1996) accurately observes that the systems-contingency approach became the dominant paradigm and there was a considerable period of doing 'normal science' (a term taken from Kuhn), and designating the testing of evidence and replication of studies within a particular framework. He argues that though challenged by critics, such as Child's concept of strategic choice (see Chapter 5) and by institutional theory (see Chapter 6), structural contingency theory has provided effective refutations or can cope with the addition of new variables. It is certainly true that most of the organisation theory done during the 1950s and 1960s can be contained under the heading 'systems rationalism' (Barley and Kunda, 1992). While not all its components could be described in terms of systems theory, operations research, decision-making theory and process theories of motivation shared an emphasis on controlling organisations through managing the boundaries between sub-units and the interface between inputs and outputs. In such theorising 'employees were largely absent' (Barley and Kunda, 1992: 380), which is another way of saying that agency had been squeezed out of the picture.

However, not all of the challenges are easily absorbed. Take the rise of institutional theory. It is true that a key emphasis is on the symbolic properties of systems. Successful adaptation to the environment in terms of legitimacy and resources depends significantly on fit with dominant institutional and state-influenced practices (such as employment policies) and social norms (Meyer and Rowan, 1977). While in one sense this is adding culture as an adaptive variable, institutional theory challenged the way in which efficiency and rationality were understood in the systems approach. As Tolbert and Zucker (1996) observe, organisations and particular structures could survive despite relatively limited efficiency, and rational decision-making is normatively bounded. Despite these advances, such approaches did little to move beyond the determinism in systems theory. Institutionalisation is characterised by habitualised action, largely taken for granted by the actor.

If we examine the theoretical developments since the 1970s, the problem of determinism has been the key factor offsetting Donaldson's (1998) view that orthodoxy could comfortably contain or incorporate criticism. He is open about the unwillingness or inability to offer explanations at the level of the human actor, preferring to talk of systems imperatives constraining managerial action to a high degree, influencing only the timing of structural change; but he underestimates the significance of a failure to do so. Individual behaviour is seen as 'determined by and reacting to structural constraints that provide organisational life with an overall stability and control' (Astley and Van de Ven, quoted in Mills and Murgatroyd, 1991: 5). The new wave of theorising was set to react against these images of orderly entities and passive people.

23 Critical Alternatives

Social action theory

The most significant sign of a major alternative to mainstream perspectives emerged with an attack on the dominant systems theory by Silverman (1970). He brought together elements of an approach described as the *action frame of reference*, or social action theory. It was not new, drawing on the phenomenological writings of Schutz (1967) and Berger and Luckman (1967). In fact its methods can partly be traced back to Weber's conception of a social science, rather than his writings on bureaucracy. For Weber, such a science begins from interpreting social action, and the subjective meanings and purposes attached to it. This rests on a distinction between the natural and social worlds, but retains an attempt to situate individual action within material structures. Donaldson recognises another, 'interpretative' Weber, and remarks that the approach works by 'gaining insights into the subjective world of actors and constructing a model of motivated actions of the typical actor in a particular social setting' (1985: 107). His complaint is merely that those who take this up ignore the 'structural', deterministic Weber.

In renewing an action perspective, Berger and Luckman popularised the concept of *social construction of reality*. Rather than conceiving of people as products of systems and institutions, they view them as 'actors' who create these patterns through their own meaningful activity. However it was accepted that the products of their action, for example organisational structures, appear to them as exterior 'things' with an independent existence. Social construction was one of the aspects of a dialectical approach discussed in Chapter 1, and it puts a necessary stress on the possibility of change through purposeful reflection and action.

Silverman was able to apply these kind of ideas more specifically to organisations, considering them as social constructs produced and reproduced through their members' activities. This was largely neglected in systems theory, which regards organisations as part of the natural world governed by laws concerning their structures and effects on behaviour. Hence, as we have argued, they have reified organisations and taken their basic features for granted. Silverman did not ignore structure, recognising that *roles*, as systematic patterns of expectations, were developed in the interplay between organisations and their environments. His study was largely theoretical, but others were of a more empirical nature, utilising the concept of organisations as *negotiated orders* (see Day and Day, 1977). By the early 1960s Strauss *et al.* (1963) had been analysing the negotiated order in hospitals, while other notable studies included those concerned with police and legal practices (Bittner, 1967; Cicourel, 1968), and welfare agencies (Zimmerman, 1971). A recurring theme was that controls exercised through rules in formal organisations were inevitably incomplete and unsuccessful. Any degree of effective co-ordination and co-operation is dependent on constant reworking of rules and goals, and formal and informal negotiation processes involving all participants. The subsequent customs and practices in any workplace act as a constraint on management.

The critique developed through action theory challenged the consensual and objective images of organisations that were often based on 'favoured' managerial definitions. By focusing on the realities of multiple goals and competing groups, dimensions of organisational life, such as work patterns and practices, could be demystified. It also shed light on why organisations do not operate as they are supposed to. As we saw in Chapter 3, this latter emphasis tied into empirical work by *neo-Weberians* who were also concerned with the bending of bureaucratic rules through the value-systems of employees (Blau, 1955; Gouldner, 1955). Indeed, Silverman utilises some of these studies extensively. He notes, for example, how Gouldner shows that industrial relations in a gypsum mine had been based on an 'indulgency pattern': implicit rules rooted in give and take rather than formal codes. When management attempted to introduce changes that clashed with the established values and practices and reasserted formal rules, it generated grievances and strike activity.

In organisation theory as such, the action perspective made its impact through Child's (1972) concept of strategic choice, which was directed against the environmental determinism of contingency theory, and was discussed in detail in Chapter 5. The theoretical significance is drawn out by Brown: 'This criticism emphasises "agency" as against "structure", that is the role of actors – managers, workers, or whoever – in choosing to pursue certain goals and/or follow certain lines of action albeit within constraints set by the actions of others and the context within which they are placed' (1992: 36).

Meanwhile, during the 1970s Silverman and other writers shifted the action approach in the more 'radical' direction of *ethnomethodology*. Though 'translated' as people-centred, it is actually only concerned with the production of a common sense world and eschews any attempt at analysis of causation which would impose external categories. Nor is it concerned with the relation between ideas and interests, or social and organisational structures present in the Weberian tradition. It restricts itself to accounting for the processes through which members construct their everyday life. Structures tend to be viewed at best as temporary patterns created by interpersonal action and based on available stocks of knowledge. While some useful material on the 'organisational work' of reinterpreting these stocks of knowledge and routine practices was generated (Silverman and Jones, 1976), it soon became difficult to locate any notion of *organisation* in the traditional sense. Phenomena such as power or control, which are expressed through relatively durable structures beyond specific situations and face-to-face interactions and meanings, are simply outside its frame of reference.

Though taken to extremes in ethnomethodology, these weaknesses were inherent in action theory. In Silverman's earlier work he argued, contrary to contingency theory, that technological and market structures were meaningful only in terms of the understandings and attachments of participants. Though structures require the involvement of actors in their reproduction, something like a product or labour market does have a structural existence partly independent from how particular individuals think or act – as anyone who has lost their job, or a fortune on the stock exchange, will testify. Concepts such as 'role' that were used to link subjective action and structure are useful but not substantial enough to carry the burden of explaining organisational behaviour. The more disconnected action theory became from wider concerns, the more it became 'buried in an obsessive concern for the minutiae of "everyday life" as exemplified in the intricacies of organisational routines' (Reed, 1985: 48). This is linked to a further problem limiting its capacity to act as a critical resource. Despite the emphasis on empirical studies, as we raised earlier and as Silverman has admitted, the approach is aimed at providing a method of analysis, rather than a theory of organisations. Nevertheless, Silverman and social action theory continue to be a focus for discussion (Hassard and Parker, 1994) and influence (Tsoukas, 1994c). Empirical studies utilising a negotiated order framework have been undertaken in the last decade with respect to kitchen workers (Fine, 1996) and environmental inspectors (Fineman, 1998).

Social action theory is also a resource for critical psychology, in this case because of the stress on the intersubjective nature of social behaviour as a form of negotiated order. The useful contribution of social action theories is, first, in the methodological emphasis maintained in rooting their work in accounts of subjective experience; and second, in the linking of accounts of how subjectivity is constructed to structures of control, culture and ideology in organisations. In relation to organisational psychology they represent that part of the domain of analysis characterised by subjective, partly rational action processes based on phenomenological, social constructionist models. They provide a link to the ethnomethodological tradition in sociology and to symbolic interactionism that has been influential in both sociology and social psychology.

Symbolic interactionism, following from Mead (1934), has long been the area where an interface between sociological and socio-psychological conceptions of identity has existed. The construction of identity and the social milieu within which individual identity exists is, in this model, dependent on interaction with others and through others with the self. Subjectivity, then, is mainly a product of intersubjective processes and is constructed through the negotiation of social rules and conventions. The social production of subjectivity, though acknowledged, is addressed through an understanding of how the formal and informal processes of culture and ideology impinge upon individual functioning. This phenomenological emphasis on situated meaning in the construction of subjectivity is a necessary methodological focus in providing a reflexive account of organisational behaviour, and informs much of our account of the securing and reproduction of identity in Chapter 21. What it lacks is the framework for understanding the social order that conditions action inside the organisation. Indeed neither critical social psychologies nor social action theories present consistent theories of either subjectivity or its structural location.

Radical structuralism

To escape the limits of an action approach, theory must move beyond how organisations and their environments are subjectively constituted to some kind of structural explanation of the dynamics of organisational development within capitalist societies. This section examines some of the resources that can be found for that purpose by reworking and extending the concepts provided by Marx and Weber. Following Burrell and Morgan (1979), we use the common heading of radical structuralism to signify that such theorising begins from an account of the structural framework of organisational behaviour, but is directed towards a critical explanation of the processes of regulation and change.

Marx and labour process theory

Marx had little to say about issues of administrative or even political organisation, and even less about the specific question of bureaucracy. As Goldman and Van

Houten note, 'Systematic study of the sociology of organisations is almost absent in the classical and modern Marxist traditions' (1977: 110). Those wishing to generate a discussion from Marx have had to rely on fragments of a critique of the Prussian bureaucracy and writings on the Paris Commune of 1871 as a model of the possibility of elimination of bureaucracy through a fully democratic administrative system (Marx, 1984). When he made observations about bureaucracy, they were very Weberian, with references to systematic division of labour, hierarchies of knowledge and mechanisms of formal behaviour (Sayer, 1991: 78). Marxist theory has tended to focus on the dynamics and contradictions of capitalism as a whole, and issues concerning the distribution of the surplus product, neglecting changes in productive processes, organisational forms and occupational structures. Some Marxist concepts have been influential, if often misunderstood, notably his account of the alienation of labour; but they have remained unconnected to any systematic organisational analysis.

However, during the last two decades Marxist-influenced theory and research has had a profound effect on all of the disciplines concerned with work organisation. This trend worries Donaldson (1985: 127), who argues that 'Marxism is a theory of society therefore it cannot be a theory of organisation'. Clegg (1988: 10) makes the apposite response that applying the same criteria to Weber would place his work on bureaucracy outside the level appropriate to organisation theory. There is a different point to be made. It is not the full apparatus of Marxist theory of history and society that has been influential, but a narrower set of ideas, though these are still central to his account of the working of capitalist production. That vehicle has been *labour process theory*, set in motion by Braverman's (1974) reworking of Marx's analysis of capitalist production. (For a full account of labour process debates see Thompson, 1989; Thompson and Smith, 2000.) We discussed this mainly in Chapter 8 as the framework for an explanation of control. Here we examine the deeper theoretical context.

Though more obviously influential in industrial sociology, labour process theory has provided conceptual tools observable in a wide range of critical organisation writers. Among the first were Clegg and Dunkerley, who began *Organization, Class and Control* (1980) by defining the theoretical object of organisational analysis: 'For this volume we have proposed as such an object the concept of organisation as control of the labour process' (1980: 1). What enables such an argument to be made? Marx may not have been interested in an understanding of organisations per se, but he was centrally concerned with issues of work and its organisation. By this we mean a combined emphasis on work organisations as the site of key economic processes and contradictions, and the meeting place of capital and labour; as well as organisation of work in terms of questions including the division of labour, relations of authority and control, and the distribution of rewards.

Donaldson also rightly observed that 'To qualify as distinctly neo-Marxian one would need to show the connection between work life in the organisation and change at the societal level' (1985: 128). That is exactly the strength of labour process theory, which Donaldson misses because the 'Marxism' he attacks is an earlier, much more general and less successful application to the sphere of work organisation. Marx defined the form of a society and economy in a manner strongly conditioned by an understanding of work relationships. Each mode of production gives rise to class relations, which under capitalism are based on the sale and purchase of labour power. The partial antagonism between capital and labour as collective classes arises from the exploitation and appropriation of the surplus labour by capital, based on its ownership and control of production. This is a far cry from the notion of fair exchange implied in mainstream theory. Work relations therefore cannot be analysed in general, but only as they are shaped by the demands of a specific system of production. As we explained in Chapter 8, the central characteristic of this process is the nature of labour as an active and indeterminate commodity. In other words, when it is purchased by capital, the outcomes remain mere potential. The goal of profitable production may be thwarted by workers asserting their own needs and self-organisation. In many ways this is a more sophisticated account of what industrial relations and other disciplines call the *wage–effort bargain*, the exchange of effort for reward, which has at its core the employment relationship (Edwards and Scullion, 1982).

The above processes cannot be understood within the confines of one organisational unit. Competition between enterprises and the conflict within the employment relationship create an accumulation process that compels capital constantly to reorganise production. Certain general features of work organisation and organisation of work tend to follow.

1   Employers need to exercise control over labour, both at the level of general directive powers and over working conditions and tasks. At the same time it is necessary to motivate employees and gain some level of consent and co-operation. Meeting these diverse and sometimes contradictory needs is the function of management systems and agents.
2   There are constant competitive pressures to cheapen the costs of production, notably labour. This may take place through deskilling, relocation of plant, work intensification or some other means; though it is subject to constraints, including worker resistance and market variations.
3   Control and cost reduction structure the division of labour, involving the design of work and division of tasks and people to give the most effective control and profitability. This is sustained by hierarchical structures and the shaping of appropriate forms of science and technology.

Let us restate this and spell out the consequences with more specific reference to organisations.

1   Work organisations are distinct from other organisations and can only be properly understood by locating the labour process within more general trends in the accumulation of capital. This 'political economy' is a bigger picture than the mainstream conception of 'the environment', but takes into account not just global patterns of ownership and competition, but how markets are shaped institutionally at regional, national and local level.
2.   'Organisations are structures of control' (Salaman, 1981: 143). This involves more than control over uncertainty, monitoring objectives or means of getting work done. They are administrative apparatuses concerned with control over productive activity in order to maximise the surplus. Managerial agency, though inherently variable and multi-layered, develops in this context.
3   In advanced capitalist societies large-scale organisations are strategic units acting as mechanisms which integrate economic, political, administrative and ideological structures (Burrell, 1980: 99).

4   Organisational structures and processes; including management and worker organ-
     isation, control and reward systems and job design, therefore are shaped by power
     relations and involve political issues, decisions and choices.
5   Organisations do not embody any universal rationality, but rather contested ration-
     alities arising from the partly antagonistic relation of capital and labour, as well as
     from other conflicts, notably that of gender relations. Organisational change will
     reflect the subsequent dialectic of control and resistance.

This is not merely a question of the 'seamy side' of otherwise excellent organisations,
as Gareth Morgan appears to believe (1986: 316–7). Relations of exploitation and
domination are integral to capitalist and other class-divided forms of work organisation. Nevertheless the underlying principles of the relations between organisations and
capitalist society are conceptualised at a very general level. Reference to class pertains
to relations between capital and labour as workplace actors, with any connections to
societal changes being conditional and requiring a broader frame of analysis. Similarly,
while radical structuralism shares a language of structural imperatives with systems
theory, it does not try to identify specific causal relations between forms of work organisation and environmental variables. Within labour process theory, there are no laws
or functional imperatives concerning *specific* forms of control, organisational structures, management strategies or job designs. While structural imperatives shape and
constrain the parameters of action, all these and other matters are empirical questions
to be determined by research and the unfolding of real events.

It is true that a reading of Braverman's (1974) emphasis on deskilling and Taylorism
as dominant tendencies can give the impression of determinism. However, second-wave
and subsequent labour process theory has made a considerable effort to give a more
complex account of structure and agency, in part by identifying a variety of levels of
influence on action, including global, state and sector: 'the objective is to examine structures and actors at different *levels*, without reducing the workplace to a mirror expression of these processes, or providing over-arching schemas of determination such as the
deskilling thesis, post-Fordism or control schemas from earlier labour process research'
(Thompson, Smith and Ackroyd, 2000: 1153).

In more general terms, such thinking parallels frameworks such as Giddens' (1984)
concept of *structuration* (though see Layder, 1987 and Whittington, 1991b for criticisms). Structures are conceived of as sets of formal and informal rules that generate common expectations and sanctions, and resources consisting of material goods and services
that affect life chances. But these are conceived of not as 'external' forces, but as things
on which people draw in their social interactions. Structures become both the medium
and outcome of that interaction. Action is conceived more precisely as agency. Agents
deploy a range of causal powers, sometimes on behalf of others who command greater
resources, sometimes to bend and break rules, but always purposeful and reflexive.

We can illustrate this way of thinking about the reciprocal interaction of structure
and agency through the example of the role of management. As we saw in Chapter 7,
there is a tendency in mainstream literature, particularly of the popular variety, to
see managers as free-floating individuals, always able to shape the destiny of their
organisation. To conceive of managers as an agency of others, as a set of activities
locked into structural constraints, goes against the grain. Yet that is the nature of the
relations between ownership and control in a capitalist economy. This view, taken in the
book, is often caricatured. Weir refers to 'the vulgar Marxist rhetoric of the inevitable

polarisation of organisation between the two fundamental classes of bourgeoisie and proletariat. The managers are simply a muddle in the middle according to this way of thinking' (1993: 16). Or try Watson talking about the managers at ZTC: 'They were indeed interested in control, but it was control over their own circumstances. . . . Managers were not seeking control on behalf of other groups' (1994: 85). Such explanation is all agency and no structure. Yes, managers are individuals with their own identities and values, struggling to make sense of their world and fight their corner within it. That makes a difference, but what they may seek and what they can do are often two different things, as Watson's own fascinating case makes clear. Managers are an agency of control, but the interesting questions start there, because that has to be achieved in the messy reality of particular firms with particular employees, in particular economies, governed by particular parties. A sense of management as agency is not about any simple functional necessities but, as Armstrong's work demonstrates (see Chapter 8), it is about the struggles of different professional or occupational groups to become the key core group in the workings of the enterprise. Any account of contemporary organisation must be at least *capable of* illuminating all levels, from the broader institutional constraints, through the sectional conflicts and down to real flesh and blood individuals.

The renewal of Marxist and labour process theory has generated or influenced a tremendous amount of historical and contemporary research at a more 'micro' level. These share features of rich description of everyday working life with ethnomethodological and negotiated order frameworks, but seek to situate such action within a broader structural context. (See Thompson and Warhurst, 1998 for a recent collection of articles.) The selective and qualified use of Marx suggested here and by other theorists has inevitably led to accusations that labour process theory is no longer Marxist (Cohen, 1987; Rowlinson and Hassard, 2000). This may be true, though authentic affinity with Marxism is only of concern to those who zealously guard orthodoxy and the sacred text. Even more importantly, even if the resource provided by labour process theory is valuable, there are still many gaps in explanations of key organisational processes. Some of this can no doubt be remedied by further research, but it is important to recognise the limits inherent in the perspective. It sets organisations specifically in the context of capitalist production, which is both strength and weakness. Among the gaps are the following.

1   Though the labour process is the core of productive activity, it does not encompass all aspects. Any theory of the role of organisations in capitalist society must deal with the *full circuit of capital* (Kelly, 1985; Nichols, 1986), including its realisation through the sale of commodities on the market, financial issues and the prior purchase of labour (see Chapter 8 for a full discussion of this). It would be very misleading for any critical theory to proceed on the assumption that organisational processes and managerial activities were based solely on the control of labour, neglecting factors such as sales and marketing, financial controls, supply of components and product quality. Even the employment relationship, though intimately connected to the labour process, is constituted on a far wider basis (Littler, 1982). Institutions such as the state and the family, plus different cultural values and patterns in a given society, shape the distinctive character of employment relationships, as can be seen by observing examples from Japan or farm work. Labour process theory is thus only a partial contribution to such analyses, though paradoxically it is in some ways ideally suited to organisation

studies, given that the dominant managerial theories are also overwhelmingly concerned with 'the labour problem'.

2   Not all work organisations are based on commodity production, or are capitalist in character. Those in health, education or other parts of the public sector are, at least for the moment, concerned with services for use, not profit. It is possible to construct a labour process or Marxist-oriented analysis which shows the links between the various types of public and private sector within the totality of capitalist society (Johnson, 1972; Heydebrand, 1977; Cousins, 1987). But it remains the case that not all organisational processes or forms of work activity can be understood solely through a theory whose categories are geared to explaining capitalist production, despite distorted attempts to do so, such as Bellaby and Orribor's (1977) analysis of the health service.

3   Non-profit-making organisations in capitalist societies, and forms of administration and enterprise in 'socialist' ones such as those in China and the former Soviet bloc countries, also show evidence of bureaucracy, power hierarchies and work fragmentation: 'contemporary socialist societies appear to be at least as bureaucratic and with as much of a self-perpetuating bureaucracy as capitalist ones' (Dunkerley and Salaman, 1986: 87). This suggests that the dynamic of bureaucratisation is partly independent of capital–labour relations, and that critical theory requires concepts that enable us to focus on that problem.

With respect to points 2 and 3, Weber provides a necessary corrective and additional resource. On the one hand, his work points to the distinctive ethos and 'regime values' of bureaucratic public administration, a reflection largely of the political environment within which it operates (du Gay, 2000: 7). On the other, Weber provides a broader account of bureaucratic rationalisation that is a necessary part of explaining its spread beyond market relations. For example, he perceptively predicted that state socialist systems would be more bureaucratic than capitalism, because of the absence of countervailing power structures between the state and markets. In a command economy, the power of bureaucratised management would increase, as would the dictatorship of the official (Sayer, 1991: 145–6).

Radical Weberianism

As Burrell (1996: 643) notes, while a conservative reading of Weber provided the perfect defence of bureaucratic hierarchy, the relevance of a left Weberianism has been largely ignored. Though some defenders of orthodoxy such as Donaldson recognise a radical Weber, many critical theorists, particularly those of a Marxist persuasion, have been hostile to the Weberian tradition (Marcuse, 1971; Johnson, 1980). Their objections relate to many of the points raised elsewhere in this book. This includes the tendency to argue that there is a bureaucratic imperative obliterating organisational differences within and between societies; that there is an inherent rationality of technique; and the identification of rationality with capitalism and the market. Also there are genuine limits to Weber's own categories, for example the emphasis on the bureaucratic hierarchy of offices has less relevance to shop-floor employees. Nevertheless there are radical Weberian perspectives, and critical writers who aim at some kind of synthesis of key aspects of Marx and Weber's analysis of work organisations (Salaman, 1979, 1981; Littler, 1982). They rightly point to common concerns with control and domination by management and bureaucratic élites: 'For both Marx and Weber the major elements of the structure of modern large-scale organisations stem from the efforts of those who own, manage and design the organisation, to achieve control over the members' (Salaman, 1979: 20–1). Despite this, mainstream accounts excluded domination from their reading of Weber (Shenhav, 1999: 8).

From a radical viewpoint, Weber's insights allow us to focus on a number of key areas. Work organisations operate on different levels, and in some of these, formal control procedures are important. Power is frequently constructed and legitimised through 'rationalisation', particularly through the expertise associated with science and technology, and what Weber described as 'control based on knowledge'. Even where analyses differ in focus and content, they are often complementary. Weber recognised that control rested on the 'complete appropriation' of all the material means of production by owners. Whereas Marx provides insights from an analysis of the consequences of the private ownership of the means of production, Weber identified the problem of concentration of power through the *means of administration*:

> The bureaucratic structure goes hand in hand with the concentration of the material means of management in the hands of the master. This concentration occurs, for instance, in a well-known and typical fashion, in the development of big capitalist enterprises, which find their essential characteristics in this process. A corresponding process occurs in public organisations. (Weber, 1984: 33)

In addition, both attempt to explain organisational dynamics within wider social and political structures rather than as independent, isolated phenomena, subject to their own 'laws'; though clearly the analysis of structural contexts differs. Marx's account of alienated labour and Weber's emphasis on the 'iron cage of industrial labour' share a concern for the fragmented and dehumanised nature of work. Weber saw that maximum formal rationality favoured economically powerful groups and their ability to use superior resources to dictate terms and conditions in what may appear as a freely-made contract of legal equality (Brubaker, 1984: 42–3). Social tensions and sectional conflicts between different interest groups were therefore inevitable.

Overlaps are less surprising than they appear. Both theorists shared a similar view of the necessity for modernity to sweep away the traditional social relations based on conceptions of natural order, personalised power and patriarchy. Capitalism was a flawed but dynamic system compelled constantly to revolutionise production and all social spheres. The difference, as Sayer observes, was that for Marx, 'what makes modernity modern is, first and foremost, capitalism itself' (1991, 12). In contrast, for Weber, 'capitalism is but one theatre among others where the drama of rationality is played out' (1991: 134). Weber was surely right in this, but, as we shall see later, wrong in some of the ways he understood the relationship between capitalism, rationalisation and modernity.

Key aspects of work organisation are not reducible to capitalism and its imperatives. As Littler (1982) points out, Weberian categories are especially important in understanding the employment relationship, and the career structure of employees in particular. Bureaucratic procedures and rules are relevant to the analysis of processes such as recruitment, reward and promotion. On a broader canvas, modern states and enterprises involve complex functions, management of competing interests, and performance of problematic tasks according to observable rules and norms. Some of these processes are created by and reflect specific relations of production, as in layers of supervision whose sole function is labour control and discipline. Certain functions may be artificially expanded, and new ones absorbed by bureaucrats themselves as a form of self-preservation. But as Polan notes, bureaucratic forms are a necessary object of analysis in their own right: 'Only as a result of conceding to the bureaucracy its genuine, legitimate and distinct functions can one begin to determine the boundaries of its powers and construct political control procedures that may successfully police those boundaries' (1984: 71).

Part of this legitimacy, as du Gay (2000: 4) demonstrates, is to recognise that attributes of the 'good bureaucrat' – adherence to procedure, expertise, impersonality and hierarchy – constitute 'a positive moral and ethical achievement in its own right' with respect to the particular requirements of equitable treatment of citizens and workers by public administration. For these and other reasons, radical Weberian analysis can act as a corrective to some of the more utopian aspects of the Marxist tradition in which bureaucracy and efficiency are simply reduced to specific class interests. This utopianism is reinforced by giving alternative socialist production relations a utopian capacity to avoid bureaucratisation altogether in a model of 'total democracy', based on:

> the election of everyone above the level of ordinary worker, with no fixed hierarchy and no-one having the right to give commands (except insofar as this right is temporarily delegated, with the commands always subject to the review of the group as a whole). Moreover, instead of a plethora of rules and an illusory focus on bureaucratically defined expertise ... regulations are reduced to a minimum, freedom is maximised, and everyone becomes technically competent to do the work.
> (Clawson, 1980: 16–17)

More realistic radical models emphasise feasible levels of task-sharing, egalitarian reward systems, democratic controls and participation and co-operative cultures (see Sirriani, 1984; Rothschild and Allen Whitt, 1986; K. Ramsay and Parker, 1992). This would result in what might be described as a *minimal bureaucracy*. Only by recognising certain necessary and distinct functions for bureaucracy can we begin to control and transform them. Clegg and Higgins comment that such arrangements:

> will neither eliminate rules nor the division of labour; in this sense it will not eliminate bureaucracy at all. To presume to do so would be chimerical. What we will achieve is a form of bureaucracy – administration by office and rules – which is not premised on hierarchy, but on collectivity; not on authoritarianism but on democracy; a new ideal type of a bureaucratic, democratic and collectivist organisation.
> (Clegg and Higgins, 1987: 217)

Radical Weberian perspectives are, however, divided on how much scope there is to modify and democratise hierarchical organisations. Orthodox Weberian analysis, by treating rationalisation and bureaucracy as independent, inexorable forces, risks losing sight of the specificity that location within particular modes of production or market systems creates. This insight is the central dividing line between one strand of radical Weberians and orthodox interpretations, for it brings with it a rejection of Weber's *fatalism* about the relations between bureaucracy and industrial societies. Radical Weberians believe that bureaucracy is not necessarily universal or inevitable, but rather a pervasive tendency that takes specific forms and therefore can and must be countered.

Like some contemporary labour process theorists, there is more emphasis on bureaucratic control as a *management strategy* (Edwards, 1979; Burawoy, 1979; Clawson, 1980). Though not unique to any system of production, bureaucracy has to be explained through its relations with that wider formation. Capitalist social relations are the primary influence on the imperative to appropriate the means of production from workers, though the outcomes are shaped by processes of bureaucratic rationalisation.

A second strand of radical Weberianism retains the traditional pessimism, but combines it with a powerful critique of the negative of rationalisation. This is particularly associated with the influential work of George Ritzer, discussed earlier, particularly in Chapter 13. In *The McDonaldization of Society* (1993), Ritzer attributes these insights solely to the modern application of Weber's idea of formal rationality. Elsewhere, however, he notes that, 'This discussion of the exploitation of customers (and workers) in McDonaldized settings serves to bring together the two great theories in the history of sociology – Weber's theory of rationalisation and Marx's theory of capitalist expansion and exploitation' (Ritzer, 1998: 73). He also acknowledges that his descriptions of the growth of routinised, deskilled 'McJobs' parallels Braverman's analysis of the degradation of labour, while adding an emphasis on service work, the involvement of customers and broader commercial trends not present in labour process theory.

This and other studies of the bureaucratisation of services are radical both as a powerful antidote to fashionable post-bureaucratic discourses, and as a critique of the irrational excesses that happen when formal rationality is taken to dehumanising extremes. Ritzer therefore reminds us of the distinction between formal and substantive rationality that is lost in mainstream readings of Weber. However, he also inherits and reproduces the weaknesses of a purely Weberian approach, notably its pessimistic fatalism. Rejecting the Marxian idea that there is a core of creative labour that can resist the rationalised and exploitative character of work, 'McDonaldization becomes the kind of iron cage described by Weber from which there is no escape and, worse, not even any interest in escaping' (Ritzer, 1998: 67). All we are allowed to do is 'rage' against the destructive, anti-social character of McDonaldized systems, mitigating their worst excesses through personal gestures in the sphere of consumption (1996: 304–5). This kind of dystopian radicalism brings to mind many of the contemporary applications of Foucault (see Chapter 8). This is not surprising because both frameworks remove labour as an active agency, or at least one that is capable of substantial dissent and resistance. Indeed, O'Neill (1986) argues that one can trace the idea of disciplinary society, with its imagery of loyal workers and committed citizens in prison, factories, hospitals and school, directly from Weber to Foucault. Whether this is accurate or not, as Smart (1999) and other essays in his edited collection make clear, Ritzer neglects and underestimates the varieties of consumer, worker and ecological resistance to McDonaldization.

This is merely one of the reasons why Ritzer's claims for the supposed inexorability of rationalisation are one-sided and unconvincing. Much of the evidence for the 'inevitable expansion' of McDonaldization is other fast food operations. When it strays from that territory, we get fleeting and fragmentary examples from dumbed-down newspapers, assembly-line pornography, and bureaucratised birth and death (1996: 294–302). Yet, as he later admits, counter-examples, even within the same processes, can easily be identified. The central problem is twofold. First, while fast food is an important sector, it cannot be used as the *template* for economic development in a globalising economy. Paradoxically, while Ritzer *does* add useful insights, his thesis is at its strongest when it is describing classic labour process concerns such as fragmented work and the separation of conception and execution through scripted service interactions. When moving onto a broader terrain, he is constrained, by both his largely American focus of experience, and the separation of rationalisation and capitalism we identified earlier. Locating the former within the latter would reveal that fast food is only one template of rationalisation. Not only does labour act as a constraint to rationalisation, national and regional patterns of competition produce diverse market rationalities and competing models of production.

Smart suggests that Ritzer fails to make sufficient distinction between fast food and formal rationality on the one hand, and rationalisation and commodification on the other. Much of the expansion of standardised products and services can be explained predominantly by the 'relentless pursuit of capital accumulation' into new global markets (1999: 4). Kellner (1999) makes a similar warning against excessive dependence on Weber, and calls for a synthesis with Marxian analysis in order to comprehend the combined instrumental rational of production and consumption. A thesis with a bit more Marx and a little less Weber also has the additional benefit that economic rationalisation need not be presented as the 'irrationality of rationality', but as the normal pursuit of profit within the capitalist mode of production (Smart, 1999: 16).

These weaknesses should not detract from the achievements of even a pessimistic Weberian analysis. As we argued in Chapter 12, there is a strong case that a modified and updated Weberian analysis of bureaucracy and rationalisation remains indispensable for an understanding of contemporary work organisation. With the relevant elements derived from a Marxist tradition, they emphasise the continuity in social relations in and beyond large-scale organisations in a capitalist society. It is precisely this notion of continuity that has been under attack in the last decade.

The postmodern challenge to rationality

Postmodernism is the least cohesive of the general social theories we have examined in this part of the book, the term being loosely applied to an overlapping set of ideas about society and knowledge deriving from French social theorists such as Baudrillard, Lyotard and Derrida, which have become increasingly influential in organisation theory in recent years (Clegg, 1990; Parker, 1992; Hassard and Parker, 1993). It lays claim to be the most radical break from orthodoxy, but the orthodoxy is different from the systems and related ideas we have talked about so far. Anything with 'post' automatically specifies its opposite, so the orthodoxy must be *modernism*. This may appear puzzling: after all, existing social theories have not traditionally been defined by that label. But as we indicated in Chapter 12, for Clegg (1990: 2), now having shuffled off his Marxist coil, organisation theory is a 'creature' of modernity. Similarly, Gergen (1992, 211–12) includes almost the full range of organisational and behavioural theories in the 'modernist' camp.

So, what is modernity? In some usages, it designates a type of society or epoch (the ontological dimension); at its simplest, industrialism in which the dominant feature is the large-scale, hierarchical bureaucracy concerned with rationality and planning throughout social and economic life. Willmott sums up the argument thus: 'Its ideal is the expertly designed, perfectly ordered and controlled world in which all ambivalence and indeterminacy are attenuated, if not wholly eliminated' (1992: 70). But within such conceptions we see the seeds of another designation, modernism as a way of thinking, a way of representing knowledge about society and organisations (the epistemological dimension). Above all, it is held to be characterised by a concern for developing the 'grand narrative', a coherent story about the development of the social and natural world, revealed through the application of reason and science (Cooper and Burrell, 1988). Modernism is thus equated with positivism, the pursuit of objective truths through a 'logico-scientific mode of knowing' in which events are explained in terms of general laws and clear cause and effect relations (Czarniawska, 1999).

Postmodernists develop a dual challenge in both these dimensions of what society is (ontology) and how we should look at it (epistemology). We have already outlined the basis of the former in Chapter 11. Rapid social change, the shift from a society based on production to one based on information, the emergence of segmented markets dominated by more discerning consumers, and turbulent environments are said to be demanding diversity and flexibility from work organisations which are released from their bureaucratic iron cage. Though it is not their exclusive property, postmodernists concerned with the workplace embrace the notion of the post-bureaucratic organisation in which the old specialised division of labour and centralised control no longer holds sway. (See Palmer and Hardy, 2000.) In turn, social theorists with a broader societal remit use this tenuous evidence of 'debureaucratisation' and 'reprofessionalisation' to sustain a broader vision of postmodernisation (Crook, Paluski and Waters, 1992). We have made an extensive critique of such claims in Chapter 12, so for most of this section, we will concentrate on the other, epistemological, dimension of postmodernism. Arguably, this discussion is directed at the issues that postmodern thinking is having greatest influence on in organisation and management theory. For example, Fournier and Grey's (2000) useful and influential account of postmodern influences on 'critical management studies' confirms the view that critical scholarship is moving away from challenging what society and organisations look like, towards alternative ways of seeing. (See Thompson, 2001 for a discussion of this.)

At the heart of this is the postmodern rejection of the grand narrative. The search for the coherent story (Braverman's theory of the degradation of the labour process in the twentieth century), or the total picture (Weber's account of the interrelated processes of rationalisation) is both pointless, because of the fragmentation of economic and cultural life, and dangerous, because it submerges diverse voices and the multiplicity of 'local' phenomena. Difference, incoherence and fluidity are preferable and more realistic because meaning cannot be fixed; it is what we make it through language that constructs, rather reflects, reality.

One variant of this kind of thinking can be seen in Baudrillard and his concept of *hyperreality*. In a media-saturated world which thrives on spectacle and encourages politicians to employ 'spin doctors' to put a twist on events before and after they happen, it becomes impossible to distinguish between the real and fictive. We cannot refer to distortion of reality, because there are too many realities for anything to be measured against. Similarly, Alvesson and Deetz (1996) argue that, as society becomes more fragmented and hyperreal, discourses multiply, reality becomes virtual and any forces that stabilise identity are lost. To return to Baudrillard, his most (in)famous claim was that during the Gulf conflict, it was impossible to know whether any events had taken place. This was literally a war of words in which all our information was second-hand, simulated and structured through media manipulation (for a critique see Norris, 1992).

While some postmodernists seek a softer version that 'recognises the ontological existence of the social world, however precarious and fluid' (Palmer and Hardy, 2000: 265), the core view remains that there is no way of distinguishing between representation and reality, with 'truth' becoming merely a product of language games. We have Derrida's 'nothing exists outside the text', taken as the interplay of different discourses (Hassard, 1994: 9). In this context, the task of the social theorist is not to construct the authentic explanation, but to *deconstruct* texts in order to reveal the contradictions, origins, instabilities and gaps. For example, this process of rereading may uncover the silences on gender issues in the classics of 'malestream' organisation theory (Calás and Smircich, 1992). While such treatment is 'exposed' to public gaze, it may be regarded as inevitable, for discourse always bears the imprint of the social identity of its producers. This notion – labelled 'perspectivism' – adds a further layer to the conception of multiple viewpoints and realities. In one sense it is an absolute relativism, moving beyond a contingent explanation for being unable to access the real (because it is too fragmented) to an all-purpose one ('truth' is merely the will to power). The outcome is, nevertheless the same – truth claims cannot be adjudicated: 'all knowledge is self-referential, coherent only in terms of its own discourse, since there exist no meta-justification agencies, no higher external authority, by reference to which claims to knowledge may be judged' (Coleman, 1991: 26).

In our previous discussions in this book, an emphasis on the primacy of language and discourse emerged most strongly in Chapter 9, through an examination of the ideas of Foucault and poststructuralism on power. Here, power is not a thing possessed by sovereign agents, but operates through discourses that produce knowledge and disciplinary practices which define and constrain the identities of workers, consumers and citizens. As we argued there, the danger is that any subject of action is lost in the interplay of discourses (Newton, 1994). But perhaps the most famous illustration in organisation theory of the abandonment of the search for the truth lying beneath the surface of social relations is Morgan's *Images of Organisation* (1986). Morgan does not just analyse organisational life in terms of a series of metaphors – the machine, the psychic prison, the tool of domination – but treats those images as of equal validity. Despite representing contradictory 'claims', they are all 'true' in their own terms; their 'cognitive power and empirical veracity can only be assessed in terms of the purposes for which they are constructed and used . . . reality is what you make of it' (Reed, 1990b: 36).

Also influential in applications of postmodern and poststructural epistemology is the shift of concern from analyses of control and rules to the construction of organisational life through cultural and symbolic resources, as we saw in Chapter 13. Alvesson and Deetz argue that as economic activity shifts from manufacturing to services, issues of corporate culture and identity rise up the managerial agenda, and that 'Objects for management control are decreasingly labour power and behaviour and increasingly the mindpower and subjectivities of employees' (1996: 192). In a period where lean production and downsizing have been the primary means of corporate rationalisation, this judgement looks particularly misplaced. But it also reveals the tension between postmodernism as epoch and epistemology. Logically, an approach that rejects narrative and totalising pictures should be hostile to or uninterested in an alternative conception of society. Alvesson and Deetz are sensitive to the problem of 'proclaiming a new postmodern epoch', given weak empirical indicators and the danger of re-labelling old ideas. At the same time, and within two paragraphs, they cannot resist justifying their claims of shifting managerial practices by reference to 'new social conditions' (1996: 192). Such writing is unfortunately typical of a new form of cultural historicism in which the source of evolutionary development is no longer technological and economic imperatives, but the management of values and engineering of the soul (Reed: 1996). As Reed goes on to note, the appeal of cultural historicism is primarily ideological: it provides a new vocabulary of motive for organisational change in circumstances where old managerial and corporatist rationales lack legitimacy.

There is, admittedly, a difference between those theorists such as Clegg who have been quite happy to use conventional tools of rational enquiry to develop accounts of postmodernity, and those such as Cooper and Burrell (1988: 106) who, in their own words, prefer the discursive 'production of organisation' to the 'organisation of production'. But the distinction is not as clear-cut as it seems. Continuities and commonalities arise in a variety of ways. In both dimensions there is a shared language of fragmentation and fracturing of the theoretical and practical order (Reed, 1991: 125). This imagery is taken from the origins of postmodernism as a perspective in art and culture, where eclecticism, stylistic promiscuity, paradox and mixing of modes replace hierarchical judgements of value and distinctions between high art and popular culture (Featherstone, 1988). They are also linked by a rejection of the 'false promises' of rational design, the idea that knowledge should offer methodologies for defining the most rational means of controlling complex, large-scale organisations (Hassard, 1994, 4). Finally and most importantly, there is the inconvenient and much observed fact that postmodernism is itself a meta-narrative (Boyne and Rattsani, 1990: 39–40). The need to create pictures of reality is inescapable in the illustrative and conceptual acts of theorising, and there is ample evidence that writers such as Lyotard, Morgan and Baudrillard draw on post-industrialism, information society and other models which take as their starting point some kind of epochal break. (For a critique, see Thompson, 1993.) Even those who have most resolutely avoided any engagement with the empirical cannot resist reference to 'the changing conditions of modern life', to justify their calls for conceptual shifts in the body of organisation theory, or in this case the theory of the organisational body (Dale and Burrell, 2000: 25).

In practice, then, the post-bureaucratic organisation located in the postmodern epoch is a rival narrative to those traditions deriving from Marx and Weber. As we saw in Chapter 14, the evidence for any substantial presence for such a mode of organising is either absent or misunderstood. Postmodern theorists appear to see little problem in sharing the agenda and language of popular management texts on such issues. (See Clegg and Hardy, 1996: 11.) Organisations may not be the 'tightly-coupled' rational machines beloved of systems theory, but when Hassard argues that 'Above all, we should seek to explode the myth of robust structural relations through establishing the fragile character of organisational life' (1994: 16), this is merely standing orthodoxy on its head, rather then a realistic picture of the modern firm.

Just as there is considerable continuity in capitalist relations of production and in rationalisation processes, large-scale organisations are considerably more durable and able to marshal powerful resources than postmodernists allow. In attacking the second edition of this book, along with the work of Salaman, Dale and Burrell (2000: 20–4) object to any reference to organisations as regular, patterned activities and corporate entities with powers over and above their members. It remains our view that power converts ambiguity into order, though the latter is not synonymous with the equilibrium of systems theory, because it is always contested and disrupted. New forms of theorising are in danger of moving so far away from rationality that they are unable to conceptualise *organisation* at all, particularly at a macro level. As Reed (1996: 42) notes, postmodernism, paradoxically reinforced by post-industrial images of decentred,

378 of WORK ORGANISATIONS

fragmented economies, has retreated into local aspects and small pictures of organisational life. Willmott makes a similar point when observing that a focus on local diversities, for example in the work of Clegg, can distract from the broader 'patterning of process of economic and organisational development' (1995: 41).

This is not just a question of the nature of contemporary structure and agency, but of the equally flawed alternative ways of seeing. As Reed comments:

> The theoretical glue once provided by an assumed epistemological commitment to rational analysis of 'organised rationality' has given way under the pressure exerted by a cacophony of voices which celebrate the reality of multiple and contested organisational rationalities which cannot be assessed or evaluated in any coherent way. (Reed, 1993: 181)

It is true, as we have continually stressed in this book, that there are conflicting ends and means pursued by rival organisational actors, and a diversity of organising logics and institutional settings. But contested practical rationalities need to be understood on rational grounds. How can we debate the *character* of organisational life if we cannot compare and evaluate theoretical claims or Morgan's 'images'? If these remain self-contained, self-referential discourses, as Reed notes elsewhere (1991: 38), organisation theory just becomes a supermarket where metaphors or other means of representation are purchased according to preference and power.

There is an increasing and dangerous tendency in organisation theory to treat management strategy, corporate culture, Taylorism, Fordism and so on, only or even primarily as discourses. When presented to us as texts, the subsequent deconstructions and rereadings are sometimes illuminating, but at the cost of confinement to the world of inter-textuality. The interplay of agency and structures has a real material existence. In his critique of postmodernism, Tsoukas persuasively illustrates the point:

> It is because actions are not taken and voices not uttered, in a vacuum that *not* all accounts are equally valid. No matter how much I shout at my bank manager he is not likely to lend me money if I am unemployed. This is not a figment of my imagination. Others also tell me they have had similar experience. (Tsoukas, 1992: 644)

It is because we need to understand these similarities of experience and their institutional underpinnings that some form of theoretical narrative is necessary. What we know is inherently incomplete, but we require a capacity to generate generalisable knowledge and to identify trends, if not laws; and we need empirical work that can help distinguish between rhetorics of the powerful and the realities of power. We will return to the question of evidence and truth claims in the discussion of paradigm incommensurability.

A masculine logic?

There is a final challenge to rationality when postmodernism is combined with some perspectives within feminism to argue that the dominant Weberian conceptualisation of rationality is a male one. Explanations have overlapping emphases. Some (Martin, 1990; Bologh, 1990; Putnam and Mumby, 1993) refer to the stress on instrumentalism, logic and calculability in the public sphere and the exclusion of emotionality, intuitive experiences and the private realm. Others lean towards a version of perspectivism in which masculinity is the driving force. For example, Hearn (1992) argues that it is mostly men who manage the introduction of rational method and men and masculinities that will be affected by it; while Bologh (1990: xv) addresses the ghost of Weber thus: 'Your vision, extensive and expansive as it is, is the vision from your body inscribed with your gender, your place, your time'. She shows that he had a patriarchal perspective based on ideas of mastery, control and impersonality.

The result is often projected as a distinction between male and female types of social action or rationality; the former embodied in authoritarian methods of control or hierarchical ways of decision-making, the latter in ways of organising dependent on emotional connection, nurturance, intimacy and co-operation (Ferguson, 1984; Grimshaw, 1986; Bologh, 1990). The glass ceiling is left intact in favour of construct-ing an entirely different kind of building – a 'womanspace' (Calás and Smircich, 1996: 227). That alternative, most forcefully put in Ferguson's (1984) *The Feminist Case Against Bureaucracy*, is influenced by relationships developed in the private realm, or friendship relations in small-scale women's movement structures such as rape crisis centres and bookstores which run on the basis of personal relations, skill sharing and egalitarianism, rather than formal rules and power games. Both attack liberal feminism (Kanter, 1993) for pursuing female interests within existing organisations.

Such distinctions can also be epistemological. Coleman invites us to 'consider organisational thinking from a specifically woman-centred perspective'(1991: 6), which rejects 'propositional knowledge' and embraces the feeling element of the learning process. Such specific 'feminist perspectives' are held to be coherent with current developments in postmodern theory. She says that it is 'ironic' that all the postmodern philosophers who write in ways that develop feminist positions are men. Ironic or not, it is difficult to see how it is possible to hold both views at the same time. Modes of thinking are either gender-specific or they are not.

Though normally distinguished from biological determination, such arguments are flawed and dangerous. Witz and Savage (1992: 20) and Due Billing argue that Ferguson's work is not established on any secure analytical basis. Due Billing observes that 'There is a tendency in Ferguson's text to operate with an ideal (essentialistic) notion of "woman" and to equate femaleness with an ideology about female values' (1994: 177). Some of the mistaken outcomes of such thinking were seen in Chapter 11, in which a number of contemporary management writers were asserting the existence of specifically female ways of managing without any convincing evidence. Similar prob-lems have been identified with essentialist and determinist perspectives that assert that technology is in its essence masculine. As Gill and Grint note, 'it is not necessary to argue that technologies *embody* gender relations in order to highlight the relevance of the wider matrix of meanings ascribed to technologies for gender relations' (1996: 7, original emphasis; and see Webster, 1996: 22–32). In principle, poststructuralist perspectives should be wary of such thinking, given their emphasis on the social *construction* of knowledge. However the strong pull of perspectivism and the desire to identify mod-ernism with a particular conception of rationality mean that talk of *masculine* institutions (Hassard *et al.*, 2000: 9) and reason (Dale and Burrell, 2000: 17) are commonplace.

To return to Weber: as a man of his times, he may well have been guilty of 'masculinism', though the stereotype of a lack of interest in the emotional may be more complicated (Albrow, 1992). More importantly, concepts and practice are distin-guishable from context. The production of knowledge is an undoubtedly gendered one.

Connections between masculinity, male privilege and the reproduction of organisation in the public sphere has been (Hearn, 1992) and still is strong (Roper, 1994). However, ideas of an essentially male rationality are static and deterministic, given that the overlay of rationality with masculinity is itself historically and socially produced. The fact that men have dominated women or had systematic advantages within the division of labour within bureaucracies does not make bureaucracies male. Some of the same objections can be made to previously-identified arguments that there is an alternative feminist mode of organising to an inherently male bureaucracy. A very effective critique of these views is developed by Due Billing (1994; see also Witz and Savage, 1992). Not only it is impossible to evade power, even in 'friendship organisations', women have been changing bureaucracies and successfully challenging their gender bias and male cultures. As we saw in Chapter 10, women as well as men can and do benefit from bureaucracy, and can pursue successful struggles within rule-governed, instrumental processes. This may not be as strange as it seems: 'Weber regards the "formalistic impersonality" of bureaucratic administration – its instituted blindness to inherited differences in status and prestige – as a source of democratic equalisation' (du Gay, 2000: 42). For this and other reasons, 'Rules could also be viewed as an asset for the people working in the organisation' (Due Billing, 1994: 183). For whatever the limits of formal equal opportunity policies or sexual harassment codes (Cockburn, 1991), it remains the case that they are an advance on the informal culture and rules of the game within which male power operates. As du Gay (2000: 55–7) notes, in this context, postmodern calls to 'repersonalise' the public realm are both naively romantic and practically dangerous.

Bureaucracy cannot just be set aside as alien practical and conceptual territory, because it is not just a discourse. Rationalisation was and is a fundamental principle of life in industrial societies and does not 'belong' to men. For example, calculable rules, whether applied to feelings, job specifications or financial reporting systems, can be initiated and operated by women as employers and managers, and experienced at the receiving end by men and women. The task of organisation theory, is surely, as Ramsay and Parker (1992) argue, to plot the *intersection* between patriarchy, rationality and bureaucracy, not to collapse each into the other.

A further 'intersection' that has been a central theme of the book is that between the sociological/structural and psychological dimensions of action. Our view has been that different modes of analysis are needed to deal with the complexities and levels of human behaviour. People are constituted as individual subjects at the level of their identities, emotions and self-directed actions. But that process is informed by the same 'structural' phenomena that shape managerial strategies or job design, such as the social relations of production between capital, labour or gender. The next chapter examines some of the theoretical resources we have engaged with, in a similar manner to the previous discussion.

24 Critical Social Psychologies

Mainstream theory has long included a psychological component, but has tended to treat people in organisations as 'psychologically determined entities' with abstractedly and individually defined needs. In addition the 'sciences' of organisational behaviour have managed to produce better ways of manipulating the identities and behaviour of employees, but have not succeeded in addressing the problems that make such manipulation necessary. A redefinition of the traditional agenda of organisational psychology requires that individual, group and organisational behaviour be placed in a wider context, particularly the social relations of production and gender relations. Specifically, this would account for subjective experience, while avoiding the over-utilisation of rational-cognitive explanations which focus on the individual determinants and constraints of purposive activity. Instead we seek to maintain a focus on how subjectivity is constructed and reproduced within organisational structures.

Given these requirements and the limitations of existing perspectives, it is understandable that over time we have seen the development of a variety of critical social psychologies. This label covers a multiplicity of radical viewpoints which have utilised concepts from mainstream western social psychology, Marxist and humanist perspectives and Freudian theory. The attempts to formulate 'Marxist psychologies' (Schneider, 1975; Seve, 1978; Volpert, Hacker and Von Cranach, 1982; Leonard, 1984) are of particular interest to us because the explanation of social behaviour is located specifically in an understanding of work organisations. This production of subjectivity and consciousness in the wider social world is also explored by Henriques et al. (1984) through an articulation with psychoanalysis and discourse theory that attempts to move beyond both individual and social determinisms. The more recent developments in poststructuralist and postmodern critique, heavily influenced by Potter and Wetherall's (1987) Discourse and Social Psychology, are themselves as varied as anything that has gone before.

Internal critique

Social psychology has historically encompassed a wide variety of critical traditions differing mainly in their concerns for internal critique of methodology and content, as opposed to a broader critique of the sociocultural relations of the knowledge they produce (Wexler, 1983). From work such as that of Moscovici (1972), Gergen (1973) and Rosnow (1981), we gain a focus on the methodological limitations of social psychology and its lack of relevance to social issues. These are essentially calls for reform, which in their understanding of social relations in terms of relatively fixed characteristics and roles follows the liberal tradition of social emancipation through individual transformation. Alternatively we have the vein of critique characterised by Armistead (1974), Archibald (1978) and Larsen (1980), which focuses on examining radical alternatives within social psychology. Although not always consistent with each other, these critiques maintain a perspective on the repressive nature of socially-organised relationships. Appealing to both humanist and Marxist theory, they are concerned with social transformations leading towards human emancipation, and like the more conventional methodological critique, they also appeal to internal procedural reform. Being essentially theoretical critiques, their focus tends to enshrine critique as a principle in itself.

There have been specific developments in internal critique that are more recognisant than the mainstream previously was of the sociocultural relations of knowledge. Though still disparate in perspective, these approaches place an emphasis on factors such as social networks, cognition and identity, albeit with the more prosaic aims of reforming the discipline rather than the subject or the client. This is exemplified in Hollway's (1991) proposals on a movement towards a work psychology reflexive of the relations of knowledge, power and practice, and also in Hosking and Morley's (1991) cognitive/political psychology of organising. Hosking and Morley (1991) in their focus on entitative approaches to persons and organisations (see Chapters 14 and 19), implicitly recognised reification as impacting on attempts to study organisational behaviour. They are keen to articulate what they term the 'skilful organising processes' with which actors 'mutually create' the networks through which they pursue their personal projects.

Wider developments in social cognition are exemplified in Augoustinos and Walker's (1995) attempts to integrate American individualism with the more ideological concerns for identity found in European social psychology. They emphasise linkages between individual and collective processes, and discuss at length the consequences of the 'anti-cognitive rhetoric associated with discourse analysis and the antipathy of the mainstream's response to the "turn to language"' (1995: 285). This anti-cognitivist stance leads others such as Haslam (2000) largely to ignore the kinds of critique coming from postmodern and discourse analysis as discussed in Chapter 25. Their focus is instead on the extent to which paradigmatic conceptions of organisation, social context and psychological processes can be integrated through the social identity approach as summarised in Figure 26.1.

Though neither radical in comparison to Armistead and others, nor expressly critical, these approaches represent a shift in line with that from micro towards macro organisation behaviour, as identified by Nord and Fox (1996, see Chapter 15). It remains to be seen whether a coherent critical social and organisational psychology can be carved out at this meso level. However the willingness of such an approach to engage with essentialist theory and positivist data in a pragmatic fashion may make it a more solid foundation for a critical psychology than the Marxist and postmodern approaches we will discuss below.

Marxist psychology?

Marxist contributions to psychology, in their understanding of subjectivity at work, begin with the concept of alienation, the estrangement of creative capacities which means that 'work is external to the worker, that it is not part of his nature, and that, consequently, he does not fulfil himself in his work but denies himself' (Marx, 1963: 124–5). The reference to a 'human nature' is not to an eternal set of values or behaviours such as aggression or jealousy beloved of reactionary thinkers, but rather to certain characteristics which distinguish man's species-being, such as the capacity for purposeful and reflective action.

Differences between organisational paradigms in terms of their attention to social and psychological dimensions of organisational life   *FIGURE 24.1*

Source: reproduced with permission from S. A. Haslam (2000) *Psychology in Organizations: The Social Identity Approach*, London: Sage.

Alienation is given specific and concrete form by its location in the capitalist labour process; individual needs and capacities are subordinated to the requirements of capital accumulation, with the psychological consequence that the worker feels a stranger in his or her work. Management, though, still needs to engage the subjectivity and tacit skills of the workforce at some level to ensure profitable production, for example through quality circles. Linked to the concept of alienation is that of *commodity fetishism*. The socially-constructed relations between labour and capital embodied in the organisation of production and exchange are experienced as an alien power and as the natural order of things. This is then reinforced by the dominant ideologies which proclaim, for example, that the operation of the market is determined by laws of supply and demand beyond human planning and control.

The problem with constructing a critical psychology from Marxism is that there are no adequate tools for understanding how alienated social relations are subjectively experienced and acted on by the individual. Marxism tends to deal with individuals only as bearers of economic categories such as labour and capital, and many social scientists influenced by Marxism have explicitly rejected any psychological explanation, as with Clegg and Dunkerley's (1980) work. It is certainly necessary to have an account of the material structures which shape our experiences and personalities. But this does not mean that people are simply 'bearers' or that attitudes and behaviour can be 'read off' from material circumstances (Leonard, 1984: 25). A purely structural analysis, even where it allows for human action and resistance, fails to get sufficiently inside those routine every-day experiences in which people react, adapt, modify and consent to work relations.

Knights and Collinson (1987) recognise that Marxist and labour process literatures tend to produce critiques of social structures and institutions that take as given the behavioural practices reproducing our concerns with identity. Such structures are both consequences of, and give rise to, the behavioural routines through which we generate secure identities for ourselves. Without accounts of identity, then, analysis of structures and the power relations and strategies through which they are maintained will always be incomplete. 'The absence of this social psychology from labour process theory means that it is unable to recognise how individuals . . . seek security either through control-ling, and/or subordinating themselves to, others', (Knights and Collinson, 1987: 171). In Marxist psychologies this often goes further, with the labelling of individuals who do not recognise their common class interests as manifesting false consciousness. This denies the validity of what people think or feel, merely because they do not correspond to a set of imputed interests they are supposed to have.

The dearth of an analysis of identity helps explain why Marxists have had a tendency to try a forced marriage with Freudianism. This led to the appropriation of ideas such as that of the unconscious and the dynamic model of personality (Schneider, 1975; Deleuze and Guattari, 1977), though for some this was always an attempt to reconcile the irrec-oncilable (O'Neill, 1985). More recently Ibanez and Ininguez' (1997) *Critical Social Psychology*, a series of readings, has claimed to bring the diverse trends of poststruc-turalist and postmodern critique together with debates over the possibilities of a Marxist psychology. However what the contributors show us mainly is that the appropriation of identity by relativists has meant that debate has focused on more fundamental issues.

> The more recent relativist fetish in social psychology simultaneously transforms and reproduces, celebrates and laments the impossibility of truth and the fragility of analysis. Relativism appears to be radical, but mirrors empiricism in traditional psychology (Parker, 1997: 164).

Parker, though willing to engage with postmodernism, is more concerned to promote a critical realism, but at the same time gets caught up in debates surrounding ego psychology and psychoanalysis. Others, such as Rosier (1997: 108) are suspicious of any attempts to produce compatibility between Marxism and postmodernism, while Reicher (1991) notes that the anti-essentialist stand of the relativists makes it difficult for them to admit the commonality of pluralism that they share with Marxists. The difficulty here is the lack of Marxism in the Marxist psychology, characterised by moves towards humanism rather than back to materialism. Any optimism in these readings over the possibility of real contributions to Marxist psychologies seems to stem from conceptions of collective identity and action. As Spears notes:

> Collective identity thus evokes a potentially powerful social reality beyond the individual and prevents agency dissolving into individualistic idealism. In these terms political resistance and change transcend the agency/structure dualism, by demonstrating the social dimensions of self, and the agency of social structure. (Spears, 1997: 19)

Parker and Spears' (1996) collection of readings gives a more comprehensive account of developments in radical and Marxist psychology. However, as indicated in the previous section, what may prove more fruitful in the long term would be a close consideration from Marxist perspectives of the social cognition/identity approach. For example Klandermans and Oegma's (1992, in Haslam, 2000: 280–1) schematic of social identity in different phases of collective action gives indications of how this might be begun.

What Marxist psychologies teach us is that the search for a secure identity or sense of solid self can be self-defeating. This is either because the individual occupies a range of positions or has interests that pull identity in different directions (Henriques *et al.*, 1984), or because identities, like commodities, become fetishised (Willmott, 1989), treated as a thing to which there is no alternative. This may lead individuals to a self-defeating project of continual reinvestment in the search for security, which in turn reproduces the very institutions that constrained their experiences in the first place. But at the same time, such perspectives can over-state trends of this kind. Employees' pursuit of identity, whether social, occupational, class or gender, has always been tied to formal and informal self-organisation in the labour process. Thus not only do we generate positive meaning and attachments in social and superordinate identities, the collective action and 'misbehaviour' generated becomes a continual problem for management, and the legitimation a problem for the continued development of technologies of regulation.

From critical theory to postmodernism

There is also a strand of critique which stems from the fact that psychological knowledge and technique continues to be an important operational element of organisational strategy regardless of the relative lack of success in generating intrinsic motivation and commitment. Psychological knowledge is assumed to provide both theoretical legitimacy and technical assistance to projects aimed at the control and utilisation of the 'human resource' in a rational-efficient manner. The 'real' psychology here is simply in the name: once you internalise the discourse constructing people as human resources, the rest is just window dressing.

Such a focus characterises much of the postmodern contribution to social psychology, drawing from the 'anything goes' methodology of Feyerabend (1975) and tradition of the Frankfurt School. The common theme in the latter, for example in the work of Horkheimer, Adorno, Marcuse and latterly Habermas, was the examination of the role of ideologies in the production of our knowledge of the social contexts in which we exist. This enabled a self-reflexive critique of how social psychology both operates to uphold the current social order, and at the same time works against the possibility of a socially-transforming discipline. The image produced (see Thompson and McHugh, 1995: 321–5, 385) is of an instrumentalised culture where psychology, in servicing and refining control procedures, acts to blind individuals to their capacities and lock them into dependence on commodity relations by presenting these as the inevitable 'natural order'. However desirable and probably necessary, a psychology based on this variant of critical theory will probably not provide a great deal of competition to current practices in terms of their influence on and role in HRM strategies. Indeed Spears (1997: 4) notes that the putative 'critical' paradigm in social psychology could not, in its 'isolated critique', challenge the 'paper mills of positivism' in terms of the production of practices. Criticism, when elevated to an emancipatory practice in itself, cannot compete with the packaged solutions and prescriptions of the mainstream, reducing further the chance that alternative conceptual frameworks will lead to effective practices.

This limitation is reproduced in more recent critiques influenced by postmodernism. In line with the project of reviewing and 'reconnecting' the current state of critical social psychology, the contributors to the Ibanez and Ininguez text discussed above raise questions and produce much in the way of methodological speculation, but in the end come no closer to any real integration. What we find is largely an iterative debate over realism versus relativism and their respective takes on social construction and political/ideological action.

> Just as realism can be seen to buttress positivist science and all of the sins of certainty and reification, so can relativism be seen to signal an absence of any political commitment or critique, or at least a solid platform (a foundation) on which to ground action. (Spears, 1997: 9)

In the end it is the lack of engagement with the traditional topics of social psychology that is most disappointing here. There is more concern for metatheory and the 'reflexively moderated criticism' (Potter, 1997: 48) of pseudo-methodologies such as *critical polytextualism*, than for critical evaluation of what mainstream and radical approaches might have to offer. Critical social psychology is rightly reflective of the desire to democratise research and transform subjects into participants, but has taken this so far that it loses all relevance to everyday experience: 'At best we can hope to have not helped to launch a textual chlorofluorocarbon – a compound that eats the very flux in which we live!' (Stainton-Rogers and Stainton-Rogers, 1997: 51)

What we have here is a desire for critique that at best does no harm and indeed is not capable of doing any, in that it is indecipherable to any but its acolytes. Much of critical social psychology has lost the desire to be critical of anything but itself and its own roots, reducing both structural and cognitive accounts to mere objects of self-reflexive literary criticism. We might see this as a case of cutting off your nose to spite your face, except that it is more one of cutting off your body to spite your head.

While the mainstream agenda in organisational behaviour continues with its traditional concerns, labour process theory and critical organisational psychology have grasped the nettle of subjectivity with some enthusiasm. This has been boosted by the previously-discussed rise of postmodern challenge and its meta-spirals of reflexive discourse. This is not to say that the values inherent in 'new thinking' (Burrell, 1994) are not welcome, and indeed they provide a crucial route for the incorporation of issues of subjectivity into organisational behaviour.

The focus on management found almost everywhere today produces an appearance that the workforce is steadily becoming unreachable as a subject of study, except perhaps in case studies of organisational 'success'. This is especially true of attempts to research what Corbett calls the 'dark side' of organisational behaviour in issues such as 'drug use, unethical behaviour, the secret workings of organisational cabals and violent behaviour' (1994: 5). Corporate discourses envision these as irrational and irrelevant to the construction of corporate harmony regardless of their role in the everyday experience and identity work of organisational participants. It remains the role of critical organisation theory to get beneath these surface appearances of organisational life.

In using identity as a linking concept, we are in no way claiming that it is the complete answer to understanding issues connected to the 'subjective factor'. Rather, it is one means of taking our understanding further. Nor do we claim that it is possible at this stage to use identity or any other means to produce an integrated critical social psychology. Unfortunately in redefining the agenda there is no new and improved magical ingredient that will wash away all the contradictions between these perspectives and provide us with a realistic, emancipatory paradigm to proceed with. What we have tried to do in Part II of the book is use the discussion of identity and subjectivity to address issues that arise in and across mainstream and critical theories and research, reassessing and integrating material within some consistent focus. The approach taken, though focusing mainly on the experiential level, is, we believe, compatible with the structural framework deriving from the perspectives informed by labour process and Weberian concepts in Part I.

25 Theory, Knowledge and Practice

Paradigm diversity or closure?

In previous chapters we have tried to set out the main general resources available for theorising about work organisations. Our own prime resources have been labour process theory, radical Weberianism and elements of critical social psychology. It would be difficult to argue that these and other components of a critical approach could, or even should, be easily or adequately synthesised into a unified and coherent explanation of work organisations.

However, despite differences and sometimes flatly opposed explanations, they can be drawn on as a resource for understanding the complexity of issues involved. In part, this is because there is some common ground. Referring to action theory and the more radical structuralist perspectives, Dunkerley and Salaman observe: 'Both seek to undermine the notion of inevitability in organisational structure; both seek to insert active human beings and groups and their values and interests into the complex processes which give rise to organisational structures' (1986: 93). Complementarity is often more feasible than synthesis, for example when labour process and radical Weberian analyses illuminate power and control through the discussion of means of production and of administration.

This rather pragmatic view of theorising will be opposed by those who believe that theories can and must operate from within hermetically sealed boxes. For one of the assumptions made by Burrell and Morgan (1979) about the paradigms with which we began the chapter is that they are incommensurable. In other words, their differences about knowledge and the world are so basic that theory can only be developed within each framework, which would then do battle with the others. As paradigms frame and define relevant interpretation, 'any observations that do not seem to fit in a particular approach belong in some other paradigm' (Ackroyd, 1994: 278). Ackroyd is rightly sceptical about the origins and consequences of the mentality of paradigm closure. Yet it is difficult for paradigms to 'speak' to one another, when they not only make different 'reality assumptions', but develop highly distinctive 'languages' of their own. It is, in fact, one of life's little ironies that many of those who believe most strongly in the constitutive power of language cannot write a sentence that can be understood without a dictionary, a gin and tonic and a great deal of patience. The problem of theoretical communication is compounded by the very different national traditions in organisation theory, as accounts of the past and present in North America (Aldrich, 1992) and Francophone analysis (Chanlat, 1994) reveal.

The paradigm wars have, however, moved on, with Clegg and Hardy observing that we now have a 'three-cornered debate' (1996: 5). The first position – incommensurability – is less popular than it was. This may be that the main defensive rationale for closure – that it would provide a space for alternative perspectives outside the functionalist-positivist orthodoxy – is less of an issue now that a variety of critical theories compete robustly in the lecture hall and through the pages of journals. Nevertheless, some paradigm warriors, notably Jackson and Carter (1991, 2000), continue to argue that communication is impossible because of the unique character of each paradigm, and dangerous given the 'intellectual imperialism' of the still-powerful orthodox voices. Such fears have been fed by some of those on the opposite side of the (non-existent) bridge. Pfeffer (1993) reasserts the need for paradigm consensus. Though there is an obvious pre-existing belief that knowledge is produced in a cumulative, developmental manner, capable of leading to agreement on methods, research questions and outcomes, Pfeffer's main worry is that organisational analysis will lose any influence it has unless it can demonstrate a degree of integration and unity that are the hallmarks of any 'mature science' (see also Donaldson, 1998).

Given the highly contested nature of organisational theory, such pleas will undoubtedly fall on deaf ears. Yet it is interesting to note that on both sides the arguments appear to be driven as much by expediency as by principle. A more positive pragmatism can be seen in a third and increasingly influential camp: those who assert the need for paradigm diversity, or multi-paradigm thinking. Gareth Morgan has certainly shifted his stance in this way and now talks about the need to 'harness the possibilities which they offer' (1990a: 27). A multi-paradigm perspective is primarily influenced by postmodernists trying to draw back from extreme relativism and seek greater dialogue. In part this may reflect the diverse and multi-faceted nature of reality which no single approach can grasp (Schultz and Hatch, 1996). Similarly, Kamoche argues that unless human resource management is analysed from within each paradigm, we may be 'ignoring the insights that other perspectives have been shown to yield' (1991: 13). A more concrete version of the same thing is offered by Hassard (1991), who interprets empirical data on the fire service in the UK through the paradigmatic 'eyes' of each of Burrell and Morgan's original quartet.

Such arguments are superficially attractive. Who, after all, could be against dialogue, or resist the call for greater 'democracy' in organisation theory? (Hassard, 1991: 296). In addition, there is no doubt that such exercises are fruitful individual exercises in collective and individual learning. But, as Parker and McHugh (1991) observed of Hassard's effort, the ability to hop between languages is not the same as demonstrating its analytical usefulness. The practice of multiple paradigm analysis tends to be closure by any other name, for each speaks from behind its own walls. Indeed, Hassard (1988) treats meta-theories as distinct language games in which we can be trained. The normal purpose of dialogue is to resolve issues or move beyond disagreements. This is difficult for postmodernists given their denial of any grounds against which to make judgements. It may be true, as Kamoche says, that paradigms generate different insights, but what if those insights are based on competing claims, for instance about the relative weight of hard and soft HRM in contemporary work-place practice? The relativist twist that everything is of equal value merely adds to the problem, and is open to the same objections that were raised by Reed of Morgan's use of metaphors: that we end up taking products down from the shelf as uncritical consumers, rather than promoting rigorous debate and research.

With these observations in mind, it seems to us that multi-paradigm or perspective approaches do not fully address the limits of incommensurability. To express a concern for the limits of multi-paradigm thinking is not to say that it is impossible or unnecessary for theories and theorists to engage with one another. This may not be as difficult as it appears. It is possible to have reservations about the strategic exchange theory of Watson (1994) or the discourse analysis of Pringle (1989), but still find their books to be exciting and revealing accounts of managerial and secretarial work. Sometimes it is necessary to get behind the different languages and explore whether writers are saying substantively similar things. As Ackroyd (1992, 1994) reminds us, a lot of the best research is not led by a commitment to paradigms, or is stimulated by 'boundary exchanges' between them. Ritzer (1975) also refers to the capacity of the classical sociological theories to bridge paradigms. Some differences can be put down to the level of analysis.

It is perfectly legitimate to have a more structural or a more micro emphasis on management or some other aspect of organisational life, or to creatively combine micro and macro. The key is not to analytically close off the possibilities of 'seeing' the other dimension, and to ensure that observations made about action and structure at different levels – workgroup, organisational, societal – are compatible with one another (Ackroyd, 2000). A multi-dimensional approach was one of the principles of good analysis set out in Chapter 1. To go further, it is possible to argue that such dimensions are sometimes most effectively addressed by different perspectives. Kellner (1999: 194) says that 'McDonaldization is a many-sided phenomenon and the more perspectives that we can bring to its analysis the better grasp of the phenomenon one will have'. This 'more the better' outlook may be overdoing it, but Kellner does persuasively argue that postmodern concepts can successfully be deployed to explain a later development of McDonaldization, when a modernist emphasis on mass production was complemented by a set of practices around consumption and management of global identities.

Our view is that there is an implicit fourth position in the paradigm wars: one that rejects incommensurability, but sees grounds, not only for dialogue, but for some kind of knowledge progression within a social-science framework. Reed (1993) notes that the pendulum has swung back from postmodern excesses towards recognition of historical continuities, narrative patterns and accumulated knowledge and procedures. Such a position admittedly leaves some of the most difficult problems unresolved. Theoretical pluralism is certainly here to stay, and that is welcome. However, the sharp theoretical disagreements will remain, not so much because of different paradigms, but because of rival claims being made about organisations and society. Ultimately the key problem is not paradigm, but reality incommensurability. For example, organisations, or at least particular types, cannot be at the same time becoming more and less bureaucratic. That might seem obvious, but the current fashion for relativism makes it difficult to take the issue any further. In other words, as we noted earlier, under the influence of postmodernism, a large number of scholars of organisation believe that it is impossible to either make truth claims or resolve them: 'Any interpretation is temporary, and specific to the discourse within which it is produced . . . the postmodern argument liberates me: my discourse is as valid as any other' (Coleman, 1991: 26–7).

In order to sustain this kind of thinking, postmodernism tends to treat science purely as 'conversation', whose logic of enquiry is rhetorical (Czarniawska, 1999: 10). Much of the force of this argument comes from a reading of the philosopher of science, Thomas Kuhn (1962, 1970 2nd edn), referred to at the start of this part of the book with reference to the idea of paradigms. He challenged the accepted, positivist view that science was based on the linear, patient, disinterested collection of facts, leading to hypotheses that were then tested or 'falsified' until the truth was discovered.

In the process of discovery, the protagonists are not merely comparing findings to the real world, but making judgements about what is acceptable in their own professional domain. Science, then, is not wholly rational, and is shaped by ideologies and power.

Given the undeniably greater ideological influences on subjects such as management and organisation studies, postmodernists were now able to argue that 'a plurality of legitimate and competing perspectives is to be expected in all sciences, but especially in the social ones' (Burrell, 1996: 648). This reading of Kuhn is, however, debatable. Kuhn argued that though observation and experiment drastically restrict the range of admissible belief, progress takes place in the state of knowledge, and that the distinction between the scientific and non-scientific is real. In short, scientific judgements involve the comparison of paradigms both with nature and with each other. Science may not be wholly rational, but it has a rational core.

This does *not* mean that the ability to make definitive statements about the natural world transfers to the social. The difference between the two is, after all, the starting-point of a critique of positivism that is shared by most organisational theorists. But having misrepresented science, postmodernists go on to do the same thing with social explanation. This is done primarily by constructing stereotypical oppositions. As Ackroyd and Fleetwood note:

> Here we arrive at the commonly held position that there are two basic perspectives on offer: either the world is objectively and unproblematically available and capable of being known by the systematic application of the empirical techniques common to positivism, or it is not knowable objectively at all; and in the place of claims to objectivity, we find that what is known is merely the product of discourses. (Ackroyd and Fleetwood, 2000: 3–4)

Our knowledge is inherently constrained and shaped by the social process of its production, but there is an alternative, middle ground between positivism and relativism. As a philosophy of science, *critical realism* accepts that social structures and the meanings actors attribute to their situation have to be recognised in the way we construct explanations. However, entities such as labour markets and gender relations exist independently of our perceptions and investigations of them (Bhaskar, 1989; Collier, 1994). As Ackroyd and Fleetwood (2000) argue, the ontological question, 'what exists?' is often confused with the epistemological one, 'how can we know what exists?' Hence, as our knowledge is bound up with our conceptions, the misleading conclusion is drawn that all that exists is our concepts or discourse. The difficulties of establishing absolute certainty should not be used to assert that we can make *no* 'truth claims'. In his defence of postmodern epistemology, Newton asks, 'How can we be sure that we have found "the real"?' (1996: 22). The short answer is that we cannot be totally sure, but that is a far cry from not knowing anything: realists 'want to hold that better and worse forms of knowledge exist and that there are reliable procedures for producing knowledge of things and events' (Ackroyd and Fleetwood, 2000: 3–4).

There cannot be an exact correspondence between reality and our representations of it, but good research aims to grasp the real with as much accuracy and complexity as is feasible. For example, we know that the vast majority of studies of empowerment demonstrate, through a variety of quantitative and qualitative methodologies, a massive gap between managerial claims of delegated decision-making and workplace outcomes. Similarly, and to return to an issue raised earlier, while politicians and generals devise forms of representation that make events such as the Gulf and Balkan wars difficult to grasp, as time unfolds and practices unravel, knowledge of what really happened on the ground does emerge into the public domain and becomes accepted as real (see Norris, 1992). Not only can we attempt to distinguish between representation and reality, it is fundamental to a healthy social science and democratic polity that we seek to do so.

When it is fashionable for social science to problematise everything, the focus is always on what we don't know rather than what we do. Whether organisational theory embraces critical realism or not, the question of addressing the real is inescapable. As we demonstrated in an earlier chapter, many postmodernists deny that it is possible to make truth claims, yet litter their discussions of contemporary organisational life with references to 'new realities', though often with quotation marks to indicate ironic distance. In other words, such theorists presuppose access to the real in order to make claims about the postmodern world (Kellner, 1988). If truth claims are inevitable, we need to have transparent, shared ways of discussing and resolving them, however partial and limited they may be. Postmodern epistemology may be 'liberating' for the individual theorist; but it is not very useful for the body of organisational theory.

However, the uses of knowledge are themselves disputed and contested. This seems a useful point to move towards a broader consideration of relations between management, theory and knowledge.

Management and theory

If we examine the interaction between theories and practices described in previous chapters, no mechanical and few direct relationships can be found. As with the approach to theorising by academics, organisational theories are a resource for practitioners, mostly of course employers and managers. Taylor and Mayo, for example, were great synthesisers of ideas and practices in a way that management found useful, not just as a guide to action but as a way of clarifying and legitimating their role. Yet theorists, and Taylor was a prime case, frequently rail against companies that do not swallow their whole package but rather apply them selectively. As Chandler (1977: 277) observes, 'No factory owner . . . adopted the system without modifying it'. This should come as no surprise. Employers and managers are pragmatists and, with some exceptions such as the Quaker-owned companies in the UK, seldom show any intrinsic interest in ideas in themselves, but rather for their 'use value' or, as one senior manager is quoted as saying in Gowler and Legge (1983: 213), 'There's no good ideas until there's cash in the till'.

This is one of the main reasons why, as Watson (1986: 2) correctly notes, there will never be a full and generally acceptable organisational or management theory. But it is not merely a case of a plurality of competing perspectives. The *partiality* of such theories is inherent in their use in control and legitimation processes. It is in the nature of theories of and for management that they give incomplete pictures. The perspectives and accompanying prescriptions only address aspects of the basic contradictions in capitalist and hierarchical work organisation. Therefore, at one level both theorists and practitioners respond within a continuum that has Taylor's minimum interaction model at one end and varieties of human relations at the other. Employers, of course, would like it both ways. Bendix gives an example of a management journal in 1910 calling for 'absolute authority as well as the willing co-operation of the workers' (1956: 272).

To some extent they can do this by *combining* theories and practices within the continuum. So we saw in Chapter 3 that human relations did not challenge Taylorism on its own terrain of job design and structures, but rather sought to deal with its negative effects and blind spots. That story of combination to deal with different dimensions of organisational experience is repeated through every period and sector. It is, of course, the case that management is not only trying to deal with the contradictory aspects of utilising human labour. Variations in strategy and practice reflect broader problems, such as harmonising different functions and sites of decision-making. But the resultant difficulties in managing the contradictions are similar: different routes to partial success and failure, as Hyman noted in Chapter 8.

It would be wrong to give the impression that the choice and use of theories are solely internal matters. This would reinforce the erroneous view that organisational theories are a historical sequence of 'models of man', the new naturally replacing the old as grateful managers learn to recognise the more sophisticated account of human needs and behaviour. Ideological conditions are influential, as evidenced by the spillover of entrepreneurial values from the political to the managerial sphere. Selectivity is also conditioned by *circumstances*, involving a number of key 'macro' and 'micro' dimensions. At the broadest level, organisational theories interact with the political economy of broad phases of capital accumulation. Taylorism and classical management perspectives emerged at a time when the scale and complexity of organisations and of markets were undergoing a fundamental change. The globalisation of markets and intensified competition, particularly from Japan, stimulated major shifts in management thinking in the more recent period. At a micro-level, the choices made by particular companies reflect even more complex factors. In particular, the *sector*, with its specific product market and labour market, technological framework and political context, is a vital consideration. Each country, too, has its own unique configuration of intellectual, social and economic conditions mediating the form and content of organisational change.

But just as there are global markets for products, so there are increasingly for ideas. This process is enhanced by the spread of pop-management and 'airport lounge' books, as the success of the excellence genre is testament. Unfortunately it reinforces the tendency for academics to form alliances with sections of management around particular perspectives or techniques as solve-all solutions. So much ideological investment is made in the process that the chosen vehicle can seldom meet the burden placed on it: hence burn-out, cynicism and later fortunate loss of memory, until, that is, a new solution comes along! But why do managers so often become locked in this fatal embrace? This is an underdeveloped area (Huczynski, 1993; Thompson and O'Connell Davidson, 1994; Furusten, 1999), but part of the explanation is that as an interest group, management requires a means of defining and expanding its activities. Referring to the spread of interest in corporate culture, Thackray comments, 'Culture is particularly seductive because it appears to open up a new frontier of managerial activism' (1986: 86). This option is particularly attractive to the personnel or human resource teams of large corporations, reminding us that the adoption of theories and practices is also likely to be affected by the internal fissures within the managerial labour process. With the demise of the great practitioner-theorists such as Taylor and Fayol, and the growth of more specialised academic production, management is also in a more *dependent* position.

But the attraction is also a reflection of the fact that the meaning of management is inseparable from the management of meaning (Gowler and Legge, 1983). Organisational theories become part of a language and a sub-culture through which management tries to understand itself and legitimate its activities to others, even when those ideological resources are used in a contradictory and rhetorical way. The essence of these points is that regardless of the social influences, organisational and management theory has a level of autonomy and its own rhythm of development. Regardless of the cycles of interest in ideas and proneness to fads and fashions, theories have their own very real effects. And as they are grappling with genuine problems it is possible to draw positive lessons, even for those of us who want to take the process of organisational change much further.

Beyond criticism?

Some time ago, Lex Donaldson described a new generation of radical commentators as demonstrating 'a supreme indifference in the fate of actual people in real organisations ... If there was a genuine interest, then this would indeed lead to wanting to know how to make organisations better' (1989: 250). He had a point, but spoilt it by arguing that betterment required valid knowledge about the effects of different structures and the systematic elimination of ambiguity in casual explanation. In other words, to do the right thing, theorists would have to enter into the closed paradigm of positivist-functionalism.

Nevertheless, critical scholars have had a problem about practice. In the 1960s and 1970s the view of management and rationality as neutral technique was replaced by an equally unhelpful hostility that failed to distinguish between particular forms of authority expressed through existing structures and systems, and the necessity for co-ordination and control of resources. Or, as Landry *et al*. put it:

> There is a vital distinction to be made between 'management' and those people who hold managerial positions, and 'management' as an assortment of integrative functions which are necessary in any complex organisation – planning, harmonising related processes, ensuring appropriate flows of information, matching resources to production needs, marketing, financial control, linking output to demand, etc. (Landry *et al*., 1985: 61)

This is part of an excellent dissection of the weaknesses of many community and other organisations in the radical movements in this period. Frequently they rejected any form of specialised division of labour, skills and expertise, and formal structures of decision-making, in favour of informal methods and rotation of all responsibilities. The result was seldom democratic or efficient. Even those collective and democratic forms of organisation, such as worker co-operatives, that have proved more durable have also remained small in number and relatively marginal in importance.

For these and other reasons, we now have something of a paradox: interest in critical perspectives on management and organisation has increased in inverse proportion to the actual existence of any practical alternatives. This could be problematic in that a critique of theoretical and practical orthodoxy that simply knocks everything down is limited and dangerous. To paraphrase Gouldner's comment for other purposes, critical social scientists have too often been morticians who bury people's hopes. We believe that it is important for critical theory not just to proclaim the limits of existing organisational forms and practices. Those constraints arising from dominant relations of wealth, power and control are real enough, as observation of the very partial progress of empowerment programmes or employee participation illustrates. But solely 'negative learning' implies an essence to work organisation under capitalism that denies it any significance.

The search for profitability involves innovations in technology, co-ordination of resources and utilisation of people's skills and knowledge that offer positive lessons relevant to any more democratic and egalitarian social order at work. This is not the same as the orthodox Marxist view, expressed by the founders of the Soviet Union, that a socialist society simply 'adds on' the techniques of capitalist work organisation to new property relations. Those techniques rather have to be added to, rethought and resituated in a new context of a more democratic and egalitarian economy. For job enrichment or teamworking, however flawed, are also indicators of the great potential of human labour to create more efficient and satisfying forms of work. To argue that all this is mere superficial window dressing is to fly in the face of the reality that we all find some work situations more creative and rewarding than others.

A further reason for not regarding the worlds of today and tomorrow as wholly sealed off from one another is that there is much to learn from the existing practices of employees. As Brecher (1978) rightly says, there is a massive 'hidden history of the workplace' which needs to be recognised and uncovered. That history is based on the self-organisation of workers trying to resist and transform work relations. Admittedly that was easier to see when craft labour was dominant and many workers genuinely felt that they could run the factories better than their bosses. Old-style movements for workers' control are no longer feasible in a world of transnationals, global production and semi-skilled labour. But there remains a wealth of untapped experience and knowledge in employees' informal job-controls and patterns of organisation (see Ackroyd and Thompson, 1999), as well as in progressive practice in the public sector (Goss, 2001).

Finally, we need to note that what Donaldson identified as armchair theorising has been given greater intellectual weight by the increased influence of postmodernism. It has become more difficult to move beyond criticism in circumstances where more and more academics have abandoned belief in 'narratives of progress' or progress through any type of rational action or design. In the previously referred to article on 'Critical Management Studies', Fournier and Grey (2000) argue that a stance against performative intent is one of its three defining boundaries. Performativity is taken to be that which is aimed at contributing to the effectiveness of management practice. In effect, given the nature of existing organisations and the postmodern rejection of progress, this quickly slips into *any* practice. So, they make a distinction between legitimately invoking notions of power, inequality and control, and the illegitimate invocation of efficiency, effectiveness and profitability. Yet why is this illegitimate in itself? In any feasible economic relations, some organisations or practices will be more effective and efficient than others, though how this is measured and what action follows from it will always be open to dispute.

Productivity matters to employees as well as managers. It is reasonable to argue that HRM or equal opportunity can be positive for efficiency, as long as this is not the only criterion on which progressive practices are advocated. While a reflexive attitude is a feature of any critical approach, hyper-reflexivity in which everything is deconstructed or problematised, while solving nothing, is ultimately arid and self-defeating. There are still practices and a world to remake.

References

ACAS (1988) *Labour Flexibility in Britain: The 1987 ACAS Survey*, ACAS Occasional Paper 41, London: ACAS.

Acker, J. (1990) 'Hierarchies, Jobs, Bodies: A Theory of Gendered Organizations', *Gender and Society*, 5: 390–407.

Acker, J. and Van Houten, D. R. (1992) 'Differential Recruitment and Control: The Sex Structuring of Organizations', in A. J. Mills and P. Tancred (eds) *Gendering Organisational Analysis*, London: Sage.

Acker, S. (1992) 'Gendering Organisational Theory', in A. J. Mills and P. Tancred (eds) *Gendering Organisational Analysis*, London: Sage.

Ackers, P. and Black, J. (1991) 'Paternalist Capitalism: An Organisation in Transition', in M. Cross and G. Payne (eds) *Work and the Enterprise Culture*, London: Falmer.

Ackroyd, S. (1992) 'Paradigms Lost: Paradise Gained? Notes on the Discovery of Meta-Theory in Organisational Analysis', in M. Reed and M. Hughes (eds) *Rethinking Organisation: New Directions in Organisation and Analysis*, London: Sage.

Ackroyd, S. (1994) 'Recreating Common Ground: Elements for Post-Paradigmatic Theories of Organisation', in J. Hassard and M. Parker (eds) *Towards a New Theory of Organizations*, London: Routledge.

Ackroyd, S. (1995) 'On the Structure and Dynamics of Some Small, UK-Based Information Technology Firms', *Journal of Management Studies*, 32. 2: 141–61.

Ackroyd, S. (2000) 'Organisational Constitution and Societal Structuration', in S. Ackroyd and S. Fleetwood (eds) *Realist Perspectives in Management and Organisation*, London: Routledge.

Ackroyd, S., Burrell, G., Hughes, S. and Whitaker, A. (1987) 'The Japanisation of British Industry', *Industrial Relations Journal*, Spring 1988, 9. 1.

Ackroyd, S. and Crowdy, P. A. (1990) 'Can Culture be Managed? Working with "Raw" Material: The Case of English Slaughtermen', *Personnel Review*, 19. 5: 12–13.

Ackroyd, S. and Fleetwood, S. (eds) (2000) *Realist Perspectives in Management and Organisation*, London: Routledge.

Ackroyd, S. and Lawrenson, D. (1996) 'Knowledge Work and Organisational Transformation: Analysing Contemporary Change in the Social Use of Expertise', in R. Fincham (ed.) *New Relationships in the Organised Professions*, Aldershot: Ashgate.

Ackroyd, S. and Proctor, S. (1998) 'British Manufacturing Organisation and Workplace Industrial Relations: Some Attributes of the New Flexible Firm', *British Journal of Industrial Relations*, 36. 2: 163–83.

Ackroyd, S. and Thompson, P. (1999) *Organisational Misbehaviour*, London: Sage.

Adair, J. (1979) *Action-Centred Leadership*, London: Gower.

Adams, J. L. (1979) *Conceptual Blockbusting*, 2nd edn, New York: W. W. Norton.

Adams, J. S. (1965) 'Injustice in Social Exchange', in L. Berkovitz, *Advances in Experimental Social Psychology, vol. 2*, New York: Academic Press.

Adkins, L. (1992) 'Sexual Work and the Employment of Women in the Service Industries', in A. Witz and M. Savage (eds) *Gender and Bureaucracy*, Oxford: Blackwell.

Adkins, L. and Lury, C. (1994) 'The Cultural and the Sexual and the Gendering of the Labour Market', paper presented to the BSA Conference on Sexualities in Their Social Context, University of Central Lancashire, March.

Adler, N. and Bartholomew, S. (1992) 'Managing Globally Competent People', *Academy of Management Executive*, 6. 3: 52–65.

Adler, N. J. (1994) 'Competitive Frontiers: Women Managing Across Borders', in N. J. Adler and D. N. Izraeli (eds) *Competitive Frontiers: Women Managers in a Global Economy*, Oxford: Blackwell.

Adler, N. J. and Izraeli, D. N. (1988) *Women in Management Worldwide*, Armonk, NY: M. E. Sharpe.

Adler, P. (1997) 'Work Organisation: From Taylorism to Teamwork', *Perspectives on Work*, 1. 3: 61–5.

Adler, P. and Borys, B. (1996) 'Two Types of Bureaucracy: Enabling and Coercive', *Administrative Science Quarterly*, 41: 61–89.

Adler, P. S. (1993) 'Time-and-Motion Regained', *Harvard Business Review*, Jan.–Feb.: 97–107.

Adler, P .S. (1995) 'Democratic Taylorism: The Toyota Production System at NUMMI', in S. Babson (ed.) *Lean Work: Empowerment and Exploitation in the Global Auto Industry*, Detroit, Mich.: Wayne State University Press.

Aglietta, M. (1979) *A Theory of Capitalist Regulation*, London: New Left Books.

Aichholzer, G. and Schienstock, G. (1985) 'Labour in Conflict: Between Capital Interests and the Maintenance of Identity', paper presented to the 20th Annual Meeting of the Canadian Sociology and Anthropology Association, University of Montreal.

Ajzen, I. (1988) *Attitudes, Personality and Behaviour*, Milton Keynes: Open University Press.

Ajzen, I. and Fishbein, M. (1980) *Understanding Attitudes and Predicting Social Behaviour*, Englewood Cliffs, NJ: Prentice Hall.

Albrow, M. (1973) 'The Study of Organizations –– Objectivity or Bias?' in G. Salaman and K. Thompson (eds) *People and Organizations*, Harlow: Longman.

Albrow, M. (1992) 'Sine Ira et Studio – or Do Organizations Have Feelings?', *Organisation Studies*, 13. 3: 313–29.

Alderfer, C. P. and Smith, K. K (1982) 'Studying Intergroup Relations Embedded in Organizations', *Administrative Science Quarterly*, 27: 35–65.

Aldrich, H. E. (1979) *Organizations and Environments*, Englewood Cliffs, NJ: Prentice Hall.

Aldrich, H. E. (1992) 'Incommensurable Paradigms? Vital Signs from Three Perspectives', in M. Reed and M. Hughes (eds) *Rethinking Organisation: New Directions in Organisation and Analysis*, London: Sage.

Aldrich, H. E. and Pfeffer, J. (1976) 'Environments and Organizations', in A. Inkeles *et al.* (eds) *Annual Review of Sociology 2*, Palo Alto: Annual Reviews.

Aldrich, H. E. and Stabler, U. (1987) 'Organisational Transformation and Trends in US Employment Relations', paper presented to the Labour Process Conference, Aston-UMIST.

Alker, L. and McHugh, D. (2000) 'Human Resource Maintenance? Organisational Rationales for the Introduction of Employee Assistance Programmes', *Journal of Managerial Psychology*, 15. 4: 303–23.

Allen, J. and Henry, N. (1994) 'Fragments of Industry and Employment: Contract Service Work and the Shift Towards Precarious Employment', paper presented to the Conference on Work, Employment and Society in the 1990s, September, University of Kent.

Allen, S. and Workowtiz, C. (1987) *Homeworking: Myths and Realities*, London: Macmillan.

Allport, F. H. (1991) *Pattern and Growth in Personality*, London: Holt-Rinehart and Winston.

Alvesson, M. (1985) 'A Critical Framework for Organisational Analysis', *Organisation Studies*, 6. 2: 117–38.

Alvesson, M. (1988) 'Management, Corporate Culture and Corporatism at the Company Level: A Case Study', *Economic and Industrial Democracy*, 13. 12: 347–67.

Alvesson, M. and Billing, Y. (1992) 'Gender and Organisations: Towards a Differentiated Understanding', *Organisation Studies*, 13. 12: 73–102.

Alvesson, M. and Billing, Y. (1997) *Understanding Gender and Organisations*, London: Sage.

Alvesson, M. and Deetz, S. (1996) 'Critical Theory and Postmodern Approaches to Organisational Studies', in S. Clegg, C. Hardy and W. Nord (eds) *Handbook of Organisation Studies*, London: Sage.

Alvesson, M. and Willmott, H. (1992) 'Critical Theory and Management Studies', in M. Alvesson and H. Willmott (eds) *Critical Management Studies*, London: Sage.

Amin, A. (1989) 'A Model of the Small Firm in Italy', in E. Goodman and J. Bamford (eds) *Small Firms and Industrial Districts in Italy*, New York: Routledge.

Amin, A. (1991) 'Flexible Specialisation and Small Firms in Italy: Myths and Realities', in A. Pollert (ed.) *Farewell to Flexibility?* Oxford: Blackwell.

Amsden, A. H. (1992) *Asia's Next Giant: South Korea and Late Industrialisation*, Oxford: Oxford University Press.

Anderson, N. R. and King, N. (1993) 'Innovation in Organizations', in C. L. Cooper and I. T. Robertson (eds) *International Review of Industrial and Organisational Psychology*, vol. 8, Chichester: Wiley.

Andreff, W. (1984) 'The International Centralisation of Capital and the Reordering of Work Capitalism', *Capital and Class*, 22: 58–80.

Anker, R. (1997) 'Theories of Occupational Segregation by Sex: An Overview', *International Labour Review*, 1366. 7: 315–40.

Anthony, P. D. (1990) 'The Paradox of the Management of Culture or "He Who Leads is Lost"', *Personnel Review*, 19. 4: 3–8.

Appelbaum, E., Bailey, T., Berg, P. and Kalleberg, A. L. (2000) *Manufacturing Advantage: Why High Performance Work Systems Pay Off*, Ithaca, NY: Cornell University Press.

Appelbaum, E. and Batt, R. (1994) *The New American Workplace: Transforming Work Systems in the United States*, Ithaca, NY: ILR Press.

Archibald, W. P. (1978) *Social Psychology as Political Economy*, Toronto: McGraw Hill Ryerson.

Argyle, M. (1974) *The Social Psychology of Work*, Harmondsworth: Penguin.

Argyris, A. (1967) 'Today's Problems with Tomorrow's Organizations', *Journal of Management Studies*, 4. 1: 31–55.

Argyris, C. (1960) *Understanding Organisational Behaviour*, Homewood, Ill.: Dorsey Press.

Argyris, C. (1976) 'Leadership, Learning and Changing the Status Quo', *Organizational Dynamics* (Winter): 29–43.

Argyris, C. and Schön, D. A. (1978) *Organisational Learning: A Theory of Action Perspective*, Reading, Mass.: Addison-Wesley.

Arias, M. E. (1993) 'MNCs, Organisational Models, and Local Firms in Developing Countries: The case of the Pharmaceutical Industry in Ecuador', paper presented to the 11th EGOS Colloquium, Paris.

Armistead, N. (1974) *Reconstructing Social Psychology*, Baltimore: Penguin.

Armstrong, M. (1987) 'Human Resource Management: A Case of the Emperor's New Clothes?' *Personnel Management*, 19. 8: 30–5.

Armstrong, P. (1984) 'Competition between the Organisational Professions and the Evolution of Management Control Strategies', in K. Thompson (ed.) *Work, Employment and Unemployment*, Milton Keynes: Open University Press.

Armstrong, P. (1986) 'Management Control Strategies and Inter-Professional Competition: The Cases of Accountancy and Personnel Management', in D. Knights and H. Willmott (eds) *Managing the Labour Process*, Aldershot: Gower.

Armstrong, P. (1987a) The Divorce of Productive and Unproductive Management', paper presented to the Labour Process Conference, Aston-UMIST.

Armstrong, P. (1987b) 'Engineers, Management and Trust', *Work, Employment and Society*, 1. 4: 421–40.

Armstrong, P. (1988) 'The Personnel Profession in the Age of Management Accountancy', *Personnel Review*, 17. 1: 25–31.

Armstrong, P. (1989) 'Management, Labour Process and Agency', *Work, Employment and Society*, 3. 3: 307–22.

Armstrong, P. (1991) 'The Influence of Michel Foucault on Historical Research in Accounting: An Assessment', paper presented to the Academy of Accounting Historians Research Methodology Conference, University of Mississippi, December.

Armstrong, P., Marginson, P., Edwards, P. and Purcell, J. (1994) 'Divisionalisation, Trade Unionism and Corporate Control: Findings from the Second Company-Level Industrial Relations Survey', paper presented to the 12th Annual International Labour Process Conference, Aston.

Arnold, J., Cooper, C. and Robertson, I. T. (1998) *Work Psychology: Understanding Human Behaviour in the Workplace*, London: Financial Times/Pitman.

Arnold, J., Robertson, I. T. and Cooper, C. (1991) *Work Psychology: Understanding Human Behaviour in the Workplace*, London: Pitman.

Aronoff, J. and Wilson, J. P. (1985) *Personality in the Social Process*, NJ: LEA.

Aronson, E. (1972) *The Social Animal*, San Francisco: W. H. Freeman.

Asch, S. E., Block, H. and Hertzmann, M. (1938) 'Studies in the Principles of Judgements of Attitudes: I. Two Basic Principles of Judgement', *Journal of Psychology*, 5: 219–51.

Atkinson, J. (1984) 'Manpower Strategies for Flexible Organizations', *Personnel Management*, August.

Atkinson, J. (1985) *IMS Report* no. 89, Institute of Management Studies, Sussex: Falmer.

Atkinson, J. and Gregory, D. (1986) 'A Flexible Future: Britain's Dual Labour Force', *Marxism Today*, April.

Augoustinos, M. and Walker, I. (1995) *Social Cognition: An Integrated Approach*, London: Sage.

Azjen, I. and Madden, T. J. (1986) 'Prediction Of Goal-Related Behaviour: Attitudes, Intentions, and Perceived Behavioural Control', *Journal of Experimental Social Psychology*, 22: 453–74.

Bacharach, S. B., Bamberger, P. A. and Sonnenstuhl, W. J. (1996) 'MAP's: Labor-Based Peer Assistance in the Workplace', *Industrial Relations*, 35. 2: 261–75.

Bacharach, S. B. and Lawler, E. J. (1980) *Power and Politics in Organizations*, London: Jossey Bass.

Bachrach, P. and Baratz, M. S. (1982) 'Two Faces of Power', *American Political Science Review*, 56: 947–52.

Badham, R. (1997) 'Towards an Ethnography of Politics', unpublished paper, University of Wollongong.

Bain, P. and Taylor, P. (2000) 'Entrapped by the Electronic Panopticon? Worker Resistance in Call Centres', *New Technology, Work and Employment*, 15. 1: 2–18.

Baines, S. (1999) 'Servicing the Media: Freelancing, Teleworking and "Enterprising" Careers', *New Technology, Work and Employment*, 14. 1: 18–31.

Baldamus, W. (1961) *Efficiency and Effort: An Analysis of Industrial Administration*, London: Tavistock.

Baldock, R. (1999) *The Last Days of the Giants?* London: Wiley.

Bales, R. F. (1950) *Interaction Process Analysis: A Method for the Study of Small Groups*, Reading, Mass.: Addison-Wesley.

Bandler, R. and Grinder, J. (1976) *The Structure of Magic II*, Palo Alto, Calif.: Science and Behaviour Books.

Bandura, A. (1977) *Social Learning Theory*, Englewood Cliffs, NJ: Prentice Hall.

Bandura, A. (1986) *Social Foundations of Thought and Action: A Social Cognitive Theory*, Englewood Cliffs, NJ: Prentice Hall.

Bandura, A. and Walters, R. H. (1963) *Social Learning and Personality Development*, New York: Holt, Rinehart and Winston.

Banton, R., Clifford, P., Frosh, S., Lousada, J. and Rosenthall, J. (1985) *The Politics of Mental Health*, London: Macmillan.

Barham, K. and Rassam, C. (eds) (1989) *Shaping the Corporate Future: Leading Executives Share Their Vision and Strategies*, London: Unwin Hyman.

Baritz, L. (1960) *The Servants of Power*, Middletown: Wesleyan University Press.

Barker, J. R. (1993) 'Tightening the Iron Cage: Concertive Control in Self-Managing Teams', *Administrative Science Quarterly*, 38: 408–37.

Barker, J. R. (1999) *The Discipline of Teamwork: Participation and Concertive Control*, London: Sage.

Barker, R. and Roberts, H. (1993) 'The Uses of the Concept of Power', in D. Morgan and L. Stanley (eds) *Debates in Sociology*, Manchester: Manchester University Press.

Barley, S. (1996) *The New World of Work*, pamphlet, British–North American Committee: London.

Barley, S. R. and Kunda, G. (1992) 'Design and Devotion: Surges of Rational and Normative Ideologies of Control in Managerial Discourse', *Administrative Science Quarterly*, 37: 363–99.

Barnard, C. (1938) *The Functions of the Executive*, Cambridge, Mass.: Harvard University Press.

Baron, R. A. and Byrne, D. (1997) *Social Psychology*, 8th edn, Needham Heights, Mass.: Allyn and Bacon.

Bartlett, C. and Goshal, S. (1990a) *Managing Across Borders*, Boston: Harvard University Press.

Bartlett, C. and Goshal, S. (1990b) 'The Multinational Corporation as an International Network', *Academy of Management Review*, 4.

Bartlett, C. and Goshal S. (1992) 'What is a Global Manager?' *Harvard Business Review*, Sept.–Oct.: 124–32.

Bass, B. M. (1985) *Leadership and Performance Beyond Expectations*, New York: Free Press.

Basset, P. (1989) 'All Together Now', *Marxism Today*, June.

Batt, R. (1999) 'Work Organisation, Technology and Performance in Customer Service and Sales', *Industrial and Labour Relations Review*, 52. 4: 539–64.

Baum, J. A. C. (1995) 'The Changing Basis of Competition in Organisational Populations: The Manhattan Hotel Industry 1898–1990', *Social Forces*, 74: 177–205.

Bavelas, A. (1950) 'Communication Patterns in Task-Oriented Groups', *Journal of the Acoustical Society of America*, 22: 725–30.

Beck, U. (1992) *Risk Society: Towards a New Modernity*, London: Sage.

Becker, G. (1985) 'Human Capital, Effort and the Sexual Division of Labour', *Journal of Labor Economics*, 3. 2: 33–58.

Becker, H. S., Geer, B., Hughes, E. C. and Strauss, A. (1963) *Boys in White*, Chicago: University of Chicago Press.

Beech, H. R., Burns, L. E. and Sheffield, B. F. (1982) *A Behavioural Approach to the Management of Stress: A Practical Guide to Techniques*, Chichester: Wiley.

Beer, M., Spector, B., Lawrence, P., Quin Mills, D. and Walton, R. (1985) *Human Resource Management: A General Manager's Perspective*, Glencoe, Ill.: Free Press.

Beirne, M., Ramsay, H. and Pantelli, N., (1998) 'Developments in Computing Work: Control and Contradiction in the Software Labour Process', in P. Thompson and C. Warhurst (eds) *Workplaces of the Future*, London: Macmillan.

Belbin, M. (1981) *Management Teams*, London: Heinemann.

Bell, D. (1960) *The End of Ideology*, New York: Collier Macmillan.

Bell, D. (1973) *The Coming of Post-Industrial Society*. Harmondsworth: Penguin.

Bellaby, P. and Orribor, P. (1977) 'The Growth of Trade Union Consciousness Among General Hospital Nurses', *Sociological Review*, 25.

Benders, J. and Huigen, F. (1999) *On the Incidence of Group Work: Results from a European Survey*, EPOC Report, Dublin

Bendix, R. (1956) *Work and Authority in Industry*, New York: Harper and Row.

Beneria, L. (1995) 'Response: The Dynamics of Globalization', *Labor and Working Class History*, 47: 45–52.

Benne, K. D. and Sheats, P. (1948) 'Functional Roles of Group Members', *Journal of Social Science*, Spring: 41–9.

Benson, J. K. (1977) 'Innovation and Crisis in Organisational Analysis', in J. K. Benson (ed.) *Organisational Analysis: Critique and Innovation*, London: Sage.

Benson, J. K. (ed.) (1977) *Organisational Analysis: Critique and Innovation*, London: Sage.

Berg, M. (1985) *The Age of Manufactures*, London: Fontana.

Berger, P. L. and Luckman, T. (1967) *The Social Construction of Reality*, London: Allen Lane.

Berggren, C. (1993) 'Lean Production: The End of History?', *Work, Employment and Society*, 7. 2: 163–88.

Berggren, C. (1996) 'ABB: Local Presence and Cross-Border Learning within a Multi-national', in J. Storey (ed.) *Blackwell Cases in Human Resource Management and Change*, Oxford: Blackwell.

Berkeley Thomas, A. (1993) *Controversies in Management*, London: Routledge.

Berle, A. A. and Means, G. C. (1935) *The Modern Corporation and Private Property*, New York: Macmillan.

Berridge, J. Cooper, C. L. and Highley-Marchington, C. (1997) *Employee Assistance Programmes and Workplace Counselling*, New York: Wiley.

Best, M. (1990) *The New Competition: Institutions of Industrial Restructuring*, Cambridge, Mass.: Harvard University Press.

Beynon, H. (1975) *Working for Ford*, Wakefield: E. P. Publishing.

Beynon, H. (1987) 'Dealing with Icebergs: Organisation, Production and Motivation in the 1990s', *Work, Employment and Society*, 1. 2: 247–59.

Bhaskar, R. (1989) *Reclaiming Reality*, London: Verso.

Biddle, B. J. (1979) *Role Theory: Expectations, Identities and Behaviours*, London: Academic Press.

Biewener, J. (1997) 'Downsizing and the New American Workplace: Rethinking the High Performance Paradigm', *Review of Radical Political Economics*, 29. 4: 1–22.

Biggart, N. W. (1989) *Charismatic Capitalism: Direct Selling Organizations in America*, London: University of Chicago Press.

Birchall, D. and Lyons, L. (1995) *Creating Tomorrow's Organisation*, London: Financial Times/Pitman.

Bittner, E. (1967) 'The Police on Skid Row: A Study of Peace Keeping', *American Sociological Review*, 32. 5: 699–715.

Bittner, E. (1973) 'The Concept of Organisation', in G. Salaman and K. Thompson (eds) *People and Organizations*, Harlow: Longman.

Blackler, F. (1982) 'Organisational Psychology', in S. Canter and D. Canter (eds) *Psychology in Practice: Perspectives in Professional Psychology*, Chichester: Wiley.

Blackler, F. (1995) 'Knowledge, Knowledge Work and Organizations: An Overview and Interpretation', *Organisation Studies*, 16. 6: 1021–46.

Blackler, F. and Shimmin, S. (1984) *Applying Psychology in Organizations*, London: Methuen.

Blair, H., Taylor, S. G. and Randle, K. (1998) 'A Pernicious Panacea: A Critical Evaluation of Business Process Re-engineering', *New Technology, Work and Employment*, 13. 2: 116–27.

Blakemore, K. and Black, R. (1996) *Understanding Equal Opportunities Policies*, London: Prentice Hall/Harvester Wheatsheaf.

Blau, G., Linnehan, F., Brooks, A. and Hoover, D. K. (1993) 'Vocational Behaviour 1990–1992: Personnel Practices, Organisational Behaviour, Workplace Behaviour and Industrial/Organisational, Measurement Issues', *Journal of Vocational Behaviour*, 43: 133–97.

Blau, P. M. (1955) *The Dynamics of Bureaucracy*, Chicago: University of Chicago Press.

Blau, P. M. (1964) *Exchange and Power in Social Life*, New York: Wiley.

Blau, P. M. (1970) 'A Formal Theory of Differentiation in Organizations', *American Sociological Review*, 35: 201–18.

Blau, P. M. and Schoenherr, R. A. (1971) *The Structure of Organizations*, New York: Basic Books.

Blau, P. M. and Scott, W. (1963) *Formal Organizations: A Comparative Approach*, London: Routledge and Kegan Paul.

Blauner, R. (1964) *Alienation and Freedom*, Chicago: University of Chicago Press.

Bluestone, B. and Bluestone, I. (1992) *Negotiating the Future: A Labor Perspective on American Business*, New York: Basic Books.

Blyton, P. and Turnbull, P. (1992) *Reassessing Human Resource Management*, London: Sage.

Blyton, P. and Turnbull, P. (1998) *The Dynamics of Employee Relations*, 2nd edn, London: Macmillan.

Boddy, D. and Buchanan, D. (1992) *Take the Lead: Interpersonal Skills for Project Managers*, London: Prentice Hall.

Bolman, L. G. and Deal, T. E. (1994) 'The Organisation as Theater', in H. Tsoukas (ed.) *New Thinking in Organisational Behaviour*, London: Butterworth and Heinemann.

Bologh, R. (1990) *Love or Greatness: Max Weber and Masculine Thinking -- A Feminist Inquiry*, London: Unwin Hyman.

Bolton, S. (2000) 'Emotion Here, Emotion There, Emotional Organisations Everywhere', *Critical Perspectives on Accounting*, 11: 155–71.

Bordieu, P. (1977) *Towards a Theory of Action*, Cambridge: Cambridge University Press.

Bordieu, P. (1994) 'Structures, Habitus and Practices', in *Polity Reader in Social Theory*, Cambridge: Polity.

Boreham, P. (1980) 'The Dialectic of Theory and Control: Capitalist Crisis and the Organisation of Labour', in D. Dunkerley and G. Salaman (eds) *Control and Ideology in Organizations*, Milton Keynes: Open University Press.

Boreham, P. (1992) 'The Myth of Post-Fordist Management: Work Organisation and Employee Discretion in Seven Countries', *Employee Relations*, 14. 2: 13–24.

Boulding, K. (1953) *The Organisational Revolution*, New York: Harper and Brothers.

Bowles, M. L. and Coates, G. (1993) 'Image and Substance: The Management of Performance as Rhetoric or Reality?' *Personnel Review*: 3–21.

Boyer, R. and Drache, D. (eds) (1996) *States Against Markets: The Limits to Globalisation*, London: Routledge.

Boyne, R. and Rattsani, A. (eds) (1990) *Postmodernism and Society*, London: Macmillan.

Bradley, H. (1986) 'Work, Home and the Restructuring of Jobs', in K. Purcell, S. Wood, A. Watson and S. Allen (eds) *The Changing Experience of Employment, Restructuring and Recession*, London: Macmillan.

Bradley, H. (1996) *Fractured Identities: Changing Patterns of Inequality*, Oxford: Polity.

Bramble, T. (1988) 'The Flexibility Debate: Industrial Relations and the New Management Production Practices', *Labour and Industry*, 1. 2.

Bramble, T., Parry, K. and O'Brien, E. (1996) 'Middle Management in an Era of Corporate Restructuring: A Case Study of Retailing', *Labour and Industry*, 7. 2: 79–102.

Brannen, P. (1983) *Authority and Participation in Industry*, London: Batsford.

Braverman, H. (1974) *Labor and Monopoly Capital: The Degradation of Work in the Twentieth Century*, New York: Monthly Review Press.

Brazier, M., Lovercy, J., Moran, M. and Potton, M. (1993) 'Falling From a Tightrope: Doctors and Lawyers between the Market and the State', *Political Studies*, 92: 197–213.

Breakwell, G. M. (1986) *Coping with Threatened Identities*, London: Methuen.

Breakwell, G. M. (1987) 'Identity', in H. Beloff and A. M. Colman (eds) *Psychology Survey 1987*, Leicester: British Psychological Society.

Brecher, J. (1978) 'Uncovering the Hidden History of the American Workplace', *Review of Radical Political Economics*, 10. 4, Winter.

Brenner, O. C., Tomkiewicz, J. and Schien, V. E. (1989) 'The Relationship Between Sex Role Stereotypes and Requisite Management Characteristics Revisited', *Academy of Management Journal*, 32. 3: 662–69.

Brewis, J. and Kerfoot, D. (1994) 'Selling Our "Selves"? Sexual Harassment and the Intimate Violations of the Workplace', paper presented to the BSA Conference Sexualities in their Social Context, University of Central Lancashire, March.

Briggs, P. (1987) 'The Japanese at Work: Illusions of the Ideal', paper presented to the Conference on Japanisation of British Industry, UMIST, also in *Industrial Relations Journal*, Spring 1988, 19. 1.

Briner, R. B. and Reynolds, S. (1993) 'Bad Theory and Bad Practice In Occupational Stress', *Occupational Psychologist*, 19: 8–13.

Broad, G. (1987) 'Beyond Quality Circles: A Critical Review of Employee Participation in Japanese Industry', paper presented to the Conference on Japanisation of British Industry, UMIST.

Brotherton, C. (1999) *Social Psychology and Management: Issues for a Changing Society*, Milton Keynes: Open University Press.

Brown, A. and Keep, E. (1999) *Review of Vocational Education and Training Research in the United Kingdom*, SKOPE, University of Warwick.

Brown, G. (1977) *Sabotage*, Nottingham: Spokesman.

Brown, H. (1980) 'Work Groups', in G. Salaman and K. Thompson (eds) *Control and Ideology in Organizations*, Milton Keynes: Open University Press.

Brown, R. (1965) *Social Psychology*, London: Collier-Macmillan.

Brown, R. (1992) *Understanding Organizations: Theoretical Perspectives in Industrial Sociology*, London: Routledge.

Browne, K. R. (1998) *Divided Labour: An Evolutionary View of Women at Work*, London: Weidenfeld and Nicholson.

Brubaker, R. (1984) *The Limits of Rationality: An Essay on the Social and Moral Thought of Max Weber*, London: Allen and Unwin.

Bruner, J. S. (1968) *Towards a Theory of Instruction*, New York: Norton.

Bryman, A. (1984) 'Organisation Studies and the Concept of Rationality', *Journal of Management Studies*, 21: 394–404.

Bryman, A. (1993) 'The Nature of Organisation Structure: Constraint and Choice', in D. Morgan and L. Stanley (eds) *Debates in Sociology*, Manchester: Manchester University Press.

Buchanan, D. (1986) 'Management Objectives in Technical Change', in D. Knights and H. Willmott (eds) *Managing the Labour Process*, Aldershot: Gower.

Buchanan, D. (2000) 'An Eager and Enduring Embrace: The Ongoing Rediscovery of Teamworking as a Management Idea', in S. Proctor and F. Mueller (eds) *Teamworking*, London: Macmillan.

Buchanan, D. and Badham, R. (1999) *Power, Politics and Organisational Change: Winning the Turf Game*, London: Sage.

Buchanan, D. and Huczynski, A. (1985) *Organisational Behaviour: An Introductory Text*, London: Prentice Hall International.

Buford, B. (1991) *Among the Thugs*, London: Secker.

Burawoy, M. (1979) *Manufacturing Consent: Changes in the Labour Process Under Monopoly Capitalism*, Chicago: University of Chicago Press.

Burawoy, M. (1985) *The Politics of Production*, London: Verso.

Burchell, B. J., Day, D., Hudson, M., Ladipo, D., Mankelow, R., Nolan, J. P., Reed, H., Wichert, I. C. and Wilkinson, F. (1999) *Job Insecurity and Work Intensification*, London: Joseph Rowntree Foundation.

Burchell, S., Clubb, C. and Hopwood, A. (1985) 'Accounting in its Social Context: Towards a History of Value-Added in the United Kingdom', *Accounting, Organizations and Society*, 10. 4: 381–413.

Burgess, J. and Strachan, G. (1999) 'The Expansion in Non-Standard Employment in Australia and the Extension of Employers' Control', in A. Felstead and N. Jewson (eds) *Global Trends in Flexible Labour*, London: Macmillan.

Burgess, S. and Rees, H. (1996) 'Job Tenure in Britain 1975–92', *Economic Journal*, 106. 435: 334–44.

Burgoyne, J. G. (1993) 'The Competence Movement: Issues, Stakeholders and Prospects', *Personnel Review*, 22. 6: 6–13.

Burke, R. J. (1997) 'Are Families Damaging to Careers?' *Women in Management Review*, 12. 8: 320–4.

Burnham, J. (1945) *The Managerial Revolution*, Harmondsworth: Penguin.

Burns, J. M. (1978) *Leadership*, New York: Harper and Row.

Burns, T. (1982) 'A Comparative Study of Administrative Structure and Organisational Processes in Selected Areas of the National Health Service' (SSRC Report, HRP 6725), London: Social Science Research Council.

Burns, T. and Stalker, G. M. (1961) *The Management of Innovation*, London: Tavistock.

Burrell, G. (1980) 'Radical Organisation Theory', in D. Dunkerley and G. Salaman (eds) *The International Yearbook of Organisation Studies 1979*, London: Routledge and Kegan Paul.

Burrell, G. (1988) 'Modernism, Post Modernism and Organisational Analysis: The Contribution of Michel Foucault', *Organisation Studies*, 9. 2: 221–35.

Burrell, G. (1992) 'Sex and Organizations', in A. J. Mills and P. Tancred (eds) *Gendering Organisational Analysis*, London: Sage.

Burrell, G. (1994) 'Foreword' to H. Tsoukas (ed.) *New Thinking in Organisational Behaviour*, London: Butterworth and Heinemann.

Burrell, G. (1996) 'Normal Science, Paradigms, Metaphors, Discourses and Genealogies of Analysis', in S. Clegg, C. Hardy and W. Nord (eds) *Handbook of Organisation Studies*, London: Sage.

Burrell, G. and Morgan, G. (1979) *Sociological Paradigms and Organisational Analysis*, London: Heinemann.

CAITS (1986) *Flexibility, Who Needs It?* London: CAITS.

Calás, M. and Smircich, L. (1992) 'Rewriting Gender into Organisation Theorising: Directions from Feminist Perspectives', in M. Reed and M. Hughes (eds) *Rethinking Organisation: New Directions in Organisation and Analysis*, London: Sage.

Calás, M. B. and Smircich, L. (1996) 'From the "Woman's" Point of View: Feminist Approaches to Organisation Studies', in S. Clegg and C. Hardy (eds) *Handbook on Organisations*, London: Sage.

Calder, B. J. (1977) 'An Attribution Theory of Leadership', in B. M. Staw and G. R. Salancik (eds) *New Directions in Organisational Behaviour*, Chicago: St. Clair.

Callaghan, G. and Thompson, P. (2001) 'Edwards Revisited: Technical Control and Worker Agency in Call Centres', *Economic and Industrial Democracy*, 22: 13–37.

Callaghan, G. and Thompson, P. (forthcoming, 2002) 'We Recruit Attitude: The Selection and Shaping of Call Centre Labour', *Journal of Management Studies* (March).

Callan Hunt, G. (1992) 'Men and Women in Nontraditional Jobs: An Exploratory Study of Men in the Pink Ghetto', *Association of Management*, August.

Callinicos, A. (1989) *Against Postmodernism: A Marxist Critique*, Cambridge: Polity.

Campbell, A. and Currie, B. (1987) 'Skills and Strategies in Design Engineering', paper presented to the Conference on the Labour Process, Aston-UMIST.

Campbell, G. (1994) 'The Languages of Workplace Reform', paper presented to the 12th International Labour Process Conference, Aston.

Campbell, J. P. and Dunnette, M. D. (1968) 'Effectiveness of T-Group Experiences in Managerial Training and Development', *Psychological Bulletin*, 70: 73–104.

Cappelli, P. (1995) 'Rethinking Employment', *British Journal of Industrial Relations*, 33. 4: 563–602.

Carchedi, G. (1977) *On the Economic Identification of the Middle Classes*, London: Routledge and Kegan Paul.

Carey, A. (1967) 'The Hawthorne Studies: A Radical Criticism', *American Sociological Review*, 32: 403–16.

Carroll, M. (1996) *Workplace Counselling*, London: Sage.

Carroll, M. and Walton, M. (1997) *Handbook of Counselling in Organisations*, London: Sage.

Carter, P. and Jeffs, P. (1992) 'The Hidden Curriculum: Sexuality in Professional Education', in P. Carter, T. Jeffs and M. Smith (eds) *Changing Social Work and Welfare*, Milton Keynes: Open University Press.

Carter, R. (1985) *Capitalism, Class Conflict and the New Middle Class*, London: Routledge and Kegan Paul.

Casey, B. (1991) 'Survey Evidence on Trends in "Non-Standard" Employment', in A. Pollert (ed.) *Farewell to Flexibility?*, Oxford: Blackwell.

Casey, C. (1995) *Work, Self and Society*, London: Routledge.

Casey, C. (1996) 'Corporate Transformations: Designer Culture, Designer Employees and "Post-Occupational" Solidarity', *Organization*, 3. 3: 317–39.

Castells, M. (1996) *The Rise of the Network Society: The Information Age – Economy*, Oxford: Blackwell.

Cattell, J. M., Eber, H. W. and Tatsuoka, M. M. (1970) *Handbook for the 16PF*, Colombia: IPAT.

Cave, K. (1997) 'Close to the Core: Zero-Hours Working Surveyed', *Flexible Employment*, 2. 3: 21–3.

Cavendish, R. (1982) *Women on the Line*, London: Routledge and Kegan Paul.

Chandler, A. (1962) 'Strategy and Structure: Chapters in the History of the Industrial Enterprise', Cambridge, Mass.: MIT Press.

Chandler, A. (1977) *The Visible Hand*, Cambridge, Mass.: Harvard University Press.

Chandler, A. D. (1990) *Scale and Scope: the Dynamics of Industrial Capitalism*, Cambridge, Mass.: Harvard University Press.

Change Partnership (1999) *The Changing Culture of Leadership: Women Leaders' Voices*, London: Tavistock Institute.

Chanlat, J-F. (1994) 'Francophone Organisational Analysis (1950–1990): An Overview', *Organisation Studies*, 15. 1: 47–80.

Chell, E. (1993) *The Psychology of Behaviour in Organisations*, 2nd edn, Basingstoke: Macmillan.

Cheng, C. (ed.) (1996) *Masculinities in Organizations*, London: Sage.

Cherrington, D. J. (1989) *Organisational Behaviour: The Management of Individual and Organisational Performance*, Boston: Allyn and Bacon.

Cherry, L. (1978) 'On the Real Benefits of Eustress', *Psychology Today*, March: 60–70.

Child, J. (1969) *British Management Thought*, London: Allen and Unwin.

Child, J. (1972) 'Organisation Structure, Environment and Performance: The Role of Strategic Choice', *Sociology*, 6. 1: 1–22.

Child, J. (1984) *Organisation: A Guide to Problems and Practice*, 2nd edn, London: Harper and Row.

Child, J. (1985) 'Managerial Strategies, New Technology and the Labour Process', in D. Knights, H. Wilmott and D. Collinson (eds) *Job Redesign: Critical Perspectives on the Labour Process*, London: Gower.

Child, J. (1987) 'Organisational Design for Advanced Manufacturing Technology', in T. D. Wall, C. W. Clegg and N. J. Kemp (eds) *The Human Side of Advanced Manufacturing Technology*, Chichester: Wiley.

Child, J., Fores, M., Glover, I. and Lawrence, P. (1983) 'Professionalism and Work Organisation: A Reply to Kevin McCormack', *Sociology*, 20. 4: 607–14.

Child, J. and Rodrigues, S. (1993) 'The Role of Social Identity in the International Transfer of Knowledge through Business Ventures', paper presented to the 11th EGOS Colloquium, Paris, July.

Child, J. and Smith, C. (1987) 'The Context and Process of Organisational Transformations – Cadbury Limited in its Sector', *Journal of Management Studies*, 24. 6: 565–93.

Chorover, S. L. (1979) *From Genesis to Genocide: Meaning of Human Nature and the Power of Behaviour Control*, Cambridge, Mass.: MIT Press.

Cialdini, R. B. (1988) *Influence: Science and Practice*, 2nd edn, London: Harper Collins.

Cialdini, R.B. (2001) *Influence: Science and Practice*, 4th edn, Boston, Mass.: Allyn and Bacon.

Cicourel, A. V. (1968) *The Social Organisation of Social Justice*, New York: Free Press.

Clairmonte, F. and Cavanagh, J. (1981) *The World in Their Web: The Dynamics of Textile Multinationals*, London: Zed.

Clark, D. D. and Hoyle, R. (1988) 'A Theoretical Solution to the Problem of Personality–Situational Interaction', *Personality and Individual Differences*, 9: 133–8.

Clark, H., Chandler, J. and Barry, J. (1994) *Organisations and Identities*, London: Chapman and Hall.

Clarke, T. and Clegg, S. (1998) *Changing Paradigms: The Transformation of Management Knowledge for the 21st Century*, London: Harper Collins Business.

Clawson, D. (1980) *Bureaucracy and the Labour Process: The Transformation of US Industry, 1860–1920*, New York: Monthly Review Press.

Clegg, S. (1977) 'Power, Organisation Theory, Marx and Critique', in S. Clegg and D. Dunkerley (eds) *Critical Issues in Organizations*, London: Routledge and Kegan Paul.

Clegg, S. (1988) 'The Good, the Bad and the Ugly', *Organisation Studies*, 9. 1: 7–13.

Clegg, S. (1989) *Frameworks of Power*, London: Sage.

Clegg, S. (1990) *Modern Organizations: Organisation Studies in the Postmodern World*, London: Sage.

Clegg, S., Boreham, P. and Dow, G. (1987) *Class, Politics and the Economy*, London: Routledge and Kegan Paul.

Clegg, S. and Dunkerley, D. (eds) (1977) *Critical Issues in Organizations*, London: Routledge and Kegan Paul.

Clegg, S. and Dunkerley, D. (1980) *Organisation, Class and Control*, London: Routledge and Kegan Paul.

Clegg, S. R. and Hardy, C. (1996) 'Introduction: Organisations, Organisation, Organising', in *Handbook on Organisations*, London: Sage.

Clegg, S. and Higgins, G. (1987) 'Against the Current: Organisational Sociology and Socialism', *Organisation Studies*, 8. 3: 201–21.

Clutterbuck, D. (ed.) (1985) *New Patterns of Work*, Aldershot: Gower.

Cochrane, A. and Dicker, R. (1979) 'The Regeneration of British Industry: Jobs and the Inner City', in Community Development Project, *The State and the Local Economy*, Newcastle.

Cockburn, C. (1983) *Brothers: Male Dominance and Technological Change*, London: Pluto.

Cockburn, C. (1985) *Machineries of Dominance: Men, Women and Technical Know-How*, London: Pluto.

Cockburn, C. (1990) 'Men's Power in Organizations: "Equal Opportunities" Intervenes', in D. Morgan (ed.) *Man, Masculinities and Social Theory*, London: Unwin Hyman.

Cockburn, C. (1991) *In the Way of Women: Men's Resistance to Sex Equality in Organizations*, London: Macmillan.

Cohen, S. (1973) *Folk Devils and Moral Panics*, London: Paladin.

Cohen, S. and Taylor, L. (1978) *Escape Attempts: The Theory and Practice of Resistance to Everyday Life*, Harmondsworth: Pelican.

Cohen, Sheila (1987) 'A Labour Process to Nowhere?' *New Left Review*, 107: 34–50.

Coleman, G. (1991) *Investigating Organisations: A Feminist Approach*, Bristol: SAUS.

Colgan, F. and Ledwith, S. (1996) 'Women as Change Agents', in S. Ledwith and F. Colgan (eds) *Women in Organisations: Challenging Gender Politics*, London: Macmillan.

Collier, A. (1994) *Critical Realism*, London: Verso.

Collins, D. (1998) *Organisational Change: Sociological Perspectives*, London: Routledge.

Collins, R. (1986) *Weberian Sociological Theory*, Cambridge: Cambridge University Press.

Collinson, D. (1992) *Managing the Shopfloor: Subjectivity, Masculinity and Workplace Culture*, Berlin: De Gruyter.

Collinson, D. (1994) 'Strategies of Resistance: Power, Knowledge and Subjectivity in the Workplace', in J. Jermier., W. Nord and D. Knights (eds) *Resistance and Power in the Workplace*, London: Routledge.

Collinson, D. and Collinson, M. (1989) 'Sexuality in the Workplace: The Domination of Men's Sexuality', in J. Hearn, D. L. Sheppard, P. Tancred-Sheriff and G. Burrell (eds) *The Sexuality of Organisation*, London: Sage.

Collinson, D. and Collinson, M. (1994) '"It's Only Dick": The Sexual Harassment of Women Managers in Insurance Sales', *Work, Employment and Society*, 10. 1: 29–56.

Collinson, D. and Hearn, J. (1994) 'Naming Men as Men: Implications for Work, Organisation and Management', *Gender, Work and Organizations*, 1. 1: 2–22.

Collinson, D., Knights, D. and Collinson, M. (1990) *Managing to Discriminate*, London: Routledge.

Considine, M. (1996) 'Market Bureaucracy? Exploring the Contending Rationalities of Contemporary Administrative Regimes', *Labour and Industry*, 7. 1: 1–28.

Collinson, D. L. and Collinson, M. (1997) '"Delayering Managers": Time–Space Surveillance and its Gendered Effects', *Organisation*, 4. 3: 375–407.

Control Data Corporation (1985) 'Telecommuting', in D. Clutterbuck (ed.) *New Patterns of Work*, Aldershot: Gower.

Cooper, C. L. (1984) 'What's New In . . . Stress', *Personnel Management*, June: 40–4.

Cooper, C. L. and Smith, M. J. (1985) *Job Stress and Blue Collar Work*, Chichester: Wiley.

Cooper, D. (1994) 'Productive, Relational and Everywhere? Conceptualising Power and Resistance Within Foucauldian Feminism', *Sociology*, 28. 2: 435–54.

Cooper, R. and Burrell, G. (1988) 'Modernism, Postmodernism and Organisational Analysis: An Introduction', *Organisation Studies*, 9. 2: 91–112.

Coopey, J. and Hartley, J. (1991) 'Reconsidering the Case for Organisational Commitment', *Human Resource Management Journal*, 1. 3: 18–32.

Corbett, J. M. (1985a) 'The Design of Machine-Tool Technology and Work: Technical Science and Technical Choice', unpublished draft, Sheffield: MRC/ESRC Social and Applied Psychology Unit.

Corbett, J. M. (1985b) 'Prospective Work Design of a Human-Centred CNC Lathe', *Behaviour and Information Technology*, 14. 1: 201–14.

Corbett, J. M. (1994) *Critical Cases in Organisational Behaviour*, London: Macmillan.

Coriat, B. (1980) 'The Restructuring of the Assembly Line: A New Economy of Time and Control', *Capital and Class*, 11: 34–43.

Cornforth, C. (1988) 'Patterns of Cooperative Management: Revising the Degeneration Thesis', paper presented to a Conference on New Forms of Ownership and Management, Cardiff Business School.

Cousins, C. (1987) *Controlling Social Welfare: A Sociology of State Welfare Work and Organisation*, Brighton: Wheatsheaf.

Cousins, C. (1999) 'Changing Regulatory Frameworks and Non-Standard Employment: A Comparison of Germany, Spain, Sweden and the UK', in A. Felstead and N. Jewson (eds) *Global Trends in Flexible Labour*, London: Macmillan.

Coventry, Liverpool, Newcastle and N. Tyneside Trades Councils (1981) *State Intervention in Industry: A Workers' Inquiry*, Newcastle: Spokeman.

Cressey, P. and Cousins, C. (1986) 'The Labour Process in the State Welfare Sector', in D. Knights and H. Willmott (eds) *Managing the Labour Process*, Aldershot: Gower.

Cressey, P. and Jones, B. (1991) 'A New Convergence?' *Work, Employment and Society*, 5. 1: 493–5.

Cressey, P. and MacInnes, J. (1980) 'Voting for Ford: Industrial Democracy and the Control of Labour', *Capital and Class*, 11: 5–37.

Crompton, R. (1997) *Women and Work in Modern Britain*, Oxford: Oxford University Press.

Crompton, R. (with N. Feuvre) (1996) 'Paid Employment and the System of Gender Relations', *Sociology*, 30. 3: 427–46.

Crompton, R. and Jones, G. (1984) *White Collar Proletariat*, London: Macmillan.

Crook, S., Paluski, J. and Waters, M. (1992) *Postmodernization*, London: Sage.

Cross, M. (1985) 'Flexible Manning', in D. Clutterbuck (ed.) *New Patterns of Work*, Aldershot: Gower.

Crouch, C. (1999) 'The Skills Creation Triangle Out of Balance', *Renewal*, 7. 4: 60–71.

Crouch, C., Finegold, D. and Sako, M. (1999) *Are Skills the Answer? The Political Economy of Skill Creation in Advanced Industrial Countries*, Oxford: Oxford University Press.

Crowther, S. and Garrahan, P. (1987) 'Invitation to Sunderland: Corporate Power and the Local Economy', paper presented to the Conference on Japanisation of British Industry, UMIST, also in *Industrial Relations Journal*.

Cully, M., O'Reilly, A., Millward, D., Forth, N., Woodland, S., Dix, G. and Bryson, A. (1998) *The 1998 Workplace Employee Relations Survey: First Findings*, Department of Trade and Industry, London: HMSO.

Cummings, T. and Blumberg, M. (1987) 'Advanced Manufacturing Technology and Work Design', in T. D. Wall, C. W. Clegg and N. J. Kemp (eds) *The Human Side of Advanced Manufacturing Technology*, Chichester: Wiley.

Cummings, T. and Cooper, C. L. (1979) 'A Cybernetic Framework for the Study of Occupational Stress', *Human Relations*, 32: 395–419.

Cutcher-Gershenfeld, J., Nitta, M., Barrett, B., Belhedi, M., Bullard, J., Coutchie, C., Inaba, T., Ishino, I., Lee,

S., Lin, W-J., Mothersell, W. and Rabine, S. (1994) 'Japanese Team-based Work Systems in North America: Explaining the Diversity', *California Management Review*, 37. 1: 42–63.

Cutler, T. (1992) 'Numbers in a Time of Dearth: The Use of Performance Indicators to "Manage" Higher Education', paper presented to the 10th International Labour Process Conference, Aston.

Cyert, R. M. and March, J. G. (1963) *A Behavioural Theory of the Firm*, Englewood Cliffs, NJ: Prentice Hall.

Czarniawska, B. (1999) *Writing Management: Organisation Theory as a Literary Genre*, Oxford: Oxford University Press.

Dahl, R. (1957) 'The Concept of Power', *Behavioural Science*, 2: 201–15.

Dahl, R. (1958) 'A Critique of the Ruling Elite Model', *American Political Science Review*, 52.

Dahler-Larsen, P. (1994) 'Corporate Culture and Morality: Durkheim-Inspired Reflections on the Limits of Corporate Culture', *Journal of Management Studies*, 31. 1: 1–18.

Dahrendorf, R. (1959) *Class and Class Conflict in Industrial Society*, London: Routledge and Kegan Paul.

Dale, K. and Burrell, G. (2000) 'What Shape Are We in? Organisation Theory and the Organized Body', in J. Hassard, R. Holliday and H. Willmott (eds) *Body and Organisation*, London: Sage.

Damanpour, F. (1996) 'Organizational Complexity and Innovation: Developing and Testing Multiple Contingency Models', *Management Science*, 42. 5: 693–716.

Dandeker, C. (1990) *Surveillance, Power and Modernity: Bureaucracy and Discipline from 1700 to the Present Day*, Cambridge: Polity.

Danford, A. (1997) 'Teamworking and Labour Regulation: A Case Study of Shop-Floor Disempowerment', paper presented to the 15th International Labour Process Conference, March, Edinburgh.

Daniel, W. W. and McIntosh, N. (1972) *The Right to Manage?* London: MacDonald.

Daniel, W. W. and Millward, N. (1983) *Workplace Industrial Relations in Britain*, London: Heinemann.

Dankbaar, B. (1988) 'New Production Concepts, Management Strategies and the Quality of Work', *Work, Employment and Society*, 2. 1: 25–50.

Davidson, M. and Cooper, C. (1992) *Shattering the Glass Ceiling*, London: Paul Chapman.

Davis, K. (1991) 'Critical Sociology and Gender Relations', in K. Davis, M. Leijenaar and J. Oldersma (eds) *The Gender of Power*, London: Sage.

Davis, K., Leijenaar, M. and Oldersma, J. (eds) (1991) *The Gender of Power*, London: Sage.

Dawson, P. and Webb, J. (1989) 'New Production Arrangements: The Totally Flexible Cage?' *Work, Employment and Society*, 3. 2: 221–38.

Dawson, S. (1986, 2nd edn 1992) *Analysing Organizations*, London: Macmillan.

Day, R. A. and Day, J. V. (1977) 'A Review of the Current State of Negotiated Order Theory: An Appreciation and a Critique', *Sociological Quarterly*, 18, Winter: 126–42.

De Cindio, F., De Michaelis, G. and Simone, C. (1988) 'Computer-Based Tools in the Language/Action Perspective', in R. Speth (ed.) *Research into Networks and Distributed Applications*, Amsterdam: North Holland.

de los Reyes, P. (2000) 'Diversity at Work: Paradoxes, Possibilities and Problems in the Swedish Discourse on Diversity', *Economic and Industrial Democracy*, 21: 253–66.

De Vroey, M. (1975) 'The Separation of Ownership and Control in Large Corporations', *Review of Radical Political Economics*, 7. 2: 1–10.

Deal, T. and Kennedy, A. (1988) *Corporate Cultures: the Rites and Rituals of Corporate Life*, Harmondsworth: Penguin.

Deaux, K. and Emswiller, T. (1974) 'Explanations of Successful Performance on Sex-Linked Tasks: What is Skill for the Male is Luck for the Female', *Journal of Personality and Social Psychology*, 24: 30–85.

Deery, S., Iverson, R. and Walsh, J. (2000) 'Work Relationships in Telephone Call Centres: Understanding Emotional Exhaustion and Employee Withdrawal', paper to International Industrial Relations Association Conference, Tokyo, May–June.

Deetz, S. (1992) 'Disciplinary Power in the Modern Corporation', in M. Alvesson and H. Willmott (eds) *Critical Management Studies*, London: Sage.

Dejoy, D. M. (1994) Managing Safety in the Workplace: An Attribution Theory Analysis Model', *Journal of Safety Research*, 25. 1: 3–17.

Delamarter, R. T. (1988) *Big Blue: IBM's Use and Abuse of Power*, London: Pan.

Delbridge, R. (1998) *Life on the Line in Contemporary Manufacturing*, Oxford: Oxford University Press.

Delbridge, R., Lowe, J. and Oliver, N. (2000) 'Worker Autonomy in Lean Teams: Evidence from the World Automotive Components Industry', in S. Proctor and F. Mueller (eds) *Teamworking*, London: Macmillan.

Delbridge, R., Turnbull, P. and Wilkinson, B. (1992) 'Pushing Back the Frontiers: Management Control and Work Intensification Under JIT/TQM Regimes', *New Technology, Work and Employment*, 7: 97–106.

Deleuze, G. and Guattari, F. (1977) *Anti-Oedipus: Capitalism and Schizophrenia*, New York: Viking.

Dent, M. (1993) 'Professionalism, Educated Labour and the State: Hospital Medicine and the New Managerialism', *Sociological Review*, 41. 2: 244–73.

Despres, C. and Hiltrop, J-M. (1995) 'Human Resource Management in the Knowledge Age: Current Practice and Perspectives in the Future', *Employee Relations*, 17. 1: 9–23.

Deutsch, M. and Gerard, H. B. (1955) 'A Study of Normative and Informational Social Influences upon Individual Judgement', *Journal of Abnormal and Social Psychology*, 51: 629–36.

Devanna, M. A., Fornbrun, C. J. and Tichy, N. M. (1984) 'A Framework for Strategic Human Resource Management', in C. J. Fornbrun, N. M. Tichy and M. A. Devanna (eds) *Strategic Human Resource Management*, New York: Wiley.

Dews, P. (1987) *Logics of Disintegration*, London: Verso.

Dex, S. (1985) *The Sexual Division of Work*, Brighton: Wheatsheaf.

Di Maggio, P. and Powell, W. (1983) 'The Iron Cage Revisited: Institutional Isomorphism and Collective Rationality in Organizations', *American Sociological Review*, 48: 147–60.

Di Tomaso, N. (1989) 'Sexuality in the Workplace: Discrimination and Harassment', in J. Hearn, D. L. Sheppard, P. Tancred-Sheriff and G. Burrell (eds) *The Sexuality of Organisation*, London: Sage.

Dicken, P. (1992) *Global Shift*, London: Paul Chapman.

Dickens, P. and Savage, M. (1988) 'The Japanisation of British Industry? Instances from a High Growth Area', *Industrial Relations Journal*, Spring, 19. 1.

Dickson, T. *et al.* (1988) 'Big Blue and the Unions: IBM, Individualism and Trade Union Strategy', *Work, Employment and Society*, 2. 4: 506–20.

Dill, W. R. (1962) 'The Impact of Environment on Organisation Development', in S. Mailick and E. H. Van Ness (eds) *Concepts and Issues in Administrative Behaviour*, Englewood Cliffs, NJ: Prentice Hall.

Ditton, J. (1974) 'The Fiddling Salesman: Connivance at Corruption', *New Society*, 28 Nov.

Domhoff, G. (1967) *Who Rules America?*, Englewood Cliffs, NJ: Prentice Hall.

Donaldson, L. (1985) *In Defence of Organisation Theory: A Reply to the Critics*, Cambridge: Cambridge University Press.

Donaldson, L. (1989) 'Reflections in Organisational Analysis', *Australian Journal of Management*, 14. 2: 243–54.

Donaldson, L. (1996) 'The Normal Science of Contingency Theory', in S. Clegg, C. Hardy and W. Nord (eds) *Handbook of Organisation Studies*, London: Sage.

Donaldson, L. (1998) 'The Myth of Paradigm Incommensurability in Management Studies: Comments by an Integrationist', *Organisation*, 5. 2: 267–72.

Donovan, Lord (Chairman) (1968) *Report on the Royal Commission on Trade Unions and Employers' Associations*, London: HMSO.

Doray, B. (1988) *A Rational Madness: From Taylorism to Fordism*, London: Free Association.

Drago, R. and McDonough, T. (1984) 'Capitalist Shopfloor Initiatives, Restructuring and Organising in the '80s', *Review of Radical Political Economics*, 716. 4: 52–77.

Drake, R. I. and Smith, P. J. (1973) *Behavioural Science in Industry*, London: McGraw-Hill.

Drucker, P. (1955) *The Practice of Management*, New York: Harper and Row.

Drucker, P. (1959) *Landmarks of Tomorrow*, New York: Harper and Row.

Drucker, P. (1968) *The Age of Discontinuity*, New York: Harper and Row.

Drucker, P. (1977) *People and Performance*, London: Heinemann.

Drucker, P. (1979) *Management*, London: Pan.

Drucker, P. (1981) *Managing in Turbulent Times*, London: Pan.

Drucker, P. (1992) 'The New Society of Organizations, *Harvard Business Review*, Sept.–Oct.: 95–104.

Drummond, H. (1996) *Power: Creating It, Using It*, London: Kogan Page.

du Gay, P. (1991a) 'The Cult[ure] of the Customer', *Journal of Management Studies*, 29. 5: 615–33.

du Gay, P. (1991b) 'Enterprise Culture and the Ideology of Excellence', *New Formations*, 13: 45–61.

du Gay, P. (1992) 'Numbers and Souls: Retailing and the De-Differentiation of Economy and Culture', paper presented to the Employment Research Unit Annual Conference, Cardiff Business School, September.

du Gay, P. (1996) *Consumption and Identity at Work*, London: Sage.

du Gay, P. (2000) *In Praise of Bureaucracy*, London: Sage.

Due Billing, Y. (1994) 'Gender and Bureaucracies: A Critique of Ferguson's "The Feminist Case Against Bureaucracy"', 1. 4: 173–93.

Duenas, G. (1993) 'The Importance of Intercultural Learning in the International Transfer of Managerial and Organisational Knowledge', paper presented to the 11th EGOS Colloquium, Paris, July.

Dumaine, B. (1990) 'Who Needs a Boss?' *Fortune*, 7 May: 40–7.

Dunford, R. and McGraw, P. (1987) 'Quality Circles or Quality Circus? Labour Process Theory and the Operation of Quality Circle Programmes', paper presented to the Conference on the Labour Process, Aston–UMIST.

Dunkerley, D. and Salaman, G. (eds) (1980a) *The International Yearbook of Organisation Studies 1979*, London: Routledge and Kegan Paul.

Dunkerley, D. and Salaman, G. (eds) (1980b) *The International Yearbook of Organisation Studies 1980*, London: Routledge and Kegan Paul.

Dunkerley, D. and Salaman, G. (eds) (1982) *The International Yearbook of Organisation Studies 1981*, London: Routledge and Kegan Paul.

Dunkerley, D. and Salaman, G. (1986) 'Organizations and Bureaucracy', in M. Haralambos (ed.) *Developments in Sociology vol. 2*, Ormskirk: Causeway.

Dunning, J. H. (1986) *Japanese Participation in British Industry*, London: Croom Helm.

Easterby-Smith, M. (1992) 'Creating a Learning Organisation', *Personnel Review*, 19. 5: 24–8.

Easterby-Smith, M., Thorpe, R. and Lowe, A. (1991) *Management Research: An Introduction*, London: Sage.

Eby, L. T. and Dobbins, G. H. (1997) 'Collectivistic Orientation in Teams: An Individual and Group Level Analysis', *Journal of Organizational Behaviour*, 18: 275–95.

Eccles, R. G. and Nohria, N. (1992) *Beyond the Hype: Rediscovering the Essence of Management*, Boston, Mass.: Harvard Business School Press.

Economic Progress Report (1986) 'A More Flexible Labour Market', no. 182, HM Treasury.

Edquist, C. and Jacobsson, S. (1988) *Flexible Automation: The Global Diffusion of New Technology in the Engineering Industry*, Berkeley, Calif.: University of California Press.

Edwardes, M. (1978) *The Dark Side of History: Magic in the Making of Man*, St. Albans: Granada.

Edwards, P., Armstrong, P., Marginson, P. and Purcell, J. (1996) 'Towards the Transnational Company?' in R. Crompton, D. Gallie and K. Purcell (eds) *Corporate Restructuring and Labour Markets*, London: Routledge.

Edwards, P. K. (1989) 'Understanding Conflict in the Labour Process: The Logic and Autonomy of Struggle', in D. Knights and H. Willmott (eds) *Labour Process Theory*, London: Macmillan.

Edwards, P. K. and Scullion, H. (1982) *The Social Organisation of Industrial Conflict: Control and Resistance in the Workplace*, Oxford: Blackwell.

Edwards, R. (1979) *Contested Terrain: The Transformation of the Workplace in the Twentieth Century*, London: Heinemann.

Edwards, R., Reich, M. and Gordon, D. M. (1975) *Labour Market Segmentation*, Lexington, Mass.: D. C. Heath.

Egan, G. (1994) *Working the Shadow Side: A Guide to Positive Behind-the-Scenes Management*, San Francisco: Jossey Bass.

Egri, C. P. (1994) 'Working with Nature: Organic Farming and Other Forms of Resistance to Industrialised Agriculture', in J. Jermier, D. Knights and W. Nord (eds) *Resistance and Power in Organisations*, London: Routledge.

Ehrenreich, B. and Ehrenreich, J. (1979) 'The Professional-Managerial Class', in P. Walker (ed.) *Between Labour and Capital*, Brighton: Harvester.

Eiser, J. R. (1986) *Social Psychology: Attitudes, Cognition and Social Behaviour*, Cambridge: Cambridge University Press.

Elbaum, B. and Lazonick, W. (eds) (1986) *The Decline of the British Economy*, Oxford: Clarendon.

Eldridge, J. E. T. and Crombie, A. D. (1974) *A Sociology of Organizations*, London: Allen and Unwin.

Elger, T. (1987) 'Flexible Futures? New Technology and the Contemporary Transformation of Work', *Work, Employment and Society*, 1. 4: 528–40.

Elger, T. (1990) 'Technical Innovation and Work Reorganization in British Manufacturing in the 1980s', *Work, Employment and Society* special issue, May: 67–101.

Elger, T. (1991) 'Task Flexibility and Intensification of Labour in UK Manufacturing in the 1980s', in A. Pollert (ed.) *Farewell to Flexibility?* Oxford: Blackwell.

Elger, T. and Smith, C. (1994) 'Global Japanisation? Convergence and Competition in the Organisation of the Labour Process', in T. Elger and C. Smith (eds) *Global Japanisation*, London: Routledge.

Elliot, D. (1980) 'The Organisation as a System', in G. Salaman and K. Thompson (eds) *Control and Ideology in Organizations*, Milton Keynes: Open University Press.

Elliot, K. and Lawrence. P. (1985) *Introducing Management*, Harmondsworth: Penguin.

Eros, F. (1974) 'Review of L. Garai's *Personality Dynamics and Social Existence*', *European Journal of Social Psychology*, 4. 3: 369–79.

Esland, G. (1980) 'Professions and Professionalism', in G. Esland and G. Salaman (eds) *The Politics of Work and Occupations*, Milton Keynes: Open University Press.

Esland, G. and Salaman, G. (eds) (1980) *The Politics of Work and Occupations*, Milton Keynes: Open University Press.

Etzioni, A. (1961) *A Comparative Analysis of Complex Organizations*, New York: Free Press.

Etzioni, A. (1988) *The Moral Dimension: Towards a New Economics*, New York: Plenum.

Evden, D. (1986) 'OD and Self-Fulfilling Prophecy: Boosting Productivity by Raising Expectations', *Journal of Applied Behavioural Science*, 22. 1: 1–13.

Eysenck, H. J. (1947) *Dimensions of Personality*, London: Routledge and Kegan Paul.

Eysenck, H. J. and Wilson, G. (1975) *Know Your Own Personality*, Harmondsworth: Penguin.

Farnham, D. and Horton, S. (eds) (1993) *Managing the New Public Services*, London: Macmillan.

Farnham, D. and Horton, S. (1993) 'The New Public Service Managerialism: An Assessment', in D. Farnham and S. Horton (eds) *Managing the New Public Services*, London: Macmillan.

Featherstone, M. (1988) 'In Pursuit of the Postmodern: An Introduction', *Theory, Culture and Society*, 5: 195–215.

Feldman, D. C. and Klich, N. R. (1991) 'Impression Management and Career Strategies', in R. A. Giacolone and P. Rosenfeld (eds) *Applied Impression Management: How Image-Making Affects Managerial Decisions*, Newbury Park, Calif.: Sage.

Felstead, A. (1994) *Corporate Paradox: Power and Control in Business Franchise*, London: Routledge.

Felstead, A. and Jewson, N. (1999) 'Flexible Labour and Non-Standard Employment: An Agenda of Issues', in A. Felstead and N. Jewson (eds) *Global Trends in Flexible Labour*, London: Macmillan.

Felstead, A. and Jewson, N. (eds) (1999) *Global Trends in Flexible Labour*, London: Macmillan.

Ferguson, K. (1984) *The Feminist Case Against Bureaucracy*, Philadelphia: Temple University Press.

Ferner, A. and Edwards, P. (1995) 'Power and the Diffusion of Organisational Change Within Multinationals', *European Journal of Industrial Relations*, 1. 2: 229–57.

Fernie, S. and Metcalf, D. (1997) '(Not) Hanging on the Telephone: Payment Systems in the New Sweatshops', *Centre for Economic Performance*, London: London School of Economics.

Festinger, L. (1957) *A Theory of Cognitive Dissonance*, Calif.: Stanford University Press.

Fevre, R. (1986) 'Contract Work in the Recession', in K. Purcell, S. Wood, A. Watson and S. Allen (eds) *The Changing Experience of Employment, Restructuring and Recession*, London: Macmillan.

Feyerabend, P. (1975) *Against Method: An Outline of an Anarchistic Theory of Knowledge*, London: NLB.

Fiedler, F. E. (1967) *A Theory of Leadership Effectiveness*, New York: McGraw-Hill.

Fiedler, F. E. (1978) 'Situational Control: A Dynamic Theory of Leadership', in B. King, S. Steufert and F. Fiedler (eds) *Managerial Control and Organisational Democracy*, Washington: Winston and Wiley.

Filby, M. (1992) 'The Figures, The Personality and The Bums: Service Work and Sexuality', *Work Employment and Society*, 6. 1: 23–42.

Findlay, P., Marks, A., McKinlay, A. and Thompson, P. (2000a) 'Flexible if it Suits Them: The Use and Abuse of Teamwork Skills', in F. Mueller and S. Proctor (eds) *Teamwork*, London: Macmillan.

Findlay, P., Marks, A., McKinlay, A. and Thompson, P. (2000b) 'In Search of Perfect People: Teamwork and Team Players in Scottish Spirits Industry', *Human Relations*, 53. 12: 1549–74.

Fine, G. A. (1996) *Kitchens: The Culture of Restaurant Work*, London: University of California Press.

Finegold, D. (1999) 'Creating Self-Sustaining High-skill Ecosystems', *Oxford Review of Economics*, 15. 1: 60–81.

Fineman, S. (ed.) (1993) *Emotion in Organizations*, London: Sage.

Fineman, S. (1998) 'Street Level Bureaucrats and the Social Construction of Environmental Control', *Organisation Studies*, 19. 6: 953–74.

Finke, R. (1990) *Creative Imagery: Discoveries and Inventions in Visualization*, London: Lawrence Erlbaum.

Finlay, P. (1985) 'Control', in K. Elliot and P. Lawrence (eds) *Introducing Management*, Harmondsworth: Penguin.

Finn, D. (1986) *Training Without Jobs*, London: Macmillan.

Fischer, F. and Sirriani, C. (eds) (1984) *Critical Studies in Organisation and Bureaucracy*, Philadelphia: Temple University Press.

Fisher, D. (1993) *Communication in Organizations*, 2nd edn, St. Paul, Minn.: West Publishing.

Fisher, S. (1986) *Stress and Strategy*, London: Lawrence Erlbaum.

Fiske, S. T. and Taylor, S. E. (1991) *Social Cognition*, 2nd edn, New York: McGraw-Hill.

Fleishman, E. A. (1974) 'Leadership Climate, Human Relations Training and Supervisory Behaviour', in E. A. Fleishman and A. R. Bass (eds) *Studies in Personnel and Industrial Psychology*, New York: Dorsey.

Fligstein, N. (1990) *The Transformation of Corporate Control*, Cambridge, Mass.: Harvard University Press.

Florida, R. and Kenney, M. (1991) 'Organisation vs. Culture: Japanese Automotive Transplants in the US', *Industrial Relations Journal*, 2. 2: 181–96.

Fontana, D. (1985) 'Learning and Teaching', in C. L. Cooper and P. Makin (eds) *Psychology and Managers*, London: BPS and Macmillan.

Ford, M. E. (1992) *Motivating Humans, Goals, Emotions and Personal Agency Beliefs*, Newbury Park, Calif.: Sage.

Fores, M. and Glover, I. (1976) 'The Real Work of Executives', *Management Today*, Sept.

Fores, M., Glover, I. and Lawrence, P. (1992) 'Management Thought, the American Legacy and the Future of European Labour Processes in 1992', paper presented to the 10th International Labour Process Conference, Aston.

Forsgren, M. (1990) *Managing the Internationalisation Process: The Swedish Case*, London: Routledge.

Foucault, M. (1972) *The Archaeology of Knowledge*, London: Tavistock.

Foucault, M. (1977) *Discipline and Punish: The Birth of the Prison*, Harmondsworth: Penguin.

Foucault, M. (1984) *The History of Sexuality: An Introduction*, Harmondsworth: Peregrine.

Fournier, V. and Grey, C. (2000) 'At the Critical Moment: Conditions and Prospects for Critical Management Studies', *Human Relations*, 53. 1: 7–32.

Fowler, A. (1985) 'Getting into Organisational Restructuring', *Personnel Management*, 17. 2: 24–7.

Fox, A. (1980) 'The Meaning of Work', in G. Esland and G. Salaman (eds) *The Politics of Work and Occupations*, Milton Keynes: Open University Press.

Francis, A. (1986) *New Technology at Work*, Oxford: Oxford University Press.

Fraser, N. (1989) *Unruly Practices: Power, Discourse and Gender in Contemporary Social Theory*, Cambridge: Polity.

Freedman, D. (1992) 'Is Management Still a Science?' *Harvard Business Review*, Nov.-Dec.: 26–37.

Freedman, M. (1984) 'The Search for Shelters', in K. Thompson (ed.) *Work, Employment and Unemployment*, Milton Keynes: Open University Press.

French, J. R. P. and Raven, B. H. (1959) 'The Social Bases of Power', in D. Cartwright (ed.) *Studies in Social Power*, Ann Arbor: University of Michigan Press.

Frenkel, S., Korczynski, M., Donohue, L. and Shire, K. (1995) 'Re-Constituting Work', *Work, Employment and Society*, 9. 4: 773–96.

Frenkel, S., Korczynski, M., Shire, K. and Tam, M. (1999) *On the Front Line: Pattern of Work Organisation in Three Advanced Societies*, Ithaca, NY: Cornell University Press.

Frese, M. (1982) 'Occupational Socialisation and Psychological Development: An Underdeveloped Research Perspective in Industrial Psychology', *Journal of Occupational Psychology*, 55: 209–24.

Fridenson, P. (1978) 'Corporate Policy, Rationalisation and the Labour Force: French Experiences in International Comparison, 1900–29', paper presented to the Nuffield Deskilling Conference.

Friedman, A. (1977) *Industry and Labour: Class Struggle at Work Monopoly Capitalism*, London: Macmillan.

Friedman, A. (1987) 'The Means of Management Control and Labour Process Theory: A Critical Note on Storey', *Sociology*, 21. 2: 287–94.

Friedman, A. (1990) 'Managerial Strategies and the Labour Process', in D. Knights and H. Willmott (eds) *Labour Process Theory*, London: Macmillan.

Frost, P. J., Moore, L. F., Louis, M. R., Lundberg, C. C. and Martin, J. (eds) (1985) *Organisational Culture*, Beverley Hills/London: Sage.

Fucini, J. and Fucini, S. (1990) *Working for the Japanese: Inside Mazda's American Auto Plant*, New York: Free Press.

Fuller, A. and Saunders, M. (1990) 'The Paradox of Open Learning at Work', *Personnel Review*, 19. 5: 29–33.

Fuller, L. and Smith, V. A. (1991) 'Consumers' Reports: Management by Customers in a Changing Economy', *Work, Employment and Society*, 5. 1: 1–16.

Fuller, S. R. and Aldag, R. J. (1998) 'Organizational Tonypandy: Lessons from a Quarter Century of the Groupthink Phenomenon', *Organizational Behaviour and Human Decision Processes*, 2. 3: 163–4.

Furnham, A. (1997) *The Psychology of Behaviour at Work: The Individual in the Organisation*, Hove: Psychology Press.

Furusten, S. (1999) *Popular Management Books*, London: Routledge.

Gabriel, Y. (1988) *Working Lives in Catering*, London: Routledge.

Galbraith, J. K. (1967) *The New Industrial State*, Harmondsworth: Penguin.

Garnsey, E., Rubery, E. J. and Wilkinson, F. (1985) 'Labour Market Structure and Workforce Divisions', Unit 8 of Open University Course *Work and Society*, Milton Keynes: Open University Press.

Garrahan, P. and Stewart, P. (1992) *The Nissan Enigma: Flexibility at Work in a Local Economy*, London: Mansett.

Garrahan, P. and Stewart, P. (1993) 'Working Leaner but Smarter, or Meaner and Harder?: New Management Practices and the Recomposition of Employee Attitudes – The Case of the Auto Industry in Britain', paper presented to the American Sociological Association 88th Annual Meeting, Miami Beach, Florida.

Geary, R. (1985) *Policing Industrial Disputes: 1893–1985*, London: Methuen.

Gecas, V. (1986) 'The Motivational Significance of Self-Concept for Socialisation Theory', in E. J. Lawler (ed.) *Advances in Group Processes*, vol. 3, Greenwich, Conn.: JAI.

George, M. and Levie, H. (1984) *Japanese Competition and the British Workplace*, London: CAITS.

Geras, N. (1983) *Marx and Human Nature: Refutation of a Legend*, London: Verso.

Gergen, K. (1992) 'Organisation Theory in the Postmodern Era', in M. Reed and M. Hughes (eds) *Rethinking Organisation: New Directions in Organisation and Analysis*, London: Sage.

Gergen, K. J. (1973) 'Social Psychology as History', *Journal of Personality and Psychology*, 26. 2: 302–20.

Gerhardi, S. (1996) 'Gendered Organisational Cultures: Narratives of Women Travellers in a Male World', *Gender, Work and Organisation*, 3. 4: 187–201.

Giacolone, R. A. and Greenberg, J. (eds) (1997) *Antisocial Behaviour in Organizations*, London: Sage.

Giacolone, R. A. and Rosenfeld, P. (eds) (1991) *Applied Impression Management: How Image-Making Affects Managerial Decisions*, Newbury Park, Calif.: Sage.

Gibson, J. W. and Hodgetts, R. M. (1986) *Organisational Communication: A Managerial Perspective*, Orlando: Academic Press.

Giddens, A. (1982) 'From Marx to Nietzsche? Neo Conservatism, Foucault and Problems in Contemporary Political Theory', in *Profiles and Critiques in Social Theory*, London: Macmillan.

Giddens, A. (1984) *The Constitution of Society*, Cambridge: Polity.

Giles, E. and Starkey, K. (1987) 'From Fordism to Japanisation: Organisational Change at Ford, Rank Xerox and Fuji Xerox', paper presented to the Conference on Japanisation of British Industry, UMIST.

Gill, C. (1985) *Work, Unemployment and the New Technology*, Cambridge: Polity.

Gill, J. and Johnson, P. (1991) *Research Methods for Managers*, London: Paul Chapman.

Gill, R. and Grint, K. (1996) *The Gender–Technology Relation,* London: Taylor and Francis.

Giordano, L. (1985) 'Beyond Taylorism: Computerisation and QWL Programs in the Production Process', paper presented to the Conference on the Labour Process, Aston-UMIST, also published in D. Knights and H. Willmott (eds) (1988) *New Technology and the Labour Process*, London: Macmillan.

Glenn, E. K. and Feldberg, R. L. (1979) 'Proletarianising Office Work', in A. Zimbalist (ed.) *Case Studies on the Labour Process*, New York: Monthly Review Press.

Glover, I., Kelly, M. and Roslander, R. (1986) 'The Coming Proletarianisation of the British Accountant?' paper presented to the Conference on the Labour Process, Aston-UMIST.

Glucksman, M. (1990) *Women Assemble: Women Workers and the New Industries in Inter-War Britain*, Routledge, London: Routledge.

Goffmann, E. (1959) *The Presentation of the Self in Everyday Life*, New York: Doubleday Anchor.

Goffman, E. (1961) *Asylums*, New York: Doubleday.

Goffman, E. (1971) *The Presentation of Self in Everyday Life*, Harmondsworth: Pelican.

Goldin, L. and Applebaum, E. (1992) 'What was Driving the 1982–88 Boom in Temporary Employment? Preferences of Workers of Decisions and Power of Employers', *Journal of Economy and Society*, 51.

Goldman, P. and Van Houten, D. R. (1977) 'Managerial Strategies and the Worker: A Marxist Analysis of Bureaucracy', in J. K. Benson (ed.) *Organisational Analysis: Critique and Innovation*, London: Sage.

Goldman, P. and Van Houten, D. R. (1980) 'Uncertainty, Conflict and Labor Relations in the Modern Firm 1: Productivity and Capitalism's Human Face', *Economic and Industrial Democracy*, 1: 63–98.

Goldsmith, W. and Clutterbuck, D. (1985) *The Winning Streak*, Harmondsworth: Penguin.

Goodrich, C. (1975) *The Frontier of Control*, London: Pluto.

Gordon, D. (1988) 'The Global Economy: New Edifice or Crumbling Foundations?' *New Left Review*, 168, March–April: 24–65.

Gordon, D. M., Edwards, R. and Reich, M. (1982) *Segmented Work, Divided Workers*, Cambridge: Cambridge University Press.

Goss, S. (2001) *Making Local Government Work: Networks, Relationships and the Management of Change*, London: Palgrave.

Gouldner, A. (1955) *Wildcat Strike*, London: Routledge and Kegan Paul.

Gouldner, A. W. (1954) *Patterns of Industrial Bureaucracy*, New York: Free Press.

Gowler, D. and Legge, K. (1983) 'The Meaning of Management and the Management of Meaning: A View From Social Anthropology', in M. J. Earl (ed.) *Perspectives on Management: A Multidisciplinary Analysis*, Oxford: Oxford University Press.

Granovetter, M. (1985) 'Economic Action and Social Structure: The Problem of Embeddedness', *American Journal of Sociology*, 91. 3: 481–510.

Granovetter, M. (1994) 'Problems of Explanation in Economic Sociology', in N. Nohria and R. G. Eccles (eds) *Networks and Organizations*, Boston, Mass.: Harvard Business School Press.

Grant, W. (1983) 'Representing Capital', in R. King (ed.) *Capital and Politics*, London: Routledge and Kegan Paul.

Green, E. and Cassell, C. (1994) 'Women Managers, Gendered Cultural Processes and Organisational Change', paper presented to the 12th Annual International Labour Process Conference, Aston University, March.

Greenbaum, J. (1979) *In the Name of Efficiency*, Philadelphia: Temple University Press.

Greenbaum, J. (1998) 'The Times They are A'Changing: Dividing and Recombining Labour Through Computing Systems', in P. Thompson and C. Warhurst (eds) *Workplaces of the Future*, London: Macmillan.

Greenslade, M. (1994) 'Managing Diversity: Lessons from the United States', *Personnel Management*, December, 28–33.

Grenier, G. J. (1988) *Inhuman Relations: Quality Circles and Anti-Unionism in American Industry*, Philadelphia: Temple University Press.

Grey, C. (1994) 'Organisational Calvinism: Insecurity and Power in a Professional Labour Process', paper presented to the 12th Annual International Labour Process Conference, Aston, March.

Grey, C. and Mitev, N. (1995) 'Re-Engineering Organizations: A Critical Appraisal', *Personnel Review*, 24. 1: 1–18.

Grieco, M. and Whipp, R. (1985) 'Women and Control in the Workplace: Gender and Control in the Workplace', in D. Knights and H. Willmott (eds) *Job Redesign: Critical Perspectives on the Labour Process*, Aldershot: Gower.

Griffin, S. (1984) *Women and Nature: The Roaring Inside Her*, London: Women's Press.

Grimshaw, J. (1986) *Feminist Philosophers*, Brighton: Wheatsheaf.

Grint, K. (1995) *Management: A Sociological Introduction*, Oxford: Polity.

Grint, K. and Gill, R. (eds) (1996) *The Gender–Technology Relation: Contemporary Theory and Research*, London: Taylor and Francis.

Gronhaug, K. and Falkenberg, J. (1994) 'Success Attributions Within and Across Organizations', *Journal of European Industrial Training*, 18. 11: 22–9.

Grossman, R. (1979) 'Women's Place in the Integrated Service', *Radical America*, 14. 1: 29–48.

Guest, D. (1998) 'Human Resource Management, Trade Unions and Industrial Relations', in C. Mabey, G. Salaman and J. Storey (eds) *Strategic Human Resource Management*, London: Sage.

Guest, D. E. (1987) 'Human Resource Management and Industrial Relations', *Journal of Management Studies*, 24. 5: 503–21.

Guest, D. E. (1989) 'Personnel and HRM: Can You Tell the Difference?' *Personnel Management*, January: 48–51.

Guest, D. E. (1990) 'Human Resource Management and the American Dream', *Journal of Management Studies*, 27. 4: 377–97.

Guest, D. E. (1992) 'Right Enough to be Dangerously Wrong: An Analysis of the In Search of Excellence Phenomenon', in G. Salaman (ed.) *Human Resource Strategies*, London: Sage.

Guest, D. E. (1999a) 'Human Resource Management: When Reality Confronts Theory', paper presented to a conference of the Netherlands HRM Network, Rotterdam, November.

Guest, D. E. (1999b) 'Human Resource Management: The Workers' Verdict', *Human Resource Management Journal*, 9. 3: 5–25.

Gummeson, E. (1991) *Qualitative Methods in Management Research*, London: Sage.

Gutek, B. (1985) *Sex and the Workplace*, London: Jossey Bass.

Habermas, J. (1971) *Toward a Rational Society*, London: Heinemann.

Habermas, J. (1987) *The Philosophical Discourses of Modernity*, Cambridge: Polity.

Hacker, W., Volpert, W. and Von Cranach, M. (eds) (1982) *Cognitive and Motivational Aspects of Action*, Amsterdam: North Holland.

Hackman, J. R. and Oldman, G. R. (1980) *Work Redesign*, Reading, Mass.: Addison-Wesley.

Hakim, C. (1990) 'Core and Periphery in Employees' Workforce Strategies: Evidence from the 1987 ELUS Survey', *Work, Employment and Society*, 4. 2: 157–88.

Hakim, C. (1995) 'Five Feminist Myths About Women's Employment', *British Journal of Sociology*, 46. 3: 429–55.

Hakim, C. (1996) *Key Issues in Women's Employment: Female Heterogeneity and the Polarisation of Women's Employment*, London: Athlone.

Hales, C. P. (1986) 'What do Managers Do? A Critical Review of the Evidence', *Journal of Management Studies*, 23. 1: 88–115.

Hales, C. P. (1988) 'Management Processes, Management Divisions of Labour and Managerial Work: Towards a Synthesis', paper presented to the Conference on the Labour Process, Aston-UMIST.

Hales, C. (1993) *Managing Through Organisation*, London: Routledge.

Hales, C. (2000) 'Management and Empowerment Programmes', *Work, Employment and Society*, 14.. 3: 501–19.

Halford, S., Savage, M. and Witz, A. (1997) *Gender, Careers and Organisations*, London: Macmillan.

Hall, P. A. (1986) 'The State and Economic Decline', in B. Elbaum and W. Lazonick (eds) *The Decline of the British Economy*, Oxford: Clarendon.

Hall, R. H. (1977) *Organizations: Structure and Process*, 2nd edn , Englewood Cliffs, NJ: Prentice Hall.

Hallet, S. (1988) 'Privatisation and the Restructuring of a Public Utility: A Case Study of BT's Corporate

Strategy and Structure', paper presented to the Conference on New Forms of Ownership and Management, Cardiff Business School.

Hallier, J. and James, P. (1997) 'Middle Managers and the Employee Psychological Contract: Agency, Protection and Advancement', *Journal of Management Studies*, 34. 5: 703–28.

Hamel, G. and Prahalad, C. K. (1996) 'Competing in the New Economy: Managing Out of Bounds', *Strategic Management Journal*, 17: 237–42.

Hamilton, G. G. and Biggart, N. W. (1988) 'Market, Culture and Authority: A Comparative Analysis of Management and Organisation in the Far East', in C. Winship and S. Rosen (eds) 'Organizations and Institutions', *American Journal of Sociology*, 94, supplement, Chicago: University of Chicago Press.

Hamilton, P. (1980) 'Social Theory and the Problematic Concept of Work', in G. Esland and G. Salaman (eds) *The Politics of Work and Occupations*, Milton Keynes: Open University Press.

Hammer, M. and Champy, J. (1993) *Re-engineering the Corporation*, London: Nicholas Brearly.

Hammond, V. and Barham, K. (1987) *Management for the Future: Report on the Literature Search*, Herts: Ashridge Management College.

Hampden-Turner, C. and Trompenaars, F. (1993) *The Seven Cultures of Capitalism*, New York: Doubleday.

Handy, C. (1976; 1980; 1985) *Understanding Organizations*, Harmondsworth: Penguin.

Handy, C. (1984) *The Future of Work*, London: Blackwell.

Handy, C. (1989) *The Age of Unreason*, London: Business Books.

Handy, C. (1994) *The Empty Raincoat*, London: Hutchinson.

Handy, C. (1995) *The Future of Work*, W. H. Smith Contemporary Papers 8.

Hannan, M. T. and Carroll, G. R. (1992) *Dynamics of Organisational Populations: Density, Competition and Legitimation*, New York: Oxford University Press.

Hannan, M. T., Carroll, G. R., Dundon, E. A. and Torres, J. C. (1995) 'Organisational Evolution in a Multi-national Context: Entries of Automobile Manufactures in Belgium, Britain, France, Germany and Italy', *American Sociological Review*, 60: 509–28.

Hannan, M. T. and Freeman, J. H. (1977) 'The Population Ecology of Organizations', *American Journal of Sociology*, 82: 929–64.

Hardy, C. (1996) 'Understanding Power: Bringing About Strategic Change', *British Journal of Management*, 7, special issue: S3–16.

Hardy, C. (1998) 'The Power Behind Empowerment: Implications for Research and Practice', *Human Relations*, 51. 4: 451–82.

Harley, B. (1998) 'The Myth of Empowerment: Work Organisation, Hierarchy and Employee Autonomy in Contemporary Australian Workplaces', Department of Management Working Paper, University of Melbourne.

Harris, R. (1987) *Power and Powerlessness in Industry: An Analysis of the Social Relations of Production*, London: Tavistock.

Harrison, B. (1994) *Lean and Mean: The Changing Landscape of Corporate Power in the Age of Flexibility*, New York: Basic Books.

Harrison, E. and Marchington, M. (1992) 'Corporate Culture and Management Control: Understanding Customer Care', paper presented to the Employment Research Unit Annual Conference, Cardiff Business School, September.

Harrison, R. G. (1984) 'Reasserting the Radical Potential of OD', *Personnel Review*, 13. 2.

Hartley, J. F. and Stephenson, G. M. (eds) (1992) *Employment Relations*, Oxford: Blackwell.

Harwood, (1996) 'Work and its Future', *Left Business Observer*, 72, internet edn.

Haslam, S. A. (2000) *Psychology in Organizations: The Social Identity Approach*, London: Sage.

Hassard, J. (1988) 'Overcoming Hermeticism in Organization Theory: An Alternative to Paradigm Incommensurability', *Human Relations*, 41. 3: 247–59.

Hassard, J. (1991) 'Multiple Paradigms and Organisational Analysis: A Case Study', *Organisation Studies*, 12. 2: 275–99.

Hassard, J. (1994) 'Postmodern Organisational Analysis: Towards a Conceptual Framework', *Journal of Management Studies*, 31. 3: 1–22.

Hassard, J., Holliday, R. and Willmott, H. (2000) 'Introduction', in J. Hassard, R. Holliday and H. Willmott (eds) *Body and Organisation*, London: Sage.

Hassard, J. and Parker, M. (1993) *Postmodernism and Organizations*, London: Sage.

Hassard, J. and Parker, M. (eds) (1994) *Towards a New Theory of Organizations*, London: Routledge.

Hassard, J. and Pym, D. (eds) (1990) *The Theory and Philosophy of Organizations*, London: Routledge.

Hawkins, K. (1978) *The Management of Industrial Relations*, Harmondsworth: Penguin.

Hearn, J. (1992) *Men in the Public Eye*, London: Routledge.

Hearn, J. and Parkin, W. (1987) *Sex at Work: The Power and Paradox of Organisation Sexuality*, Brighton: Wheatsheaf.

Hearn, J. and Parkin, W. (1992) 'Gender and Organizations: A Selective Review and a Critique of a Neglected Area', in A. J. Mills and P. Tancred (eds) *Gendering Organisation Analysis*, London: Sage.

Hearn, J., Sheppard, D. L., Tancred-Sheriff, P. and Burrell, G. (1989) (eds) *The Sexuality of Organisation*, London: Sage.

Heckscher, C. (1995) *White Collar Blues: Management Loyalties in an Age of Corporate Restructuring*, NY: Basic Books.

Heckscher, C. (1997) 'The Changing Social Contract for White Collar Workers', *Perspectives on Work*, 1. 1: 18–21.

Heckscher, C. and Donnellon, A. (eds) (1994) *The Post-Bureaucratic Organisation*, London: Sage.

Heider, F. (1946) 'Attitudes and Cognitive Organisation', *Journal of Psychology*, 21: 107–12.

Heider, F. (1958) *The Psychology of Interpersonal Relations*, New York: Wiley.

Held, D. (1984) 'Central Perspectives on the Modern State', in D. Held (ed.) *States and Societies*, Oxford: Martin Robertson.

Henderson, G. (1993) 'Industrial Policy for Britain: Lessons From the East', *Renewal*, 1. 2: 32–42.

Henderson, J. (1989) *The Globalisation of High Technology Production*, London: Routledge.

Henderson, J. (1992) 'Global Economic Integration, Business Systems and States in East Asian European Development', paper presented to the First European Conference of Sociology, Vienna, August.

Hendry, C., Pettigrew, A. and Sparrow, P. (1988) 'Changing Patterns Of Human Resource Management', *Personnel Management*, Nov.

Henriques, J., Hollway, W. and Urwin, C. (eds) (1984) *Changing the Subject: Psychology, Social Regulation and Subjectivity*, London: Methuen.

Herriot, P. and Pemberton, C. (1994) *Competitive Advantage through Diversity*, London: Sage.

Hershey, R. (1993) 'A Practitioner's View of Motivation', *Journal of Managerial Psychology*, 8. 3: 10–13.

Herzberg, F. (1966) *Work and the Nature of Man*, Cleveland, Ohio: World Publishing.

Herzberg, F. (1968) 'One More Time, How Do You Motivate Employees?' in S. J. Carroll, F. T. Paine and J. B. Miner (eds) (1977) *The Management Process*, 2nd edn, New York: Macmillan.

Herzberg, F., Mauser, B. and Snyderman, B. (eds) (1959) *The Motivation to Work*, New York: Wiley.

Heydebrand, W. (1977) 'Organisational Contradictions in Public Bureaucracies; Toward a Marxian Theory of Organisations', in J. K. Benson (ed.) *Organisational Analysis: Critique and Innovation*, Contemporary Social Science Issues 37, London: Sage.

Heydebrand, W. (1989) 'New Organisational Forms', *Work and Occupations*, 16. 3: 323–57.

Hicks, M. J. (1991) *Problem Solving in Business and Management*, London: Chapman and Hall.

Hickson, D. J. (1971) 'A Strategic Contingencies Theory of Interorganizational Power', *Administrative Science Quarterly*, 16: 216–29.

Hickson, D. J. (1973) 'A Convergence in Organisation Theory', in G. Salaman and K. Thompson (eds) *People and Organizations*, Harlow: Longman.

Hickson, D. J. (1990) 'Politics Permeates', in D. Wilson and R. Rosenfeld (eds) *Managing Organizations: Texts, Readings and Cases*, Maidenhead: McGraw Hill.

Hickson, D. J., Lee, C. R., Schneck, R. E. and Pennings, J. M. (1973) 'A Strategic Contingencies Theory of Intraorganizational Power', in G. Salaman and K. Thompson (eds) *People and Organizations*, Harlow: Longman.

Hickson, D. J. and McCullough, A. F. (1980) 'Power in Organizations', in G. Salaman and K. Thompson (eds) *Control and Ideology in Organizations*, Milton Keynes: Open University Press.

Hill, S. (1991) 'Why Quality Circles Failed but Total Quality Management Might Succeed', *British Journal of Industrial Relations*, 29. 4: 541–68.

Hilmer, F. G. and Donaldson, L. (1996) *Management Redeemed: Debunking the Fads that Undermine Corporate Performance*, Sydney: Free Press.

Hindess, B. (1982) 'Power, Interests and the Outcome of Struggles', *Sociology*, 23: 535–58.

Hinings, B. (1988) 'Defending Organisation Theory: A British View from North America', *Organisation Studies*, 9. 1: 2–7.

Hirst, P. and Thompson, G. (1992) 'The Problem of Globalisation: International Economic Relations, National Economic Management and the Formation of Trading Blocs', *Economy and Society*, 21. 4: 359–95.

Hirst, P. and Thompson, G. (1996) *Globalisation in Question*, Oxford: Polity.

Hirst, P. and Zeitlin, J. (1991) 'Flexible Specialisation Versus Post-Fordism: Theory, Evidence and Policy Implications', *Economy and Society*, 20. 1: 1–56.

Hitt, M. A., Middlemist, R. D. and Mathis, R. L. *et al.* (1986) *Management Concepts and Effective Practice*, St Paul: West Publishing.

Hobsbawm, E. J. (1975) *The Age of Capital: 1845–1875*, London: Weidenfeld and Nicholson.

Hochschild, A. R. (1983) *The Managed Heart: Commercialisation of Human Feeling*, London: University of California Press.

Hochschild, A. R. (1993) 'Preface' to S. Fineman (ed.) *Emotion in Organizations*, London: Sage.

Hofstede, G. (1980) *Cultures Consequences: International Differences in Work Related Values*, Beverley Hills, Calif.: Sage.

Hofstede, G. (1986) 'Review of E. H. Schein, Organisational Culture and Leadership: A Dynamic View', *Organisation Studies*, 7. 2.

Hofstede, G. (1990), 'The Cultural Relativity of Organisational Practices and Theories', in D. Wilson and R. Rosenfeld (eds) *Managing Organizations: Texts, Readings and Cases*, Maidenhead: McGraw Hill.

Hofstede, G. (1991) *Cultures and Organisations: Software of the Mind*, Maidenhead: McGraw-Hill.

Hofstede, G. and Søndergaard, M. (1993) 'Transfer of Management Ideas to Eastern European Business Organisations', paper presented to the 11th EGOS Colloquium, Paris.

Hogg, M. A. and Abrams, D. (1990) 'Social Motivation, Self-Esteem and Social Identity', in D. Abrams and M. A. Hogg (eds) *Social, Identity Theory: Constructive and Critical Advances*, Hemel Hempstead: Harvester Wheatsheaf.

Hogg, M. A. and Abrams, D. (eds) (1990) *Social Identity Theory: Constructive And Critical Advances*, Hemel Hempstead: Harvester Wheatsheaf.

Holland, S. (1975) *The Socialist Challenge*, London: Quartet.

Hollander, E. P. (1964) *Leaders, Groups and Influence*, New York: Oxford University Press.

Holloway, J. (1987) 'The Red Rose of Nissan', *Capital and Class*, 32: 142–64.

Hollway, W. (1984) 'Fitting Work: Psychological Assessment in Organizations', in J. Henriques, W. Hollway and C. Urwin (eds) *Changing the Subject: Psychology, Social Regulation and Subjectivity*, London: Methuen.

Hollway, W. (1991) *Work Psychology and Organisational Behaviour: Managing the Individual at Work*, London: Sage.

Holton, R. J. and Turner, B. S. (1989) *Max Weber on Economy and Society*, London: Routledge.

Homans, G. C. (1961) *Social Behaviour: Its Elementary Forms*, London: Routledge and Kegan Paul.

Honey, P. and Mumford, A. (1982) *Manual of Learning Styles*, Maidenhead: Honey.

Hope, V. and Hendry, J. (1995) 'Corporate Culture: Is it Relevant for the Organisations of the 1990s?' *Human Resource Management Journal*, 5. 4: 61–73.

Höpfl, H. (1992) 'The Challenge of Change: The Theory and Practice of Organisational Transformations', paper presented to the Employment Research Unit Annual Conference, Cardiff Business School, September.

Höpfl, H., Smith, S. and Spencer, S. (1992) 'Values and Variations: The Conflicts Between Culture Change and Job Cuts', *Personnel Review*, 21. 1: 24–38.

Hopper, T., Cooper, D., Lowe, T., Capps, T. and Mouritsen, J. (1986) 'Management Control and Worker Resistance in the National Coal Board: Financial Controls in the Labour Process', in D. Knights and H. Willmott (eds) *Managing the Labour Process*, Aldershot: Gower.

Hopwood, A. (1974) *Accounting and Human Behaviour*, London: Prentice Hall.

Horne, J. H. and Lupton, T. (1965) 'The Work Activities of Middle Managers', *Journal of Management Studies*, 2. 1: 14–33.

Hosking, D. and Morley, I. (1991) *A Social Psychology of Organising: People, Processes and Contexts*, Hemel Hempstead: Harvester Wheatsheaf.

Hosking, D. M. and Anderson, N. (1992) *Organisational Change and Innovation: Psychological Perspectives and Practices in Europe*, London: Sage.

House, R. J. and Mitchell, T. R. (1974) 'A Path-Goal Theory of Leadership', *Journal of Contemporary Business*, Autumn: 81–98.

Howard, S. (1985) 'Big Blue's Big Family', *International Labour Reports*, March–April.

Howarth, N. and Hughes, S. (2000) 'Internationalisation, Industrial Relations Theory International Relations', *Journal of Industrial Relations*, 42. 2: 195–213.

Huczynski, A. A. (1993) *Management Gurus*, London: Routledge.

Huczynski, A. and Buchanan, D. (2000) *Organizational Behaviour: An Introductory Text*, London: Financial Times/Prentice Hall.

Hull, R. (2000) 'Knowledge Management and the Conduct of Expert Labour', in C. Prichard, R. Hull, M. Chumer and H. Willmott (eds) *Managing Knowledge: Critical Investigations of Work and Learning*, London: Macmillan.

Hunter, L. and MacInnes, J. (1992) 'Employers and Labour Flexibility: Evidence from the Case Studies', *Employment Gazette*, June: 307–15.

Huselid, M. (1995) 'The Impact of Human Resource Management Practices on Turnover, Production and Corporate Financial Performance', *Academy of Management Journal*, 38: 635–72.

Hutton, W. (1992) *The State We're In*, London: Cape.

Hyman, R. (1981) 'Whatever Happened to Industrial Sociology?' in D. Dunkerley and G. Salaman (eds) *The International Yearbook of Organisation Studies 1980*, London: Routledge and Kegan Paul.

Hyman, R. (1986) 'Trade Unions and the Law: Papering Over the Cracks?', *Capital and Class*, 31: 93–114.

Hyman, R. (1987) 'Strategy or Structure: Capital, Labour and Control', *Work, Employment and Society*, 1. 1: 25–55.

Hyman, R. (1988) 'Flexible Specialisation: Miracle or Myth?' in R. Hyman and W. Streek (eds) *Trade Unions, Technology and Industrial Democracy*, Oxford: Blackwell.

Hyman, R. (1991) 'Plus ça Change? The Theory of Production and the Production of Theory', in A. Pollert (ed.) *Farewell to Flexibility?* Oxford: London.

Ibancz, T. and Ininguez, L. (eds) (1997) *Critical Social Psychology*, London: Sage.

Ibarra, H. (1993) 'Personal Networks of Women and Minorities in Management: A Conceptual Framework', *Academy of Management Review*, 18: 56–87.

Ibarra, H. (1995) 'Race, Opportunity and Diversity of Social Circles in Managerial Networks', *Academy of Management Journal*, 38: 673–703.

Ichinowski, C., Kochan, T., Levine, D., Olsen, C. and Strauss, G. (1996) 'What Works at Work: Overview and Assessment', *Industrial Relations*, 35. 3: 299–333.

IHSM Consultants (1994) *Creative Career Paths in the NHS, Report no. 1: Top Managers*, London: Department of Health.

Inkson, K. (1993) 'Do Careers Exist? Studies of Managerial Job Change in the 90s', paper presented to the ANZAM Conference, Deakin University.

Institute of Management (1994) *The 1994 National Management Salary Survey*, London: Institute of Management.

Institute of Management (1995) *Survival of the Fittest: A Survey of Manager's Experience of and Attitudes to Work in the Post-Recession Economy*, London: Institute of Management.

Institute of Management (1996) *Are Managers Under Stress? A Survey of Management Morale*, London: Institute of Management.

IPM Digest (1986) 'Flexibility: In Search of a Definition', no. 253: August.

Israel, J. and Tajfel, H. (eds) (1972) *The Context of Social Psychology: A Critical Assessment*, London: Academic Press.

Itoh, M. (1984) 'Labour Control in Small Groups', *Radical America*, 18. 2, 3.

Izraeli, D. N. and Adler, N. J. (1994) 'Competitive Frontiers: Women Managers in a Global Economy', in N. J. Adler and D. N. Izraeli (eds) *Competitive Frontiers: Women Managers in a Global Economy*, Oxford: Blackwell.

Jackson, N. and Carter, P. (1991) 'In Defence of Paradigm Commensurability', *Organisation Studies*, 12. 1: 109–27.

Jackson, N. and Carter, P. (2000) *Rethinking Organisational Behaviour*, Harlow: Financial Times/Prentice Hall.

Jackson, P. (ed.) (1999) *Virtual Working: Social and Organisational Dynamics*, London: Routledge.

Jackson, T. (1994) 'Organisational Behaviour in International Management', Oxford: Butterworth-Heinemann.

Jacques, E. (1990) 'In Praise of Hierarchy', *Harvard Business Review*, Jan.–Feb.

Jacques, R. (1996) *Manufacturing the Employee: Management Knowledge From the 19th to the 21st Centuries*, London: Sage.

James, K., Lovato, C., Khoo, G. *et. al.* (1994) 'Social Identity Correlations of Minority Worker's Health', *Academy of Management Journal*, 37. 2, April: 383–96.

Janis, I. L. (1972) *Victims of Groupthink: A Psychological Study of Foreign Policy Decisions and Fiascoes*, Boston, Mass.: Houghton Mifflin.

Janis, I. L. and Mann, L. (1977) *Decision Making: A Psychological Analysis of Conflict, Choice and Commitment*, New York: Free Press.

Jeffreys, S. (1990) *Anticlimax*, London: Women's Press.

Jenkins, A. (1994) 'Teams: From Ideology to Analysis', *Organisation Studies*, 15. 6: 849–60.

Jenkins, C. D. (1979) 'Psychosocial Modifiers of Response to Stress', *Journal of Human Stress*, 5. 4: 3–15.

Jenkins, R. (1982) 'Management, Recruitment Procedures and Black Workers', Working Papers on Ethnic Relations, no. 18, Birmingham Research Unit on Ethnic Relations.

Jenkins, R. (1984) 'Divisions Over the International Division of Labour', *Capital and Class*, 34: 28–57.

Jenkins, R. (1986) *Racism and Recruitment: Managers, Organisations and Equal Opportunities in the Labour Market*, Cambridge: Cambridge University Press.

Jermier, J., Knights, D. and Nord, W. R. (eds) (1994) *Resistance and Power in Organisations*, London: Routledge.

Jessop, B. (1992) ''Towards the Schumpetarian Welfare State: Global Capitalism and Structural Competitiveness', unpublished paper.

Jewell, L. N. and Seigel, M. (1990) *Contemporary Industrial/Organisational Psychology*, 2nd edn., St. Paul, Minn.: West Publishing.

Jewson, N. and Mason, N. (1986) 'The Theory and Practice of Equal Opportunity Policies: Liberal and Radical Approaches', *Sociological Review*, 34: 307–34.

Johns, G. (1993) 'Constraints on the Adoption of Psychology-Based Personnel Practices: Lessons from Organisational Innovation', *Personnel Psychology*, 46: 569–92.

Johnson, I. and Moore, K. (1986) *The Tapestry Makers: Life and Work at Lee's Tapestry Works*, Birkenhead: Merseyside Docklands Community Project.

Johnson, P. and Gill, J. (1993) *Management Control and Organisational Behaviour*, London: Paul Chapman.

Johnson, T. (1972) *Professions and Power*, London: Macmillan.

Johnson, T. (1980) 'Work and Power', in G. Esland and G. Salaman (eds) *The Politics of Work and Occupations*, Milton Keynes: Open University Press.

Johnston, L. (1986) *Marxism, Class Analysis and Socialist Pluralism*, London: Allen and Unwin.

Jones, A. M. and Hendry, C. (1994) 'The Learning Organisation: Adult Learning and Organisational Transformation', *British Journal of Management*, 5. 2: 153–62.

Jones, A. N. and Cooper, C. L. (1980) *Combating Managerial Obsolescence*, Westport, Conn.: Greenwood.

Jones, B. (1991) 'A New Convergence?' *Work, Employment and Society*, 5. 1: 493–5.

Jones, B. (1997) *Forcing the Factory of the Future: Cybernation and Societal Institutions,* Cambridge: Cambridge University Press.

Jones, B. (1998) 'Whatever Happened to the Automatic Factory? A New Perspective on the Mutations of Fordism', paper presented to the Work, Employment and Society Conference, University of Cambridge, September.

Jones, C., Nickson, D. and Taylor, G. (1997) 'Whatever It Takes? Managing Empowered Workers and the Service Encounter in an International Hotel Chain', *Work, Employment and Society*, 11. 3: 541–54.

Jones, C., Thompson, P. and Nickson, D. (1998) 'Not Part of the Family? The Limits to Managing the Corporate Way in International Hotel Chains', *International Journal of Human Resource Management*, 9. 6: 1048–63.

Jones, G. (1978) 'Ideological Responses to Deskilling of Managerial Work', paper presented to the Conference on Deskilling, Nuffield.

Jones, O. (1994) 'Professionalism and Work Study: An Alternative Perspective on Subjectivity and the Labour Process', paper presented to the 12th International Labour Process Conference, Aston.

Jones, O. (1997) 'Changing the Balance? Taylorism, TQM and Work Organisation', *New Technology, Work and Employment*, 12. 1: 13–24.

Jowett, G. S. and O'Donnell, V. O. (1992) *Propaganda and Persuasion*, 2nd edn, Newbury Park: Sage.

Joyce, P. (1980) *Work, Society and Politics*, London: Methuen.

Kahle, L. R. (1984) *Attitudes and Social Adaptation*, Oxford: Pergamon.

Kamata, S. (1982) *Japan in the Passing Lane*, London: Pantheon.

Kamin, L. (1979) *The Science and Politics of IQ*, Harmondsworth: Penguin.

Kamoche, K. (1991) 'Human Resource Management: A Multiparadigmatic Analysis', *Personnel Review*, 20. 4: 3–14.

Kamoche, K. (1994) 'A Critique and a Proposed Reformulation of Strategic Human Resource Management', *Human Resource Management Journal*, 4. 4: 29–47.

Kandola, R. and Fullerton, J. (1994) *Managing the Mosaic: Diversity in Action*, London: Institute of Personnel Development.

Kanter, R. M. (1968) 'Commitment and Social Organisation: A Study of Commitment in Utopian Communities', *American Sociological Review*, 33. 4: 499–517.

Kanter, R. M. (1984) *The Change Masters*, London: Unwin.

Kanter, R. M. (1993) *Men and Women of the Corporation*, 2nd edn, New York: Basic Books.

Karasek, R. and Theorell, T. (1990) *Healthy Work: Stress, Productivity and the Reconstruction of Working Life*, New York: Basic Books.

Karmel, B. (ed.) (1980) *Point and Counterpoint in Organizations*, Hinsdale, Ill.: Dryden.

Katz, D, and Kahn, T. (1970) 'Open Systems Theory', in O. Grusky and G. A. Miller (eds) *The Sociology of Organizations: Basic Studies*, New York: Free Press.

Katz, D. and Kahn, R. L. (1966, 1978 2nd edn) *The Social Psychology of Organisations*, New York: Wiley.

Katz, F. E. (1968) *Autonomy and Organizations: The Limits of Social Control*, New York: Random House.

Katz, G. (1982) 'Previous Conformity, Status, and the Rejection of the Deviant', *Small Group Behaviour*, 13: 402–14.

Keenoy, T. (1992) 'Constructing Control', in J. F. Hartley and G. M. Stephenson (eds) *Employment Relations*, Oxford: Blackwell.

Keep, E. (2000) 'Creating a Knowledge Economy: Definitions, Challenges and Opportunities', paper presented to the Progress Conference, The 21st Century Challenge, London: Sept.

Keep, E. and Mayhew, K. (1999) 'Towards the Knowledge-Driven Economy: Some Policy Issues', *Renewal*, 7. 4: 50–59, 60–71.

Keith, B. and Collinson, D. (1994) 'Policing Gender: Barriers to Change in the Police', paper presented to the 12th Annual International Labour Process Conference, Aston University, March.

Kelley, H. (1971), 'The Warm–Cold Variable in First Impressions of Persons', *Journal of Personality*, 18: 431–39.

Kellner, D. (1988) 'Postmodernism as Social Theory: Some Challenges and Problems', *Theory, Culture and Society*, 5: 239–263.

Kellner, D. (1999) 'Theorising/Resisting McDonaldization: A Multiperspectivist App-roach', in B. Smart, *Resisting McDonaldization*, London: Sage.

Kelly, A. and Brannick, T. (1987) 'Personnel Practices and Strong Organisational Cultures in Ireland', paper presented at Conference on Japanisation of British Industry, UMIST.

Kelly, G. A. (1955) *The Psychology of Personal Constructs* (2 vols), New York: Norton.

Kelly, J. E. (1982) *Scientific Management, Job Design and Work Performance*, London: Academic Press.

Kelly, J. E. (1985) 'Management's Redesign of Work', in D. Knights, H. Willmott and D. Collinson (eds) *Job Redesign: Critical Perspectives on the Labour Process*, Aldershot: Gower.

Kelly, K. (1994) *Out of Control: The Rise of Neo-Biological Civilisation*, Reading, Mass.: Addison-Wesley.

Kelman, H. (1961) 'The Processes of Opinion Change', *Public Opinion*, 25: 57–78.

Keltner, J. W. (1973) *Elements of Interpersonal Communication*, Belmont, Calif.: Wadsworth.

Kerfoot, D. and Knights, D. (1994) 'Empowering the "Quality Worker": The Seduction and Contradiction of the Total Quality Phenomenon', in A. Wilkinson and H. Willmott (eds) *Making Quality Critical*, London: Routledge and Kegan Paul.

Kerr, C., Dunlop, J. J., Harbison, F. H. and Mayers, C. A. (1960) *Industrialism and Industrial Man*, Cambridge, Mass.: Harvard University Press.

Kets de Vries, M. R. F. and Miller, D. (1984) *The Neurotic Organisation: Diagnosing and Changing Counter-productive Styles of Management*, San Francisco: Jossey Bass.

Khandwalla, P. N. (1974) 'Viable and Effective Organisational Design of Firms', *Academy of Management Journal*: Sept.

Kieser, A. (1993) 'Review of Geert Hofstede, "Cultures and Organizations: Software of the Mind"', *Organisation Studies*, 14. 1: 85–8.

Kimmel, M. S. (1993) 'What do Men Want?' *Harvard Business Review*, Nov.–Dec.: 50–63.

King, N. and Anderson, N. (1995) *Innovation and Change in Organisations*, London: Routledge.

Kipnis, D. and Schmidt, S. M. (1988) 'Upward Influence Styles: Relationship with Performance Evaluations, Salary and Stress', *Administrative Science Quarterly*, 33: 528–42.

Kirton, G. and Greene, A-M. (2000) *The Dynamics of Managing Diversity: A Critical Approach*, Oxford: Butterworth Heinemann.

Kitschelt, W. (1992) 'Industrial Governance Structures, Innovation Strategies and the Case of Japan: Sectoral or Cross-National Comparison?' *International Organisation*, 45. 4: 163–88.

Klandermans, B. and Oegma, D. (1992) 'Potentials, Networks, Motivations and Barriers: Steps Toward Participation in Social Movements', *American Sociological Review*, 52: 519–31.

Klein, H. J. (1989) 'An Integrated Control Theory Model of Work Motivation', *Academy of Management Journal*, 14. 2: 150–72.

Knight, S. (1999) *Introducing NLP*, London: Institute of Personnel and Development.

Knights, D. and Collinson, D. (1987) 'Shop Floor Culture and the Problem of Managerial Control', in J. McGoldrick (ed.) *Business Case File in Behavioural Science*, London: Van Nystrand.

Knights, D. and Morgan, G. (1990) 'The Concept of Strategy in Sociology: A Note of Dissent', *Sociology*, 24: 475–83.

Knights, D. and Willmott, H. (1985) 'Power and Identity in Theory and Practice', *Sociological Review*, 33. 1: 22–46.

Knights, D. and Willmott, H. (eds) (1986a) *Gender and the Labour Process*, Aldershot: Gower.

Knights, D. and Willmott, H. (eds) (1986b) *Managing the Labour Process*, Aldershot: Gower.

Knights, D. and Willmott, H. (eds) (1988) *New Technology and the Labour Process*, London: Macmillan.

Knights, D. and Willmott, H. (1989) 'Power and Subjectivity at Work: From Degradation to Subjugation in Social Relations', *Sociology*, 23. 4: 535–58.

Knights, D. and Willmott, H. (eds) (1990) *Labour Process Theory*, London: Macmillan.

Knights, D. and Willmott, H. (eds) (2000) *The Reengineering Revolution*, London: Sage.

Knights, D., Willmott, H. and Collinson, D. (eds) (1985) *Job Redesign: Critical Perspectives on the Labour Process*, London: Gower.

Knoke, D. (1990) Political Networks: *The Structural Perspective*, New York: Cambridge University Press.

Kochan, T., Katz, H. C. and McKersie, R. B. (1986) *The Transformation of American Industrial Relations*, New York: Basic Books.

Kochan, T. and Osterman, P. (1994) *The Mutual Gains Enterprise*, Boston, Mass: Harvard Business School Press.

Kohn, M. L. and Schooler, C. (1983) *Work and Personality: An Inquiry into the Effects of Social Stratification*, NJ: Ablex.

Kolb, D. A. (1976) *The Learning Style Inventory: Technical Manual*, Boston, Mass.: MacBer.

Komter, A. (1991) 'Gender, Power and Feminist Theory', in K. Davis, M. Leijenaar and J. Oldersma (eds) *The Gender of Power*, London: Sage.

Kondo, G. (1990) *Crafting Selves*, Chicago: University of Chicago Press.

Kotter, J. (1982) *The General Manager*, New York: Free Press.

Kouzmin, A. (1980) 'Control in Organisational Analysis: the Lost Politics', in D. Dunkerley and G. Salaman (eds) *The International Yearbook of Organisation Studies 1979*, London: Routledge and Kegan Paul.

Kraft, P. (1999) 'To Control and Inspire: US Management in the Age of Computer Information Systems and Global Production', in M. Wardell, T. L. Steiger and P. Meiksens (eds) *Rethinking the Labor Process*, Albany: State University of New York Press.

Kraft, P. and Dubnoff, S. (1986) 'Job Characteristics in Computer Software', *Industrial Relations* (USA), 25. 2: 179–95.

Kram, K. E. (1983) 'Phases of the Mentor Relationship', *Academy of Management Journal*, 26: 608–35.

Krugman, P. (1999) *The Return of Depression Economics*, London: Allen Lane.

Kuhn, T. (1970) *The Structure of Scientific Revolutions*, 2nd edn, Chicago: University of Chicago Press.

Kumar, K. (1996) *From Post-Industrial to Post-Modern Society*, Oxford: Blackwell.

Kunda, G. (1992) *Engineering Culture: Control and Commitment in a High Tech Corporation*, Philadelphia: Temple University Press.

Kyotani, E. (1999) 'New Managerial Strategies of Japanese Corporations', in A. Felstead and N. Jewson (eds) *Global Trends in Flexible Labour*, London: Macmillan.

Labour Research Department (1986a) 'Flexibility Examined', Bargaining Report, London, LRD.

Labour Research Department (1986b) 'Franchising – Who Really Benefits?' August, London: LRD.

Labour Research Department (1988) 'Stress at Work: The Trade Union Response', London: LRD.

Landes, D. S. (1969) *The Unbound Prometheus*, Cambridge: Cambridge University Press.

Landry, C., Morley, D., Southwood, R. and Wright, P. (1985) *What a Way to Run a Railroad: An Analysis of Radical Failure*, London: Comedia.

Lane, C. (1991) 'Industrial Reorganisation in Europe', *Work, Employment and Society*, 5. 4: 515–39.

Langer, E. J. (1981) 'Rethinking the Role Of Thought in Social Interaction', in J. H. Harvey, W. Ickes and R. F. Kidd (eds) *New Directions in Attribution Research*, vol. 2, New York: Erlbaum.

Larsen, K. S. (1980) *Social Psychology: Crisis or Failure?*, Monmouth, Ore.: Institute for Theoretical History.

Lasch, C. (1985) *The Minimal Self: Psychic Survival in Troubled Times*, London: Picador.

Lash, S. and Urry, J. (1987) *The End of Organized Capitalism*, Cambridge: Polity.

Lawler, E., Mohrman, I. and Ledford, G. E. (1995) *Creating High Performance Organizations*, San Francisco: Jossey Bass.

Lawlor, E. E. (1976) 'Control Systems in Organizations', in H. D. Dunnette (ed.) *Handbook of Industrial and Organisational Psychology*, Chicago: Rand McNally.

Lawrence, P. R. and Lorsch, J. W. (1967) *Organisation and Environment*, Cambridge, Mass.: Harvard University Press.

Layder, D. (1987) 'Key Issues in Structuration Theory: Some Critical Remarks', *Current Perspectives in Social Theory*, 8: 25–46.

Layton, E. T. (1969) 'Science, Business and the American Engineer', in R. Perruci and J. E. Gersth (eds) *The Engineer and the Social System*, New York: Wiley.

Lazarus, R. S. (1966) *Psychological Stress and the Coping Process*, New York: McGraw-Hill.

Leadbetter, C. (1999) *Living on Thin Air: The New Economy*, London: Viking.

Leavitt, H. J. (1951) 'Some Effects of Certain Communication Patterns on Group Performance', *Journal of Abnormal and Social Psychology*, 46: 38–50.

Leavitt, H. J. (1965) 'Applied Organisational Change in Industry: Structural, Technological and Humanistic Approaches', in J. G. March (ed.) *Handbook of Organizations*, Chicago: Rand McNally.

Leavitt, H. J. (1978) *Managerial Psychology*, , 4th edn, Chicago: UCP.

Leavitt, H. J. and Bahrami, H. (1988) *Managerial Psychology: Managing Behaviour in Organizations*, 5th edn, Chicago: University of Chicago Press.

Ledwith, S. and Colgan, F. (eds) (1996) *Women in Organisations: Challenging Gender Politics*, London: Macmillan.

Lee, B. (1985) 'Internal Politics', in K. Elliot and P. Lawrence (eds) *Introducing Management*, Harmondsworth: Penguin.

Lee, R. and Lawrence, P. (1985) *Organisational Behaviour: Psychology at Work*, London: Hutchinson.

Leflaive, X. (1996) 'Organisations as Structures of Domination', *Organisation Studies*, 17. 1: 23–47.

Legge, K. (1978) *Power, Innovation and Problem-Solving in Management*, London: Hutchinson.

Legge, K. (1989) 'Human Resource Management: A Critical Analysis', in J. Storey (ed.) *New Perspectives in Human Resource Management*, London: Routledge.

Legge, K. (1995) *Human Resource Management: The Rhetorics, the Realities*, London: Macmillan.

Lehman, C. and Tinker, T. (1985) 'The Not-So-Great Society: The Role of Business Literature on Reshuffling Johnson's New Deal', paper presented to the Conference on the Labour Process, Aston-UMIST.

Leidner, R. (1993) *Fast Food, Fast Talk: Service Work and the Routinization of Everyday Life*, Berkeley: University of California Press.

Leonard, P. (1984) *Personality and Ideology: Towards a Materialist Understanding of the Individual*, London: Macmillan.

Lessem, R. (1985) 'The Enabling Company', in D. Clutterbuck (ed.) *New Patterns of Work*, Aldershot: Gower.

Lessem, R. (1986) *The Roots of Excellence*, London: Fontana.

Leverment, Y., Ackers, P. and Preston, D. (1998) 'Professionals in the NHS: A Case Study of Business Process Re-engineering', *New Technology, Work and Employment*, 13. 2: 129–39.

Levitt, T. (1991) 'The Globalization of Markets', in C. A. Montgomery and M. E. Porter (eds) *Strategy Seeking and Securing Competitive Advantage*, Boston: Harvard Business School Press.

Lewin, K, Lippitt, R. and White, R. K. (1939) 'Patterns of Aggressive Behaviour in Experimentally Created Social Climates', *Journal of Social Psychology*, 10: 271–301.

Lewin, K. (1947) 'Frontiers in Group Dynamics', *Human Relations*, 1: 5–41.

Lewin, K. (1951) *Field Theory in Social Science*, New York: Harper and Row.

Lewin, K. (1956) 'Studies in Group Decision', in D. Cartwright and A. Zander (eds) *Group Dynamics: Research and Theory*, 2nd edn, Evanston, Ill.: Row Peterson.

Lewis, M. (1975) 'Early Sex Differences in the Human: Studies of Socioemotional Development', *Archives of Sexual Behaviour*, 4. 4: 329–35.

Lewis, R. (1984) (ed.) *Open Learning in Action: Case Studies, Open Learning Guide 1*, London: Council for Educational Technology.

Lewis, R. A. (1991) 'Models for Managing Change', *Management Development Review*, 4. 5: 3–6.

Likert, R. (1961) *New Patterns of Management*, New York: McGraw-Hill.

Limerick, D., Passfield, R. and Cunnington, B. (1994) 'Transformational Change: Towards an Action Learning Organisation', *The Learning Organisation*, 1. 2: 29–40.

Lindblom, C. E. (1959) 'The Science of Muddling Through', *Public Administration Review*, 19: 79–88.

Linstead, S. and Grafton Small, R. G. (1992) 'On Reading Organisation Culture', *Organisation Studies*, 13. 3: 331–45.

Lipietz, A. (1982) 'Towards Global Fordism?' *New Left Review*, 132: 33–47.

Lippman, W. (1922) *Social Opinion*, New York: Harcourt Brace.

Littler, C. R. (1980) 'Internal Contract and the Transition to Modern Work Systems', in D. Dunkerley and G. Salaman (eds) *The International Yearbook of Organisation Studies 1979*, London: Routledge and Kegan Paul.

Littler, C. R. (1982) *The Development of the Labour Process in Capitalist Societies*, London: Heinemann.

Littler, C. R., Bramble, B. and McDonald, J. (1994) *Organisational Restructuring: Downsizing, Delayering and Managing Change at Work*, Canberra: Commonwealth of Australia.

Littler, C. R. and Salaman, G. (1982) 'Bravermania and Beyond', *Sociology*, 132: 33–47.

Lloyd, M. (1993) 'The (F)utility of a Feminist Turn to Foucault', *Economy and Society*, 22. 4: 437–60.

Locke, E. and Latham, G. P. (1984) *Goal Setting: A Motivational Technique that Works!* London: Prentice Hall.

Lockett, M. (1988) 'Culture and the Problems of Chinese Management', *Organisation Studies*, 9. 4: 484–97.

Lodge, D. (1990) *Nice Work*, Harmondsworth: Penguin.

Lofy, M. M. (1998) 'The Impact of Emotion on Creativity in Organizations', *Empowerment in Organizations*, 6. 1: 5–12.

Loveridge, R. (1982) 'Business Strategy and Community Culture', in D. Dunkerley and G. Salaman (eds) *The International Yearbook of Organisation Studies 1979*, London: Routledge and Kegan Paul.

Lucas, M. (1986) *How to Survive the 9–5*, Thames: Methuen.

Lukes, S. (1974/1982) *Power: A Radical View*, London: Macmillan.

Lupton, T. and Gowler, D. (1969) *Selecting a Wage Payment System*, London: Kogan Page.

Luthans, F. (1981) *Organisation Behaviour*, 3rd edn, New York: McGraw Hill.

Lynn, R. (1966) 'Brainwashing Techniques in Leadership and Childrearing', *British Journal of Social and Clinical Psychology*, 5: 270–3.

Mabey, C., Salaman, G. and Storey, J. (1998) 'Strategic Human Resource Management: The Theory of Practice and the Practice of Theory', in C. Mabey, G. Salaman and J. Storey (eds) *Strategic Human Resource Management*, London: Sage.

McArdle, L., Proctor, S. J., Rawlinson, M., Hassard, J. and Forrester, P. (1994) 'Total Quality Management and Participation: Employee Involvement or the Enhancement of Exploitation?' in A. Wilkinson and H. Willmott (eds) *Making Quality Critical*, London: Routledge.

McCabe, D. (2000) 'The Team Dream: The Meaning and Experience of Teamworking for Employees in an Automobile Manufacturing Company', in S. Proctor and F. Mueller (eds) *Teamworking*, London: Macmillan.

McCann, D. (1988) *'How to Influence Others at Work'*, London: Heinemann.

McClelland, D. (1961) *The Achieving Society*, New Jersey: Van Nostrand.

Maccoby, M. (1977) *The Gamesman*, New York: Simon and Schuster.

McCullough, A. and Shannon, M. (1977) 'Organisation and Protection', in S. Clegg and D. Dunkerley (eds) *Critical Issues and Organizations*, London: Routledge and Kegan Paul.

MacDuffie, J. P. (1995) 'Human Resource Bundles and Manufacturing Performance: Organisational Logic and Flexible Production Systems in the World Auto Industry', *Industrial and Labor Relations Review*, 48: 197–221.

McGill, M., Slocum, J. and Lei, D. (1992) 'Management Practices in Learning Organisations', *Organisational Dynamics* (Summer): 5–17.

McGregor, D. (1960) *The Human Side of the Enterprise*, New York: Harper and Row.

McHugh, D. (1997) 'Self-Serving Bias: The Attribution of Cause as a Significant Form of Managerial Labour', paper presented to the 15th International Labour Process Conference, Edinburgh University, March.

McHugh, D., Groves, D. and Alker, A. (1994) 'Cultural Heuristics and Behavioural Change: What do We Learn from a Learning Organisation?' paper presented to the Conference on the Strategic Direction of HRM, Nottingham-Trent University, December.

McHugh, D., Groves, D. and Alker, A. (1998) 'Self-Managed Learning and Behavioural Change: What do we Learn from a Learning Organisation?', *The Learning Organisation*, 5, 5.

MacInnes, J. (1987) *Thatcherism at Work*, Milton Keynes: Open University Press.

McKenna, E. (1987) *Psychology in Business: Theory and Applications*, London: Lawrence Erlbaum.

McKenna, E. (1994) *Business Psychology and Organisational Behaviour: A Student's Handbook*, Hove: Lawrence Erlbaum.

McKenna, E, (2000) *Business Psychology and Organisational Behaviour*, 3rd edn, Hove: Psychology Press.

McKinlay, A. (1999) 'Recasting the Visible Hand? Strategy, Structure and Process in UK Manufacturing, c. 1970–97', *Contemporary British History*, 13. 3: 148–63.

McKinlay, A. (2000) 'The Bearable Lightness of Control: Organisational Reflexivity and the Politics of Knowledge Management', in C. Prichard, R. Hull, M. Chumer and H. Willmott (eds) *Managing Knowledge: Critical Investigations of Work and Learning*, London: Macmillan.

McKinlay, A. and Taylor, P. (1996) 'Power, Surveillance and Resistance: Inside the Factory of the Future', in P. Ackers, C. Smith and P. Smith (eds) *The New Workplace and Trade Unionism*, London: Routledge.

MacKinnon, C. A. (1979) *Sexual Harassment of Working Women*, New Haven, Conn.: Yale University Press.

McLellan, D. (1973) *Karl Marx: His Life and Thought*, London: Macmillan.

Maddock, S. and Parkin, D. (1993) 'Gender Cultures, Women's Choices and Strategies at Work', *Women in Management Review*, 8. 2: 3–9.

Maguire, M. (1986) 'Recruitment as a Means of Control', in K. Purcell, S. Wood, A. Watson and S. Allen (eds) *The Changing Experience of Employment, Restructuring and Recession*, London: Macmillan.

Mangum, G. L. and Mangum, S. L. (1986) 'Temporary Work: The Flip Side of Job Security', *International Journal of Manpower*, 7. 1: 12–20.

Mann, S. (1999) *Hiding What We Feel, Faking What We Don't: Understanding the Role of your Emotions at Work*, Shaftesbury: Element.

Manz, C. C. and Sims, H. P. (1989) *SuperLeadership: Leading Others to Lead Themselves,*: New York, NY: Prentice Hall.

March, J. G. and Simon, H. A. (1958) *Organizations*, New York: Wiley.

Marchington, M. (1992) 'Managing Labour Relations in a Competitive Environment', in A. Sturdy, D. Knights and H. Willmott (eds) *Skill and Consent*, London: Routledge.

Marchington, M. and Parker, P. (1987) 'Japanisation: a Lack of Chemical Reaction?' paper presented to the Conference on Japanisation of British Industry, UMIST.

Marchington, M. and Wilkinson, A. (1998) 'Direct Participation', in K. Sisson and S. Bach (eds) *Personnel Management in Britain*, 3rd edn, Oxford: Blackwell.

Marchington, M., Wilkinson, M., Ackers, P. and Goodman, J. (1993) 'The Influence of Managerial Relations on Waves of Employee Involvement', *British Journal of Industrial Relations*, 31. 4: 553–76.

Marcuse, H. (1971) 'Industrialisation and Capitalism', in O. Stammer (ed.) *Max Weber and Sociology Today*, Oxford: Blackwell.

Margerison, C. J. and McCann, D. J. (1986) 'The Margerison-McCann Team Management Resource – Theory and Applications', *International Journal of Manpower*, 7. 2.

Marginson, P. (1991) 'Change and Continuity in the Employment Structures of Large Companies', in A. Pollert (ed.) *Farewell to Flexibility?*, Oxford: Blackwell.

Marginson, P., Armstrong, P., Edwards, P. and Purcell, J. (1995) 'Extending Beyond Borders: Mutinational Companies and the International Management of Labour', *International Journal of Human Resource Management*, 6. 3: 702–19.

Marglin, S. A. (1974) 'What do Bosses Do? The Origins and Functions of Hierarchy in Capitalist Production', *Review of Radical Political Economics*, 6: 60–102.

Marks, A., Findlay, P., Hine, J., McKinlay, A. and Thompson, P. (1997) 'Handmaid's Tale or Midwives of Change? HR Managers and Organisational Innovation', *Journal of Strategic Change*, 6: 469–80.

Marks, A., Findlay, P., Hine, J., McKinlay, A. and Thompson, P. (1998) 'The Politics of Partnership: Innovation in Employment Relations in the Scottish Spirits Industry', *British Journal of Industrial Relations*, 36. 2: 209–26.

Mars, G. (1983) *Cheats at Work: An Anthology of Workplace Crime*, London: Unwin.

Marsden, R. (1993) 'The Politics of Organisational Analysis', *Organisation Studies*, 14. 1: 93–124.

Martin, J. (1990) 'Deconstructing Organisational Taboos: The Suppression of Gender Conflict in Organisations', *Organisational Science*, 1: 1–21.

Martin, J. (1992) *Cultures in Organisations: Three Perspectives*, New York: Oxford University Press.

Martin, J. (1998) *Organisational Behaviour*, London: International Thomson Business Press.

Martin, J. and Siehl, C. (1983) 'Organisational Culture and Counterculture: An Uneasy Symbiosis', *Organisational Dynamics*, Autumn: 52–64.

Martin, P. (1993) 'Feminist Practice in Organizations', in E. Fagenson (ed.) *Women in Management: Trends, Issues and Challenges in Management Diversity*, Newbury Park, Calif.: Sage.

Martin, P. and Nicholls, D. (1987) *Creating a Committed Workforce*, London: Institute of Personnel Management.

Martinez Lucio, M. and Weston, S. (1992) 'Human Resource Management and Trade Union Responses: Bringing the Politics of the Workplace Back into the Debate', in P. Blyton and P. Turnbull (eds) *Reassessing Human Resource Management*, London: Sage.

Martinko, M. J. (ed.) (1995) *Attribution Theory: An Organisational Perspective*, Florida: St. Lucie.

Marx, K. (1963) *Early Writings*, trans. T. B. Bottomore, New York, NY: McGraw-Hill.

Marx, K. (1984) 'The Spirit of Bureaucracy and Beyond Bureaucracy: The Paris Commune', in F. Fischer and C. Sirriani (eds) *Critical Studies in Organisation and Bureaucracy*, Philadelphia: Temple University Press.

Maslow, A. H. (1954) *Motivation and Human Personality*, New York: Harper and Row.

Masreliez-Steen, G. (1989) *Male and Female Management*, Sweden: Kontura Group.

Mather, C. (1987) 'Disposable Workers', *New Internationalist*, July.

Mathews, J. (1993) 'Organisational Innovation: Competing Models of Productive Efficiency', paper presented to the Fifth APROS International Colloquium, Honolulu, Hawaii.

Mathews, J. (1994) *Catching the Wave: Workplace Reform in Australia*, New York: ILR.

Maurice, M., Sorge, A. and Warner, M. (1980) 'Societal Differences in Organising Manufacturing Units', *Organisation Studies*, 1. 1: 63–91.

Mayo, E. (1946) *Human Problems of an Industrial Civilisation*, New York: Macmillan.

Mead, G. H. (1934) *Mind, Self and Society*, Chicago: Chicago University Press.

Mechanic, D. (1962) 'Sources of Power of Lower Participants in Complex Organizations', *Administrative Science Quarterly*, 7: 349–64.

Meek, V. L. (1988) 'Organisational Culture: Origins and Weaknesses', *Organisation Studies*, 9. 4: 453–73.

Meindl, J. R. and Ehrlich, S. B. (1987) 'The Romance of Leadership and the Evaluation of Organisational Performance', *Academy of Management Journal*, 30: 91–109.

Meindl, J. B., Ehrlich, S. B. and Dukerich, J. M. (1985) 'The Romance of Leadership', *Administrative Science Quarterly*, 30: 78–102.

Melling, J. (1982) 'Men in the Middle or Men on the Margin', in D. Dunkerley and G. Salaman (eds) *The International Yearbook of Organisation Studies 1981*, London: Routledge and Kegan Paul.

Merton, R. K. (1949) *Social Theory and Social Structure*, Glencoe, Ill.: Free Press.

Meyer, J. W. and Rowan, B. (1977) 'Institutionalised Organizations: Formal Structure as Myth and Ceremony', *American Journal of Sociology*, 83. 2: 340–63.

Meyer, J. W. and Scott, R. W. (1983) *Organisational Environments: Ritual and Rationality*, Beverley Hills, Calif.: Sage.

Meyer, M., Stevenson, W. and Webster, S. (1985) *Limits to Bureaucratic Growth*, New York: Walter De Gruyter.

Meyer, P. B. (1986) 'General Motors' Saturn Plant: A Quantum Leap in Technology and its Implications for Labour and Community Organizations', *Capital and Class*, 30: 73–96.

Miliband, R. (1969) *The State in Capitalist Society*, London: Weidenfeld and Nicholson.

Milkman, R. (1997) *Farewell to the Factory: Auto Workers in the Late Twentieth Century,* Berkeley, Calif.: University of California Press.

Milkman, R. (1998) 'The New American Workplace: High Road or Low Road?' in P. Thompson and C. Warhurst (eds) *Workplaces of the Future*, London: Macmillan.

Miller, D. R. (1963) 'The Study of Social Relationships: Situations, Identities and Social Interaction', in S. Koch (ed.) *Psychology: A Study of a Science*, vol. 5, New York: McGraw-Hill.

Miller, E. J. and Rice, A. K. (1967) *Systems of Organisation: The Control of Task and Sentient Boundaries*, London: Tavistock.

Miller, G. A., Galanter, E. and Pribram, K. H. (1960) *Plans and the Structure of Behaviour*, London: Holt.

Miller, H. G. and Verduin, J. R. (1979) *The Adult Educator: A Handbook for Staff Development*, Houston: Gulf.

Miller, N. E. and Dollard, J. (1953) *Social Learning and Imitation*, New Haven, Conn.: Yale University Press.

Miller, P. and O'Leary, T. (1987) 'The Entrepreneurial Order', paper presented to the Conference on the Labour Process, Aston-UMIST.

Miller, P. M. (1989) 'Strategic HRM: What it Is and What it Isn't', *Personnel Management*, February.

Mills, A. J. (1991) 'Organisational Discourse and the Gendering of Identity', paper presented to the Conference on Towards a New Theory of Organisations, University of Keele.

Mills, A. J. and Murgatroyd, S. J. (1991) *Organisational Rules: A Framework for Understanding Organisations*, Milton Keynes: Open University Press.

Mills, A. J. and Tancred, P. (eds) (1992) *Gendering Organisational Analysis*, London: Sage.

Mills. A. J. and Murgatroyd, S. J. (1991) *Organisational Rules: a Framework for Understanding Organizations*, Milton Keynes: Open University Press.

Mills, C. W. (1959) *The Power Elite*, Oxford: Oxford University Press.

Millward, N. (1994) *The New Industrial Relations?* London: Policy Studies Institute.

Millward, N., Bryson, A. and Forth, J. (2000) *All Change at Work: British Employment Relations 1980–1988, As Portrayed by the Workplace Industrial Relations Survey Series*, London: Routledge.

Millward, T., Stevens, M., Smart, D. and Hawkes, W. R. (1992) *Workplace Industrial Relations in Transition, The ED/ESRC/PS1/ACAS Surveys*, Aldershot: Dartmouth.

Mintzberg, H. (1973) *The Nature of Managerial Work*, New York: Harper and Row.

Mintzberg, H. (1983) *Structure in Fives: Designing Effective Organizations*, Englewood Cliffs, NJ: Prentice Hall.

Mirchandani, K. (1999) 'Re-Forming Organisations: Contributions of Teleworking Employees', in P. J. Jackson (ed.) *Virtual Working*, London: Routledge.

Mischel, W. (1973) 'Towards a Cognitive Social Learning Reconception of Personality', *Psychological Review*, 80: 200–13.

Mitter, S. (1986) *Common Fate, Common Bond: Women in the Global Economy*, London: Pluto.

Montgomery, D. (1976) 'Workers' Control of Machine Production in the Nineteenth Century', *Labor History*, 17. 4: 486–509.

Morgan, D. and Stanley, L. (eds) (1993) *Debates in Sociology*, Manchester: Manchester University Press.

Morgan, G. (1986) *Images of Organisation*, London: Sage.

Morgan, G. (1990b) *Organizations in Society*, London: Sage.Morgan, G. (1990a) 'Paradigm Diversity in Organisational Research', in J. Hassard and D. Pym (eds) *The Theory and Philosophy of Organizations*, London: Routledge.

Morgan, G. and Hooper, D. (1987) 'Corporate Strategy, Ownership and Control', *Sociology*, 21. 4: 609–27.

Morgan, K. and Sayer, A. (1984) 'A "Modern" Industry in a "Mature" Region: The Re-Making of Management–Labour Relations', working paper, Urban and Regional Studies, University of Sussex.

Morishima, M. (1995) 'Embedding HRM in a Social Context', *British Journal of Industrial Relations*, 33. 4: 617–40.

Morris, J. (1987) 'The Who, Why, and Where of Japanese Manufacturing Investment in the UK', paper presented to the Conference on Japanisation of British Industry, UMIST.

Moscovici, S. (1972) 'Society and Theory in Social Psychology', in J. Israel and H. Tajfel (eds) *The Context of Social Psychology: A Critical Assessment*, London: Academic Press.

Moscovici, S. and Zavalloni, M. (1969) 'The Group as a Polarizer of Attitudes', *Journal of Personality and Social Psychology*, 12: 125–35.

Mueller, F. (1994a) 'Societal Effect, Organisational Effect Globalisation', *Organisation Studies*, 15. 3: 407–28.

Mueller, F. (1994b) 'Teams Between Hierarchy and Commitment: Change Strategies and the "Internal Environment"', *Journal of Management Studies*, 31. 3: 383–403.

Mueller, F. (1996) 'Internationalisation of Markets and the Externalisation of Hierarchy in MNCS', paper presented to the Conference on Globalisation of Production and Regulation of Labour, Warwick.

Mulgan, G. (1989) 'The Power of the Weak', in S. Hall and M. Jacques (eds) *New Times*, London: Lawrence and Wishart.

Mulholland, K. (1998) '"Survivors" Versus "Moves and Shakers": The Reconstitution of Management and Careers in the Privatised Utilities', in P. Thompson and C. Warhurst (eds) *The Future Workplace*, London: Macmillan.

Mullins, L. (1985) *Management and Organisation Behaviour*, London: Pitman.

Mullins, L. J. (1999) *Management and Organisational Behaviour*, 5th edn, London: Financial Times/Pitman.

Munro, R. (1994) 'Governing the New Province of Quality: Autonomy, Accounting and the Dissemination of Accountability', in A. Wilkinson and H. Willmott (eds) *Making Quality Critical*, London: Routledge and Kegan Paul.

Murakami, T. (1997) 'The Autonomy of Teams in the Car Industry: A Cross-National Comparison', *Work, Employment and Society*, 11. 4: 749–58.

Murphy, L. R. and Sorenson, S. (1988) 'Employee Behaviours Before and After Stress Management', *Journal of Organisational Behaviour*, 9: 173–82.

Murray, F. (1983) 'The Decentralisation of Production and the Decline of the Mass-Collective Worker', *Capital and Class*, 19: 74–9.

Murray, F. (1987) 'Flexible Specialisation and the Third Italy', *Capital and Class*, 33: 84–95.

Murray, P. and Wickham, J. (1985) 'Women Workers and Bureaucratic Control in Irish Electronic Factories', in H. Newby (ed.) *Restructuring Capital, Reorganisation in Industrial Society*, London: Macmillan.

Murray, R. (1985) 'Benetton Britain', *Marxism Today*, November.

Myers, C. S. (1926) *Industrial Psychology in Great Britain*, London: Jonathan Cape.

Myers, C. S. (ed.) (1929) *Industrial Psychology*, London: Thornton Butterworth.

Myers, M. T. and Myers, G. E. (1982) *Managing by Communication: An Organisational Approach*, New York: McGraw-Hill.

Nadworny, M. (1955) *Scientific Management and the Unions*, Cambridge: Mass.: Harvard University Press.

Naisbitt, J. and Aburdene, P. (1985) *Reinventing the Corporation*, London: MacDonald.

Nandhakumar, J. (1999) 'Virtual Teams and Lost Proximity: Consequences on Trust Relationships', in P. J. Jackson (ed.) *Virtual Working*, London: Routledge.

NEDO (1986) *Changing Working Patterns*, report prepared by the Institute for Manpower Studies for the National Economic Development Office in Association with the Department of Employment, London: NEDO.

Neimark, M. and Tinker, T. (1986) 'On Rediscovering Marx: Dissolving Agency–Structure in Dialectical Unity', paper presented to the Conference on the Labour Process, Aston-UMIST.

Nelson, D. (1975) *Managers and Workers: Origins of the New Factory System in the United States 1880–1920*, Madison: University of Wisconsin Press.

Newell, H. and Dopson, S. (1996) 'Muddle in the Middle: Organisational Restructuring and Middle Management Careers', *Personnel Review*, 25. 4.

Newton, T. (1994) 'Resocialising the Subject? A Re-Reading of Grey's "Career as a Project of the Self"', *Sociology*, 28. 2, Working Paper Series, Department of Business Studies, University of Edinburgh.

Newton, T. (1996) 'Postmodernism and Action', *Organisation*, 3. 1: 7–29.

Newton, T. and Findlay, P. (1996) 'Playing God? The Performance of Appraisal', *Human Resource Management Journal*, 6. 3: 42–58.

Newton, T., with Handy, J. and Fineman, S. (1995) *'Managing' Stress: Power and Emotion at Work*, London: Sage.

Ng, C. W. and Fosh, P. (2000) 'Prospects for Women Workers at East Asia Air: Sky's the Limit or Rough Climb Through Thick Clouds?' paper presented to the Employment Relations Research Unit Conference, Cardiff Business School.

Nichols, T. (1986) *The British Worker Question*, London: Routledge and Kegan Paul.

Nichols, T. and Beynon, H. (1977) *Living With Capitalism*, London: Routledge and Kegan Paul.

Nicholson, N. (1997) 'Evolutionary Psychology: Towards a New View of Human Nature and Organisational Society', *Human Relations*, 50. 9.

Nickson, D., Warhurst C., Witz, A. and Cullen, A. M. (2001) 'The Importance of Being Aesthetic: Work, Employment and Service Organisations', in A. Sturdy, I. Grugulis and H. Willmott (eds) *Customer Service*, London: Palgrave.

Noble, D. (1979) 'Social Change in Machine Design', in A. Zimbalist (ed.) *Case Studies in the Labour Process*, London: Monthly Review Press.

Nohria, N. (1992) 'Is a Network Perspective a Useful Way of Studying Organizations?' in N. Nohria and R. G. Eccles (eds) *Networks and Organizations*, Boston, Mass.: Harvard Business School Press.

Nohria, N. and Eccles, R. G. (eds) (1992) *Networks and Organizations*, Boston, Mass.: Harvard Business School Press.

Nonaka, I. and Takeuchi, H. (1995) *The Knowledge Creating Company*, Oxford: Oxford University Press.

Nord, W. R. and Fox, S. (1996) 'The Individual in Organisational Studies: The Great Disappearing Act', in S. Clegg, C. Hardy and W. Nord (eds) *Handbook of Organisation Studies*, London: Sage.

Norris, C. (1992) *Uncritical Theory: Postmodernism, Intellectuals and the Gulf War*, London: Lawrence and Wishart.

North-West Women Into Management (1987) Newsletter, Manchester: June.

Nyland, C. (1987) 'Scientific Management and Planning', *Capital and Class*, 33: 55–83.

Ó Riain, S. (1998) 'Networking for a Living: Irish Software Developers in the Global Workplace', paper presented to the Work Difference and Social Change Conference, Binghamton, May.

O'Brien, G. E. (1992) 'Changing Meanings of Work', in J. F. Hartley and G. M. Stephenson (eds) *Employment Relations*, Oxford: Blackwell: 44–66.

O'Connell Davidson, J. (1993) *Privatisation and Employment Relations: The Case of the Water Industry*, London: Mansell.

O'Connell Davidson, J. (1994a) 'On Power, Prostitution and Pilchards: The Self-Employed Prostitute and Her Clients', paper presented to the 12th Annual International Labour Process Conference, Aston University, March.

O'Connell Davidson, J. (1994b) 'What Do Franchisers Do? Control and Commercialisation in Milk Distribution', *Work, Employment and Society*, 8. 1: 23–44.

O'Donnell, M. (1996) 'Into the Mystic: Cultural Change and TQM Teams in the NSW Public Sector', *Journal of Industrial Relations* (Australia), 38. 2: 241–63.

OECD (1977) *The Development of Industrial Relations Systems: Some Implications of the Japanese Experience*: Paris: OECD.

Ogbonna, E. (1992a) 'Managing Organisational Culture: Fantasy or Reality?' *Human Resource Management*, 3. 2.

Ogbonna, E. (1992b) 'Organisation Culture and Human Resource Management: Dilemmas and Contradictions', in P. Blyton and P. Turnbull (eds) *Reassessing Human Resource Management*, London: Sage.

Ogbonna, E. and Wilkinson, B. (1988) 'Corporate Strategy and Corporate Culture: The View from the Checkout', *Personnel Review*, 19. 4.

Oldersma, J. and Davis, K. (1991) 'Introduction', in K. Davis, M. Leijenaar and J. Oldersma (eds) *The Gender of Power*, London: Sage.

Oliver, J. (1993) 'A Degree of Uncertainty', *Management Today*, June.

O'Neill, J. (1986) 'The Disciplinary Society: From Weber to Foucault', *British Journal of Sociology*, 37. 1: 42–60.

O'Neill, N. (1985) 'Marxism and Psychology', in M. Shaw (ed.) *Marxist Sociology Revisited*, London: Macmillan.

O'Reilly, C. A. and Chatman, J. A. (1996) 'Culture as Social Control: Corporations, Cults and Commitment', in B. M. Staws and L. L. Cummings (eds) *Research in Organisational Behaviour*, 18: 157–200, Greenwich, Conn.: JAI.

O'Reilly, J. (1992) 'Where Do You Draw the Line? Functional Flexibility, Training and Skill in Britain and France', *Work, Employment and Society*, 6. 3: 369–96.

Osterman, P. (1994) 'How Common is Workplace Transformation and How Can We Explain Who Adopts it?' *Industrial and Labor Relations Review*, Jan.: 175–88.

Ouchi, W. G. (1981) *Theory Z*, Reading, Mass.: Addison-Wesley.

Ouchi, W. G. and Johnson, J. B. (1978) 'Types of Organisational Control and Their Relationship to Emotional Well Being', *Administrative Science Quarterly*, 23, June: 293–317.

Palmer, B. (1975) 'Class Conception and Conflict', *Review of Radical Political Economics*, 17. 2: 31–49.

Palmer, I. and Hardy, C. (2000) *Thinking About Management*, London: Sage.

Parker, I. (1997) 'The Unconscious State of Social Psychology', in T. Ibanez and L. Ininguez (eds) *Critical Social Psychology*, London: Sage.

Parker, I. and Spears, R. (eds) (1996) *Psychology and Society: Radical Theory and Practice*, London: Pluto.

Parker, M. (1992) 'Post-Modern Organizations or Post-Modern Organisation Theory?' *Organisation Studies*, 13. 1: 1–17.

Parker, M. (1998a) 'Capitalism, Subjectivity and Ethics: Debating Labour Process Analysis', *Organisation Studies*, 20. 1: 25–45.

Parker, M. (1998b) 'Organisational Culture and the Disciplines of Organisation: The Career of a Concept', paper presented to the International Labour Process Conference, UMIST.

Parker, M. (1999) *Organisation Culture and Identity*, London: Sage.

Parker, M. and Jary, D. (1994) 'Academic Subjectivity and the New Managerialism', paper presented to the 13th International Labour Process Conference, Aston.

Parker, M. and McHugh, G. (1991) 'Five Texts in Search of An Author: A Response to John Hassard's "Multiple Paradigms and Organisational Analysis: A Case Study"', *Organisation Studies*, 12. 3: 451–6.

Parker, M. and Slaughter, J. (1988) *Choosing Sides: Unions and the Team Concept, Labor Notes*, Boston: South End Press.

Parsons, T. (1951) *The Social System*, New York: Collier Macmillan.

Parsons, T. (1956) 'Suggestions for a Sociological Approach to the Theory of Organizations', *Administrative Science Quarterly*, 1: 63–85, 225–39.

Parsons, T. (1960) *Structure and Process in Modern Societies*, Chicago: Free Press.

Pascale, R. (1990) *Managing on the Edge*, Harmondsworth: Penguin.

Pascale, R. T. and Athos, A. G. (1982) *The Art of Japanese Management*, Harmondsworth: Penguin.

Pearce, F. (1989) *The Radical Durkheim*, London: Unwin Hyman.

Pearson, R. (1986) 'Female Workers in the First and Third Worlds: The "Greening" of Women's Labour', in K. Purcell, S. Wood, A. Watson and S. Allen (eds) *The Changing Experience of Employment, Restructuring and Recession*, London: Macmillan.

Penn, R. (1985) *Skilled Workers in the Class Structure*, Cambridge: Cambridge University Press.

Penn, R. (1986) *Socialisation into Skilled Identities: An Analysis of a Neglected Phenomenon*, paper presented to the Conference on the Labour Process, Aston–UMIST.

Perlmutter, H. V. (1969) 'The Tortuous Evolution of the Multinational Corporation', *Columbia Journal of World Business*, Jan.-Feb.: 9–18.

Perloff, R. M. (1993) *The Dynamics of Persuasion*, Hillsdale, NJ: Lawrence Erlbaum.

Perrons, D. (2000) 'Living with Risk: Labour Market Transformation, Employment Policies and Social Reproduction in the UK', *Economic and Industrial Democracy*, 21: 283–310.

Perrow, C. (1961) 'The Analysis of Goals in Complex Organisations', *American Sociological Review*, 26: 854–66.

Perrow, C. (1972) *Complex Organizations: A Critical Essay*, Glenview, Ill.: Scott Foreman.

Perrow, C. (1973) 'The Short and Glorious History of Organisational Theory', *Organisational Dynamics*, Summer, 2–15.

Perrow, C. (1979) *Complex Organizations: A Critical Essay*, (2nd edn), Glenview, Ill.: Scott Foreman.

Perrow, C. (1992) 'Small Firm Networks', in N. Nohria and R. G. Eccles (eds) *Networks and Organizations*, Boston, Mass.: Harvard Business School Press.

Peters, T. (1989) *Thriving on Chaos*, London: Pan.

Peters, T. (1992) *Liberation Management: Necessary Disorganisation for the Nanosecond Nineties*, New York: Alfred Knopf.

Peters, T. J. and Austin, N. (1986) *A Passion for Excellence*, New York: Random House.

Peters, T. J. and Waterman, R. H. (1982) *In Search of Excellence: Lessons from America's Best-Run Companies*, New York: Harper and Row.

Pettigrew, A. (1973) *The Politics of Organisational Decision-Making*, London: Tavistock.

Pettigrew, A. (1985) *The Awakening Giant: Continuity and Change at Imperial Chemical Industries*, Oxford: Blackwell.

Pettigrew, A. and Whipp, R. (1991) *Managing Change for Competitive Success*, Oxford: Blackwell.

Petty, R. E. and Cacioppo, J. T. (1981) *Attitudes and Persuasion: Classic and Contemporary Approaches*, Iowa: Wm. C. Brown.

Pfeffer, J. (1981a) 'Management as Symbolic Action', *Research in Organisational Behaviour*, 3: 1–52.

Pfeffer, J. (1981b) *Power in Organizations*, London: Pitman.

Pfeffer, J. (1982) *Organizations and Organization Theory*, Boston: Pitman.

Pfeffer, J. (1987) 'A Resource Dependence Model of Intercorporate Relations', in M. S. Mizruchi and M. Schwartz (eds) *Intercorporate Relations: The Structural Analysis of Business*, Cambridge: Cambridge University Press.

Pfeffer, J. (1992) *Managing with Power: Politics and Influence in Organizations*, Boston: Harvard Business School Press.

Pfeffer, J. (1993) 'Barriers to the Development of Organisational Science: Paradigm Development as a Dependent Variable', *Academy of Management Review*, 18: 599–620.

Pfeffer, J. (1997) *New Directions for Organisational Theory: Problems and Practices*, Oxford: Oxford University Press.

Pheysey, D. (1993) *Organisational Cultures: Types and Transformations*, London: Routledge.

Phizacklea, A. (1987) 'Minority Women and Economic Restructuring: The Case of Britain and the Federal Republic of Germany',*Work, Employment and Society*, 1. 3: 309–25.

Pierson, C. (1984) 'New Theories of State and Civil Society', *Sociology*, 18. 4: 563–71.

Piore, M. J. (1986) 'Perspectives on Labour Market Flexibility', *Industrial Relations*, 25. 2: 146–66.

Piore, M. J. and Sabel, C. F. (1984) *The Second Industrial Divide: Possibilities for Prosperity*, New York: Basic Books.

Pitelis, C. (1993) 'Transnationals, International Organisation and Deindustrialisation', *Organisation Studies*, 14. 4: 527–548.

Poggio, B. (2000) 'Between Bytes and Bricks: Gender Cultures in Work Contexts', *Economic and Industrial Democracy*, 21: 381–402.

Polan, A. J. (1984) *Lenin and the End of Politics*, London: Methuen.

Pollard, S. (1965) *The Genesis of Modern Management*, London: Edward Arnold.

Pollert, A. (1981) *Girls, Wives, Factory Lives*, London: Macmillan.

Pollert, A. (1988a) 'Dismantling Flexibility', *Capital and Class*, 34, Spring: 42–75.

Pollert, A. (1988b) 'The Flexible Firm: Fixation or Fact?' *Work, Employment and Society*, 2. 3: 281–316.

Pollert, A. (ed.) (1991) *Farewell to Flexibility?* Oxford: London.

Pollert, A. (1991) 'The Orthodoxy of Flexibility', in A. Pollert (ed.) *Farewell to Flexibility?* Oxford: London.

Pollert, A. (1996) 'Teamwork on the Assembly Line: Contradiction and the Dynamics of Union Resilience', in P. Ackers, S. Smith and P. Smith (eds) *The New Workplace and Trade Unionism*, London: Routledge.

Poole, M. and Mansfield, R. (1992) 'Managers' Attitudes to Human Resource Management', in P. Blyton and P. Turnbull (eds) *Reassessing Human Resource Management*, London: Sage.

Porter, M. (1980) *Competitive Strategy*, New York: Free Press.

Porter, M. E. (1990) *The Competitive Advantage of Nations*, London: Macmillan.

Potter, I. (1997) 'Discourse and Critical Social Psychology', in T. Ibanez and L. Ininugez (eds) *Critical Social Psychology*, London: Sage.

Potter, J. and Wetherall, M. (1987) *Discourse and Social Psychology*, London: Sage.

Potterfield, T. A. (1999) *The Business of Employee Empowerment: Democracy, Ideology and the Workplace*, Westport: Quorum.

Poulantzas, N. (1975) *Classes in Contemporary Capitalism*, London: New Left Books.

Prethus, R. (1962) *The Organisational Society*, London: Macmillan.

Prichard, C. (1998) 'Identity Work – Moving the "Theory of the Subject" From "Division To Depth" in Labour Process Analysis', paper presented to the 16th Annual International Labour Process Conference, Manchester School of Management, April.

Pringle, R. (1989) *Secretaries Talk: Sexuality, Power and Work*, London: Verso.

Proctor, A. J., Rowlinson, M., McArdle, L., Hassard, J. and Forrester, P. (1994) 'Flexibility, Politics and Strategy: In Defence of the Model of the Flexible Firm', *Work, Employment and Society*, 8. 2: 221–42.

Proctor, S. and Mueller, F. (2000) 'Teamworking: Strategy, Systems and Culture', in S. Proctor and F. Mueller (eds) *Teamworking*, London: Macmillan.

Pugh, D. S. (ed.) (1971) *Organisation Theory*, Harmondsworth: Penguin.

Pugh, D. S. and Hickson, D. J. (1973) 'The Comparative Study of Organizations', in G. Salaman and K. Thompson (eds) *People and Organizations*, Harlow: Longman.

Pugh, D. S. and Hickson, D. J. (1976) *Organisation Structure in its Context: The Aston Programme 1*, London: Saxon House.

Pugh, D. S., Hickson, D. J. and Hinings, C. R. (1968) 'Dimensions of Organisation Structure', *Administrative Science Quarterly*, 13: 65–103.

Pugh, D. S., Hickson, D. J. and Hinings, C. R. (1969) 'An Empirical Taxonomy of Structures of Work Organizations', *Administrative Science Quarterly*, 14.

Pugh, D. S., Hickson, D. J., Hinings, C. R., MacDonald, K. M., Turner, C. and Lapton, T. (1963) 'A Conceptual Scheme for Organisational Analysis', *Administrative Science Quarterly*, 16.

Purcell, J. (1987) 'Mapping Management Styles in Industrial Relations', *Journal of Management Studies*, 24. 5: 535–48.

Purcell, J. (1991) 'The Impact of Corporate Strategy on Human Resource Management', in J. Storey (ed.) *New Perspectives in Human Resource Management*, London: Routledge.

Purcell, J. and Sissons, K. (1983) 'A Strategy for Management Control in Industrial Relations', in J. Purcell and R. Smith (eds) *The Control of Work*, London: Macmillan.

Purcell, K., Hogarth, K. and Simm, C. (1999) *Whose Flexibility?* London: Joseph Rowntree Foundation.

Purcell, K., Wood, S., Watson, A. and Allen, S. (eds) (1986) *The Changing Experience of Employment, Restructuring and Recession*, London: Macmillan.

Putnam, L. L. and Mumby, D. K. (1993) 'Organizations, Emotion and the Myth of Rationality', in S. Fineman (ed.) *Emotions in Organisations*, London: Sage.

Quinn Mills, D. (1993) *Rebirth of the Corporation*, New York: Wiley.

Rabinow, P. (ed.) (1991) *The Foucault Reader*, Harmondsworth: Peregrine.

Rainbird, H. (1991) 'The Self-Employed: Small Entrepreneurs or Disguised Wage Labourers?' in A. Pollert (ed.) *Farewell to Flexibility?* Oxford: Blackwell.

Rainnie, A. (1988) *Employment Relations in the Small Firm*, London: Routledge and Kegan Paul.

Rajan, A. (1999) *Employment: Bridging the Gap Between Rhetoric and Reality*, London: Centre for Research in Employment and Technology in Europe.

Ramazanoglu, C. (1987) 'Sex and Violence in Academic Life or You Can't Keep a Good Man Down', in J. Hammer and M. Maynard (eds) *Women, Violence and Social Control, Explorations in Sociology* no. 23, London: Macmillan.

Ramsay, H. (1983) 'Evolution or Cycle? Worker Participation in the 1980s', in C. Crouch and F. Heller (eds) *Organisational Democracy and Political Processes*, London: Pitman.

Ramsay, H. (1985) 'What is Participation For: A Critical Evaluation of "Labour Process" Analyses of Job Reform', in D. Knights, H. Willmott and D. Collinson (eds) *Job Redesign: Critical Perspectives on the Labour Process*, London: Gower.

Ramsay, H. (1991) 'Reinventing the Wheel? A Review of the Development and Performance of Employee Involvement', *Human Resource Management Journal*, 1. 4: 1–22.

Ramsay, H. and Scholarios, D. (1998) 'Women and Workplace Democracy: An Attitude Problem?' unpublished paper, University of Strathclyde.

Ramsay, H., Scholarios, D. and Harley, B. (2000) 'Employees and High-Performance Work Systems: Testing Inside the Black Box', *British Journal of Industrial Relations*, 38. 4: 501–31.

Ramsay, K. and Parker, M. (1992) 'Gender, Bureaucracy and Organisational Culture', in A. Witz and M. Savage (eds) *Gender and Bureaucracy*, Oxford: Blackwell.

Randle, K. (1995) 'The Whitecoated Worker: Professional Autonomy in a Period of Change', paper presented to the 13th Annual International Labour Process Conference, University of Central Lancashire, Preston.

Randle, K. and Rainnie, A. (1994) 'Control, Contradiction and Complexity in a Pharmaceutical Research Company', paper presented to the 12th International Labour Process Conference, Aston.

Randolph, W. A. (1995) 'The Empowerment Effort that Came Undone', *Harvard Business Review*, Jan.–Feb.: 20–31.

Ray, C. A. (1986) 'Corporate Culture: the Last Frontier of Control?' *Journal of Management Studies*, 23. 3: 287–97.

Reed, M. (1984) 'Management as a Social Practice', *Journal of Management Studies*, 21. 3: 273–85.

Reed, M. (1985) *Redirections in Organizational Analysis*, London: Tavistock.

Reed, M. (1990a) 'The Labour Process Perspective on Management Organisation: A Critique and Reformulation', in J. Hassard and D. Pym (eds) *The Theory and Philosophy of Organizations*, London: Routledge.

Reed, M. (1990b) 'From Paradigm to Images: The Paradigm Warrior Turns Post-Modernist Guru', *Personnel Review*, 19. 3: 35–40.

Reed, M. (1991) 'Scripting Scenarios for a New Organisation Theory and Practice', *Work, Employment and Society*, 5. 1: 119–32.

Reed, M. (1992a) 'Experts, Professions and Organizations in Late Modernity', paper presented to the Employment Research Unit Conference, Cardiff Business School.

Reed, M. (1992b) *The Sociology of Organisations*, London: Harvester.

Reed, M. (1993) 'Organizations and Modernity: Continuity and Discontinuity in Organisation Theory', in J. Hassard and M. Parker (eds) *Postmodernism and Organizations*, London: Sage.

Reed, M. (1996a) 'Organisational Theorising: A Historically Contested Terrain', in S. Clegg, C. Hardy and W. Nord (eds) *Handbook of Organisation Studies*, London: Sage.

Reed, M. (1996b) 'Rediscovering Hegel: The "New Historicism" in Organisation and Management Studies', *Journal of Management Studies*, 33. 2: 139–58.

Reed, M. (1997) 'In Praise of Duality and Dualism: Rethinking Agency and Structure in Organisational Analysis', *Organisation Studies*, 18. 1: 21–42.

Reed, M. and Hughes, M. (eds) (1992) *Rethinking Organisation: New Directions in Organisation and Analysis*, London: Sage.

Rees, T. (1992) *Women and the Labour Market*, London: Routledge.

Reich, R. (1991), 'Who is Them?' *Harvard Business Review*, March–April.

Reich, R. (1993) *The Work of Nations*, London: Simon and Schuster.

Reicher, S. (1997) 'Laying the Ground for a Common Critical Psychology', in T. Ibanez and L. Ininugez (eds) *Critical Social Psychology*, London: Sage.

Reinstein, A. and Bayou, M. E. (1997) 'Critical Thinking in Accounting Education: Processes, Skills And Applications', *Managerial Auditing Journal*, 12. 7: 336–42.

Resch, M., Hacker, W., Leitner, K. and Krogoll, T. (1984) 'Regulation Requirements and Regulation Barriers: Two Aspects of Industrial Work', in M. Thomas (ed.) *Design of Work in Automated Manufacturing Systems*, Oxford: Pergamon.

Rhinesmith, S. (1991) 'Going Global From the Inside Out', *Training and Development*, 45: 42–7.

Rifkin, J. (1995) *The End of Work: The Decline of the Global Labour Force and the Dawn of the Post-Market Era*, New York: G. P. Putnam.

Rifkin, J. (1999), *The Biotech Century*, New York: Tarcher Putnam.

Ritzer, G. (1993) *The McDonaldization of Society*, London: Pine Forge.

Ritzer, G. (1975) *Sociology: A Multiple Paradigm Science*, Boston, Mass.: Allyn and Bacon.

Ritzer, G. (1996) 'The McDonaldization Thesis: Is Expansion Inevitable?' *International Sociology*, 11. 3: 291–308.

Ritzer, G. (1996) *Sociological Theory*, 4th edn, New York: McGraw Hill.

Ritzer, G. (1998) 'McJobs: McDonaldization and Its Relationship to the Labour Process', in G. Ritzer (ed.) *The McDonaldization Thesis*, London: Sage.

Robertson, D., Rinehart, J. and Huxley, C. (1992) 'Team Concept: A Case Study of Japanese Production Management in a Unionised Canadian Auto Plant', paper presented to the 10th International Labour Process Conference, Aston.

Robinson, P. (1999) 'Explaining the Relationship Between Flexible Employment and Labour Market Regulation', in A. Felstead and N. Jewson (eds) *Global Trends in Flexible Labour*, London: Macmillan.

Roeber, J. (1975) *Social Change at Work*, London: Duckworth.

Roethlisberger, F. G. and Dickson, W. J. (1964) *Management and the Worker*, New York: Wiley.

Roethlisberger, F. G. and Dickson, W. J. (1984) 'Human Relations and the Informal Organisation', in F. Fischer and C. Sirriani (eds) *Management and the Worker*, New York: Wiley.

Roffe, I. (1999) 'Innovation and Creativity In Organisations: A Review of the Implications for Training and Development', *Journal of European Industrial Training*, 23. 4/5: 224–41.

Rogers, C. (1969) *Freedom To Learn: Studies of the Person*, Columbus, Ohio: Charles Merrill.

Rollinson, D., Broadfield, A. and Edwards, D. J. (1998) *Organisational Behaviour and Analysis: An Integrated Approach*, Harlow: Addison-Wesley.

Roper, M. (1994) *Masculinity and the British Organisation Man Since 1945*, Oxford: Oxford University Press.

Rose, G. (1978) *The Melancholy Science: An Introduction to the Thought of Theodore W. Adorno*, London: Macmillan.

Rose, M. (1986) *Industrial Behaviour*, Harmondsworth: Penguin.

Rose, M. and Jones, B. (1985) 'Managerial Strategy and Trade Union Responses in Work Reorganization Schemes at Establishment Level', in D. Knights, H. Wilmott and D. Collinson (eds) *Job Redesign: Critical Perspectives on the Labour Process*, London: Gower.

Rose, N. (1989) 'Individualising Psychology', in J. Shotter and K. J. Gergen (eds) *Texts of Identity*, London: Sage: 99–118.

Rose, N. (1990) *Governing the Soul: The Shaping of the Private Self*, London: Routledge.

Rosenberg, S. and Lapidus, J. (1999) 'Contingent and Non-Standard Work in the United States: Towards a More Poorly Compensated, Insecure Workforce', in A. Felstead and N. Jewson (eds) *Global Trends in Flexible Labour*, London: Macmillan.

Rosener, J. (1990) 'Ways Women Lead', *Harvard Business Review*, Nov.-Dec.: 119–25.

Rosenfeld, P., Giacolone, R. A. and Riordan, C. A. (1995) *Impression Management in Organizations*, London: Routledge.

Rosenman, R. H., Friedman, M. and Strauss, R. (1964) 'A Predictive Study of CHD', *Journal of the American Medical Association*, 189: 15–22.

Rosenthal, P., Hill, S. and Peccei, R. (1997) 'Checking Out Service: Evaluating Excellence, HRM and TQM in Retailing', *Work, Employment and Society*, 11. 3: 481–503.

Rosier, M. (1997) 'Postmodernism, Postmodernity and Social Psychology', in T. Ibanez and L. Ininugez (eds) *Critical Social Psychology*, London: Sage.

Rosnow, R. L. (1981) *Paradigms in Transition: The Methodology of Social Enquiry*, New York: Oxford University Press.

Rothschild, J. and Allen Whitt, J. (1986) *The Cooperative Workplace: Potentials and Dilemmas or Organisational Democracy and Participation*, Cambridge: Cambridge University Press.

Rothwell, S. (1987) 'Selection and Training for Advanced Manufacturing Technology', in T. D. Wall, C. W. Clegg and N. J. Kemp (eds) *The Human Side of Advanced Manufacturing Technology*, Chichester: Wiley.

Rothwell, W. J. and Kazanas, H. C. (1986) 'The Attitude Survey as an Approach to Human Resource Strategic Planning', *Journal of Managerial Psychology*, 2: 15–18.

Rotter, J. B. (1972) 'Generalised Expectancies for Internal versus External Control of Reinforcement', in J. B Rotter, J. E. Chance and E. J. Phare (eds) *Applications of a Social Learning Theory of Personality*, New York: Holt, Rinehart and Winston.

Rowlinson, M. (1997) *Organisations and Institutions*, London: Macmillan.

Rowlinson, M. and Hassard, J. (2000) 'Marxist Political Economy, Revolutionary Politics and Labour Process Theory', *International Studies of Management and Organisation*, 30. 4: 85–111.

Roy, D. F. (1973) 'Banana Time, Job Satisfaction and Informal Interaction', in G. Salaman and K. Thompson (eds) *People and Organizations*, Harlow : Longman.

RSA Inquiry (1994) *Tomorrow's Company: The Role of Business in a Changing World*, London: Royal Society of Arts.

Rubery, J., Smith, M. and Fagan, C. (1999) *Women's Employment in Europe: Trends and Prospects*, London: Routledge.

Rueschemeyer, D. (1986) *Power and the Division of Labour*, London: Polity.

Rugman, A. (2000) *The End of Globalization*, London: Random House.

Russ, G. S. (1991) 'Symbolic Communication and Image Management in Organizations', in R. A. Giacolone and P. Rosenfeld (eds) *Applied Impression Management: How Image-Making Affects Managerial Decisions*, Calif.: Sage.

Ryan, R. (1992) 'Flexibility in New Zealand Workplaces: A Study of Northern Employers', *New Zealand Journal of Industrial Relations*, 17: 129–47.

Sabel, C. (1991) 'Mobius Strip Organizations and Open Labour Markets: Some Consequences of the Reintegration of Conception and Execution in a Volatile Economy', in J. Coleman and P. Bourdieu (eds) *Social Theory for a Changing Society*, Boulder, Colo.: Westview.

Sabel, C. F. (1982) *Work and Politics and the Division of Labour in Industry*, Cambridge: Cambridge University Press.

Salaman, G. (1979) *Work Organizations: Resistance and Control*, London: Longman.

Salaman, G. (1981) *Class and the Corporation*, London: Fontana.

Salaman, G. (1986) *Working*, London: Tavistock.

Salaman, G. and Thompson, K. (eds) (1973) *People and Organizations*, Harlow: Longman.

Salaman, G. and Thompson, K. (eds) (1980) *Control and Ideology in Organizations*, Milton Keynes: Open University Press.

Salancik, G. R. and Pfeffer, J. (1978) 'A Social Information Processing Approach to Job Attitudes and Task Design', *Administrative Science Quarterly*, 23: 224–53.

Sandberg, A. (1993) 'Volvo Human-Centred Work Organisation: The End of the Road?' *New Technology, Work and Employment*, 8. 2.

Sandberg, A. (ed.) (1995) *Enriching Production*, Aldershot, Avebury.

Sandelands, L. E. and Srivatsan, V. (1993) 'The Problem of Experience in the Study of Organizations', *Organisation Studies*, 14. 1: 1–22.

Sargent, A. G. (1983) *The Androgynous Manager*, New York: AMACOM.

Saunders, C. S. (1981) 'Management Information Systems, Communication and Depart-mental Power: An Integrative Model', *Academy of Management Review*, 6: 431–42.

Sayer, A. (1986) 'New Developments in Manufacturing: the Just-in-Time System', *Capital and Class*, 30: 43–72.

Sayer, A. and Ray, L. (eds) (1999) *Culture and Economy after the Cultural Turn*, London: Sage.

Sayer, D. (1991) *Capitalism and Modernity: An Excursus on Marx and Weber*, London: Routledge.

Sayles, C. R. (1958) *Behaviour of Industrial Work Groups*, New York: Wiley.

Scarborough, H. and Burrell, G. (1996) 'The Axeman Cometh: The Changing Roles and Knowledges of Middle Managers', in S. R. Clegg and G. Palmer (eds) *The Politics of Management Knowledge*, London: Sage.

Schein, E. H. (1965) *Organisational Psychology*, 1st edn, Englewood Cliffs, NJ: Prentice Hall (also 1980, 3rd edn.).

Schein, E. H. (1985) *Organisational Culture and Leadership: A Dynamic View*, San Francisco: Jossey Bass.

Schienstock, G. (1991) *The Brave New World of the Multinational Corporation*, 10th EGOS Colloquium, Vienna.

Schiller, D. (1999) *Digital Capitalism Networking the Global Market System*, Boston: MIT Press.

Schlenker, B. R. (1980) *Impression Management*, Monterey: Brooks/Cole.

Schneider, M. (1975) *Neurosis and Civilisation: A Marxist/Freudian Synthesis*, New York: Seabury.

Schneider, S. C. and Barsoux, J-L. (1997) *Managing Across Cultures*, London: Prentice Hall.

Schor, J. B. (1993) *The Overworked American: The Unexpected Decline of Leisure*, New York: Basic Books.

Schultz, M. and Hatch, M-J. (1996) 'Living with Multiple Paradigms: The Case of Paradigm Interplay in Organisational Culture Studies', *Academy of Management Review*, 21: 529–57.

Schumann, M. (2000) 'The Development of Industrial Labour: New Inconsistencies', *Economic and Industrial Democracy*, 21: 97–106.

Schutz, A. (1967) *The Phenomenology of the Social World*, Evanston: North Western University Press.

Schwartz, H. S. (1983) 'A Theory of Denotic Work Motivation', *Journal of Applied Behavioural Science*, 14: 204–14.

Scott, A. (1994) *Willing Slaves? British Workers Under Human Resource Management*, Cambridge: Cambridge University Press.

Scott, J. (1979) *Corporations, Classes and Capitalism*, Hutchinson: London.

Scott, J. (1985) 'Ownership, Management and Strategic Control', in K. Elliot and P. Lawrence (eds) *Introducing Management*, Harmondsworth: Penguin.

Seivers, B. (1986) 'Beyond the Surrogate of Motivation', *Organisation Studies*, 7. 4.

Seligman, M. E. P. (1975) *Helplessness*, San Francisco: Freeman.

Selznick, P. (1949) *TVA and the Grass Roots*, Berkeley, Calif.: University of California Press.

Selznick, P. (1957) *Leadership in Administration*, Evanston: Row Peterson.

Senge, P. M. (1992) 'Building Learning Organisations: The Real Message of the Quality Movement', *Journal for Quality and Participation*, March.

Sennett, R. (1998) *The Corrosion of Character: The Personal Consequences of Work in the New Capitalism*, London: W. W. Norton.

Seve, L. (1978) *Man in Marxist Theory and the Psychology of Personality*, Sussex: Harvester.

Sewell, G. (1998) 'The Discipline of Teams: The Control of Team-Based Industrial Work Through Electronic and Peer Surveillance', *Administrative Science Quarterly*, 43: 406–69.

Sewell, G. and Wilkinson, B. (1992) '"Someone to Watch Over Me": Surveillance, Discipline and the Just-in-Time Labour Process', *Sociology*, 26. 2: 271–89.

Shaiken, H., Herzenberg, S. and Kuhn, S. (1986) 'The Work Process Under More Flexible Production', *Industrial Relations*, 125. 2: 167–83.

Shamir, B (1991) 'Meaning, Self and Motivation in Organisations', *Organisation Studies*, 12. 3: 405–24.

Sharpe, D. (1996) 'Changing Managerial Control Strategies and Subcultural Processes: An Ethnographic Study on the Hano Assembly Line', paper presented to the 14th Annual Labour Process Conference, Aston.

Sharpe, R. (1998) 'Globalisation: The Next Tactic in the 50-Year Struggle of Labour and Capital in Software Production', paper presented to the Work Difference and Social Change Conference, Binghamton, May.

Shaw, M. (1990) 'Strategy and Social Process: Military Context and Sociological Analysis', *Sociology*, 24. 3: 465–73.

Shenhav, Y. (1999) *Manufacturing Rationality: The Engineering Foundations of the Managerial Revolution*, Oxford: Oxford University Press.

Sheppard, D. (1989) 'Organizations, Power and Sexuality: The Image and Self-Image of Women Managers', in J. Hearn, D. L. Sheppard, P. Tancred-Sheriff and G. Burrell (eds) *The Sexuality of Organisation*, London: Sage.

Shotter, J. and Gergen, K. J. (1989) *Texts of Identity*, London: Sage.

Shrivastava, P. (1983) 'A Typology of Organisational Learning Systems', *Journal of Management Studies*, 20. 1: 7–28.

Shutt, J. (1985) 'Tory Enterprise Zones and the Labour Movement', *Capital and Class*, 23: 19–44.

Silver, J. (1987) 'The Ideology of Excellence: Management and Neo-Conservatism', *Studies in Political Economy*, 24, Autumn: 105–29.

Silverman, D. (1970) *The Theory of Organizations*, London: Heinemann.

Silverman, D. and Jones, J. (1976) *Organisational Work: The Language of Grading and the Grading of Language*, London: Macmillan.

Simon, H. A. (1960) *Administrative Behaviour*, New York: Macmillan.

Simpson, R. (1997) 'Have Times Changed? Career Barriers and the Token Women Manager', *British Journal of Management*, 8, special issue, June: S121–30.

Simpson, R. (1998) 'Presenteeism, Power and Organisational Change: Long Hours as a Career Barrier and the Impact on the Working Lives of Women Managers' *British Journal of Management*, 9, special issue, Sept.: S37–50.

Sims, D., Fineman, S. and Gabriel, Y. (1993) *Organising and Organisations: An Introduction*, London: Sage..

Sirriani, C. (1984) 'Participation, Equality and Opportunity: Towards a Pluralist Organisational Model', in F. Fischer and C. Sirriani (eds) *Critical Studies in Organisation and Bureaucracy*, Philadelphia: Temple University Press.

Sisson, J. (1990) 'Introducing the Human Resource Management Journal', *Human Resource Management Journal*, 1. 1: 1–11.

Sisson, K. (1997) *New Forms in Work Organisation: Can Europe Realise its Potential?* Dublin: European Foundation for the Improvement of Living and Working Conditions.

Sisson, K. and Marginson, P. (1995) 'Management: Systems, Structure and Strategy', in P .K. Edwards (ed.) *Industrial Relations: Theory and Practice in Britain*, Oxford: Blackwell.

Skinner, B. F. (1971) *Beyond Freedom and Dignity*, New York: Knopf.

Slappendel, C. (1996) 'Perspectives on Innovation in Organizations', *Organization Studies*, 17. 1: 107–29.

Slaughter, J. (1987) 'The Team Concept in the US Auto Industry: Implications for Unions', paper presented to the Conference on Japanisation, UMIST.

Sloan, M. (1987) 'Culture and Control at Salesco: A Participant Observation Study', unpublished BA Dissertation, Lancashire Polytechnic.

Smart, B. (1985) *Michel Foucault*, London: Tavistock.

Smart, B. (1992) *Modern Conditions, Postmodern Controversies*, Oxford: Polity.

Smart, B. (1999) 'Resisting McDonaldization: Theory, Process and Critique', in B. Smart, *Resisting McDonaldization*, London: Sage.

Smircich, L. (1983) 'Concepts of Culture and Organisational Analysis', *Administrative Science Quarterly*, 28: 339–58.

Smith, C. (1987) 'Flexible Specialisation and Earlier Critiques of Mass Production', paper presented to the Conference on the Labour Process, Aston-UMIST.

Smith, C. (1991) 'From 1960s' Automation to Flexible Specialisation: A Déjà Vu of Technological Panaceas', in A. Pollert (ed.) *Farewell to Flexibility?*, Oxford: Blackwell.

Smith, C. and Elger, T. (1994) (eds) *Global Japanisation? The Transnational Transformation of the Labour Process*, London: Routledge.

Smith, C. and Meiskens, P. (1995) 'System, Society and Dominance in Cross-National Organisational Analysis', *Work, Employment and Society*, 9. 2: 241–67.

Smith, C. and Thompson, P. (1992) *Labour in Transition: The Labour Process in Eastern Europe and China*, London: Routledge.

Smith, D. (1987) 'The Japanese Example in South West Birmingham', paper presented to the Conference on Japanisation of British Industry, UMIST.

Smith, V. (1990) *Managing in the Corporate Interest: Control and Resistance in an American Bank*, Berkeley, Calif.: University of California Press.

Snyder, M. and Gangestad, S. (1986) 'On the Nature of Self-Monitoring: Matters of Assess-ment, Matters of Validity', *Journal of Personality and Social Psychology*, 51: 123–39.

Søndergaard, M. (1994) 'Hofstede's Consequences: A Study of Reviews, Citations and Replications', *Organisation Studies*, 15. 3: 447–56.

Sorge, A., Hartmann, G., Warner, M. and Nicholas, I. (1983) *Microelectronics and Manpower in Manufacturing*, Aldershot: Gower.

Sparrow, P. R. and Hiltrop, J-M. (1998) 'Redefining the Field of European Human Resource Management: A Battle between National Mindsets and Forces of Business Tradition', in C. Mabey, G. Salaman and J. Storey (eds) *Strategic Human Resource Management*, London: Sage.

Spears, R. (1997) 'Introduction', to T. Ibanez and L. Iniguez (eds) *Critical Social Psychology*, London: Sage.

Springer, R. (1999) 'The End of New Production Concepts? Rationalization and Labour Policy in the German Auto Industry', *Economic and Industrial Democracy*, 20: 117–45.

Staber, U. and Aldrich, H. (1987) 'Organisational Transformation and Trends in US Employment Relations', paper presented to the Conference on the Labour Process, Aston-UMIST.

Stacey, R. D. (1996) *Complexity and Creativity in Organizations*, San Francisco, Calif.: Berret-Koehler.

Stainton-Rogers, R. and Stainton-Rogers, W. (1997) 'Going Critical?' in T. Ibanez and L. Ininguez (eds) *Critical Social Psychology*, London: Sage.

Standing, G. (1986) *Unemployment and Labour Market Flexibility:The United Kingdom*, Geneva: International Labour Office.

Stanko, E. (1988) 'Keeping Women in and Out of Line: Sexual Harassment and Occupational Segregation', in S. Walby (ed.) *Gender Segregation at Work*, Milton Keynes: Open University Press.

Starkey, K. (1992) 'Durkheim and Organisational Analysis: Two Legacies', *Organisation Studies*, 13. 4: 627–42.

Starkey, K. (ed.) (1996) *How Organizations Learn*, London: International Thomson Business Press.

Steers, R. M. and Porter, L. W. (1987) *Motivation and Work Behaviour*, New York: McGraw-Hill.

Steffy, B. D. and Grimes, A. J. (1992) 'Personnel/Organisation Psychology: A Critique of the Discipline', in M. Alvesson and H. Willmott (eds) *Critical Management Studies*, London: Sage.

Steiner, T. and Miner, B. (1978) *Management Policy and Strategy*, West Drayton: Collier-Macmillan.

Stephenson, C. (1994) 'Problem Solving in a Lean Production Scenario', paper presented to the 12th Annual Labour Process Conference, Aston.

Stewart, E. (1967) *The Reality of Management*, London: Pan.

Stewart, E. (1976) *Contrasts in Management*, Maidenhead: McGraw-Hill.

Stodgill, R. M. (1948) 'Personal Factors Associated With Leadership: A Review of the Literature', *Journal of Psychology*, 25: 35–7.

Stodgill, R. M. (1974/1976) *Handbook of Leadership*, New York: Free Press.

Stone, K. (1973) 'The Origins of Job Structures in the Steel Industry', *Radical America*, 7. 6.

Storey, J. (1983) *Managerial Prerogative and the Question of Control*, London: Routledge and Kegan Paul.

Storey, J. (1985) 'The Means of Management Control', *Sociology*, 19. 2: 193–211

Storey, J. (ed.) (1989) *New Perspectives on Human Resource Management*, London: Routledge.

Storey, J. (1992) *Developments in the Management of Human Resources*, Oxford: Blackwell.

Storey, J. (ed.) (1995) *Human Resource Management: A Critical Text*, London: Routledge.

Storlie, F. J. (1979) 'Burnout: The Elaboration of a Concept', *American Journal of Nursing*, December: 2108–11.

Strauss, A., Schatzman, L., Erlich, D., Bucher, R. and Sabshim, M. (1963) 'The Hospital and its Negotiated Order', in E. Friedson (ed.) *The Hospital in Modern Society*, New York: Macmillan.

Streek, W. (1987) 'The Uncertainties of Management in the Management of Uncertainty: Employers, Labour Relations and Industrial Adjustment in the 1980s', *Work, Employment and Society*, 1. 3: 281–308.

Stringer, P. (ed.) (1982) *Confronting Social Issues: Applications of Social Psychology*, vol. 2, London: Academic Press.

Stryker, S. (1980) *Symbolic Interactionism: A Social Structural Version*, Menlo Park, Calif.: Benjamin/ Cummings.

Sturdy, A. (1987) 'Coping with the Pressure of Work', paper presented to the Conference on the Labour Process, Aston-UMIST.

Sturdy, A. and Fineman, S. (2001) 'Struggles for the Control of Affect: Resistance as Politics of Emotion', in A. Sturdy, I. Grugulis and H. Willmott (eds) *Customer Service: Empowerment and Entrapment*, London: Palgrave.

Sturdy, A., Grugulis, I. and Willmott, H. (eds) (2001) *Servicing Consumers: Critical Studies of Consumer Service*, London: Palgrave.

Supple, B. (1991) 'Scale and Scope: Alfred Chandler and the Dynamics of Industrial Capitalism', *Economic History Review*, 44. 3: 500–14.

Sussman, L. (1991) 'Managers: on the Defensive', *Business Horizons*, Jan.–Feb.: 83.

Sweiger, D. M., Sandburg, W. R. and Ragan, J. W. (1986) 'Group Approaches for Improving Strategic Decision Making: A Comparative Analysis of Dialectical Inquiry, Devil's Advocacy and Consensus', *Academy of Management Journal*, 29: 149–59.

Swieringa, J. and Wierdsma, A. (1992) *Becoming a Learning Organisation*, Wokingham: Addison-Wesley.

Symons, G. (1992) 'The Glass Ceiling is Constructed Over the Gendered Office', *Women in Management Review*, 7: 18–22.

Taber, T. D. (1991) 'Triangulating Job Attitudes with Interpretative and Positivist Measurement Methods', *Personnel Psychology*, 577–600.

Tailby, S. and Turnbull, P. (1987) 'Learning to Manage Just-in-Time', *Personnel Management*, January.

Tajfel, H. (1982) *Social Identity and Intergroup Relations*, Cambridge: Cambridge University Press.

Tajfel, H. and Turner, J. C. (1979) 'An Integrative Theory of Intergroup Conflict', in W. G. Austin and S. Worschel (eds) *The Social Psychology of Intergroup Relations*, Monterey, Calif.: Brooks-Cole.

Tajfel, H. and Turner, J. C. (1986) 'The Social Identity Theory of Intergroup Relations', in W. G. Austin and S. Worschel (eds) *The Social Psychology of Intergroup Relations*, Monterey, Calif.: Brooks-Cole.

Taylor, F. W. (1947) *Scientific Management*, New York: Harper and Row.

Taylor, P. and Bain, P. (1998). 'An Assembly Line in the Head: The Call Centre Labour Process', *Industrial Relations Journal*, 30. 2: 101–117.

Taylor, S. (1998) 'Emotional Labour and the New Workplace', in P. Thompson and C. Warhurst (eds) *Workplaces of the Future*, London: Macmillan.

Taylor, W. (1991) 'The Logic of Global Business: An Interview with ABB's Percy Barnevik', *Harvard Business Review*, March–April: 91–105.

Taylor, W. (1994) 'Control in an Age of Chaos', *Harvard Business Review*, Nov.-Dec.: 64–76.

Teasdale, P. (2000) 'What Can We Say About the Future of Work Using Statistics that Describe the Past?' paper presented to the 15th Annual Employment Research Unit Conference, Cardiff Business School, September.

Tedeschi, J. T., Schlenker, B. R. and Bonoma, T. V. (1971) 'Cognitive Dissonance: Private Ratiocination or Public Spectacle?' *American Psychologist*, 26: 685–95.

Tennen, H. and Affleck, G. (1990) 'Blaming Others for Threatening Events' *Psychological Bulletin*, 108: 209–32.

Teulings, A. (1986) 'Managerial Labour Processes in Organised Capitalism: The Power of Corporate Management and the Powerlessness of the Manager', in D. Knights and H. Willmott (eds) *Managing the Labour Process*, Aldershot: Gower.

Thackray, J. (1986) 'The Corporate Culture Rage', *Management Today*, Feb.: 67–70.

Thackray, J. (1988) 'Flattening the White Collar', *Personnel Management*, August.

Thackray, J. (1993) 'Fads, Fixes and Fictions', *Management Today*, June.

Thomas, A. and Kitzinger, C. (eds) (1997) *Sexual Harassment: Contemporary Feminist Perspectives*, Milton Keynes: Open University Press.

Thomas, R. J. (1988) 'What is Human Resource Management?' *Work, Employment and Society*, 2. 3: 392–402.

Thompson, E. P. (1967) 'Time, Work Discipline and Industrial Capitalism', *Past and Present*, 38: 55–97.

Thompson, J. D. (1967) *Organizations in Action*, New York: McGraw-Hill.

Thompson, J. D. and McEwan, W. J. (1973) 'Organisational Goals and Environments', in G. Salaman and K. Thompson (eds) *People and Organisations*, Harlow: Longman.

Thompson, P. (1984) 'The New Vocationalism: the Trojan Horse of the MSC', *Social Science Teacher*, 13. 2.

Thompson, P. (1988) 'The End of Bureaucracy? New Developments in Work and Organisation', in M. Haralambos (ed.) *Developments in Sociology*, vol. 5, Ormskirk: Causeway.

Thompson, P. (1989) *The Nature of Work: An Introduction to Debates on the Labour Process*, London: Macmillan.

Thompson, P. (1993) 'Fatal Distraction: Postmodernism and Organisation Theory', in J. Hassard and M. Parker, *Postmodernism and Organisations*, London: Sage.

Thompson, P. (1994) 'Corporate Culture: Myths and Realities, West and East', paper presented to the Conference on Convergence versus Divergence: the Case of Corporate Culture, Dunaújváros, Hungary.

Thompson, P. (2001) 'Progress, Practice and Profits: How Critical is Critical Management Studies?' paper presented to the 19th International Labour Process Conference, Royal Holloway.

Thompson, P. and Ackroyd, S. (1995) 'All Quiet on the Workplace Front: A Critique of Recent Trends in British Industrial Sociology', *Sociology*, 29. 4: 615–33

Thompson, P. and Bannon, E. (1985) *Working the System: The Shop Floor and New Technology*, London: Pluto.

✓ Thompson, P. and Findlay, T. (1999) 'Changing the People: Social Engineering in the Contemporary Workplace', in A. Sayer and L. Ray (eds) *Culture and Economy after the Cultural Turn*, London: Sage.

Thompson, P., Flecker, J. and Wallace, T. (1995) 'Back to Convergence? Globalisation and Societal Effects on Work Organisation', in T. Boje (ed.) *The Welfare State and the Labour Market in a Changing Europe*, New York: M. E. Sharpe.

Thompson, P., Jones, C., Nickson, D. and Wallace, T. (1998) 'Internationalisation and Integration: A Comparison of Manufacturing and Service Firms', *Competition and Change*, 3. 4: 387–416.

Thompson, P. and McHugh, D. (1995) *Work Organisations: A Critical Introduction*, Basingstoke: Macmillan.

Thompson, P. and O'Connell Davidson, J. (1994) 'The Continuity of Discontinuity: Management Rhetoric in Turbulent Times', paper presented to the Conference on The Strategic Direction of Human Resource Management, Nottingham Trent University, December.

Thompson, P. and Smith, C. (1998) 'Beyond the Capitalist Labour Process: Workplace Change, the State and Globalization', *Critical Sociology*, 24. 3: 193–215.

Thompson, P. and Smith, C. (2000) 'Follow the Redbrick Road: Reflections on Pathways In and Out of the Labour Process Debate', *International Studies of Management and Organization*, 3. 4: 40–67.

Thompson, P., Smith, C. and Ackroyd, S. (2000) 'If Ethics is the Answer, You've Been Asking the Wrong Questions: A Reply to Martin Parker', *Organisation Studies*, 21. 6: 1149–58.

Thompson, P. and Wallace, T. (1996) 'Redesigning Production Through Teamworking', *International Journal of Operations and Production Management*, special issue on *Lean Production and Work Organisation*, 16. 2: 103–118.

Thompson, P., Wallace, T. and Flecker, J. (1992) 'The Urge to Merge: Organisational Change in the Merger and Acquisition Process', *International Journal of Human Resource Management*, 3. 2: 285–306.

Thompson, P., Wallace, T., Flecker, J. and Ahlstrand, R. (1994) 'It Ain't What You Do It's the Way that You Do It', paper presented to the 13th Annual International Labour Process Conference, Aston.

Thompson, P., Warhurst, C. and Callaghan, G. (2000) 'Human Capital or Capitalising on Humanity? Knowledge and Skills in Interactive Service Work', in C. Prichard, M. Chumer and R. Hull (eds) *Managing Knowledge: Critical Discussions of Work and Learning*, Basingstoke: Macmillan.

Thurley, K. and Wood, S. (1983) *Industrial Relations and Management Strategy*, Cambridge: Cambridge University Press.

Tichy, N. and Devanna, M. A. (1986) *Transformational Leadership*, London: Wiley.

Tichy, N., Fombrun, C. and Devanna, M. A. (1982) 'Strategic Human Resource Management', *Sloan Management Review*: 47–61.

Tierney, M. (1996) 'Negotiating a Software Career: Informal Work Practices and "The Lads" in a Software Installation', in K. Grint and R. Gill (eds) *The Gender-Technology Relation: Contemporary Theory and Research*, London: Taylor and Francis.

Toffler, A. (1970) *Future Shock*, New York: Bantam.

Tolbert, P. S. and Zucker, L. G. (1996) 'The Institutionalization of Institutional Theory', in S. Clegg, C. Hardy and W. Nord (eds) *Handbook of Organization Studies*, London: Sage.

Tomlinson, J. (1982) *The Unequal Struggle? British Socialism and the Capitalist Enterprise*, London: Methuen.

Tompkins, P. K. and Cheney, G. (1985) 'Communication and Unobtrusive Control in Contemporary Organizations', in R. D. McPhee and P. K. Tompkins (eds) *Organizational Communication: Traditional Themes and New Directions*, Beverly Hills, Calif.: Sage.

Torrington, D. (1989) 'Human Resource Management and the Personnel Function', in J. Storey (ed.) *New Perspectives on Human Resource Management*, London: Routledge.

Towers, B. (1987) 'Managing Labour Flexibility', *Industrial Relations Journal*, 18. 2: 79–83.

Townley, B. (1990) 'Foucault, Power/Knowledge and its Relevance for HRM', paper presented to the Employment Research Unit Annual Conference, Cardiff Business School, September.

Townley, B. (1993) 'Performance Appraisal and the Emergence of Management', *Journal of Management Studies*, 30. 2: 27–44.

Tran, V. (1998) 'The Role of the Emotional Climate in Learning Organisations', *The Learning Organisation*, 5. 2: 99–103.

Triandis. H. C. (ed.) (1980) *Handbook of Cross-Cultural Psychology* vol. 5, Boston, Mass./London: Allyn and Bacon.

Trist, E. L. and Bamforth, K. W. (1951) 'Some Social and Psychological Consequences of the Longwall Method of Coal-Getting', *Human Relations*, 4. 1: 3–38.

Trist, E. L., Higgin, G. W., Murray, H. and Pollock, A. B. (1963) *Organisational Choice*, London: Tavistock.

Tsoukas, H. (1992) 'Postmodernism, Reflexive Rationalism and Organisational Studies: A Reply to Martin Parker', *Organisation Studies*, 13. 4: 643–49.

Tsoukas, H. (1994a) 'Socio-Economic Systems and Organisational Management: An Institutional Perspective on the Socialist Firm', *Organisation Studies*, 15. 1: 21–45.

Tsoukas, H. (1994b) 'What is Management? An Outline of a Metatheory', *British Journal of Management*, 5: 289–301.

Tsoukas, H. (1994c) 'From Social Engineering to Reflective Action in Organisational Behaviour', in H. Tsoukas (ed.) *New Thinking in Organizational Behaviour*, London: Butterworth and Heinemann.

Tuckman, A. (1994) 'Ideology, Quality and TQM', in A. Wilkinson and H. Willmott (eds) *Making Quality Critical*, London: Routledge and Kegan Paul.

Tuckman, B. W. (1965) 'Developmental Sequences in Small Groups', *Psychological Bulletin*, 63: 384–399.

Turnbull, P. J. (1986) 'The Japanisation of British Industrial Relations at Lucas', *Industrial Relations Journal*, 17. 3: 193–206.

Turnbull, P (1988) 'The Limits to Japanisation: Just-in-Time, Labour Relations and the UK Automotive Industry', *New Technology, Work and Employment*, 3. 1: 7–20.

Turner, J. C. (1985) 'Social Categorization and the Self-Concept: A Social-Cognitive Theory of Group Behaviour', in E. J. Lawler (ed.) *Advances in Group Process: Theory and Research*, vol. 2, Greenwich, Conn.: JAI.

Turner, L. and Auer, P. (1994) 'A Diversity of New Work Organisation: Human-Centred, Lean and In-Between', *Industrielle Beziehungen*, 1. 1: 39–61.

Tyler, M. and Taylor, S. (1997) '"Come Fly With Us": Emotional Labour and the Commodification of Sexual Difference in the Airline Industry', paper presented to the 15th International Labour Process Conference, Edinburgh. A version of this paper was published in *Work, Employment and Society*, 14. 1: 77–95.

Ursell, G. and Blyton, P. (1988) *State, Capital and Labour*, London: Macmillan.

Urwick, L. and Brech, E. F. I. (1949) *The Making of Scientific Management, vol. 1: Thirteen Pioneers*, London: Pitman.

Van Maanen, J. (1992) 'Drinking our Troubles Away', in D. M. Kolb and J. M. Bartunek (eds) *Hidden Conflict in Organisations: Uncovering Behind the Scenes Disputes*, London: Sage.

Van Strien, P. J. (1982) 'In Search of an Emancipatory Social Psychology', in P. Stringer (ed.) *Confronting Social Issues: Applications of Social Psychology*, vol. 2, London: Academic Press.

Vargish, T. (1994) 'The Value of Humanities in Executive Development', in H. Tsoukas (ed.) *New Thinking in Organisational Behaviour*, London: Butterworth Heinemann.

Vroom, V. H. (1964) *Work and Motivation*, New York: Wiley.

Vroom, V. and Mann, F. C. (1960) 'Leader Authoritarianism and Employee Attitudes', *Personnel Psychology*, 13: 125–40.

Vroom, V. H. and Yetton, P. W. (1973) *Leadership and Decision Making*, Pittsburgh: University of Pittsburgh Press.

Wainwright, H. (1987) 'The Friendly Mask of "Flexibility"', *New Statesman*, 11 December.

Wajcman, J. (1996a) 'Desperately Seeking Difference: Is Management Style Gendered?' *British Journal of Industrial Relations*, 34. 3:333–49.

Wajcman, J. (1996b) 'Women and Men Managers: Careers and Equal Opportunities', in R. Crompton, D. Gallie and K. Purcell (eds) *Changing Forms of Employment: Occupations, Skills and Gender*, London: Routledge.

Wajcman, J. (1998) *Managing Like a Man: Women and Men in Corporate Management*, Oxford: Polity and Blackwell.

Walby, S. (1986) *Patriarchy at Work*, Cambridge: Polity.

Walker, C. R. and Guest, R. H. (1952) *Man on the Assembly Line*, Cambridge, Mass.: Harvard University Press.

Wall, T. D., Clegg, C. W. and Kemp, N. J. (eds) (1987) *The Human Side of Advanced Manufacturing Technology*, Chichester: Wiley.

Wall, T. D., Kemp, N. J., Jackson, P. R. and Clegg, C. W. (1986) 'Outcomes of Autonomous Workgroups: A Long-Term Field Experiment', *Academy of Management Journal*, 29: 280–304.

Wallace, C. (1993) 'Reflections on the Concept of "Strategy"', in D. Morgan and L. Stanley (eds) *Debates in Sociology*, Manchester: Manchester University Press.

Walton (1985) 'Towards a Strategy of Eliciting Employee Commitment Based on Policies of Mutuality', in R. E. Walton and P. R. Lawrence (eds) *Human Resource Management, Trends and Challenges*, Boston, Mass.: Harvard University School Press.

Walzer, M. (1985) 'The Politics of Michel Foucault', in D. Hoy (ed.) *Foucault: A Critical Reader*, Oxford: Blackwell.

Wardell, M. (1986) 'Labor and the Labor Process', paper presented to the Labour Process Conference, Aston-UMIST.

Warhurst, C. (1997) 'Political Economy and the Social Organisation of Economic Activity: A Synthesis of Neo-Institutional and Labour Process Analyses', *Competition and Change*, 2: 213–46.

Warhurst, C., Nickson, D. and Shaw, E. (1998) 'A Future for Globalization? International Business Organisation in the Next Century', *Research in International Business and International Relations*, 7: 247–71.

Warhurst, C. and Thompson, P. (1998). 'Hands, Hearts and Minds: Changing Work and Workers at the End of the Century', in P. Thompson and C. Warhurst (eds) *Workplaces of the Future*, London: Macmillan: 1–24.

Waterman, R. H. (1988) *The Renewal Factor*, London: Bantam.

Watson, J. B. (1930) *Behaviourism*, (2nd edn), New York, NY: Norton.

Watson, T. (1980) 'Understanding Organizations: The Practicalities of Sociological Theory', in D. Dunkerley and G. Salaman (eds) *The International Yearbook of Organisation Studies 1980*, London: Routledge and Kegan Paul.

Watson, T. (1986) *Management, Organisation and Employment Strategy: New Directions in Theory and Practice*, London: Routledge and Kegan Paul.

Watson, T. (1994) *In Search of Management: Culture, Chaos and Control in Managerial Work*, London: Routledge.

Webb, J. (1996) 'Vocabularies of Motive and the "New" Management', *Work, Employment and Society*, 10. 2: 251–277.

Webb, J. (1997) 'The Politics of Equal Opportunity', *Gender, Work and Organisation*, 4. 3: 159–69.

Webber, A. (1993) 'What's So New About the New Economy?' *Harvard Business Review*, Jan.–Feb.: 24–42.

Weber, M. (1968) *Economy and Society*, New York: Bedminster.

Weber, M. (1984) 'Bureaucracy', in F. Fischer and C. Sirriani (eds) *Critical Studies in Organisation and Bureaucracy*, Philadelphia: Temple University Press.

Webster, F. and Robins, K. (1993) 'I'll be Watching You: Comment on Sewell and Wilkinson', *Sociology*, 27. 2: 243–52.

Webster, J. (1996) *Shaping Women's Work: Gender, Employment and Information Technology*, London: Longman.

Weick, K. (1987) 'Organisational Culture as a Source of High Reliability', *California Management Review*, 39. 2: 112–27.

Weigert, A. J., Smith Teitge, J. and Teitge, D. W. (1986) *Society and Identity: Towards a Sociological Psychology*, New York: Cambridge University Press.

Weightman, J. (1999) *Introducing Organisational Behaviour*, Harlow: Longman.

Weir, D. (1993) 'Why Isn't There any Good Management Research?' *British Academy of Management Newsletter*, no. 15, June.

Weitz, S. (1977) *Sex Roles: Biological, Psychological and Social Foundations*, New York: Oxford University Press.

Wellin, M. (1984) *Behaviour Technology: A New Approach to Managing People at Work*, Aldershot: Gower.

West, M. A. (1997) *Developing Creativity in Oerganizations*, Leicester: British Psychological Society.

West, M. A. and Farr, J. L. (eds) (1990) *Innovation and Creativity at Work: Psychological and Organisational Strategies*, Chichester: Wiley.

West, P. (1994) 'The Concept of the Learning Organisation', *Journal of European Industrial Training*, 18. 1: 15–21, MCB University Press.

Westwood, S. (1984) *All Day, Every Day: Factory and Family in the Making of Women's Lives*, London: Pluto.

Wexler, P. (1983) *Critical Social Psychology*, Boston: Routledge and Kegan Paul.

Wheeler, S. and Lyon, D. (1992) 'Employee Benefits for the Employer's Benefit: How Companies Respond to Stress', *Personnel Review*, 21. 7: 47–65.

Whipp, R. (1996) 'Creative Deconstruction: Strategy and Organisations', in S. Clegg, C. Hardy and W. Nord (eds) *Handbook of Organisation Studies*, London: Sage.

Whitaker, A. (1986) 'Managerial Strategy and Industrial Relations: A Case Study of Plant Relocation', *Journal of Management Studies*, 23. 6: 657–78.

White, H. C. (1992) *Identity and Control*, New Jersey: Princeton University Press.

Whitehead, T. N. (1936) *Leadership in a Free Society*, Cambridge, Mass.: Harvard University Press.

Whitehead, T. N. (1938) *The Industrial Worker*, London: Oxford University Press.

Whitley, R. (1987) 'Taking Firms Seriously as Economic Actors: Towards a Sociology of Firm Behaviour', *Organisation Studies*, 8. 2: 125–47.

Whitley, R. (1984) 'The Fragmented State of Management Studies', *Journal of Management Studies*, 21. 3: 331–48.

Whitley, R. (1992a) *Business Systems in East Asia*, London: Sage.

Whitley, R. (1992b) *European Business Systems: Firms and Markets in Their National Contexts*, London: Sage.

Whitley, R. (1994) 'The Internationalisation of Firms and Markets', *Organisation*, 1. 1: 101–24.

Whitley, R. (1999) *Divergent Capitalism: The Social Structuring and Change of Business Systems*, Oxford: Oxford University Press.

Whittington, R. (1988) 'Environmental Structure and Theories of Strategic Choice', *Journal of Management Studies*, 25. 6: 521–36.

Whittington, R. (1991a) 'The Fragmentation of Industrial R&D', in A. Pollert (ed.) *Farewell to Flexibility?* Oxford: London.

Whittington, R. (1991b) 'Putting Giddens into Action: Evolving Accounts of Managerial Agency', paper presented to the Conference, Towards a New Theory of Organizations, University of Keele.

Whyte, W. H. (1956) *The Organisation Man*, New York: Simon and Schuster.

Wickens, P. (1987) *The Road to Nissan*, London: Macmillan.

Wickens, P. D. (1992) 'Lean Production and Beyond: The System, its Critics and the Future', *Human Resource Management Journal*, 3. 4: 75–89.

Wiener, N. (1948) *Cybernetics: Control and Communication in the Animal and the Machine*, Cambridge, Mass.: MIT Press.

Wilkinson, A. (1992) 'The Other Side of Quality: Soft Issues and the Human Resource Dimension', *Total Quality Management*, 3. 3: 323–9.

Wilkinson, A., Godfrey, G. and Marchington, M. (1997) 'Bouquets, Brickbats and Blinkers: Total Quality Management and Employee Involvement in Practice', *Organisation Studies*, 18. 5: 799–819.

Wilkinson, A., Marchington, M. and Goodman, J. (1992) 'Total Quality Management and Employee Involvement', *Human Resource Management Journal*, 2. 4: 1–20.

Wilkinson, A. and Willmott, H. (1994) 'Introduction', in A. Wilkinson and H. Willmott (eds) *Making Quality Critical*, London: Routledge and Kegan Paul.

Wilkinson, B. (1983a) *The Shopfloor Politics of New Technology*, London: Heinemann.

Wilkinson, B. (1983b) 'Technical Change and Work Organisation', *Industrial Relations Journal*, 14. 2, Summer.

Wilkinson, B. (1986) 'Human Resources in Singapore's Second Industrial Revolution', *Industrial Relations Journal*, 17. 2: 99–114.

Williams, K., Cutler, T., Williams, J. and Haslam, C. (1987) 'The End of Mass Production?' *Economy and Society*, 16. 3: 405–39.

Williams, K., Haslam, C., Williams J. and Cutler, T. with Adcroft, A. and Juhal, S. (1992a) 'Against Lean Production', *Economy and Society*, 21. 3: 321–354.

Williams, K., Haslam, C., Williams J. and Cutler, T. (1992b) 'Ford-v-"Fordism": The Beginning of Mass Production', *Work, Employment and Society*, 6. 1: 517–48.

Williams, R. (1988) 'The Development of Models of Technology and Work Organisation with Information and Communication Technologies', paper presented to the Conference on the Labour Process, Aston-UMIST.

Williamson, O. (1975) *Markets and Hierarchies*, New York: Free Press.

Williamson, O. (1981) 'The Economics of Organisation', *American Journal of Sociology*, 87: 548–77.

Willis, P. (1977) *Learning to Labour*, Farnborough: Saxon House.

Willmott, H. (1984) 'Images and Ideals of Managerial Work', *Journal of Management Studies*, 21. 3: 349–68.

Willmott, H. (1987) 'Studying Managerial Work: A Critique and a Proposal', *Journal of Management Studies*, 24. 3: 249–70.

Willmott, H. (1989) 'Subjectivity and the Dialectics of Praxis: Opening up the Core of Labour Process Analysis', in D. Knights and H. Willmott (eds) *Labour Process Theory*, London: Macmillan.

Willmott, H. (1990) 'Beyond Paradigmatic Closure in Organisational Enquiry', in J. Hassard and D. Pym (eds) *The Theory and Philosophy of Organizations*, London: Routledge.

Willmott, H. (1992) 'Postmodernism and Excellence: The De-differentiation of Economy and Culture', *Journal of Organisational Change*, 5. 1: 69–79.

Willmott, H. (1993a) 'Strength is Ignorance; Slavery is Freedom: Managing Culture in Modern Organisation', *Journal of Management Studies*, 30. 5: 515–52.

Willmott, H. (1993b) 'Managing the Academics: Commodification and Control in the Development of University Education in the UK', unpublished paper.

Willmott, H. (1994) 'Theorising Agency: Power and Subjectivity in Organisation Studies', in J. Hassard and M. Parker (eds) *Towards a New Theory of Organizations*, London: Routledge.

Willmott, H. (1995) 'What Has Been Happening in Organisation Theory and Does it Matter?' *Personnel Review*, 24. 8: 33–53.

Wilson, E. (ed.) (2001) *Organisational Behaviour Reassessed: The Impact of Gender*, London: Sage.

Wilson, F. and Thompson, P. (2001) 'Sexual Harassment as an Exercise of Power', *Gender, Work and Organizations*, 8. 1: 61–83.

Wilson, F. M. (1995) *Organisational Behaviour and Gender*, London: McGraw-Hill.

Wilson, G. (1997) 'Biology, Sex Roles and Work', in *Liberating Women from Modern Feminism*, London: Institute of Economic Affairs.

Winfield, I. J. and Kerrin, M. (1994) 'Catalyst for Organisational Learning: The Case of Toyota Motor Manufacturing UK Ltd', *The Learning Organisation*, 1. 3: 4–9, MCB University Press.

Wise, S. and Stanley, L. (1990) 'Sexual Harassment, Sexual Conduct and Gender in Social Work Settings', in *Social Work and Social Welfare Handbook*, Milton Keynes: Open University Press.

Witz, A. (1986) 'Patriarchy and the Labour Market: Occupational Controls and the Medical Division of Labour', in D. Knights and H. Willmott (eds) *Managing the Labour Process*, Aldershot: Gower.

Witz, A. (1992) *Professions and Patriarchy*, London: Routledge.

Witz, A., Halford, S. and Savage, M. (1994) 'Organized Bodies: Gender, Sexuality, Bodies and Organizational Culture', paper presented to the BSA Conference, Sexualities in their Social Context, University of Central Lancashire, March.

Witz, A. and Savage, M. (1992) 'The Gender of Organizations', in M. Savage and A. Witz (eds) *Gender and Bureaucracy*, Oxford: Blackwell.

Witz, A. and Savage, M. (eds) (1992) *Gender and Bureaucracy*, Oxford: Blackwell.

Womack, J., Jones, D. and Roos, D. (1990) *The Machine that Changed the World*, New York: Macmillan.

Wood, S. (1979) 'A Reappraisal of the Contingency Approach to Organisation', *Journal of Management Studies*, 16. 3: 334–54.

Wood, S. (ed.) (1982) *The Degradation of Work: Skill, Deskilling and the Labour Process*, London: Hutchinson.

Wood, S. (1986) 'The Cooperative Labour Strategy in the US Auto Industry', *Economic and Industrial Democracy*, 7. 4: 415–48.

Wood, S. (ed.) (1989a) *The Transformation of Work?* London: Hutchinson.

Wood. S. (1989b) 'The Japanese Management Model', unpublished paper.

Wood, S. and Albanese, M. T. (1995) 'Can We Speak of High Commitment Management on the Shop Floor?' *Journal of Management Studies*, 32: 215–45.

Wood, S. and de Menzes, L. (1998) 'High Commitment Management in the UK', *Human Relations*, 51: 485–515.

Woodward, J. (1958) *Management and Technology*, London: HMSO.

Woodward, J. (1965) *Industrial Organisation: Theory and Practice*, London: Oxford University Press.

Woolf, J. (1977) 'Women in Organisations', in S. Clegg and D. Dunkerley (eds) *Critical Issues in Organisations*, London: Routledge and Kegan Paul.

Wray, D. (1994) 'Paternalism and its Discontents: A Case Study', paper presented to the 12th International Labour Process Conference, Aston.

Wright, C. and Lund, J. (1998) '"Under the Clock": Trade Union Responses to Computer-ised Control in US and Australian Grocery Warehousing', *New Technology, Work and Employment*, 13. 1: 3–15.

Wright, S. (1994) 'Culture in Anthropology and Organisational Studies', in S. Wright (ed.) *Anthropology of Organizations*, London: Routledge.

Yakhlef, A. and Salzer-Morling, M. (2000) 'Intellectual Capital: Managing by Numbers', in C. Prichard, R. Hull, M. Chumer and H. Willmott (eds) *Managing Knowledge: Critical Investigations of Work and Learning*, London: Macmillan.

Yarrow, M. (1992) 'Class and Gender in the Developing Consciousness of Appalachian Coal-Miners', in A. Sturdy, D. Knights and H. Willmott (eds) *Skill and Consent*, London: Routledge.

Yates, D. (1986) 'Is Dual Labour Market Theory Dead? The Changing Organisation of Work: The Employer's Perspective', paper presented to the Conference on the Labour Process, Aston-UMIST.

Zeitlin, M. (1974) 'Corporate Ownership and Control: The Large Corporation and the Capitalist Class', *American Journal of Sociology*, 79. 5: 1073–119.

Zimbalist, A. (ed.) (1979) *Case Studies on the Labour Process*, New York: Monthly Review Press.

Zimbardo, P. G., Ebbesen, E. B. and Maslach, C. (1977) *Influencing Attitudes and Changing Behaviour*, 2nd edn, Reading, Mass.: Addison-Wesley.

Zimmerman, D. (1971) 'The Practicalities of Rule Use', in J. Douglas (ed.) *Understanding Everyday Life*, London: Routledge and Kegan Paul.

Zuboff, S. (1988) *In the Age of the Smart Machine: The Future of Work and Power*, Oxford: Heinemann.

Zummato, R. (1988) 'Organisational Adaptation: Some Implications of Organisational Ecology for Strategic Choice', *Journal of Management Studies*, 25. 2.

Name Index

Becker, H. S. 134, 313
Bedeaux, C. 33
Beech, H. R. *et al.* 279
Beer, M. *et al.* 52
Beirne, M. *et al.* 184
Belbin, M. 319, 332
Bell, D. 4, 149, 153, 167, 170
Bellaby, P. and Orribor, P. 370
Benders, J. and Huigen, F. 182
Bendix, R. 32, 50, 51, 214, 392
Beneria, L. 79
Benne, K. D. and Sheats, P. 268, 269
Benson, J. K. 8, 14, 17, 18, 19
Berg, M. 21
Berger, P. L. and Luckman, T. 363
Berggren, C. 81
Berkeley Thomas, A. 89
Berle, A. A. and Means, G. C. 90
Berridge, J. *et al.* 284
Beynon, H. 66
Bhaskar, K. 391
Biddle, B. J. 244
Biewener, J. 181, 185, 189
Biggart, N. 5, 10, 209
Billig, M. 349
Birchall, D. and Lyons, L. 162
Bittner, E. 363
Blackler, F. 154, 213
Blackler, F. and Shimmin, S. 351
Blair, H. *et al.* 182
Blakemore, K. and Black, R. 146
Blau, P. M. 39, 58, 60, 364
Blau, P. M. and Gouldner, A. 359
Blau, P. M. and Schoenherr, R. A. 102
Blau, P. M. *et al.* 280, 281
Blauner, R. 60
Bluestone, B. and Bluestone, I. 166
Blyton, P. and Turnbull, P. 53
Boddy, D. and Buchanan, D. 232
Bolman, L. G. and Deal, T. E. 275
Bologh, R. 378, 379
Bolton, S. 138, 287, 288
Boreham, P. 50, 182
Boulding, K. 4
Bourdieu, P. 254
Boyer, R. and Drache, D. 86
Boyer, R. and Rattansi, A. 377
Bradley, H. 108, 132
Bramble, T. 152
Bramble, T., Parry, K. and O'Brien, E. 179
Brannen, P. 26, 123
Braverman, H. 31, 34, 40, 94, 96, 103, 105, 106, 366, 368, 373, 375
Breakwell, G. M. 324, 336, 340, 341
Brecher, J. 395
Brenner, O. C. *et al.* 147
Brewis, J. and Kerfoot, K. 143, 145
Briggs, P. 178, 183
Briner, R. B. 288

Briner, R. B. and Reynolds, S. 290
Broad, G. 203
Brotherton, C. 275, 307, 314
Brown, A. and Keep, E. 171
Brown, G. 22, 28, 29, 30, 31, 32, 33, 43, 44, 47
Brown, H. 96, 322
Brown, J. S. and Duguid, P. 248
Brown, R. 313, 361
Browne, K. R. 134, 136
Brubaker, R. 358, 371
Bryman, A. 11, 12, 78, 108
Buchanan, D. 52, 112, 164
Buchanan, D. and Badham, R. 117, 122, 254
Buchanan, D. and Huczynski, A. 13, 222, 266
Buford, B. 6
Burawoy, M. 32, 65, 106, 113, 209, 319, 373
Burchell, S. *et al.* 126, 159, 160, 179, 180, 189
Burgess, J. and Strachan, G. 177
Burgess, S. and Rees, H. 179
Burgoyne, J. 93
Burke, R. J. 147
Burnham, J. 90
Burns, T. 92, 272, 273
Burns, T. and Stalker, G. M. 59, 60, 61
Burrell, G. 16, 19, 127, 130, 141, 367, 370, 386, 391
Burrell, G. and Morgan, G. 356, 365, 388, 389
Business Week 41, 156, 199

Calder, B. J. 276
Callaghan, G. and Thompson, P. 108, 115, 116, 206, 287, 288, 289, 346
Calás, M. and Smircich, L. 132, 133, 135, 137, 376, 379
Callan Hunt, G. 225
Campbell, A. and Currie, B. 109
Cappelli, P. 179, 180
Carchedi, G. 103, 105
Carey, A. 45
Carr Mill Consultants 192
Carroll, M. 284, 285
Carter, P. and Jeffs, P. 143
Carter, R. 94, 98
Casey, B. 160, 325
Castells, M. 150
Caulkin, S. 133
Cave, K. 159
Chandler, A. 27, 37, 38, 67, 70, 71, 87, 106, 110, 128, 392
Chanlat, J. F. 388
Chell, E. 264
Cheng, C. 138
Cherrington, D. J. 223, 318
Cherry, L. 279, 282
Child, J. 54, 57, 58, 63, 64, 65, 66, 67, 87, 88, 89, 90, 96, 97, 107, 110, 113, 172, 364
Child, J. and Smith, C. 65
Child, J. and Rodrigues, T. 76
Chomsky, N. 241
Chorover, S. L. 237

Cialdini, R. B. 231, 265
Cicourel, A. V. 363
Clairmonte, F. and Cavanagh, J. 68
Clark, D. D. and Hoyle, R. 233, 234
Clarke, T. and Clegg, C. 189
Clawson, D. 21, 22, 23, 24, 25, 26, 27, 28, 29, 32,
    34, 38, 128, 372, 373
Clay Hamner, W. 13
Clegg, S. 122, 124, 125, 126, 127, 130, 149, 150,
    155, 358, 366, 374, 377, 378
Clegg, S., Boreham, P. and Dow, G. 86
Clegg, S. and Dunkerley, D. 8, 14, 17, 22, 35, 37, 48,
    55, 57, 62, 76, 77, 103, 118, 123, 131, 366, 383
Clegg, S. and Hardy, C. 150, 377, 388
Clegg, S. and Higgins, G. 372
Clutterbuck, D. 159, 160
Cockburn, C. 111, 117, 118, 122, 133, 135, 136,
    139, 141, 143, 201, 380
Cohen, S. 341, 369
Cohen, S. and Taylor, L. 340, 347, 348
Coleman, G. 376, 379, 390
Colgan, F. and Ledwith, S. 139
Collier, A. 391
Collins, R. 36, 250, 251
Collinson, D. 127, 130, 141, 206
Collinson, D. and Collinson, M. 141, 143, 180, 188
Collinson, D. and Hearn, J. 132
Collinson, D. et al. 146
Considine, M. 190
Cooper, C. L. 277, 282
Cooper, D. 143
Cooper, R. and Burrell, G. 156, 375, 377
Coopey, J. and Hartley, J. 202
Corbett, J. M. 231, 258, 340, 386
Cousins, C. 370
Cressey, P. and Jones, B. 81
Cressey, P. and McInnes, J. 112
Crompton, R. 132, 147
Crompton, R. and Jones, G. 139
Crook, S. et al. 375
Cross, M. 159
Crouch, C. 17
Crouch, C. et al. 252
Crowther, S. and Garrahan, P. 173
Cully, M. et al. 165, 171, 182
Cummings, T. and Blumberg, M. 172
Cummings, T and Cooper, C. L. 280
Cutcher-Gershenfeld, J. et al. 182
Cyert, R. M. and March, J. G. 58, 91, 120
Czarniawska, B. 375, 390

Dahl, R. 119
Dahler-Larsen, P. 191, 360
Dahrendorf, R. 90
Dale, K. and Burrell, G. 377, 379
Damanpour, F. 253
Dandeker, C. 114, 115, 125, 128
Danford, A. 182, 183
Daniel, W. W. and McIntosh, N. 163

Daniel, W. W. and Millward, N. 98
Davidson, M. and Cooper, C. 134
Davis, K. 144
Dawson, P. and Webb, J. 182
Dawson, S. 122, 294
Day, R. A. and Day, J. V. 363
De Cindio, E. et al. 262
De Los Reyes, P. 146
DeVroey, M. 105
Deal, T. and Kennedy, A. 191, 193, 194, 195, 200,
    202, 208
Deaux, K. and Emswiller, T. 224
Deery, S. et al. 188
Deetz, S. 126, 127, 130
Dejoy, D. M. 228
Delamarter, R. T. 199
Delbridge, R., Lowe, J. and Oliver, N. 183, 209
Delbridge, R., Turnbull, P. and Wilkinson, B. 184
Delbridge, R. et al. 127, 128
Deleuze, G. and Guattari, F. 384
Dent, M. 188
Derrida, J. 376
Despres, L. and Hiltrop, J. M. 150, 153, 169
Deutsch, M. and Gerard, H. B. 231
Devanna, M. A., Fombrun, C. J. and Tichy, N. M. 52
Dews, P. 130
Dex, S. 132
Di Maggio, P. and Powell, W. 76, 79
Di Tomaso, N. 141
Dicken, P. 68
Dicken, P. and Savage, M. 178
Dickson, T. et al. 196, 201
Ditton, J. 352
Donaldson, L. 6, 7, 8, 9, 11, 13, 14, 16, 61, 64, 357,
    358, 360, 361, 362, 363, 366, 370, 389, 394, 395
Donovan Report 98
Doray, B. 22, 26, 33, 43, 74
Drago, R. and MacDonough, T. 341
Drake, R. I. and Smith, P. J. 316
Drucker, P. 89, 90, 95, 96, 149, 167, 199, 246
Drummond, H. 117
Du Gay, P. 192, 203, 208, 370, 372, 380
Due Billing, Y. 379, 380
Duenas, G. 83
Dumaine, B. 164
Dunford, R. and McGraw, P. 164, 181
Dunkerley, D. and Salaman. G. 370, 388
Durkheim, E. 16, 19, 194, 359, 360

Easterby-Smith, M. 249
Eby, L. T. and Dobbins, G. H. 325
Eccles, R. G. and Nohria, N. 93, 167, 189
Edquist, C. and Jacobsson, S. 79, 81
Edwards, P. K. 104, 113, 116
Edwards, P. K. and Scullion, H. 367
Edwards, P. K. et al. 181
Edwards, R. 23, 26, 27, 31, 38, 44, 45, 65, 103,
    104, 106, 107, 115, 130, 197, 373
Edwards, R. and Reich, M. 106

Subject Index

advanced manufacturing technology 151–3, 163, 168, 185, 342
information technology, influence of 81, 96, 128, 150–1, 156, 170, 174–5, 64, 99, 127, 142, 180–1, 187, 189–91
teleworking 155, 161–2, 173, 178
total institutions 127, 313–15
Toyota 58, 81, 84, 249
trade unions 24, 26, 34, 38, 45, 48, 50, 53, 66, 81–2, 112, 156–7, 196, 198, 319, 337
training 27, 50, 159, 165, 240, 260
 of management 291, 350
transaction costs 38, 67
transnational companies 68–9, 79, 81–3, 122, 137
trust, high and low relationships 53, 151–2, 156, 163, 180–2, 196

United Distillers/UDV 159, 255
United States (USA) 7–8, 23–6, 29–30, 33, 37, 43–5, 50, 70–1, 73, 133, 159, 161, 165, 170–1, 178–9, 181, 189, 214, 258, 273, 284

values, role of in organisations 11–12, 14, 22, 53, 74–5, 192–3, 208–9, 220, 228–33, 258, 277, 316–17, 326–7, 360
 and motivation 306, 308–10
Volvo 80, 163, 183, 351
 see also groups
Weberian theory 4, 15–16, 34–8, 133–6, 272, 327. 357–9, 378–9
 neo-Weberianism 39–40, 135, 364
 radical Weberianism 123, 186, 362, 370–4, 388
WERS surveys 165–6, 181–2, 196–7